Catherine of Aragon

Catherine of Aragon

An Intimate Life of Henry VIII's True Wife

Amy Licence

AMBERLEY

For Tom, Rufus and Robin.

First published 2016

Amberley Publishing

The Hill, Stroud

Gloucestershire, GL5 4EP

www.amberley-books.com

British Library Cataloguing in Publication Data.

A catalogue record for this book is available from the British Library.

ISBN 978 1 4456 5670 0 (hardback)
ISBN 978 1 4456 5671 7 (ebook)

Printed in Malta, by Melita Press.

You have left to all women in every way of life
a magnificent example.

Juan Luis Vives

Contents

Introduction

Seven pairs of Spanish slippers, corked and garnished with gold. Smocks made for childbirth. A vellum primer covered in cloth of gold, with silver gilt clasps and embroidery in gold thread. An image of the martyrdom of St Catherine. A pin cushion. Two looking glasses. Two ivory chess sets, with red and white chessmen. A horn cup with a cover and a foot and knot of ivory. A broken branch of coral, used as a baby's teether.

In 1534, an inventory was compiled of a number of items of clothing and possessions that were being held in storage at Baynard's Castle, in London. They belonged, or had formerly belonged, to Catherine of Aragon, Queen of England, first wife of Henry VIII. Singly, they illustrated some of the key aspects and themes of her identity: domesticity, childbirth, motherhood, piety, regality, Spanishness. Collectively, they formed a mosaic of a complex life which had been broken apart by forces beyond Catherine's control.

Baynard's was a place Catherine knew well, spending one of her wedding nights there and later having been granted the castle as one of her bases in the city. She was so accustomed to it that the majority of her clothing and effects had been stored there, although by 1534 she had not seen the castle for a few years, nor the objects in it. Yet these items were not being recorded for Catherine's benefit. Such inventories were usually drawn up in the case of someone's death, but at the time when the king's officials were sorting through her intimate possessions Catherine was definitely still alive; she would not die for another two years. Nor were these goods to be forwarded to her current residence of Buckden Palace, in Cambridgeshire; instead they were to be picked over by her former husband and his new wife, Anne Boleyn, who selected the items they wanted for themselves before the rest was consigned to storage.

Catherine is principally remembered in the twenty-first century as the wife that Henry divorced. This is misleading, as it casts her in the role of a victim, a poor tragic woman who failed to produce a son and was set aside for a younger model. Yet Catherine was so much more than this. She was a humanist queen, a figure of erudition, with a Spanish inheritance of learning, crusading and exploring. She was perhaps even more educated and intelligent than Henry himself, who was eulogised across Europe in his early reign as a perfect model of scholarly kingship. Erasmus certainly believed her to be more than the king's match. She was a warrior, a crusader, a scholar and a patron, the daughter of the most famous marriage in the early modern world, coming from the largest, most evolving empire, in the name of which her parents had fought cultural and religious campaigns against heresy. She had been her father's ambassador, her husband's adviser and her country's regent at the time when England won its greatest victory over the Scots. She was the figurehead of worship, a role model of piety, an archetype of beauty, the symbol of an Anglo-Spanish union that reconnected two branches of the ancient Lancastrian bloodline. Catherine was all this. Yet she is remembered today for the one thing she did not do: bear a son that survived to adulthood.

Nor was Catherine actually divorced. After the examination of religious texts and much debate, Henry decided that their marriage was invalid, had never been legitimate and therefore had never existed. She was stripped of the titles of queen and wife, her daughter declared a bastard, and was condemned as having been living in sin with Henry as the Dowager Princess of Wales, his brother's wife. And yet the Pope, along with a significant number of European universities, doctors and leading thinkers of the day, declared that the marriage was completely valid and endorsed her as Henry's true wife. Under oath, in the confessional, in private letters, in court and upon her deathbed, Catherine never wavered from her conviction that she was the true wedded wife of the king. And it was this focus, perhaps stubbornness, that made her adhere to her role unwaveringly, even when capitulation would have made life easier for herself and her daughter. Yet Catherine was not one to choose the easy road. Wearing a hair shirt under her clothing and rising at dawn to hear Mass, she saw her steadfastness as a crusade to save her husband's soul. For Henry had not just rejected her, he had turned his back on the Pope and the very tenets of the Catholic faith that had shaped their mutual devotions. Convinced Henry was heading for damnation, Catherine elected to suffer in his stead, praying that God would forgive him. Watching her supporters go to the stake, or the block, she lived her final years in the expectation of following them and was prepared to embrace the opportunity of becoming a martyr.

Catherine of Aragon was a complex, passionate, unbreakable woman whose life spanned the key years of the late Renaissance and the Protestant Reformation. She knew great joy and the depths of misery; she had loved and lost; she had been a queen and also been reduced to penury, begging for her bread. Her life was one of extremes. Her death is riddled with controversy. Her story deserves to be told for more reasons than the simple fact that she was cast aside by Henry VIII. She should not be remembered as a tragic figure, more as a majestic, humanist crusading queen, paradoxically an inspiration and a frustration. But for one small twist of misfortunc, her life might have been entirely different. She was, indeed, in the words of her friend Juan Luis Vives, a 'magnificent inspiration'. She still is.

Amy Licence
Canterbury, July 2016

Prologue

This story begins with a map. A map that depicts a world that no longer exists; a map painted on paper that has itself disappeared – burned, lost, drenched or reused at some point in more than five hundred intervening years. Its physical absence leaves a small space in history, yet paradoxically that small space is strong enough that it can be used as a stepping stone back into the past, back into the world of a Catholic humanist queen who was the product of the beliefs, cultures and developments that were captured by the cartographer's pen.

The known world in 1485 was a smaller place but it was, nevertheless, intensely colourful and exciting. In Lisbon, Portugal's centre of trade and cartography, a twenty-four-year-old Italian called Bartholomew Columbus was mixing up inks made from lamp-black and gum arabic, or Brazil wood chips and egg white. On sheets of paper carefully glued together, he was drawing up a map of every ocean and landmass from which the merchants returned with the holds of their ships groaning with spices, silks, jewels and strange fruits. No doubt he had listened to their accounts down at the harbour and plied them for details of what they had seen. And they had seen a lot. In recent years, Henry the Navigator, son of the King of Portugal, had explored the lush green archipelago of the Azores and the long African coastline; his successors had reached as far as the Gold Coast, captured Tangiers and explored the Congo River. Also, in the Portuguese royal library, there was a copy of Marco Polo's book of his travels, published in 1477. Bartholomew certainly found it and leafed through its pages with interest, as is clear from the annotations he made in its margins. At some point he passed the book on to his brother Christopher, whose handwriting also appears there, interspersed among the Venetian's adventures. Bartholomew's map recording all this no longer survives, but others that were inspired by it remain.

The lives of these cartographers prove it would be a mistake to think medieval people did not travel. Just as Bartholomew had left behind his native Genoa and was then resident in Lisbon, another map-maker, Henricus Germanus, born in Nuremberg in Germany, had relocated over eight hundred miles south to the sun-drenched city of Florence, often considered the birthplace of the Renaissance, or the 'Athens of the Middle Ages'. There, the ageing Lorenzo de Medici, known as 'the Magnificent', was commissioning works by Botticelli, Michelangelo and da Vinci, including murals in the Sistine Chapel, and expanding the library established by his grandfather. He would die in 1492, the year that Christopher Columbus landed in the New World. In the shadow of the Medici Palace, Germanus drew up his own world view, on nine sheets of paper measuring 122 centimetres by 201. Using black, blue, red and gold, he depicted misshapen versions of Europe, Asia and Africa, buffeted by the puffing faces of winds, all enclosed within a foliate border. It was the first map to incorporate the descriptions of the Cape of Good Hope, navigated by Bartholomew Diaz in 1487–8, and the existence of Japan, or 'Cipangu', albeit too far to the west. Thus the old *mappae mundi* of the medieval world, which had been created primarily to illustrate tenets of classical learning, were giving way to the more accurate portolan charts, as aids to navigation.

Maps not only aided travellers, they also travelled fair distances themselves. Copies of Germanus' work were made by Florentine artist Francesco Rosselli using copperplate engraving on vellum and were widely circulated. One reached another Nuremberg native, Martin Behaim, who used it to create the first known globe, the Erdapfel, or earth apple. This was a linen ball in two halves, reinforced by wood, covered with a map painted by illustrator Georg Glockendon, which depicts outsized versions of Europe and Asia, surrounded by empty ocean. This space is put to good use by the inclusion of illustrations and inscriptions of mythical beasts, legends, astrological symbols, superstitions and natural resources, making the globe a record of late medieval culture which extends far beyond its various landmasses. After exploring western Africa and the Azores, Behaim spent part of 1486 in Lisbon, where he was knighted by King John and served on his mathematical junta. It was during his Portuguese sojourn that the junta solved the problem of calculating latitude by taking measurements of the height of the midday sun using an astrolabe, an instrument that had been developed by medieval Islamic astrologers. Behaim would have had ample opportunities to view Bartholomew's map, or to speak with him in person, before the departing for the Azores.

In these ways, little by little, through the drawing up of a map, the circulation of literature or the meeting of scientists and travellers, the secrets of the universe were being unravelled. For centuries, thinkers had been challenging the notion that the world was flat. By the thirteenth century Thomas Aquinas assumed that his readership understood it was spherical. He knew of different methods by which this fact could be proven, by physicists observing the movement of heavy bodies towards the centre and by mathematicians studying the shapes of eclipses. The same belief was echoed through cultural and literary traditions in the work of Roger Bacon, Hildegard von Bingen, Peter Abelard, Marco Polo, Dante Alighieri, Geoffrey Chaucer, Jean de Mandeville, Christine de Pisan, William Caxton and others. In spite of this, it was still commonly believed that the earth was the centre of the universe, around which the sun, moon and other planets revolved, according to the Ptolemaic model. Another thirty years would pass before Nicolaus Copernicus circulated his seven assumptions to prove otherwise.

Alongside the creation of these maps, another revolution was taking place on paper. The first printing press, the Gutenberg Press, was set up in Mainz, Germany, with the ink drying on its maiden publication, a forty-two-line Latin Bible, in around 1454. Presses were established in most major European cities over the next two decades, and by the end of the century a thousand such places had produced a staggering eight million books. The first printer in Spain was a German immigrant named Johannes Parix, who travelled there via Italy and set up his business in 1472 in Segovia, producing eight books, starting with the *Synodal of Aguilafuental*. Soon afterwards, more books were running off the presses in Seville, Barcelona, Valencia, Zaragoza, Salamanca, Burgos and Toledo. England lagged behind by only a couple of years. In the early 1470s, the merchant William Caxton had travelled to Cologne in the service of the Duchess of Burgundy, and witnessed the process of production in the workshop of Ulrich Zel. Inspired, Caxton returned home to establish his workshop within the precincts of Westminster Abbey in 1476, printing papal indulgences before undertaking his first complete book, a translation of the *Dictes and Sayings of the Philosophers*. Other presses were set up in Oxford in 1478, St Albans in 1479 and again in London in 1480, under Wynkyn de Worde. Today, around thirty thousand incunabula, or works printed before 1501, survive, catalogued in the British Library.

The printed word spread through Europe almost as quickly as the plague had in previous centuries. It allowed for the dissemination of information on an unprecedented scale and opened up the world as surely as the expeditions of the navigators did. The contribution of printers and mapmakers to the spread of humanism and the Renaissance cannot be underestimated. Yet their audience, which means those who had access to these works as well as the ability to read them, was still limited. The population of England in 1485 was somewhere between two and three million, about half of what it had been before the Black Death. Only about ten percent of people, or fewer, were resident in towns or cities, with the others spread through the more typical villages. The average life expectancy, accommodating infant and child mortality, was thirty-five.[1] If someone was lucky enough to avoid illness, famine, plague and accident and survive into adulthood, they might even reach their late sixties or older, but this had been estimated at less than a tenth of the population.[2] Occupation and class also mattered; in the Medicis' Florence, a lay person might die in their late twenties[3] but those cloistered away in a religious life could fare better. The whole of Italy was home to around ten million people, as was Germany, while the combined territories of Spain and Portugal had seven million between them. Both inside and outside those cloistered walls, people offered prayers for their survival to a vengeful, omnipotent, omniscient God, through the channel of the pre-Reformation Catholic Church, whose autonomy would remain unchallenged for another generation.

Discovery, cartography, education, the Renaissance, humanism, the printed word, transience and religion: these were the powerful elements that shaped the world in 1485. This was the world into which Catherine of Aragon arrived in Spain that December, and her life would follow the extraordinary cultural trajectory that these combined influences set in motion.

PART ONE

A Daughter of Spain 1447–1501

1

Catherine's Roots 1447–1453

I

In the midst of a cold winter, the king and queen had retreated to the Palace of Alcalá de Henares, right in the geographical heart of Spain. Behind its thick, yellow stone walls, courtiers wrapped themselves up against the cold and huddled around blazing fires, or looked out through the horseshoe arches across the rooftops of the fortified town. The palace was located on a dry plateau, a harsh, rocky terrain. With the temperature fluctuating between extremes, wheat and vines struggled to grow, so the local farmers supplemented their crops by raising goats and sheep. In fact, 95 per cent of all Castilian subjects were agricultural workers, tied closely to the land and its seasons.[1] It had been that way for centuries. The area had once been inhabited by the Celts and Romans, then developed under the Moors, but most of the present palace dated from the fourteenth century, juxtaposing the best of early Renaissance architecture with the elegant carving, tiles and filigree work of the Mudéjar style. The interiors were hung with tapestries, velvet or painted with colourful frescoes, ornamented with silver and cloth of gold.

It was to one such ornate bedroom that the heavily pregnant queen retired to deliver a daughter, a red-haired girl who arrived on 16 December, reputed to look more like her mother than any of her elder siblings. They named her Catalina, but today she is known by the Anglicised version of her name, Catherine, and although she was equally a creation of her father's Aragonese and her mother's Castilian backgrounds, only the former is used nowadays in reference to her origins. Her veins flowed with Spanish, Portuguese and English blood, a triumvirate of influences that would shape her young life. In the days following her birth, as the queen lay recovering, a messenger brought a letter from the Italian navigator Christopher Columbus, describing his intention to sail west in order to open up new trading routes, and requesting her help. Queen Isabella summoned him at once to court. It would be Spanish money that would fund his voyage across the Atlantic when Catherine was six years old.

Catherine of Aragon lived and died a daughter of Spain. The country's temperament, its history, climate and culture, left their indelible imprint upon her character. She spent less than a third of her life there, but those were her formative years. She may have left her native land at the age of fifteen and spent the next thirty-five years on English soil. She may have been crowned queen of England and given birth to an English queen, and she may have died and been buried in English soil without ever returning home. But, despite all this, her position as the daughter of Spain's Catholic monarchs remained in her blood, particularly the example set by her mother. Like Isabella of Castile, Catherine was feisty and formidable, taking her duties and her piety to the extreme. It meant that in the coming years she remained passionate in her defence of her country and clung to her beliefs despite suffering banishment and austerity. Refusing to renounce her position, Catherine employed the elements of theatre, even melodrama, that her mother had perfected, preferring to embrace martyrdom before compromising. Her commitment was absolute, her faith unshakeable. Until her death, she lived, prayed and thought as a Spaniard, like the daughter of a queen, raised to be a queen in her own right. It shaped her ambition, her decision-making, her destiny. And that destiny was intricately entwined with the course of English history and the Reformation.

Thus the role played by Catherine's mother in shaping the young girl's mind cannot be overestimated. Isabella of Castile wrote her own chapter not just in Spanish national identity but in the story of Europe in the fifteenth century, in the discovery of the Americas, in pre-Reformation Catholicism, in Jewish history and also in the history of women. As the first female monarch of any independent province in the Iberian Peninsula, and as a product of her times, Isabella's actions were undeniably definitive. Towards the end of her life, her chaplain Pedro Martir (Peter Martyr) described her as being 'stronger than a strong man ... a marvellous example of honesty and virtue; nature has made no other woman like her'.[2] It was from her mother's rule, her character and actions, that Catherine drew her own particular blend of piety, passion and stubbornness, never forgetting she was the daughter of the woman who established the Inquisition, who recaptured Granada after eight centuries of Muslim rule and who expelled the Jews from Spain. However, Isabella remains something of a paradox for historians, her reputation chequered with what would be considered great acts of cruelty and intolerance to the modern mind. Like Catherine's, there was a dark side to her story, coloured as it was with sacrifice and sorrow, with casualties strewn along the path to glory. Therefore, the story of Catherine's life must overlap that of the Castilian queen and resonate with it, right until the very end.

Born into the house of Trastámara, Isabella was a formidable leader; driven, able and astute, her reign was described by her royal chronicler, Hernando del Pulgar, as 'a thing most marvellous, that what many men and great lords did not manage to do in many years, a single woman did in a short time, through work and governance'. She did not inherit an easy task. Isabella's kingdom was an evolving and dynamic country, fragmented in political and religious terms, multicultural, studded by mountains and Moorish palaces, raw and beautiful. Poetry composed by the early medieval prince Mohammed Ben Abad captures the atmosphere of a world where musk and camphor were strewn across the floor, where Muslim lords were summoned by trumpets to watch the bullfight, dressed in black and silver, watched by haughty-looking ladies seated behind lattice windows. He paints a picture of a chief in a turban wrought with gold, a garnet or amethyst at his brow, of girls sitting weaving at the loom, of a pair of silver earrings dropped down a well, of wrinkled, yellow melons piled in the marketplace, and of horses approaching the city gates at dusk.

It was not Spain as we know it today, but a composite of regions, divided under different rulers, of which Castile was the largest. The Aragonese Empire, meanwhile, was a scattered entity including Sicily, Naples, Sardinia, Malta, Corsica and the Balearics. Commensurate with its size, Castile had the largest population, containing at least three-quarters of the population of the entire country. To the west lay Portugal, to the north was the little enclave of Navarre, and to the south the Moorish bastion of Granada. The rulers of Castile presided over peripatetic military courts, living out of tents in the pursuit of ideals, swinging from crushing defeats to strategic victories. The plains around its walled cities were dotted with sheep, its hillsides sprouting almond blossom and olive groves, its roads worn by the feet of pilgrims and armies. Spanish society was broadly divided into three groups, defined by Francesc Eiximenis, a Catalan author who died half a century before Isabella's birth: the *maiors*, or ruling classes, were the barons, bishops, counts and knights associated with the court; the *mitjans* were the middle-class merchants and others engaged in commerce and industry, particularly of wool in Castile; while the largest group were the *menors*, farmers of the land. It was a country of high drama and conflict, war and religion.

II

Isabella of Castile would have been conscious from an early age that both Portuguese and English Plantagenet blood flowed in her veins. As the great-granddaughter of John of Gaunt, she seems to have inherited the Lancastrian looks and colouring passed down by John to her father, John II of Castile, who was 'tall and handsome, fair skinned and slightly ruddy' with hair the 'colour of a very mature hazelnut', a 'snub' nose and eyes 'between green and blue'.[3] John II had inherited the throne as an infant, on the early death of his father, and his youth was overseen by his English-born mother Catherine (Catalina), his uncle Ferdinand I of Aragon, 'the just' or 'the honest', and his *contino* or old friend Duke Álvaro de Luna. The young king displayed little of the warlike temperament of his English cousin Henry V, favouring a tolerant approach to religious minorities and devoting his time to hunting, tournaments and writing poetry. His first marriage, to his cousin Maria of Aragon, produced four children, all of whom died save for a single son, Enrique, or Henry. After Maria's death, the forty-two-year-old John took as his second wife Isabel of Portugal, niece of Henry the Navigator. Isabel was in her late teens at the time of her wedding and had been married for almost four years by the time of her first confinement.

Perhaps Isabel felt she had taken too long to fall pregnant. Perhaps she was despairing of having a child at all. Almost three years after their wedding day, 22 July 1447, Isabel made a vow to the Virgin Mary and set out on pilgrimage to Toro, in Zamora, north-west of Madrid. Apart from being John of Castile's birthplace, the town was also home to the shrine of Santa Maria de la Vega, which stood in a pine wood near the River Duero. Isabel made all, or part, of the journey barefoot, which was a common practice among pilgrims, especially women hoping that the saints would intercede for them and grant specific wishes. With its origins in the twelfth century, the shrine is a simple, plain, red-brick building, with its long, straight central section culminating in a round apse. There, Isabel would have made her devotions, offering prayers on bended knee, or prostrating herself before the shrine and perhaps leaving gifts of money and jewels, alongside the simpler flowers, herbs and eggs left by her poorer subjects. The cult of the Virgin Mary was particularly strong across medieval Europe, inspiring the devotion of aspiring mothers, and Isabel is unlikely to have visited Toro without also seeing the Collegiate Church also associated with her. Entering through the ornate Pórtico de la Majestad, with its carvings depicting the lives of Mary and her child, Isabel would have seen the thirteenth-century sculpture of the pregnant Virgin and offered up more prayers. It must have seemed to Isabel that her voice was heard as, soon after her return home[4] in July 1450, she fell pregnant.

Little is known about the actual birth. Isabel would have been attended by court physicians, and perhaps female midwives; if King John was enlightened enough, he would have benefitted from drawing on the vast medical expertise of his Muslim subjects, whose wisdom was broader than the narrow northern European practices of the time, such as are witnessed in the confinements of Isabel's contemporaries in England. Islamic texts incorporated the best of Greek and Roman methods alongside those of Syria, Persia and

India, and from the ninth century onwards, formally recognised the female profession of the experienced midwife. This role came about through practical training, with women serving an apprenticeship that took place in birthing rooms, applying traditional methods and the use of herbs and instruments, usually overseen by relatives. They were able to command a salary for their services and were often employed by the wealthy on a more long-term basis, to live in the home, helping deliver and then raise the children.[5] They were professional specialists long before midwifery was finally regulated in England in 1562 by the requirement of a centralised oath of conduct. Fifty years before the queen's confinement, Arab historian Ibn Khaldūn described them as 'the best informed about the embryo; there is nothing in the womb they do not know'.[6] Islamic midwives might have offered Isabel poppy or hemp seeds to dull the pain, or advised her to eat watermelons during her pregnancy to produce a child of good character and countenance, or to eat dates and burn incense to ensure she delivered a boy.[7]

In the end, Isabel did not deliver a boy. Her daughter's birth was later recorded by one of her private physicians, Dr Fernán Álvarez, as having taken place between four and five in the afternoon of 22 April 1451, at the royal palace in the village of Madrigal de la Altas Torres in the central-western region of Avila. In the *Chrónicon de Valladolid*, Alvarez described a bedroom on the second floor, stifling and airless, where the queen gave birth in an alcove[8] to a girl whom she named after herself. Chronicler Alfonso de Palencia refers obliquely to the queen suffering from postnatal depression following the delivery,[9] although this cannot have been first-hand information as he was then in the service of Cardinal Bessarian in Florence. The arrival of a princess was considered of little real political consequence, as although Castilian laws of inheritance did not forbid female rule, Isabella's half-brother Henry was expected to inherit the throne. By 1451 he was already twenty-six, and a married man who had won a military victory at the Battle of Olmedo. At best, Isabella might anticipate making a diplomatic marriage. This outcome became even more likely when the little girl was two and a half and her mother bore a son, who was given the name of the kings of Portugal, Alfonso. With two male relatives between her and the throne, no one anticipated that Isabella might one day become queen.

The Castilian court under Isabella's father was depicted in verse by the early Renaissance humanist poet Juan de Mena. A prolific writer who translated Homer's *Iliad*, Mena received a Master of Arts degree from the advanced University of Salamanca and travelled widely in Italy. In the 1440s, he composed an epic poem in three hundred satirical stanzas in the 'arte mayor' form of twelve syllables, or dodecasyllabic verse. The *Laberinto de Fortuna* drew on the model of Dante's *Inferno* to create 'circles' visited by the narrator, dominated by the theme of the wheel of fortune and with commentary upon the king's close advisers. Particularly singled out for praise was the influential Álvaro de Luna, who had guided John since he was a child, inspiring a devotion so deep that it prompted rumours of witchcraft among those who resented his position. There were also whispers that he had played a role in the death of John's first wife, Maria, whose suspicious end was often considered to have been the result of favouring her brothers over her husband, although this, as with all rumour, must be treated with caution. Presented to John in person by its author, Mena's poem lauds Castile as having a heroic identity, in epic style, as a rallying cry for future greatness and the king himself as a 'new Caesar' to bring about unity, with Luna's help.

However, Luna was not popular with everyone. Even though he had been the one to arrange her marriage, disregarding John's own preference for a French wife, Queen Isabel disliked the hold the minister had over her husband and struggled to disengage John from his favourite's grip. According to Pedro de Escavias, John loved his young wife 'very much'[10] but Fernán Peréz de Guzmán twice repeats rumours that Luna attempted to regulate the pair's intimate life, refusing to allow them to sleep together or spend time together, supporting claims made by Palencia of a homosexual relationship between the king and his minister. Luna believed it was the king's appetite for food and sex that led to his ill-health and restrained him 'using coercion where persuasion failed', in Palencia's words. Other witnesses claimed Luna berated the royal pair after having found them together, telling Queen Isabel, 'I married you and I'll unmarry you.'[11] In the end, it was the minister's involvement in the murder of the king's accountant that provided the excuse for his arrest and execution, in June 1453. Although Isabel had succeeded in removing her rival, it was a pyrrhic victory, as the sentence plunged the king into an irrevocable depression. John never recovered from the loss and died eight months later at the age of forty-nine. He entrusted his second family to his eldest son, but when Henry IV became the new king of Castile, his stepmother and her two children left court for the castle of Arévalo. Some accounts state this was at his request, while others claim it was Isabel's wish. The future queen, at the age of three, was plunged into obscurity.

2

Isabella of Castile 1454–1485

I

Arévalo was a quiet market town, a mere twenty miles to the east but far removed from the intrigues and sophistry of the Castilian court. It was a mixture of influences, where Catholics rubbed shoulders with Muslims and Jews in the marketplaces, overlooked by church towers and Mudéjar arches; its main site for Christian worship, the Church of San Miguel, had even been built on the foundations of a mosque. When the dowager queen and her household arrived in the summer of 1453, they found a solid, white sugar lump of a castle, dominated by an immense tower with a rounded end. The windows were small and high; the surrounding moat had long since dried up.[1] It had an unhappy history as the location where Peter the Cruel had imprisoned his young wife a century before, just days after their wedding. It was to prove unhappy for John's young queen as well; widowed at the age of twenty-seven, she rapidly descended into depression. Palencia, the previous source for Isabel's post-partum condition, blamed her new unhappiness upon an incident which appears to have been designed to undermine her as a mother. By the terms of John's will, she was to retain custody of her children so long as she remained chaste; yet, in around 1454, she was unpleasantly importuned by Pedro Girón, one of Henry's favourites with whom he was visiting

Arévalo, and, according to Palencia, this led her to close 'herself in a dark room, self-condemned to silence, and dominated by such depression that it degenerated into a form of madness'.[2] One of Isabella's biographers, Nancy Rubin, relates 'legends' that told of the widowed queen's increasing mental instability, from her belief that the castle was haunted, to the grief occasioned by her later separation from her children.[3]

Living with them was Isabel's mother, Isabel de Barcelos, a daughter of the 1st Duke of Braganza who had been married to her half-uncle John, the son of the King of Portugal. Just like John II of Castile, this John, Constable of Portugal, was a descendant of John of Gaunt, but from an older daughter. The Portuguese descent came through Philippa of Lancaster, the first child born of Gaunt's first marriage, to Blanche of Lancaster, and thus related to John of Castile, whose ancestor had been borne by Gaunt's second wife. This gave Isabella English blood on both sides, paternal and maternal. Isabel de Barcelos had been widowed in 1442 and was, by the time she arrived at Arévalo, in her fifties. She was also a strong and capable figure who had been instrumental in negotiating Henry's second marriage, to Juana of Portugal, 'a notable woman of great counsel and great help and consolation to her daughter'. And Isabella was then in great need of consolation, according to the later account of her daughter, as their income was insufficient so that they were frequently 'in extreme lack of necessary things'.[4] King Henry requested that they return to his court, but his stepmother preferred to remain away, so a royal guard of two hundred was sent to watch over the castle. This afforded them protection, but may also have contributed to the feeling that they were living a constricted life.

Despite her unhappiness, either Isabel or her mother managed to supervise the education of the children, instilling in them a formidable piety, with the support of a large enough staff to maintain their regal status. The Portuguese influence was not confined only to the children's grandmother, but was also found in other key members of the household, particularly the children's nurse Clara Alvarez and her husband Gonzalo Chacón, who was the administrator of their household, and in Isabel's lady-in-waiting Beatriz de Silva, the future founder of the Order of the Immaculate Conception. In addition, both children were championed by

Alfonso Carrillo de Acuna, alchemist Archbishop of Toledo, of noble Portuguese descent, who would later support their claims to the throne over that of close family rivals. Some historians have even speculated that due to these circumstances young Isabella's first language was Portuguese.[5] Isabella also had the company of the children of Mosén Pedro de Bobadilla, who was Governor of Arévalo Castle; his daughter Beatrice, although a decade older than Isabella, soon became her favourite.

Still being raised in anticipation of a dynastic marriage, Isabella's formal education was balanced by feminine pursuits such as needlework, painting and reading the Bible, as well as riding and hunting in the surrounding fields. Reputedly a great reader,[6] she consumed heroic stories, including Arthurian legends, more likely in the French version of Chrétien de Troyes than the Latin of Geoffrey of Monmouth. In later life, she would regret that she had not studied Latin to any significant level, but she did have the opportunity to learn from some of the leading thinkers of her time. Isabella shared a tutor with her brother, as the royal confessor, inquisitor and professor of theology, Bishop Lope de Barrientos, was charged in the will of John II to oversee the education of his two youngest children. Her later character suggests this was the case – Isabella did lean on Barrientos later in life, and his religious policies find echoes in many of her policies, particularly towards unconverted Jews and the influence of magic. Another figure who inspired certain passions in the young girl was her father's secretary, the historian and doctor of law Rodrigo Sánchez de Arévalo, a great admirer of Joan of Arc. Arévalo had been in France during the short life and career of 'La Poucella' or 'Poncella'[7] and is likely to have shared his stories of her with Isabella, as well as a copy of the anonymous *La Poncella de Francia*, with the result that the princess grew to respect Joan as the instrument of God, and moreover an active, militant figure, a female warrior. When she grew up, Isabella would use the saint's posthumous reputation as a model, presenting herself as a 'latter-day Joan', allowing a rare opportunity for a woman to adopt the role of a chivalric hero in a largely male sphere. As queen she would see herself as the deliverer of her people, and possibly aspired to the hagiographical qualities of the text, with her own posthumous reputation in mind.

Arévalo was also the author of *Compendiosa Historica Hispánica*, in which he compiled a narrative of Castile dating from the fifth-century invasion of the Visigoths through to the reign of Henry IV. The region is presented as superior to the rest of Spain and Europe, especially Portugal, France and England, much in the vein of Mena's poetry of the 1440s, fostering in Isabella a sense of destiny and importance of her country. This sense of focus, drive and 'sedateness'[8] was observed as part of Isabella's character from a young age, but also owed something to a contemporary national stereotype. She may have appeared to conform to this while also being defined by it. In the 1457 allegorical debate *Tratado* by Alfonso de Palencia the figure of Exceritio personifies one national type, that of the Spaniard who excels in physical prowess, but a traveller contrasts the national 'sad demeanour' with the 'happy blood' (*sangre alegre*) of the French. Isabella would later be known for her seriousness and intensity, even when she was able to employ a sense of spectacle, colour and drama.

In line with this 'sad demeanour' was the deep piety Isabella had developed from an early age. She chose as her patron saints John the Baptist and John the Evangelist and followed strict rules set out by contemporary writers such as Fray Pedro Cordoba's *Garden of Noble Women*, which stressed the need for purity and prayer. The castle had connections with the nearby Franciscan monastery, and Isabella later gave gifts to one of the friars, 'whom she had known well when she was growing up', and asked to be buried in a Franciscan habit. Situated just outside the town gates, the establishment had been maintained by her father John during his lifetime. It is very likely that she had access to the extensive monastic library collected by Gonzalo de Madrigal, which was under papal protection.

II

Although they were hidden away in a backwater, Isabella and Alfonso were still King Henry's half-siblings, carrying the royal blood of Trastámara in their veins. As the years passed and Henry failed to father a child, the Spanish nobles began to look to the boy and girl at Arévalo as potential future monarchs of Castile. This convinced Henry of the need to override Isabel's wishes and bring her children under his closer supervision, partly for their education but also to prevent them from becoming figureheads of opposition to his rule. His decision was enforced with little sensitivity. Later in life, Isabella wrote in a letter that she and Alfonso were 'forcibly and intentionally taken from the arms'[9] of their mother and placed in the court of their half-brother's new consort, Queen Juana, in Madrid. It has been suggested that this act contributed to the mental deterioration of Isabel, who was to remain at Arévalo for the remainder of her days. Isabella was placed in the household of her new sister-in-law, who was twelve years her senior but very different in character.

Henry's first marriage had been beset by rumours of his impotence and possible homosexuality. He had been married at the age of fifteen to Blanche of Navarre in a match designed to bring Navarre and Castile together, but it had proved personally unhappy and not just childless but unconsummated. The one thing on which the pair agreed was that they had never engaged in any sexual activity, with the king claiming he was permanently impotent with the queen but experienced no problems with other women. As evidence, Henry cited an affair he had with a Portuguese woman at court and produced two prostitutes from Segovia who swore they had slept with him. This was ironic given that in his later years Henry's Cortes de Ocana punished prostitutes with flogging and the confiscation of their clothes.[10] Blanche submitted to a physical examination that concluded she was capable of conceiving and bearing children. Such procedures were common in annulment cases and would have been conducted by a panel of matrons. Finally, Henry had appealed to Pope Nicholas V, in the belief that the marriage had been bewitched and was, therefore, canonically invalid. The Pope agreed with him. Blanche was sent home and imprisoned by her family; when she refused to remarry, she was murdered by poisoning, probably by her father or sister.

Henry had remarried in 1455 to the high-spirited, scandalous Juana of Portugal. Her love of finery and pleasure contrasted strongly with the image Henry presented upon meeting her, dressed all in black, with a hat pulled down over his face, wearing an expression that was 'not one of fiestas'. Yet, on occasion, Henry could appear with regal magnificence, dressing ostentatiously and accompanied by a Moorish guard among barges with sails of cloth of gold to meet the French at the conference of Bayonne.[11] In spite of his new marriage, the question of Henry's sexuality would not go away, and the previous doubts seemed to be confirmed when seven further years elapsed before his second wife Juana fell pregnant. Tellingly, the custom of displaying the stained bedsheets from the wedding night was eschewed in the case of both Henry's wives, despite the fact that his history might have made it expedient for him to have proven that consummation took place with Juana. When the queen finally conceived, it seemed questionable to their contemporaries that the baby was actually his. When a daughter was born in February 1462, also named Juana, it was widely rumoured that the father was the handsome royal favourite Beltrán de la Cueva, and the little girl has been remembered in history by his name as Juana La Beltraneja. Henry later banished his wife, who went on to bear two illegitimate children, before the king divorced her for having 'not used her person cleanly'. Isabella was not sorry to see the queen go; she later described Juana's court as being frivolous and pleasure-seeking, focused on clothes and costumes, pageants and dancing. Juana's behaviour, especially Cueva's suggestive championing of her in the joust, set the tone for a court to which her young niece reacted with distaste.

Amid this world, Isabella was emerging as a strong young woman who would take her destiny into her own hands instead of being manipulated by others. When Henry attempted to arrange marriages for her with the royal families of Portugal, France and England, and with a prominent Castilian nobleman, she refused, replying that her father's will had stipulated that the consent of the Castilian nobility was required for the choice of her husband. She was only eleven when she refused to make the political alliance Henry had planned for her with the thirty-four-year-old Portuguese king. She was able to do this because of the support of powerful nobles behind her – some of whom, like Chacun and Carrillo, had been with her at Arévalo and now began to scheme to replace the unsuitable Henry. With the scandal of the royal marriage followed by the king's repudiation of the queen, the precarious situation of Juana le Beltraneja as heir was the final straw for many.

Rebels led by Henry's childhood friend Juan Pacheco, Marquess of Villena, gathered in the town of Burgos in September 1464 and issued a list of grievances against Henry, among which was the accusation that 'Doña Juana, the one called the princess, is not your daughter'.[12] This was followed by a reminder that John II's will stated that if Henry left no legitimate children, his throne was to pass to Alfonso and then Isabella. Henry ignored the insult and chose to meet the rebels rather than punish them, agreeing to name Alfonso as his heir instead of his acknowledged daughter. That November, the king entrusted Alfonso to Pacheco, who was to act as his tutor, with the oath that 'the legitimate succession to these realms belongs to my brother'. Within weeks, though, Henry was uncomfortable with his decision, feeling he had been pressured into this course of action, and in February 1465 he declared his oath invalid and raised an army. That June, the rebels retaliated by staging a theatrical event known to history as the Farce of Avila. A huge wooden platform was built in the square behind the cathedral, upon which was placed a wooden effigy of King Henry in a chair, bearing a sceptre and sword, dressed in sable furs, with a crown and spurs. Another list of accusations was read out to the curious crowd that had gathered there, including charges of the king's impotency, homosexuality, pacifism and sympathy with Muslims. At each charge, the effigy was stripped of one symbol of its power before being symbolically de-crowned by the nobility and the body thrown from the platform, where it was stamped into the ground. Isabella's twelve-year-old brother was crowned king upon the chair in his place. This was an incredibly violent and significant act, attacking the sanctity of kingship and desecrating the king's image. Furious, Henry ordered the queen's household, including Isabella and Princess Juana, to relocate from Madrid to Segovia under heavy guard.

The truth of Juana le Beltraneja's real paternity may never be known. Allegations of illegitimacy were an easily and frequently employed political tool for the discrediting of enemies, and were most plausible when set within a dubious morality, such as the behaviour of the queen and the royal separation. A number of theories have been put forward about Henry's sexuality and impotence, his hormonal balance and the likelihood that he suffered from various conditions like acromegaly (excess growth hormone) or constitutional eunuchoidism (delayed puberty). However, when the king's body was exhumed from the monastery at Guadalupe in 1946, and his remains examined by surgeons and archaeologists, his skeleton was found to be normal with nothing to suggest any form of physical defect. Still, the rumours persisted, as politically useful rumours do.

Castile descended into chaos, with the private armies of the nobility taking control; there was even talk of dividing the realm in half. Isabella was brought back to Madrid, to be married to the brother of rebel leader Juan Pacheco, the forty-three-year-old Pedro Girón, the same man who had propositioned and insulted her mother at Arévalo. Preparations were made for the wedding, which was scheduled to take place in April 1466, in spite of the bride's protestations that she would rather die and Beatriz de Bobadilla's promise to stab the groom.[13] The match was not to be. En route to Madrid, beset by a flock of storks that were interpreted as an ill omen, Girón succumbed to a fatal throat abscess. His death must have seemed to reinforce Isabella's sense of destiny.

It would take one more death, though, before Isabella's claim to the throne moved from being simply theoretical to very likely. Henry's army clashed with Alfonso's at the second Battle of Olmedo in 1467, and in spite of the hostile Palencia claiming that Henry fled in cowardice,[14] the outcome was unclear. Both sides claimed victory. In the summer of 1468, Isabella and her brother were back at Arévalo, when news was brought to them of the advance of the plague. Following the terrible outbreak of the disease that had devastated Europe in the 1340s, the Black Death, or pneumonic or bubonic plague, caused by the spread of the *Yersinia pestis* bacteria, had never really gone away. A second pandemic was especially virulent in the mid-fifteenth century, and in 1466 it is estimated that 40,000 people died in Paris. Those who were able to travel to avoid it did so, especially the *maiors*, or upper classes. Isabella and Alfonso quickly left Arévalo that June, before the town was put under quarantine and the gates were permanently closed. Their destination was Avila, the capital town within the province of the same name, a distance of about thirty miles due south. Around eight miles short of their destination, they stopped for the night at Cardenosa and dined on freshly caught trout at the house of a wealthy citizen. In the morning, Alfonso was discovered in a deep coma, with his tongue black and his veins refusing to yield any blood to the surgeon. A black, swollen tongue has been historically recorded as a sign of plague, although the blood is more likely to gush from the nostrils than coagulate and there were no tell-tale buboes on his body; equally, symptoms of poisoning by arsenic include a black tongue and coma. Alfonso died on 5 July, at the age of fourteen. His body was taken back to Arévalo to be interred in the monastery, but Isabella was forbidden from accompanying him to protect her from the plague. Instead she was sent to Avila's Monastery of Saint Ana.

III

Even before her brother's death, Isabella was anticipating taking over his position as the heir to Castile. A letter she wrote on Alfonso's last night informed the people of the south-eastern town of Murcia that doctors did not expect the boy to survive and that in the event of his decease, 'the succession of the reign and the dominions of Castile and León belong to me as the legitimate heir and successor'.[15] It was probably not the only rallying cry she sent. This was more diplomatic than it was ruthless, as Alfonso had already prepared a will in which he urged her to assume his position as leader of the rebels.[16] However, his death seemed to rally support for the king as an opportunity to heal the breach, and apparently Henry was grieved at the loss. Castile was not dominated by the Salic law that prevented female succession in other parts of Spain, but it was one thing to replace Henry with a young man and quite another to prefer a young woman who had been raised in comparative obscurity, destined merely for marriage. Isabella was summoned out of monastic seclusion by Carrillo, who asked her to become the figurehead of the dissenters and be crowned Queen of Castile. Here, the princess displayed a wisdom beyond her seventeen years, replying that while Henry was alive, 'no other person had a right to the crown' and that perhaps Alfonso's death was a sign of heavenly disapproval.[17] Instead, Isabella met Henry just outside Avila, where pre-Roman men had left four stone statues of bulls. It probably helped her situation that Queen Juana's infidelity and secret pregnancy had just been exposed, again weakening the claim of La Beltraneja. Isabella promised to respect her half-brother as king, and he formally recognised her as his heir, with income and properties suitable to her position. Isabella was then sworn in as Princess of Asturias and his legitimate heir. Representatives of the three estates, clergy, nobility and commoners, kissed her hand and swore allegiance, and Henry issued decrees to be dispatched across Castile naming her as his heir.

The Castilian inheritance secure, Isabella turned to the business of finding herself a husband. Although many of them had been old enough to be her father, not all the candidates suggested by Henry over the years had been abhorrent to her; in fact, she now returned to a suitor whose name had first been raised back when she was a mere five or six. Her second cousin Ferdinand was then sixteen, a figure of similar abilities and commitment who had ruled his region for a year on behalf of his ailing father. Aragon was a smaller region than Castile but at the height of its powers its rule extended over the Balearic Islands, southern Italy, parts of the south of France and Greece, giving it a wide and powerful Mediterranean coastline. Its capital city was Zaragoza, dominated by its two cathedrals, the twelfth-century one dedicated to the Saviour, where the kings of Aragon were traditionally crowned, and the other, known as the Basilica of Our Lady of the Pillar, reputedly built on the spot where the Virgin appeared to St James. Ferdinand was the son of John II of Aragon, of the house of Trastámara, and his second wife, Juana Enriquez, a Castilian noblewoman. His birth in March 1452 made him less than a year younger than Isabella and the proximity of Castile and Aragon being conducive to unity, he was as keen to marry her as she was him. However, in the intervening years, Henry had changed his mind about this connection and, having staked his own right to veto any suitor he disliked, was making tentative offers to Edward IV of England, proposing a marriage between Isabella and Edward IV's younger brother, the future Richard III. Isabella knew that if she wanted Ferdinand she would have to marry him in secret, present it as a *fait accompli* to Henry and potentially incur his wrath. However, she did have the support of a large Aragonese faction at court, headed by Carrillo and supported by agents of the potential groom's father, King Juan, who was prepared to offer large bribes to Castilian officials.[18]

Isabella wrote to Ferdinand's father, Juan, on 1 November 1468, stating her intentions to marry. The King and Prince of Aragon reacted swiftly, aware of the prize they were being offered. Two months later, on 7 January, Ferdinand signed a series of concessions at Cervera:

> I, Lord Ferdinand, by the Grace of God, King of Sicily along with His Majesty, my very honourable father, with whom I rule and reign jointly the said kingdom of Sicily; heir of all his kingdoms and lands, governor general, Prince of Gerona, duke of Montblanc, Count of Ribagorza, lord of the city of Balaguer; for the reason that between me and Her Majesty Lady Isabella, crown princess and heiress of the kingdoms and domains of Castile and León, it is hoped by the grace of our Lord to contract matrimony.[19]

He solemnly agreed to uphold his identity as a Catholic king, to obey the Pope, be at the disposal of the prelates and bishops of his country and show all due honour and respect to the Church. He would also uphold justice, help the poor and needy, grant his people audiences and 'treat them with love and clemency'. The laws and customs of Castile would be respected by Ferdinand, who would maintain the ruling councils and not cause the nobles, knights and grandees 'any real or personal affront without cause'.[20] It was clear from the start who was to be the dominant partner in the marriage, with Ferdinand swearing to reside in Castile and not to leave it, nor remove their future children from it, without Isabella's consent, nor would he gift any lands that she had not agreed, although she was able to do so freely, and he would consider them as gifts he had made himself. All letters, privileges and documents, all appointments and decisions, all treaties of peace and war, in fact all moves, every step he took, would be jointly considered. Before they had even met, Isabella and Ferdinand established a basis for marriage that was a union of two crowns, a formal pooling of resources with an inbuilt respect for the position and authority of a future queen, a union that appears to overturn the usual patriarchal dominance in recognition of the status and abilities of the parties involved. Some might have seen it as humiliating for Ferdinand to make such concessions to a woman; Ferdinand clearly thought Isabella was worth it. This formal union would also develop into a match of mutual passion and respect, with the pair adopting a chivalric approach to each other, to emphasise their individual and combined roles as the masculine and feminine entities of power. He would be her loyal knight and she would be the brains and organisation, the inspiration and support behind his success. It was a formula that their daughter Catherine would hope to emulate in England.

Isabella and Ferdinand did not meet until shortly before their wedding day. She escaped from Ocana on the pretext of visiting her mother in Arévalo, while he rode incognito across the border from Aragon.[21] They met at Valladolid in October 1469, over two hundred miles from Zaragoza. She would have seen a tall, thin youth with dark hair, full lips and a slight cast in one eye, but the story that she spotted him from a window and declared, 'That is he!'[22] is likely to be apocryphal. A portrait of him in middle age, painted by Isabella's favourite artist, the Flemish Michael Sittow, shows a fleshy-faced man with a large nose, narrow brown eyes and full cheeks. Chronicler Pulgar described him as having a friendly manner and unusual charm 'so that anyone who spoke with him at once loved him and desired to serve him', but he was also focused and ruthless, to the extent that Machiavelli would use him as a model for his infamous creation in *The Prince* in 1513. In a letter, the Renaissance politician described the king as 'more crafty and fortunate than wise and prudent' and believed him a perfect example of the concept of the ends justifying the means.[23]

Ferdinand was greeted by a short, curvaceous, red-haired young woman who was no great beauty but whose round face, plump cheeks and pursed red lips were by no means unattractive. Possibly the most famous portrait of Isabella, showing a young woman with long, rippling, red-gold hair, crowned and seated on a throne with a book open on her lap, has been attributed to Gerard David. David was certainly a contemporary of Isabella, being born in the mid-1450s in Utrecht, in the Netherlands, but the details of his early life are unclear. By 1484, he was working in Bruges and he certainly contributed to a book of hours presented to Isabella in 1496, and perhaps to another created in 1486, now held in the sixteenth-century Escorial Palace near Madrid. Yet there is no definite evidence that he ever travelled to Spain or saw Isabella in person, and his painting bears significant resemblance to those he painted of the Virgin Mary. His elegant young beauty may actually be more generic than realistic. Another portrait of Isabella, by Juan de Flanders, is more trustworthy as he was resident at the Spanish court from at least 1496, when he first appears on their records, and was promoted to court painter two years later. His Isabella is pale and sombre-faced, with blue eyes and a bowl of dark hair smoothed down either side of a centre parting, topped by a small cap. She wears a brown embroidered dress, with a white kerchief over her breast and necklace in the shape of a golden diamond with four grey-blue stones, perhaps pearls.

The ceremony took place at once, either in the chapel or great hall at the Palacio de los Vivero, the Palace of the Vivero family, in Valladolid on 19 October 1469. Technically, there were still certain obstacles remaining, although these were set aside with a certain laissez-faire indicative of their determination to succeed. The couple's affinity as descendants of John I of Castile required a papal dispensation, but it appears Isabella and Ferdinand were not prepared to wait for this, perhaps fearing Henry may intervene to prevent it being issued, or halt proceedings before it arrived. They went ahead using a forged document, with the name of the Pope given incorrectly as Pius II instead of Paul II. By 1469 Pius had been dead for five years, but the dispensation was accepted by Isabella's leading minister Pedro González de Mendoza, Bishop of Toledo. Perhaps they felt that, presented as a *fait accompli* with the union consummated, they were unlikely to be challenged. Yet as it was consciously done it was a triumph of personal power over canon law; not even the question of divine law was allowed to stand in their way. The couple were formally bedded before witnesses, to the sound of trumpets and drums, and the following morning the bloodied bedsheets were displayed in stark contrast to the scenes after Henry's two wedding nights. Her half-brother must have felt the intention.

Soon after the marriage Isabella dispatched a conciliatory letter to Henry, stating her loyalty and explaining the wisdom of the match, but the king was slow to respond other than in his confiscation of the town of Arévalo and its lucrative revenue, taking it from the dowager queen and giving it to the Count of Plasencia instead. It was the birth of Isabella's first child, a daughter named Isabella, on 9 October 1470 that prompted Henry to take hostile action, refuting Isabella's claim to the throne and reinstating Juana. His proclamation denounced Isabella as a dissolute woman who had acted against Castilian law to marry an enemy to whom she was closely related without a proper dispensation. Technically this was true, but Isabella replied that she had removed herself from Henry's immoral court, that she had acted on the advice of the country's nobles and had satisfied her conscience. Reconciliation did not take place until the end of 1473, when the pair met at Segovia, dined, sang together and rode through the streets side by side.

Now aged forty-nine, Henry had been ailing for a while, vomiting blood but rejecting the advice of his doctors, whom he considered to be incompetent. His end came swiftly, in December 1474, without him receiving the last rites or making a will. The news reached Isabella the following day and she acted swiftly and decisively. She was in Segovia, far from the court at Madrid, but she dispatched a letter containing instructions for the king's funeral and her own accession. Then she employed the persuasion of theatre to stage something of a 'rebirth' to mark her passage to queenship; dressed in the white of Spanish mourning, she processed to the Church of San Miguel and heard Mass for her brother before reappearing on a stage in the plaza to the sound of trumpets and drums, her funereal clothing replaced by the image of a queen in gold and colourful clothing, studded with jewels. All present were required to kneel before her and swear an oath of allegiance before she departed for the palace, riding under a canopy with the sword of state drawn before her. Just six days after Henry's death, the council met at Avila and approved her claim.

Even as a teenager Isabella displayed a rare political acumen, which led the statesmen of Castile to accept this technically invalid marriage and approve her claim to the throne over that of the girl who was technically their late king's heir. La Beltraneja was disinherited on the basis of rumour and her mother's behaviour, with the weight of support behind Isabella, whose parentage was not in doubt and whose character and abilities proved convincing. Yet in spite of Isabella's credentials and the approval of her council, La Beltraneja did not lack followers. Juana called on the help of her uncle Alfonso V of Portugal and he promptly invaded Castile and married the young girl, who was then thirteen. The question was decisively settled in 1476, when the armies of Isabella's new husband Ferdinand met the Portuguese at Toro, after which Juana's opposition crumbled. The new Queen of Castile was secure.

IV

By 1485, Isabella had borne five children, four of whom had survived. The eldest, Isabella, was then fifteen; John, or Juan, was seven; Juana, or Joanna, was six; and Maria was three. That autumn she entered the third trimester of her final pregnancy, but her focus was firmly on her duties as a queen, on politics and religion instead of the nursery. She was determined to pursue her aim of eradicating almost eight centuries of Moorish rule from her kingdoms, and so instead of retreating to await her confinement, Isabella seized the chance to attack the poorly defended town of Moclín, which she could use as a gateway to the Muslim stronghold of Granada. In September she installed her court in the ninth-century gothic castle at Baena, with its seven towers, and dispatched her general, the Count of Cabra, who had recently defeated and captured Sultan Muhammad of Granada, also known to the Castilians as Boabdil. There, feeling her child move, the queen watched the road to the south as she passed through the rocky mountains and river valleys. Her determination to continue in her role of warrior queen right up until the moment she gave birth was typical of Isabella and would also shape the attitude of the child she carried.

When news came, it was catastrophic. Cabra had attempted to take the town without waiting for the reinforcements promised by Isabella's husband, and instead had marched his men through the night into an ambush. Anticipating their arrival, the Moors had hidden in the hills surrounding the valley, armed with stones and poisoned arrows. Their sudden attack, followed by a charge down the hillside, led to a great slaughter of the Castilian troops. In the moonlight, Cabra's order to his armies to retreat came too late; at least 1,000 men lay dead and the rest were captured. The Spanish humanist and historian Hernando del Pulgar, who had been appointed royal chronicler by Isabella in 1481, wrote that she should thank God for having 'conquered more cities in three years than … any of the former kings acquired in two hundred'. But there was compensation for the military-minded queen. Before the end of the month, the couple had united their talents to achieve a victory. Ferdinand's armies laid siege to two Moorish castles near Jaén, supported by Isabella's meticulous planning and provisioning. There, on 27 September, the victorious king was reunited with his wife. Side by side, they rode in triumphant procession around the city. With the time of her lying-in approaching,

Isabella retired to the palace of Cardinal Mendoza at Alcalá de Henares. She delivered Catherine there on 16 December.

One of the most oft-repeated stories about Isabella is not the steely determination of her religious campaign but her refusal to admit to feeling pain during the ordeal of childbirth. Unable, as a woman, to lead her troops into battle, Isabella displayed her stoicism and bravery in the birth chamber instead, suffering with 'marvellous fortitude' and never complaining, according to her ladies.[24] There would have been little on offer for her in terms of pain relief, with the usual herbal and talismanic remedies offering more of a placebo effect; no doubt Isabella would have used prayer, religious artefacts and relics to focus during her ordeal. While monarchs across Europe tended to hope for the arrival of sons, a fourth daughter did not concern Isabella. The baby girl was received with 'great delight' and Cardinal Mendoza hosted a banquet in her honour.

Yet Isabella could not forget Moclín. Just seven months after giving birth, she launched a second campaign, gathering a huge army of 52,000 men[25] that stormed nearby Loja and Illora, before riding to meet her men in person. It was an occasion that perfectly illustrates the character of the woman who was to shape the mind of Catherine of Aragon: feminine yet strong, reflective yet active, learned yet theatrical, sexual yet virtuous, iconic yet accessible. In many ways, both women were a mass of paradoxes. Isabella enacted her own version of Elizabeth I's Tilbury speech, proving she had the heart and stomach of a king, a century before her grandson's armada was launched against the English. On a plain outside Moclín, she greeted her troops from the back of a chestnut mare which was trapped in crimson cloth with gold embroidery. The colours matched those of the queen, whose velvet Andalusian skirt, Moorish mantle and black hat trimmed with gold contributed to her iconic status as a great warrior queen, a descendant of the Trastámara line, a crusader in a holy war backed by the Pope, as venerable as the Virgin Mary. Even more than this, she was a real woman, who then removed her hat, shaking out her cascading red hair in front of the waiting men.[26] Three days later, Moclín fell. Isabella entered the city to witness the consecration of mosques as churches. According to a local legend, she and her husband gave the town a gift of a large cloth painting depicting Christ bearing the cross. Brought into the city amid a swathe of bloodshed, it later became renowned for its healing properties.

3

Childhood 1485–1492

I

A few details about baby Catherine's early life were recorded by Isabella's treasurer, Gonzalo de Baeza, in his *Libros de Asentios*, or account books. Baeza clearly kept copious records, as is shown by his frequent requests for *manos* (hands) of paper, which were fractions of reams. Soon after her arrival, Catherine was christened by the Bishop of Palencia, for which occasion she had a gown of white brocade trimmed with gold lace and lined with green velvet. When she was put down to sleep in her cot, on a brand-new mattress stuffed with two pounds of fresh cotton, she wore a nightgown of fine Olanda linen imported from Holland and lay her head upon a pillowcase of Breton naval linen. As she dreamed, the new royal baby was watched over by a maid, Elena de Carmona, who had a new bed set beside the cradle for the purpose. When Catherine woke, she was washed in a brass basin and sprinkled with perfume before being dressed in scarlet cloth from Florence.[1] She would be fed by a wet nurse, because European queens chose to resume their duties rather than tie themselves to a regular routine of breastfeeding.

And Isabella had considerable duties to attend to. Catherine was only few weeks old before her parents were on the move again. The Spanish court, although sometimes based in Madrid or

Segovia, was really a peripatetic establishment, following the king and queen and existing wherever they had cause to be. Usually women remained in confinement for around a month before rising for their churching ceremony. Isabella must have left her bed fairly swiftly, as she went from Alcalá de Henares, north-west to Arévalo and Madrigal de las Altas Torres, before turning south to the monastery at Guadalupe, a round trip of just under three hundred miles. The party arrived there during Lent and, with Easter Sunday falling on 4 April that year, it was a fairly punishing schedule for a woman who had just given birth. It is unclear whether or not baby Catherine was with her parents, as in the coming years she would sometimes travel with them and sometimes remain with a nurse. If she did accompany her family on this occasion, her nursery entourage would have gone too. Isabella stayed at Guadalupe, commissioning a new oratorio and hostelry, while Ferdinand went to lay siege to the Moors in Loja. Isabella was suffering from a fever when she wrote to him in May, mentioning that the children were well. This might have referred to her eldest daughter and son, or may indicate the presence of them all.

That June, when Catherine was six months old, we catch sight of her mother riding into the village of Illora. Lying just twenty miles to the west of the Muslim stronghold of Granada, and only ten miles from Moclín, it had just fallen to Ferdinand's armies. Entering newly conquered territory, Isabella knew she was inching closer and closer to her goal. Her husband rode out to meet her, dressed in yellow satin, a brocade robe, a crimson vest and plumed hat, holding the weapon of his enemies, the scimitar. Isabella had a retinue of around forty attendants. She rode a mule, which was the usual practice for women, on a richly gilded silver saddle, draped in embroidered golden satin. Her dress of velvet and brocade was topped by a scarlet cloak in the Muslim style and her hair was caught in a silk net, under a broad-brimmed black hat. From there, she and Ferdinand took their eldest daughter, the fifteen-year-old Princess Isabella, north to Santiago de Compostela, leaving Catherine and the younger children behind at Jaén. It is likely that the nursery entourage stayed in the Castillo de Santa Catalina (Castle of St Catherine), with its five defensive towers set on a hill overlooking the town. One of them contained a shrine to the fourth-century martyr St Catherine, famous for her death upon the wheel and central to the medieval cult of virginity. It would have been an appropriate location for the young Catherine, Juana and Maria, with writers such as Christine de Pisan lauding the saint as an exemplar for girls.

The entire family were together at Córdoba the following March, once one of the largest cities in Europe, reclaimed from the Moors back in the thirteenth century. It was to be their base as Ferdinand laid siege to Vélez-Málaga, and when it surrendered at the end of April Isabella again went to join him, leaving the children behind. Catherine was then fifteen months old, probably taking her first steps in the Alcázar de los Reyes Cristianos (Castle of the Christian Monarchs), with its complex of Moorish courtyards and gardens. The spring weeks passed for the children in their nursery routine of play, food and sleep, with Juana, aged seven, and Maria, aged four, undertaking their lessons, perhaps reading and writing a little. Young Catherine might have joined them in their prayers, learning how to place her small hands devoutly together and concentrating upon the rhythm of the words. Then the news reached the castle of an assassination attempt made upon their parents. A Muslim holy man had mistaken two members of the royal court for the king and queen and had attempted to attack them with a dagger. Ferdinand was sleeping at the time, and Isabella was not present. The assassin was immediately dispatched but it served as a reminder of the danger of their situation, and that despite their power, success and all the shows of majesty they could muster, Catherine's parents were still only human. In the autumn, another threat arose when plague arrived in Córdoba. Mindful of her brother's death, Isabella lost no time in relocating her family. The nursery was packed up and the girls travelled almost thirty miles east to Montoro.

Catherine's early years were spent in an atmosphere of education, religion and the strength of her parents' collaboration. There is no question that Ferdinand and Isabella fell deeply in love and enjoyed a passionate relationship, or that they were a very efficient team. They complemented each other with their differences, just as the deaf Castilian Teresa de Cartagena wrote that men and women were designed to, in a proto-feminist poem around the time of their birth. In 1488, nineteen years after their wedding, royal chaplain Pedro Martir commented that Isabella and Ferdinand were two separate and mortal bodies 'animated by one spirit and one mind'.[2]

Their motto, '*Tanta monta, monta tanta*', translating as 'equal opposites in balance' or 'each is worth the other', was embroidered on Isabella's clothing.[3] As a further sign of their unity, the pair had commissioned their joint arms, featuring a crowned eagle, a symbol of power that began to appear on municipal buildings from around 1475. It proved to be a recurring motif, forming the subject of a sermon delivered by Talavera in the year of Catherine's birth, with the bird as a metaphor for royal virtues and renewals, as well as being the symbol of one of Isabel's chosen saints, John the Evangelist. Catherine would have been used to seeing the eagle symbol, on buildings, shields and coins; she would also have been accustomed to her mother's bundle of arrows, or 'flechas', featuring alongside the letter 'F', and Ferdinand's yoke, or 'yugo' with the letter 'Y', which began his wife's name in Spanish.[4] When Catherine was six, they added the symbol of the pomegranate, or *granada*, following their conquest of the city of that name. A decade later, their daughter chose it as her personal device.

As a baby, Catherine's daily contact would have been with her wet nurse and governess, but very quickly her mother would have become the most influential person in her life, frequently present while Ferdinand was campaigning, and an enthralling presence. Outside the heavens themselves, there can hardly have been a female role model to whose example the growing princess could aspire. The deference of their contemporaries only added to the prestige of Catherine's mother. Historian and teacher Pedro Martir asked rhetorically, 'Beyond the Virgin Mary, mother of God, what other woman could you point to among all those that the church venerates in the catalogue of saints who [exceeds] her mercy, purity and virtue?'[5] Lofty in her bearing, the queen rejected the fashions and make-up of other court women, reminiscent as it was of the reign of the disgraced Juana, but when the need arose she was well able to outshine them all in a show of majesty, dazzling in cloth of gold and large jewels. Jeronimo Munzer, who visited Spain in 1494–5, described the discrepancy between Isabella's personal charms and her warlike nature: according to him, she had an 'agreeable countenance' and was deeply devout, spending 'great amounts of money' on gifts to churches, and of such 'a sweet disposition that one would struggle in vain to sing the praises that her virtues deserved'. Munzer praised her knowledge of the arts of peace and war. Her confessor, Fray Hernando de Talavera, described her as being a 'very wise Deborah in her counsel, her help and her intervention' and 'like another very beautiful Judith with her petitions and prayers raised to God'.[6] Even before her marriage, Martin Alonso de Cordoba had dedicated his *Jardin de las nobles Doncellas*, or *Garden of Noble Maidens*, to Isabella, commissioned by her mother Isabel, which gives a history of women, followed by an outline of their virtues, providing literary and biblical examples of good wives, mothers and rulers. Isabella was clearly in possession of considerable talents, both natural and acquired, and her contemporaries saw her as the successor of this female legacy. It was a role that the queen embraced, seeking wherever possible to facilitate the learning and cultural exchanges of both Spanish and, more generally, European women.

II

While planning a suitable education for her children, Isabella focussed upon completing a programme of study of her own. Regretting her own shortcomings, she engaged for herself a Latin tutor, Beatriz Galíndez, known as La Latina, an erudite and exceptional scholar, understanding that a knowledge of the language was key to female participation in the academic world. For decades, humanist debate had sought to clarify the role of women in society, manifesting a literary genre known as the *querelle des femmes*; those females able to participate were largely an exceptional educated elite, but many and most went silent or retired upon marriage. Nowhere was this truer than in the life of Venetian-born Cassandra Fedele, with whom Isabella entered into a correspondence. Born in 1465, Fedele had been taught Latin by her enlightened father, who also arranged tuition for her in Greek, philosophy, logic and natural sciences. While still very young, and considered something of a prodigy, she lectured at the University of Padua and to the Venetian Senate and Doge, four of her lectures being published in a single volume when she was twenty-two. Her extensive correspondence included heads of European states, university chancellors and other Renaissance thinkers; Isabella encouraged the possibility that Fedele might take up an academic position in Spain, or join her court, but her early biographers claim she was forced to refuse as the Doge forbade her from emigrating.[7] There was also Juana de Mendoza, the wardrobe mistress of the queen's eldest daughter, Isabella, who was a patron of the arts, with a reputation for her erudition and frequently the recipient of poetic dedications. While the fertile exchange of ideas resulted in the movements of men across Europe, it was a different story for women.

The queen also established a school of Classics within her palace and donated much of her library to it, in an attempt to educate young noblemen and women, albeit probably in separate classes. From 1492, Pedro Martir was put in charge of overseeing the pupils. Prince Juan's tutor, Fray Diego Deza, came from the University of Salamanca to teach the pupils, as did the historian and classicist Lucio Marineo Siculus, along with other Spanish and Italian humanist scholars, but there were also female teachers, including the philosopher and linguist Cecilia Marello, the mathematician Alvara de Alba and the classicist and Erasmus disciple Isabel de Vergara. The royal chronicler Pulgar related how Isabella brought high-born orphaned girls to court to be educated, then married them off 'to learned men'.[8] The Spanish philosopher Juan Luis Vives, who would later be closely connected with Catherine and would travel to England at her request, attended a similar school in his native Valencia. New statutes drawn up there in 1499 outlined a curriculum of grammar, logic, natural and moral philosophy, metaphysics, canon and civil law, poetry and 'other subjects such as the city desires and requires'.[9] His description of the atmosphere there captures the mood of impassioned debate that characterised the Renaissance:

> Even the youngest scholars are accustomed never to keep silence; they are always asserting vigorously whatever comes uppermost to their minds, lest they should seem to be giving up the dispute. Nor does one disputation, or even two a day prove sufficient, as for instance at dinner. They wrangle at breakfast; they wrangle after breakfast; they wrangle before supper and they wrangle after supper. At home they dispute, out of doors they dispute. They wrangle over their food, in the bath, in the sweating room, in the church, in the town, in the country, in public, in private. At all times they are wrangling.[10]

Catherine would have benefitted from the existence of this elite royal school, perhaps taking part in it, even if she did not directly participate in every lesson. Historians have recognised Isabella's patronage of education as a significant marker in the path of the Renaissance, as there had never before 'been such a numerous and select retinue of ladies under previous sovereigns' and 'the fuller participation of women was one of the chief differences of the Spanish Renaissance'.[11] This sparked a trend for the establishment of '*colegios de doncellas*' or schools for girls, with Galíndz founding one in Madrid and Cardinal Ciseros starting another in Alcalá de Henares.[12] Isabella was preparing her daughters to take leading roles in a changing world, where they needed to be at least the equals of their male peers, and perhaps even their superiors.

Catherine studied Latin, history, civil and canon law, Scripture, classical and devotional literature, along with the courtly pursuits of riding, hunting and falconry; her education also took in weaving, spinning, sewing and embroidery, dancing, music, drawing and cooking. It was her mother's practice of sewing Ferdinand's shirts by her own hand that inspired Catherine to do the same for her future husband. The princess also benefitted from her mother's patronage of a number of practical manuals. Such books followed the joint ideals of humanism and the Renaissance for personal self-improvement, by which individuals could aspire to become more like the Italian concept of the '*uomo universale*', learned and ready for any situation. In particular, Antonio de Nebrija's *Introduction to Latin* and his *Castilian Grammar*, along with Alonso de Palencia's *Universal Vocabulary in Latin and in Romance*, were aimed at the ladies at Isabella's court, including her daughters.[13]

The royal couple made the Spanish court into a hub for humanist thinkers of both genders but it also helped to nurture them. The Catalan poet Juan Boscán was the son of a court official and benefitted from the humanist syllabus offered by Ferdinand and Isabella's school. Born in 1490, he was inspired by Siculus' teaching and introduced the Petrarchan poetic form into Spain, going on to translate Baldassare Castiglione's *Book of the Courtier* into Spanish. Two more sons of court officials were Hernán Núnez de Toledo y Guzmán and Garscilaso de la Vega, who may have been Guzman's nephew, being the son of Sancha de Guzman and Pedro Suarez de

Figueroa. Hernan was born in 1475, educated at Valladolid and Bologna, devoting himself to the study of ancient literature. He was recruited by Cisneros to work on a project undertaken by the University of Alcalá, a Complutensian polyglot Bible intended to revive the study of the Scriptures, which ran from 1502 until the publication of six hundred copies in 1514. In addition, he wrote a glossary of Mena's poem, the *Laberinto de Fortuna*, which had lauded Castilian superiority. Vega was twenty-five years his junior and pursued a military career despite his talent for poetry. His work was published by Juan Boscan after his premature death from injuries sustained in battle.

Ferdinand and Isabella sought teachers for their children and pupils from among graduates from the University of Salamanca, as well as for the administration of Spanish territories in the New World. One in particular would have been a familiar figure to Catherine while she was growing up. Francisco Ximenes (or Jimenes) de Cisneros graduated in Law from the University of Salamanca in the 1460s but then followed a religious calling and became a Franciscan friar. He became Isabella's confessor on invitation in 1492 and led an ascetic life at court, being promoted to Bishop of Toledo in 1495 and given a commission to examine all the clergy under the aegis of the Inquisition. He took a reforming view of the Church, wanting it to have a fresh start, led by meritocracy and devotion rather than the old aristocratic network. In 1499 he founded the University of Alcala as a base for training these future leaders, forming an alternative capital of culture and education alongside the religious centre of Toledo and the political one in Madrid. He was known for his extreme piety, living as an anchorite, sleeping on the bare floor, wearing a hair shirt and doubling his fasts, as well as his inflexibility towards heretics who would not convert. His extreme practices impressed Isabella, and probably her young daughter too.

By 1490, Catherine's eldest sister, Isabella, was nineteen years old. She was probably the closest to her mother of all the children, having been her only child for eight years and frequently travelling with her on campaign. Her future had already been decided for a decade, when the Treaty of Alcáçovas had been signed with Portugal following the end of the conflict with Juana la Beltraneja. This not only settled the War of the Castilian Succession by the placing of Juana in a convent, but it resolved disputes over territories such as the Canary Islands and Azores, and the control of the seas divided between Spain and Portugal. The young princess had been betrothed to Alfonso, son and heir of King John II, who was five years younger than her. The princess had even spent three years in her childhood living in the Portuguese town of Moura with Alfonso, under the regime of his grandmother Beatrice, Duchess of Viseu, who was a daughter of Isabel of Barcelos and thus Queen Isabella's aunt. However, the princess had returned home to Castile before Catherine's birth. Although Ferdinand and Isabella attempted to substitute another of their daughters for Isabella in the marriage plans, wanting to keep her with them as their heir, the Portuguese would not agree. Arrangements were made for the wedding to take place, and the four-year-old Catherine would have watched them unfold.

Queen Isabella was not prepared to let her daughter go without a costly show of magnificence and power. In May there was a two-week public festival, with pageants and jousting. Knights from all across Spain attended and the Castilian-Aragonese courtiers were dressed in cloth of gold and coloured silks. A proxy wedding ceremony was held in Seville's Cathedral of Santa Maria de la Sede on Easter Sunday, officiated by Cardinal Mendoza, with the royal women dressed in gold, studded with jewels and accompanied by a train of seventy ladies-in-waiting and a multitude of torchbearers. The cathedral was almost complete, after a lengthy building programme that had started far back in 1411. With the nave, stalls, east end and doorway all in place, it was about to become the largest cathedral in the world. The celebrations were probably divided between the site and the thirteenth-century Archbishop's Palace located on its north-eastern side, with the city draped in silk banners and flowers.[14] Catherine would have been present, dressed in similar finery. Isabella finally departed with nine female attendants that November, riding with her parents and brother John to Córdoba, before Cardinal Mendoza took her to the Portuguese border. Pulgar's chronicle relates that the princess's trousseau included dozens of gowns made from velvet, silk and brocade, fifty linen chemises, twenty brocade coats, six silk robes 'edged with pearls and encrusted with gold', silk-threaded tapestries, beds and other items of clothing and furniture, to the tune of 5.3 million maravedís.[15] Some 1,500 mules and oxen were required to carry it all to her future home.

The wedding took place at the fourteenth-century royal palace in Évora, to which a new wing and gardens were added for the occasion. A Portuguese chronicler, Garcia de Resende, related the details of splendid celebrations, including banquets at brocade-covered tables where the guests were served roast peacock and roast mutton carried in on golden carts. There was dancing and jousting, and a dumb show, or mummery, where Isabella's father-in-law, King John, dressed as the Knight of the Swan, entering the hall in a pageant of a ship, affixed with waves and foam made of painted cloth. Rigged with gold and silk and bearing sails of purple and white, the ship carried flags bearing the arms of the newly-weds.[16]It was a dazzling start to the wedding.

Just eight months later, disaster struck. The Portuguese royal family had been visiting Santarem, situated on the bank of the River Tagus, along which the sixteen-year-old Alfonso was riding when he was thrown from his horse. By some accounts they were hunting, although in his 1846 *A History of Portugal*, J. M. Neale describes how it was the custom to bathe in the river in the evening, and when Alfonso was reluctant to join his father in the river they rode a race instead.[17] A contemporary chronicle written by Portuguese Rui de Pina included the detail that the boy was dragged along under the horse, while Neale states it fell on him. He adds that Alfonso was carried into the hut of a fisherman, while his mother and wife came rushing down from the nearby palace. Isabella's grief was intense. She may have interpreted it as divine punishment for religious policies pursued by her parents or by Portugal. She cut off her long hair, refused to eat and would only wear sackcloth and a veil. Isabella and Ferdinand hurried to meet her at Illora, dressed in deep mourning, to bring her home. Catherine would have noticed the difference between the beautiful, happy young woman to whom they had recently bid farewell and this quiet, colourless and withdrawn widow. It was a harsh lesson that even the happiest of marriages between two young people, made as a result of long-term plans, might go so terribly wrong.

III

Spain was changing in other ways, too. Catherine's early years were to witness the paradox of dark acts of faith taking place alongside the illumination of the Renaissance. The country had always been a religious melting pot, reflecting centuries of Muslim occupation in the architecture of every town, in their history, cuisine, art and the golden jewellery and ornaments favoured by the royals. Back in the eighth century the invading Moors had been welcomed by Spanish Jews, who had fought alongside them, adopting Arabic words and numerals, seeing their homeland as a place of opportunity and tolerance. The eleventh-century Alfonso VI of Castile had even incurred the wrath of the Pope because of his favouritism of the Jews, 40,000 of whom fought for him at the Battle of Sagrajas, while Alfonso VIII angered the nobility in the following century through his love affair with a beautiful Jewess. But by 1485 the country was on the brink of religious apocalypse. The actions of Catherine's parents raise some challenging questions for modern readers, but must be interpreted within the context of their times and as an influence upon their daughter's faith.

Over the years, Ferdinand and Isabella had been inching closer to the city of Granada. The capital of an autonomous region in the south, stretching along the coastline facing North Africa, it had been occupied by the Moors since the eighth century, but Muslims, Jews, Christians and others lived alongside each other in harmony. They also benefitted from a certain cultural sophistication and municipal advantages well ahead of their time. In the early medieval period, the nearby city of Córdoba was the most modern city in Europe, boasting streetlights that extended over ten miles of raised pavements, and almost a thousand public baths. There were at least seventy public libraries in Moorish Spain, housing thousands of manuscripts of philosophy, chemistry, physics, mathematics and other topics. One by one, Jaén, Baza, Moclín, Loja, Marbella and Vélez-Málaga fell, but in 1489, after the captures of Baza, Almería and Guadix, Isabella and Ferdinand were finally at the gates of Granada.

That June, Isabella and her children arrived at Los Ojos de Huécar, the location on the outskirts of the city where Ferdinand had encamped his army. Catherine would have helped them celebrate her brother John's thirteenth birthday, a coming-of-age for which he was knighted by his father and received a chainmail coat, helmet and dagger, along with a symbolic twelve doubloons.[18] Catherine also travelled with her mother and siblings to the village of Zubia, where she issued the Duke of Cadiz with orders and observed the city properly for the first time. Shortly afterwards, the family had a lucky escape when the royal tents caught alight and most of their camp burned to the ground. Catherine would have remembered being woken in the early hours, with the flames being fanned by strong wind, and her father, wielding his sword, hurrying them all to safety in their nightshirts. When the tents were replaced in the coming days by houses made of brick and tile, the watching Granadans knew the Christian army did not intend to give up.

The last ruler of the city, Emir Muhammad XII, Abí Abdilehi, known to the Christians as Boabdil, had little choice but to negotiate. From October 1491, terms of surrender were drawn up. The city was to surrender peacefully after a term of forty days, with five hundred people, the children and siblings of the important leaders of the town, being held as hostages for a period of ten days to ensure there were no deceptions or violence. The residents were encouraged to relocate to Africa, being offered free and safe passage on seven ships for their families and all their movable goods, including 'merchandise, jewels, gold, silver and all types of weapons'. Islamic laws, customs and places of worship were to be respected and, significantly, 'no Moor shall be forced to become a Christian against his will'.[19] The official surrender took place on 2 January 1492.

Isabella, Ferdinand and their children made a formal entrance together into the city four days later. They made for its citadel of power, the fourteenth-century palace of the Alhambra, built on top of an old Roman site out of red clay and white alabaster stucco work in the elegant filigree and ornamentation of the Mudéjar style. It was essentially a small city in itself, with several palaces, halls, towers, bath houses with hot and cold running water, gardens full of lemons and myrtles, courtyards, pools and irrigation systems. Inside, Catherine would have walked through rooms decorated with calligraphy and arabesques, dark wood and colourful carved panels. She would have found shady gardens with marble columns and alabaster basins, where white marble fountains spurted water on the hour, overhung by the filigree work of pavilions and beautiful mosaic patterns underfoot. There was a great reception hall in the shape of a square, projecting out of the palace walls, giving views over the city on three sides. A grand throne, recently vacated by the last emir, sat reproachfully under the domed ceiling, which stretched up seventy-five feet above their heads. Catherine and her family gazed about in wonder. That day they only explored, returning to the Spanish camp; their first night in the palace would not be until April. Isabella's royal court chaplain, Juan de Anchieta, composed a Mass upon the city's surrender.

Isabella appointed her royal confessor, the graduate of Salamanca University Fernando de Talavera, as Archbishop of Granada, with the aim to gently encourage conversion of those who remained. This was a long-term, slow process based in education, but by 1499, Cisneros, Bishop of Toledo, had lost patience with this method, and under the aegis of the Inquisition began a program of 'miraculous conversions' and forced baptisms. The terms of the peaceful, respectful Alhambra Decree had lasted only seven years. This course was widely approved by that great admirer of Ferdinand's, Niccolò Machiavelli, who saw Ferdinand's religious message as a screen to his political ambition, a cynical tool for self-advancement: 'A prince still reigning whom it would not be fitting for me to name, never talks of anything but peace and good faith, yet he had ever observed either he would have several times observed his credit and his faith.'[20] Ferdinand might have typified the realpolitik of Renaissance rule but actions such as these raise difficult questions for modern historians.

In the same year that Granada fell, Ferdinand and Isabella became determined to convert the Jews among their subjects to Christianity and establish a new, 'pure' Jerusalem on Spanish soil. Like their slow encircling of Muslim territories, this was the culmination of years of segregation. The facts are difficult to read today. Driven by a pious fervour, they were absolute in their mission, forcing the Jews into ghettos from as early as 1480 onwards, compelling some to leave the country and others to buy their freedom, while those who did convert were still regarded with suspicion and hostility. The papal inquisition had already been established in Castile, but in 1478 Isabella and Ferdinand gained permission from Pope Sixtus IV to appoint their own inquisitors, beginning a reign of terror by which anyone of suspicious bloodline was identified and arrested, enduring torture and imprisonment that could last for years.

The accused were forced to testify without legal representation, without being informed of the charges against them, and a refusal to cooperate was considered tantamount to an admission of guilt. While the Dominican Friars running the Inquisition officially 'forgave' those charged, they were then passed on to the State, which was less lenient. Many endured horrific *autos-da-fé* or acts of faith, public deaths by burning or garrotting.

Ironically, it was a descendant of converted Jews, Tomás de Torquemada, who was appointed first Inquisitor General for Castile in 1483. Described by one historian as an 'inhuman' zealot, it has been estimated that Torquemada was responsible for the deaths of between 2,000 and 9,000 'suspects' by formal execution, with a further 100,000 perishing in his dungeons.[21] The nephew of a theologian who had written in defence of the '*conversios*' in Rome, Torquemada had been Isabella's confessor when she was a child living at Henry's court in Segovia, and wrote his own rules for the Inquisition to follow, the *Instrucciones*, completed in 1486. In turn, it was Torquemada who employed the man whose assassination sparked a swell of popular support in favour of the Inquisition and a backlash against the Jews. The crucial event took place just months before Catherine's birth, in September 1485, when the Priest Pedro de Arbués, the Head Inquisitor of Aragon, was killed while kneeling in prayer in the cathedral of Zaragoza. The building itself was a symbol of religious oppression and duality: having once been a mosque, it retained the typical filigree and ornament of the Mudéjar style, with recent archaeology suggesting the ghost of a domed minaret, removed upon its conversion to Catholicism in 1121. The Inquisition had been received in Aragon as an attack upon local values and the mutual tolerance that had existed between two such interconnected cultures, but this shocking death was met with cries that Arbués was a martyr and sparked riots that led to the deaths of at least twenty Aragonese Jews in retaliation. Arbués' canonisation in 1867 remains controversial.

Catherine was six when the decisive blow was struck. Torquemada and his bishops drew up a decree ordering all Jews to leave Spain within four months, upon pain of death, because of the 'evil and harmful' acts they practised daily. Ferdinand and Isabella signed it on 31 March, as the culmination of their policy to curb what they saw as the social and political influence of the Jews. The specific threat they believed was being posed was that of the conversion of Christians to Judaism, the apostasy and 'subverting and stealing' of faithful Christians as a deliberate policy. Isabella and Ferdinand had been informed by agents of the Inquisition that 'great injury has resulted and still results' because the Jews were holding meetings to teach their faith, were distributing religious books and advocating that Christians should observe certain festivals and practices, such as the circumcision of male children. They were also sharing unleavened bread and 'meats ritually slaughtered' from their homes and had been successful 'according to the weakness of our humanity and by diabolical astuteness'.[22] In other words, the Jews were welcoming and teaching those who expressed an interest in converting to their faith, either willingly or as part of the Inquisition's methods to entrap. Yet Christians in Spain actively encouraged, even demanded, the same behaviour on their terms: the conversion of people of different faiths, employing a similar method of sharing information, holy texts and teachings, to bring their new followers to the light.

It is anachronistic and futile to raise questions of hypocrisy and tolerance here. To the Catholic monarchs, their conviction and their duty were absolute. Catholicism was the only true faith and all others were damned; there was no room for such modern concepts as tolerance, their mission was to serve God through this process of cleansing, to protect their faith and save the souls of the damned through enforced conversion. If that failed, the only path to redemption was through fire. As far removed as this may seem from the liberal values of the twenty-first century, it underscores how completely were Isabella and Ferdinand the embodiment of their times, but also that such views have resurfaced in every century since their lifetimes, and still have a foothold in the modern world. This religious absolutism, this utter immersion in one's faith and crusading devotion, this conviction of salvation and the desire to convert, coupled with the sense of regal majesty and the complete refusal to compromise, formed an essential part of Catherine's childhood. Her parents were nothing less than God's missionaries, with a direct personal connection to the divine and answerable only to Him, fighting in His name.

The only remedy, according to the edict, was to 'prohibit all interaction between the said Jews and Christians', so they ordered 'all Jews and Jewesses ... along with their sons and daughters, menservants and maidservants, Jewish familiars, those who are great as well as the lesser folk, of whatever age they may be, to depart and never to return'.[23] Some elected to remain and undergo baptism and conversion, but as a result of the Alhambra Decree up to 300,000 left Spain in 1492, heading to refuge in France, Germany, Morocco and the Ottoman Empire. Their property and fortunes were confiscated and their synagogues were destroyed or adapted for alternative uses, with only three surviving in Spain that date from this period.[24] Once the deadline had passed, the Inquisitors stepped up their campaign against those who had professed to renounce their faith, claiming that they could be identified by a difference in smell, while their houses were searched for non-kosher foods and they were forced to eat ham. This was by no means an isolated incident. If anything, the Jews in Spain had escaped a more widespread European anti-Semitism that had led to their expulsion from England in 1290. Persecution had been spreading since they had been scapegoated for the proliferation of the plague in 1348–9, triggering attacks in Seville in 1391. They were evicted from France in 1394, Austria in 1421, Provence in 1430 and Lithuania in 1445. This reminds us just how far Catherine, her parents, her future husbands and subjects were products of their time, a critical difference that modern historians and readers must bear in mind at all times.

IV

1492 was to be a significant year for Spain. The crusading zeal of Catherine's parents extended beyond the walls of the Alhambra and the racial cleansing of the Jews. On 13 July, they signed a deal with Alonso Fernández de Lugo for the conquest of the final remaining Canary Islands, La Palma and Tenerife, which he would take in 1493 and 1496. Just three weeks later, though, on 3 August 1492, Christopher Columbus set sail across the Atlantic with a crew of a hundred in three ships, caravels named the *Nina*, the *Pinta* and the *Santa Maria*. His mission was to find a passage to India and China by sailing west, rather than east. Six weeks later, as supplies were running low, they sighted land and, on 12 October, set foot on an island in the Bahamas, which he named

San Salvador, or 'Holy Saviour', later known as Watling Island. It was five miles wide and thirteen miles long and, tantalisingly, only around three hundred nautical miles from the tip of Florida. As Columbus discovered, the island was already inhabited by peaceful and vulnerable natives adorned with gold jewellery, whom he might easily conquer and govern with fifty men. He recorded in his diary that 'they ought to make good and skilled servants, for they repeat very quickly whatever we say to them. I think they can very easily be made Christians.' Indeed, he acted on this notion, taking six natives back to Spain with him as slaves. After San Salvador, he landed on Cuba, Haiti (Hispaniola) and the Dominican Republic.

A year after his departure, Columbus returned to Spain and visited Ferdinand and Isabella's court. Catherine may have been present to hear his extraordinary tales about the 'Indies': of islands and savages who believed the explorers were Gods, of hurricanes and ships swept apart by the tides, of exotic fruit and spices, parrots and strange flowers, of sunsets over Haiti and the quest for gold. To her parents, his stories were a sort of divine justification, confirmation of their position and favour in God's eyes. In one earlier letter to him, they wrote, 'We have taken much pleasure in learning whereof you write, and that God gave such a result to your labours, and well guided you in what you commenced, whereof He will be well served and we also.'[25] Columbus travelled in procession to the court, drawing great crowds to see the natives he had enslaved, with their golden ornaments and painted bodies, and the exotic specimens and trays of cotton and gold. His hosts took the unusual step of allowing him to be seated in their company, in order to recount his travels and answer their many questions, a process which took hours. He remained with them in Barcelona for weeks as an honoured royal guest, hunting with Ferdinand and feasting. Pedro Martir described him as having 'given light to the hidden half of the world'. As he began to plan his second voyage, Catherine's parents rewarded him with titles and rights, including a new personal coat of arms which displayed the Castilian castle and lion in gold and purple. Their reception of the explorer was one example of the way that Ferdinand and Isabella interpreted everything within the context of their faith, whether success or failure, as part of their wider Christian mission.

And it seemed that in the early 1490s God was very pleased with his Spanish crusaders.

The triumphant Ferdinand and Isabella were at the height of their powers. However, their conquests in the New World may have been responsible for one unwelcome arrival in Spain that was to have far-reaching consequences. It seems to be more than coincidental that the first cases of syphilis were recorded in Spain. A bacterial disease that is transmitted through sexual contact, or from mother to foetus, it develops from lesions and ulcers to a rash and fevers before the tertiary stage, in which the nervous system comes under attack. Ultimately it can prove fatal. Not a single case was recorded in Europe before 1492, and no evidence of it has been found on any bodies exhumed dating to before that time. It may have been brought back by the sailors returning from the New World, China or India, but there is no evidence of it there either. The first cases were recorded in Barcelona in 1493 according to a physician who treated them, and in 1494 the French army suffered an outbreak while besieging Naples. In 1497, Pope Alexander VI's physician described the treatment of seventeen cases, calling it 'the French disease', while a year later, a Latin humanist poet called it '*las buvas*', an illness with genital sores.[26] Edicts issued by the town council of Aberdeen in 1497 show that the 'Naples Sickness' had spread as far north as Scotland by then.

Young Catherine may have been on campaign with her parents but she would have been brought up carefully, shielded from such sexual dangers and scandals. And there were many to shield her from, right under her nose and as part of her parents' policies. Isabella and Ferdinand used prostitution as a political tool to reward their loyal servants, giving them the right to own or control a brothel. In 1486, they rewarded the loyal service of Alonso Yanez Fajardo '*el putero*' (the pimp) with the control of all the bordellos in unconquered Granada, six years before they actually took the city. In total he held the title of Lord of the Brothels for a decade.[27] Prostitutes who operated openly were favoured over those who worked in secret but there were advantages to each. When the king and queen imposed a tax upon all members of the profession in 1476, those private workers had to pay twice the amount of their counterparts, but they did not have to live in penury, renting a room in a brothel, buying their own food and clothing at whatever price the house's owner might set. Some brothels were granted by Ferdinand and Isabella to religious houses so that they might use the proceeds for the maintenance and operation of their holy work.[28]

There were scandals within her parents' marriage too. Devoted as Ferdinand was to Isabella, this did not prevent him from indulging in other women. This did not sit well with Isabella, who according to Pulgar was 'jealous beyond all bounds'; if she thought his eye had landed upon any woman at court 'with a betrayal of desire', she would discreetly have them removed from office. Ferdinand largely kept his amours out of sight, but he did father a handful of illegitimate children, who were sometimes brought to court and publicly acknowledged. His son Alfonso was born in 1470, to a Catalan noblewoman named Aldonza Ruis de Ivorra, given a humanist education and appointed as Archbishop of Zaragoza at the age of five. Two of Ferdinand's daughters by the name of Maria entered nunneries, while Juana of Aragon, born around 1471, married Bernardino Velasco, Duke of Frias, and bore him a daughter. With these illegitimate children often at court in the company of the queen, young Catherine may have been aware of their true identities. She would also have seen how her mother maintained her regal façade in public and turned a blind eye.

4

Negotiations 1489–1499

I

Plans for Catherine's marriage started early. As far back as the spring of 1489, Ferdinand and Isabella had received a delegation sent by Henry VII of England, seeking her as a bride for his son. That March, the royal family were at the castle of Medino del Campo, a red, blockish medieval fortress situated on a mound dominating the town, to hear the culmination of a year's worth of offers and promises, conditions and stipulations, about the futures of two small children. Catherine was then three years old, a small, sturdy princess with auburn hair who was accustomed to travel, having been brought up half on the road and half in the magnificent Mudéjar interiors of hill-top castles. Her prospective husband was barely out of the cradle. Henry VII's eldest son, Arthur, was the first-born child of a new dynasty, and nine months Catherine's junior at two and a half. Yet his position, and that of his parents, was a precarious thing.

For decades England had been torn apart by civil war, with the Lancastrian descendants of Edward III pitted against their cousins who believed that their senior line of inheritance had been usurped. The last Yorkist king, Richard III, had been killed in battle four months before Catherine's birth, and the victor of the famous encounter at Bosworth Field had been crowned as the first Tudor monarch. The lean, ascetic Henry Tudor was then twenty-seven, a shrewd and cautious man who had been in exile half his life. The only child of a short-lived marriage, his mother, Margaret, just like Isabella herself, was the great-granddaughter of John of Gaunt, while his father was the product of a secret marriage made by the mother of Henry VI to her Welsh squire Owen Tudor. Born when his mother was just thirteen years old, Henry had been forced to flee England at a similar age, only returning at the head of an invasion fleet. Within six months of his victory at Bosworth he had taken as his wife the beautiful Yorkist princess Elizabeth, whose first son had arrived in September 1486, half York and half Lancaster. It was a big legacy, especially considering the additional dimension Henry added by naming him Arthur, deploying the popular legends of the once and future king, the son of a white queen and red king. Henry had even arranged for his birth to take place at Winchester, where the round table commissioned by Edward III still hung. Much was expected of this prince.

At first it seemed that the weather was against the match taking place. Unless the English ambassadors were prepared to take the laborious land route across a hostile France, they had to brave the Channel, followed by the Celtic Sea around the tip of Brittany, and finally the famously extreme conditions of the Bay of Biscay. Thomas Savage, a doctor of law, and Sir Richard Nanfan, newly knighted by King Henry, endured three false starts to their trip due to terrible winds buffeting the south coast. Tossed about on the waves, they had been forced to turn back twice before embarking from Falmouth on 12 February, but although they crossed the Channel safely, their ordeal was not yet over. As they approached the Spanish coast, the weather was so extreme that those aboard expected to be drowned and fell to their knees on deck to pray for their salvation. When the ship finally limped into Laredo, a small port between Santander and Bilbao, a heavy snowstorm kept them prisoner for a week and they found lodgings difficult to procure. The final stage of their journey was across the mountainous terrain of northern Spain, taking them over two hundred miles directly south. After this less than auspicious start, Savage and Nanfan finally arrived at Medina del Campo on 14 March. It was not until the evening that they were admitted to the presence of Isabella and Ferdinand, accompanied by torchbearers through the falling dusk across the drawbridge and through the archway into the courtyard, from where they were led into the hall.

What struck the ambassadors as they entered was the dazzling display of gold. 'The Kings', as they referred to Ferdinand and Isabella, were seated under a canopy bearing their coat of arms, resplendent in the royal colour. Catherine's mother shone in a dress of gold cloth covered in jewels, with a red satin cloak and black velvet collar slashed with gold and more gems, suspended from which were ribbons bearing more stones including a huge ruby, 'a thing so rich no man has ever seen the equal'. Around her neck was a necklace, again made from gold, featuring enamelled red and white roses and a single huge jewel in the centre. Her hair was pulled back under a gold net. Her visitors were no strangers to finery, with Savage having been appointed as Henry VII's chancellor of the earldom of March and royal chaplain, and Nanfan being Sheriff of Worcestershire. In a letter to Henry they estimated that the queen's clothing cost around 200,000 crowns, but, as Isabella defended herself to her confessor, who had objected to the extravagance, the cost was nothing beside the political message: it was her costume of state, designed to impress the King of England. And impress it did. At her side, Ferdinand matched Isabella's opulence in a long golden gown trimmed with fur. That first evening, the ambassadors delivered dispatches from the King of England, and Dr Savage made a long oration in Latin.

A few days of celebrations followed, with bullfighting and jousting, tilting and feasting, along with more displays of wealth to impress the ambassadors. Finally, Savage and Nanfan were allowed to meet the three-year-old Catherine, the subject of their negotiations and the reason for them having endured such a nightmarish journey. On 24 March they attended the service of Compline, or evening prayers, to mark the arrival of Lady Day on the morrow, followed by an audience with the royal family in a gallery lined with tapestries. Ferdinand and Isabella were seated, with Prince Juan at their feet and their daughters arranged around them 'very richly dressed'. The gallery must have been crowded, as the ambassadors noticed that the two younger girls, Maria and Catherine, each had fourteen ladies-in-waiting present, all of 'noble lineage' and all dressed in cloth of gold.[1] Presumably the older children, Isabella, John and Juana, as well as their parents, had more attendants. There was a further opportunity for the English to see Catherine the next day when she attended a spear tournament, dressed in a gown of brocade studded with jewels. They reported back to Henry VII that 'it was beautiful to see how the queen held up her youngest daughter, the Infanta Doña Catherine, [who was to be] Princess of Wales'.[2]

After the preliminaries, serious discussions regarding Catherine's future began. The groundwork had already been done by the Spanish Ambassador, Rodrigo Gonzalez de Puebla, who had been sent out to England two years before, but now the terms were laid out in detail in the Treaty of Medina del Campo. Firstly, there were general points about the mutual support and benefit to national security, trade and shipping that accompanied the main clause. An alliance between England and Spain was to be 'observed henceforth', with the promise to 'assist one another in defending their present and future dominions against any enemy whatsoever'.[3] Neither party was to assist or sign peace treaties with their mutual enemy, Charles VIII of France, nor any other hostile prince, but was to provide support to their allies within three months of it being requested. Spanish and English vessels using the ports of their allies were to give security for their good behaviour, injured parties could demand redress from the monarch and the terms were to be proclaimed in each town and seaport six months after the signing.

Then Ferdinand and Isabella came to the marriage itself. As both parties were underage, it was to be contracted *per verba de futura*, a verbal promise that made a binding contract, and as soon as possible by the words of those present, *per verba de praesenti*, either by Arthur and Catherine themselves or those representing them in proxy. After that, the union was to be consummated as soon as possible, once the two parties had reached the necessary age. Ferdinand and Isabella were to 'employ all their influence with their children that the marriage be contracted as stipulated'.[4] The marriage portion that the Spanish were obliged to give to England was set at 200,000 scudos, half of which was to be paid when Catherine arrived at Henry's court and the other half within two years of that time. The value of a single scudo was set at four shillings and two pence in English sterling. To put this in perspective, there were twelve pennies in a shilling and twenty shillings in a pound. A thatcher working in England in the 1490s received around five pence a day in wages while a lawyer might receive around £300 a year; a yard of tawny wool cost sixpence, as did a pair of boots, while a hat might set you back ten pence.

Ferdinand and Isabella pledged all their goods and revenues, and those of their subjects, in order to pay the marriage portion, but there was some disagreement about what form this might take. De Puebla, the Bishop of Exeter and Lord Privy Seal agreed that a quarter of this could be paid in jewels, ornaments and artefacts belonging to the princess, although the English ambassadors had not agreed; this was to be significant later. Catherine was to be sent to England 'decently apparelled and provided with ornaments and jewels becoming her rank'. The wedding was to take place within a month of her arrival. In return, Henry would provide her with an income drawn from the revenues of the duchies of Wales, Chester and Cornwall, to a value between 23,000 and 25,000 crowns, although this would increase if she was to become Queen of England. The date of her departure remained to be fixed.[5] On 27 March the ambassadors left court with Ferdinand and Isabella's signatures upon the agreement and 'laden with rich presents', but Henry VII was not so swift to sign. Ever the diplomat, he was watching the shifting European climate, hoping for a reconciliation with the Holy Roman Emperor Maximilian I or with France for the restoration of Plantagenet lands lost during the Hundred Years War. Nine months passed. The following January, Isabella wrote to Henry insisting that he 'must sign the marriage treaty without any alteration, even of a single word'. She added that they had entered the agreement because they knew of Henry's 'many virtues' and that 'their good opinion of him [was] a better security than all the pledges they could give'. If the English king required further assurance, she suggested he might appeal to the Pope. Yet Henry did not sign.

It was something of a battle of wills, the proud Isabella pitted against the sceptical Henry. Yet Isabella did not know that Henry was playing a wider diplomatic game rather than waiting on further Spanish reassurances. In spite of his promises to the contrary, Henry was treading a difficult line between France and Brittany; it was only when his French plans fell through that he signed two treaties at Woking, one to confirm his friendship with Maximilian and the second to ratify the Treaty of Medina del Campo. A further clause was added, clarifying that Catherine was to be sent to England 'as soon as she had completed the twelfth year of her age'. This took place in September 1490, a full eighteen months after the terms had been agreed. No doubt Ferdinand and Isabella were relieved that Henry had finally committed to the treaty, but his delay raised alarm bells in the Spanish court.

II

While Catherine's future hung in the air, Ferdinand and Isabella had other marriages on their minds. Firstly, there was a proposed union for Ferdinand's illegitimate daughter Juana with the new King of Scotland, James IV. Ambassador De Puebla had been attempting to negotiate this from England but his efforts had only served to irritate. In fact, he had made a diplomatic faux pas with the potential for serious consequences. The monarchs wrote sternly to him in January 1490 to clarify that 'De Puebla [had] certainly acted with the best intentions but it was not wise to say that Doña Juana was a legitimate daughter [of Ferdinand] by a clandestine marriage ... he must tell the Scotch Ambassadors the truth before they leave'. She was a 'natural daughter, born before marriage'.[6] If the rumour got around that Ferdinand had been contracted, promised or secretly married before 1469, the legitimacy of Catherine and her siblings would be called into question and the likelihood of their own marriages and succession in doubt. It would appear that this was an invention of De Puebla's to aid the girl's chances, but it was a political gaffe of a serious nature. The lowborn De Puebla would later be responsible for negotiating the final stages of Catherine's alliance and he would not prove popular with the young princess. In the end, the illegitimate Juana became the wife of a Spanish nobleman, the Duke of Frias.

The marital future of Catherine's brother Juan, or John, Prince of Asturias, was also being planned. One potential candidate was the thirteen-year-old Anne, Duchess of Brittany, who declared herself enthusiastic for the match and was the ruler of the duchy in her own right. While Ferdinand and Isabella were happy to approve her as a daughter-in-law in 1490, they had concerns about sending their young son and heir into Brittany to be raised there. They also suspected that Henry, or 'other persons', had 'proposed their son ... in order to draw off' the duchess from a less desirable match. By 1494, the year when John turned sixteen, they were exploring a double alliance with France's other enemy, the Burgundians. The Holy Roman Emperor, Maximilian of Austria, had two children: a daughter, Margaret, who would marry John; and a son, Philip, a likely heir to the imperial title, intended as a husband for Juana. The following summer, as the negotiations were nearing their conclusion, Isabella wrote to De Puebla to dismiss any concerns Henry might have about this and to reassure him of her friendly intentions: 'If Henry resent the alliance, and the relation ... with the King of the Romans, De Puebla is to tell him that there is no ground for displeasure. They are bent on making Henry and the King of the Romans friends, and averting all danger from England.'[7]

John, his mother's 'angel', had been given an education tailored to his needs and preferences, with a particular emphasis on theology and the music which he loved and demonstrated a talent for. As well as singing, he enjoyed playing the clavichord, flute and violin, and took his lessons alongside the other aristocratic young men in Isabella's royal school under the direction of Pedro Martir. However, he appears to have never really enjoyed robust health, with Munzer suggesting he may have had a problem with his tongue and lower lip, and adding that his daily routine included an early morning visit from his doctors, to see how he had slept and to monitor his diet. Isabella sent him treats that were associated with good digestion, including quincemeat, strawberry jam and sugared sweets,[8] suggesting he may also have suffered from stomach complaints.

His sister Juana, or Joanna, was sixteen months younger, and had been educated alongside her younger sisters Maria and Catherine. Her first tutor had been the Dominican priest Andres de Miranda, followed by the Latin scholar Beatriz Galindo, and she had excelled in law, languages, music, classics and theology. Juana later gained a reputation for insanity, although the nature and diagnosis of this raise more questions about her marriage and the treatment she received at the hands of her husband and father than they do about her mental health. Described as melancholy and infatuated with her spouse, she was considered to be 'cowed' and controlled by him into submission and was later deprived of her inheritance and ended her days in seclusion, in a manner reminiscent of her maternal grandmother, Isabel of Portugal. Madness is a social construct, a label applied to those whose behaviour does not conform to expected norms. It is difficult to discern exactly when the labelling of Juana began; although much of it is clearly a function of her marriage, whether it predates that is unclear. It seems unlikely that Emperor Maximilian would have accepted a bride for his only son who was considered tainted by madness, although this was not always an impediment in dynastic cases, where a woman's dowry and prospects, along with her potential for childbearing, could override similar concerns. Catherine's biographer Patrick Williams suggests that a reason for the delay of her marriage might be parental concern 'about her mental stability',[9] but acknowledges that it may also have been due to the ongoing war with France. Nancy Rubin, Isabella's biographer, speaks of Juana's 'difficult temperament ... sulks, temper tantrums and insistence upon having her own way', an analysis deduced in part from the girl's 'pouting portraits'.[10] Although her letters do not survive, snatches of her conversation do, and it has been suggested that Juana's recorded comments imply wit and a scepticism about religion. If this is the case, such questioning would constitute a 'difference' in Juana from the zeal that her siblings shared with their parents. When Catherine met her sister again, a decade after Juana left Spain, she was deeply shocked and saddened by the change she observed in her.

As it happened, Juana's marriage took place first out of the two. The Treaty of Antwerp was signed on 20 June 1495 by Maximilian, Philip and Margaret, and the Spanish Ambassador Francisco de Rojas. Christopher Columbus was called upon to advise upon the fleet that would carry Juana on the dangerous sea route across the Bay of Biscay, round the tip of Brittany, through the English Channel and across the North Sea. True to Spanish style, she was equipped with a huge retinue of 4,610[11] people including Moorish slave girls from Malaga, divided between twenty-two ships, provisioned with 4,000 barrels of wine, 1,000 chickens, 200 cattle[12] and 2,000 eggs.[13] Catherine accompanied her parents in escorting Juana north to the port of Laredo, from whence she embarked on 21 August 1496. Her wedding took place on 20 October, having been brought forward because the bridegroom was unable to control his desire and demanded to consummate the match at once.

The same fleet that had carried Juana then escorted Margaret of Austria through stormy seas back to Spain for her wedding to John. Catherine was at Santander with her parents to welcome the bride when she arrived the following March. Princess Margaret charmed them all with her wit, intelligence and looks, especially the eighteen-year-old John, who fell passionately in love with her. The wedding ceremony took place on 3 April 1497 in Burgos Cathedral. Six months later Prince John was dead of an unspecified wasting illness, although some attributed his waning strength to the ardour of the young couple. Pedro Martir had written to Isabella in July suggesting that they should not be allowed to spend so much time together, but this advice had not been taken. Margaret had become pregnant early on in the marriage but she miscarried her child and plunged into intense grief. Whatever the nature of John's final illness, the popular assumption that overenthusiastic sexual activity had resulted in exhaustion and death was a sinister warning that would return to haunt Catherine five years later.

Worse for Catherine, though, was the fact that Juana's marriage presented a possible threat to her own by creating a new diplomatic divide. Although he had won the throne of England by right of conquest, Henry VII was still defending his rule against a series of challenges and pretenders. He had defeated a number of the old Yorkist vanguard, and their child figurehead, Lambert Simnel, at the Battle of Stoke in 1487, but a new, more dangerous claimant soon emerged. The identity of the man known to history as Perkin Warbeck remains uncertain. Under duress he admitted to being the child of a Flemish couple living in Tournai, but in 1490 he was presenting himself as a son of the first Yorkist king, Edward IV, making him a brother of Henry's wife and the rightful heir to the English throne. Thus, he would have been the younger of the two Princes in the Tower, who disappeared in the summer of 1483 and whose fate has never been satisfactorily resolved. Warbeck posed a threat to the Tudor regime, and the Spanish were not keen to unite themselves with a dynasty that could potentially be ousted in the coming years. Additionally, if Warbeck's claim were true, it meant that he was related to Isabella, on the side of her paternal grandfather. It was as a kinsman that Warbeck wrote to the queen in September 1493, hoping to gain her support. Having explained that he was rescued by a sympathetic guard following the assassination of his elder brother, he hoped to inspire Isabella's assistance against the 'iniquitous conduct' and 'wicked tyranny ... of the usurper, Henry Richmond',[14] the very Henry whose son Isabella intended to secure as a husband for Catherine:

> Most serene Princess, Lady and Cousin, since on account of our relationship and your renowned virtues ... you ought no less than other Princes to compassionate our condition and succour us with pious love, I pray and implore your Majesty will use your influence with your Serene Spouse that, together with your clemency, he may be induced to pity the numerous calamities of our family, and in my right, which is also yours, to further me and mine, with his favour, aid and assistance. For I promise, if the Divine Grace should restore me to my hereditary kingdom, that I will continue with both your Majesties in closer alliance and friendship ... ever ready to fulfil your pleasure, no less than your own realms.[15]

Isabella made no response to the letter. She wrote instead to reassure Henry that she had written to Margaret, Duchess of Burgundy, Warbeck's reputed aunt, 'showing her that the whole affair was an imposture' and not to 'the so-called Duke of York'. Margaret did not reply but continued to support Perkin, whom some claimed was her own illegitimate son. He had received support from James IV of Scotland and, in 1495, from Emperor Maximilian himself. When an alliance was proposed between the Holy Roman Empire, Spain and England, Maximilian wished to include a clause that forbade Ferdinand and Isabella from assisting Henry if he was to act against Warbeck. The emperor went as far as supplying him with a fleet of fourteen ships, although his attempt to invade was a failure when his ships were repelled off the coast of Kent. When Warbeck was arrested in 1497, he made a formal confession that he was an imposter, but it was only with his execution in 1499 that the arrangements for Catherine's marriage truly progressed.

More tragedy loomed on the horizon for the family of Isabella and Ferdinand. After years of persuasion, their eldest daughter Isabella had finally agreed to remarry, to Manuel I of Portugal, who had succeeded her former father-in-law, John. Following the example set by her parents, Princess Isabella insisted on the condition that Manuel expel from Portugal all Jews who would not convert. The wedding took place in September 1497. Isabella fell pregnant within weeks, giving birth to a son, Miguel, the following August, but she died shortly afterwards. The little boy did not live to see his second birthday, dying in the arms of his grandmother Isabella in Granada in 1500. After the many triumphs of the early 1490s – the expulsion of the Jews, the conquest of the final Muslim enclave in Spain and the colonial expansion across the Atlantic – when God had seemed to have been favouring Ferdinand and Isabella, the series of personal tragedies at the end of the decade suggested He had deserted them. Isabella would never fully recover, clinging to her final youngest daughter Catherine, especially after Princess Maria was dispatched to Portugal to be a replacement bride for Manuel. That wedding took place on 30 October 1500, and the marriage produced ten children.

III

Over the final years of the century, as Catherine approached her teens, her future marriage inched closer. A series of family portraits painted by the Flemish artist Juan de Flanders show similarities between Isabella and her daughters Catherine and Juana. Trained in Ghent, Flanders was employed in the Spanish court from at least 1496 until after Catherine's departure for England. His early Renaissance style shows similar chiaroscuro effects, composition and style to Da Vinci's *Lady with an Ermine* and *Ginevra de' Benci*. Flanders' painting of Queen Isabella, with her bell of dark hair, plain and devout appearance, narrow eyes, long face and nose, small pursed lips and double chin, has much in common with those of her daughters. Two portraits of young girls of a similar age have given rise to much discussion about their identities. Both feature young women on the verge of puberty, and the similarities are evident but the differences are strong enough to suggest two related sitters, in fact two sisters. The elder girl wears a low-cut, square-necked dress, designed to expose her chest, edged with gold and laced over a darker insert panel. Her right hand is raised, index finger extended, and her hair is fairer than that of the second sitter. She has the features of many an early Renaissance Madonna, with her golden colouring and glowing pale skin, but her long nose and slanting eyes mark her out as Isabella's daughter, while her expression is alert and direct, almost confrontational. As traditional identifications have concluded, this is most likely to be Juana. The younger sitter, clearly still a child, wears a simpler garment, covering her chest. Her hair is slightly darker, redder than Juana's, and her eyes are more docile. This portrait of Catherine, her hair still loose down her back, her fingers clasping a flower, indicates a girl on the verge of womanhood. And that womanhood was to play out on an international stage.

In September 1496, Isabella wrote to de Puebla in London with instructions to conclude the arrangements for Catherine's marriage. She insisted on a few slight alterations to the Treaty of Medina del Campo, which had been signed over seven years before. The percentage of the marriage portion to be paid in ornaments was increased, the value of the scudo was clarified and the size of the princess's retinue, Isabella declared, was to be no less than 150. The agreement was signed in London on 1 October by de Puebla and Thomas Savage, who had been promoted to Bishop of London since his trip to Spain. The new terms stated that as soon as Arthur turned fourteen, the marriage would be celebrated *per verba de praesenti*, either by the bride and groom themselves or those whom they nominated to be their proxy. As soon as this had taken place, Catherine was to be sent to England, at her parents' expense, and the details of her marriage portion and dower were to remain the same as previously outlined.[16] A copy of the agreement was sent to Spain, where, on 1 January 1497, Ferdinand and Isabella added their signatures to it, and, for the first time, so did Princess Catherine. That act of committing her name to the bottom of the document, of inscribing her identity and her agreement in ink, was a symbolic act, a rite of passage for a young girl indicating that she was leaving her childhood behind. In Burgos on the same day, she empowered de Puebla to take her role in the forthcoming procedures in England.

The formal betrothal took place at Woodstock Palace on 15 August 1497. Set in the Oxfordshire countryside, it had been a hunting lodge built for Henry I, comprising several courtyards, gardens, menagerie, park, stone walls and gatehouse. Although nothing of the original building survives, buried under the Baroque symmetry of Blenheim Palace, early drawings suggest a fairly compact series of buildings with two crenelated towers. By this time Arthur was approaching his twelfth birthday, 'taller than his years would warrant, of remarkable beauty and grace, and very ready speaking in Latin'.[17] His bride was represented by de Puebla, who spoke the words of the promise, making the match legally binding. The ambassador took the bride's role seriously, holding Arthur's right hand, sitting on his right side during the feasting and providing a nominal presence in the formal bedding ceremony.

The next formal step was marriage by proxy. On 19 May 1499, which fell upon Whit Sunday, the ceremony *per verba de praesenti* was held at Tickenhill Manor, near Bewdley in Worcestershire. This was one of Arthur's main residences, along with Ludlow Castle, both of which came to him through his mother's descent from the Mortimer line. Tickenhill had recently been redeveloped and extended from a manor into a palace to accommodate the Council of the Marches, which the young Arthur oversaw. Proceedings began in the chapel there at about nine in the morning, after first Mass had been held. Once again de Puebla stood in for Catherine, repeating her vows and joining his right hand with that of Arthur, and accepted him as the princess's husband. Arthur replied in a 'loud and clear voice' that 'he was very much rejoiced to contract with Catherine ... in indissoluble marriage, not only in obedience to the Pope and King Henry, but also for his deep and sincere love for the princess, his wife'. A papal dispensation had been acquired for Arthur to say his vows, as he was still four months off his fourteenth birthday. De Puebla was given a seat of honour at the banquet that followed and ate from the best dishes, to his great delight. From that moment forward, Catherine was officially styled 'Princess of Wales' but although she and Arthur were legally married, they were still in separate countries.

While they waited, the young pair wrote to each other enthusiastically, even passionately. Some of the terms of endearment may have been fairly formulaic, taken from the Latin texts taught to Arthur by his tutor, the humanist biographer and historiographer Bernard André, but they were sincerely meant. There is something touching about the young man's efforts to prove the lover. In October 1499, Arthur thanked Catherine for her 'sweet letters', from which he had 'easily perceived your entire love for me' and conveyed his own 'urgent desire' to see her. He complimented Catherine, saying that her letters 'written by [her] very own hand evoked her presence and even her embrace'. Taking an even more intimate tone, he continued, 'I cannot tell you what an earnest desire I feel to see your Highness, and how vexatious to me is this procrastination about your coming. Let it be hastened, that the love conceived between us and the wished-for joys may reap their proper fruit.' Some royal advice was also conveyed to Catherine by de Puebla, which originated from her future mother-in-law, Elizabeth of York, and Arthur's grandmother, Margaret Beaufort. The ambassador wrote that they recommended Catherine should converse in French as much as possible with her new sister-in-law, John's wife Margaret. It was necessary because the English ladies 'do not understand Latin, and much less, Spanish'. Catherine was also advised to get used to drinking wine as 'the water of England is not drinkable, and even if it were, the climate would not allow it'.[18] Sadly, Catherine's letters to Arthur have not survived.

As Arthur's fourteenth birthday approached, Catherine should have been preparing to depart for England. Yet she would not actually leave Spanish shores for another year. One of the reasons for this appears to have been concerns on both sides about the ability of Arthur to consummate the match, and also for his general health. According to the interpretations of modern historians, Arthur was either tall for his age or shorter than Catherine, who stood only a little over five foot; he may have been a full-term baby, or premature a month or two, and his childhood may have been healthy and normal, or else plagued by weakness and constant illness. The truth is hard to recover. The facts, though, state that he was born eight months after his parent's wedding day, although this still allows for a pregnancy of almost thirty-six weeks, and both his father and Ferdinand did express concerns about the physical aspects of their wedding. Contemporary wisdom about the nature of sexual relations varied, and although fourteen was generally held to be the age of maturity, it was recognised that this could be overridden as the need arose in individual cases. Generally, they appear to have been guided by the onset of puberty rather than by numbers. Too much sexual activity too young was thought to drain the strength and pregnancy before a girl was fully mature and could impede her chances of bearing subsequent children or result in her death.

On 3 June, Thomas Savage wrote to Ferdinand and Isabella that 'the marriage between the Prince and Princess of Wales is now concluded, and there remains nothing to be done but that the Princess should come to England'. He added that it was 'impossible to describe how much he and the whole nation desire to see her' and that 'in all parts of the kingdom preparations are making [*sic*] for her festive reception'.[19] Just three days later, though, Catherine's parents wrote back to insist on a change in the clause of the settlement. Given the tragedy that had befallen their own son, the physical aspect of the match was clearly weighing on their mind. Whereas the agreement had previously specified that Catherine's dowry was to be paid ten days after the wedding, the Spanish now wanted it to be paid 'ten days after the consummation of the marriage',[20] implying that a lapse of time might occur between the ceremony and the couple first sharing a bed. On 27 June, de Puebla added another dimension to this question, writing to inform his employers that Henry had 'intimated … that his intention is to keep the Prince and Princess of Wales, during the first year of their marriage, about his person and at court'.[21] A second Spaniard in London, Don Pedro de Ayala, technically the ambassador to Scotland, disagreed, saying Catherine should be sent to England at once in order to learn to appreciate the 'manners and customs' of her new home.[22]

More detailed information reached the Spanish monarchs from another source. Unsure of the trustworthiness and abilities of de Puebla, who seemed to frequently tie himself in diplomatic knots, Ferdinand dispatched Gutierre Gómez de Fuensalida to London for an initial two months during this tricky period of negotiation, although he would later return for longer. Part of Fuensalida's brief was to spy on his fellow countryman. Ferdinand and Isabella had been concerned to hear that Henry was meeting with Archduke Philip, Juana's husband, in Calais, possibly to try to match Arthur with Philip's sister and John's widow, Margaret of Austria. Fuensalida met with Henry's council, who were critical of de Puebla, before having a lengthy meeting with the king himself. He wrote to his employers that he understood 'from a reliable source' that Henry had decided 'the prince will know his wife sexually on the day of the wedding and then separate himself from her for two or three years because it is said in some way the prince is frail'. This suggested a compromise, so that the match was legally binding but a full sexual relationship was delayed. 'The King told me,' Fuensalida continued, 'that he wanted to have them [Arthur and Catherine] with him for the first three years so that the prince should mature in strength.'[23] In light of this, given the approaching autumn and the dangerous sea conditions, it was agreed to delay Catherine's departure until had the following summer. In addition, it was not safe for her to travel because of prolonged rebellion from the Muslims around Granada, who fled into the Alpujarra mountains, forcing Ferdinand to launch military attacks against them which would last into early 1501. So Catherine settled in for a final winter. This meant she was at home to witness the disgrace of the man her parents had once heralded as a hero.

Since his triumphant return to Spain carrying parrots and gold, spices and slaves, Christopher Columbus had undertaken two more voyages to the New World, through the Antilles and Canary Islands, back to Cuba and Hispaniola, making new discoveries along the coast of South America. However, his methods as governor of these new territories raised questions, with reports of torture and mutilation to subdue mutinous and lawbreaking natives reaching Ferdinand and Isabella. It cannot be denied that the Spanish Inquisition had operated by using similarly brutal techniques, but in the perception of the Catholic Monarchs, Columbus was not persecuting heretics but controlling conquered territory; similar levels of cruelty might have been employed, but the context differed. The conquistador was judged as having acted too harshly, which numerous complaints against him seemed to confirm. Yet perhaps Ferdinand and Isabella might have seen this coming. In 1499 Columbus had sent a message back to court to ask for a royal official to assist him in his rule, as he was increasingly suffering from debilitating health, and the colonies were rebelling. Instead of sending help, they removed him from office, and Francisco de Bobadilla was sent out to investigate and succeed Columbus as second governor of the Indies. Christopher and his brothers, including the mapmaker Bartholomew, were sent back to Spain in chains and imprisoned for six weeks. Catherine and her parents were at the Alhambra when they finally summoned the disgraced explorer and allowed him a hearing. After listening to his explanations, they restored his position and even agreed to fund a fourth voyage, but Columbus would never be appointed as governor again.

It appears to have been at the insistence of the Spanish that another wedding was held for Catherine and Arthur once the boy had turned fourteen. Perhaps they were experiencing doubts over the rumours that Henry was seeking a Burgundian bride for his son, or they might have believed de Puebla's statement that it was quite within the English character to change the mind. Although the proxy wedding at Tickenhill eighteen months before had been entirely legal, and a dispensation had been secured to cover Arthur's age, a second ceremony was held at Ludlow on 22 November 1500, two months after the prince had turned fourteen. Henry considered another wedding superfluous, but clearly Ferdinand and Isabella wanted to avoid a situation where the arrangements were revoked at the last minute or, worse still, that Catherine was sent to England and returned unwed. This had been the case with their daughter-in-law Margaret of Austria, whose first betrothal to the future Charles VIII of France resulted in a long residence at the French court before the Valois king repudiated her and sent her home, only to pave the way for her marriage to John, Prince of Asturias. Ultimately, whatever they professed to the contrary, the Spanish did not trust Henry. And yet, in spite of all their care to make it legal, the Bishop of Lincoln, one William Smyth, objected to performing the Ludlow ceremony because he considered the match to be 'clandestine' and felt it should be performed by a secular lord. He was persuaded to cooperate by de Puebla, but seeds of doubt had been sown.

IV

As the spring of 1501 advanced, preparations were being made for Catherine's departure for England. Isabella wrote to de Puebla of her delight to hear that Henry was planning a huge reception for her daughter, 'because it shows the magnificent grandeur of my brother and because demonstrations of joy at the reception of my daughter are naturally agreeable to me', although she urged the king to keep the expenses moderate as 'the substantial part of the festival should be his love'.[24] Catherine was equipped with 100,000 gold ducats, forming half her dowry, which was to be paid at the time of her wedding, and another 50,000 ducats' worth of plate and jewels that would remain in her keeping for the following year. The final 50,000 would be paid six months after her arrival. An elaborate trousseau was prepared, with brocades and laces, blackwork, hooped skirts and veils sewn with gold lace and silks, and adorned with pearls and jewels. Catherine was to appear every inch the daughter of Isabella and Ferdinand and her entire bridal wardrobe was reputedly valued at half the value of her dowry.[25] She chose as her motifs the pomegranate of Granada, split open to reveal the seeds inside, with all the connotations of fertility this implied, and a sheaf of arrows, symbolic of her parents' martial achievements. Ever hopeful, her mother also packed a christening gown.[26]

Optimistically, Isabella began planning a large entourage for her daughter, drawn from familiar faces at the Spanish court. This included the Count and Countess of Cabra, who were to run her state chamber, her chaplain Alessandro Geraldini, her chamberlain Juan de Diero, the Archbishop of Santiago, the Bishop of Majorca, a troop of knights and archers, and a number of Muslim slaves. Her duenna and first lady of honour was Doña Elvira Manuel, a well-born woman of the same age as Isabella who had the queen's complete trust, along with her husband Pedro Manrique, Catherine's chamberlain, and their son Inigo, who was to be the master of her ceremonies and master of her pages. Elvira had a female companion of her own, a Doña Martina Mudarra, and two other servants, plus Katherine Cardenas, who was to attend to the princess's private needs. Catherine was also accompanied by Inez (or Agnes) de Venegas, the daughter of a woman of the same name who had been governess to her and Princess Maria. A handful of other children raised at the Spanish royal court now travelled to England with the princess, including Inez and Maria de Salinas, whose father Juan had been secretary to Catherine's eldest sister Isabella; three women named Francisca de Silva, Beatriz, daughter of Blanca and Martina, daughter of Salazar; a niece of Cardinal Mendoza; a niece of the treasurer Morales; and Maria de Rojas, the daughter of a Spanish diplomat. The master of her hall was to be the Knight Commander Antonio de Esquivel, her chief cupbearer the son of Francisca de Silva, her laundress the wife of Andreas Martines, her secretary was named as Pasamonte and her chaplain was Pedro Morales. She also had four equerries, a comptroller, a quartermaster, a keeper of the plate, a clerk, Ambres Martinez the baker, a purser, a sweeper and Hieronimo de Vega the cook.[27]

Predictably, Henry objected to Catherine's planned entourage. Where Isabella believed that her daughter's status and dignity demanded that she be accompanied by a minimum of 150 attendants, Henry now 'made great difficulties' and refused to consider certain officials which to the Spanish were indispensable, including the Lord High Steward, Lord Treasurer, Lord High Gentleman in Waiting[28] and others. Such a large party would be expensive but also, he argued, it would prevent Catherine from having to learn English. Instead, he issued Fuensalida with a list of twenty positions that would constitute her future household: three ladies of noble rank who were virgins with one servant, one matron who was a widow, a lady to be a porter, a doctor with servant and stablehand, two chaplains with two servants and stablehands, a cook with servant, a child for her chamber and two children to be stablemates.[29] Henry specified that the ladies-in-waiting should be 'of gentle birth and beautiful or, at the least, by no means ugly'.[30] In the end, Catherine left the Alhambra on 21 May with a household staff of fifty-five, including maids, cooks, cupbearers and others, as well as the bishops, knights and archers that were to accompany her to the coast. Most were to return home within weeks of her arrival.

De Puebla wrote to Ferdinand and Isabella that preparations had been made to receive Catherine, whose arrival was anticipated from 25 May. All the Lords of England, Ireland and Wales had been summoned to London and further invitations had been sent to France, Flanders and Brittany, to any knights wishing to come and take part in the celebratory jousts. These were planned to last for forty days in London, which was 'perfectly healthy now', and the challengers were three dukes and three earls, with whom the combatants were invited to break three lances and exchange three blows. The nobles would 'vie with each other in splendour' and, to continue the theme 'of olden times' for which he had named his son, Henry expected a total of 230 knights 'of the round table' to attend.[31] It promised to be a magnificent occasion, fitting for any future queen of England.

Henry had not heeded Isabella's request for the spending to be modest. The preparations made in the last year alone had cost more than 100,000 rubles, 'but the English do not mind that', and the projected expenses for the wedding celebrations 'will be much greater'.[32] In March 1501, perhaps mindful of the lavish descriptions his ambassadors had brought back from Medina del Campo, Henry spent £14,000 on jewels to adorn himself and his family during the coming festivities,[33] and a printed pamphlet was commissioned by the royal household, 'The Traduction of Ladie Kateryne', containing instructions for her reception.[34] More was poured into planning the wedding itself, preparing lodgings, cleaning up the city and on the food, pageants, dances and entertainments. All southern towns, villages and seaports were in a state of readiness, with Catherine's arrival being anticipated at either Southampton or Bristol, as the two safest and closest locations. Thomas Savage, now promoted from Bishop to Archbishop of York, travelled to both places to oversee their plans, but the other coastal towns were also on alert, given the unpredictability of tides and weather. Henry ordered that two ships should be rigged and equipped, along with other barges and great boats, to accompany her 'the more easily and the more assured' to the shore. Catherine was to be transferred into the hands of Henry's Lord Steward, Lord Willoughby de Broke, a Wiltshire-born man who had been one of the king's chief commanders in putting down Perkin Warbeck's last rebellion in the south-west. He would have nine knights at his disposal 'for the ordering and receiving of the Princess from the water, for the first meeting on land, for her conveying, lodging and dislodging'. They were reminded of the details of precedence, that servants 'be not suffered to ride before' the important arrival and her guests, but instead to send a party ahead 'to be ready to receive them', and between them they were to devise and rehearse this method. Others were appointed to supply chairs, horses, palfreys and litters, two of the latter being required; a plainer one to conduct her to Croydon, then an ornate one for her entry into London.[35] In St Paul's Cathedral, workmen were busy constructing a wooden platform along which the young couple would walk, high above the heads of onlookers. When the time came, England would be ready.

Catherine lingered in Spain as long as possible, caught in a web of bad weather and bad health, uprisings and obligations. She was suffering from a 'low fever' in April, which may have been caused by her imminent separation from her family, and in May she had an 'ague,' an unspecified complaint that could be a cover-all for a range of illnesses. Isabella judged that this made it 'imprudent [for] her to expose herself to the fatigue of quick travelling'. Along with the rebellion of the Moors, which delayed Ferdinand's return to Granada until 15 May, this encouraged the queen to retain her daughter for another month or two, promising Henry that she would 'be in England as soon as possible'.

Finally, the day of Catherine's departure could no longer be delayed. As they said their farewells, on 21 May 1501, the princess knew it was unlikely that she would see her parents again. Ferdinand and Isabella were then aged forty-nine and fifty and were loath to let go of Catherine, who had become a consolation to them through their recent losses and the queen's recurring bouts of illness. When Juana had sailed for Burgundy in 1496, her mother had spent two days aboard ship with her and wept copiously when she finally sailed. No doubt there were similar emotional scenes inside the Alhambra. All Isabella's children had died or left and she was also devastated that following the death of her grandson Miguel the joint crowns of Castile and Aragon would be divided, with Castile passing to the son Juana had borne in Burgundy in 1500, the future Charles V. Initially, Isabella had planned to travel with her youngest daughter to the port of Corunna, where Catherine would embark for her new home, but increasing ill-health dictated that she remained in Granada instead. Catherine was fifteen when she said goodbye to her parents. She was travelling to a foreign land to become the bride of a young man she had never met and, eventually, to rule over people whose customs and culture were very different from her own. Although brides did return home, like Isabella and Margaret of Austria, that only occurred in tragic circumstances, and Catherine did not anticipate returning to Spain. She would not see her parents again.

On the day of Catherine's departure, Isabella's secretary Miguel Perez de Almazan had written to de Puebla that the entourage of the princess was under instructions to 'travel as fast as possible', and the queen herself wrote to the ambassador that they had not accompanied her 'because she will travel quicker if left alone'.[36] On 5 July Catherine arrived at Guadalupe, a distance of around 270 miles north of Granada, taking advantage of her time there to visit the monastery's shrine to the Virgin, with its famous black Madonna. As her parents related to de Puebla, she was travelling 'as quickly as possible' but the heat was so great that she could not make long journeys.[37] She also stopped for a time in Zamora, a further 200 miles on, where the town feasted her on twelve dozen fowl, three bulls, ten calves and eight casks of wine.[38]

Catherine's journey then took her north-west, through Toledo, Valladolid and on to Santiago de Compostela, visiting the cathedral as a pilgrim among the many who flocked to visit the reputed tomb of St James. The city would have been busy as it was a jubilee year, meaning that special indulgences, or pardons, were being distributed, but a dramatic incident made it memorable for more than religious reasons. It is reputed that during Catherine's visit the huge censer, one of which is still swung in the church today, broke loose from its chain but luckily swung out of one of the conveniently placed windows. However, this provides a fortuitous conclusion to an event that in reality may have caused more damage, and may have been aligned with her visit as an 'omen', according to the hindsight of those who saw her embarkation to England as doomed. Ferdinand and Isabella had anticipated that their daughter would arrive on the coast in mid-July, but she did not reach Corunna until a month later. On 17 August her fleet put to sea, but the conditions in the Bay of Biscay were so severe that all but one were beaten back with torn sails and leaking hulls. Catherine was forced to wait at Laredo until the weather improved. Informed of this, Henry sent one of his best captains, Stephen Butt, or Brett, to await the appearance of her ships and guide her into port.

The Spanish finally set sail on Monday 27 September. As Licentate Alcares wrote to Isabella, they weighed anchor at five in the afternoon and, although the weather 'was favourable at first, it changed after midnight' when they were overtaken by thunderstorms and huge waves. After that, there was a storm every few hours. Alcares reported that 'it was impossible not to be afraid', but they sailed on for another six days through the notorious Bay of Biscay and around the tip of Brittany. After that, they entered the channel and the coast of England came into sight. On Saturday 2 October, at around three in the afternoon, the Spanish fleet drifted into harbour at Plymouth.

The Catherine who stood on deck was a short, curvaceous fifteen-year-old, blue-eyed and with red-gold hair; she was very much her mother's daughter. The first third of her life, arguably the most influential, had been spent absorbing the dry plains and mountain ranges of dusty Spain, where old Moorish castles sat on the tops of hills overlooking walled towns punctuated by the tolling bell towers of magnificent cathedrals and monasteries. Her days had been passed in the saddle, under colourful tents or in palace rooms that were dazzling in their ornament; under circular domes, gazing at elaborate carvings and tiles in black, gold, blue, red and white; among the shade of paradise gardens where water trickled through fountains. Her nights had seen festivities, where foreign dignitaries and princesses danced and the darkness was lit by thousands of blazing torches, as if the king and queen were so powerful they could banish shadows and make midnight bright as noon. She had seen her country redefined through acts of her parents' will, the population forced to submit along religious and ethnic lines; the Jews had been expelled, the Moors had been enslaved and natives halfway round the world had become the playthings of the Spanish court. She had tasted exotic fruits and spices from the New World and heard parrots sing. She had seen her parents lauded by the Pope, dressed from head to foot in gold, heralded by their people as the instruments of God upon earth, as his crusaders, cleansing their realm and pushing their boundaries, employing new thinkers, claiming centres of learning, criss-crossing their country in journeys of hundreds of miles, god-like themselves.

And yet Catherine had also seen the darker side to this glory, the shadow that lined the gold. She was aware of her mother's struggle to gain the throne, of her unlikely rise to power and the precedence of men and vulnerabilities of women, of the problems caused by weak rulers and rival factions, the necessity for swift action and strength and the constant threat from one's enemies. She had benefitted from the broad and deep humanist education her mother had never received, but she had learned more from Isabella than mere book learning and tales from the past. She had seen her mother majestic and regal, resolute and determined in the face of danger, undaunted in spirit and committed to a path that she had chosen but that was also her calling. She had observed the way Isabella had organised and provisioned Ferdinand's military campaigns, how she had headed her court in his absence with great strength and fortitude, how she drew leading academics, thinkers, artists and musicians to her court to make it a cultural centre, along with her patronage of the universities and monasteries. Catherine had seen her mother in the role of a great conquistador queen but also as a wife and mother, as a woman. Isabella had made her own marriage and committed herself to making it a success. Her daughter was aware of the tiny marks of affection and deference, the personal touches between man and wife, which saw Isabella take care of Ferdinand, mending his shirts herself and ordering his favourite foods. Most powerfully of all, Catherine had seen the tide of fortune turn against her mother. The woman who could unite and subdue a nation had been broken by personal loss, as each of her children in turn slipped through her fingers. In the last few years, especially the last twelve months, when Isabella had only Catherine left, she had seen the queen's determination to continue, going through the business of running court and country even though she was heartbroken and physically frail. She had seen her mother grit her teeth and carry on. Her daughter would never forget those lessons of commitment to duty and dogged perseverance above all. Later she would become Queen of England, but first and foremost she was a daughter of Spain.

PART TWO

Arthur
1501–1502

5

First Impressions 1501

I

England stretched before Catherine, damp, green and fertile, with gently undulating hills dotted with sheep and mines full of tin – at least that was the way another foreign visitor found it, an anonymous Venetian who recorded his impressions of the country and its people in around the year 1500. He described a land very different in climate and appearance to that which the Spanish princess was accustomed, full of lush 'beautiful valleys ... agreeable woods and extensive meadows', with less severe winters and milder summers than his native Italy. 'This,' he explained, was 'owing to the rain' which had fallen almost every day through June, July and August during his visit, adding to the 'great abundance of large rivers, springs and streams' and 'every description of tree' including almost 'all our fruit trees, with the exception of the olive and the orange'.[1] As the Spanish fleet sailed into the Channel, closing in upon the Devon coast, they could only have distinguished colours and outlines; a cliff face and shingle beach, rolling fields, the odd spire and, perhaps, banks of cloud. Just eighty miles from the most south-westerly tip of the British Isles lay the port and town of Plymouth, where Catherine was to get her first taste of England and the English.

A map of Plymouth in 1540 shows an extensive sea wall and defences, with a square tower marking the entrance of the bay, dotted with cannons. The Spanish fleet would have sailed into Sutton Pool, a safe haven protected by fortifications and an entrance which could be closed off by chain. This was the main resting place for ships before the construction of Plymouth docks. It is unlikely to have been so well defended in 1500. The first major landmark Catherine would have seen from the water was Plymouth Castle, built on a mound immediately to the west to help defend against the frequent raids by the French during the Hundred Years War. It was unusual in being a municipal, civic building run by the mayor and aldermen, with four imposing towers maintained by the four wards over which they had jurisdiction. Behind it, the town stretched away to the north and west, bounded by two parish churches. The map shows four ships at anchor, their bowsprits pointing towards the quay, but Catherine probably had to walk down a gangplank or disembark into a small vessel which conveyed her to dry land. A delegation met her on the quayside, headed by the mayor and aldermen, with the townspeople lined up and banners fluttering in the cobbled streets behind. As Alcares wrote to Isabella, her daughter 'could not have been received with greater rejoicings if she had been the saviour of the world'.[2] No doubt the colourful Spanish entourage, with their strange fashions and their Muslim and African servants, caused a stir.

Catherine's first request was to be taken to the parish church 'as soon as she left the boat',[3] where she went in procession with her party, in order to give thanks for their safe arrival. The church was St Andrews, originally a Saxon building, with a new Lady chapel and stone tower in the early Perpendicular style completed as recently as 1490. Photographs of the old interior of the church before its destruction by a bombing raid in 1941 show a simple traditional nave with two aisles, fairly plain altar and main window, with simple beams above. When Catherine knelt there to regain a little equilibrium after being tossed on the waves, it would have been far more colourful and ornate. Like Spain, England was a Catholic country, devout and particularly dedicated to the cult of the Virgin. While the rest of her surroundings may have felt unfamiliar, the rituals and trappings of her faith would have provided Catherine with a connection to home. The Italian visitor also remarked upon the devotion of the English, stating that they attended Mass daily, giving liberal alms, reciting verses and carrying rosaries, but he sounded a note of caution that there were 'many who have various opinions concerning religion'.[4] This was to resonate later in Catherine's life. Watching her, Alcares hoped that God would give her 'the possession of all those realms for such a period as would be long enough to enable her to enjoy life, and to leave heirs to the throne'.[5]

After prayers, the princess was taken through the streets to be feasted by the mayor. The earliest surviving building in Plymouth, Prysten House, or the Priest's House, in Finewell Street, gives an impression of the first English streets Catherine laid her eyes on. Built in 1498 from local limestone and granite from Dartmoor, it appears rather castle-like today with its wide expanse of pale stone and small windows, save for one, large and protruding, set in a first-floor bay above the entrance. Originally built for a merchant named Thomas Yogge just a short walk from St Andrews, the docks and the Hoe, it must have been typical of the wealth such men had acquired through trade, with its oak gallery and courtyard. The feast may have been held in a similar building or in the castle itself, but what Catherine made of her first taste of English food went unrecorded. According to the Venetian visitor, meal times held a particular significance as the people of England 'think that no greater honour can be conferred, or received, than to invite others to eat with them'. When they dined, they took 'great pleasure in having a quantity of victuals and also in remaining a long time at table'; they were 'great epicures' and liked to 'indulge in the most delicate fare'. Foreigners like the Italian had been surprised when presented with a certain dish of freshwater mussels to discover that they contained tiny pearls.[6] He also remarked that there were no good wines made in England, so they imported those, but instead made their own beer and ale, which were not 'disliked by foreigners after they have drunk them four or six times'.[7] Given the timing of their arrival, it is likely that Catherine and her party stayed in Plymouth that night.

The next stage of the journey saw Catherine travelling to the cathedral city of Exeter, just over forty miles to the east, a route that would have taken them along the bottom of Dartmoor for most of the way. This probably took three or four days, as the entourage was moving slowly, necessitating stops along the way in great houses, monasteries, inns or whatever could be prepared to house such a number of guests. Heralds riding ahead would have secured lodgings or erected tents, which would have been necessary in October. Studies of rainfall on the moors over a period of thirty years from 1971–2000 give an average rainfall of just over twenty-one centimetres and a minimum daytime temperature of 6.4 degrees Celsius for that month.[8] Upon reaching Exeter, Catherine was lodged in the Old Deanery, a long building of dark-red stone which still stands beside the cathedral. Local legend has it that she was unable to rest due to the noise of a weathervane positioned on top of nearby St Mary Major, so a servant was sent to remove it. No doubt during her visit Catherine took the opportunity to pay her first visit to an English cathedral, where she witnessed the opulent apogee of the English Catholic Church in all its glory. As the Venetian commented, there was 'not a parish church in the kingdom so mean as not to possess crucifixes, candlesticks, censers, patens and cups of silver ... besides many other ornaments'. England's churches, he found, were 'more like baronial palaces than religious houses' and the larger ones contained the 'splendid tombs of saints'. Many monasteries, apparently, also had in their possession 'unicorn's horns of an extraordinary size'.[9] At Exeter, Catherine may have been shown the holy relics of which the community were deeply proud: a piece of the candle which the angel of the Lord lit in Jesus' tomb and a bit of the bush from which Christ spoke to Moses.

Around 19 October, a delegation from Henry's court arrived in Exeter, bringing her a letter of welcome from the king. It was warmly written, expressing the joy at her 'noble presence, which we have often desired'. Henry requested that she regarded him 'henceforth as your good and loving father, as familiarly as you would do the king and queen your parents, for on our part we are determined to treat, receive and favour you like our own daughter, and in no wise more, or less dearly, than any of our own children'. They also brought 'viands [food], horses, and carriages, as every other necessary'. It may also have been at Exeter where Catherine was welcomed by the Earl of Surrey and his second wife, the Duchess of Norfolk, Agnes Tilney, aged twenty-four, bringing 'with her a goodly company of countesses, baronesses, and many other honourable gentlewomen ... [who] kept her continual company'.[10] Other sources state that the duchess met her at Amesbury in

Wiltshire. King Henry's servant, William Holybrand, was chosen to read aloud a long welcoming address in Spanish, as he had spent time in Catherine's homeland.

This was Catherine's first contact with the English court. Hearing of her arrival, the nobility of the south-west hurried to attend her from Plymouth to Exeter, 'with godly manner and haste ... with right honourable gifts to repair to that noble princess',[11] but now she had an escort for the 200 miles to London, headed by Henry's Lord Steward, Baron Willoughby de Broke. Now she met a number of urbane, fashionable courtiers, with their formal manners and rich clothes in velvet, silk and furs, the men 'wearing gowns called doublets plaited on the shoulders, reaching half-way down the leg ... caps with one or two ornaments [and] short hair like priests',[12] and women in square-necked gowns, with fur-lined kirtles and turned-up sleeves. The Venetian observer found the English to be rather proud of their own appearances and manners, being 'extremely politic in their language' and doing each other the 'incredible courtesy of remaining with their heads uncovered whilst they talked'. He found the English 'for the most part, handsome and well-proportioned' but also 'great lovers of themselves and of everything belonging to them: they think that there are no other men than themselves and no other world but England'. If they happened to see a good-looking foreigner, they would remark that he looked like an Englishman 'and that it is a great pity that he should not be' one.[13]

The Dutch humanist Erasmus, still an impoverished tutor in 1500, found the welcome of the English to be remarkable in another respect: 'there are nymphs here with divine features, so gentle and kind ... wherever you go, you are received on all hands with kisses; when you leave you are dismissed with kisses ... wherever a meeting takes place there is kissing in abundance ... if you had once tasted how sweet and fragrant those kisses are, you would indeed wish to be a traveller, not for ten years ... but for your whole life, in England'.[14] Other foreign visitors found the English to be vain, 'proud without any respect, and claim[ing] superiority over all other nations', or changeable and difficult to deal with being 'devout as angels' in the morning but 'after dinner they are like devils'.[15] No doubt the fifteen-year-old Catherine was presented with a polished retinue on their best behaviour. John

Leland cited a contemporary account that emphasised the nature of her welcome, in which she was saluted 'with right honourable gifts, and in goodly and with all required points and feats of courtesy … entertaining her with her pleasures, presents and attendances … waiting and guiding' her upon her journey.[16]

From Exeter, Catherine's party headed east, through Honiton and Crewkerne, where Somerset gentry Sir Hugh Lutterell of Dunster and Sir Amyas Paulet of Hinton St George waited to receive her and conduct her along the next stage, to Sherborne. Their route lay through Shaftesbury, Amesbury and Andover, where they spent the night of 3 November in the Angel Inn, which still stands in the High Street.[17] They reached Basingstoke in Hampshire on 4 November and two days later arrived at Dogmersfield House, owned by the Bishop of Bath and Wells, with a handsome 1,000-acre park and fish ponds. Meanwhile, Henry could not conceal his impatience to meet the princess over whose marriage he had been wrangling for years. It may have been more than just the desire to see her, as the pamphlet Henry commissioned to described Catherine's arrival suggested. *The Receyt of the Ladie Kateryn* states that the king was 'not soo intensifly satisfied with the chere, servyce and diligente attendans', so set off to make his own welcome.[18] Arthur departed from Ludlow Castle at the same time as his father left Richmond; they met at a royal hunting lodge near Easthampstead in Berkshire and headed south together to meet Catherine. The weather was terrible and they arrived the following day, in the afternoon or evening, while the visitors were resting after their arrival. But this was not the main problem. Their presence took the Spaniards by surprise, as they were under 'strict injunction and commandment' from Ferdinand and Isabella that Catherine should have no 'manner of communication or company' with Prince Arthur and his family, or to be seen unveiled, until the morning of the wedding day.[19]

Unperturbed, Henry then spent some time considering his position, on 'certain musing of the mind of this King of Spain', and called a meeting of his men in the field, asking them 'whether they thought it most reasonable and agreeable to incline to this declared purpose, or that he should, as he intended, maintain his passage to that Lady'. It was concluded that Spain and Spanish customs had no jurisdiction in England, as 'since the princess and her attendants were so far entered into the empire and realm of England, they should seem to be in part discharged against their sovereign ... and that the pleasure and commandment of her seemed to lie in the power, grace and disposition of our noble King of England'.[20] Henry returned to the manor house and insisted upon an interview. Catherine's first lady, Elvira Manuel, was horrified at the thought of their custom being broken and insisted that 'the princess was in her rest', to which Henry replied that 'if she were in her bed he would see and commune with her, for that was the mind and intent of his coming'. The moment might have turned sour, with a clash of Spanish protocol and English might, except for Catherine's diplomatic sensitivity and response to the insistence of her new father and lord. She consented to see him, asking for a little time to prepare herself.[21]

The man that Catherine met on the evening of 6 November 1501 was approaching forty-five and had been on the English throne for sixteen years. He was described extensively by the Italian humanist Polydore Vergil, who first came to England in 1502, just months after Catherine's arrival, and was welcomed at court with ample opportunity to observe the king at this time in his life. Henry was above average height, with a slender but strong and well-built body. Vergil judged him to be 'remarkably attractive' in appearance 'and his face was cheerful, especially when speaking'; his eyes were 'small and blue', his complexion sallow and by this age his hair was grey, turning white, his teeth 'few, poor and blackish'. Two years earlier, his clothing had been described by Trevisa, another foreign visitor, who was impressed that 'his Majesty wore a violet-coloured gown, lined with cloth of gold, and a collar of many jewels, and on his cap was a large diamond and a most beautiful pearl'. Vergil also commented at length on Henry's character, finding his 'spirit distinguished, wise and prudent, his mind was brave and resolute and never, even at moments of the greatest danger, deserted him'. He had a good memory and was shrewd and prudent, so that 'no one dared to get the better of him through deceit or guile' and knew well how to maintain his royal majesty 'in every time and place'. No doubt he made Catherine feel welcome, as Vergil claimed him to be 'attentive to his visitors and easy of access', adding that 'his hospitality was splendidly generous [and] he was fond of having foreigners at his court and he freely conferred favours on them'.[22]

Vergil was also critical of Henry's harsh treatment of transgressors and his avarice, but these would only become relevant to Catherine in the coming years.

Henry was pleased with the young woman who unveiled herself before his critical eye and gave him an 'honourable meeting'. Happily for Catherine, her looks conformed to the contemporary English standards of beauty, which favoured pale skin and red-gold colouring, blue eyes and rosebud lips, of the kind depicted in early Renaissance images of the Madonna, such as those painted by Perugino in 1500 and Raphael in 1505. In fact, Catherine is likely to have been the sitter for two religious portraits, of the Virgin Mary and Mary Magdalen, painted by Michael Sittow before she left Spain. The exquisite portrait of the Magdalen, depicting a girl in her early teens, captures the delicate colouring of Catherine's features, set in a round, pale face, with large, heavy-lidded downcast eyes, full red lips and small round chin with a dimple. Her head is bare and her long, wavy golden hair cascades down brightly, matching the gold chalice she holds between long, tapering fingers. Her expression is demure, serene and pious. The same face appears in the depiction of the Virgin and child, on the left-hand panel of a diptych that has now been divided. From the folds of her clothing to the strand of hair across her forehead, the sitter is easily identifiable, although one is likely to have been painted from a sketch made for the former. Nevertheless, they both capture the idealisation of the young princess not only in terms of character and appearance but also in the identification of royal and religious femininity, with Catherine emulating those pious qualities considered and acting as a conduit between kingdoms spiritual and temporal. Sittow was to visit London in the coming years, when he would produce his most famous portrait of Catherine.

Henry was delighted with what he saw, although communication proved a little difficult. He hurried away to bring Arthur to her side and, finally, after years of correspondence, planning and anticipation, the young pair stood face to face. It was not how Catherine had imagined it, thinking she would first see her husband at the altar, dressed in her wedding finery, lifting her veil when the vows had been exchanged. Into the room came a boy who did not look unlike his father, with a long, thin face and dark eyes, sensitive mouth and fashionably cut dark hair, if his portrait of around 1499 is to be believed. In that, he poses with a white rose between his fingers, dressed in a gown of cloth of gold lined with fur over a red doublet with gold edging, a jewelled pendant of black stones set in gold and a black hat and jewel, from which hang three pearls. Painted in oil with gold leaf on a wooden panel, it is the only surviving portrait painted during the boy's lifetime, the closest impression of what Catherine saw at Dogmersfield. An altarpiece depicting Henry's family which was painted a couple of years after Arthur's death shows a youth with a somewhat generic face, the copy of his father's long dark hair and eyes, wide mouth and strong nose. Other contemporary images, in a Guild Book of Ordinances and at prayer in a window at Great Malvern Priory, are similarly general and lacking in personal detail, even touched up in later years. A final image of Arthur from the 1520s depicts a more mature face, with strong nose and small mouth, the sitter wearing a gold chain of office and a red hat with a pilgrim badge, his empty right hand open before him, where the previous portrait had held a flower. From these three images, it seems likely that the fifteen-year-old Arthur was dark in colouring, with a longish, slender face and nose, thin lips and a sensitive expression; a young king-in-waiting, wearing his learning and legacy as visibly as the marks of his status. There are definite facial similarities with a 1509 portrait of Arthur's younger brother Henry, the future Henry VIII, about the eyes and mouth, with the boys having the same blunt, straight-cut bobbed dark hair under a black hat in Arthur's 1499 portrait and the red gown with brown fur shown in the 1520 work. One key difference is the flower held between Henry's fingers, which is red rather than white, emphasising his Lancastrian roots. There is no evidence to suggest that Arthur was in anything other than good health, or that his health during childhood had been poor: he was a tall, slender boy who elicited nothing but compliments from his contemporaries.

Prince Arthur had been born in 1486, eight months after his parents' wedding. He had spent his early years in a nursery at Farnham under the careful eye of his governess, rocked in his cradle and fed by a wet nurse, taking his first steps and celebrating his first birthdays before being invested as Prince of Wales at three and established at the head of his household, a tiny king-in-waiting, at the age of only five. His upbringing had been very different from that of his siblings Margaret, born in 1489, Henry, born in 1491 and Mary, born in 1496. Three other siblings, Elizabeth, Edward and Edmund, had died before Catherine's arrival in England. While the others were raised together at Eltham Palace, Arthur's future role had seen him distanced from his family, undertaking a careful regime of education under tutors such as John Rede, headmaster of Winchester College, who also acted as his chaplain, and the blind poet Bernard Andre, both of whom had connections with a circle of humanists who were patronised by the boy's grandmother, Margaret Beaufort. They included men that would shape English thinking at the turn of a new century: Thomas Linacre, who had been taught alongside the Medici children at Bologna; John Fisher, Margaret's chaplain and doctor of sacred theology; William Grocyn, lecturer in Greek at Oxford; William Lily, the grammarian who had been on pilgrimage to Jerusalem; John Colet, lecturer at Oxford and later dean of St Paul's; and Thomas More, then a student at Lincoln's Inn. Erasmus described them at the end of the century, in delight at the climate of intellectual debate he had found in England:

> When I listen to my friend Colet, I seem to hear Plato himself. Who would not marvel at the perfection of encyclopaedic learning in Grocyn? What could be keener or nobler or nicer than Linacre's judgement? It is marvellous how thick upon the ground the harvest of ancient literature is here everywhere flowering forth.[23]

According to Andre, Arthur was fluent in French and Latin and was able to recite a number of key Roman texts, as well as the tenets of humanist education: theology, grammar, rhetoric, logic, history, poetry, mathematics and music, at which the prince appears to have excelled. William Caxton dedicated his version of Virgil's *Aeneid* to Arthur in 1490 and Andre composed a number of texts for his education, including St Augustine's *City of God*. Andre praised his intelligence with a biblical comparison: 'That famous utterance of the Apostle Paul has been proved true of me: Apollo planted, I watered, God has given the increase.'[24] He had been appointed Head of the Council of the Marches while still young, and it was initially run for him by his uncle Jasper Tudor, but by fifteen he was taking an active part in its administration. In terms of their education, Catherine and Arthur were well matched.

In terms of their language, they were less suited. Catherine spoke no English and her guests spoke no Spanish. They made themselves understood as best they could with the help of translators and Latin pronounced with different accents: as the *Receyt* states, 'thrugh thenterpretacion of busshoppis of bothe contrethis be the meane of Latin were understonden'. Among the princess's attendants, Alonzo de Fonesca, Archbishop of Santiago, and Antonio de Rojas, Bishop of Mallorca, were on hand to help. That evening, Henry retired to dine, leaving Arthur behind with Catherine.[25] Yet there was no opportunity for intimacy; the Spanish minstrels played at Dogmersfield and the young pair danced, but not together. Arthur partnered Lady Guildford while Catherine took the floor with some of her ladies. While the Spanish were prepared to bow to the English king's wishes and relax their rules over contact before the wedding ceremony, dancing together would not have been appropriate for the young couple, even though they were technically man and wife already. It may also have been that they did not yet know a dance they could perform together, with Catherine executing Spanish steps and Arthur performing an English favourite. No record remains of this meeting, of Catherine's response to the youth she had been raised to consider her husband, with whom she would be intimate, who would father her children, by whose side she would sit as he ruled England. On a dynastic level, the pair's responses were insignificant, as they would not alter the commitment they had already made to live as man and wife. On a personal level, though, each must have been relieved to find the other attractive, personable and educated. There is every reason to suppose that Catherine and Arthur were pleased with each other. In fact, Arthur would write to Ferdinand and Isabella that he had 'never felt so much joy' in his entire life as when he 'beheld the sweet face of his bride' and that 'no woman in the world could be more agreeable to him'.

After their evening together, Henry and Arthur left for London, with Catherine's retinue following on slowly behind. Their likely route towards the capital probably lay to the south of the present-day M3, passing instead through Farnborough and Woking, which was the site of a royal palace formerly home to Margaret Beaufort.

The next known stop on the itinerary was Chertsey, where the Spanish probably enjoyed the hospitality of Chertsey Abbey, before pressing on to Kingston upon Thames. There, Edward's friend and cousin Edward Stafford, Duke of Buckingham, was waiting at the head of a party of several hundred horsemen, dressed in black and red, to escort her into the city. As England's wealthiest aristocrat and the only duke in the country at that time, Buckingham at the age of twenty-three was one of the most flamboyant figures at the Tudor court, a dazzling and arrogant figure whose trajectory Catherine would witness ending in tragedy.

II

Catherine's destination was London, England's capital, the hub of government and finance, of foreign trade, the centre of culture and religion, the seat of prosperity and rebellion, the home to which the peripatetic court continued to return. The points on its skyline were the spires of churches and towers of palaces, the great oriel windows of merchants' houses and the sloping roofs of tenements, crosses in marketplaces, gallows and the masts of ships at the docks. The city's mayor of a century before, the real Dick Whittington, who held office in 1397, 1406 and 1419, had not exactly found the streets to be paved with gold, but an Italian visitor in 1500 found 'one single street, named the Strand ... [where] there are fifty-two goldsmiths' shops, so rich and full of silver vessels' it could not be rivalled by 'all the shops in Milan, Rome, Venice and Florence put together'. John Stowe, born in the heart of the city in 1525, later described it as being responsible for 'the propagation of learning, the maintenance of arts, the increase of riches'.

The city into which Catherine rode for the first time in November 1501 was a place of constant variety, where rich and poor alike lived in close proximity, in buildings made of timber and brick, and where narrow lanes of tall, thin houses gave way to wide thoroughfares. Wealthy citizens built themselves large, sprawling houses with long gardens along the waterfront, or else took over entire blocks, constructing buildings around courtyards; traders lived above their shops or slept in backrooms, while their apprentices slept on truckle beds if they were lucky, or whatever they could find in their workspace, bound as they were to serve for seven years.

London was full of religious houses; much of its land and property was owned by the Crown or the Church and saints' days and holy festivals defined the working day and year. The riverside thronged with merchants, sailors and travellers from across Europe and further, bringing furs, timber, copper and flax over the North Sea, wines, carpets and textiles from the Netherlands, leather, fruit and alum from Spain, glassware, oil and salt from the Mediterranean, spices and ceramics from the Holy Lands and ivory, gold, almonds and coral from Africa. As a Venetian of 1500 observed, the ebb and flow of the River Thames meant that 'vessels of a hundred tons burden' could sail right up to the docks in the heart of the city 'and any ship within five miles of it'. The city's population, falling within the approximate square mile from Newgate in the west to the Tower in the east, was somewhere between 50,000 and 100,000, roughly one hundred times smaller than in the census taken five centuries later. It was mostly confined to the north bank, with a single bridge spanning the river, famous for its nineteen arches and the many buildings, including public latrines and a chapel dedicated to St Thomas.

The Venetian observed that 'persons of low degree and artificers ... [had] congregated there from all parts of the island, and from Flanders and from every other place'. The 'alien subsidies' or foreigners' tax returns paid between 1480 and 1510 confirm there was indeed a wide spectrum of nationalities resident in the city during this time. By far the largest group, at 795 individuals, were those classified as 'Teutonic' (German), closely followed by Scots at 236 and Flemings at 189. There were 44 Zeelanders, 43 French and 37 Dutch, 12 Hollanders, 7 Lombards and 6 Icelanders, along with a sprinkling of Florentines, Welsh, Danes, Brabanters, Saxons, Greeks, a Frisian and a Pomeranian.[26] It was largely a pale-skinned, northern European demographic. Where non-white faces did appear on English streets, they would have stood out, like the Indians Benedictus and Antonia Calman who were recorded living in Bishopsgate Ward in June 1483, or Jacobus Black, also Indian, who arrived in Devon on 24 July 1484. They would have found their way to England across land, heading west to Turkey or Greece, or perhaps into the Holy Lands; from there they could have continued across Europe, or boarded a merchant ship at one of the Mediterranean ports. Like Catherine, Jacobus Black's arrival on the

Devon coasts suggests he had sailed around the tip of Gibraltar, up the Spanish coast, through the Bay of Biscay, straight up to the first English port available.

There were, however, a few Spaniards resident in England, dating back to the end of the reign of Arthur's Yorkist grandparents. A Castilian, John Sans or Sancius de Venesse, from Fuenterrabia was recorded as resident on 3 July 1482, but appears to have been a merchant as he is listed as returning to England on 17 January 1486, in a ship named the *Maria de Fontarabia*. A goldsmith from Catalonia, Augustinius Grace, who had arrived in June 1483 with three apprentices named Lucas, Clemens and Jacobus Cok, all resident in Aldgate Ward, may have been Moorish émigrés from Catherine's homeland. Two residents of Long Melford, Suffolk, that August appeared to have come from Aragon. A surgeon, Fernandy Pedro, appears in the records on 12 December 1488; a Sebastian de Mosica, Spaniard, on 10 January 1497; and a Francis Dyas, Spaniard, on 27 May of that year.[27] In 1494, King Henry made a payment of £4 to 'Spaniard, the tennis player', who may have been coaching him in the old-style real tennis which he loved to play.

The Spanish party was conducted by the Duke of Buckingham for ten miles from Richmond, through Richmond Park along the riverbank, past places like Putney and Clapham, which were then mere villages. On 12 November he brought them to Lambeth Palace, the London residence of the Archbishop of Canterbury, an important location in a religious and legal sense, but geographically significant as it stood on the south bank, still on the margins of the city, which befitted Catherine's status. She might have been married already and welcomed by the king and her future husband as a legal member of the family, but she was still symbolically an outsider. Her entrance into the city had been planned for over a year and this stop on the south bank, and the trains of colourfully clothed attendants in their well-rehearsed stages along the route, give the impression of the princess being both the guest of honour and the star of a play with whose scenes and lines she only had a vague familiarity. She went into it willingly, bravely, perhaps even excitedly and proudly, thinking of this as the culmination of her parents' wishes, and of herself as their ambassador. From witnessing the marriages of her siblings she understood that all did not necessarily run smoothly, but the signs in London were auspicious that autumn.

At Lambeth, Catherine passed through the newly completed redbrick gateway, built by the recently deceased Cardinal John Morton. It was a prime example of the newest architecture of the time, with its five towers featuring a diaper, or diamond, design in black header bricks and the rooms inside decorated with linen-fold wooden panelling. Inside, the Spanish were received in the medieval Great Hall, where up to 5,000 people could be feasted. It was probably in this hall of red brick and timber buttresses that Catherine and her party dined, although in the coming years she would witness ceremonial feasts being held in the Great Chamber and in Morton's Tower. Catherine was lodged in the palace itself, enjoying the hospitality of the Bishop of Rochester while her entourage were found places to sleep in the surrounding houses and inns of Lambeth.

On the morning of Friday 12 November, the Spanish party rode to St George's Field, which was the meeting point for the entry into the city itself. Here, the Mayor Sir John Shaa was waiting to greet them and the guests were lined up to be paired with an English courtier of equal rank. Here, also, Catherine was to meet the person who was to have the greatest impact on her life. She cannot have known it when the ten-year-old Prince Henry rode up, confident in the saddle, enthusiastic about his role in the day's proceedings. Tall, sturdy and fair-haired, he would have appeared every inch the young prince, his precocious abilities and easy grace already noted by Erasmus and Thomas More, who had visited him in the schoolroom at Eltham. There was already something exuberant in his high spirits, his flamboyance and dexterity in handling his horse, having been riding since at least the age of three. To Catherine that November he was a future brother-in-law, perhaps destined for the Church, or as a powerful ally with a family of his own, once she and Arthur became king and queen of England. From St George's Field, with the princess mounted on a mule, the long procession began its journey to London Bridge.

The very fabric of London itself had become a stage set for the most important performance of Catherine's life so far. A lot of planning had gone into the decorations, music, references and designs for six separate pageants, or set-pieces, along the route, intended to glorify and flatter the young couple, to place their marriage within a cultural and mythological context, and to hint at expectations for their future together. England had a long, rich history of such pageantry, to welcome returning kings and foreign brides or to celebrate weddings. Queen Elizabeth had been brought to her coronation in 1487 by barges shaped like dragons breathing fire. There was always a mixture of serious symbolism, religion and pantomimic elements, largely derived from the traditions of courtly entertainment and the miracle and morality plays staged by city guilds. Accounts left by some of the guilds outlined the extent to which they committed their time and funds in creating, painting and erecting scenery and scaffolding, making props, learning lines, training singers and sewing the costumes some of their members would wear on the day. The dominant theme of the celebrations planned for Catherine was 'honour'. The city of London turned out en fête on 12 November, to do honour of their own to the Spanish princess who had come to marry their Arthur. Although traditionally it fell to the mayor, aldermen and guilds to prepare the city, on this occasion Henry appointed two courtiers, Sir Reginald Bray and George Neville, Lord Bergavenny, to oversee the arrangements. Henry himself took a keen interest in the preparations, ordering the Master of the Revels, Henry Wentworth, to pack all the pageants and costumes up and send them to Richmond for his inspection.[28]

As she approached London Bridge from the south, the first pageant came into view. It was a structure with two storeys, painted blue and gold, decorated with the symbols of Tudor heritage: red English lions, Beaufort portcullises, ostrich feathers of the Prince of Wales and the Lancastrian rose. Catherine was met by her own namesake, the figure of St Catherine, announcing her presence as 'Kateryn of the Court Celestyall' and claiming the princess's long-standing devotion to her from the day of her christening. Since then, the saint had been her 'shild and proteccion' and would now oversee her entry into London, suggestive of a second baptism into a new city and country, a new role and life. More than this, Catherine was now to be a bridge between the spiritual and temporal realms, as the wife of both Arthur and Jesus himself, although she was exhorted to always put her God first. These lines were of great significance for the daughter of Ferdinand and Isabella, whose similar attitude towards religion and marriage provided Catherine's model for the couple united in wedlock and in the service of God:

And as I halp you to Crist, your first make [mate]
So have I purveid a Second spowse trewe
But ye for hym the first shall not forsake
Love your first spouse chief, and after that your newe.[29]

St Catherine was joined by a British saint, Ursula, who reminded the princess of her Lancastrian roots and created another connection, claiming that the saint herself was of the same blood. Thus, Ursula and Catherine were presented as sharing noble descent from John of Gaunt, as Arthur did, through his paternal grandmother. If Ursula had real historical roots, she was associated with the west of England, possibly the daughter of a king of Dumnonia (Cornwall, Devon, Dorset and Somerset) who was martyred along with 11,000 virgins on her way to be married in Brittany, in the fourth or fifth century. This mattered little, however, beside the potential for symbolism that she offered. The Ursula of the pageant claimed descent from the mythological King Arthur and stated that Catherine's imminent marriage to the new Arthur created a sort of kinship between them. The cult of St Ursula was particularly strong in Wales too, with one surviving version of her life being written in the rare medieval Welsh, creating an additional connection with the prince. The two saints then conducted the princess to the first pageant, which represented the Castle of Policy.

Rather like a medieval miracle or morality play, the Policy pageant contained a panel of characters, some historical, some biblical and others as abstract virtues. Thus the qualities of Virtue and Nobleness sat alongside Job and Boethius, Catherine's ancestor Alphonse and the Archangel Raphael, patron of marriage and procreation. Together, they combined to offer the princess lessons on 'policy' or how to rule, as without their 'help all they that think to reign, or long to prosper, labour all in vain'.[30] A vision of Catherine and Arthur seated side by side in the court of Honour promised the rewards of their efforts to employ the lessons offered by this political wisdom. The visual aspects of these displays must have been powerful, containing shorthand and codes for identities, such as the association of St Catherine with the wheel, or the familiar blue and white in which the Virgin Mary was, and is, always depicted. The actual castle itself was decorated with the red roses of Lancaster and the portcullises of the Beaufort family and was at least two storeys, hung with blue and red cloth of tissue. Before it stood two great posts, painted with the arms of England and gilded, along with gold and azure decoration.

Yet the question of the princess's understanding cannot be avoided. As yet, Catherine could barely speak English. The words of these characters, so skilfully chosen and set to rhyme, probably by the court poets Skelton and Andre, would have completely passed her by. From the instructions given by Elizabeth of York for Catherine to practise her French, it seems impossible that Henry, Bray and Neville were unaware of her limitations with the language. As an educated Catholic and humanist princess, having drawn from the same pool of key classical texts as Arthur's tutors, no doubt she could decode some of the clues and understand the pageants' messages on some level. It would have helped that each one was accompanied by a short Latin inscription. No doubt she was convinced of their welcome, their goodwill and their aspirations for her: perhaps the specific details did not matter. Yet, there were clearly many attempts to tease out obscure references, virtues and connections that were specific to the identity and lineage of the Spanish princess. It is impossible to know now just how much of them she understood fully. However, they are likely to have made a powerful impact upon the intelligent ten-year-old Henry at her side, witnessing his first ever such experience and consolidating his belief in Catherine's worth and destiny.

The procession crossed the bridge, over Stone Gate, over the drawbridge that allowed the passage of tall ships, past the chapel and down into Bridgestrete. A surviving map from 1520 allows a detailed description of the landmarks Catherine passed, of the buildings that formed her first view of the busy, cosmopolitan city. To her right, the Church of St Magnus the Martyr, the guild church of the Worshipful Company of Fishmongers, was a reminder of one of the city's crucial trades and also an important place in the city, where news was disseminated, criminals were punished and notices were read out. To her left, separated from the church by the road, was the churchyard, where important figures such as Henry Yevele, master cathedral builder, lay at rest. Catherine crossed over Thames

Street, a major thoroughfare running parallel with the river, leading off to Billingsgate market a few blocks to the east, and headed north up New Fysshestrete. The road was lined with the homes and shops of merchant and fishermen, with alleyways leading between them into the central courtyards or gardens inside each block. They had barely passed four or five such properties before another church appeared, that of St Margaret's, sitting inside its own grounds, surrounded by tombs. Later destroyed in the Great Fire of London, it stood on the site of the present-day Monument, also serving the community of fishermen and their families. A little further ahead along the same street was the final church of Bridge Ward, St Leonard's, Eastcheap, also a casualty of the 1666 fire. Then, just past the crossroads of Estchepe [*sic*] and Graschestret, close by the stone house that had housed Catherine's Lancastrian great-great-great-uncle, the Black Prince, the second pageant was waiting.

The history embodied in this second performance was more recent and more visual. Catherine was greeted by the union rose, a combination of the red rose of Lancaster and the white rose of York; this was a clever piece of propaganda on the part of the Tudor regime, building bridges between the warring families of the previous century. The princess can hardly have failed to understand its symbolism. Built across the Great Conduit, just past the Tabard in the centre of Gracechurch Street, this pageant included two elaborate gateways. In order to pass through them, Catherine had to accept the terms offered by Policy, that 'this sound castle is for virtue, not for nobility, but without me no entrance lies open in this place'. The conduit itself was new, having been built in 1491 by former Mayor Thomas Hill. From there, Catherine headed up Gracechurch Street Hill, passing St Benet's Church with its newly completed south aisle on the right, where the road met Fenchurch Street and All Hallows Church on the left, almost on the corner of Lombard Street. This area was often used as a corn market, but there would have been no trace of it as Catherine passed by.

The procession headed onwards, past the rows of densely packed houses, separated by the occasional alley, like Offele Alley, which likely got its name from the animal waste once dumped there. To their right lay Leadenhall Market, dating from the fourteenth century, which had until recently been used for the weighing and sale of cloth and wool, before Henry designated it in 1488 as solely for the handling of leather. Opposite and further along sat the Church of St Peter upon Cornhill, the highest point in London. From here, the Spaniards would have had a view down over the rooftops of the city, turning to see it all stretching out behind them down to the Thames. Here, they turned left into Cornhill, a major thoroughfare and division in the city, where foreign bakers were restricted to a small area for selling their wares so that they didn't compete with the locals. If they required any deterrent, the pillory set halfway along, close to Longhornes Alley, offered an unpleasant, public form of shame.

Cornhill was long enough to boast three conduits. The third pageant was situated at the main one of these, where a cistern had stood in 1401, developed into a castellated stone fixture by a Robert Drope in 1475. Atop its solid fortifications, King Alfonso the Wise of Castile prophesised that the royal marriage would produce many offspring, as it had been foretold in the stars that 'a goodly pryncess yong and tender' would marry a 'noble prince'.[31] Over the sphere rode Arthur's chariot, and above that the figure of God himself. Amid this panorama, the young couple took on an astrological significance, with Arthur associated with Arcturus, the brightest star in the northern sky, and Catherine with Hesperus, the evening star, or planet Venus, the 'bright sterre of Spain'. This may have been a play on the old Roman name for Spain, Hispania or Hesperia. The chroniclers described this as the most impressive of all the pageantry that day, 'ffer excedyng the othir in cost and cunnyng of dyvyse' with its three red-and-green pillars framing a stage with a backcloth painted to look like stonework. Above various royal devices was a recreation of the heavens, the stars, astrological signs and information about the waning and waxing of the moon, all covered over by a cloth painted in white and green checks.[32]

Again, Catherine was reminded of her higher allegiance, this time by the figure of Job:

> Alfons hath shewed you the hevenly bodies
> For your comfort, and of your spouse a figure.
> But now, Madam, loke up above all this
> And ye shall find a more special pleasure

To knowe and beholde the Great Lord of Nature
Almighti God, that creatyd and wrought
Arthure, Hesperus, and all the heven of nought.

It was a lesson that she scarcely needed, already having learned from her mother the higher authority of God, but a lesson that would prove poignant later in her life.

Passing along Cornhill, in front of the Cardinal's Hat inn, the party rode into a junction where the road met Lombardetrete, Bradstrete and Le Pultrye, or the Poultry, where chickens and other fowl were sold. This was considered to be the exact middle of the city, where the Stocks Market, the largest of all London's fish and flesh markets, had been built in the late thirteenth century to raise funds to assist the building and maintenance of the bridge. Diagonal to it, beyond Scalding Alley, was the recently rebuilt St Mildred's Church and the entrance to the grand Grocer's Hall with its extensive gardens, a row of almshouses and a convent, also with a garden. This gave into Cheapside, where the 'cheaps', or markets, a major hub of commerce and activity, sold everything from wood, milk, soap and bread to honey. Here the people had gathered in large numbers to see the Spaniards but were restrained behind wooden railings to prevent any disturbance.

The fourth pageant stood at the east end of the street, on the Eastchepe conduit, which had been rebuilt by Thomas Ilam in 1480 from its original 1261 form. Behind it was the thirteenth-century Hospital of St Thomas of Acon, which was then in the hands of Richard Adams, who was steadily accruing debts that would amount to over £718 by 1510.[33] It was also the location where the Mercers' Guild met. Here, Prince Arthur was presented as the Sun King, whose brightness illuminated the earth and who dispensed wisdom and justice. The pageant itself was a tall construction with pillars supporting Welsh dragons and English lions, against a backdrop painted with stars, angels and clouds. A mechanised wheel carried more astrological symbols and was turned by three young boys, before the figure of Arthur appeared in a chariot.

A little further along Cheapside stood the King's Head and St Mary-le-Bow Church, whose bells could be heard as far away as Hackney Marshes. In the centre of the street, opposite Honey Lane, near the Standard Inn, stood a conduit and 'standard', which was also a fountain and a significant location in terms of civic justice. Various beheadings had taken place there, along with the burning of official rolls and the striking off of criminals' hands. On this day, though, the sight was more welcoming. Here, the fifth pageant was entitled 'The Temple of God', with the figure of the Lord adorned in gems and pearls, seated on a throne surrounded by burning candles and singing angels. A huge red rose was borne aloft by heraldic beasts. More comparisons were made between King Henry and the deity, during which a 'prelate of the church' spoke on the holy union of marriage, expanding the earlier theme of Catherine's two husbands and the parallel of earthly and spiritual connection:

> The maryage of God to the nature of man
> This mariage was so secret a mystery
> That oure Blissid Savyour, Crist Jhesus
> Compared it to a maryage erthely
> To make it appiere more open and pleyn to us
> By a parabill or symylitude, seyeng thus:
> The Kyng of Heven is like an erthely kyng
> That to his sonne prepareth a weddyng.

Yet while she was watching this pageant unawares, Catherine was herself being observed. Arthur, Henry, his wife and his mother had taken over 'a howys wheryn that tyme dwelled Wylliam Geffrey, haberdasher' and stood in the windows, 'not in very opyn sight ... beholdynge the persones, their raise, ordre and behavynges of the hole companye, bothe of Englonde and of Spayne, as well of their apparell and horsis'.[34] At this point a description of the princess is also recorded, reminiscent of her mother's appearance on ceremonial occasions, with 'her here hanging down abowt her shulders, which is faire auburne, and in maner of a coyfe betwene her hede and her hatt of a carnacioun colour, and that was fastenyd from the myddis of her hed upwards so as men might weell se all her here from the myddill parte of her hid downwards'.[35] Also watching her pass was the young lawyer Thomas More, then a twenty-three-year-old student in Lincoln's Inn. He wrote to his friend John Holt that Catherine had 'thrilled the hearts of everyone' and that she possessed 'all those qualities that make for beauty in a very charming young girl'. 'Everywhere she receives the highest of praises,' he went on, 'but even that is inadequate. I do hope this highly publicised union will prove a happy omen for England.'[36]

More reacted quite differently to Catherine's entourage, which contained a number of African or Muslim servants, 'ridiculous, tattered, barefooted pygmy Ethiopians, like devils out of hell'. As cosmopolitan as London may have been with all its foreign trade, such faces were still relatively unfamiliar on its streets. The entire Spanish party must have seemed exotic and unfamiliar, led along by the princess' musicians playing their shawms and sackbuts, the women dressed in long headdresses of black lace. A twist of fate meant that each pairing of English and Spaniard rode side-saddle back to back, instead of facing each other. Alongside their English counterparts, who had dressed in cloth of gold and dazzling colours, the darkness of the Spaniards must have proved quite a contrast.

From here, Catherine entered the final stage of her journey. She passed the White Bear Inn and Goldsmith's Row, which had so impressed the Venetian with its dazzling arrays of silver cups. It must have impressed Catherine as a display of London's wealth, an effect which is conveyed well by John Stowe later in the century: 'a most beautiful frame of houses and shops, consisting of tenne faire dwellings, uniformly builded foure stories high, beautified towards the streets with the goldsmiths' arms and likeness of Woodmen ... riding on monstrous beasts, all richly painted and gilt'. Catherine rode on past the gilded cross that had been raised in 1290 as a memorial to Edward I's queen, Eleanor of Castile, and the church of St Peter Westcheap, past Saddler's Hall and the Mitre Inn, to her final stop, which was the conduit at the west end of the street, before the gate that led into St Paul's Cathedral. Up a set of seven steps each of the cardinal virtues was represented, with two vacant thrones at the top awaiting Arthur and Catherine. At the door of St Paul's, the mayor, aldermen and guildsmen presented her with their traditional gifts, including 'basins and pots filled with coin to a great sum' and other treasures. Catherine thanked them all in a 'most-learned manner' and entered the cathedral.

After all the noise, activity and colour outside, the cool, dark quietness of St Paul's must have provided a contrast, if not relief. The cathedral Catherine entered was one of the longest and tallest in Europe, easily comparable to anything she had seen in Spain and breathtaking with its gothic Perpendicular arches, vaulted nave and exquisite stained glass, especially the rose window which found its way into Chaucer's *Canterbury Tales* as a standard of beauty. Catherine made her way to the building's most famous shrine, that of St Erkenwald, a seventh-century Bishop of London and the subject of a famous fourteenth-century poem, possibly written by the same author of *Pearl* and *Sir Gawain and the Green Knight*. The poem describes the awakening of a long-dead pre-Christian who laments his fate and is baptised by a single tear shed by Erkenwald, enabling him to enter Heaven. The popularity of the poem and the saint's cult combined to make St Paul's a focus for medieval pilgrimage, and Catherine would have seen the splendid shrine in all its glory. Rebuilt in 1339 by three London goldsmiths who dedicated an entire year to its beautification, the shrine was a pyramid in shape, covered in gold, silver and jewels, with an altar for offerings. An engraving by the seventeenth-century artist Wenceslaus Holler shows a tomb-like box surrounded by railings, topped by a three-arch structure, over which the decorated pyramid sits. By a twist of fate, Catherine's wedding day was scheduled to take place on St Erkenwald's day, 14 November. This made it particularly poignant that the cathedral and the saint's centuries-old association with the city of London were being employed on the princess's behalf.

While she was there, Catherine would also have taken in the wooden tabernacle to the side, which contained a portrait of St Paul and the pillar on which a beautiful image of the Virgin was displayed, above a constantly lit lamp. The nave, known as St Paul's walk, was long and impressive. In the choir lay Catherine's ancestor John of Gaunt, forefather of the Lancastrian dynasty and his first wife, Blanche. The cathedral was laid out in the shape of a Greek cross, with four equal parts converging on a central cross. It was also the repository of a number of relics, including a stone from the spot of the Ascension, a piece of wood from the True Cross and, reputedly, some bones from the 11,000 virgins who had accompanied Saint Ursula.[37] The Princess was blessed by the Archbishop of Canterbury and left her own offering to St Erkenwald. She would also have given thanks for her safe arrival in the city; just like her mother, Catherine was used to the juxtaposing of lavish celebrations and piety. Finally she was led through a private door to the adjacent Bishop of London's Palace, where she was to pass the night, disappearing for a while from the public stage.

The map of 1520 shows the location of the palace, to the north-west of the cathedral, with its own gardens and courtyard, bordered by the Atrium, Paternoster Rowe and Ave Maria Alley. The bishop's lodgings had been re-glazed in Catherine's honour. Four blocks to the south, King Henry, Queen Elizabeth and Prince Arthur settled in for the night at Baynard's Castle on the river. The streets of London began to return to normal. The pageants were taken down, as were the wooden railings; banners and flags were untied and rolled away; the swept cobbles began to accumulate mess and dirt again, as animals strayed and feet criss-crossed the path where the princess had travelled. Soon the citizens would be summoned to worship, and after that the ceremonial spaces would be filled again by markets. The conduits would run with water instead of wine. As the night of Friday 12 November slipped into the early hours of Saturday morning, the king, prince, mayor and guildsmen could reflect that the reception of their future queen had been a success. With her voluptuous beauty and long auburn hair, Catherine had made a positive impact upon the London crowd. It was to be the start of a long relationship during which she would be held in great affection by her subjects.

6

The Wedding
November 1501

I

Baynard's Castle was an imposing sight to those passing along the Thames. With its massive octagonal towers topped by little turrets and its extensive glazed windows, with four wings standing around a courtyard of trapezoid shape, it was clearly a residence worthy of royalty. Before the arrival of Henry Tudor it had been in the hands of Queen Elizabeth of York's family and had witnessed the crown being offered to her father, Edward IV, in 1461, and her uncle, Richard III, in 1483. In recent years, Henry had transformed it from a largely defensive building into a venue 'farre more beautifull and commodious for the entertainment of any Prince or Great Estate'[1] and that November it was chosen for further interaction between the English and Spanish, with its high walls offering a degree of privacy for the sensitive tasks ahead.

On Saturday 13th, Henry hosted the Spanish party at Baynard's, receiving them while sitting in state with his two sons on either side. This was a visit of business rather than pleasure, and both boys sat and watched as the Spanish presented the terms of the forthcoming match and gave the king assurances from Ferdinand of his daughter's virginity.[2] This was more than a formality, although at this stage of the proceedings Catherine's untouched state was taken for granted. Even more than her status as a daughter of

Spain, virginity was the measure of her worth, as a dynastic vessel for childbearing and her suitability as a bride for Arthur and a future queen of England. There could be no question of Spain attempting to provide Henry with an impure woman, or worse, one who might already be pregnant. Sexual history, or 'good fame', was the foundation stone on which women's reputations and marital careers were built. On one hand, the state of Catherine's innocence was a private, intimate matter, confided secretly behind the walls of Baynard's Castle from one father to another, but it was also symbolic of the centrality of the female body to the success of royal dynasties and international relations. The topic might be delicate, but it was also one of politics and state. Catherine did not have to endure the display of bloodstained sheets after her wedding night that had been the custom in Spain, but the assurances of her virginity were made in earnest before senior officials and the Tudor royal family. She had to be untainted. The impression this made upon Arthur, aged fifteen, and Henry, aged ten, was one of an inescapable rite of passage. Women's good reputations were indispensable and the act of marriage marked their transition between innocence and sexual experience. It was a very clear line in the sand, drawn and valued by men, with the princess as the commodity over which they were bargaining. Catherine herself was notably absent from the discussion.

Later that afternoon, the princess was conveyed down the hill to Baynard's, where she was received by her future mother-in-law, Elizabeth of York. The eldest daughter of the popular first Yorkist king, Elizabeth was then thirty-five and still bearing the traces of beauty inherited from both her parents that not even the births of six, perhaps seven, children could eradicate. The product of a secret love match, she had been raised amid the turbulence of the Wars of the Roses, fleeing into exile with her mother when the Lancastrians had displaced them, and again in the aftermath of Edward's death when she and her siblings had been declared illegitimate by their uncle, who then succeeded as Richard III. The solution to the rivalry and fighting had been her marriage to Henry, the victor of Bosworth, uniting the houses of York and Lancaster, in January 1486. And yet, unlike anyone else in Henry's small family, there was something different, something 'other' about her. As an only child, born posthumously, Henry had only his mother Margaret and his uncle, Jasper Tudor, as close relatives to rely on. His children would continue that bloodline but his wife represented the old reigning dynasty, of which other members had gradually been removed as threats. Yorkists such as the Pole brothers, Elizabeth's cousins, were still young but proved to be sources of future trouble, and she had already seen the execution of another male claimant, Edward, Earl of Warwick, son of her father's brother. In spite of this, there was never any question of Elizabeth's loyalty. Her commitment to her husband and children was absolute, even when various pretenders to the throne claimed kinship, but her Yorkist history gave her another dimension, making her an outsider on the inside, which may have created a connection between her and Catherine.

For the daughter of Isabella of Castile, Elizabeth offered a very different model of queenship to that with which she had grown up. Instead of the imposing figure of leadership whose drive and fervour had led to the conquest of Granada and the expulsion of the Jews, the organiser behind Ferdinand's campaigns and the master of dramatic performance and dress, Elizabeth of York appeared placid and gentle, but those were the very strengths of her appeal. Her role was a supportive one, taking a clear second place to her husband, who had claimed the throne by right of conquest rather than by alliance with her bloodline. Henry was clearly the driving force in the relationship, aided by his formidable and capable mother, and Elizabeth deferred to him, forging her own identity as the face of compassion, piety and supplication. Hugely popular with the people, she was the recipient of their regular gifts, with surviving accounts from 1502–3 indicating a steady stream of fresh fruit, vegetables, eggs, meat, flowers and delicacies being brought to her palaces whenever she was in residence. Through her motherhood she was associated with the cult of the Virgin Mary, an earthly embodiment of divine maternity and a conduit to heaven by virtue of her anointed position. Her accounts betray her warmth and charity, rewarding old servants, assisting those who were ill or in need, or who undertook pilgrimage on her behalf. She was an accessible figure, submissive, obedient and passive, mild and self-effacing, personifying her motto 'humble and reverent', with daughters of her own just a couple of years younger than Catherine.

It is not clear how long the two women shared each other's company, or what passed between them. The *Receyt* describes a merry tone to events, with 'pleasure and goodly communication, dancing and disports' but the nature of the communication is not stated. Elizabeth may simply have been hosting her imminent daughter-in-law, as Margaret Beaufort had held a feast for the Spanish party, creating an occasion for a formal introduction. Yet there may have been a more intimate, personal note if the queen took the opportunity to try and speak to the girl, using translators, about their expectations of her. Just as Henry would describe himself as a new father figure for Catherine, it is quite in keeping with what is known about Elizabeth's character that she would adopt a maternal role towards her son's wife. Whether or not she recognised it at the time, Catherine had a potential ally in the queen, who would have been a considerate and welcoming figure, a friend to the young girl so newly arrived in a foreign land, a sympathetic ear, even an advocate to steer her amid the male-dominated world of politics. At the least it is likely that Elizabeth outlined the arrangements for the following day, for the wedding itself, which was to be the costliest of Henry's entire reign and the most significant for the Spanish visitors. From the first plans that had been made for the children as infants, fourteen years of anticipation and negotiation were to come to fruition in the morning. One chapter of Catherine's life, and one identity, would close and a new one would begin. Catherine would return to her lodgings in the Bishop's Palace by torchlit procession, conscious of the significance of the moment.

II

Catherine woke the following morning in the shadow of St Paul's Cathedral, perhaps even to the sound of its bells. Henry's choice of location was not an idle one. His own wedding had taken place at Westminster, but at this point in London's history the palace and abbey were removed from the main city, a considerable distance outside the walls, far from the mass of citizens whom he had hoped to impress with pageantry and ceremony. For Henry had secured a daughter of Spain for his son. All the effort he had invested in establishing his own royal credentials found validation in Isabella and Ferdinand's choice to send him their daughter, making an alliance for England with the most formidable power of the late fifteenth century. Catherine brought his regime validity on the European stage and the might of the conquistadors in the face of future challenges; he wanted news of this wedding to have an international spread, and for this he needed an audience.

Geographically, St Paul's sat at the heart of the city, at its middle point and at its peak, on top of the original London Hill. The many markets clustering round it ensured a constant throng of locals and visitors, engaged in the exchange of money and goods. By 1501 it had also become the centre of the dissemination of news, through printed pamphlets and notices posted there and the gathering of gossips to pass information by word of mouth. Three 'folkmote' (folk meetings) a year had traditionally been held on the green to the east of the cathedral, to which the citizens had been summoned by bells, and the stone cross was used as a location for the delivery of sermons, papal bulls, excommunications and punishments. It had been the location in June 1483 where Elizabeth of York and her siblings had been publicly denounced as illegitimate in order to clear the way for Richard III to the throne. The historian Carlyle later went as far as to refer to St Paul's as 'a kind of *Times* newspaper of the day', such was its centrality in the history of communication, while Bishop Earle likened it to Babel with its 'confusion of languages' and as a 'market for young lecturers'.[3] St Paul's was large enough to accommodate vast numbers of people, central enough for them to attend and established enough to be suitable for a wedding. Henry wanted to employ the tongues of his Londoners to praise the occasion and ensure that it would never be forgotten. It meant maximum exposure for Catherine, too.

On the morning of Sunday 14 November, Doña Elvira and the other Spanish ladies helped Catherine to dress. Even this early on, there was a clear difference between the fashions of the Spanish and English courts, a cultural clash which would take a little time to overcome. While the English courtiers draped themselves in colourful silks, cloth of gold, jewels and gold chains, the Spanish women favoured heavy black-lace mantillas and a kind of embroidery known as blackwork. Catherine's wide-brimmed red hat, held in place with gold lace, had caused comment during her arrival, being considered strange and similar to that of a cardinal. Most of all, though, her wedding dress was to attract attention because of its strangeness. It was the first time that England had seen the farthingale, or vardingale, named for the Spanish word 'verdugos' after the supple green twigs used to create hoops that made the distinctive shape of the skirt. The fashion was thought to have begun a generation before, described by Palencia as an attempt by Juana of Portugal, wife of Isabella's brother Henry IV, to conceal a pregnancy. One Spanish monk described the shape created, making women 'ugly, monstrous and deformed until they ... look like bells'.[4] The fashion had been banned in Italy in 1498 and must have created an impact in England, which was used to the female form being draped in long, loose gowns over the traditional kirtles. The differences were clearly identifiable enough to replicate in pageantry as early as the day of the wedding, when a woman appeared dressed 'in the style of Hispayne', and the style would establish itself for centuries to come.

Catherine chose to be married in white. The colour would not become an established tradition for weddings until the Victorian period, so it is interesting that the princess selected it, with its associations of innocence and purity, over the costly brocades and gold that were favoured at her parents' court. The symbolic message, the significance of the ceremony, appears to have overridden the opportunity to dazzle with colour and jewellery. She wore a long white satin skirt over her farthingale, pleated in folds, creating a hooped effect, and her face was covered by a white veil, edged in gold, embroidered with pearls, almost a prototype for what was to become a conventional bridal outfit. Her long hair hung loose as a further symbol of her virginity, as was traditional for a bride, and her long train was carried by the queen's sister, Lady Cecily Welles. To some English eyes, the effect was rather masculine, concealing the female form, her dress being 'very large, both [in] the sleeves and also the body with many pleats ... much like men's clothing'.[5] It was perhaps coordinated that Arthur was also dressed in white satin, as was his brother Henry, who was to give away the bride. This conjured an unusual visual reference between husband, wife and brother that was prophetic of years to come.

Even inside the cathedral, Henry intended that the young couple should be seen. To this effect, he set them upon a stage of their own, a wooden platform that had been erected along the entire 350 feet from the choir door to the west door, standing four feet high and twelve feet wide. Covered in red cloth, it included a raised platform and was railed along each side to keep onlookers at bay. Catherine and Arthur were literally to be centre stage, elevated over the heads of Londoners, in something like the culminating pageant of the recent days, only in the flesh instead of in representation. This replacement of the symbolic with the real was a reminder that the earthly and divine came together in the person of royalty and that such figures were an actual, visible presence in the capital and among their people. And because it was Catherine and Arthur's day, King Henry observed the ceremony from behind a screen, so that he, his wife and his mother would not upstage the young pair in terms of precedence.

Prince Henry and the Duke of Cabra escorted Catherine from the Bishop's Palace to the west door of the cathedral. The Archbishop of Canterbury, Henry Deane, was waiting for her there with eighteen bishops and abbots, and led her inside to the sound of trumpets. Arthur had travelled there from his lodgings in the Great Wardrobe, just to the south of the cathedral, and, dazzling in white satin, took his place at Catherine's side to repeat their wedding vows before the congregation. The agreement between England and Spain was read aloud, after which the princess was endowed with the titles and lands Henry had bestowed on her as her settlement in becoming his daughter-in-law. After they were formally pronounced man and wife, the pair turned to acknowledge the crowd 'so the present multitude of people might see and behold their persons'[6] and walked along the length of the platform, hand in hand. One observer described them as a 'lusty and amorous couple'. They were blessed and the Mass was read, before they retired from public gaze back into the Bishop's Palace. After all the years of waiting, Arthur and Catherine were now officially man and wife, side by side in the flesh.

The newly-weds were greeted at the west door by another pageant. King Henry himself had almost caused a civic uproar when he commissioned the display then tried to bill the city aldermen over £100 for it. In a play upon his former title, Earl of Richmond, and his newly built palace at Sheen, Henry had requested a mountain, or rich mount, running with wine, on which grew three trees. Each tree represented a king, of England, Spain or France, identifiable by their arms and iconography, such as Henry's own red Lancastrian rose and Welsh dragon. The mountain sparkled with greyhounds, harts and lions of amber, coral and jet, trees budded with gold flowers, roses and oranges, while fountains ran with wine. A little gate allowed the people to approach the spectacle and fill their cups.

After pausing in appreciation, Catherine and Arthur entered the palace's great hall, where the wedding feast was to be served to over a hundred guests. The theme for the feast was 'all the delicacies, dainties and curious meats that might be purveyed or got within the whole realm of England'[7] which were served up in three courses of twelve, fifteen and eighteen dishes respectively. As the honoured guest, Catherine sat at the high table with the 'Bishop of Spain' as the English termed Antonio de Rojas Manrique, Bishop of Mallorca, later Archbishop of Granada. Arthur was seated separately with his siblings, surrounded by cupboards displaying gold plate and expensive hanging tapestries. As was the custom during such important events, they were waited on by the lords of the English court, dressed in their finery, 'wonderful ... to behold'.[8] The Duke of Buckingham wore a fantastically expensive embroidered gown set upon cloth tissue furred with sable, Sir Thomas Brandon, Master of the King's Horse, wore an equally pricy gold chain, and that of the king's Master of the Hawks, Guillaum de Rivers, cost £1,000. Another courtier wore a gown of purple velvet set with pieces of gold so thick that it was reputed to be worth the same amount even without the silk and furs.[9] Two of the young men closely associated with Arthur's household served him at table, with Maurice St John, a relative of Margaret Beaufort, carving the meat, and Thomas, Marquis of Dorset, a grandson of Queen Elizabeth Woodville, serving the drinks. The feasting went on until four or five in the afternoon.

III

Catherine and Arthur's bedding ceremony followed. In the intervening five centuries it has become the most famous bedding ceremony of all time, although no one could have anticipated this on that autumn evening as the sheets were being laid down and the room strewn with herbs. Thirty years later, exactly what happened between these two inexperienced teenagers behind closed doors on the night of 14 November 1501 would be analysed and dissected for every nuance. It became of the utmost national importance. Witnesses were recalled from retirement in foreign countries, all to establish just how intimate Arthur and Catherine had been when left alone in their chamber with their attendants waiting in the anteroom beyond. Catherine went towards it willingly as a young bride, little fathoming how it would return to haunt her and redefine her life.

Before the end of the feast, Catherine's ladies and the Earl of Oxford departed for Baynard's Castle to make the necessary arrangements. A normal part of the ritual, the ceremony combined elements of the public and private, with physical consummation essential to consolidate the vows spoken earlier by the couple in the cathedral, marking the final stage of the ceremony. The bed was inspected and tested by the earl, who sat on each side to ensure it was comfortable and that no concealed blades had been smuggled into the chamber. Catherine and Arthur travelled from the Bishop's Palace to the castle, where they were changed and prepared for bed at around eight in the evening. A small crowd gathered to offer good wishes and prayers and to corroborate that events actually took place. In the words of *The Receyt of Ladie Kateryn*, 'Lords and ladies accompanied the pair with thentent to have the oversight and apparament of the chamber and bedde that the prince and Princes, aftir the condicion of wedlock, shuld take in their reaste and ease ... Aftir the goodly disportes, dauncynges with pleasure, myrthe and solas before usyd, [Arthur] departid to his said arrayed chambre and bedde, wheryn the princes bifore his comyng was reverently leied and reposed ... And thus thise worthy persones concludid and consummat theffecte and compliment of the sacrament of matrimony.'[10]

As the *Receyt* indicates, the princess was brought in first, dressed in her nightgown and laid 'reverently' in bed. Then she had to wait. Arthur stayed up longer, drinking and celebrating with his gentlemen, but finally they carried him in, singing and making merry, possibly reciting some of the many bawdy songs associated with the charivari, or rude music, associated with such events. References to sex and fertility would not have been out of place, or too crude, even for a royal wedding. The pageantry had already alluded to the couple's anticipated fecundity, which was again raised in the blessing and prayers recited by the Bishop over the couple in bed. Then, at last, the guests withdrew and the pair were left alone. They might have spent their entire lives being trained to endure the public gaze but in private how well equipped were they for the anticipated consummation of their marriage? To put it bluntly, the question that confounded England in the 1530s and has been wrangled over by historians ever since is this: how likely is it that Catherine and Arthur had sex?

The following morning, Arthur appeared flushed and thirsty, 'good and sanguine', calling for a drink as he had spent the night 'in the midst of Spain' and saying that it was a 'good pastime to have a wife'. These words have to be understood in the context of political and masculine expectations, from the pageantry references to the proof of virginity at Baynard's Castle, the bawdiness of his friends and the expectations on his shoulders that he would live up to his part in the most expensive and magnificent occasion of his life. Arthur's role to that point had been kept to a minimum. He had met Catherine briefly, in private, but otherwise had taken a backseat, behind his father or overlooking events while the princess took centre stage. The public gaze had fallen on her throughout, as a foreigner and guest of honour, and even Arthur's presence at her side in St Paul's and at the wedding feast was designed to complement her, in white satin, rather than to eclipse her. Still, despite all the various ceremonies they had been through, the marriage was incomplete. Only Arthur could claim his bride in the physical, binding sense that would ensure the full, undisputed union of England and Spain, rendering the match indissoluble in the eyes of the Church. The nuptial night was the first time that the lead was handed over to the prince. This was his moment, with this single act to perform, when the traditional gender roles dictated the submission of Spain to conquering England. There must have been considerable pressure on him to perform.

Then there was the additional need for Arthur to prove himself a man. As a future king of England, a youth verging on the threshold of manhood, he could not be seen to fail this test. His duty was to achieve intercourse, and definitions of his masculinity, his prowess and fitness to rule rested upon his success or failure.

Robust heterosexuality was considered an essential component of masculine health, and previous kings whose sexuality was dubious, such as Catherine's great-uncle Henry IV of Spain, Edward II or the Lancastrians Richard II and Henry VI, had been perceived as weak and effeminate, unsuitable as monarchs. There was also the precedent of the prince's own conception, which had taken place on his parents' wedding night, or soon afterwards. Arthur had absorbed the cult of his own identity that his father had begun to weave since before his birth: the associations with the mythical warrior king, and by extension his advocate, the fecund Edward III; the symbols of fertility and flowering; the parallels with historical and biblical figures. His father had been an only child and the dynasty was in its infancy. Arthur had to complete the carefully constructed picture himself by passing the challenge of masculine sexuality, of successfully penetrating a woman and proving his ability to father sons. The marriage would not have gone ahead had he been too young, or weak, or if he had not yet undergone puberty, as some historians have speculated; it had already been delayed after the threshold age of fourteen and Henry must have given the Spanish assurances of his son's normal physical development. Delivered from the hands of the young bucks at court, with their bawdy words ringing in his ears, the fifteen-year-old Arthur knew it was his job to claim the virginity that had been guaranteed by his father-in-law. In the morning, his friends would have been looking for confirmation that he had.

Was he successful? Catherine later swore that they didn't have sex, and she never wavered from this position thereafter. The following morning, she was quiet and subdued, remaining with her ladies. In the depositions dating from the 1520s, the voice of Juan de Gamarra stands out. As a twelve-year-old boy, he had slept in her antechamber on the wedding night, literally adjoining Catherine's bedroom, and stated that 'Prince Arthur got up very early', perhaps even before the princess herself woke, 'which surprised everyone a lot'; when he went into her room, he found Catherine's dresser and confidante, Francesca de Carceres, appearing sad and informing the others 'that nothing had passed between Prince Arthur and his wife, which surprised everyone and made them laugh at him'.[11] Hence the need for Arthur's boast. Catherine's first lady, Doña Elvira, was convinced that the princess was still as pure as she had been when she left her mother's womb, and she imparted this belief to Ferdinand, who did not doubt her. In addition, Catherine's doctor later deposed that Arthur had not been capable of the act, having been 'denied the strength necessary to know a woman, as if he was a cold piece of stone, because he was in the final stages of phthisis [tuberculosis]' and he had never before seen a man whose limbs were so thin. Convincing as this may sound, though, it does belong to a perspective of hindsight, from a man who treated the prince on his deathbed.

Arthur never stated implicitly that they had slept together, although his bawdy request for drink was designed to imply that consummation had taken place. This line could be taken at face value, or it might have been the bravado of a young man giving assurance that he had not failed in his duty, especially if he had failed and could feel the disappointment of the Spaniards. His words must be taken in the context of political and gendered expectations. It was all part of the performance of the last few days, of the keeping up of appearances and the appropriate behaviour of those who ruled. Arthur's request for drink, even though it related to something intimate, was a function of his public identity, and did not necessarily bear relation to private truths. If consummation had not taken place, this did not make his words a lie, as he did not explicitly state that penetration had taken place. His chosen phrase, 'in the midst of Spain', with its obvious physical implication, could equally refer metaphorically to Catherine's company, and her body as the symbolic representation of Spain. As the pageants had enforced, she was the embodiment and representative of Spain, as he was of England. The non-sexual experience of her physicality, including her appearance and clothing, her accent and language, was being used by Arthur as something of a metaphysical conceit, akin to those later used by John Donne, that had translated their bedchamber into a little enclave of Spain, where Arthur had to fulfil the role of diplomat. It implied sex but it also did not confirm it; the bawdiness lay in its suggestion rather than its actuality. Arthur could hardly have behaved as Catherine did the following morning: he had to define himself differently, as opposite as masculinity was from femininity, as active rather than passive, as boastful and swaggering rather than quiet and subdued. If his gentlemen took his words to mean that Arthur had fulfilled his manly duties and confirmed his masculinity, then so much the better.

A closer look at the gentlemen of Arthur's company also sheds light on the nature of their 'manly' interactions and the extent of the information available to Arthur about what he was to expect that night. These young men were his audience, the judges of his performance far more than his virginal bride, but just how informed were they and how ready to believe his boast? A large number of them were still young, unwed and had not yet fathered a child. Of the names that appear in the 1528 depositions concerning that night, most were slightly older than the prince but not by much. Anthony Willoughby, son of Baron de Broke, was the man of whom Arthur had requested his cup of ale, and while his exact date of birth is unknown, it had to be after that of his elder brother in 1472; he appears to have died unmarried without issue. Then there was Gruffydd ap Rhys ap Thomas, born around 1478, who fathered his first child in 1508; Anthony Poyntz, born in 1480, whose eldest son arrived in 1510; Robert Ratcliffe, born in 1483 and married in 1505; and Gerald Fitzgerald, one year younger than the prince, who was married in 1503 and became a father a decade later. What marks out all these young men, and explains why they were chosen for the role, is their youth and inexperience. It is possible that none of them were sexually experienced, or that their encounters were limited to illicit pre-marital relations. It is likely that they had little actual advice to offer the young prince; perhaps they were even looking to him to report back, to be the pioneer among their innocent group. Other, sexually mature men attended the wedding, such as the Earl of Oxford, who was almost sixty, and Thomas Boleyn, already a father, but Boleyn at least was not present the following morning to witness Arthur's reputed post-coital performance. In 1528, George, Earl of Shrewsbury, who had been married at the age of thirteen, stated his belief that Arthur had consummated the match 'because himself knew his wife being not sixteen', just as Thomas, Duke of Norfolk asserted that 'himself also at the same age did carnally know and use'. But such anecdotal, associative fallacies overlook the specific, personal nature of biology: just because one or two fifteen-year-old males were sexually active, it did not mean that all were.

Between Catherine's denial and Arthur's suggestion lies much grey area for interpretation. Of course, by the late 1520s it was in Catherine's interests to say that the marriage had not been consummated, but it was also crucial to her in the spring of 1502, when the question first arose in a formal context. In addition to the events of the wedding night, a complete lack of consummation meant the pair would have never achieved full sex during the entire four and a half months of their marriage. Understandably this scenario is less credible simply because of the greater opportunities afforded the couple once they were established in their own household, but Catherine still maintained that she had shared a bed with Arthur on only seven occasions and he had never 'known' her. Arthur's gentleman Maurice St John contradicted this, claiming that they had slept together at Shrovetide, the day before Lent began, which fell on 19 February that year, after which 'the prince began to decay and was never so lusty in body and courage until his death'.[12]

Regardless of all the views expressed later by Arthur's servants who had accompanied him to her bed, or overheard his quip, or Mary, Countess of Essex who helped Agnes, Duchess of Norfolk prepare the bed, or Catherine's confessor Alessandro Geraldini who believed consummation must have taken place, there were only two people in the bedchamber of the Prince and Princess of Wales that night. Only those two people knew what had passed between them, although it is possible that the inexperienced teenagers had actually come to very different conclusions about their degree of success. Yet plenty of other people have formed an opinion on it, including the chronicler Edward Hall, who was four years old at the time although still able to state in the 1540s that 'this lusty prince and his beautifull bride were brought and ioyned together in one bed naked, and there dyd that acte, whiche to the performance and full consummacion of matrimony was moost requisite and expedient'. However, this, along with all the others, can only be speculation.

So what really happened? It is not possible to know for certain, but nor is it necessary to accuse either the prince or princess of telling falsehoods. Historians have often reduced this delicate situation to two possible interpretations: either the couple did sleep together and Catherine lied about it, or they didn't and

Arthur's boast was intended to mislead. However, a third option is possible. Amid the fumblings of two inexperienced but pressured teenagers, who did not share a common language, they might both have been right. Arthur may have believed that full intercourse had taken place while Catherine, arguing in the 1520s from a standpoint of sexual experience, knew that it had not. How might this have come about?

With the closing of the chamber door and the footsteps of the court receding, Catherine and Arthur were truly alone. Lying side by side in their perfumed sheets, with the fire burning in the grate, they both understood the significance of the occasion, but without hindsight they also believed that there was no rush. They were still young and thought they had the next thirty or forty years together, hardly guessing that the metaphorical clock was already ticking for their short-lived union. Communication cannot have been easy; looks, smiles, touches and goodwill must have made up the shortfall of language between them. The exchange of words was not essential for intercourse to take place, but it would have helped establish an intimacy between two people who were virtual strangers. They must have been tired, and Arthur had been drinking, but they could not share what they had been through in the last few days and weeks. There is also a chance that as the date was a major saint's day, and a Sunday, the couple behaved like the good Catholics they were raised to be, and abstained. However, given the pressure on Arthur, it would seem more likely that consummation was attempted.

Incredible as it may seem to a modern reader, Arthur may have mistakenly believed he had acted sufficiently to relieve his bride of her virginity. To address a sensitive question directly, just how far was penetration required in order to constitute a successful consummation? There may have been some form of foreplay, or else Arthur may have achieved some shallow degree of penetration that was not sufficient to rupture her hymen, leaving her technically a virgin. It is also possible that on what must have been his first sexual encounter, Arthur experienced premature ejaculation upon, or soon after, penetration. Catherine's quietness the following morning might indicate the embarrassment and discomfort of a bungled effort at intercourse rather than complete non-consummation. In later years, when she was forced to defend her virgin state, she did so from a position of comparison with the robust lovemaking of her second husband. It is perfectly possible that Arthur thought he had experienced full sex, or at least taken his wife's virginity, while she thought he had not. The court took it for granted that he had. Catherine had no way of knowing that the question would ever be raised again.

7

Man and Wife? 1501

I

The new Princess of Wales spent Monday 15 November closeted away in seclusion with her ladies and 'no access utterly was suffered to be had'.[1] An exception was made for a single guest, Henry's chamberlain, the Earl of Oxford, who brought her a gift and message from the king, who 'wished above all things to be of good comfort to her and that he waited impatiently for the time when he might see her to his great joy and gladness'.[2] He did not intend to wait long. The next day, Catherine was brought to Henry for a private audience, in which they met with 'right pleasant and favourable words, greetings and communications'. From Baynard's Castle they all took to the Thames, in 'so many barges (more than forty) so as heretofore have not been seen'. As they sailed along, Catherine had her first glimpse of some of the landmarks that were to feature in her life as princess and queen. At Baynard's steps they climbed into barges that were painted and adorned, probably hung with bells, to recline upon cushions and steer their way between the many flocks of wild swans that the visiting Venetian had noticed the previous year. Just past Baynard's they would have seen the thirteenth-century Dominican friary at Blackfriars, with its grounds sloping down to the river and bounded on the west by the Fleet River, where the intimate details of Catherine's marital bed would later be aired in public. After that they passed the site of the old St Bride's Inn, near a well dedicated to the saint, which would soon be razed to create the splendid Bridewell Palace.

The next stretch of the north bank was full of greenery as garden succeeded garden: the trees and plants of the Carmelite friary gave way to New Temple Gardens, then the formally laid beds of the inns owned by the bishops of Exeter, Bath and Wells, Llandaff, Chester and Worcester, and that of the Strand Inn. After that, they passed the location of the old Savoy Palace, owned by their mutual ancestor John of Gaunt and razed to the ground during the Peasant's Revolt of 1381. Very soon, the king would start to redevelop the site, laying the first stone of the Hospital of St John the Baptist in 1505, to accommodate 100 poor men. Then, as the river began to veer south, Catherine would have had her first sighting of the fourteenth-century Durham House, vaguely monastic-looking with the roof of its large hall and chapel visible behind the private apartments that onto faced the river. She might have admired its solid walls, little suspecting that within months this house was to take on sinister associations for her. Just past it sat York House, soon to be transformed beyond recognition into the Palace of Whitehall. Next along the bank was Scotland Yard, as yet devoid of any legal connections but rather literally the place where the Scottish would stay when visiting London; many Scots were soon to arrive, to negotiate the marriage of James IV with Catherine's new sister-in-law Margaret Tudor. After this, the boats began to pull towards shore as the landing steps for Westminster came within range. Catherine would have seen the long building of the Star Chamber flanking the river's edge, the ridge of the great hall and spire of St Stephen's behind, all in front of the majestic rise of the grey stone abbey.

Westminster had been carefully prepared for the royal party's arrival. They passed the night in the riverside apartments, where the lack of comments relating to Arthur and Catherine's arrangements suggest that no bed sharing took place. On Thursday 18th, the festivities began again. The 'large space' between the palace and abbey had been cleared, gravelled and sanded for jousting and tilting. In the traditional English style, a fake tree had been set up there, painted with leaves, flowers and fruit, where the arms of the competing knights were hung. A gallery had been built for the spectators, with hangings and cushions of gold for the royals, where women sat on one side and men on the other. The mayor and aldermen were opposite and a number of seats were rented out at high prices to Londoners, affording the rabble another glimpse of their future queen.

Once again, the ambitious and indiscreet Duke of Buckingham drew attention to his royal blood, riding a horse with blue velvet trapping depicting the castle motif of Castile and sporting the Prince of Wales' ostrich feathers in his helmet. His pavilion alone was a breathtaking construction of towers and turrets, covered with silk in the Tudor colours of white and green, set with red roses, his servants in his own black-and-red livery, riding horses with gold spangles.[3] Along with the duke, Sir George Herbert, Sir Rowland Knights and John Bourchier, Lord Berners, made up the four challengers. Their opponents arrived in equal, if more tactful, splendour on the other side of the field: Guillam de Rivers in a pageant of a ship borne aloft by his men, Sir John Pechey in a pavilion of red silk, Lord William of Devonshire in a red dragon led by a giant that carried a tree, and Henry Bourchier, Earl of Essex, atop a mountain of plenty, accompanied by a beautiful lady with loose hair.[4] They jousted, or broke staves, before the crowd, so that 'such a justs and Field Royall, so nobly and valiantly done, hath not been seen ne heard' before.[5]

The following day, Friday 19th, a great feast and disguising were held in Westminster Hall. The walls were hung with richly coloured arras and cupboards were erected to display glittering plate, and after the king and queen were seated under the cloth of estate, the pageants were wheeled out. These had been specially commissioned from William Cornish, although it is not clear whether this was the elder, who died in 1502, or, as is more likely, his son, the Master of the Children of the Chapel Royal, composer and poet to Henry's court, who often took performance roles in his creations. Whichever Cornish it was, he was assisted by John Atkinson and John English, as well as Jacques Hault and William Pawne, who created 'moresques', Moorish or Morris dances, in honour of the guests.[6] The first pageant was a castle upon wheels, pulled by four beasts with gold chains: a gold lion, a silver lion, a hart with gilt horns and an elk. A child dressed as a maiden sat in each of the castle's four towers, and inside it were eight 'goodly and fresh ladies'. The second was a ship, fully rigged, carrying a 'goodly and a fayre lady, in her apparell like unto the princess of Spayne' and setting its anchor beside the castle. It bore a message for the ladies in the Tower, carried by the figures of Hope and Desire, sent from eight gentlemen from the mount of Love, which then appeared as the third pageant. The knights, with their banners unfurled, laid siege to the castle and the ladies submitted and agreed to dance with them. After the pageant had ended, Arthur danced with his aunt Cecily and Catherine danced with one of her ladies. Then, Duke Henry took to the floor with his sister Margaret and, 'perceiving himself to be accombred with his clothes, sodainly cast off his gown and daunced in his jackett', to the delight of his parents.[7] Then came the voidee, a banquet of spices and wine to fortify the guests. On the Saturday it rained, and on Sunday another banquet was held in the Parliament Chamber, followed by more dancing and disguisings, including an arbour containing knights and a great ball covered in lawn and lit from within by candles so the ladies within were visible in shadow. The following week unfolded in a similar fashion, with more tournaments, pageants and feasts, music and disguisings. Then the party headed to Richmond, Henry's newly built architectural fantasia, a royal playground for the final stage of the celebrations.

As they approached the palace by water, Catherine caught her first sight of the impressive collection of turrets topped with domes, the long chapel and castellated walls surrounded by extensive gardens. The original palace had burned down in 1497 and the rebuilding had incorporated elements of French and Burgundian design[8] set amid the quiet English countryside. Alighting from her barge, Catherine was ushered into 'an erthly and secunde paradise in our region of Englond' with 'bewtyouse exemplere of all proper lodgynes'. The author of the *Receyt* described the grounds as being the height of horticultural fashion, as 'moost faire and pleasaunt gardeyns with ryall knottes alleyed and herbed, many marvellous beastis, as lyons, dragons and such othir of divers kynde, properly fachioned and corved in the ground'. Around these heraldic statues there grew 'many vynis, sedes and straunge frute right goodly besett, kept and norrisshed with motche labour and diligens'. They passed through an outer court lined by galleries with large windows and into an inner court paved with marble where a fountain played in the centre. To the right lay the great hall, covered with tiles and featuring statues of kings in golden robes. Opposite sat the chapel, well paved, glazed and hung with cloth of arras. Passages and galleries, glazed and decorated with carved roses, portcullises and bags of gold, led to the king's chambers and the chambers where Catherine was lodged, hung with rich hangings. Hidden away from view, according to the *Receyt*, the houses of office – the pantry, buttery, cellars, kitchen and scullery – were preparing to cater for the many guests. The palace was designed as a royal playground, containing 'pleasaunt dauncyng chambers and secrett closettes ... housis of pleasure to disport inn at chesse, tables, dise, cards, bowling alleys, buttes for archers, and goodly tennes plays',[9] and Catherine's Spanish 'tumbler', or acrobat, held them all spellbound by his ingenious antics, hanging by his teeth from a suspended rope.

After dining in the hall they were treated to more pageants, including a tower, drawn in by seahorses on wheels, accompanied by mermaids and mermen, to the singing of the children of the chapel. Eight gallants inside the pageant set free 'many quick coneys' (rabbits), who 'ran about the hall and made many great disportes', before eight ladies released white doves, which created much amusement and laughter. This was followed by dancing and a voidee before the company retired to bed. And thus it went on for several more days, with more acrobatics, dancing and sports, and the Count de Cabra shooting deer in the park, until the day came for part of Catherine's Spanish retinue to return home. Some had been intended as part of her future household but others were visitors, merely accompanying her to her new life and helping celebrate the wedding. For a young girl who spoke little English, in a new and unfamiliar land, married to a young man with whom she could not communicate and had probably not been intimate, this represented a significant loss. She had always known it would happen, but when the time came to say goodbye, marking the end of the festivities and the start of her life as Arthur's wife, Catherine's spirits must have been low.

Henry compensated with gifts. The leading figures of the Spanish court were given several hundred marks' worth of gold and silver plate, and in the library at Richmond he offered Catherine and her ladies their choice of jewels to 'increase gladness, mitigate sorrow, refresh and comfort the spirits'. According to the author of the

Receyt, this method worked and Catherine 'assuaged her heaviness and drew herself into the manner, guise and usages of England'. Henry and Arthur also acknowledged the receipt of 100,000 scudos, or half Catherine's dowry, in a sworn statement before a Spanish notary, and the king wrote to the Spanish monarchs in praise of their daughter's beauty 'as well as her agreeable and dignified manners'. The friendship between their two countries, he added, was now 'intimate and indissoluble'. Certain that they would be missing Catherine, he wrote as one parent to another, begging them to 'banish all sadness from their minds', as although they 'cannot now see the gentle face of their beloved daughter, they may be sure that she has found a second father who [would] ever watch over her happiness and never permit her to want anything that he [could] procure for her'. Arthur also wrote to reassure them that he would make a good husband.[10] Copies of the *Receyt* went back to Spain when the princess's retinue departed on 29 November and would have been read avidly by Ferdinand and Isabella, keen to learn the nature of the reception the English had given their daughter. So far, so good.

II

Then the question of money reared its ugly head. For all his gifts of plate and jewels, his warm welcome, fatherly affection and praise, Henry had not yet received the additional 35,000 scudos of Catherine's dowry that he had been promised in the shape of gold, silver, jewels and tapestries, which de Puebla now encouraged him to request. What followed was deeply embarrassing for the English king, who demanded these items from Juan de Cuero, Master of Catherine's Wardrobe, only to be told these were to remain in the Spaniard's possession and that Cuero was to weigh, value and guard them and that he desired a receipt for them. The incident was reported to Ferdinand and Isabella by their Ambassador to Scotland, Pedro de Ayala, then resident in London, whose general tone towards de Puebla shows there was little love lost between the two fellow countrymen. Ayala claimed that 'some altercations' took place on the subject and that Henry felt both 'affronted' that his will had been thwarted but also ashamed, as he felt he had been tricked by de Puebla into asking for them ahead of time. Henry felt obliged to explain himself to Catherine, visiting her in her chamber to explain that de Puebla's plan had been to insist that the princess use her own jewels, so that they could not later be counted as part of the dowry. The king informed her of the ambassador's 'crafty design' and distanced himself from it, saying he was 'exceedingly sorry he had asked for the jewels in question' and would 'not consent that [the idea] be attributed to' him. He asked her to write to her parents to explain this 'artful trick' and was 'afraid to be thought a miser', adding that 'if it were necessary ... he could spend a million of gold without contracting a debt'.[11] Initially, this seemed to be a straightforward case against de Puebla, who had offered the English king a means of obtaining more money from the Spanish, which his sense of honour had refuted. However, on reflection, Henry could see the plan's merits.

The next day, Henry summoned Ayala into his presence. He wanted to discuss the question of Catherine and Arthur living together as man and wife, as it had become necessary to send the prince into Wales to head the Council of the Marches. The question was whether or not Catherine should accompany him. Henry's initial plan had been to allow the couple to consummate the match, making it legal in the eyes of the Church, then to allow Arthur to return alone while Catherine remained with the court in London, until they were both a little older and more mature. Then, when the parents judged the time was right, they would set up their own household and live as man and wife. Some members of the royal council, and of Arthur's council, disagreed with this. Ayala advised that Catherine should remain in London, where she would 'more easily bear being separated and their abstinence from intercourse'[12] with the king and queen to distract her, rather than waiting for the prince alone at Ludlow. Also he expressed the reservations of the Spanish, mindful of the fate of their own son, that 'knowing the tender age of the prince, [they] would rather be pleased than dissatisfied if they for some time did not live together'.[13] The next day, Henry consulted with Catherine, who replied diplomatically that 'neither in this nor in any other respect had she any other will than his, and that she would be content with whatever he decided'. After several days, during which the question was repeated, Catherine refused to commit, but waited to learn the king's wishes. In the meantime, Doña Elvira attempted to establish exactly what arrangements had been made for provisioning the princess's household in Wales, a role which had been assigned to de Puebla. Although de Puebla had previously reassured the Spanish on this point, he now 'was much surprised, and said that such a demand was an entirely new thing to him'[14] and that Catherine would be provided for by her husband, although as Ayala wrote, there was not so much 'as a pin' assigned to the prince's new wife by Henry. She would need to live closely with Arthur, taking her meals with him, denying her considerable autonomy, and condemning her to penury during his necessary absences at sessions of the Council of the Marches. Thus it transpired that if Catherine did accompany Arthur to Wales, she would be forced to use her own jewels and plate to pay her expenses, invalidating them as part of her dowry and necessitating further payment from Ferdinand and Isabella. De Puebla's crafty plan, from which Henry had seemed so keen to distance himself, appeared to be working in the king's financial favour after all. 'His intention,' Ayala concluded, 'for no other can be found, is to procure her an occasion to use the said things, in consequence of her journey, and thus by what he ordered, to attain his ends.'[15]

The question of Arthur and Catherine's married life was a genuine one, regardless of Henry's aims concerning her plate and jewels. It is likely that the king had real concerns about the wisdom of allowing the couple to commence married life at once, which may or may not have been grounded in Arthur's health. Contemporary medical opinion was divided when it came to sexual relations between young newly-weds. While a physical relationship was considered beneficial in physical and emotional terms, with the denial of natural urges leading to health problems and temptation, the timing was critical. It was a common practice among aristocratic families for marriages to be made while the bride and groom were still underage, as Catherine and Arthur had experienced, but the exact moment of consummation could be delayed for several years after the pair had begun to live together. This contained risks, as the premature death of one of the parties prior to the physical act meant that the bereaved partner had no claim upon dowry payments and financial support.

For weeks, the question of Arthur and Catherine's married life hung in the air. Presumably no one was better placed to judge the prince's strength and physical development than his father, but Henry still sought advice from members of the Spanish household, including Ayala and Doña Elvira, who spoke in favour of a separation, and Catherine's confessor Alessandro Geraldini, who argued that 'on no condition in the world should [Henry] separate them, but send her with her husband' or else the princess would be in 'great despair'. During the time that elapsed since their wedding, at Westminster and Richmond, such discussions and references to the 'princess's chamber' suggest that the pair were given separate rooms and had not been openly encouraged to share a bed. It is possible that Arthur visited Catherine at night, but this does not arise in the depositions of 1520, when it surely would have provided critical evidence of attempted consummation. The silence implies that the young couple were living apart, coming together for the festivities and feasts, in anticipation of the king's ruling about their future. After all, there was no hurry; so far as they knew, the pair had the rest of their lives to perfect their union and produce children. Yet Henry swung away from caution, perhaps influenced by de Puebla's argument regarding the princess's plate and jewels. It was a decision that would come to haunt him. Eventually, against the advice of the Spanish and much of his council, the king ruled that Catherine would accompany Arthur into Wales at once. They departed for Ludlow on 21 December, five days after the princess turned sixteen.

Arthur's business in the Welsh Marches must have been pressing indeed if the pair could not wait to celebrate Christmas in London, or for better weather to arrive. With Arthur riding on horseback and Catherine sitting in a litter, they spent three or four days covering the 130 miles to reach Bewdley, on the River Severn, described by Leland as 'so comely a man cannot imagine a town better'. They passed Christmas at Tickenhill Manor, set on a ridge overlooking the town, where Catherine would have had the chance to see the chapel where she had been married to Arthur by proxy in 1499. No doubt they observed the holy day there and dined in the 100-foot-long hall on the south side of the house, which had been given new doorways and windows of stone tiles and repaired with local timber in recent years. Nothing of the old palace now remains, which was set amid extensive gardens and hunting grounds, although Catherine and Arthur were unlikely to have had much time, or sufficiently clement weather, to take advantage of the park. Given their rate of travel, they would only have needed an additional day or two to cover the twenty miles due west to Ludlow. Depending on how long they remained at Tickenhill, the pair probably arrived at their destination around New Year.

As the Prince of Wales, head of the Council of the Marches and a newly married man, Arthur could have anticipated a warm welcome. Ludlow Castle sat at a high point along the River Teme, its solid stone walls encircling the outer bailey, where artisans served the inhabitants, and an inner bailey with apartments, hall and free-standing round chapel. Away to the west the Welsh hills were a purple ripple on the horizon, and to the east lay the rolling green lands of Shropshire and Herefordshire. They would have approached through the walled town, entering through the Gladford Gate or Old Gate, progressing up the hill past the rows of timber framed buildings into the wide marketplace, which gave access to the castle gatehouse. The townsfolk and Welsh magnates turned out to welcome them, and Catherine would have been ushered into the hall, where members of their new household were waiting to be introduced. Some of her male Spanish staff had been demoted to the positions of ushers as Henry had judged their roles unnecessary, and no doubt there was some awkwardness as they now faced those in senior positions in the prince's household. Here were men such as Sir Richard Pole, a relative of Margaret Beaufort who was Arthur's chamberlain; Sir Richard Croft, his steward, whose family had been associated with Ludlow for generations; Arthur's chancellor, John Arundell; governor and treasurer Sir Henry Vernon; comptroller of the household Sir William Uvedale; almoner and confessor Dr Edenham; John Nele, dean of the chapel; and Bishop William Smyth, president of the Council of the Marches.

The rooms in which Catherine would spend the next few months were clustered in a line to the north-west, with the large thirteenth-century solar sitting over the castle's cellars. This gave onto the great hall with its three trefoil windows and central hearth, which in turn led through to the first-floor chamber block, about sixteen feet long, and a four-storey tower containing bed chambers and storerooms. Catherine and Arthur would have had separate chambers, as was the custom, which dictated that a husband would initiate relations by visiting his wife; otherwise, their establishments were quite separate. The great kitchen and pantry, or Oven Tower, stood separately, close to the central well and chapel of St Mary

Magdalene, which between them would cater for the couple's spiritual and culinary needs. Ludlow was built from a local red-grey limestone, developed piece by piece since the eleventh century, with some sections of the solar and great hall finished in a hurry. To a princess accustomed to the elegant, breath-taking complexity of the Alhambra, it must have seemed a little crude.

By 6 January, news of the couple's safe arrival had reached de Puebla in London, who had in turn written to inform Ferdinand and Isabella of the facts. On that day, they composed a reply from Seville, as his tidings had 'given them much pleasure', requesting that he give them a 'full relation of all that has taken place'. Catherine was also writing to them, as was Doña Elvira, although their letters do not survive, but news had already reached Spain of the demotion of Elvira's husband Don Pedro, in whose cause they urged de Puebla to entreat the king that such an affront should not be made.[16]

With Arthur resuming his duties, Catherine's days passed quietly as she settled in to her new home. They would have come together for meals, but otherwise the prince's work required him to travel and undertake long days of work in the government of Wales. They did not have much time together to become acquainted, although Anthony Willoughby later remarked that they had slept together at Shrovetide, 19 February, and that he had frequently accompanied Arthur to his wife's chamber door at night. This sits in direct opposition to Catherine's rebuttal that they shared a bed on only seven occasions throughout the four and a half months of marriage.

Catherine had her lady mistress and her familiar ladies-in-waiting, but among the English women she made a new friend in Margaret Pole, the wife of Arthur's chamberlain. The cousin of Queen Elizabeth, she was the elder sister of Edward, Earl of Warwick, whom Henry had beheaded in 1499, and had never been pronounced illegitimate as Elizabeth and her siblings had. She was technically next in line to the Yorkist throne and Countess of Salisbury in her own right, but her gender made her less of a threat than her de la Pole cousins, the sons of the Duchess of Suffolk. Margaret was then twenty-eight and had been married to a half-nephew of Margaret Beaufort, bearing five children and strengthening ties between the York and Lancaster dynasties. Although Margaret was that much older than the princess, they were drawn together by circumstances and character, forming a connection that would prove to be lifelong. Other visitors to Ludlow included Sir John Blount and his wife Catherine, of Kinlet, which lay fifteen miles to the east, and just five miles from Bewdley. Catherine met their pretty blonde daughter Bessie, for whom she would find a position in her household in the coming years.

At the end of March, Catherine and Arthur both fell ill. The prince's last public engagement was during the celebrations for Maundy Thursday on 24 March. He may have been distributing money to the poor, or even assisting in the traditional foot-washing. It seems more than coincidence that both husband and wife succumbed at the same time, suggesting that they contracted a virus, perhaps as Arthur came into close bodily contact with the people on this last occasion. Unfortunately, no evidence remains to confirm whether or not other members of their household were affected, which would have been a likely outcome of this scenario. At the time, it was recorded that a 'great sickness' was in the area, which may have been the plague, or possibly the sweat, a particularly virulent and dramatic illness that had arrived in England in 1485 and was known to kill within hours. Symptoms of the illness included cold shivers, headaches, muscle pain, dizziness and exhaustion, which quickly gave way to a high temperature and the heavy sweating that was the main characteristic for sufferers. Thirst, delirium and palpitations followed, after which there was a final exhausted collapse.

While the cause of the sweating sickness is still unknown, contemporaries blamed poor sanitation, and sources describing the outbreak at Ludlow referred to a 'malign vapour which proceeded from the air'. Isabella, who never visited the town, described it from Castile as an 'unhealthy place', which may refer to information contained in lost letters from her daughter, or recounted in retrospect after her illness. It was true that outbreaks of the sweat usually occurred in the summer months and went into abeyance with the frosts of winter, so perhaps an unusually mild spring followed the terrible weather that marked the start of 1501. Typically, it seems to have affected upper-class adults, and the cramped, dirty living conditions in castles supports claims that it was related to hygiene. The curse of poor sanitation and water was avoided in Henry's London palaces by the peripatetic nature of the court, but the prince and princess had then been in residence at Ludlow for three uninterrupted months.

Among Catherine's retinue was a French apothecary, John de

Soda or Soto, a native of Perpignan, former capital of Roussillon in the south-west of France, and a Spanish physician, Dr Alcarez. At the end of her life, Isabella was tended by a Nicolas de Soto, so there was probably a family connection in the royal service. They had probably anticipated catering for the princess's needs during pregnancy and childbirth, but as March turned into April, they would have been sourcing whatever herbs and cures they could to deal with this mysterious malady. The plague was well known, as were the various treatments and prayers employed in the often futile attempt to fight it, but then, as now, numbers of theories about the cause and nature of the sweat have yet to provide a satisfactory answer. Given that it first appeared in England in 1485, when Henry arrived with foreign mercenaries among his army, it may have been imported just as syphilis was from the New World, although this might equally just be coincidence. The sudden influx of a group of Spanish visitors into a regional border town might also have created havoc in terms of immunities and illness as different germs came into contact. A scourge of the early Tudor period, the sweat burned itself out and was not recorded in England again after the late 1550s. That, however, was too late for Arthur.

On the evening of Saturday 2 April, while Catherine languished in bed, her young husband died. He was fifteen and a half. Examining the body, Dr Alcarez diagnosed his condition as 'tisis' or 'phthisis', pulmonary tuberculosis, which was common during this period, especially among children, and could become severe very quickly. Indeed, some of the symptoms were similar to those of the sweat. Yet if Arthur had been suffering from this disease on a long-term basis, his weakness should have surfaced before this point, and the king and queen would not have consented to his marriage or his return to Ludlow. According to modern understanding, the disease is spread in the air by bacteria when people who have the active form of tuberculosis cough and sneeze. Arthur might have come into contact with an infected person during his work in the Welsh Marches, or picked it up at court, perhaps even from his father, whom the same illness would claim seven years later. Only one in ten cases progresses from latent to acute, triggering symptoms of coughing, fever, weight loss and sweating. It can then kill very rapidly. Clearly Catherine and Arthur did not both have tuberculosis, but if the prince was entering an acute phase of illness, during which he had been losing weight, he would have been too weak to fight off any virus from which an otherwise healthy person might recover. Thus, when both young people were infected with a virulent strain of sickness that March, perhaps as a result of his work on Maundy Thursday, Catherine was able to fight it off, but Arthur's recent decline left him too weak. This is a plausible explanation for their joint sickness and the difference in outcome, only there are no accounts of rapid decline in the boy in the spring months of 1502. To be fair, though, there are no surviving accounts of their time at Ludlow at all, so conclusive answers cannot be drawn. It is equally possible that the prince was suffering from some form of testicular cancer that also prevented him from consummating his marriage or an inherited illness that would also afflict his nephew Edward VI. All that can be stated with certainty is that Arthur died and Catherine survived.

III

The author of the *Receyt*, who had recently described all the vivid detail of the couple's wedding pageantry, had not expected to follow it so soon with the account of a funeral. Yet, book four of the five concludes Arthur's brief moment in the spotlight with these details, enclosing his short life and ending a chapter of Catherine's. It paints a picture of the boy's last valiant battle, against 'a moost petifull disease and sikeness, that with so soore and great violens hedde battilid and driven in the singler partise of him inward; that cruell and fervent enemye of nature, the dedly corupcion, did utterly venquysshe and overcome the pure and frendfull blood without almoner of phisicall help and remedy'.[17]

It is not clear exactly when Catherine learned the terrible news. It may have been broken to her that same evening, but as she continued unwell for some time afterwards she may have been protected from the truth. That would account for the delay in the boy's funeral. However, letters were written at once to the king by Richard Pole and other members of Arthur's council, and a messenger was dispatched for Greenwich. He covered the 150 miles in just two days. The news was broken to Henry by his confessor early the following morning, Tuesday 5 April, and the king sent for his wife so that they might 'take the Painefull sorrows together'. After comforting each other, Elizabeth concealed her pain long enough to remind Henry that they still had healthy children and were still young enough to create more. The loss was severe, and both parents felt it deeply, but their eldest son had been taken to God and the dynasty rested on the shoulders of a ten-year-old. Within weeks the queen would fall pregnant again.

With Catherine upstairs on her sickbed, Arthur's body was prepared for burial. An account of his funeral was made by John Writhe, Garter King at Arms, who was on hand to record the details. First, the prince was seared and dressed in spices and other sweet stuff, so that his body did not leak, but was instead sewn into good black cloth with a white cross on top. At his request, his bowels were buried in the little Ludlow chapel of St Mary Magdalene. Arthur lay in his chamber under a table that was covered over with rich cloth of gold and bearing a cross and silver candlesticks and wax tapers. Four other large tapers were set to burn in his room. Writhe mentions his alms folk, who sat about the corpse, day and night, holding torches and keeping vigil, possibly those whom he had attended on Maundy Thursday. He remained there for three whole weeks until St George's Day, 23 April, on the afternoon of which he was removed to the church. Arthur's yeomen of the chamber carried him into the hall at Ludlow, draped in black cloth of gold with a cross of white cloth of gold, and rested him on a trestle, where three bishops censed the body and sprinkled it with holy water. Noblemen then came to pay their respects, including the principal mourners, the earls of Surrey, Shrewsbury and Kent, dressed in black hoods and robes; Lord Grey of Ruthven; Baron Dudley; Lord Powys; Sir Richard Pole, Arthur's chamberlain; and other members of his household. A canopy was carried over the corpse, with banners at every corner, depicting the Trinity, the Cross, Our Lady and St George, while a banner of Arthur's own arms was carried before him by Sir Griffiths ap Rhys. Before them were two Spaniards 'of the best degree' from Catherine's household, behind the pursuivants, who were officials from the College of Arms, then the churchmen, bishops, abbots and priors, parsons, priests and friars, flanked by eighty poor men in black mourning bearing torches.

Arthur was carried into the choir of the parish church of St Laurence, where he would lie for the next two nights. A dirge was sung for his soul and readings given by the bishops of Lincoln, Salisbury and Chester; the following day there were more masses, songs and offerings, then alms were given to the poor. Finally, Arthur was placed on a chariot drawn by six horses trapped in black cloth with escutcheons of gold. The vehicle was covered in black velvet, with a white cross of cloth of gold, banners at each corner and surrounded by mourners in black hoods. On St Mark's Day, 25 April, the procession left Ludlow for Tickenhill, in Bewdley, but the weather was so terrible, battering them with wind and rain, that the horses were substituted for oxen, to drag the hearse through the rutted streets. From there, they proceeded to Worcester in better weather, being met at the city gates and drawn through the streets by fresh horses, with dignitaries and churchmen on either side. The Norman Worcester Cathedral, formerly a priory, had been designated by Henry as his son's resting place. The following day the ceremony proper began, with the man-at-arms riding a charger into the choir, carrying a poleaxe pointing downwards, followed by lords and officers who laid palls of cloth of gold tissue across the hearse. A sermon was read, more alms distributed, more incense waved and, amid much weeping, the members of Arthur's household broke their staffs of office and cast them down into the grave.[18] Catherine was not present.

Arthur's household had been a court in waiting, anticipating a time when the youth would become king and they his leading men. From its small nucleus of regional loyalties and the Spanish marriage, an impressive individual should have emerged to rule England, educated along humanist lines and experienced in the ways of government, with a network of allegiances and a wife and children at his side. His death represented the loss of a future king and his reign, the loss of years of investment in his education, his guidance and in the prince as an individual. When Henry VII died, in April 1509, Arthur would have been twenty-two and married for eight years, potentially the father of several surviving children. The Tudor dynasty might have had a responsible, shrewd adult king and heirs to the throne, devoted to the new learning and devout in their Catholicism. Catherine would have been an established wife and mother, secure in her position as she approached her coronation. They would have been another Ferdinand and Isabella, united in their shared destiny in steering England's course through the challenges of the sixteenth century, perhaps for three or four decades to come. Instead, years of uncertainty, unhappiness and penury awaited the widow. If ever a death changed the course of history, it was that of Arthur Tudor, Prince of Wales, the king England never had.

PART THREE

The Widow 1502–1509

8

Aftermath 1502–1504

I

Spring arrived in Ludlow. The rough-hewn walls, great hall and chapel must have seemed empty when Catherine was well enough to rise from her bed. Her young husband's body was already interred in Worcester Cathedral, his staff reduced to a minimum, and his chambers were quiet. Still weak from her illness and dressed in the deepest mourning, the princess was fully aware of the change in her status and just how much of a diplomatic problem she now presented. She may have assumed that she would soon be returning home to Spain, as her elder sister Isabel had done, but a realisation that this would require Henry to return her 100,000 scudos may have made the move less likely. It may be that a match with Arthur's younger brother had already occurred to her, as it did to her parents almost at once, but Catherine was not able to take charge of her own destiny. She had to sit and wait while the key players at the courts of England and Spain negotiated terms. They, in turn, were waiting to see whether or not the princess was pregnant. No doubt Catherine mourned the loss of Arthur, for whom she had been intended since the age of three, but after such a short marriage, she was unlikely to really have known him well. Perhaps more poignantly, she mourned the loss of their future, the potential of their union and the uncertainty of her situation. She wrote to her parents and waited for their reply.

In Spain, Ferdinand and Isabella had been distracted by the consequences of another death. The loss of their grandson Miguel meant that the throne of Castile passed to their eldest surviving daughter Juana and her controlling husband, Philip of Austria. Dressed in their colourful splendour but deeply anxious concerning the duke's loyalty, the Spanish monarchs prepared vast and elaborate festivities to welcome him, which would culminate in a ceremony investing the new heirs. Juana and Philip had arrived in the country at the end of January, travelling on to Vitoria, Burgos, Miraflores, Valladolid, Medina del Campo, Segovia and Madrid, a round of festivities that lasted the duration of Catherine's time at Ludlow. Ferdinand and Isabella had been to Seville and were making their way towards Toledo, where the court was awaiting Philip's arrival, but the duke was an ungracious guest, making no effort to conceal his lack of interest in Spain. Anxious for the pregnant Juana and the future of Castile, they had travelled as far as Puente del Arzobispo, a distance of around seventy-five miles, by 15 April, when they wrote to de Puebla in England that they were 'glad to hear that the King and Queen of England, with the Prince and Princess of Wales, are in good health'.[1] In fact, Arthur had been dead almost two weeks by this time but the news had not yet arrived. Nor had it four days later, when they wrote from Talavera, another twenty miles further along the road, to support Henry in his attempt to oust the Yorkist Edmund de la Pole, Duke of Suffolk, from his Burgundian exile. They were preoccupied by Philip developing measles at the end of the month when the tragic news finally reached them from England on 3 May. Isabella was so unwell that Ferdinand kept it from her for a week.

But the news could not be kept from the Castilian queen forever. By 10 May she had recovered sufficiently to be told that her youngest daughter was now a widow and the hard-fought alliance with England was in jeopardy. Ferdinand and Isabella gathered their thoughts and sent instructions to de Puebla, by the hand of a new ambassador, Ferdinand, Duque de Estrada, whose daughter had borne the king an illegitimate son. De Puebla was ordered to obey the duke in every detail, as he was empowered 'in their name and in the name of the Princess of Wales'. A difficult and contradictory task lay ahead of Estrada, for which de Puebla was clearly not trusted given his recent record of gaffes and crafty devices. Firstly, Estrada was to confront the question of Catherine's widowed status, by demanding the return of the 100,000 scudo dowry already paid and to insist that she receive the lands assigned to her at the time of her wedding. He was to ask Henry to return the princess to Spain 'in the best manner, and in the shortest time possible', and, if necessary, the king was to 'superintend for himself the arrangements for her departure'. He was to do this in 'such a way that he may believe we are desirous of it, for in this manner the business may best be furthered'.[2]

But Catherine's return to Spain was not ultimately what her parents hoped to achieve. Hoping that Henry would not wish to return the 100,000 scudos or lose the alliance with the most powerful European monarchy, they urged Estrada to 'conclude with Henry, in their names … a marriage between their daughter Catherine and his son Henry, Prince of Wales'.[3] It was not until 12 May that they sent their official condolences to de Puebla, telling of their 'profound sorrow', coupled with the statement that 'the will of God must be obeyed'. The Spaniards must have received other letters, from Catherine herself, or from Doña Elvira, which have since been lost, outlining their daughter's miserable conditions at Ludlow, as Ferdinand and Isabella wrote to de Puebla that 'the Princess of Wales is suffering [and] must be removed, without loss of time, from the unhealthy place where she is now'. On the same day, a solemn requiem Mass was held for Arthur in the church of San Juan de los Reyes, in Toledo, attended by Ferdinand, Isabella, Juana and the newly recovered Philip.

More tales of woe must have reached Spain from Ludlow, as Catherine's parents wrote again to de Puebla on 29 May, in anticipation that Henry would 'lose no time in fulfilling all his obligations towards the Princess of Wales'. They could not believe that the king was 'capable of exposing [her] in this her time of grief, to want and privation' and repeated their former request for Catherine to receive what was due to her from her dower lands. It was 'not to be supposed that such a Prince as the King of England would break his word and much less … whilst the princess is overwhelmed with grief'. They had probably been informed of the content of Arthur's will, in which all his possessions were left to his elder sister Margaret and no provision had been made for his widow. Her parents added that Catherine must not borrow money, as some in England had advised her, as this would 'reflect great dishonour on Henry', citing the examples of her sister Isabel and sister-in-law Margaret being supported by their countries of adoption in the event of their widowhood. De Puebla was instructed to write to Doña Elvira that she must inform Juan de Cuero to 'keep all the gold, silver, jewels etc of the princess with the greatest care'. Not even the smallest portion of them was to be sold and no new servants were to be engaged in her household.[4] Henry responded that year by granting Catherine an annual income of £83 6*s* 8*d*, roughly equal to that of an English nobleman.

It was the queen who came to Catherine's rescue. Elizabeth dispatched a litter of black velvet fringed with valance and ribbon to bring her back to London. Her accounts for the end of May included a payment to Ellis Hilton for two and three-quarter yards of satin of Bruges black for the covering of a saddle for the princess and a yard and a quarter of black velvet to trim it.[5] Under the direction of Doña Elvira, the Spaniards packed up their possessions, including Catherine's controversial jewels and plate, and departed from Ludlow, never to return. They travelled slowly, probably retracing the route that had only recently marked the princess's triumphant post-marital journey at what they assumed was the start of her new life. On 14 June, her parents were able to write to de Puebla that they had been informed that the king 'has already removed her from the unhealthy situation where she was staying, and that she has come to a place nearer London'.[6] That place was one of the riverside mansions Catherine and Arthur had sailed past on their journey to Westminster. The princess may have noticed Durham House, or Place, six months earlier, and admired its great hall abutting the river and its two acres of garden, little suspecting that it would soon become her home. For the next three years this was to be her principal residence, sandwiched between the Thames and the Strand, flanked on either side by York House and Ivy Lane beside the Strand, in the parish of St Margaret.

The sixteen-year-old widow and her Spanish entourage found themselves in a large thirteenth-century house, traditionally the London residence of the Bishop of Ely, a position then held by Richard Redman. The heart of the palace was the main hall, formerly used as a courtroom for petty cases, and described at the end of the century as 'stately and high, supported with lofty marble pillars'. There was a first-floor chapel with door leading to a solar, both of which extended over the vaulted cellar beneath and flanked a sizeable courtyard. According to Stowe's account, the house hosted the May Day revels of 1540, during which it accommodated the king, queen and her ladies, the entire court, six challengers dressed in white velvet, forty-six defendants, the knights and burgesses of the House of Commons, the mayor, aldermen and their wives. It would have been considerably quieter during Catherine's residence. Perhaps she was also received at court, welcomed back and comforted by the family she had just joined, by her mother-in-law, or Arthur's grandmother and sisters, perhaps by the ten-year-old boy whose future had just altered as dramatically as her own. Durham House sat on the bend of the Thames, just a short ride away from Westminster, with its own landing stage to access the palace by river. Yet it was a symbolic distance: Catherine was not being drawn back into the heart of the court as she had been in November, as the focus of its celebrations. As a widow in an awkward situation, she was being kept at arm's length.

The Privy Purse accounts of Elizabeth of York for 1502–3 give an insight into the life of the Tudor court from which Catherine was excluded, but they also represent the model of queenship espoused by Elizabeth and her character. On Maundy Thursday, while Arthur washed the feet of the poor at Ludlow, the queen's almoner, Richard Pain, paid out 114 shillings for her to distribute among thirty-seven local women. She also made offerings on Good Friday and every day of Easter week, along with gifts to St Albans, Windsor, Eton, Reading, Caversham, Cockthorpe, Hailes, Northampton, Walsingham, Sudbury, Woolpit, Ipswich, Crowham, Canterbury, Dover, Barking, Willesdon, St Paul's, Stoke Clare and, ironically, Worcester. Many of these locations were associated with the cult of the Virgin Mary, the particular favourite of English queens, and established a pattern of piety and patronage that Catherine was to follow. In terms of court life, Robert Fairfax was paid for setting an anthem to music, and minstrels were rewarded, as were the kitchens, scullery, porters and saucer. Payments were given to those who brought the queen gifts, such as a carp from her son Henry's fool, apples, pears and a sole brought to her at Richmond, and almond butter at Hampton Court. On 31 March, she received the gift of some oranges from a 'servant of the prothonotarye of Spain'. The bill of a saddler named Nicholas Major was settled for £10, 'for making of certain stuff of his occupation against the marriage of the prince'. After the news broke, the court went into mourning. Elizabeth's accounts contain payments to a William Botery for black tinsel satin for the 'making of an edge of a gown of blake velvet for the queen'.[7] From the windows of Durham Place, Catherine might have seen Arthur's family being rowed past on their way to Greenwich or the Tower and back again past Westminster to Richmond or Windsor.

Soon after their return to London, Catherine was troubled by an upsetting betrayal. Having insisted that her marriage had not been consummated, the princess learned of a letter written to her parents by her confessor Alessandro Giraldini, who had been with her at Ludlow, insisting that Arthur and Catherine had slept together. The letter was possibly supported by their doctor. His motive for this is unclear, and it surely must be taken as an act of conscience, however correct or incorrect that may have been. The impact of a confessor's testimony would be irrefutable and implied secret knowledge that the princess had imparted to him in the confessional. Perhaps she had attempted to describe the couple's struggles with intimacy during the long winter months in the round chapel at Ludlow. Perhaps she had said enough to convince the man of her husband's success. Whatever Catherine had confessed, the priest now broke her confidence. The result was that Giraldini was recalled to Spain, and the princess was so furious she would not receive him on his return fifteen years later. Isabella referred discreetly to the letter, of which she enclosed a copy, when writing to de Puebla on 14 June. 'Be on your guard about it,' she urged, fearing it might damage Catherine's prospects, 'in order that they may do no harm when … the affair of the marriage shall be agreed upon.'[8] The Spaniards were secretly concerned because such disagreements would dictate whatever arrangements and dispensations were required for the future. 'Be careful also to get at the truth as regards the fact whether the prince and Princess of Wales consummated the marriage,' the king wrote to Estrada two days later, 'use all the flattering persuasions you can to prevent them from concealing it from you.'[9] By the following month,

Ferdinand and Isabella had been convinced by Doña Elvira that Catherine 'remains as she was here'.[10]

Through the summer months, Ferdinand and Isabella continued to press for a betrothal between Catherine and young Henry, who was officially termed Prince of Wales from that June onwards. Estrada was to appear nonchalant and make arrangements for the return of the princess to Spain in order to push the English to commit, but the king simply refused to be drawn on the matter. Catherine's brief moment of triumph, with all its expensive pageantry, seemed to have been forgotten amid the plans for another forthcoming marriage, that of Arthur's sister Margaret to James IV, King of Scots. The wedding had taken place, by proxy, on 25 January, but the twelve-year-old princess was still too young to be sent away to live with her adult husband. Queen Elizabeth, in the early stages of her final pregnancy, was occupied with the purchase of items for her daughter and the ordering of clothes.

The days must have passed quietly for Catherine and her ladies, walking in the gardens, praying in the chapel, sitting in their apartments overlooking the river, reading, writing letters and sewing. Perhaps they allowed themselves the consolation of acrobats, fools and minstrels, or even dancing the low Spanish bass steps, despite their mourning status. At the end of August, one of the queen's ladies, Anne Percy, was reimbursed for £20 which she had lent to 'a Spanyarde that camme from the princess', and that September Elizabeth sent her daughter-in-law some books.[11] On 28 October, a payment of five shillings was made to Lady Dorothy Verney, so that she might pay an individual named 'Carnevelle ... for his costs riding to the princess', which might relate to Catherine. Perhaps the approaching anniversary of her wedding stirred memories and consciences, as on 6 November 1502 a payment appears for 'conveying the princesse in the queen's barge with xvi rowers from the Bisshop of Duresme Palace to Westminster and from Westminster again'.[12] There are no indications in the Privy Purse accounts of Catherine's seventeenth birthday being acknowledged that December, or that she was present at court at any time during the Christmas season. The year 1502, which had begun so auspiciously, drew to a close for Catherine in loneliness and uncertainty, possibly in neglect.

While the days ticked past slowly at Durham House, the march of Renaissance discovery continued apace. Since the creation of Bartholomew Columbus's maps in 1485 and Behaim's Erdapfel, or the first globe of the known world in 1492, cartography had been forced to expand as the conquistadors sailed further west. The first map to include the Americas was painted on parchment by a Spaniard, Juan de la Cosa, in around 1500, showing traffic across the Atlantic. De la Cosa was sent to Portugal by Isabella at the head of a delegation to protest about Portuguese attempts to gain Spanish territories but he was imprisoned there and only released in 1502 with the queen's help. In recent years, the Portuguese had discovered Brazil, Newfoundland and Madagascar and Vasco da Gama established a colony at Cochin, in China, but their rivalry with the Spanish conquistadors had not abated. They produced their own latitude map, now known as the Cantino Planisphere, charting all their discoveries up to 1502. That May, around the time that Catherine arrived at Durham Place, Christopher Columbus was embarking on his final mission, having been restored to favour in the eyes of Ferdinand and Isabella. He would travel to Honduras, Panama and Costa Rica, before being shipwrecked off Jamaica and marooned there for a year. When he returned to Spain, he brought cocoa beans.

In 1502, Nicolaus Copernicus was puzzling over the heavens as canon of Frauenberg Cathedral, Lucas Cranach the elder arrived in Vienna, and in Florence Leonardo da Vinci was drawing plans for seemingly impossible bridges of 720 feet in length. The following year, as Catherine waited patiently, he began to sketch the twenty-four-year-old Lisa Gherardini, the wife of a silk merchant, who would become known to the world as *La Giaconda*, or the *Mona Lisa*. In Nuremburg, Albrecht Durer began work on a series of seventeen illustrations of *The Life of the Virgin*, while the Dutch Hieronymus Bosch was working on his triptych *The Garden of Earthly Delights*. In the south, Giovanni Bellini was painting Madonnas and crucifixion scenes, in Florence Sandro Botticelli was engaged on the ambitious four paintings of the life of Zenobius that would complete his long career, and in the Perugian countryside Raphael de Urbino was adorning local churches with coronations, weddings and crucifixions. A 1502 Italian translation of Herodotus' *Histories* was published in Venice, while in 1503 the *Imitations of Christ* by the German canon Thomas à Kempis was published posthumously in English. Machiavelli issued his *Discourse on the Provision of Money* and Erasmus published a *Handbook of a Christian Soldier*. That year, in which Catherine might have anticipated bearing Arthur's first child, the notorious French apothecary Nostradamus was born.

In spite of new ideas about religion and learning, the rulers of the Renaissance still measured their worth in terms of material status symbols and patronage. Henry commissioned the Flemish merchant Peter van Aelst to supply tapestries to Richmond Palace, one of which was delivered in 1502 as 'oon pece of arras of tholde lawe and newe and nyne bordoures of the same wrought with fyne golde'. He supplied tapestries of the Veneration of the Virgin to Juana and Philip of Austria in the same year, and his son would later become court painter to their son Charles. Not to be outdone, Ferdinand and Isabella commissioned Donato Bramante to create the Tempietto, a small temple in the Renaissance style, to stand in the courtyard of St Peter's in Rome, perhaps to celebrate the passing of a decade since their religious achievements. Isabella had also set her court painter, Juan de Flandres, to work on a polyptych of twenty-seven religious images that would later be known by her name. Two of them were worked by the Flemish Michael Sittow, but his departure for England at this time would result in the creation of the most famous portrait ever painted of Catherine.

Perhaps Sittow visited Catherine at Durham Place, or else she was allowed to sit for him at Westminster. The painting captures the stillness and sorrow of the young widow, in suitably funereal tones of black and brown. The princess's large circular headdress is almost lost against the dark background, and her black hood would be difficult to make out if it had not been fringed in gold. Her square-necked dress is a rich, warm brown, but the intensity of this colour is only visible where the light catches it, otherwise it is dulled by shadow. Her jewellery stands out amid the gloom: the round necklace of linked squares that bears the initial of her name, and the longer, heavier gold chain where several strands appear wound together in complex design. Gold studs edge her bodice, and the edge of a white chemise or under-layer with delicate pattern is visible, being almost the same colour as her pale skin. The effect of this Renaissance chiaroscuro is to throw Catherine's young face into relief. Pretty and demure, her eyes are cast down as in former portraits, perhaps as she reads while posing. Her cheeks are full, her mouth pink and plump, her chin and nose rounded. The expression on her face is one of serenity, even passivity and resigned acceptance, although it is difficult to disassociate the image from its context at this point in her life. Above her slender, arched eyebrows her red-gold hair is smoothed down on either side of a centre parting, bright and radiant among the darkness, as if to juxtapose the humanity of her features with her status as a precious commodity, a rare creature that embodied the riches of Spain.

II

At the end of January, Queen Elizabeth went into labour 'suddenly' at the Tower of London. She may have been caught unawares, with the child arriving early, as indications suggest she had planned her confinement to take place at Richmond, which was far quieter and more suitable. With the exception of her first two labours, Elizabeth had favoured the countryside locations of Richmond and Greenwich with, historically, the Tower of London rarely ever being chosen by queens, unless under duress. Her accounts reveal the visits of nurses in the late autumn, perhaps as routine, but plausibly because of the concerns raised during her penultimate delivery, when she bore a son named Edmund in 1499, who had lived only sixteen months. Elizabeth bore a daughter on Candlemas Day, 2 February, to whom she gave the name Katherine, perhaps as a favour to the princess, or in reference to the queen's own sister of the same name who features more frequently in her accounts. But something went wrong. Doctors were summoned but the queen died nine days later, on her thirty-seventh birthday, followed shortly afterwards by her infant. The loss of Elizabeth as a queen, wife and mother, as well as the gentle kindness which may have softened Catherine's hardship, was a severe blow for the royal family. Prince Henry, then aged eleven, described the news as 'hateful' to his ears, while the king made the arrangements for her elaborate funeral before shutting himself away at Richmond to mourn. The Princess of Wales lost a potential advocate, a model for queenship and a guide through the pitfalls of childbirth, as well as a relationship that the circumstances never allowed to develop into friendship or anything deeper. With hindsight there is no doubt that Elizabeth's death changed the king in unanticipated ways, but when Henry emerged from seclusion a few weeks later it was with the realisation that he might now make a new, diplomatic marriage of his own. He could set aside his personal grief and find a second wife, perhaps even father another son. And there was already a young, beautiful princess from one of the most powerful dynasties in Europe waiting patiently in his kingdom.

Isabella wrote from Alcalá de Henares on 12 April to offer her condolences to the English king on the loss of 'our sister'. She told Estrada that 'these tiding have ... caused us much grief' and instructed him to 'administer' consolation according to her instructions, but added indignantly that the suggestion of a match between Catherine and the king was a 'very evil thing, one never before seen and the mere mention of which offends the ears ... we would not for anything in the world that it should take place'.[13] Determined to prevent the match, she redoubled her command that the princess should return home as soon as possible, even if it meant that Catherine should join a fleet of Spanish merchants then conducting business in Flanders. 'In this way,' Isabella wrote, 'the king will be deprived of his hope of marrying her', which was a 'barbarous and dishonest' act. Worse still, she considered it a personal affront, dishonourable and strange:

> For, it certainly seems a very grievous and strange thing to us that, after having conducted ourselves in this business with so much love and frankness towards the King of England, and with such pure heart and such a good will to preserve and increase the bonds of relationship and amity between ourselves, him, and our successors, he should desire to conclude the negotiation in the manner he does, especially when we consider his former wishes in regard to it. For, what he now requires, is neither that which in reason ought to be between such Princes, nor will our honour, nor that of the Princess of Wales, our daughter, permit that he should make use of such crooked expedients in these negotiations.[14]

The proposed marriage would have translated the widowed Catherine into an immediate queen, but it would have been a short-lived victory, as the age gap meant that most of her life would be spent as a queen dowager. Also there was little chance of her bearing a future monarch, as any child of the union would take second place to the Prince of Wales. Letters would have been delivered by Estrada to Durham House, containing instructions for Doña Elvira and her husband Pedro, for Juan de Cuero and for Master of the Hall Alonso de Esquivel, to prepare for departure. Catherine's thoughts on the subject do not survive but her obedience and duty to her parents was never in question. Isabella's outrage, though, had the desired effect.

In June 1503, Prince Henry was a tall, robust child of almost twelve, confident in himself and in company, fond of his studies, riding and dancing. A bust by Guido Mazzoni, which is thought to depict him in around 1498, shows a laughing and mischievous little boy, with round cheeks and ready smile, half turning away from the viewer as if distracted by a joke or toy. Yet the losses of recent years had taken their toll. A recently discovered illumination in the *Vaux Passionale* manuscript, created soon after the death of Queen Elizabeth, has been thought to represent Henry grieving for his mother. Two princesses, his sisters Margaret and Mary, are seated facing each other, reading before a blazing fire as the figure of a boy in green leans over what appears to be a table, his fair head bent over his folded arms. It may well portray the depths of sorrow of a young boy who had lost a close, loving mother. While Arthur had been sent away to Ludlow, Henry had seen Elizabeth regularly and she had taught him to read and write, being a constant presence in their London palaces and a visitor to the nursery at Eltham.

As the new heir to the throne, the choice of Henry's future spouse had suddenly assumed greater significance, yet by the same age Arthur had already been betrothed for a decade. The king had previously suggested a match between the prince and Eleanor, daughter of Juana and Philip of Austria, Catherine's niece. Born in November 1498, Eleanor was then only four, so another decade would have to pass before the marriage could be solemnised, and ultimately the king did not want to lose the Spanish alliance. On 23 June a treaty of betrothal between Catherine and Prince Henry was signed, and two days later a formal ceremony was held at the London palace of the Bishop of Salisbury. Referred to as Salisbury House or Dorset House, this sat between Bridewell and Whitefriars, a short ride for Catherine along the Strand and into Fleet Street, or else a quick trip downriver. She set aside her mourning clothes in favour of a white dress[15] and, standing beside the glowing youth and repeating her vows, she must have felt a great sense of relief.

And yet, the terms on which the marriage rested, the papal dispensation to dissolve their affinity, was to come back to haunt Catherine later. A certain sensitivity prevented direct communication about her wedding night with Arthur and, coupled with conflicting accounts of their marriage, the Spanish thought it best to allow for the possibility that consummation had taken place. This, they hoped, would prevent any problems from arising in the future. Both sides acknowledged that the paperwork was required, 'because the said princess had ... on a former occasion contracted a marriage with the late Prince Arthur, brother of present Prince of Wales, whereby she became related to Henry ... in the first degree of affinity, and because her marriage with Arthur was solemnised according to the rites of the Catholic Church, and afterwards consummated'.[16] Following assurances from Doña Elvira and Catherine herself, Ferdinand was in no doubt regarding his daughter's innocence. He believed she remained 'as intact and incorrupt as when she emerged from her mother's womb', adding that 'although they were wedded, Prince Arthur and Princess Catherine never consummated their marriage. It is well known that the princess is still a virgin, but as the English are much disposed to cavil, it has seemed to be more prudent to provide for the case as though the marriage had been consummated ... the right of succession depends on the undoubted legitimacy of the marriage.'[17] The monarchs of both countries wrote to the Pope, which was Alexander VI until August 1503, then Pius III for three weeks before the inauguration of Julius II that October, but the wheels of papal machinery moved slowly. Inevitably, the question of Catherine's jewels and plate arose again, being incorporated in the new dowry arrangements. Her gold and silver plate had been valued by London silversmiths at 15,000 scudos and her jewels, pearls and ornaments at 20,000, which was to form a portion of the 100,000 the king now expected, along with an additional 65,000 worth of gold coin. The wedding was to take place once Prince Henry had reached the age of fourteen, in the summer of 1505.

Catherine had every reason to be optimistic as the year 1504 arrived. On 18 February, Henry was invested as Prince of Wales and Earl of Chester, although there was no formal ceremony at that point, just a verbal declaration by his father at Westminster. This was made official when Parliament passed an Act of Recognition confirming the prince to be 'now the king's heir apparent'. As his betrothed, Catherine was sometimes allowed to visit court and travelled downriver to Greenwich that summer, a favourite family residence which the king was rebuilding. She would have seen the new gallery, tower, kitchens and garden walls, for which the final payments were made that year.[18] She was also taken by the king to Richmond and from there on to Windsor, where 'they stayed twelve or thirteen days, going almost every day into the park and the forest to hunt deer and other game'.[19] After that she had spent another week back at Richmond, which must still have held powerful memories for them all of her wedding celebrations and happier times. Prince Henry was there too, but the king and Catherine left him behind when they went on to Westminster and then to Greenwich.[20] However, the princess did have Henry's younger sister Mary with her as a companion. Born in March 1496, Mary was then eight years old, and Catherine may have been something of a substitute elder sister for her following the departure of Princess Margaret, Queen of Scots, in the summer of 1503.

That August, though, Catherine fell ill during her stay at Greenwich. Whereas on 1 July Henry had been able to write to Estrada of his pleasure to hear she was in 'such good health',[21] a month later he dispatched his 'most trusty servants' to care for her as he loved her 'as his own daughter'. He was 'ready to do all in his power for her'.[22] Estrada gave further details of her condition to her mother a week later, on 10 August; after a week or so at Greenwich, 'the princess had been unwell for three days, suffering from ague and derangement of the stomach'. She returned to Durham House but was 'rather worse' when she got there, suffering alternately from sweating and chills, losing her appetite, developing a cough and her complexion changing 'completely'. The physician, who Estrada knew as skilful and who 'generally bleeds well', purged her twice and made two attempts to bleed her, with no success. The king had been obliged to depart for Kent with the prince, but was very solicitous for Catherine's comfort, sending 'messages to her very often' and offering to visit.[23] By 27 August,

Henry had received a letter from Catherine, delivered by Estrada, and rejoiced to hear 'that she had recovered'.

Estrada also showed concern over the papal dispensation which had not yet appeared. Henry ordered an investigation into its whereabouts, to be conducted by Adriano Castellesi, who made a report on 4 January 1504 that the matter was still under consideration. Castellesi was an Italian who had first arrived in England as far back as 1488 to try to smooth its relations with Scotland, but on proving himself to be a dedicated Anglophile he was appointed to the bishopric of Hereford, then of Bath and Wells. His deputy was Polydore Vergil, the humanist scholar and 'father of English history', who came to England in 1502 and remained to serve Henry and his son, penning an immense chronology that provides much detailed information about the country. Castellesi returned to Italy, where he unsuccessfully continued to seek the dispensation. Pope Julius claimed to have granted it 'by word of mouth', but Isabella believed that he was awaiting the arrival of an English embassy. Henry's ambassador did arrive in Rome on 20 May, and was championed by Castellesi, but returned home again empty handed. In July, the Pope wrote to King Henry explaining that he had not intended to delay the issue of the paperwork, only to afford it the proper 'mature consideration'[24] and the 'brief' for the dispensation arrived in England that August. By that October, the all-important paperwork had still not been dispatched, a fact which de Puebla mused may have been caused by the ambassador being ill or the machinations of the French.[25] When the actual papal bull finally arrived it was dated to December 1503, indicating the level of procrastination or 'consideration' it required, although it is not impossible that it may have been backdated.

That summer there were also problems among Catherine's servants at Durham House. Money was tight: she had an income from Henry, overseen by William Holybrand, but her household of fifty Spaniards proved hard to maintain on this amount. This contributed to the squabbles between Doña Elvira, her husband Pedro and the treasurer Juan de Cuero, none of whom liked De Puebla, which became so bad that Catherine asked Henry to intervene. This was impossible, Henry replied, as they were Spanish subjects not English ones, and recommended that she appeal to her parents. However, in secret he did take steps to help her, although 'not, for a great deal, would he have the princess learn that he had known about, and taken part in this business'.[26] De Puebla wrote to reassure Isabella that while Doña Elvira had the 'reins of government' of the princess's household in her hands, 'your highnesses are right in feeling no anxiety' and that de Cuero should account to the Lady Mistress for his spending. He requested that Elvira be rewarded for her efforts by her son Inigo receiving the Order of Santiago, as the Pope had given Ferdinand responsibility for the administration of the order in 1499. Yet he hinted that Catherine was not able to control such personalities, as 'the liberality of the princess is so great'.[27]

III

By the autumn, Catherine was 'in perfect health'. That November, she stayed at Westminster Palace and the attendants were ordered to treat her and Princess Mary the same. Catherine wrote separately to her parents, hearing they had been ill, saying that she had not heard from them for so long – her father for 'the whole of last year' – and could not be 'satisfied or cheerful' until she received word from Spain. Juana had been writing to her with news of their mother's 'daily attacks of ague, and the fever which followed the ague'. Catherine had 'no other hope or comfort than that which comes with knowing that her mother and father are well'.[28] The letters were composed on 26 November and entrusted to de Puebla, who sent them with a protest at the arrest of his daughter by the Inquisition. They were destined to go unread by Isabella. On that very day, the Queen of Castile died at the age of fifty-three in Medina del Campo.

Isabella's health had been poor for a long time. She had been gravely concerned about passing on the crown of Castile to Juana and Philip, the breaking of the connection with Aragon and about continuing hostilities between France and Spain. The strain of caring for Juana in 1503 through her depression and fourth pregnancy after Philip had returned to Burgundy pushed Isabella to the point of collapse. In June she suffered from a fever and pains, and purging only made her weaker; her doctors feared for her life that night. Isabella rallied but Juana's dramatic scenes, alternating weeping with silence, attempting to escape barefoot and refusing to eat, continued for another nine months until she left Spain in March 1504. Ferdinand insisted that Isabella retire from the world briefly to recuperate over Easter at the hermitage of La Mejorada near Olmedo. In August, Ferdinand and Isabella were back at Medina del Campo where they both fell ill from fevers. Ferdinand recovered but Isabella declined, finding breathing difficult and with her body beginning to swell with dropsy. Pedro Martir wrote on 3 October that 'the fever has not yet disappeared and seems to be in her very marrow. Day and night she has an insatiable thirst and loathes food. The deadly tumour is between her skin and her flesh.'[29] She signed her will nine days later. The document acknowledged that Juana was her mother's legal successor, but also contained provision for potential problems that would arise as a result of her rule. If Juana, 'heiress … to my kingdoms, lands and signories, may be absent from them, may be obliged to leave them again, or that, although being present, she might not like or might be unable to reign and govern … it would be necessary to provide that the government should be nevertheless carried on'.[30] In such an eventuality, she nominated Ferdinand to 'reign, govern and administer the said kingdom, lands and dominions' in Juana's name, until her eldest son Charles was capable of ruling. The following January the Cortes would follow Isabella's wishes by swearing allegiance to Juana only to immediately declare her unfit to rule, placing Ferdinand in the role of regent.

According to a letter written the following January by the Bishop of Worcester, a secret copy of the papal dispensation for Catherine's marriage had been sent to the queen 'for her consolation, when on her deathbed'. Coming after all the concerns over Juana and Castile, it may have provided Isabella with some comfort, some degree of closure, some sense of security for the future of her youngest child. On the night of 25 November, amid a terrible storm, it became clear that she was dying. The Queen of Castile, who had forged her own marital and martial destinies, who had fought a crusade on her own territory and who had claimed much of the New World, the mother whose influence shaped the core of Catherine's belief, breathed her last at around noon the following day. She was buried in the Alhambra, later being moved into the chapel royal that was erected there by her grandson Charles.

Ferdinand had lost his wife less than two years after King Henry.

He described his grief as 'boundless', 'the greatest affliction' and 'piercing his heart'. On the same day, however reluctantly, he went out into the marketplace at Medina del Campo and stood on a platform to renounce his claim to the Castilian throne in favour of his daughter and son-in-law. Then he wrote to the other widower in England that it had 'pleased God' to take Isabella to glory, but her death was 'the greatest affliction that could have befallen him'. He did not doubt that Henry would feel her loss 'as a brother'. On 5 December Catherine was at Westminster, where she had been for a month, and de Puebla was still writing to Ferdinand and Isabella, so the news had clearly not reached London yet of the queen's death. She is likely to have heard later that month, although her response was not recorded.

Isabella's contemporary Antoine de Lalang, Senor de Montigny, wrote that her death was a 'loss to all Christendom'. Although Catherine had not seen her mother in over three years, the demise of the queen robbed her daughter of her chief advocate and confidante, the woman who had shaped and defined her, who provided her with the robust and complex model of queenship and wifedom that Catherine was to follow all her life. In Isabella, Catherine had observed the blend of martial fortitude and organisation, a sense of vision and determination to carry her desires to fruition, an absolute faith in the Catholic Church and the crusading zeal that saw her relentless in her pursuit of heretics. She had witnessed her mother's combination of regality and maternity, the soft side she showed to her husband and children beside the steely determination to crush her enemies. The queen may have endured Ferdinand's affairs but nothing had shaken her marriage; until the day of her death the pair had remained devoted partners in their mutual cause. This was the model of matrimony Catherine would attempt to recreate in England.

But Isabella's death was not just a personal loss for Catherine, breaking a thread with her homeland, it was instrumental in redefining her status. Just as she had embodied the Spanish nation, being a physical symbol in England for the unification and might of the two monarchs and all they had achieved, the princess now represented the disintegration of that nation and its future uncertainty. Where Spain had recently been the most powerful country in Europe, with its monarchs dazzling in gold from the

New World, it was now dangerously divided, a football between warring spouses, an enclave of the Burgundians. Catherine was no longer the daughter of the monarchs of Spain, she was now merely the daughter of Aragon, a much smaller entity of far less significance on the European stage. If Henry wanted to court Spain, he needed to build his relationship with Castile's new king, Philip of Austria. Suddenly, Philip's daughter Eleanor was looking a far more attractive prospect than the nineteen-year-old Catherine. Her vision of being the Isabella of England was fading.

9

Potential Spouses 1505–1507

In spite of her loss, Catherine had a wedding to look forward to. Sitting by the window at Durham House, she could imagine the magnificent pageants that would be devised in her honour, the feasts laid in the great halls of palaces, Londoners turning out in their finery to wave and cheer, the whole city en fête as the conduits ran with wine. Henry was younger than her by five and a half years but he was strong, long-limbed and handsome. As the spring of 1505 slipped into summer, and the evenings lengthened in the park at Richmond, the approach of the prince's fourteenth birthday meant an impending change for Catherine. She had been a widow for over three years, existing in a sort of limbo on the edges of court life, watching as the boy grew into a youth, anticipating their new life together. Soon, she would be a wife – and hopefully a mother.

The past years had revealed to Catherine just how far her future depended upon the willingness of her father and father-in-law to negotiate. Along with Isabella, they had forged her first match, wading through the details of dowry payments, plate and jewels, arrangements and arrivals. There had been setbacks and postponements but the mutual interests of England and Spain had prevailed. Although the onus now fell entirely upon the shoulders of Ferdinand of Aragon to speak on Catherine's behalf, his interactions with Henry through the month of June gave his daughter every reason to hope that she would soon become a wife for the second time. On 11 June, Henry wrote to Ferdinand from

Richmond Palace that he was 'ready to confirm the new ... alliance and [was] contented with the marriage portion of the princess' and would have 'more deliberations with de Puebla on these subjects' soon.[1] Ferdinand sent his reply from Segovia eleven days later, to 'inform the King of the pleasure the marriage has given him' and instruct that Doña Elvira must guard the princess's plate and jewels so that it could again form part of her dowry. The remaining 65,000 scudos would be delivered when Henry reached the age of fifteen.[2] But all was not to run smoothly.

On the eve of the prince's birthday, just as the preparations should have been coming together, the groom repudiated his bride. In the 'eastern portion' of 'one of the lower chambers' of Richmond Palace, Henry made a declaration in front of Richard Foxe, Bishop of Winchester, protesting 'against his marriage with Princess Katharine [*sic*] of Spain'. As he stated, they had been 'contracted in marriage during his minority' but now that he was 'near the age of puberty' he would not 'ratify the said marriage contract, but, on the contrary, denounce[d] it as null and void'.[3] In case there was to be any doubt, it was signed by six witnesses and presumably endorsed by the king, whose name is conspicuously absent from the paperwork. The declaration took place on 27 June. The following day, Henry celebrated his fourteenth birthday.

Catherine's response to this is not recorded. After the long years of waiting, which had seemed with such certainty to be nearing a conclusion, disappointment may have been unavoidable; but it all depends on whether or not Catherine was actually informed of this change by the king, or his son, and offered any sort of explanation for it. It is difficult not to see the hand of Henry VII driving the youth to renounce a match that had devalued in English eyes, in the hopes of concluding a better deal. Yet the exchange of letters between Henry and Ferdinand suggest that the deal was imminent, even anticipated, right up until the weeks preceding the significant date. Unless Henry was bluffing in this correspondence, his change of heart was rapid, perhaps occasioned by pique over the terms Ferdinand offered. Because the princess had been over the age of consent when the betrothal vows were exchanged, they remained legally binding for her, but the prince's juvenility meant that he was under no obligation to fulfil his promise. King Henry wanted to keep Catherine tied to him in case he later decided to honour the match, and to free his son for a more lucrative offer.

That lucrative offer was personified in the figure of Margaret, or Marguerite, of Angoulême. A sister of the future King Francis I of France, Marguerite was potentially a more realistic wife for Prince Henry than Eleanor of Castile, having been born just ten months after him. Being raised in Cognac, where the Italian Renaissance was revered, Marguerite's family gave a home to Leonardo da Vinci for the last four years of his life; she would become a significant patron and writer, as well as an advocate of religious reform, and would bear Henri II of Navarre two children. Her most famous work, the *Heptameron*, was a collection of stories using the same structure as Boccaccio's *Decameron*, which was published posthumously and incomplete in 1558. She would outlive Henry by two years: in many ways she would have made an ideal wife for him. The King of England's interest in her as a potential daughter-in-law represented a shift in allegiance away from his former alliance with Spain to Valois France.

The year 1505 was something of a turning point for King Henry in terms of his international focus; the old alliances were crumbling and he was looking towards Europe with fresh eyes, even hoping to remarry with the intention of fathering another son now that the dynasty was resting on the shoulders of the prince alone. The father's choice was the widowed Joanna of Naples, who, ironically, had been suggested to him by her aunt Isabella of Castile before she died. It may have been Isabella's intention to steer Henry's interest away from Catherine and to keep him close to the Aragon–Castile alliance. That June, shortly before the prince repudiated Catherine, English ambassadors arrived in Valencia to answer a detailed list of questions Henry had devised in order to gauge the attractiveness of the widow. They were able to reassure the king that she was demure in appearance with clean, fair skin and good teeth, comely neck and full breasts, arms of good length and soft hands, without hair on her lips and of a sweet savour. Yet this marriage came to nothing. 1505 was the year when Henry and his son might have both taken wives, establishing a new Tudor family unit that could have produced more heirs. Had the king fathered another surviving son, the course of the prince's life and that of the dynasty would have altered beyond recognition. But such visions belong to fiction. Juana stayed in Spain, and Catherine languished at Durham House.

King Henry was keeping a discreet eye on Ferdinand. That July he sent three ambassadors, James Braybroke, Francis Marsin and John Stile, to visit the widower 'to endeavour in the most wise and secret ways they can use, to learn the state the King of Aragon hath stood in since the death of his queen'. Their first meeting with him suggested that Ferdinand knew nothing of the prince's repudiation of his daughter, as he said that 'the conclusion of the disposal betwixt the noble lord, the Prince of Wales, and his daughter ... had been greatly to his comfort'.[4] He went on to enquire about her English and was told 'she could speak some, and understand much more' and that she had 'great affection for her father'. Ferdinand replied that she had 'ever loved him more than his other children' and that he 'greatly desired that she should be an Englishwoman'. Then they spoke specifically about the match between Catherine and Henry, at which 'the king and his nobles greatly rejoice' and 'every man and woman in the realm [of England] favour the lady Princess above any of the king's other children'.[5] It would appear that Ferdinand and Catherine knew nothing of the prince's repudiation, that King Henry was ensuring his son's freedom while maintaining a diplomatic façade. Equally, the repudiation was not publicly known and Catherine's popularity in the realm exceeded that of the prince and his sisters. By mid-September, Henry was writing to Ferdinand to assure him that the marriage would soon take place.[6]

Yet that year did see a wedding take place in Catherine's immediate family. On 19 October 1505, less than a year after Isabella's death, Ferdinand of Aragon signed a new marriage contract. His new wife was to be Germaine de Foix, a niece of King Louis XII of France who, at eighteen, was almost two years younger than Catherine. She was also Ferdinand's great-niece, as the granddaughter of his half-sister Eleanor of Navarre. Catherine wrote to her father that December, hoping his marriage would 'soon be concluded and ... secure the peace of Christendom'. At the time of the wedding, on 18 March 1506, the groom was fifty-five, but this was no stereotypical case of an older man lusting after a younger woman. Ferdinand's motivation was of the utmost dynastic and political imperative to save Aragon. Conscious that his death would mean his inheritance passing to Juana and Philip, he was anxious to father a son who would supersede his sister in the succession. With Juana's behaviour becoming increasingly erratic and Philip's arrogance and controlling tendencies rendering him incapable of concealing his disrespect of Ferdinand and Spanish history, the king was making a last-ditch attempt to prevent Aragon going the same way as Castile. This new marriage, a ramification of her mother's death, revealed to Catherine just how dependent dynasties were upon the production of healthy heirs, especially sons. Germaine did bear Ferdinand a son, John, Prince of Girona, in 1509, but he did not live long enough to assist the Aragonese succession.

The ambassadors also presented their interpretations of Catherine's father at this time, as a 'goodly personage, right lusty for his age', of a 'gross, strong nature', with a 'smiling countenance' and 'lisps because of a tooth he had lost before'. Like Henry VII, Ferdinand had 'a little cast' in one eye. Reputedly, he rose daily before 6 a.m. and had heard two Masses by eight, after which he would go to dine alone. Despite never sitting at table for more than a half-hour, he was 'a good feeder' and drank two draughts of water and wine. He was believed to be 'very rich', as he was during Isabella's lifetime, having no need to dip into the coffers of Aragon, and was held in high esteem by his people. The visitors also met the Duque de Estrada, who had returned to Spain and was judged to be 'an honest, wise gentleman'. However, they reported that Estrada had been chided by Isabella before her death for 'taking too much rule in the Princess of Wales' household'. The queen had told him, upon his arrival, that she had 'sent him to England as her ambassador and not to rule her daughter'.[7] However, now that Catherine had lost her mother, some assistance and direction, some guidance, even some 'rule', was exactly what the princess needed.

II

This was the turning point where things started to go downhill for Catherine. As the summer weeks passed, she became increasingly aware that no wedding was being planned. She may have blamed it on a rumpus that erupted in her own household at the same time, which saw her loyalties divided between her sister and father as tension over the Castilian inheritance reached a height.

With the support of Doña Elvira, who was no fan of Ferdinand, Catherine's brother-in-law, Archduke Philip, began to write her letters proposing that they meet and sent ambassadors to meet her at Durham House. Catherine responded and Philip continued to address her as 'my dearly beloved sister', while Elvira's brother at the Burgundian court was actively encouraging the Yorkist Duke of Suffolk, an exiled claimant to the English throne. The woman who had been running Catherine's household for the last four years attempted to manipulate the naïve princess into helping create an alliance between Henry and Philip that would unseat Ferdinand in Castile. The plot was uncovered by de Puebla, ever loyal to Ferdinand, who confronted Elvira and explained the danger to the princess, that they 'intended to do injury to her royal father, and to the queen her sister, by means of it'. Catherine had already written to the English king proposing they meet with the Burgundians somewhere on the Continent. Now she was deeply embarrassed and wrote out what de Puebla dictated, to beseech him to 'value the interests of her father, the king of Spain, beyond those of any prince in the world'.[8] Although she had never liked de Puebla, whom the incident had reduced to tears, Catherine had to recognise that Doña Elvira was a traitor and the formidable woman was dismissed from her service. The occasion was later described by Catherine's Master of Hall, Alonso de Esquivel, as a 'horrible hour'. It also came to light that there were 'five pieces of silver and different other things missing' from the princess's coffers. De Puebla wrote to Ferdinand that Elvira and Ayala had persuaded Catherine to give some of these items away. This was in direct contradiction to Catherine's marriage agreement, by which these items formed part of her dowry.

Henry was displeased. He summoned de Puebla for a private audience and addressed 'a great many reproached full of venom to him', blaming him for the loss of 100,000 scudos of Catherine's dowry, as well as her jewels and ornaments, her gold and silver. De Puebla weathered the storm, although 'the words which came from his mouth were vipers' and he 'indulged in every kind of passion'[9] before quietly leaving the king alone. As this episode played out, Henry also felt that he could not trust Catherine, expressing his astonishment that she should feel 'such partiality' for Philip and that he 'did not like to speak to the princess about this matter, for the princess would have directly communicated it to Doña Elvira, and Doña Elvira to her brother'. Although she had been the unwitting dupe in the machinations of Burgundy and the Manuels, permanent damage had been done.

The king disbanded Catherine's household at Durham House and installed her in an out-of-the-way corner of Richmond Palace. Even before this change Catherine was in financial trouble, as she was not receiving enough income to provide her with a basic standard of living, let alone one worthy of her status. Back in March, she had complained to de Puebla of 'the misery in which she lives', which will 'reflect dishonour' on Henry's 'character if he should entirely abandon his daughter'. She explained that if she had 'contracted debts for luxuries, the king might have reason not to pay them' but she had been 'forced to borrow, otherwise she would have had nothing to eat'.[10] On 22 June, Ferdinand wrote to de Puebla, instructing him to find out whether Henry would 'undertake to pay the salaries of the princess's household' and endeavour to ensure that everything necessary was provided for her. As all her expenses 'will be defrayed by the king', her father counselled that she should revere Henry, being 'very obedient' to him 'as is her duty, and as being a means of making him love her more, and of doing more for her'.[11] But Henry was not meeting Catherine's expenses. That September she wrote to her father on behalf of her ladies. Six of them had come with her from Spain and 'have served her right well, without her giving them a single maravadi' and she had nothing to offer them as dowries.[12] By December, she was describing herself as 'destitute' and unable to buy clothing. It was said that 'each day her troubles increase', and she had 'lost her health'.[13]

Then, in January 1506, the meeting Catherine had longed for actually happened – by accident. Sailing from Burgundy to Spain to claim the throne of Castile, Philip and Juana were forced to shelter at Melcombe (now Weymouth) in Dorset to avoid their fleet being drowned in a storm in the Channel. The monarchs and their crew had been through a terrible ordeal, with the 'pilots and crew utterly bewildered' and giving 'themselves up for lost'; Philip was flung into the hold by waves of such violence that he was believed dead.[14] Henry sent Prince Henry[15] and Sir Thomas Brandon, the Master of the Horse,[16] to welcome him, while Juana travelled more slowly behind, seeing the English countryside in the same way as Catherine had upon her arrival in 1501. The archduke was then twenty-seven and, for all his arrogance and controlling behaviour, still cut a dash as something of an ideal Renaissance prince, being tall, athletic, powerful and strikingly handsome. The Venetian ambassador, Quirini, meeting him the previous year, described him as 'above the middle stature, of fair proportions … of a most pleasing appearance and most gracious both in manner and language'.[17] Henry met him at Winchester, where the new arrivals were being entertained by Richard Foxe. The young prince was very impressed, greeting Philip so warmly that on 'seeing them together you would have thought that they were brother and good friends',[18] and was to see the older man as a role model for manhood and kingship, writing to him after his departure asking for news 'from time to time, of his health' and hanging Philip's portrait in his closet.

Philip met the King of England at Windsor on 31 January 'saluting each other with glad and loving countenances',[19] Henry VII acting as if the visitor was as dear to the king 'as my own son who is here present'.[20] Philip was lavishly entertained with 'recreation' such as hunting, jousting and tennis, before being invested with the Order of the Garter on 9 February. On the same day, a treaty of alliance was drafted, whereby Henry agreed not to assist Philip's enemies or anyone who might behave towards him in a way that was 'prejudicial', upon which England would send an army of assistance. Nor would Henry allow any exiles or fugitives from Castile to shelter in his kingdom, but that they would be arrested and delivered to Philip. According to the eighth clause, the King of Castile issued Henry with a list of similar promises, prompting him to swear an oath of support upon a fragment of the True Cross.[21] But the protestations of support also had another effect, which Henry had clearly been hoping for. Six days later, Philip offered to hand over the exiled Yorkist Duke of Suffolk, Edmund de la Pole, the 'White Rose', a rival claimant to the throne. The English traitor would be returned from Burgundy as long as Henry swore an oath that he would not be harmed. The king kept his word and imprisoned the duke, but his son, watching the proceedings, was not required to make such a promise.

Catherine was invited to Windsor on the day of Philip's arrival and entertained her brother-in-law by performing a Spanish dance in national dress, before Princess Mary danced with one of her attendants. The occasion became awkward, as while King Henry and Philip were talking, Catherine approached them and asked Philip to dance. He made an excuse and she asked again, whereupon he dismissed her brusquely. After the warmth of his letters the previous year, encouraging her to meet him, it was a calculated snub to remind Catherine that she had chosen to side with her father. In that moment, she saw a flash of the vindictive, controlling side of Philip, with which her sister had to live. Her response was to withdraw quietly and sit with Mary, but neither her father-in-law nor her betrothed responded in Catherine's defence.

Juana arrived on 10 February and Catherine was invited from Richmond to dine with the sister she had not seen for a decade. In contrast with the lavish welcome mounted for Philip, Juana was literally ushered in by a back door, entering 'secretly ... by the backside of the castle unto the king's new tower'. The king was waiting to greet her 'and kissed and embraced her', and in spite of Philip's attempts to keep them apart, Juana made a favourable impression upon Henry. Then she was brought to Catherine, who would, undoubtedly, have seen a change. Apart from having borne five children in the last seven years, Juana's mental health had deteriorated and her relationship with Philip continued to be tempestuous. The sisters had only a little time together, during which they were supervised, before Juana departed, seemingly of her own volition. She and Philip had quarrelled, and while Catherine returned to Richmond, where her brother-in-law was to join them, her sister headed instead for the coast. Catherine was disappointed, writing later of the 'great pleasure it gave me to see you and the great distress which filled my soul, a few hours afterwards, on account of your hasty and sudden departure'.[22] The sisters would never see each other again.

Another agreement was reached during Philip's stay in England regarding a marriage for King Henry. The bride was to be none other than Princess Margaret of Austria, Philip's sister, who had been the youthful wife of Catherine's short-lived brother John of Asturias. Thus it was intended that her former sister-in-law should become her mother-in-law. Just five years older than Catherine, Margaret had been a bright, intelligent, fun-loving young woman when she arrived in Spain in 1497, but the loss of her husband, followed by a miscarriage, had changed her. She had remarried, in 1501, to Phillibert II, Duke of Savoy, who had also died young, after just three years. She bore him no children and swore that she would never marry again. This resolution did not deter her brother or the King of England, who must have assumed they could easily change her mind as they thrashed out the details for a nuptial agreement. William Warham, the new Archbishop of Canterbury, Richard Foxe, Bishop of Winchester and Thomas Dockwra, Prior of St John in Jerusalem, were appointed as ambassadors to conclude the deal on 20 March.[23] The dowry was to be 300,000 crowns, with a third payable within fifteen days of Margaret departing for England, or by the end of August 1507, and the rest in six instalments.[24] Henry was still hopeful of fathering children, and provided for them in the treaty, which guaranteed their inheritances in Spain, Flanders or anything to which Margaret was entitled. Everyone signed and the agreement was ratified by Henry at Windsor on May 15.

Yet Margaret did not marry Henry. In fact, she refused to remarry at all, being later named by her court poet as Dame de Deuil, or Lady of Mourning. On 24 September, her father, Emperor Maximilian, wrote to Henry that he had 'not yet been able to persuade his daughter' to marry and was going to visit her with that intention.[25] The following day, though, the emperor's family was to completely change. Philip and Juana had arrived safely in Spain, but then, at Burgos, the new King of Castile caught typhoid fever, rapidly declined and died. Poisoning was suspected but nothing was proven. His widow was distraught, refusing to eat, sleep or change her clothes, setting out to transport the body to its burial place in the Alhambra, but only travelling by night so that none should see he was dead and leaving the coffin open so that she could embrace Philip and kiss his feet. Ferdinand quickly intervened to put a stop to such behaviour. Philip's death and Juana's grief put power firmly back in his hands. After this she would be queen in name only, with her father incarcerating her in a convent in Torsedillas. Henry VII would consider marrying her, little caring about her instability next to her impressive fertility record, but Juana would remain at Santa Clara for her remaining fifty years.

10

Solace in the Church 1507–1509

I

Back in 1502, the first stone had been laid on Henry VII's magnificent Lady chapel at Westminster Abbey. The space at the east end of the church had previously been occupied by two chapels, one already dedicated to Our Lady and the other to St Erasmus, but the king believed himself justified in dismantling the monuments of the past, as well as a tavern adjoining them, in order to raise his religious and architectural legacy. The first foundations were laid on this spot in January 1503, just six weeks before the death of Elizabeth of York, and over the next nine years it grew into one of the most spectacular and elegant monuments to late medieval Catholicism. With its fan-vaulted ceiling, hanging pendants and statues of angels, martyrs and apostles, the Lady chapel would become a symphony in stone to the glory of Catherine's religion and something of its final hurrah. Martin Luther's ninety-five theses that triggered the Reformation might still be a decade off, but voices of dissent were already being raised against Catherine's way of worship.

Only fifteen years had passed since Catholicism's triumphant year when Ferdinand and Isabella had expelled the Moors from Granada and the Jews from Spain. Such religious absolutism demanded an unwavering faith, an absolute conviction of authority and divine approval. This new country may have felt unfamiliar at the time of Catherine's arrival in England, but the reassuring paraphernalia of the church, gold and glittering with flickering candles lighting the statues of saints, would have been welcoming. Although the interiors of English and Spanish churches differed in their detail, in essence late medieval Catholicism offered Catherine a fairly homogenous experience; the rituals of prayer and the Mass, the celebration of saints' days, the structure of daily observance and the decorated missals provided continuity between her two homes. When her marriage failed to take place, her friends betrayed her and the king refused to support her, it is little wonder that Catherine turned to religion, a connection with her mother and homeland.

By 1500, the Catholic Church in England was incredibly powerful and all-pervasive. Its ritual of feasts, fasts and observances defined the calendar and the structure of the seven sacraments to mark transitional stages in life: baptism, confirmation, communion, confession, marriage, ordination and extreme unction. It was a demanding religion, peopled by a host of saints, each with their own special affiliation and story, some significant by region, others by gender, age or vocation. Although Catholics were familiar with a wide range of saints, and celebrated their feast days as they appeared inked in red on the calendar, they would have had special connections to a handful, including that of their parish church, perhaps the patron of a guild or those who had particular personal appeal and relevance. By a long way, the most popular of all the late medieval saints' cults was that of the Virgin Mary, to whom the largest percentage of English churches were dedicated. It struck a particular chord in the English psyche, but pilgrims from all round the world also travelled to visit the shrines along the East Anglian Marian route such as Bury St Edmunds, Willesden, Ipswich, Woolpit and Walsingham. The fame of certain statues or images of Mary spread, assuming a value of their own like the Willesden black Madonna, the golden lady at Warwick and the Mary in the four-poster chair at Lincoln.[1]

Churches were also the repositories of hundreds of relics, such as the bones of saints, hair, clothing, girdles, objects, milk, tears, nails, fragments of the cross and similar. It was a tactile, sensory religion, as pilgrims approached shrines barefoot, or on their knees, to witness shrines operated by pulleys, sunshine streaming through stained glass, and smell the incense, kiss relics and hear the chanting. Little differentiation was made between religion, magic and superstition; pseudo-religious rituals and chants existed for every aspect of life: to deliver a healthy baby, to ensure crops grew, to safeguard you on a journey. One constant of late medieval life was uncertainty: illness, loss, war, famine, bad weather, the plague and premature death. Without the support of modern medicines and the explanations of logic and science, every action and reaction was part of a religious framework, to give people the illusion of understanding and interpreting their world. Catholicism was not a passive religion, either; worshippers could undertake pilgrimage, buy indulgences, attend more Masses, say more prayers and make offerings of whatever they could to secure good fortune. There were undoubtedly abuses endemic in the Church by the arrival of the sixteenth century, but these were often overlooked in favour of the wider sense of comfort and belonging for those who believed that heavenly figures were watching over them and wishing them well. For some, though, this was not enough. Progressive thinkers began to anticipate the Reformation by questioning the interpretation and practice of religion.

Catherine would certainly have heard of the martyred Italian friar Girolamo Savonarola. Excommunicated and condemned for prophesying the deaths of leading Florentine nobles, Savonarola had preached against the abuses of the papacy from the time of Catherine's parents' campaigns. Presenting himself as the visionary mouthpiece of the Virgin Mary, he urged through laws to penalise moral transgressions and vices, such as drunkenness, adultery, homosexuality and extravagant clothing, as well as being deeply critical of behaviour in the Vatican. Eventually the Pope's patience ran out and the friar was hanged, then burned, in 1498, when Catherine was twelve years old. Savonarola might have been silenced but his words would resurface soon, when they were taken up by the German reformer Martin Luther.

Among the voices of dissent in England was that of Desiderius Erasmus, so recently impressed by the young Prince Henry, who had written *The Handbook of a Christian Knight* in 1501, exhorting the faithful to act in accordance with the spirit of Christianity rather than simply going through the motions of religious rituals. In 1513, Erasmus visited Walsingham and Canterbury, using satire in his second volume of *Colloquies* to expose what he perceived to be the follies of blind, unquestioning faith. A pilgrim to St James at Compostela thought that the saint had responded to him by giving a smile and nod of the head; at Walsingham the darkness and scent were very 'conducive' to religion, as were the glittering jewels, gold and silver. The canons were not permitted to show themselves for fear that 'while they are serving the Virgin, they lose their virginity' but the pilgrims were less likely to give donations if there was not someone watching over them, while some even stole from the shrine without retribution. Erasmus' character noted that a great many things such as holy water and milk of the Virgin were 'forged for the sake of getting money', the milk looking remarkably like beaten chalk, tempered with egg white. At the shrine of St Thomas the pilgrim was shown the special relics of Canterbury Cathedral because of his friendship with the archbishop, and his friend caused general embarrassment by asking why the treasures of the generous saint were not being shared among the poor. The piece questioned why the Church needed so many golden fonts, images and candlesticks when our 'brothers and sisters ... are ready to perish for hunger and thirst'.[2]

It was an attitude with which Catherine would have sympathised, given that the members of her household were all but about to perish for hunger. In April 1506, she had written to her father that despite sending him many other letters, she had received no reply and her state of penury continued. Henry would not support her, although she had 'asked him with tears', placing her now in the 'greatest anguish' with her people 'ready to ask alms and herself all but naked'.[3] Additionally, she was in need of spiritual support, begging her father to send her a confessor 'as she cannot understand English, and has been for six months near death'.[4] Catherine sent out other requests for help when Ferdinand proved sullen and silent. She appealed to Juan Lopez in Valladolid, a trustee of Queen Isabella, asking for assistance. Lopez wrote to Ferdinand that he had done 'all in his power to remedy' her embarrassment but that he was only in possession of two crown jewels and a collar, which he did not think wise to send to England. He implored her father to help her, as 'his child', stating that 'the poverty of the princess reflects dishonour on his, and on the late Queen's name. If she had been alive, she would not have suffered it.'[5] It was the duty of a king, Lopez continued, 'to succour a young princess who is living in a foreign land without protection and exposed to such dangers as the Princess of Wales'.[6] In October 1406, Catherine wrote to Juana that she had been suffering from more attacks of fever but had recently improved and was in better spirits. She thought 'it right to let her know this'.[7] By the end of the month, she was ill again and Henry offered her the use of a house in Fulham, so that she might be nearer court if it would help her improve. By December, she was asking her father to pay the Genoese physician 'who had restored her to life in a great sickness she had had'.[8] Even her Master of the Hall, Alonso de Esquivel, tried to help, writing that Catherine was 'in great want of assistance',[9] as did her physician Johannes, who urged Ferdinand that her 'only hope is in his royal and paternal solicitude'.[10] Again, Ferdinand neglected his daughter.

II

Her father may not have honoured Catherine's many financial requests but he did heed her request for spiritual consolation. It was around this time that Fray Diego Fernandez arrived in her household. He was a young Observant Franciscan from Castile, a product of the new education and opportunities advocated by Isabella, having ability but being of humble origins and yet managing to go to university. He appeared in Catherine's life just at the time she was seeking an emotional raft to cling to, having lost her mother, being neglected by her father, suffering ill health and poverty and with no indication that her marriage to the prince was forthcoming. In fact, Ferdinand was now blaming Philip's death for the failure of Catherine's marriage portion to arrive in England, as it was now technically Juana's money and she was too distressed to sign the paperwork. Nor had Catherine even set eyes on Prince Henry for four months.[11] With Doña Elvira having betrayed her, Catherine was susceptible to the influence of a strong character coming into her life, in whom she was encouraged to confide and who provided her with a channel to an authority higher than that of the King of England. The role of confessor was an intimate thing; the fact that the princess would never forgive Geraldini's betrayal, even at the special request of the Pope, goes to show just how sacred that confidence was. Yet it could also encourage an unhealthy dependence, a personal connection during which deep vulnerabilities were exposed, so it is little wonder that Catherine clung to her new confidant. But the relationship of client and confessor could be exploited by the unscrupulous. This is exactly what happened to the insecure princess in 1508–9.

Catherine had already demonstrated a propensity to take her religious observations to the extreme. Regular prayer and fasting were central to the lives of pious Catholics, with many, like Henry VII's own mother, Margaret Beaufort, opting to lead lives of semi-religious retirement, following monastic regimes in their own homes and embracing chastity. Later in life Catherine would be well known for her observances, remaining on her knees in prayer for hours, rising in the small hours of the night to celebrate Lauds, the moment of daybreak, with all its significance for the resurrection of Christ. There were also key events in the calendar such as Lent, and the semi-fasts of Wednesday, Friday and Saturday, when eating meat was forbidden. Taken to the extreme, this could damage the health of a young woman, especially one who was not well nourished and frequently experienced fevers and agues. At one point Catherine's menstruation was known to have stopped for several months, and it could prove erratic on other occasions, which might incur problems if she later hoped to conceive and bear healthy children. Catherine would also take to wearing a sackcloth shift of St Francis under her clothing, as an act to mortify her flesh and a constant reminder of the suffering of Christ. For the princess, this created a parallel with her own pain and deprivation; at difficult times in her life, this intense religious passion would offer her a connection with God, just as her mother had felt, creating a tendency to embrace further pain, to martyr herself, as a release and the only method of control over her life. In 1505, the signs were already there, as Pope Julius II wrote to the Prince of Wales[12] granting him permission to restrict her 'excessive religious observances which are injurious to her health'.[13] Obviously, young Henry did not wish his future wife's piety to affect her fertility. It was an early sign of the way Catherine's religion could become an all-consuming power in her life, transcending that of earthly authority and cares.

Very quickly, Diego de Fernandez became a trusted member of the princess's small household. Although the secrets of her confessional have remained so, it seems almost impossible that Catherine did not take the opportunity to unburden herself of the details of her financial, marital and health problems to Fernandez. Shortly before his arrival she was complaining that 'no woman of whatever station in life can have suffered more than she has' and none of the promises made to her had been fulfilled. Her servants had 'never received the smallest sum of money since they were in England and have spent all that they possessed'. She could not think of them, their six years of services and sacrifices, 'without pangs of conscience'.[14] She had also found 'the English [to be] very different from any people in the world, and very dilatory in negotiating'.[15] No doubt by this point Catherine had formed other impressions of England and the English, which she could only share with her fellow Spaniards. She had certainly seen two sides to Henry VII, who on the one hand prided 'himself in his magnanimity' in waiting for the payment of final marriage portion', although actually, 'he loses nothing by it ... he is the gainer under the present circumstances' and considered himself and the prince not to be bound by the treaty. 'Hers is always the worst part,' Catherine complained. Henry's 'words are kind but his deeds are as bad as ever' and she was receiving 'nothing from him'.[16] And yet, Henry was urging Catherine to write on his behalf to the man who had been her mother's confessor, Cardinal Ximinez de Cisneros, to try to bring about the king's marriage to Juana. In Fernandez, the princess must have found a sympathetic ear, a protector and conduit to the Divine, even an alternative father figure. Perhaps he was something more.

Their association did not come to light until Fernandez clashed with the new Spanish ambassador, Gutierre Gomez de Fuensalida, a forceful character who had already spent a decade at the Burgundian court. Having arrived in England in February 1508, he based himself in the house of the Italian banker Francesco Grimaldini, who was then in the process of wooing one of Catherine's ladies, her dresser Francesca de Carceras. Francesca soon supplied Fuensalida with the intimate news of Catherine's household, including the influence of her confessor over her. Soon the ambassador was writing to warn Ferdinand that 'now the household is governed by a young friar, whom the princess has for confessor, and who, being in my view and in that of everyone unworthy of having such a charge, causes the princess to commit many errors'. It was Fuensalida's opinion that the friar was taking advantage of her goodness and conscience, by making 'a sin of all acts, of whatever kind they may be, if they displease him'. He found the man 'young and light, and haughty and scandalous in an extreme manner' and reported that Henry VII had already been forced to have 'very strong words' with the princess about him. Knowing that Fuensalida disliked him, the friar had managed to influence Catherine against the ambassador 'that if I had committed some treason she could not have treated me worse'.[17] Fernandez defended himself, saying that there were 'evil tongues slandering him', which enraged the ambassador to the point that he was 'almost beyond power of restraint from laying hands upon him'.[18] Even worse, Fuensalida complained, in spite of her poverty Catherine spent whatever little money she had 'buying books and other things for him' and had sold some of her dowry plate 'and would have sold more had she not been prevented by her servants, in order to satisfy the follies of the friar'.[19]

From Richmond, Catherine wrote to her father in her own defence. Her tone was desperate:

> Things here become daily worse and my life more and more insupportable, I can no longer bear this in any manner ... It is impossible for me any longer to endure what I have gone through and am still suffering from the unkindness of the king and the manner in which he treats me ... My necessities have risen so high that I do not know how to maintain myself, for I have already sold my household goods, as it was impossible to avoid it ... Some days ago, speaking with the king, he said to me that he was not bound to give my servants food, or even to my own self, but the love that he bore me would not allow him to do otherwise. From this your highness will see to what a state I am reduced, when I am warned that even my food is given me almost as alms.[20]

She quickly turned to praise of Fernandez:

> What afflicts me most is that I cannot in anyway remedy the hardships of my confessor, whom I consider to be the best that ever woman of my position had, with respect to his life, as well as to his holy doctrine and proficiency in letters ... it grieves me that I cannot maintain him in the way his office and my rank demand, because of my poverty, during which he has always served me

> with such labour and fatigue as no one else would have done. He is very faithful in his office ... in giving good advice and a good example.[21]

The heavy-handedness of Fuensalida had prompted Fray Diego to offer to leave the princess's household:

> As I am in great want of such a person as he [Diego] is, I implore your highness to prevent him [from leaving] ... and to beg him that for the love of your highness he should be very well treated and humoured ... for the greatest comfort in my troubles is the consolation and the support he gives me ... I send almost in despair ... to implore you not to forget I am your daughter and how much I have suffered for your service and how much my sufferings continually increase. Do not let me perish in this way ... I was obliged to sell from my wardrobe. I do the same always when I am unwell during fasting time, for in the house of the king they would not give meat to anyone, even if he were dying and they look upon anyone who eats it as heretics.[22]

In March 1509, an incident occurred from which Fuensalida could not refrain writing to Ferdinand about, as it had proved damaging to Catherine's relationship with King Henry and resulted in her refusing to follow his orders against her father's wishes. Because Catherine was 'so submissive to a friar whom she has as a confessor ... he makes her do a great many things which it would be better not to do' and 'many things happen in her house which have need of amendment'. On this particular day, Catherine and Princess Mary were due to leave the 'lonely house which is in a park', where they were staying and relocate to Richmond to meet the king. Catherine had been sick the night before and the friar forbade her from leaving the house, even though Mary was waiting and Catherine professed herself well enough to go and unwilling to stay there alone:

> He said, 'I tell you upon pain of mortal sin you do not go today.' The Princess contended that she was well ... the friar however, persevered so much that the Princess, so as not to displease him, determined to remain. When Madame Mary had been waiting

> for more than two hours, she sent to tell Madame Mary to go, but that she did not feel well. The English who witnessed this, and had seen the Princess at mass and at table, rode off ... whilst the Princess remained alone with her women ... There is no need to speak of the provisions the Princess had that night, for as the contingency was not expected it was not provided for.[22]

King Henry took the matter personally and did not issue another request for Catherine to attend him, assuming she had 'been staying in such company as suited her', but it was noted at court that he was 'very much vexed'.[23] The following day Catherine did go to Richmond, accompanied by three women on horseback, the chamberlain D'Esquivel, her waiter and Fernandez. Henry would not see her, and had not done so for twenty days at the time the account was written, nor did he send to enquire after her health.[24] The advice of Fray Diego was putting Catherine in a difficult position, but by citing her fear of mortal sin he had even greater leverage over her than the king did. In March 1509, Fuensalida wrote to Henry that he wished Diego was in a monastery, because 'if he is here much longer he will bring greater injury on her highness'.[25] Worse still, he implied that Catherine might be in danger of a different kind of corruption, with Fray Diego 'scandalous in an extreme manner' and he hated to see the friar 'so continually about the palace and amongst the women'. Fernandez would later be dismissed from Catherine's service for sleeping with a woman in her household, so, while exercising the caution of hindsight, it would seem likely that the ambassador had grounds for criticising Fernandez's moral conduct. Although the friar described her in 1510 as 'the most beautiful creature in the world', and has been likened by some historians to Rasputin in terms of his influence,[26] it is deeply improbable that there was any form of physical relationship between them given Catherine's sense of propriety and desire to be married. Although the princess was clearly devoted to him, any attempted seduction on Fray Diego's part would have cost him his position. The friar's hold over her was an emotional one, a passionate religious one, and it was all the more powerful for being physically chaste.

Catherine's sense of despair only increased over her postponed marriage to Prince Henry, who was now well past the age of consent. In October 1507, when the boy was sixteen, de Puebla's opinion had been that there was 'no finer a youth in the world than the Prince of Wales'. He was 'already taller than his father, and his limbs are of a gigantic size' and 'is as prudent as to be expected from a son of Henry VII'.[27] Yet the recent years had been marred by disputes over the payment of the dowry, with the king rejecting Fuensalida's bills of guarantee and falling out with the ambassador, whose heavy-handed tactics resulted in him being denied access to court. In June 1508, while Eleanor of Austria was still being considered a potential English bride, the Prevost of Cassel wrote to the Archduchess Margaret that it was 'said that the Prince of Wales is not much inclined to the match'.[28] His wording is a little ambiguous, but it appears to refer to Henry's repudiation of the princess rather than a dislike of Eleanor. That August the king decided that he would only accept 100,000 scudos in gold, without taking any part of Catherine's plate or jewels as payment – plate and jewels she had been forced to use and sell in order to survive, due to the complete lack of financial support from either her father or father-in-law. Ferdinand wrote furiously about this 'very unjust' act 'in not keeping the promise he made' and feared that Henry would still not honour the match even if he received the money, and that he might cheat them and prevent Catherine from leaving England.[29] In addition, Henry arranged a marriage between his younger daughter Mary and Charles, the son of Philip and Juana, and Catherine could not help feeling[30] that this represented a connection for England with the new Spain, rendering her alliance obsolete.

There is no question that during the latter years of her widowhood Catherine was treated shamefully by the two men who should have been protecting her, and who each had it in their power to alleviate her situation. She knew it, and the many letters and pleas made on her behalf show that her contemporaries knew it. Her tone alternated between misery and apology, loathing the undignified position she had been put in, still writing to her father as late as March 1509 that she was 'grieved to have to thus trouble him, and always have to write him such annoying letters'.[31] Her terrible penury and health, in a foreign country, along with her youth and inexperience, meant that she could do nothing to prevent herself becoming a political football between the two men. Both professed their love, yet each was content to see her suffer shamefully. It is little wonder that as the years passed she became increasingly desperate and clung to those few friends she could trust.

By the spring of 1509, a potential crisis was brewing for Catherine. Fuensalida repeated his claim for Fray Diego to be withdrawn, in strong terms that could leave Ferdinand in no doubt that his influence was dividing her from the king and prince as well as threatening her popularity: 'He is with her highness against the will of all the English, and especially against the will of the King and his Highness.'[32] Nor had the friar anything to commend him, although Catherine clearly found him amenable. 'May God destroy me,' wrote the ambassador, 'if I see in the friar anything for which she should have so much affection, for he has neither learning, nor appearance, nor manners, nor competency, nor credit, and yet if he wishes to preach a new law they have to believe it.'[33] Yet Fuensalida's list overlooks the vital qualities the friar possessed which the princess was in such need of: friendship and company, and a sympathetic ear. These things are independent of learning, looks and manners, but they were exactly what the lonely Catherine needed in her time of neglect. At the thought of Fray Diego leaving, she wrote to her father, she was 'in such a state she feels almost desperate', and if Ferdinand did not help, she feared 'something may happen which neither he nor king Henry would be able to prevent'.[34] Her confessor was her 'only consolation' in her 'miserable life' and she would 'perish' without him. She begged her father to help 'before [her] life was sacrificed, as she fear[ed] it would be soon, owing to the trials she [had] to endure'.[35] Lastly, she threatened to 'do something desperate'.[36]

Catherine's threat seems to point to one interpretation. Was this devout, obedient Catholic princess really threatening to do herself harm? What exactly did she mean by this 'desperate act'? The fear of eternal damnation would have been strong, as she would have shared Hamlet's belief that the Everlasting had 'fix'd his canon 'gainst self-slaughter'; perhaps the desperate princess had something else in mind entirely. Coupled with her frequent references to her own imminent death, albeit through penury or ill health, Catherine was using the only currency she had left in a last-ditch attempt to alleviate her situation. Her letters give the impression that she was on the verge of a breakdown, friendless, comfortless and at the end of her tether. With a new boldness, or desperation, she demanded to inspect the original marriage treaty made for her and Arthur, but the infirm Henry, already angered by her failure to obey his summons, refused to comply. In fact, as the princess wrote to Ferdinand, he was so angry that he said 'things which are not fit to be written to your highness'.[37] For the first time, Ferdinand wrote back with a solution.

In April 1509, the King of Aragon was about to send a new ambassador to Spain. His detailed instructions for Miguel Perez Almazan contain the fear that Henry VII had changed his mind about Catherine's marriage and the dishonour this would bring. The ambassador was to liaise with Fuensalida as soon as he arrived, and if Henry could not be persuaded to agree to the match, perhaps making it dependent upon that of Princess Mary with Charles of Burgundy, they were to secretly prepare her to leave England. 'Her own honour and the honour of Spain would suffer if under such circumstances she was to remain,' Ferdinand wrote, 'but if she were to return to Spain, her long suffering would be at an end and she would soon find opportunity for another very acceptable marriage.'[38] Ships were to be hired to bring the princess, her ladies, Fuensalida, Esquivel, her treasurer Morales and his wife, home to Spain, along with the plate and jewels that now belonged to Catherine. He believed that Henry might attempt to keep Catherine in England 'against her will', so the new appointee must 'employ all his powers of persuasion in order to dissuade' him from 'this iniquitous design'. He was also poised to send a new physician and an 'aged and learned' confessor, whom he hoped would be 'well received and well treated' in England. He also included the possibility, which was always the ultimate aim, that the marriage would still go ahead, in which case he expected that all would 'be arranged in such a way that the princess can live in comfort and at ease'.[39] Ferdinand did not know it, but Henry VII may already have been dead as he wrote these words. Everything was about to change for Catherine.

III

In January 1509, Henry VII had turned fifty-two. His health had been poor for a number of years, and he had suffered from a range of respiratory problems which usually manifested as bad coughs, worsening in the spring. He was 'very ill' at Wanstead in 1503[40] and the following year at Eltham, before becoming dangerously unwell in October 1507, with what seems to have been tuberculosis. He recovered, only to fall ill again the following February, with his condition being worsened by failing eyesight and gout. Fuensalida had been keeping Ferdinand up to date about the state of Henry's health, as in July 1508 the Spanish had heard that he was 'in the last stage of consumption' and so there was little point attempting to negotiate Catherine's match 'before the death of the king'. Ferdinand's patience was coming to an end and he wrote privately to Fuensalida commenting on 'how badly the Princess of Wales is treated' and that 'in all these matters Henry has shown extreme covetousness and but little love for him, the Queen of Castile [Juana] and the Princess of Wales'. Ferdinand was inclined to 'have no longer any brotherhood or amity with him, only that he trusts the Prince of Wales will show himself to be more amenable to reason'.[41] A change was in the air and much was expected of the tall, athletic young prince in the final months of his father's decline.

But Henry VII was not dead yet. The diplomatic game still had to played. When news arrived in Spain that summer that he had rallied, Ferdinand wrote to express his relief and 'much pleasure' as 'the news of his illness had caused him much anxiety'.[42] However, any bout of recovery Henry may have experienced was followed just as quickly by a more weakened state, as on 17 August 1508 a report reached Venice via a letter sent to Milan that he 'was very ill and in extremis'.[43] The king might have been ill but he wasn't quite at death's door at that point, growing stronger through the autumn and spending Christmas at Greenwich and Richmond. However, the following spring saw a return of an illness so severe that it was clear that he was approaching death. The Venetian ambassador was correct when he wrote on 29 March that Henry was 'very ill and utterly without hope of recovery'.[44] The king himself recognised it and confided in his servants that if 'it pleased God to send him a new life, they would find him a new changed man'.[45] But there was to be no new life for the old king.

Henry retired to Richmond, the one palace that, of all his royal residences, really represented his favourite retreat at important moments in his reign. He had rebuilt it almost entirely, creating out of its medieval ruins something of a pleasure palace unrivalled in England at the time. It had witnessed the wedding celebrations of Arthur and Catherine, and had happy memories associated with his wife, as well as being the place where he chose to withdraw after her death. The ageing king now paid little attention to the marble-lined courtyard or the heraldic beasts in the garden, or the tennis courts and bowling alley his family had enjoyed; he devoted himself instead to prayer and hearing Mass several times a day and 'wept and sobbed' as he sought absolution.[46] On 6 March, when ambassadors arrived from Burgundy, they did not even lay eyes on the king; Prince Henry met them and took charge of all the necessary arrangements regarding the marriage of his sister Mary and Catherine's nephew Charles. This was the occasion when Henry summoned Catherine and Mary to Richmond, wishing for their company, when the princess was forbidden by Fray Diego from attending that day. Although she did not realise it at the time, it was probably the last chance Catherine had to see her father-in-law, as he did not see her again after this, being so close to death. This casts the friar's behaviour in an even more disparaging light and suggests that the princess and king did not get to say their farewells, and that the last interaction between them had been one that created annoyance.

Henry completed his thirty-seven-page will on the last day of March. Thousands of Masses were being sung for him daily. His mother, Margaret Beaufort, then aged sixty-five, arrived at Richmond, along with her best bed and various kitchen implements that were rowed downriver for her from Coldharbour House.[47] Prince Henry was also at his father's bedside, and during this time much must have passed between them about the youth's future. The prince later stated that this was when his father urged him to fulfil the Spanish treaty and marry Catherine. Also present at Richmond were Richard Foxe, Bishop of Winchester; John Fisher, Bishop of Rochester; probably William Warham, Archbishop of Canterbury; and the young Thomas Wolsey, who had been in the service of Sir Richard Nanfan until his master's death in 1507, then becoming Foxe's secretary and royal chaplain. On Easter Sunday, 8 April, Henry crawled from his bed into his privy closet to receive the sacrament, and on the 16th he issued a general pardon, but after that point he went into rapid decline.

Two weeks later, on 20 April, Henry VII began his final struggle, which lasted a little over twenty-four hours. A sketch was made of him on his deathbed by Sir Thomas Wriothesley, Garter Knight at Arms, who recorded those waiting around his canopied bed, including clerics and physicians and those of noble blood. These men were to manage the transition to the next reign and take their role in the household and government of Catherine and Henry VIII. There was the twenty-one-year-old George Hastings, Earl of Huntingdon since 1506, who had been created a Knight of the Bath at Arthur's wedding, and Richard Weston, then in his mid-forties, who would become Henry VIII's treasurer. There was also Richard Clement of Ightham Mote, in Kent, who had started as a page in the king's privy chamber and had become a gentleman of the court by 1509; he was to become a gentleman usher in the next reign. Beside him was Matthew Baker, then almost sixty, who had shared Tudor's exile in Brittany as a young man and would not long outlive him, and John Sharpe and William Tyler, grooms of the chamber. Finally, there were Hugh Denys of Osterley, aged almost seventy, who was Henry VII's groom of the stool, and William FitzWilliam, the young Earl of Southampton, who had been raised as a companion to Prince Henry. One of the tonsured clerics may have been Thomas Wolsey, and Henry's physician Giovanni Boerio may have been one of the figures clasping a flask. The prince and Margaret Beaufort are likely to have been present, although they do not feature in the image, nor do Foxe, Warham and Fisher, the latter of whom was definitely there, as he placed the lighted taper in the king's dying hands and recorded his end. Foxe may have been the one holding the cross that Henry kissed and embraced before breathing his last at eleven at night on 21 April.

For the next three days, the king's death was kept a secret. Life at Richmond continued as before, with fires being lit in the king's chambers and meals being prepared and brought to the door, while those in the know made the arrangements for the smooth transition from one reign to the next. Three days later, on St George's Day, the news was announced by heralds riding through the streets with trumpets, and Prince Henry proceeded solemnly to the royal lodgings in the Tower. Catherine was presumably still at Richmond, having arrived there at the end of March. Her last letters that month were written from there, probably from her apartments above the stables. She is likely to have been in residence at the palace when Henry died, but was she taken into the confidence of Prince Henry regarding the real date of the king's death? It seems likely that she was not informed while the important decisions were still to be made, including that of her own future. Catherine probably learned of her father-in-law's death at the same time as the rest of the court, on 24 April. She was included in a list of mourners that were given an allowance of black cloth for mantles and kerchiefs, along with her two ladies Dame Agnes Vanegas and Dame Maria de Gavara, her four gentlewomen Katerina Fortes, Maria de Salinas, Kateryn Montaya and the wife of John de Quero, along with two chamberers, Kateryn de Gavara and Isabel de Vanegas. The accounts also contain payments for her saddlery – suggesting that she was to ride as part of the funeral procession, or at least attend the occasion in person – and livery for her servants 'against the interment'.[48]

The king's magnificent Lady chapel at Westminster was not completely finished by 1509, but this did not prevent Henry VII from being laid to rest there. His funeral took place on 9 May, when seven large horses in black velvet drew the chariot on which the coffin rested, covered with black cloth of gold. On top of it, Henry's effigy lay on golden cushions, dressed in his parliamentary robes, wearing the crown and carrying the orb and sceptre in its hands. Six hundred torches were carried behind him on the journey from Richmond to St George's Fields in Southwark. There, in a parallel of Catherine's own arrival eight years before, Henry's body was met by the lords, commons and religious figures all dressed in black. From there, the procession travelled through the streets of London, over the bridge to St Paul's, probably taking the same route that had previously been filled with colourful decorations and cheering Londoners. First came the sword-bearer and vice chamberlain, followed by messengers, trumpeters and minstrels, then foreigners, ushers, chaplains and squires; after them were the aldermen and sheriffs, two heralds and Sir Edward Darrell, mounted on a horse trapped in black velvet, carrying the king's standard. But this was just the beginning. Behind them were Knights of the Bath, deans, councillors, justices, friars, canons, lords and barons, then three knights bearing the king's helmet with crown, his harness and battleaxe, and his armour embroidered with the English arms;

the Mayor of London carried his mace. Then came the hearse carrying the body, followed by the Duke of Buckingham and four earls, leading the Knights of the Garter, with Sir Thomas Brandon, Master of the Horse, leading the other gentlemen.[49]

Henry's body stayed at St Paul's overnight, under a 'stately hearse made of wax'[50] while sermons were read and Masses performed, before heading along Fleet Street to Charing Cross where it was censed, and on to Westminster. There, he was set in a hearse of lights as Masses were said, after which the staves of office were broken and a 'sumptuous entertainment' was held in the palace. Later, the Florentine sculptor Pietro Torrigiano, a rival of Michelangelo, was commissioned to produce the bronze sculpture of Henry VII and Elizabeth of York that still adorns their tomb. Finally completed in 1517, it sat on a base of black marble adorned with six bronze medallions of saints, with coats of arms held up by cherubs. The portrait of Henry, probably taken from his death mask, shows the face of the man Catherine would have known, with high cheekbones and gaunt face, his eyebrows rounded above smallish eyes, a firm chin and flowing shoulder-length hair.

Henry's reign had been unexpected and unpredictable. His surprise victory at Bosworth Field had catapulted him unprepared onto the throne of a country from which he had been exiled all his adult life. An unlikely monarch, he had been quick to establish himself as wise and cautious when it came to decision-making, as a shrewd player on the international stage and a clever propagandist, understanding the power of symbols and iconography. His reign had seen a flourishing of intellectual culture in a time of peace and he had also sponsored the expeditions of John Cabot to the north coast of America. Through his marriage to Elizabeth, Henry's children had inherited the Yorkist blood of the popular Edward IV and for seventeen years he had been the head of a large family, with a dutiful wife at his side. Her loss was something he never fully recovered from, and his character darkened subsequently, no longer tempered by the queen's softness and kindness – something which might have made a real difference to Catherine. In addition, his fiscal policies and ways of extracting money may have led to a huge increase in the royal coffers, but it was often at the expense of the respect of his people. That respect turned to fear, where loans were forced out of the aristocracy; indeed, his chief instruments,

Richard Empson and John Dudley, were to be the first casualties of the new reign. The new king may have removed the hated financial ministers, but this was not going to stop him from enjoying his father's fortune.

Over the course of twenty-four years Henry VII had seen off a number of threats and challenges, some real, some potential, but the greatest danger to his dynasty had been the loss of his sons Arthur and Edmund, the latter having died before the age of two. Perhaps his greatest legacy was that he handed his kingdom peacefully to a legitimate male heir who had come of age. He was the first king to have done this since Henry V's death in 1422. With the support of his council, Henry's seventeen-year-old son became king unchallenged. Within weeks Henry VIII had decided to marry the princess he had repudiated four years earlier. It was to prove one of the most famous and controversial marriages in history and it was to alter the course of English culture and religion, even national identity. After the union of Henry and Catherine, England would never be the same again.

PART FOUR

The Honeymooners 1509–1513

11

Wife and Queen 1509

I

With the Richmond coffers overflowing and the new king brimming with youth and energy, Henry VIII's reign began with excess, with an enthusiasm and optimism, a sense of chivalric glory and celebration, of relief and joy, of parties and pleasure. In 1509, as the century was still new, the reign of his father was consigned to the past, to the world of dynastic conflict and challenge, to old ways of thinking, archaic methods of explaining the world and worshipping God. The plaudits of the poets in 1509 seem too genuine, too universal, to suppose they were merely flattering the new king. Chronicler Edward Hall wrote of the people's 'great reuerance, love and desire'[1] for Henry's kingship; Lord Mountjoy wrote to Erasmus that Heaven and Earth were rejoicing ('everything is full of milk and honey and nectar') and that Henry was not inspired by 'gold, or gems or precious metals, but virtue, glory, immortality', but rather his character was 'almost divine'. Avarice was expelled from the country and liberality 'scatters wealth with bounteous hand'.[2] Thomas More, composing verses for the coronation pageant, promised that such a king would free them from slavery, 'wipe the tears from every eye and put joy in place of our long distress'. Fuensalida concurred that the English were 'very happy and few tears' had been shed for the old king; 'instead people are as joyful as if they had been released from prison'. When Henry wrote to

Ferdinand that his people's joy was 'immense' and their 'applause most enthusiastic',[3] he was witnessing the expressions of hope in more than just a new reign, but a new era, a new century. More than this, he was the embodiment and the spirit of this new age. In the euphoric summer of 1509, England was looking to this 'perfect model of manly beauty'[4] to create a new world for them.

It was indeed a time of revelation and creation, as the High Renaissance really burst into bloom. Michelangelo was climbing into his wooden scaffolding under the ceiling of the Sistine Chapel in the Vatican and painting his Noah and the fate of Humanity directly onto the drying plaster, before touching it up with gold leaf and lapis lazuli. Italian mathematician Fra Luca Pacioli was developing his theories on the golden ratio in his work *De Divinia Proportione*, published in Venice in 1509 with illustrations by Leonardo da Vinci. Da Vinci himself was also working on his immense collection of scientific writings, later known as the *Codex Leicester*, including his thinking on hydraulics, meteorology and astronomy, with theories about the effects of water in motion, why fossils might be found on mountains and the luminosity of the moon, way ahead of his time.

At the end of May, William Warham, Archbishop of Canterbury, offered Erasmus 150 nobles if he would 'come and spend the rest of his life in England'[5] and William Blount, Lord Mountjoy, also added his voice to request the presence of his former teacher, certain that Erasmus would 'cease to mourn when he learns that Henricus ... Octavius [had] succeeded his father'. If he could 'see how nobly, how wisely the prince behaves, is sure he would hasten to England. All England is in ecstasies.'[6] Mountjoy reported that he had enquired of the king whether he intended to patronise great men, to which Henry replied that England 'could hardly live without them'. Warham praised Erasmus' *Adagia* and promised him a living, along with £5 for his journey, to which Mountjoy added the same amount to cover his journey. Erasmus accepted their offer. He returned to England in August and made his way to the home of his friend Thomas More, The Barge, in Bucklesbury, a lane off Cheapside. There, in the summer of 1509, he began work on his most famous book, *In Praise of Folly*, a satirical attack on the Catholic Church and superstitions. Soon, some of his criticisms were to begin to seep into English culture.

Henry VIII's newly inherited royal printer, Richard Pynson, brought out two English translations of Sebastian Brandt's German *Ship of Fools*, criticising the various vices and follies of contemporary society. Also published in Brandt's home country was a chapbook recounting the picaresque adventures of the legendary figure Fortunatus, through Cyprus, Egypt, Flanders, France and England, where the lessons he learns are focused on the emerging modern, capitalist world rather than the old feudal system. Ferdinand of Aragon appointed Amerigo Vespucci as Spain's chief navigator, and in Nuremberg clockmaker Peter Heinlen was working on the first pocket watch. The Dutch emigrant Wynkyn de Worde set out the typeface in his workshop on Fleet Street and printed a translation of Antoine de Sale's *The Fyftene Joyes of Maryage*, perhaps in celebration of the new king's nuptials.

Henry and Catherine were married quietly at Greenwich on 11 June. It was a small, private affair in comparison to her first wedding, when she walked in her farthingale high above the heads of the crowds on the red platform in St Paul's, surrounded by hangings of cloth of gold. In the last few weeks, events had moved rapidly forward. Fuensalida had already begun arranging Catherine's departure to Spain in the belief that Henry would never marry her, when he received a surprising summons by the council on 3 May. He hurried to Richmond to be told that the new king intended to make the princess his wife. Ferdinand had written without a trace of irony on 18 May that he was thankful to hear of the marriage as he loved Catherine 'more than any of his other children' and she had always been 'a dutiful and obedient daughter to him'. Her match was a 'very grand and very honourable one', he said, and there had been 'no possibility, in the whole world, of marrying her to anyone but her present husband'.[7] The main voice of opposition to the match had been raised by William Warham, Archbishop of Canterbury, who believed Catherine's former marriage to Arthur would create problems and that the papal dispensation was flawed. However, the weight of opinion, including that of the new king, was against Warham, and he was obliged to issue a marriage licence on 8 June, allowing the match to take place after only one reading of the banns, rather than the usual three. Less than seventy-two hours later, Catherine had achieved that aim for which she had been intended since the age of three, and became the wife of the King of England. Those early summer months must have seemed rather unreal, exciting, even magical.

Henry's motives were a mixture of the personal, political and dynastic. Apart from his father's reputed deathbed wishes, the new king wrote to Ferdinand that even if he were free he would have chosen Catherine anyway. This might point to his true motivation, belying his belief that he was already committed to the Spanish match, ethically if not legally. The ceremony may have taken place quickly so that the king and queen could share their coronation day, two weeks later, in which case it was a generous step on the part of Henry, who might have easily enjoyed being the centre of attention alone and delayed his wedding until after the event. Instead, the fact that he wanted Catherine at his side, crowned along with him so that they could begin their reigns together, suggests his respect for her and his conviction that she was more than a worthy partner to him. There is no doubt that Catherine was suitable in terms of her pedigree and education. A marriage to her would preserve the connection with Ferdinand, who was now the effective ruler of Castile as well as Aragon. This would maintain the old alliance against France, which the young king immediately perceived as his enemy, declaring his intention to invade. Catherine was also beautiful. Despite her recent sufferings, and her comparatively older age of twenty-three, she conformed to the contemporary ideals of appearance and colouring. She was suitable in every respect and she was available and accessible. As Henry wrote to Cardinal Sixtus de Rovere, he had taken 'into consideration the high virtues of the princess Catherine.'[8] Not only that, she had come from a family where the women had proven themselves fertile, at a time when it was crucial for a queen to provide heirs. It cannot be discounted that over the years a degree of affection had sprung up between the pair, both aware that they represented the future as Henry VII had aged. Perhaps there was also a chivalric element to the feelings of a young man fond of reading historical romances and playing the role of the ardent lover, in rescuing a princess who had spent many years in distress. There is also the possibility that the new king wished the union to be accomplished before any further objections could be raised to the bride. Ferdinand had already written to remind him that the dispensation made all 'perfectly lawful' and that Catherine's own sister Maria had married her former brother-in-law and borne many children. Chronicler Hall gives a more cynical explanation, that Henry was moved 'by some of his counsail that it should be honourable and profitable to his realme' to marry Catherine who had 'so great a dowrie', lest she should 'marry out of the realme, whiche should be unprofitable to him'.[9] Probably all these motives combined to create a compelling case for Henry.

Henry chose Greenwich as the location for the ceremony, rejecting his father's long and now gloomy association with Richmond Palace. As well as being his own birthplace and newly renovated, Greenwich was private and secluded, allowing the vows to be exchanged without the knowledge or congregation of the huge crowds that had thronged the streets of London to see Arthur and Catherine, and even Henry VII and Elizabeth of York. The location would also have been amenable to Catherine, given her affiliation and that of her mother with the order of Greyfriars. A new gallery connected the Burgundian-style palace, completed in 1504, to the nearby House of the Observant Friars. Their church at Greenwich had been founded by Edward IV, who obtained permission from Pope Sixtus IV, and the first stone had been laid on 2 July 1482, on a place 'where the game of ball used to be played'.[10] Henry VII had then founded a convent on the site and drew up plans for the inclusion of a stained-glass window in 1502–3; in his will he had left them £200 to enclose their garden and orchard with a brick wall, plus an additional £100. By the time of the royal wedding, the friars had changed their former London russet habits for white grey, because it was cheaper, and Henry VIII could not commend them enough for their 'strict adherence to poverty, their sincerity, charity and devotion' and their assiduous battle 'against vice'.[11] Catherine would have approved.

The ceremony was conducted by Archbishop Warham before a small gathering of witnesses, which probably included some of Catherine's ladies, along with George Talbot, Earl of Shrewsbury, and William Thomas, Groom of the Privy Chamber, whom the princess would have known well as a former member of Prince Arthur's household. Their words had been arranged in advance, with Warham asking the king,

> Most illustrious Prince, is it your will to fulfil the treaty of marriage concluded by your father, the late King of England,

> and the parents of the Princess of Wales, the King and Queen of Spain; and, as the Pope has dispensed with this marriage, to take the Princess who is here present for your lawful wife?[12]

Henry answered, 'I will', whereupon a similar question was put to Catherine and she answered with the same words. She could not have been happier. Soon after the wedding, her confessor described her as being in 'the greatest gaiety and contentment that ever there was.'[13]

The recent building programme at Greenwich had created a palace along domestic rather than defensive lines. After the ceremony, the couple and their guests retreated to the hall that flanked the middle court and into the royal lodgings overlooking the river to partake of a banquet and entertainment. By nightfall, Henry's gentlemen and Catherine's ladies would have withdrawn to make the necessary arrangements in the bedchamber, which was situated on the first floor of the five-storey royal apartment block. It was a very different process from the public bedding Catherine had undergone with Arthur, being characterised instead by privacy and discretion. No doubt the bed was still carefully made and checked by yeomen and grooms of the chamber, with the mattress spread with bed of down covered by fustian and no man being permitted to touch it until the first sheet was laid. The yeomen were to lie upon this, and add 'such pyllows as shall please the kyng', although they were to kiss the bed and make the sign of the cross wherever their fingers came into contact with it. The curtains at either side were checked and let down, and the king's sword was set at the head of the bed, before all those involved were rewarded a loaf of bread and a pot of ale or wine. All except one, who was left behind with a light to guard the bed 'unto the tyme the kynge be disposed to goo to yt'.[14] Henry and Catherine are likely to have taken wine and spices, a voidee, before they met in bed, as this was thought to increase the heat in the body and encourage the libido. There is no doubt surrounding this wedding night as there had been with Arthur. Catherine's second marriage was consummated fully.

II

Preparations began at once for the coronation. A 'Device for the Manner and Order of the Coronation' was drawn up, with instructions for the order of proceedings, the wording, clothing, protocol and the roles of those involved. It would have been inspired by that of Henry VII in October 1485, but also, still within living memory, by the coronation of Richard III and his queen, Anne Neville, which was even more relevant for providing a model for a joint crowning of a husband and wife. Double the usual work began in the royal wardrobe, offices and kitchens. With 'pain, labour and diligence',[15] the tailors, embroiderers and goldsmiths undertook to make clothes for the lords and ladies, as well as the decking for decoration and trappings for the horses and carriages, and 'for a suretie, more riche no more straunge nor more curious works hath not been seen' than those prepared for the ceremony.[16] Instructions were issued for all those in attendance to repair to Westminster, and for twenty-six 'honourable persons' to be at the Tower on the night of 22 June, to serve him dinner and afterwards to be dubbed Knights of the Bath. Two of them, Edward Stafford, Duke of Buckingham, and Henry Bourchier, Earl of Essex, had been nominated by Catherine.[17] The day before, Henry left Greenwich and rode to London, crossing over the bridge and heading up into Gracechurch Street, where he was greeted by the Duke of Buckingham, dressed in a gown entirely covered by goldsmiths' work, in the company of other worthy gentlemen. Hall seems to suggest the king stayed there, and makes no mention of Catherine. Perhaps she came to the capital more slowly, or travelled by river, as they were both present at the Tower on 22 June, on the occasion when the knights were dubbed.

On around 4 p.m. on the afternoon of Saturday 23 June, Catherine and Henry left the Tower of London for the coronation procession to Westminster. The streets were railed and barred, hung with tapestries and cloth of arras, even with cloth of gold along Cornhill and Cheapside. Henry rode before Catherine on a horse draped in damask gold, under a canopy of gold, dressed in a crimson velvet robe edged in ermine, a placard studded with gems, a jacket of raised gold and a necklace of rubies. He was 'much more handsome than any other sovereign in Christendom' and 'most invincible', with such qualities that the Venetian ambassador considered him to 'excel all who ever wore a crown', making the country 'blessed and happy' in 'having as its lord so worthy and eminent a sovereign'.[18] Hall's praise was fulsome despite stating that the king's charms needed no description:

> The features of his body, his goodly personage, his amiable visage, his princely countenance, with the noble qualities of his royall estate, to every men needeth no rehearsal ... I cannot express the giftes of grace and of nature, that God hath endowed him withal.[19]

The Duke of Buckingham followed, making his presence felt as a person of the royal blood, the only duke in the land, in a coat of gold and silver thread, sparkling with diamonds. Perhaps Catherine could see the back of him as he rode between her and her husband, his head held high as he looked out over the sea of faces from astride his white horse. There was also Sir Thomas Brandon, Master of the Horse, wearing the baldrick of gold, 'great and massy', that he had been given by Henry VII for his loyalty the previous year. Loyalty ran in the Brandon family blood, as Thomas had fought for the Tudors at Bosworth, alongside his brother William, who had been cut down by Richard III as he bore Henry's standard aloft. William's son Charles, who was twenty-five at the time of the coronation, was already one of the new king's closest friends and would soon become his brother-in-law.

The queen's retinue came next, with 'lords, knights, esquires and gentle menne in their degrees, well mounted and richly apparelled in tissues, cloth of gold, of silver, tinsels and velvets, embroidered, fresh and goodly to behold'.[20] A total of £1,536 16*s* 2*d* had been spent on preparations for Catherine's coronation, only a little less than the £1,749 8*s* 4*d* required by the king.[21] Warrants were issued for gowns for the ladies in her train, some of whom came from her existing household, while others were to form her new entourage as queen. 'Lady Doña Agnes', or Agnes de Venegas, Katerina Fortes, Mary or Maria de Gavara and Maria de Salinas were among those of her 1501 party to be honoured, along with her Master of Hall, Alonso de Esquivel, Juan de Cuero, her treasurer and Master of her Wardrobe and her confessor, which must have been Fray Diego. The long, hard years of penury must have seemed worth it as Catherine saw them decked out in their new clothes. There were also new faces already in position, Robert Hasilrig and Oliver Holand, yeoman ushers with the queen, John Varney her chief sewer, the server of her drinks, and her new ladies-in-waiting, including some whose names would become significant in years to come, Lady Elizabeth Stafford, Lady Anne Percy, Lady Lisle, Dame Elizabeth Boleyn, Mrs Anne Weston and Catherine's former friend from Ludlow, Dame Margaret Pole.[22]

Catherine herself was carried in a litter drawn by two white palfreys trapped in cloth of gold. She wore a dress of white embroidered satin, with a 'rich mantle of cloth of tissue',[23] her red-gold hair loose 'hangyng donne to her backe, of a very great length, bewtefull and goodly to behold' and a coronet set on her head, made from 'rich orient stones'.[24] From the Tower they rode west, probably along Tower Street past All Hallows, Barking, past St Dunstan's in the East and St Margaret Pattens diagonally opposite, and past the church of St Andrew Hubbard, standing in the middle of the main thoroughfare of Eastchepe, on through Billingsgate ward, before they reached Gracechurch Street. Here, they picked up the route which had been Catherine's first view of the city of which she was now queen. They travelled almost all the way up the hill before bearing left into Lombard Street. There, as she passed the well-known tavern called The Cardinal's Hat, the heavens opened and a sudden, unexpected summer shower almost destroyed the silken canopy over her litter and sent Catherine hurrying for cover under the awning of a draper's stall.

Once the rain had cleared, they pressed on into Cheapside, where representatives of all the guilds had gathered, along with the mayor and aldermen and virgins in white carrying white wax tapers. They passed the place where Arthur had watched his fifteen-year-old bride arrive, where Margaret Beaufort and Princess Mary now watched, past the Standard, past the Cheapside Cross, past the towering edifice of St Paul's where Catherine had first become a wife, and out of the city walls at Ludgate into Fleet Street and into the Strand. On the verge of becoming England's anointed queen, how did Catherine feel as she passed the gates to Durham House, the scene of so much misery and uncertainty? That night she dined and slept in Westminster Palace, watched over by the statues of previous monarchs, warmed by roaring fires and soft feather mattresses, nourished by the finest foods the kitchens could prepare. It was Midsummer's Eve, a time when, traditionally, bonfires were lit in the streets after sunset to purge the air, with the wealthy setting out tables 'with sweet bread and good drink ... with meats and drinks plentifully, whereunto they would invite their neighbours and passengers also to sit and be merry with them in great familiarity, praising God for his benefits bestowed on them'.[25] The doors of English homes were also adorned with green birch, fennel, white lilies and similar plants, with 'garlands of beautiful flowers' and 'lamps of glass with oil burning in them all the night'.[26] As the couple prayed together in the chapel of St Stephen that night, the city must have been flickering with light, the air filled with the tang of smoke, as the sun finally set on Catherine's long journey.

At eight in the morning on Midsummer's Day, Henry and Catherine were dressed in crimson robes and took their place in long procession from the palace to the abbey along a striped ray cloth strewn with flowers. Writing his coronation verses for the occasion was Thomas More, then aged thirty-one and the father of four small children living off Cheapside. Having been struck by Catherine's beauty in 1501, he was full of praise for her as Henry's wife and queen:

> In her you have as wife one whom your people have
> been happy to see sharing your power,
> one for whom the powers above care so much that they
> distinguish her and honour her by marriage with you ...
> In her expression, in her countenance, there is a remark-
> able beauty uniquely appropriate for one so great and good.

In typical Renaissance style, More compared Catherine to classical examples: she was more devout than the ancient Sabine women, more dignified than 'the holy, half-divine heroines of Greece', more eloquent than the 'well-spoken' Cornelia and more loyal to her husband than Penelope, the long-suffering wife of Odysseus. He continued to praise her patience and devotion, referring to her long years of waiting, her ancestry and their anticipated family:

> This lady, prince, vowed to you for many years, through a long
> time of waiting remained alone for love of you.
> Neither her own sister nor her native land could win her from her
> way; neither her mother nor her father could dissuade her.
> It was you, none other, whom she preferred to her mother, sister,
> native land, and beloved father.

> This blessed lady has joined in lasting alliance two nations, each of them powerful.
> She is descended from great kings, to be sure; and she will be the mother of kings as great as her ancestors.
> Until now one anchor has protected your ship of state— a strong one, yet only one.
> But your queen, fruitful in male offspring, will render it on all sides stable and everlasting.
> Great advantage is yours because of her, and similarly is hers because of you.
> There has been no other woman, surely, worthy to have you as husband, nor any other man worthy to have her as wife.

Two empty thrones awaited them in Westminster Abbey, on a platform before the altar. Henry swore his coronation oath first and was anointed by Archbishop Warham before the crown of Edward the Confessor was lowered onto his head. Catherine's ceremony was shorter and her crown was lighter, being a golden coronet set with rubies, pearls and sapphires. She was anointed on the head and chest and given a ring to wear on the fourth finger of her right hand, a sort of inversion of the marital ring, as a mark of her marriage to her country. She would take this vow very seriously. A contemporary woodcut depicts them seated side by side, looking into each other's eyes and smiling as the crowns were lowered onto their heads, a poignant image of the moment, suggestive of a couple in love, as equals, embarking on a journey together. Above Henry's head was a huge Tudor rose, a reminder of his heritage and England's recent conflicts, while Catherine's image was topped by her chosen device of the pomegranate, symbolic of the expectations of all Tudor wives and queens: fertility and childbirth. In Christian iconography, it also stood for resurrection, featuring in Renaissance paintings of the baby Jesus by Botticelli and da Vinci. It was eminently suitable for the process of rebirth that Catherine had been through, surviving years of widowed penury to return as England's queen.

In Westminster Hall, the newly crowned king and queen sat down to a three-course feast. It was a meal of 'plentifull abundance ... whiche was sumptuous, with many subtelties, strange devices ... and many deintie dishes' served 'admirably'. The Duke of

Buckingham announced the courses, riding into the hall on a charger trapped in embroidered gold, and Sir John Dimmock, the king's champion, rode in wearing a helmet topped with a plume of ostrich feathers, to call for drink. He demanded to know of the hall whether there was any person there present who challenged the right of Henry VIII as the 'natural inheritor' of the realm and offered to fight in his stead. When no opposition was mounted, the king sent him a gold cup to drink from and the heralds made proclamations in all four corners of the hall. After the tables were cleared, dishes of wafers were served and the Mayor of London, Sir Stephen Jenyns, served the king with hippocras wine in a golden cup. After that, they departed for their chambers.

The celebrations continued on the following days. To provide shelter for the king and queen during the tournaments and jousts, a 'faire house' was erected, covered with tapestries and hung with rich cloth; outside a castle was erected over a fountain which was topped with a royal crown, alluding to the heraldic device of Castile, the battlements covered with gilded roses and pomegranates and the castle wound about by a vine with golden leaves and grapes. The sides of the castle were painted in white and green lozenges, each featuring different image; a rose, pomegranate, sheaf of arrows, an H or a K for 'Kateryn'. Red and white wine ran out of the mouths of 'certain beasts' and gargoyles, while Thomas Howard and his 'young gallants' dressed in the Tudor green and white to match the castle's colours and were presented to the king by Pallas Athene, the goddess of wisdom, against the challengers, the knights of Diana, in blue velvet, gold and silver, representing love, who were presented to Catherine. They announced they had 'come to do feats of arms for the love of ladies' and fought a mock tourney, or tournament; their leader, Cupid, presented Catherine with his spear and asked her permission to join in. The combat was only halted by the king when night was 'commyng on'.[27] The following day, 28 June, was Henry's eighteenth birthday. More celebrations followed, including a pageant during which huntsmen, dressed in green, entered a park enclosed by railing in the Tudor colours and filled with artificial trees. Live deer were released into the park where greyhounds were set upon them and the carcasses presented to the queen. Catherine was asked to give permission for the hunters to accept a challenge from Pallas' knights, but

Catherine passed the question to Henry, who gave his permission. When the knights fought again, love and wisdom proved unable to defeat each other, so that Henry drew it again to a close and distributed prizes 'to every man unto his deserts'.[28]

These coronation celebrations established a pattern of deference and symbolism towards Catherine as queen that was to persist for the next two decades. In the elaborate play of court ritual, she was the chivalric focus of male aspiration, the earthly personification of inspiration, whose favour and approval was always the central part of any regal event. The extent of her involvement was limited. She was definitely an observer rather than a participant, the presiding goddess over the arena of masculine strength and violence and, by implication, the figure with authority over life and death, at the feet of whom dead offerings were lain. This tells us much about concepts of queenship in 1509. In one sense, Catherine was still something of a medieval icon, harking back to troubadour stories of courtly love, symbolic as a figurehead almost in the way that the statues of the Virgin Mary were the passive recipients of prayers and offerings at shrines across the nation. Henry would soon adopt the name 'Sir Loyal Heart' in the lists, declaring his devotion to his wife and leading the way for the worship of Catherine by his courtiers. The Queen of England was the recipient of the devotion offered by her subjects, but it was her passive presence that such tournaments demanded, being satisfied with a mere word or gesture in order to initiate the next phase of the action. The body of Catherine was enough, dressed in its velvets, gold cloth and jewels, just as she had been the passive audience to the pageants of her first wedding day; she was metonymic for queenship, for loyalty, for England. In this way, it was an impersonal, distant sort of queenship, similar to that pursued by Henry's grandmother Elizabeth Woodville and his mother Elizabeth of York. But Catherine was to break this model. She would not be content to be the silent beauty at her husband's side, worshipped for her femininity and royal blood. She was an educated humanist princess, a scholar who had read the classics, who had grown up at a court that prioritised Renaissance debates, an expert in canon law and soon to prove herself a warrior queen like her mother. She was not a woman to keep her mouth shut when it came to matters of state or to accept such a passive, ceremonial role for long. Catherine understood the importance of ceremony and accepted the deference of the knights of Pallas and Cupid as her due, but after the long years of waiting, she was to fully and actively embrace her role as queen.

III

The day after Henry's birthday, news came of the death of his grandmother, Lady Margaret Beaufort, aged sixty-six. She had made her will that January, suggesting that she had not been in the best of health, leaving Catherine a bequest of £202 10*s*.[29] However, her death on 29 June was unexpected, as she was taken ill after eating cygnet, perhaps at one of the royal banquets. Her physicians brought waters and powders to revive her but her condition worsened during the night and she was pronounced dead at Cheneygates, the lodgings of the Abbot of Westminster. Ultimately, the cause of her death is unknown. Margaret's body was moved to the abbey refectory on 3 July, where candlelit vigils were held and Masses were said for her soul. She was laid to rest in her son's Lady chapel and, like his, her golden effigy was designed by Pietro Torrigiano, adorned with Beaufort and Tudor symbols, depicting her in her widow's weeds, with a hood and mantle, and her head resting on two pillows. Also carved on her tomb were the arms of Henry VIII and Catherine, as the new rulers and hopefully the continuers of her bloodline.

Over the years since her arrival, Catherine had little to do with this stalwart survivor of the Wars of the Roses, who had lately embraced a life of contemplation but still remained involved in politics and humanist developments in religion. The king's mother had played a role in the celebrations of 1501, hosting the Spanish party at her London home at Coldharbour House on the eve of the wedding, but there is no surviving evidence to show that she had much contact with Catherine after that, or that any sort of connection was made between the women. Margaret was a shrewd politician and may have been playing her cards close to her chest, or simply reluctant to involve herself in what she perceived to be her son's business. Yet she had shown an interest in the visit of Philip and Juana in 1506, ordering a pamphlet to be drawn up for her describing the details of their visit, suggesting that she was not present in person. Margaret was also a key transitional figure in the arrival of English humanism. She commissioned a number of manuscripts to be printed, including the 1489 French romance *Blanchardin and Eglantine* from William Caxton, and was the dedicatee of Walter Hilton's *Scale of Perfection*, produced in 1494 by Wynkyn de Worde, as well as being the patron for his editions of the *Nicodemus Gospel*, a *Life of St Ursula* and the *Parliament of Devils*. Margaret's own writing included a translation of the French text *The Mirror of Gold for the Sinful Soul*, and the fourth book of Thomas à Kempis' *Imitation of Christ*. Margaret took young scholars into her circle and educated them in her own court at Collyweston along the lines of merit rather than birth, and rooms were made available for noblewomen who required her protection like Cecily, Lady Welles and Elizabeth Neville, Lady Scrope. Perhaps it was outside her remit to extend such an opportunity to Catherine during her penury, or that the princess's status did not permit it. Margaret gathered around her a group of learned men, connected through Cambridge University, such as Bishop Morton, Thomas More and the doctor of theology John Fisher; she founded Christ's and St John's colleges, establishing a Lady Margaret Professorship of Divinity at both locations. It was her confessor and friend Fisher who wrote and delivered her glowing funeral elegy.

Margaret Beaufort was a woman into whose shoes Catherine may have aspired to step. Learned, dignified, religious and wise, she represented an intellectual influence that was difficult for members of the female sex to achieve at the time, from constraints of literacy and opportunity. In this respect, Margaret may have reminded Catherine of her own mother's efforts to spread the tenets of humanism through education and patronage, being 'bounteous and liberal to every person of her knowledge and acquaintance'. As Catherine would do in later life, Margaret had worn a hair shirt under her clothing, lived temperately and modestly, making her confession every three days. Almost four centuries after her death, she would be described by biographer Charles Henry Cooper as 'the brightest example of the strong devotional feeling and active charity of the age in which she lived' who 'stepped widely ... out of the usual sphere of her sex to encourage literature by her patronage and her bounty' with the 'exercise of a mind at once philosophic and humble'. Cooper's contemporary Caroline Amelia Halsted praised Margaret as a role model to whom 'the females of

Britain look with duty and affection, with pride as women, with devotion as subjects'. Catherine may not have spent large amounts of time in Margaret's company, yet by 1509 she could not have failed to be aware of her reputation. Furthermore, Margaret's death left a particular space at the heart of the court into which the younger woman could now step undaunted, to occupy the position of queen, of patroness and of female authority at the side of a powerful king. If Margaret's death was loss for Catherine, it was also an opportunity to come out of the shadows, to come into her own.

12

Queen of Hearts 1509–1511

I

There is no doubting Catherine's happiness in that exhilarating summer of 1509. But it was a happiness in which the personal joy she felt in her marriage was the pinnacle of something bigger, of the political and international achievement of uniting England and Spain. She wrote to her father from Greenwich on 29 July in response to his letter, unable to 'express her delight' at the knowledge that Ferdinand had always held her in esteem as his true daughter and servant. Her letter makes clear that her loyalties still lay very much with Spain. Ferdinand's favour was the 'only thing she value[d] in this life' and the reason why she loved Henry so much was 'that he is so true a son' to Spain. She hinted that England was now under Ferdinand's control, writing that 'these kingdoms [England and Spain] of your highness' were 'in great tranquillity' and showed herself and Henry 'great affection'. Henry himself, she added, put himself 'entirely' in his father-in-law's hands. He regarded Ferdinand as 'his new father' and preferred 'an alliance with him to any alliance with other princes', not hesitating 'to reject them all in order to preserve his friendship … like a dutiful son'. Catherine had performed, 'as desired, the office of her father's ambassador'.[1]

And yet, Catherine was experiencing the most exciting time of her life, with the next six months representing something of a honeymoon period, full of pleasure and joy, as an exciting future stretched out before her. Finally she was a wife and queen, but, even better, she and Henry found great personal happiness together. Even Fray Diego could see it, writing to Ferdinand that 'the king my Lord adores her'. Suddenly, it had gone from a politically expedient union to a love match. 'The time passes in continual feasting,' Catherine continued, as the long summer days at Greenwich were spent hunting in the park, watching tournaments, banqueting and dining. She asked her father to send three horses, a Spanish jennet, a Sicilian and one from Naples, as gifts for her husband 'by the first messenger'.[2] Henry wrote to Ferdinand that he was 'diverting himself with jousts and will shortly go birding and hunting', although he also intended to get down to business and 'visit divers parts of [his] realm and look to public affairs'.[3] Ferdinand replied that he was 'exceedingly glad to hear that she and the king her husband are well and prosperous, and that they love one another so much'. He hoped their happiness would 'last as long as they lived' for, as he knew, 'to be well married is the greatest blessing in the world'. A good marriage, he wrote, 'is not only an excellent thing in itself but the source of all other kinds of happiness'. Catherine and Henry had much to look forward to, as 'God shows favour to good husbands and wives'. She had good cause to believe his words, as by the time he wrote them in September Catherine was already pregnant.

In 1509, Catherine presided over a young, passionate court of newly-weds. Love, romance and dalliance set the tone of Sir Loyal Heart and his Lady. Of Catherine's eight ladies in waiting, five had been married within the last five years. Two others even married in 1509. Mary Scrope had become the wife of Edward Jerningham, and Anne Stafford married George Hastings that December. Anne's sister Elizabeth had been wife to Robert Radcliffe for four years, the same length as Anne Hastings' marriage to the Earl of Derby, and Elizabeth Scrope had become the second wife of the Earl of Oxford in 1507. The other three ladies were the older Anne Talbot, Countess of Shrewsbury; Mary Say, Countess of Essex and wife of Henry Bourchier, the son of Anne Woodville, Henry's great aunt; and Agnes Tilney, the second wife of the Duke of Norfolk. One of Catherine's original Spanish entourage also found herself a husband soon after her mistress. On 30 July, Henry wrote to

Ferdinand that one of Catherine's ladies of the bedchamber, Agnes de Venegas, had been married to William, Lord Mountjoy. Henry thought it 'very desirable that Spanish and English families should be united by family ties' and requested that Agnes receive a legacy left to her by Isabella of Castile, and that some of her property be sent to England.[4]

Catherine's household transformed in two stages. From the small, restricted group of Spaniards whose wages she could not afford and who quarrelled amongst themselves, it expanded to forty-four people after the death of Henry VII, and then to a total of one hundred and sixty to wait on her as queen. She was suddenly the head of a bustling, busy world overseeing the lives of her servants, taking young women under her wing, heading a small crowd in front of, and behind, the scenes. Besides her ladies-in-waiting there were ladies of the bedchamber, whose husbands were often in the service of the king, and a group of maids of honour. The women were organised by rank, with ladies, countesses, baronesses, gentlewomen and knight's wives, with thirty-three named in total in the coronation accounts. Thomas Butler, 7th Earl of Ormonde, was appointed as her chamberlain, but as he had then reached the age of eighty-three it was more a nominal appointment, lasting only three years, with much of the work being fulfilled by the vice-chamberlain, Sir Robert Poyntz. Fray Diego was still part of Catherine's household, although he was now termed her chancellor as well as her confessor and she had six other chaplains. A Dr Beckensall, Richard Hert and William Dawtre served as her almoners, Richard Decons was her secretary in English, while John de Scutea was her secretary 'for the Spanish tongue'.

When Catherine dined in the hall, Edward Jernyngham bore her cup, Alexander Frognall and William Knevett were her carvers, George Beckensall and John Verney her sewers, or servers, in charge of the napery, or linen, and the laying of the table, with three gentlemen ushers. When she dined in her chamber, she was served by Anthony Polen and John Moreton, assisted by six squires attendant and two yeoman ushers. Although she would have eaten with Henry often, Catherine would have had her own kitchens and staff for those occasions when she was apart from the king, or dining in private in her rooms. John Adams was her 'groom for the mouth', in charge of her bakehouse, Richard Brampton and Nicholas Clyff ran her pantry, and her cellars were overseen by a team of four. The ewery, responsible for water, vessels and washing up, was the preserve of John Awrey, Richard Amer and George Wrey, while the buttery, or butler, in charge of alcoholic drinks, was William Fytton. The man responsible for storing meat, otherwise called the office of the acatry, was Thomas Tylley, while a separate position overseeing the larders was given to Thomas Astley. The kitchen had a team of four men working under the master cook William Bryce. Her wardrobe was cared for by Ellis Hilton and her bedchamber overseen by William Hamerton, along with grooms, pages and porters of the chamber. Her stable was run by Sir Thomas Tirrell, her master of the horse, along with a number of grooms, clerks, saddlers, yeomen of the chair, pages, palfrey men and a master of the aviary.

The queen's household was a separate body within the court with its own set of rooms, sometimes operating in conjunction with that of the king and sometimes independently. The focus was always Catherine's own royal apartments, a set of chambers designated for her in each royal residence, usually comprising bedroom, presence chamber and one or more other retiring rooms. There is likely to have also been at least one privy closet, which might be used for ablutions, for storage or even for prayer. If her rooms contained no suitable small corner for the celebration of Mass, she might rely upon a portable altar, popular among the aristocracy, especially given the peripatetic nature of the court. Although Catherine's chambers represented a retreat for the queen from the public eye, where she might rest, or dine, read, or enjoy some entertainment, they were still busy and crowded. Their privacy would have increased the further she passed through the rooms, with her attendants only being allowed through certain doors, so that the inner sanctum where she slept was peopled only by her most trusted servants. When the king chose to visit his wife at night, it was never a private occasion. He would be led through the corridors from his apartments by his grooms, clearing and lighting the way, before being ushered in by Catherine's ladies, who had to vacate their positions and find alternative sleeping arrangements in antechambers. Privacy was a luxury that few could afford, but it was also not much valued as a commodity when royal lives were spent so much in the public eye.

From the start, Catherine and Henry appear to have enjoyed a strong physical relationship. The rapidity with which she was able to conceive suggests they were frequently together and that this was not simply in the expectation of conceiving an heir. Contemporary manuals such as *Jacob's Well* and the *Book of Vices and Virtues* outlined the importance of female enjoyment during sex if a woman was to fall pregnant. Although there were restrictions placed by the Church upon exactly when a couple should be intimate, such as fast and feast days, it was recognised that moderate, appropriate sex within marriage was necessary to guard against original sin. 'For wedlock truly knit, truly kept and used in order, is of such virtue ... if you use your wife or husband as your sweetheart in intent, only for lust ... not for love, nor the fruit of wedlock, nor to be honest, but as an unreasonable beast ... beware of the fiend!'[5] Nor had the years of ill health affected the queen's ability to conceive. As Ambassador Caroz later wrote, Catherine's menstruation could be very erratic, so it was difficult to tell when she was in the early stages of pregnancy. It was believed by one French doctor that both partners should be aware of the moment of conception, as a man would feel an 'extraordinary contentment' and a 'sucking or drawing at the end of his yard', while a woman would feel a sensation of 'yawning or stretching' in the womb, a shaking or quivering not dissimilar to passing water, followed by a chill and a rumbling in the belly as her womb contracted around the seed. The doctors might examine a woman's urine or ask her to drink certain herbs, but in most cases pregnancy could only be diagnosed with certainty once the baby quickened in the womb, at around four or five months. Catherine's pregnancy was announced to the court on 1 November.

By this point, Catherine would already have consulted her physicians. She would have been advised to eat bland food and avoid spicy dishes and certain meats, especially from 'animals that could beget', roebuck and venison, which led to melancholy; roast hare, which caused excessive urination; peacock and crane, which created bad blood; and fatty food, fish and salty or sweet tastes. The queen would have been advised to consume the flesh of young creatures, especially milk-fed lambs and piglets, fattened turtledoves and pigeons, and to drink wine and beer. Henry wrote to Ferdinand that 'the child in her womb is alive' and that Henry and his kingdom 'rejoice at this good news'.[6] His father-in-law replied with his own recommendations, and his concern may have been sharpened by the fact that he had lost his own infant son, by Germaine de Foix, that May:

> Her pregnancy is a great blessing, since she, her husband, and the English people have wished it so much. May God give her a good delivery. Will continually pray the Almighty to grant his prayers till he is informed that she has given birth to her child. Begs her to be careful of her health. During her pregnancy she must avoid all exertion, and especially not write with her own hand. With the first child it is requisite for women to take more care of themselves than is necessary in subsequent pregnancies.[7]

Catherine was clearly confiding in Fray Diego regarding her health and the pregnancy, as Ferdinand wrote directly to the friar on 28 November alluding to his letter, dated three weeks earlier. Far from being a figure of suspicion, Fernandez was now being thanked by the Spanish king for 'his communications regarding the health of the queen'. Ferdinand added that 'no news, of whatever kind it might be, could afford him so much pleasure as the tidings of the pregnancy of the queen'.[8]

As her pregnancy advanced, Catherine was still playing the role of ambassador for her father. As part of the continuing Italian wars, the Emperor Maximilian was laying siege to Padua, in Italy, causing the leaders of neighbouring European kingdoms to take sides. Henry and Catherine both believed that they and Ferdinand should ally with Maximilian, but that they should seek peace to prevent the destruction of Venice, which would harm their trade and part of the Aragonese empire. That Catherine was playing an important role in communicating developments and influencing her husband is clear from the way her father wrote to her at the end of November. He urged her to impress upon Henry the need to write all his letters in code, as she herself had done: 'Secrecy is necessary in great enterprises and that nothing should be written except in cipher.' Ferdinand suggested to Catherine that 'the king likewise enter secret negotiations with the Pope and the King of the Romans' and that he might approach Margaret, Maximilian's daughter, as 'a fit person to negociate [*sic*] the alliance'. It had to be brought about by subtle means, 'not by means of ambassadors, but by secret agents, men who are trustworthy and discreet, and who are travelling ostensibly for other purposes'.[9] The letter also contained advice about Henry's attitude towards the French. In Ferdinand's opinion, a recent answer made to England by Louis XII 'seems wanting in courtesy' but that 'the king must not show any resentment yet' as the French would never attack England so long as Ferdinand was alive. However, he advised Catherine that French may try to ally with the Scots, but as Henry's sister Margaret was married to James IV, they should be at peace. Ferdinand counselled Catherine to suggest Don Luis Caroz to her husband as a likely negotiator of peace north of the border.[10] Catherine was clearly already influencing her husband behind the scenes, as early in December Ferdinand wrote, without irony, that he was 'very glad to hear that the opinions of the King of England exactly coincide with what he had written to England before he knew the wishes of the king'.[11] A treaty of peace between England, France, Spain and the Emperor was signed on 12 December at Blois. Thus the model for Machiavelli's *The Prince* was giving the young King of England lessons in statecraft through the medium of his queen.

The royal couple returned to Richmond for their first Christmas and the festivities continued. The twelve days lasting through New Year to Epiphany were traditionally a time of games, jests and disguises, where order could be overturned, boy bishops crowned and a Lord of Misrule reigned over the proceedings. Henry particularly revelled in this kind of play, this carnival where masks and costumes allowed for role reversal, acting and surprises, which increasingly became a theme in his early reign. On 12 January, a traditional joust was held before the palace gates, on what is now Richmond Green, and Henry competed for the first time in public, but with his identity concealed. If anybody was fooled by the gargantuan proportions of the knight breaking lances against Sir William Compton, Henry's identity was revealed as he whipped off his mask when Compton was injured. The unveiling and the resulting surprise was just as important a factor in the process as the secrecy and thrill conveyed by the disguise. When the court returned to Westminster, Henry and his gentlemen put on costumes of Kentish green, with bows and arrows, 'like out lawes or Robyn Hodes' men',[12] and burst into Catherine's apartments, where they danced with the 'abashed' ladies before casting off their masks to the women's mock surprise. Perhaps Henry's exuberance was a reaction to his years of upbringing under his father's careful nurturing and watchful eye, which had led Fuensalida to comment that he was being cossetted as if he were a young girl. The unmasking of the king, the revealing of his identity, made a symbolic parallel with the sudden position he found himself thrust into upon Arthur's death and the process of rebirth following the old king's death. He was suddenly stepping out of the shadows into the limelight, throwing off an old identity for a new one; but he found that the disguise also afforded opportunity for intrigue, especially with women. Again, Catherine's role was a passive one, to be an audience for Henry's performance, a foil for his playfulness, to enter the spirit of the joke and never to admit she had recognised her husband but to be surprised and delighted when he revealed himself. She never wore a costume to conceal her identity, but she wore her jewels and her regal smile as a way of concealing her emotions.

II

As the days passed, Catherine may have been beginning to anticipate her lying-in, or at least been trying to make herself more comfortable. On 26 November, Henry issued a warrant to the Great Wardrobe on behalf of 'our most dear wife the queen' to send to her at Greenwich 'these parcels' containing eight fine pillows.[13] Catherine had chosen this favourite location as the place of her lying-in, and her apartments there were prepared in accordance with the guidelines set down by Margaret Beaufort in 1486. The rooms were cleaned and swept, hung with tapestries depicting calm scenes, furnished with beds and cradles, supplied with linen and blankets, cushions and sundries. The silver font from Canterbury Cathedral was shipped up the Thames in preparation for the christening, candles were piled up and holy relics requested, such as the girdle of the Virgin that Elizabeth of York had used in labour. The queen would be attended entirely by her women, her midwife and the 'god-sips' or gossips, whose job it was to keep her cheerful during the days of waiting. The royal surgeon, Jehan Veyrier, a native of Nimes in France, would be on standby, but his help would only be sought in an emergency. In December, the department of the Great Wardrobe issued him with lengths of black chamlet for a new gown. Catherine would retreat into a closed-off little world, a dark, womb-like place, symbolic for the process of birth, from which she would emerge triumphant, having delivered a son and heir. That, at least, was the theory.

By the end of January, Catherine would have been around seven months pregnant, assuming that she conceived soon after her wedding night and given the announcement of her quickening on 1 November. On the evening of 30 January, she felt a little pain in one knee which seemed innocuous enough, but the following day she went into premature labour. The pain was so intense that she made a vow to make an offering of a rich headdress she owned to the shrine of St Peter the Martyr of the Franciscan Order,[14] but she miscarried her child, which appears to have been a daughter. She must have been alone, or in comparative seclusion at the time, as only Henry, two Spanish ladies, Fray Diego and the surgeon knew anything of it for months. Over the next few days, the queen's belly did not begin to go down as expected and the surgeon surmised that she had been carrying twins, one of which remained in her womb, ready for delivery in March. It is little surprise that Catherine allowed herself to be convinced by those whose job it was to read the signs of her body. The weight of her hopes, coupled with those of Henry, disposed her to believe that she was still carrying a viable foetus, the fleshly embodiment of their marital and dynastic success. No one at court was any the wiser as she returned to the public gaze with a rounded belly, the preparations for her lying-in chambers being completed.

On 20 February, the Sunday before Shrove Tuesday, Catherine was the guest at a banquet hosted by Henry at Westminster Palace. After 'making chere' and ensuring his guests were comfortable, Henry mysteriously disappeared, to return dressed as a stranger in Turkish costume, wearing 'bawdkin', a weave of gold thread and silk, powdered with gold, with a scimitar and a red velvet hat that had great rolls of gold. His gentlemen wore different costumes: white, yellow and red silk to represent Russia, with grey fur hats, shoes with the toes turned up and carrying hatchets; crimson velvet laced over the breast with silver chains, short cloaks of red satin and dancers' hats with pheasant feathers as a Prussian costume; and the torchbearers all dressed in red and green, with their faces painted black to depict Moors. This final detail must have been a response to Catherine's influence, to her heritage and the presence of Africans like the drummer John Blanke in her retinue. According to the chronicler Hall, the king brought in a 'mummery' or dumb show for the audience to watch, perhaps where the Russians and Prussians engaged against the Moors, to echo Ferdinand's current campaigns in North Africa. Henry may even have taken part, as the mummers were members of the court and soon departed to return dressed in their usual apparel. The tables were cleared and dancing began, but Henry soon disappeared a second time, to return to the sound of drummers dressed in white and green damask, followed by others in blue and grey carrying torches. Henry had put on a costume comprising 'one suit of short garments' of blue velvet and long sleeves, slashed to show gold beneath, the clothes embroidered with Catherine's motifs of the castle of Castile and her personal sheaf of arrows. After them came ladies, two of whom wore crimson and purple satin decorated with the fleur-de-lys of France, while two others in the same colours were embroidered with a vine of pomegranates. Princess Mary danced one of these parts, with her arms, neck and face covered in Lombardy black, to appear as a Moor. These costumes and symbols may have been deliberate allusions to the current political tensions in Europe, representing the conflicts of Spain and England and, no doubt, dancing out their recent and anticipated successes. It suggests that Henry himself played a key role in devising it, planning the costumes, roles and action. Through this act of mimesis, art imitated life as a compliment to the influence of Catherine, for whom the entertainment had been devised.

A week later, Catherine formally entered her confinement, confident that she would soon deliver the second, surviving twin. She took Mass, then processed with her ladies and members of the king's court to partake of wine and spices in her chambers, as the beds were blessed. Then, the company retreated and the doors were closed, leaving the queen with her gossips to wait out the time. Reading, dice and cards would have helped while away the time, as would playing music and singing, or watching her ladies dance; no doubt Catherine would also have prayed each day and spent some time in contemplation. The Spanish were also particularly good at the fashionable blackwork stitch that was used to adorn cuffs and collars, and with Catherine keen to sew all of Henry's shirts she had plenty of time for such gentle work, providing the dim light allowed it. As March progressed, there was no sign that her labour was beginning. April arrived and Catherine may have assumed her baby was late, praying for the onset of delivery and taking herbal remedies to trigger contractions. Still no baby came, and by May she was probably confused and ashamed, embarrassed about the misdiagnosis and having to return to court without having produced the expected child.

At the end of May, Fray Diego wrote to Ferdinand. 'I did not dare write to your highness of the condition of the queen,' he explained, 'in order not to annoy her and because all the physicians deceived themselves until time was the judge of the truth.' He confessed all the details of the miscarriage in January, adding that in order to conceal the earlier loss, Catherine 'did not guard herself against the cold' and her belly was so swollen as was never seen in pregnant women: '*uterus intumuit* so much as never was seen in *gravida muliere*'.[15] Catherine believed herself to be pregnant, he explained, until God acted as her physician to decrease her uterus. Catherine also wrote to her father, explaining that she had not previously informed him of events because the English considered a stillbirth to be unlucky. She and Henry were cheerful, she added, and she thanked 'God for such a husband'. However, there was also good news to relate. As it turned out, Catherine was actually pregnant again. It appears she and Henry had been intimate during her term of lying-in, or else very soon afterwards, as by the time she emerged into the public eye again, she was visibly pregnant. Fray Diego informed Ferdinand that 'her Highness cannot deny it, because she is already, by the grace of our Lord, very large, so much so that all the physicians know and affirm it and a Spanish woman who is in her private chamber told me the same thing from secret signs that they have'.[16] He went on to say that she had conceived three months ago, although the new Spanish ambassador, Luis Caroz, wrote that the queen herself told him she was no more than nine weeks.[17] Diego described Catherine as 'very healthy' and 'the most beautiful creature in the world, with the greatest gaiety and contentment that ever was'. Henry, Diego admitted, 'adores her, and her Highness him'.[18] And yet, out of this new pregnancy, and in spite of the depth of love between the king and queen, would come the pair's first serious quarrel.

III

Luis Caroz de Villaragut had arrived in England amid the confusion of Catherine's phantom pregnancy. A very different character from Fernandez, with whom he immediately clashed, and the now departed Fuensalida, his letters presented a different side of the story, and a sympathetic one. Caroz wrote at once to give Ferdinand his full impressions of the situation at the English court, stating that he had believed a misdiagnosis to be the case after hearing that Catherine's menstruation had begun again during her confinement. 'When I saw the bringing forth delayed,' he added, 'I felt sure of that which I suspected.' He left it to Ferdinand to decide 'how excusable to error was ... to make her withdraw publicly for her delivery' although the King's privy councillors were 'very vexed and angry at this mistake' and were blaming 'the bedchamber women who gave the queen to understand that she was pregnant whilst she was not'. Caroz suggested that the king and council 'should console and comfort the queen, who perhaps might be sad and disconsolate, as she had desired to gladden the king and the people with a prince'. He also counselled them to 'think of the account' that was to be given to the wider world, which was waiting expectantly for news of a prince.[19]

Caroz also had concerns about Catherine because, although she had 'a pretty and most healthy colour in her face', she still did not appear to have adjusted to the English palate, although that might have been accounted for by her condition, or the still-recent change in her diet from pauper's plate to fine dining. Caroz recorded that there was some 'irregularity in her eating and the food which she takes causes her some indisposition'. He was certain that this was the cause of her irregular menstruation, '*quod non menstruat bene, quœ res principalis est causa non concipiendi*', which was essential, as he pointed out, for conception to take place. He had been told that she was eating without care and her advisers wished she would 'go out and be no longer withdrawn', which rather sounds as if Catherine was not taking care of herself or was suffering from depression, although this is not confirmed or even hinted at by any other correspondence of the time. Fray Diego had told Caroz a lot of 'extravagant follies',[20] so it would be quite understandable if Catherine was unsure who she might trust in those days. As her pregnancy advanced through 1510, it seemed that even her husband might be keeping secrets from her. Caroz's long letter contained the account of another domestic incident at court that blew up at the time of his arrival.

Before Catherine had emerged from her confinement, Henry's eye might have been taken by one of her ladies. With his wife absent from the elaborate joust that took place at Greenwich, the king needed an audience to admire his skill, a focus for his chivalry, without which there was little point. On 1 May, 'beynge yonge and not willing to be idell', Henry had risen early and gone out dressed in white satin into the woods to shoot arrows and collect green boughs.[21] As Caroz wrote, the king and queen were 'young and cannot be without novelties'.[22] One of these novelties for Henry was the attention of other young women at court, particularly Anne, the sister of the Duke of Buckingham. In her late twenties, Anne had recently been married for the second time, to George Hastings, while her elder sister Elizabeth was around thirty, and already the wife of Robert Radcliffe, Earl of Sussex. According to Caroz, Anne was 'much liked by the king, who went after her', although he acknowledged that there was another interpretation of the situation, in which it was actually Henry's close friend William Compton who was wooing Anne with the king's collusion. The more 'credible version' in the ambassador's eyes was that Compton was the go-between, pursuing Anne for the king, which he believed because of Henry's 'great displeasure' at the unfolding of events.[23]

The intrigue soon attracted attention at court, and Anne's elder sister, who was a 'favourite of the queen', became very anxious and confided her concerns to their brother, the Duke of Buckingham, and Anne's husband. The duke waited in Anne's rooms until Compton arrived, whereupon he 'intercepted him, quarrelled with him, and the end of it was that he [Compton] was severely reproached in many and very harsh words'. Compton reported back to the king, who was 'so offended' that he 'reprimanded the Duke angrily', with the result that Buckingham immediately left court, vowing never to return, followed by the departure of Hastings, who carried Anne away and 'placed her in a convent sixty miles from here, that no one may see her'.[24] But this was not the end of the matter. In a rage, Henry turned Elizabeth and her husband away from court, believing her to be the cause of all the trouble, and would have sent away more 'tale-bearers' who were 'insidiously spying out every unwatched moment', except that he feared a 'great scandal'.[25] Of course it did not take long for Catherine to find out about this and question her husband as to why he had dismissed Elizabeth, leading to their quarrel. Afterwards, 'almost the whole court knew that the queen was vexed with the king, and the king with her', and so the 'storm' between them continued.[26] Caroz was angered by the role that Fray Diego had taken in the matter, encouraging the queen and, as a 'married man and having often treated with married people in similar matters', telling the friar he 'ought to have behaved himself'. Fernandez was most indignant and attempted to deny responsibility, but Caroz found him stubborn and 'the English ladies of this household as well as the Spanish who are near the queen, are rather simple'. Caroz feared Catherine might behave 'ill in this ado', and had done so already as she 'by no means conceals her ill-will towards Compton', which greatly angered Henry. Whatever the truth of the matter, whether or not the king did have an affair with Anne Hastings, or was tempted to, Catherine was hurt by these actions and articulated her feelings. It seems from the ambassador's accounts that Henry, more than anything else, was angry that she had allowed a private matter to become public. It was a wake-up call for the queen and marked the end of their honeymoon period.

IV

During the summer of 1510, Catherine stayed at Eltham Palace while Henry went on progress. At the end of June, instructions were being issued to the Great Wardrobe to provide coverings for carts carrying Henry's 'closet stuff' and his buckhounds. Horse harnesses were to be delivered, along with a hundred riding jackets for the king's guard.[27] Hall relates how he celebrated Pentecost at Greenwich, then passed the summer days at Windsor, 'exercysing hym self daily in shooting, singing, daunsyng, wrestling, casting of the barre, playing at the recorders, flutes, virginals, and in setting of songes, making of ballettes (ballads) as well as hearing two masses a day'.[28] By mid-July he was still at Windsor, where a riding coat for the king was requested,[29] but by 26 July he was at Reading Abbey, requesting another harness and, five days later, a coat for one of the sewers of his chamber.[30] In early August he was in Hampshire, at Romsey Abbey,[31] then Southampton; two weeks later he was at Beaulieu Abbey in the New Forest.[32] By September he had ridden east, through Sussex into Kent, and was signing grants from Otford and Knole.[33] During his absence, his despised ministers Empson and Dudley were executed in the Tower for loyally serving Henry VII's fiscal policies – sacrifices for the sake of Henry's popularity.

Given Catherine's former experience, they probably judged it wise that she remain in seclusion and not travel about so much. Eltham Palace had been a great favourite of Henry's Yorkist grandfather, Edward IV, who had undertaken renovations there in the 1470s, building new kitchens and an impressive hammer-beamed hall. Situated in north Kent, in what is now the overspill of London, Eltham was then close enough to be accessible but far enough away to be in the countryside. It had special memories for Henry, as he had spent most of his childhood there and would invest considerable time and money into the property during his reign. A surviving floor plan from 1547 shows the main building, surrounded by the great park and ringed by a moat, accessible by two bridges. The privy bridge led from the park into a small court surrounded by kitchens adjoining the central hall. The king's lodgings fronted the moat in the north-east corner, linked to the queen's along the east wing, and had access to the chapel, which projected out into the largest courtyard, parallel with the hall. A separate base court was situated beyond the moat, where the offices of the poultry, bakehouse and scalding house were located with the spicery, pastry and coal house; beyond them lay the woodyard, orchard, great garden and, after 1517, a tilt yard.[34]

Catherine would have spent the summer months quietly at Eltham before being reunited with her husband in October, when they went to Greenwich. There, in the park, Henry devised an entertainment at which men fought each other with battleaxes, himself taking on a German giant while the queen and her ladies looked on. From there, they sailed the next morning along the Thames to the Tower, where the king gave gifts of gold valued at 200 marks to all the competitors, the money being put towards the preparations for a banquet. This was held at the Fishmonger's Hall in Thames Street, where all twenty-four knights wore the same livery, all dressed in yellow satin in the German fashion, with yellow hose and shoes, and bonnets with yellow feathers, all cut and lined with white satin, which was also wound about their scabbards. When they had finished, they made a torchlit procession along Thames Street back to the Tower, to show their costumes to Henry and Catherine, who 'took pleasure to behold them'.[35] On 8 November they went to Richmond, where payments were made to the wardrobe for costumes for revels in which Charles Brandon and William Compton answered all challengers, tilting with spears and tourneying with swords.[36]

The preparations for Catherine's lying-in at Richmond were already underway. On 29 September, instructions were given to the Great Wardrobe for furnishing the royal nursery with eight yards of purple velvet and two yards of green say.[37] Towards the end of December, lengths of blue say, hooks and curtain rings were sent to the palace[38] around the time that the queen entered her confinement. Catherine would have been acutely aware of the dynastic and political significance of this birth, and her desire to produce a healthy child would have been acute. Memories of her recent experiences must have been fresh as her labour pains began on the last day of the year. Her ladies would have encouraged her to walk around in the early stages, and other superstitious practices would have been observed, like the loosening of all laces, ties and fastenings, as these were thought to create a connection in sympathy in the natural world, echoing potential barriers to the child. Even sitting with arms or legs crossed was considered a risk to the birth. Catherine would have prayed and held religious artefacts, or recited charms and used amulets, shells and certain stones, which were thought to ease the pain. Some of the herbal remedies favoured by midwives did have some basis in fact, such as the use of willow bark, which contains the pain-killing ingredients of modern aspirin, but other methods would have had a placebo effect, perhaps calming the labouring queen by creating the illusion of control. As her contractions grew stronger, Catherine would have taken to the pallet bed, with its many sheets and cushions, before a roaring fire in her darkened room. There, on Wednesday 1 January, she delivered her child. To her absolute delight, it was a healthy boy.

The beginning of 1511 must have been a euphoric time for Catherine. As she lay back in bed, exhausted after her ordeal, she could reflect that she finally had everything she wanted. After long years of uncertainty she was England's queen, married to a young husband who adored her, in a peaceful and prosperous country where she was popular with the people, and she now had a son. Her happiness at the time could not have been increased; in fact, this moment was probably the happiest of her entire life. Henry felt the same. He rode to the shrine of Our Lady at Walsingham to give thanks and commissioned a window for the chapel there to be made by the royal glazier, Bernard Flower. England rejoiced in the news of the arrival of a prince: church bells rang, prayers were said in parish churches, bonfires were lit, conduits ran with wine and the cannon at the Tower of London were fired to mark 'the great gladness of the realm',[39] while letters confirming the boy's arrival were dispatched all over Europe.

Catherine would not have attended his christening, which was held in the nearby Church of the Observant Friars on 5 January. Protocol forbade it, so the task was entrusted to the prince's godparents, William Warham, Archbishop of Canterbury, and the absent King Louis XII of France and Margaret of Savoy, who were represented by members of the court. Barriers and rails were erected to hold back the onlookers alongside a twenty-four-foot-wide path, strewn with rushes and topped with gravel so that no one would slip. Cloth of arras was hung all along the south side of the way and also inside the church, where the prince was baptised using water from the silver font from Canterbury. The King of France made a gift of a salt cellar and a cup of gold and £10 to the midwife.[40] The Venetian representative, Andrea Badoer, reported back to the Doge that, along with the ambassadors of France, Spain and the Vatican, he was permitted to visit the queen in her confinement afterwards and congratulate her.[41] Nor did Catherine attend the banquet held on the next day in Richmond's great hall, as she was still recovering, but her ladies may have brought her news of the pageant depicting a mountain, glistening with gold and precious stones, topped with a golden tree hung with gold roses and pomegranates, surrounded by children dancing, dressed as Moors. The queen underwent her ceremony of purification, her churching, at Candlemas, on 2 February, for which the Great Wardrobe supplied purple and crimson velvet,[42] after which she re-emerged into the world in order to enjoy the celebrations that followed, which were, after Henry's coronation, the most expensive single event of his reign.

Leaving baby Henry behind at Richmond, Henry and Catherine travelled by river to Westminster. Henry had been planning the joust since the christening, with notes and sketches dating from 5 January surviving with the names of the competitors and methods of scoring.[43] By 11 February all was in readiness, with six illustrated plates and the rules drawn up, which survive in the State Letters and Papers along with verses written for the occasion:

Owre Ryall Rose now reignyng, rede and whyte,
Sure graftyd is on grounde of nobylnes
In Harry the viij owr joye and our delyte
Subdewer of wronges mayntenar of rightwysnes
Fowntayne of honer exsampler of larges.
Our clypsyd son now cleryd is from the darke.
By Harry owr Kyng, the flowr of natewr's warke.[44]

The illustrated plates show the entire procession with those who took part in their various roles, with the knights and challengers, the trumpeters, officers, masters of arms and others. It was on one of these images that the face of John Blanke, or Blacke, was depicted; he was the Moorish trumpeter who had come to England in Catherine's entourage in 1501 and entered the service of Henry VII, and then Henry VIII, receiving 8*d* a day for his trouble. In the Westminster Tournament Roll, Blanke is shown twice, riding a black horse dressed in gold and purple – another reminder, along with the embroidered pomegranates, that Catherine brought her past with her. He pops up again in the accounts on 14 January 1512, when Henry wrote from Greenwich to instruct the Great Wardrobe to issue him with a gown of violet cloth, including a bonnet and a hat, 'to be taken as our gift against his marriage'.[45] What became of the Moorish trumpeter and his wife, whoever she was, is unknown.

Once again, it fell to Catherine to take on the symbolic role of audience and distributor of prizes. On the first day, 11 February, she rewarded Sir Thomas Knivett, or 'Valiant Desire', and Richard

Blount with 200 crowns each, but the next day the prizes fell to the king, as Sir Loyal Heart, and Edmund Howard.[46] Fifteen banners with tassels were provided for the king's trumpeters and there was a pageant of a forest, comprising many different props, peopled by foresters in green velvet, around a castle made of gold. Also among the trees and rocks were a number of wildmen, or woodhouses, 'their bodies, heddes, faces, hands and legges covered with grene sylke', along with four armed knights, their tappers embroidered with golden pomegranates. The pageant was pulled in by the usual mythical beasts, fittingly coming to rest in front of the queen, where trumpets sounded and the action unfolded. On the second day it was again to Catherine that each of the knights presented their petition for permission to take part. Dressed as pilgrims or hermits, Charles Brandon, Henry Guildford, Thomas Boleyn and others were each granted their licence to compete and joined the lists. That evening, after supper and evensong, an interlude was performed and there was singing and dancing in the hall. Finally, a pageant was wheeled in, depicting a garden of pleasure with an arbour of gold. The lords and ladies within were 'moche desirous to shew pleasure and pastime to the Quene and ladies' and Catherine answered their request, saying that 'she and all the other there were most desirous to see their pastime'. As Sir Loyal Heart, dancing out his allegory of love, Henry's excitement was so great that he insisted the people watching might help themselves to the gold spangles sewn onto his costume. In the free-for-all that followed, the royal guards had to intervene to ensure that the king and queen got away to safety: 'The rude people ranne to the pagent and rent, tare and spoyled the pagent, so that the Lord Stuard nor the head officers could cause them to abstaine, except they shoulde have foughten and drawen bloude and so was this pagent broken.' Henry and Catherine merely retreated to a banquet in the royal apartments and 'all these hurtes were turned laughyng and game'.[47]

But soon there was bad news from Richmond. The baby prince had died fifty-two days after his birth, on 22 February. Catherine's grief was extreme and visceral; 'like a naturall woman, [she] made much lamentacioun' while Henry deliberately downplayed his grief and 'dissimuled the matter ... the more to comfort the queen'. But Catherine could not recover from this so quickly, and although it was 'by the kings good persuasion and behaviour [that] her sorrow was mitygated', it was 'not shortlye'.[48] Henry in the meantime set about the one office he could do for his son, and five days later payments were made for his funeral, including 186 yards of black cloth to cover three barges, over 5,000 lb of wax for candles on the hearse and for the torches, for banner-painters and for gowns, palls and a canopy.[49] The chief mourners included Henry Stafford, Earl of Wiltshire, brother to the Duke of Buckingham; Henry Bourchier, Earl of Essex; and Thomas Grey, Marquis of Dorset, while Sir Thomas Boleyn was one of the pallbearers. There were also gentlemen ushers, grooms, knights of the pall, singing children, gentlemen of the chapel, chaplains, yeomen and all those who had been in attendance on the boy during his short life.[50] He was laid to rest in Westminster Abbey.

Exactly what caused the death of the prince is not known. It may have been an infection, or what is now known as a cot death, but to Catherine it was an unexplained and sudden loss, the shattering of what had seemed to be perfect happiness. As a good Catholic, she knew that such acts could only be interpreted as the will of God, yet she had seen how similar divine interventions had darkened the latter part of her mother's life. She consoled herself with the thought that she and Henry were still young and might have other children. In the meantime, she had to find the strength to carry on and face the challenges ahead.

13

The Ferdinand and Isabella of England 1511–1513

I

As a young king full of chivalric notions and crusading zeal, eager to prove himself on the international circuit, Henry was seduced by the achievements of Catherine's parents. Having hero-worshipped the suave Philip of Burgundy, the young Tudor looked towards Ferdinand as more than a replacement father, as the Christian king who had unified Spain politically and religiously, as a great Renaissance man. With Ferdinand's daughter at his side, Henry wanted to emulate that glorious reputation, to win victories in battle, to be a champion of Catholicism and part of a power couple for the new century, setting national and cultural trends. He was the new arrival, the fresh blood in an established triangle of old men, thirsty to reopen the wounds of the Hundred Years War and be as great as that former national hero Henry V. This led him to ally himself firmly, trustingly and unquestioningly with Spain, so that Henry VII's alliances of peace were rejected and Spain's enemies also became the enemies of England. Of course his wife shared his vision. As her father's ambassador and the inheritor of her mother's genes and ambitions, Catherine was uniquely positioned to ensure that England continued her parents' legacy, following the Spanish model to stamp their mark upon Europe. In the event, though, it was Catherine rather than Henry who was to achieve the great military victory of the reign.

In May 1510, Luis Caroz informed Ferdinand that Henry had shown 'great joy and became visibly excited in his desire to show his great readiness to serve' him. The first opportunity to do so came when the King of Aragon launched an offensive against the Moors in Africa. Thomas, Lord Darcy was dispatched in March 1511 to be Admiral of the Fleet and assist 'against the infidel'.[1] Henry wanted to go too, but contented himself with sending 1,000 archers, embarking from Falmouth in mid-May.[2] Upon meeting Ferdinand, Darcy was to present him with letters from the king and make the following speech, before entreating the King of Aragon to 'use him as his own subject':

> The King's Highness his good son, which as entirely loveth the said King of Aragon his good father as though he were his own natural son, and no less mindeth, pondereth and desireth the wealth, prosperity, surety and honor of his said good father and his prosperous successes in all his affairs, than he doth the wealth, prosperity, surety and honor of his own royal person, having knowledge, by his orator resident within his realm, that his said father, of his devout mind and catholic purpose, to his great laud and honor in this world and immortal reward in Heaven, now intendeth in his own person to make a noble voyage with a great army against the Moors and Infidels, enemies of Christ's faith; and being desired on his behalf by his said orator, hath sent him with his company and retinue to his Highness, and straitly commanded him to give his attendance upon him.[3]

On 24 May, Henry signed a treaty with Ferdinand under the eyes of Luis Caroz and Thomas Ruthall, Bishop of Durham. The intent was to form a more 'intimate alliance' with 'the treaties of peace and alliance between King Ferdinand and the late Queen Isabella, on the one part, and the late King Henry of England, on the other part, remaining in full force', because 'the sovereigns who, by the marriage of Queen Catherine with the King of England, have become so nearly related'.[4] A few days later, Caroz wrote 'the King and Queen rejoice much at the good tidings they have received respecting the victory in Africa. The English believe it to be the beginning of very great things, they pray for him, and hope that in his lifetime all the Infidels will be conquered.'[5]

That September, Ferdinand knighted Henry Guildford and Wistan Browne for their 'prowess exhibited in the African Wars'. At the palace of Burgos, he touched them on each shoulder with his drawn sword and allotted them the escutcheons of a pale pomegranate on a white field and a black eagle on a white field, respectively.[6] However, this was something of a sham; the truth was far less glamorous. When Darcy had arrived in Spain, there was no sign of Ferdinand. He wrote to the King of Aragon on 6 June asking for orders, but no orders came, only the answer that Darcy and his company 'were shortly to be dispatched to England without doing any enterprise or battle against the Moors'.[7] The war had been postponed. With nothing else to do, the English troops misbehaved and the whole fiasco cost Henry £1,000. The king was not pleased, but still, the idea of Ferdinand slaying infidel Africans had fired his imagination and ambition. He had been spending his time tilting at the ring, dancing and dressing up 'like knights of olden times'[8] but now he wanted a real adventure. Yet the naïve young Henry did not realise he was being misled. Ferdinand was duping him, and his own daughter, using Africa as a smokescreen. He conveyed his real intentions in a secret letter to Ramon de Cardona, his viceroy in Naples, to whom he explained that he had, 'under the pretext of a war with the Moors, provided everything that was necessary for a war with France'. Ferdinand wanted certain territories back, and he was not above using his 'dear son' as a means to help him recover them.

By the spring of 1512, Ferdinand had convinced Henry that they would invade Aquitaine together, tempting him with the promise that it was historically an English property. 'The world shall know,' wrote Ferdinand, bombastically, 'that the King of England and he will not permit anyone to trample the church underfoot.'[9] This was fighting talk, and allowed Henry to flatter himself that he was Ferdinand's new military partner in Europe, standing shoulder to shoulder with him, just as Isabella once had. Furthermore, Pope Julius II promised that in the event of a French defeat the titles and realms of Louis XII would be transferred to Henry, harking back to the claim of Henry VI that kings of England were also kings of France. Catherine's husband would also receive the title of 'Most Christian King', a clear incentive to equal the similar epithets bestowed upon Ferdinand and Isabella.

Convinced, Henry dispatched 6,000 men to Spain under Admiral of the Fleet Sir Edward Howard, who would join Ferdinand in the north-east and cross the border into France with him. Howard's salary was set at 10*s* a day, and that of his other captains at 1*s* 6*d*, and he was to have the command of eighteen ships, including the 1,000-tonne *Regent,* which could take 700 soldiers, and the smaller *Mary Rose* and *Peter Pomegranate*, at 500 and 400 tonnes, right down to the little *Genet* at 70 tonnes.[10] 200 little flags were ordered from the Great Wardrobe, to be made of buckram, in Tudor white and green, embroidered with a red rose, surmounted by a yellow imperial crown, which were to 'be set on the carriage of our treasure of war',[11] while the trumpeters were equipped with green-and-white coats.[12] In early May Henry was down at Southampton to inspect the fleet, now with an additional 12,000 under Sir Thomas Grey, and found the men 'marvellously encouraged' by a papal indulgence he gave them to absolve them from sins during the war; they were 'likely to do great things'.[13] However, they never got the opportunity. The same thing happened as before. Ferdinand had his eyes firmly on recovering his former territories in Navarre. The English troops arrived in Fuenterrabia to await the arrival of the King of Aragon, but Catherine's father was seventy miles to the south in Navarre. While Henry and Catherine ordered riding coats of black and purple velvet[14] and caroused at Greenwich in beds made of white and green satin,[15] their troops sat waiting, running out of supplies and being made ill by the local wine.[16] A witness wrote home that 'discipline was so badly kept they might at any time have been crushed' and that 'victuals were untruly served'.[17]

Thomas Grey remained in position for twenty-five days, awaiting reinforcements, but then a disagreement arose between the leaders, with Howard arguing that 'he would endure this winter war, and gladlier he would die for the honor of his master, the realm, and himself, than, contrary to the King's commandment, with rebuke and shame, return into England'.[18] After this, 'great uproar ensued', things were 'out of order' and the king 'unlovingly served' in some quarters.[19] Howard was overruled and the armies returned home in October, despite Henry's attempts to make them stay. On 31 October, Pedro Martir wrote that 'the King of England's stringent command to his men to put themselves at the order of Ferdinand came too late, for they had already sailed'.[20]

Ferdinand wrote to his son-in-law at once, giving 'very detailed accounts of all that has happened', but proceeding to blame Thomas Grey for returning home, even though the Spanish had been waiting in the Pyrenees to 'render the passage of the mountains safe' and guard their rear. Ferdinand wrote that he was 'very much astonished and offended at seeing such an exhibition of fickleness', with Grey changing 'all his plans within a few days' and missing 'an easy and brilliant conquest'. The English, Ferdinand stated, had not remained long enough for the engagement to take place and 'such conduct would have been interpreted as springing either from want of resources or from lack of energy.' 'Either interpretation,' he continued, 'would have been very prejudicial to them in their future enterprises against France.' Worse still, Ferdinand accused them of duplicity. 'Many Spaniards have their suspicions, or firmly believe, that some of the persons who served in the [English] army, entertained a secret understanding with the French.' He stated that he was unable to believe this but had, nevertheless, ordered an investigation which concluded that the English had 'obstinately refused to acknowledge' anything that was not of immediate benefit to them, that they 'did not know how to behave in a campaign' and were 'inclined to self-indulgence and to idleness'.[21] The upshot was that Ferdinand declined to send an army Henry had requested to help him stave off the threat from the Scots, and that Spain was making a six-month truce with France.

These developments must have been agony for Catherine, who was torn between her indignant father and her insulted, shamed husband. Ferdinand dispatched Martin de Muxica, his chief paymaster, to England with long instructions, and he and Caroz were to request an audience with Henry. Ferdinand wrote tersely to his daughter that they 'have something to say on his behalf to the King of England which they are commanded to communicate to her', and begged 'credence for them'.[22] Catherine was to take a central role through the crisis, as diplomat and politician, in an attempt to restore the friendship between her home country and her adopted one. Muxica contacted Catherine upon his arrival, but she correctly told him it was not proper for them to have an audience until the ambassador had first formally met with the king. However, Catherine did write 'and advised him to wait, letting him know that he king was already informed how shamefully the English had behaved, and that he was very angry with them'. When he finally met with Henry and Catherine, Muxica handed over letters and explained the Spanish position, to learn that the English agreed their commanders had behaved badly. The captains were brought before the Privy Council to explain their actions on their knees, blaming poor provisions, increasing mutiny and the bad decision of Thomas Grey, who was then summoned to answer charges. It also emerged that Grey was intending to arrange a marriage for himself to the daughter of the late King of Navarre, which cast no glory upon him. Catherine championed the view of the injured Spanish and advised Henry and his council to continue to fund Ferdinand's war.[23]

Catherine's role in this was a significant one. She was walking a fine line between her husband's ambition and reputation and her father's position, even though he had just signed a treaty with the French. She did not hesitate to take on the role of negotiator and adviser, comfortable at the heart of politics on an international scale, mediating with ambassadors, shaping interpretations of events and influencing decision-making. Her nationality and her comparative maturity made her the natural person for Henry to turn to, but it is also an indication of the nature of their relationship that she was the young king's main confidante and that he was willing to take her advice. They were still clearly very close, with a Spanish delegation who met them at Winchester in 1512 reporting that Henry kissed and embraced his wife in public, 'treating her with care and affection', and all those present were 'amazed at the great love the king professed towards the queen'.[24] More than that, Henry clearly respected Catherine. The decision he took next reveals just how highly he thought of his wife. That October, it was agreed that he would lead the next expedition in person 'with fire and sword' to provide leadership and ensure no such thing happened again. During his impending absence, who better was there to rule the country than his partner and equal, the capable, driven Catherine?

II

In 1513, Henry began to plan his invasion of France. Catherine approached the Venetian ambassador in the hope of hiring Italian ships for the purpose, being 'very warm in favour of this expedition', as Badoer wrote to the Doge and Senate. She 'would fain to have four large galleasses and two bastard galleys from the Signory, and enquired of him the monthly cost of a galley afloat'. The king was 'bent on war', he added, and while the council were opposed to it, 'the queen wills it'.[25] Moreover, there was now a religious reason for the invasion, as Louis XII had recently been excommunicated for trying to oust the Pope. Catherine painted the war as a holy crusade, describing Henry's mission as being against 'the foes of the church' and that he was 'determined never to rest or desist until their king be utterly destroyed'.[26] Ferdinand advised against their actions, framing them as being likely to 'prove very difficult and dangerous when undertaken by the king of England alone', especially as Spain already had plans for a joint invasion. But the time had passed when Henry would blindly accept his father-in-law's advice.

This decision led Henry and Catherine directly into conflict with the leading thinkers in England, many of whom had been part of Margaret Beaufort's circle or were the king's personal friends. The humanists were pacifists, seeing war as a sin, a scandal and a folly. Desiderius Erasmus, John Colet, William Grocyn, John Fisher, Thomas Linacre and Hugh Latimer espoused the new learning as a way to establish education, to encourage peace and purify religion through reforms. In 1513, they voiced their collective concerns in *Treaty Against War*. To a man of the new learning, who was not a fallen, corrupt creature but a work of God, Erasmus wrote, warfare was 'naturally repugnant'. His frame was 'weak and tender', and he is 'born to love and amity', with the aim of cooperating with other like-minded men 'in the pursuit of knowledge'. War, wrote Erasmus, came from ignorance and led to contempt for virtue and godly living, being waged mainly for 'vain titles or childish wrath' and did not foster any of the 'nobler excellences'.[27] At this point, Henry and Catherine's martial desires to replicate the glory of her parents were in direct conflict with the English leaders of the new learning, but this would be just the first instance of how complex the early sixteenth century was to prove for the individual, assailed by various conflicting influences.

In 1513, when Henry was embarking on his martial programme, John Colet, dean of his newly founded St Paul's School, preached at court against war as something 'barbarous and unchristian' which did not spare kings or popes 'who dealt otherwise'.[28] Henry summoned Colet to explain himself, quizzing him about whether he saw all wars as unjustifiable, but the humanist was not prepared to become a martyr; taking a suitably statesmanlike approach, he gave an answer that satisfied the king. Three years later, Thomas More condemned wars of aggression in *Utopia*, his vision of an ideal society. It was not to be the last time he would defy the king. Ultimately, Henry and Catherine were king and queen, so no one, not even the humanists they valued so highly nor members of Henry's council, could prevent them from going to war if that was what they wanted to do so. Erasmus left England that year to set up permanent residence in Basel. However, out of all this dissent, one rising man made the decision to abandon his humanist pacifist principles and simply deliver the king's wishes.

Thomas Wolsey emerged as a serious political figure as a result of the French war, and as he rose, with Henry increasingly trusting and relying upon him, Catherine would find herself gradually pushed out. Just as his father had done, Henry liked to reward commoners of ability instead of the over-mighty nobility ,who often had their own motives and affiliations at heart. Wolsey came from humble origins, being the son of a butcher or cattle trader from Ipswich, but a sound education underpinned the genius for organisation and complete dedication to service that caused his meteoric rise. After Oxford, he was ordained as a priest, joined the service of the Archbishop of Canterbury, became Henry VII's chaplain and then secretary to Richard Foxe and finally, in 1509, Henry VIII's almoner. Known for his readiness to take on mundane and tedious tasks, Wolsey soon became indispensable at court, and his influence on the king suddenly increased when he backed, and then meticulously organised, the 1513 campaign against France.

On 11 June, Henry appointed Catherine 'Regent and Governess of England, Wales and Ireland during the king's absence in his expedition against France, for the preservation of the Catholic religion and recovery of his rights'. Although she would still be supervised by the council, headed by Archbishop Warham, she was given 'power to issue commissions of muster', to give assent to Church elections, to 'appoint sheriffs, to issue warrants under her sign manual' and other powers. John Heron, Treasurer of the Chamber, was instructed to pay 'any sums of money ordered by the queen ... to whatever persons she may appoint for defence of the kingdom'. Her servants were exempted from service in order for her to be 'suitably attended', with her chamberlain and chancellor both being mentioned,[29] which was especially important as she was by now four months pregnant. Catherine also had the seasoned veteran Thomas Howard, Earl of Surrey, who had fought at Bosworth and quashed rebellions in the north, in the event of any invasion or rebellion. Little did she know how soon she would be calling on his support.

On 15 June, Catherine left Greenwich with Henry at the head of a train of 600 guards dressed in liveries of white and green with silver spangles and embroidery.[30] They made a slow procession through Kent, reaching Canterbury five days later, where they stayed in the royal forest of Blean on a hill overlooking the city, before heading down to make their offerings at the cathedral's shrine to St Thomas Becket. Catherine was presented with a cup of silver and gilt, weighing over thirty-one ounces and engraved with the city's arms, filled with coins. The royal trumpeters, heralds, henchmen and footmen were all given 6*s* 8*d* each and Catherine's footmen received 5*s*. They lingered in the city until midsummer, from where Henry made payments of £2,000 for wages to his guard and the comptroller of the king's works, and 100 marks for rigging and other necessaries for the king's ship.[31] Five days later, on Henry's twenty-second birthday, they arrived at Dover Castle, set high on a windswept hill overlooking the channel. They spent the night there, probably in the solid stone keep built by Henry II in the centre of the complex, with its thick stone walls and long, spacious rooms hung with tapestries. Below them, spread out in the bay in front of the town, flanked by the white cliffs, the ships were waiting for a favourable tide. In the morning, Catherine watched as Henry departed in a carrack called the *Mary Lorett*. They landed in the English-held Calais that same evening.

On the day Catherine and Henry had reached Dover, the new Pope, Leo X, wrote to Henry's brother-in-law, James IV of Scotland, expressing his annoyance that in spite of two warnings from the Vatican James was still preparing to invade England. As Catherine rode back towards London, now as regent of her adoptive country, she had little idea of the storm clouds gathering above her head. She returned to Richmond, from where she wrote to Thomas

Wolsey, as she was not likely to hear from her husband so often, 'for the great business in his journey that every day he shall have'. She urged Wolsey to 'write by her messengers successively of the king's health', and as they neared the enemy she would 'never be at rest till she often have letters' from the almoner.[32] She was pleased to see the involvement of the Pope, who had issued Henry with instructions, knowing that 'all the business that the King hath was first the business of the church', and trusted that he would return home soon with 'as great a victory as ever Prince had'.[33] Wolsey clearly did write to Catherine as requested, as her surviving letters thank him for taking 'payne' to do so. Yet for all the almoner's assurances, Catherine could not refrain from worrying about her husband, and on 1 August she wrote from Windsor to Margaret of Savoy, asking her to send a physician to attend upon Henry.[34] Catherine's own advancing pregnancy was also a concern. In spite of their disagreements over the war, Ferdinand wrote to his envoy Diego de Quiros, saying that he would send Catherine a Spanish physician once he could find one who was willing to go and live in England.[35]

The absence of the king from England was a concern that Catherine must have fully understood, but even more worrying for her was the fear that Henry might die in battle, or as the result of accident, injury, sickness or shipwreck. The twenty-two-year-old king ran a huge risk in waging war before he had left an heir to his kingdom; had he not returned, the crown of England would have likely passed to the heirs of his eldest sister, Margaret, Queen of Scots. It had also clearly been on Henry's mind, too, as a grant for the fulfilment of his latest will was made at Richmond in early September.[36] Catherine had good reason to be anxious, but soon reports arrived of his successes. Henry had met with the Emperor Maximilian, in a tent of cloth of gold, with the English king dressed all in gold, and having gold bells hung from his horse. Despite receiving only a disappointing 2,000 men from Maximilian, the English went on to win a victory at the Battle of the Spurs, before taking the towns of Thérouanne and Tournai. Thomas Wolsey would be rewarded with the title of Bishop of Tournai the following year, after the death of the existing incumbent. Henry also captured a French duke, Louis d'Orleans, Duc de Longueville, and sent him back to Catherine, who housed him in the Tower.

These were significant victories for the young English king, with Catherine describing them as 'none such hath been seen before',[37] but once these towns were won they posed a problem of how they should be defended and retained.

By early August, it was clear that the Scots were intent on taking advantage of Henry's absence to invade England. Catherine put the country on alert, but some were slow to respond. She was forced to write a second time to the mayor and sheriffs of Gloucester, surprised to have had no reply to her former letter and commanding them to supply her with information about the men and arms in their towns.[38] She took a more laissez-faire approach in a letter to Wolsey on 13 August, claiming that it was a mere diversion to her and that she was 'very glad to be busy with the Scots, for they take it for [a] pastime.' 'My heart is very good to it,' she added, 'and I am horribly busy with making [of] standards, banners, and badges.'[39] But in reality, the knowledge that she was going to have to hold the country in the event of a full-scale invasion must have occupied her mind day and night. She met with her council to discuss England's defences and their plan to repel the Scots, as part of which levies were imposed and sanctions threatened against anyone who disobeyed. In addition, all Scotsmen living in England were to be deemed enemies, though those married to Englishwomen might remain at the cost of half their possessions; all others were to 'have their goods seized and their persons banished, under penalty of their lives'. For good measure, all French people living near the coast were thrown into prison.[40] Mindful of the paraphernalia of war that her mother had employed, she requested the Great Wardrobe to release certain banners and standards, including those bearing the arms of England and Spain, the lion, the cross imperial and the cross of St George.[41]

On 2 September, Catherine wrote to Wolsey from Richmond Palace that she was sending the Duc de Longueville to the Tower for now, 'especially the Scots being so busy as they now be, and I am looking for my departing every hour'.[42] News reached her the following day that they had already crossed the border and captured Norham Castle, the property of Thomas Ruthall, Bishop of Durham, who was also absent in France as Henry's secretary. Surrey's troops, including his sons Edmund and Thomas, were ready and waiting at Newcastle; in the earl's absence, as a Marshal of England, Catherine gave a commission of array to Thomas Lovell to raise troops in the Midlands and to hear the legal cases of murder, treason and other crimes committed during this period.[43] She had to prepare for the eventuality that Surrey might be defeated and that the Scots would march into England and need to be repelled. Catherine travelled north from Richmond to Buckinghamshire, and it is likely that this was where she addressed assembled troops, much as her mother had used to, 'making a splendid oration to the English captains', reminding them that 'the Lord smiled upon those who stood in defence of their own' and that 'English courage excelled that of all other nations'. The writer of this description was none other than Peter Martyr, or Pedro Martir, of Spain, who had never set foot in England but certainly, as Isabella's chaplain, witnessed her speeches to troops on the eve of battles. Catherine certainly intended to look the part, as the royal goldsmith, Robert Amadas, was paid for 'garnishing a head piece with a golden crown', the precious metal reminiscent of her mother's style. Both queens understood that when under attack, the first recourse was to dress in gold.

The armies engaged near the village of Branxton in Northumberland on 9 September. James was killed within a spear's length of Surrey. Catherine was at Woburn Abbey in Bedfordshire, midway between St Albans and Northampton, when the news reached her seven days later. She wrote to Henry from there on 16 September:

> My Lord Howard hath sent me a letter, open, to your Grace, within one of mine, by the which ye shall see at length the great victory that our Lord hath sent your subjects in your absence. Thinks the victory the greatest honor that could be. The King will not forget to thank God for it. Could not, for haste, send by Rouge Cross 'the piece of the King of Scots coat which John Glyn now bringeth. In this your Grace shall see how I can keep my promys, sending you for your banners a King's coat. I thought to send himself unto you, but our Englishmen's hearts would not suffer it. It should have been better for him to have been in peace than have this reward. All that God sendeth is for the best'. Surrey wishes to know the King's pleasure as to burying the King of Scots' body. Prays for his return; and for the same is going to our Lady at Walsingham, that I promised so long ago to see.[44]

From Woburn Abbey, it was a journey of little over a hundred miles to the north Norfolk town of Walsingham. Henry had previously undertaken a pilgrimage there in 1511 to give thanks for the birth of their son Prince Henry, but it was now to offer thanks for the outcome of the battle that Catherine travelled the route. She arrived there on 23 September. The centre of the Marian cult in East Anglia, and the culmination of many pilgrim routes, the shrine of the Virgin had been founded in 1061 and came to be known as 'the English Nazareth'. A priory had been built beside it in 1150 and royal patronage increased its popularity to the extent that the value of jewels and offerings before the shrine was so great by 1346 that it needed to be locked overnight. When Erasmus visited in 1512, the shrine was surrounded on all sides with gold, silver and gems, 'some of them larger than a goose's egg',[45] shining brilliantly in the gloom. Mary's statue was draped in fine silk, set with precious stones, with a lace veil edged in pearls. It was customary for pilgrims to halt at the slipper chapel and remove their shoes, before walking the final mile and approaching the shrine. Catherine had an additional motive for visiting: to ask for a successful delivery for the child she was carrying.

Exactly when Catherine lost her third child is unclear. Some accounts give this date as early as 17 September, but this cannot be the case because Catherine was on the move between Woburn and Walsingham, so if she had given birth or suffered a late miscarriage, she would have entered the lying-in period of recovery and thus be unable to continue her journey. It seems more likely that she delivered this child on her way home, or soon after her arrival. On 8 October, the Imperial agent James Bannissius reported to Lord Albert of Carpi that 'the queen has given birth to a son',[46] but made no comment about the child's survival. The fact that he was given a name, Henry, suggests that he was born alive but did not survive, as opposed to a stillbirth or late miscarriage, such as the queen had suffered back in 1510. Yet there is a silence in Catherine's own correspondence, and that of the king. When Henry returned to England at the end of October, he headed to Richmond to be reunited with his wife. Their meeting was 'so loving' that the bystanders 'rejoiced' to see it.[47] It is possible that Catherine was not pregnant at all, or it is equally possible that the relevant letters have not survived, or that they chose to draw a veil of silence over their personal grief.

Flodden was a great personal victory for Catherine. Although Surrey had won the battle, in her husband's absence she had steered the country through a crisis, taking over practical arrangements and making critical decisions. It also marked a move away from Spain, with Catherine choosing to follow her husband and England over her father's plans, showing that Henry and Catherine were united in their ambition and no longer prepared to be the dupe of Machiavellian politics. Henry was unwell on his return and took to his bed at Richmond, and it was here, according to Victorian historian W. H. Dixon, that he finally reached a 'true perception of Ferdinand, in his nature and his purpose [and] the schemes of that great criminal, to whom the Borgias seemed like puppets, were unrolled before his eyes'. He perceived, according to Dixon, that Ferdinand was prepared to sacrifice him and the reason why he had been 'forced into wedlock' with Catherine.[48] This certainly goes too far, as nothing supports the notion that Henry married against his will, and most evidence indicates the contrary, but it is correct that both Henry and Catherine had their eyes opened as a result of the past years' dealings with Ferdinand. This, coupled with the victory over the Scots, gave them greater autonomy and credibility than ever before. Henry would now veer away from Spain towards their former enemy, France.

Catherine also spared time to think of her sister-in-law Margaret, Queen of Scots, who was now a widow, sending a Friar Langley north to comfort her in her hour of need.[49] Margaret replied on 11 November, thanking Catherine 'for her sympathy in the misfortune fallen upon her' and hoping that Catherine would 'keep her brother in remembrance of her, that his kindness may be known'.[50] Margaret was then twenty-three and had borne five children to James IV, although only one of them had survived. At the time of Flodden, she was around four to six weeks pregnant, although she may well not have been aware of this herself. The Scottish Parliament appointed her regent over her young son, but this was an unpopular act given that James V was not yet eighteen months old, meaning a long tenure. It was one thing for Catherine to take over the helm during the absence of an adult king, but quite another for a woman to be in charge of a country for, conceivably, the next twelve years. Catherine had not seen Margaret since she departed from Richmond Palace in June 1503 as a thirteen-year-old bride, and now they were technically enemies, with her husband killing Margaret's, but Catherine still extended support to the widow as a fellow queen, perhaps also as a woman who had experienced similar losses. If nothing else, their devout faith united them, as well as indicating that it was spiritual consolation that Catherine thought to be of greatest value amid Margaret's grief. For the Queen of England, just like her mother, the Catholic faith was always the answer, the comfort, when faced by any problem.

III

A key part of Ferdinand and Isabella's legacy had been their intolerance of heresy, pursued by the Inquisition. It was his earnest wish, Henry wrote, 'to restore Christ's religion to its primitive purity'.[51] There were no Jewish or Moorish populations in England for Henry and Catherine to pursue but they did take seriously any case of heretical belief that might undermine the Catholic Church. The example of Christopher Grebill and his parents, of Cranbrook in Kent, which came to light in 1511, highlights this aspect of their rule, as well as illustrating some of the criticisms of the Church that were changing attitudes in England on the eve of the Reformation. Christopher was then twenty-two, the son of John and Agnes Grebill, who was examined by the ecclesiastical court on 30 April upon the teaching of his mother on six key topics. He admitted that Agnes had told him that the bread of the sacrament did not literally turn into the body of Christ, which would prove to be one of the critical tenets of the reformed faith. This was the difference between transubstantiation, a literal transformation, and consubstantiation, a symbolic one. As well as rejecting infant baptism and confirmation, Agnes vowed that confession should be made directly to God, without the intermediary of any saints or icons, and that pilgrimage had no effect at all. Two decades later Henry would come round to these ideas, but to the young Catholic king of 1511 and his pious wife they were abhorrent. On 2 May, at the Archbishop of Canterbury's residence of Knole in Kent, Agnes Grebill was convicted of heresy and her punishment was handed over to the secular court.[52] In a decision reminiscent of the Inquisition, she died in an act of faith, being burned at the stake.

In fact, the Kent Heresy trials of 1511–12 include many more cases of individuals speaking out against established beliefs, and illustrate the extent of what Catherine and Henry would have seen as a crusade within their own country, just as Ferdinand and Isabella had fought theirs. A spate of investigations and trials scared the community enough to elicit almost fifty additional penances and followed a similar pattern to Spain's informants, whereby neighbours, friends and family members reported each other's heresies, such as William Baker's deposition that John Browne had denied the existence of purgatory, stating that 'aftir that a man was decessit he shulde goo straight to heven or to hell'.[53] Many of these religious questions, for which Catherine's subjects were to pay with their lives, were to be echoed in the writings of Erasmus in 1513 and the theses of Martin Luther in 1517, which would shake Catholicism to its core. While Erasmus was composing his arguments, Catherine was admitted, in her absence, to the monastery of St Mary in Guadalupe, in the Order of St Jerome, in the diocese of Toledo, from which she could enjoy 'all the spiritual benefits'.[54] In response to the challenges of her life, and those theological schisms ahead, Catherine's faith, her consolation, her inheritance, would always remain rock solid.

14

Maternity 1514–1516

I

As part of his new-found autonomy when it came to international affairs, in 1514 Henry decided to marry off his younger sister. Princess Mary had been a long-standing fixture at court, appearing with Catherine on many occasions and staying with her in various royal properties since the death of Prince Arthur. Nine years younger than Catherine, Mary had been the one to console her when Philip of Burgundy rudely rejected her invitation to dance, and it was Mary who had been awaiting Catherine on the occasion when Fray Diego forbade her from going to court. The two young women were treated similarly in the account books, with payments and arrangements for their households being replicated, 'same as the princess' or 'same as the Queen of Castile'. They also considered themselves to be closely connected in terms of their future alliance. From an early age Mary had been intended for Catherine's nephew Charles, the son of Philip and Juana, and was known at court by his titles; Mary and Charles would be an important young couple on the dynastic stage, taking over the legacy of Ferdinand and Isabella in Spain, crucial allies for England in the future. In February 1514, when Mary was seventeen and Charles reached his fourteenth birthday, the wedding date was finally set. That May she would become his wife in Calais, where elaborate jousts and celebrations were being planned as late as 21 March.[1] But May arrived, then

June, and no wedding took place. On 19 June, Mary was being considered as a potential bride by the General of Normandy, a man 'said to be a great lord', as she was 'promised to the Prince of Castile but is still here unmarried'.[2]

Pedro Martir summed up the root of the problem in a letter written from Valladolid on 8 June:

> The sister of the King of England was betrothed to Prince Charles on condition that he should marry her when he passed the age of fourteen. Henry is urgent to have the marriage completed, as the Prince was of the age required on the 24 Feb. last. Maximilian and Ferdinand require its postponement, as Charles is naturally of a feeble constitution. Henry is exceedingly angry, and threatens to make terms with France.[3]

In a fit of pique against Ferdinand, Henry threw away an excellent alliance for his sister and for England. He ignored the letter from Margaret of Savoy on 20 June, that the moon was prolonging Charles's illness, but that he was improving.[4] Breaking with Spain and allying himself instead with France, he chose the ageing Louis XII, newly widowed fifty-two-year-old, as his sister's new bridegroom. Mary and Catherine must have both been aghast, not just at the personal dimension, as large age gaps were not uncommon in dynastic matches, but at the rejection of such a powerful and significant political alliance, one which would have seen something of a restoration of the legacy Isabella had died believing she had lost. Yet Catherine wisely did not question Henry's choice openly; she obediently followed his lead in the recognition that her loyalty was owed to him above all others, and that marital harmony required it. She had also announced her fourth pregnancy that June, another good reason to opt for a quiet life without disagreements over matters she could not change.

That month, Catherine was by Henry's side when he showed the visiting Imperial ambassadors John Colla and Gerard de Pleine around his new great ship of 1,500 tonnes, and then when he granted them an audience at Eltham Palace. There, he read Maximilian's letters and was 'not pleased with the contents', nor was he happy at Baynard's Castle to hear of various truces being made by Ferdinand that 'treated [him] like a boy'.[5] De Pleine wrote to Margaret of Savoy about the princess on 30 June, still considering that the match was to go ahead:

> Had refrained from writing about the Princess [Mary] till he had seen her several times. Has never seen so beautiful a lady. Her deportment is exquisite both in conversation and in dancing, and she is very lively. If Margaret had seen her she would not rest till she had her over; she is very well brought up, and appears to love the Prince wonderfully. She has a very bad picture of him, and is said to wish to see it ten times a day, and to take pleasure in hearing of him. She is not tall, but is a better match in age and person for the Prince than he had heard say.[6]

De Pleine also mentioned Catherine, whom he stated was believed to be with child, and was so, as far as he could judge. She was 'of a lively and gracious disposition; quite the opposite of the Queen her sister [Juana] in complexion and manner'.[7]

A month later, though, Mary's formal renunciation of her betrothal to Charles, in front of witnesses at Wanstead, put an end to Ferdinand's and Maximilian's hopes. Catherine cannot have liked the new arrangements, but she was obediently dressed in ash-coloured satin, with gold chains and a gold cap, to attend the proxy wedding that followed two weeks later at Greenwich. She was present alongside Henry to witness Louis' proxy, the Duke of Longueville, take Mary by the hand and read the French king's vows before the assembled crowd. However, the Spanish ambassadors stayed away, feeling 'quite dispirited', and were reportedly not on speaking terms with their French counterparts.[8] The Venetian ambassador added that the 'English abuse Spain excessively for her bad faith in making truce with France',[9] with Luis Caroz adding that, as late as December 1514, Henry continued to behave 'in the most offensive and discourteous manner whenever his affairs [King Ferdinand's] are treated' and that Spanish sea captains were being maltreated. The situation was so bad, in fact, that the ambassador begged to be withdrawn from England, as he was 'of no use'.[10]

Despite remaining loyal to Henry, Catherine must have felt a degree of discomfort at the way the relationship with her homeland had soured. Worse still, Italian gossip suggested that Henry was intending to divorce her and take a new wife, although he is hardly likely to have rejected his queen while she was pregnant, and other evidence suggests he was still in love with her. Fray Diego advised Catherine to 'forget Spain and everything Spanish in order to gain the love of the King of England and the English' and later reported that Henry had 'badly used' his wife.[11] When Mary departed for France that October, Catherine lost her companion of a decade, and perhaps a friend and ally. Now the queen represented the past alliance with Spain, something that was broken, and a cause of resentment to Henry. She had fought so long for her marriage, and tried to use what she had learned as a daughter of Spain, when it came to leading and defending her realm, that she was not about to despair. In comparison with the warmth and popularity of her welcome in 1501, and then again at her coronation in 1509, the mood for Catherine had turned decidedly chilly. Only twelve months before, she had led the country to victory against the Scots; now there were rumours of her being divorced. It must have been distressing. The situation forced her to choose between her father and husband, and she chose Henry.

Behind the scenes, Ferdinand was dismayed at having lost his ambassador in England. He sought a closer adviser for Catherine, to make her once again the advocate of his interests, and Caroz became his instrument for this in England. Writing to Friar Juan de Eztuniga of Aragon on 6 December, Caroz's assessment of Catherine's current situation was that she 'greatly requires some discreet and intelligent person who could take care, as well of her soul as of the government of her house and her person, and who could give her advice how to behave towards the English and towards the Spaniards, and how she could best further the interests of the King of Spain'.[12] The friar was to report to Ferdinand his observations of Catherine's treatment of Caroz and her disposition to help her father again. She had, he believed, 'the best intentions, but there is no one to show her how she might become serviceable to her father'. Caroz blamed Fray Diego for this for his advice to turn her back on Spain, and she had 'become so much accustomed to this idea that she will not change her behaviour, unless some person who is near her tells her in every case what she ought to do'.[13] Nor were the members of her Spanish household any use, as they 'prefer to be friends with the English and neglect their duties as subjects of the King of Spain', the worst influence being Maria de Salinas, who dictated how Catherine behaved. Caroz revealed the true Spanish attitude towards Henry when he told Ferdinand that if he did not 'put a bridle on this colt … it will be afterwards found impossible to control him'.[14]

If things were uncomfortable for Catherine that summer and autumn, they were about to get worse. With such tensions and rumours flying round between the ambassadors, and with England's alliance with Spain now rejected, it was even more important that the queen proved her personal worth, as a woman and a wife. She might have no longer represented Henry's current international intentions, but she hoped that she might be able to bear him an heir. Arrangements were made in October for her lying-in, including a cradle lined with scarlet and lengths of blue material. Wolsey wrote to Louis XII that the queen 'looks to lie in shortly' and was pleased to hear that if she 'bears a son, Louis will gladly be godfather'.[15] Just before she entered her confinement, Catherine may have attended the marriage of a daughter of one of her ladies-in-waiting. Margaret Bryan, *née* Bourchier, had been present at Henry and Catherine's wedding and served in her household since. Now her fourteen-year-old daughter Elizabeth married one of Henry's gentlemen and fellow jouster, Sir Nicholas Carew, after receiving a grant of £500 from the king. It has been suggested that Elizabeth and Henry were lovers, but if Catherine was aware of it, she did not let it influence her treatment of the girl's family, nor did she think the time was right for her to create a scene with Henry such as that which had followed the departure of Anne Hastings from court. Soon, Catherine would require Lady Bryan's services as lady governess in the household of her child, but it would not be just yet.

At some point in December or January, Catherine lost her fourth child. According to Hall, 'in November, the queen was delivered of a prince which lived not long after', and by the end of December, Pedro Martir in Spain wrote that 'the Queen of England had given birth to a premature child' and was in no doubt that it was 'through grief … for the misunderstanding between her father and husband'. He added that Henry had 'reproached her with her father's ill faith'.[16] This timescale is confused somewhat by a letter written in October 1515, from Catherine to Ferdinand, in which she refers to losing a child after Candlemas, which falls on 2 February. Assuming the translation and dating of this letter is correct, this discrepancy is difficult to explain, unless Catherine was again not being strictly accurate with the information she was feeding Ferdinand. She appears to have lost her child before Christmas, and a subsequent conception and loss would have been very swift, almost impossibly so. Catherine had emerged from her chamber by Twelfth Night, or 6 January, when revelry was held at Greenwich, consisting of a pageant depicting wildmen dressed in moss who fought fiercely with knights. It must have been difficult to accept this loss, seemingly at full term, or almost so, in the climate of the moment. The sense of political and personal failure, of four children lost in five years, must have weighed heavily on the queen. But she did not give up. Four months later she would conceive again.

II

By October 1514, the breach between England and Spain was healing. A treaty had been signed, sworn in the chapel at Greenwich, concessions made and gifts of 'splendid presents and jewellery' exchanged. Henry's wounded pride was quickly won over by these expensive gifts, although 'he values them principally because they show his [Ferdinand's] love and benevolence towards him'; he was certain 'no one could send such presents who is not animated by the most sincere and tender love towards him'.[17] Suddenly Henry loved Ferdinand 'as much and as sincerely as he ever did before, and even more', having 'forgotten all the disagreeable things which had passed between them'. In addition, Ferdinand had sent a Spanish physician, the 'very distinguished' Jewish doctor Hernando Lopez, who may have attended on Catherine during her pregnancy.

Catherine wrote happily to Ferdinand now that the dispute had been solved and her loyalties were no longer divided. She echoed her husband's sentiments about the presents he was very proud of and assured her father that this treaty would be better observed than the last, as the former contained clauses the English could never agree to and were not profitable to Ferdinand either. She also made an observation about the English character, which had become 'very visible in the last transactions', that 'there [were] no people in the world more influenced by the good or bad fortunes of their enemies than the English. A small success of their enemies prostrates them, and a little adversity of their antagonists makes them overbearing.'[18] It seemed also that by this point, Fray Diego had left Catherine's service, as she recommended him to her father, as he had gone to Spain. Although she wrote that he had 'served her very faithfully all the time he was in England ... much better than certain persons pretend' and 'had he remained in England things would not have come to so bad a pass as they did'.[19]

Fray Diego's time in England had ended badly, with accusations of gross misconduct being made against him by members of Catherine's household. Henry summoned him to hear the accusations, upon which he commented that if he was badly used, 'the queen was more badly used', which defiance did his cause no favours. He was convicted of fornication by an ecclesiastical court and left England, never to return. But Fray Diego did not go quietly. In a long Latin letter to Henry, he railed against his 'ill-informed' accusers who hoped to 'defame and depose' Henry's true subject, and especially a religious man, but stated Catherine's treasurer and his wife had always hated him, which was why they made a statement against him. The charges were 'unheard of' and 'detestable' 'evil' against him, made by people of appetite and envy, who were 'not committed' to Henry's service nor that of the queen, who 'took witness against' him and made 'devious' oaths that he had had carnal knowledge of women at Windsor. He added that he ought to know what their replies had been to his denials and swore to God that he had done no harm. He said, 'with tears', that his services to England had been seen, but he was still condemned and 'because such a judgment was made with the greatest cruelty, and cruelly so sudden, and now against the sight of my mistress'. It was the loss of Catherine's trust that he appeared to lament most, but her mention of him to her father is brief. She must have believed the charges, or at least believed in the possibility of them, as she did not make any attempt to clear his name or retain his services. It would have meant opening a division in her household, as his accusers were presumably servants whom she trusted. There was also an unpleasant edge to Fray Diego's letter, as he added, 'My lord, O king, I do not wonder how you were not afraid of me, out of the kingdom of you by knowing all the secrets of God ... I know all your secrets', and further desperation, as he was prepared to return to the 'upright' in such a condition that the hearing might assign to him, and was 'so wretched he wished to die'.[20] His letter did not have its desired effect. Fray Diego was replaced by the Spanish Observant friar Jorge de Atheca, who had previously acted as Catherine's clerk.

Fray Diego's disgrace was forgotten amid the court revels that took place that spring. The Twelfth Night pageant had set a high standard, with eight dancers entering Catherine's chambers with lighted torches, dressed in blue velvet lined with cloth of silver or gold, designed to imitate the Savoyard and Portuguese styles. Among the four ladies was Elizabeth Blount, a relative of Lord Mountjoy, the newly arrived daughter from a family Catherine had known during her brief marriage in Ludlow. The fair-haired Elizabeth, or Bessie, had been just a baby at that time, but now she was an accomplished fourteen and had been given a place as a maid of honour in Catherine's household. Bessie's partner for the dance was the king himself. If Catherine picked up on any signs that her husband found the young woman attractive, she followed her mother's example and did not voice them in public. She would not have been mistaken, though, as on at least one occasion, four years later, Henry and Bessie would sleep together. At New Year 1514, however, the queen was so delighted with their performance that she 'hartely thanked the kynges grace for her goodly pastime and kyssed him'.[21]

Soon after the merrymaking came to an end, news arrived at court of the death of Louis of France on 1 January. Just four days earlier, the king had written to Henry that 'his 'satisfaction with the queen his wife was such that Henry might be sure of his treating her to her own and to his satisfaction'. As a beautiful widow of eighteen, and a Queen of France, Mary was potentially prey to the advances of possible suitors, including the new King of France, the suave young Francis I, who already had something of a reputation for his love of women. Mary could not leave until it had been firmly established that she was not pregnant, so she sat out the weeks in close confinement, considering her fate. Wolsey wrote to her on 10 January, sounding a note of caution, for as she found herself 'during her heaviness … among strangers', she should not forget that Henry 'would not forsake her' and should 'do nothing without the advice of his grace' and listen to no other offers of marriage.[22] Henry and Catherine had moved from Eltham to Greenwich before Henry wrote formally to congratulate the new king of France on 14 January, at the same time as he dispatched Sir Charles Brandon to fetch his sister home. Yet Henry had not reckoned with the promise Mary had extracted from him at Dover the previous October, that if she went through with the French marriage she should be able to choose her second husband for herself. She chose Charles Brandon, 'comely of stature, high of courage', a great jouster raised alongside

Henry, and married him in secret. Aware that he would incur the king's wrath, in particular in jeopardising the dower payments he had been sent to collect, Brandon wrote to Wolsey for help in early March. Apparently Mary had been insistent and had 'never let [him] be in rest till (he) had granted her to be married'; they had lain together so much, Brandon added, that he feared that 'sche by wyet child'. Knowing the king well, he suggested that 'the Mirror of Naples', a diamond with a big pearl, should be sent him by Mary, to smooth their return to England. Wolsey went straight to the king. Henry was furious when he learned what had taken place, unable to believe it at first, then taking it 'grievously and displeasantly', but Mary was clearly in love, having 'always been of a good mind' towards Brandon, as she expected the king to know, and was now 'so bound to him that for no earthly cause could she change'.[23] She was also aware that Henry might go back on his promise and try to make a match for her elsewhere.

Mary had done her duty, and now begged for her brother's goodwill. She also made a public gift of 'all such plate and vessel of clean gold' and jewels that Louis had given her, to Henry VIII. Did Catherine speak on her sister-in-law's behalf, or was she as horrified and disappointed as her husband at this rash match of affection? It was the duty of those born into the royal line to make advantageous marriages, not to follow their hearts. If they were lucky, like Henry and Catherine or Ferdinand and Isabella, love might grow between them, but otherwise there was a clear division between the destinies of princesses and the secrets of their hearts. Mary and Brandon arrived at Dover on 2 May. Wolsey met them and conducted them to the home of Lord Abergavenny, where Henry was waiting. An agreement was reached whereby Mary would repay her brother £2,000 a year until her debt was paid, after which the couple were married again at Greenwich. Catherine had been at Richmond at the end of April, but travelled downriver to Greenwich to be reunited with her sister-in-law and to attend the ceremony on 13 May 1515.[24]

Catherine was still playing an ambassadorial role when it came to international politics and one of a cultural focus at court. On 1 May she met the visiting Venetian Sebastian Giustinian, and went out riding with him before he was granted a private audience with Henry. They dined together, after which the king jousted, winning fulsome praise from his guests, as a 'very expert in arms, most excellent in his personal endowments, so adorned with mental accomplishments of every sort, he has few equals in the world. He speaks English, French and Latin; understands Italian; plays almost every instrument; sings and composes; and is free from all vice.'[25] Afterwards they made a point of visiting the queen again, where one of them 'addressed her in Spanish, knowing it would please her', to which Catherine replied in her native tongue, speaking about her mother.[26] This shows the extent to which it was understood that the queen had influence over her husband and was a figure worth pleasing in her own right, as well as to gain further favour with the king. One Nicholas Sagudino was also a witness to the splendour of the court at this time, observing Henry dining on gold and silver plate of great worth, seated on a table alone, before he addressed the ambassadors in French, Latin and Italian. He was, according to Sagudino, 'very handsome, courageous and an excellent musician'; no such court had been witnessed in England for fifty years. This parallel between Henry's court and that of his grandfather Edward IV would have pleased the king. On May Day, Sagudino saw Catherine 'richly attired' and accompanied by twenty-five ladies on white palfreys, 'their dresses slashed with gold lama'. They rode into the woods, where they were met by 'the king and his guard in green liveries, with bows in their hands, and in the woods were bowers filled with singing birds'.[27] Afterwards they dined, played music and jousted, where Henry reputedly 'looked like St George on horseback' and Sagudino had never seen 'such a beautiful sight', although he also commented rather harshly that 'the queen is rather ugly than otherwise and is reported to be with child'. Similar bucolic imagery was used in an event held after the wedding of Mary and Brandon, recounted by Edward Hall, except this one took place at Shooter's Hill, where Henry and Catherine together were welcomed by a Robin Hood figure in green, a popular motif for Henry's early entertainments. Again there were arbours with sweet herbs and flowers, and the ladies were dared to enter the woods, where they found the 'outlaws' breakfasting on venison.[28]

In the summer of 1515, Henry went on progress into the west of England. Given her condition, and precedents for previous summers, it is likely that Catherine remained in residence at Greenwich or Eltham. By July, Henry was at Otford Palace, the residence that William Warham was in the process of rebuilding to rival the property being built by Wolsey at Hampton Court. Situated on the River Darent, near Sevenoaks, it was a symbol of the struggle for supremacy between the two ministers that had come to a head in the last few years. Where Warham had criticised the king's intentions to go to war, Wolsey had supplied the royal needs and run his campaigns without question. And 1515 was to prove Wolsey's year. Eventually, William Warham resigned as chancellor and Henry appointed the younger man in his place; then, to crown his rise, Wolsey became a cardinal on 10 September. As Hall relates, the red hat arrived from Rome and was brought through Kent to London 'with suche triumphe as though the greatest prince of Christendom had come into the realme'.[29]

III

With Henry's third parliament being dissolved shortly before Christmas, Henry and Catherine celebrated the season at Eltham, where a great pageant of a castle was held on Twelfth Night, followed by dancing and a banquet of a hundred dishes.[30] While the suite of rooms was being prepared for Catherine's lying-in at Greenwich, news came from Scotland about the health of Margaret Tudor, who had remarried to Archibald Douglas, 6th Earl of Angus, and borne him a child in October 1515. This daughter was Margaret's seventh child, but only the second to survive, and it must have had particular resonance for Catherine to read that her sister-in-law was suffering from a 'great infirmity' with 'intolerable pain' in her right thigh, 'at the seat of sciatica', unable to stir, and only capable of eating broth, pottage, almond milk and boiled meats with any degree of comfort. After her recovery, Margaret returned to England for a year, being 'received joyously' by Henry, Catherine and Mary at Greenwich and 'feasted royally'.[31]

With her confinement rapidly approaching, Catherine left Eltham to travel the four miles north to the Thames where Greenwich Palace was situated. She made a ceremonial withdrawal into confinement at the end of January, processing to her rooms, praying and partaking of wine and dishes of spices with her chamberlain, Lord Mountjoy, before bidding him farewell. Then the doors closed behind her and the waiting began. Just before dawn on 18 February, she gave birth to a daughter, a healthy child whom she named Mary. Henry was so relieved that he stated hopefully that he and Catherine were both still young and that 'if it was a daughter this time, by the grace of God, the sons would follow'. After all, Catherine's mother and sister Juana had both delivered girls before they went on to have sons. Venetian ambassador Giustinian wrote to the Signory two days later 'would offer the due congratulations on behalf of the State; had an heir male been born, would have done so already'.[32]

It was only then, after her ordeal was safely over, that Catherine was informed of the death of her father. Ferdinand had died in the village of Madrigalejo, while travelling to Andalusia, on 23 January. He was sixty-three and his inheritance bypassed Juana, who had been incarcerated in a convent for the past six years, and was settled upon her son Charles. The old triumvirate of Henry VII, Ferdinand and Louis XII had now been completely replaced by Henry VIII, Charles I and Francis I, and Henry now found himself the most experienced of the three. A memoir of Ferdinand's last acts and intentions, perhaps recorded by a witness to his final hours, laid out his thoughts on the international situation, and indicate the path he would have followed. He named the French as a threat to the peace of Christendom, always trying to 'conquer and tyrannise over as many countries as they can', and with 'an instinctive hatred of the Spaniards'. He wanted Emperor Maximilian and Henry to enter an alliance with the Swiss in order to keep the French threat under control. Henry agreed to a Swiss alliance so long as Spain contributed if they invaded France, which matters Ferdinand had been considering upon his deathbed. He was a 'friend of peace', wrote the anonymous author of the piece, always seeking a diplomatic solution but, failing that, prepared to gain security 'by forcible means', with this 'in common with the king of England and with his other allies'. But influential as he had been in life, and reputedly 'peace-loving', not even Ferdinand could influence affairs from beyond the grave.[33] He was laid to rest beside Isabella in the Royal Chapel at Granada.

It must have been Henry who took the decision to keep the news from Catherine until the child had been born. Giustinian confirms this, writing on 20 February that he had 'just heard of the death of Ferdinand of Aragon [which] was kept secret for some days, as the queen was on the verge of her delivery'.[34] Catherine had been aware of her father's ill-health the previous October, being pleased to hear news of Ferdinand's recovery after he had been 'so ill'.[35] But any recovery had been short-lived, as on 27 November Pedro Martir noted that Ferdinand was no stronger and 'his asthma grows worse'.[36] The king's refusal to rest or slow down was considered dangerous, with Pedro

Martir commenting as early as November 1514 that it would kill him along with his old French rival. He was proved correct in both cases:

> Unless Ferdinand throws off two of his appetites he must soon go the way of all flesh. He is 63, and, besides his asthma, never lets his wife from his side. It is now winter, and the country is very cold, yet he talks like a young man of going to the mountainous country of Leon, because he hears that bears are to be found there. If he does not part with one rib, he will lose all. Charon will carry in his boat both him and Louis if they are not careful. The Frenchman went out to meet his bride like a gay bridegroom, perched elegantly on a fine Spanish war-horse, 'semicevens', licking his lips and gulping his spittle. If he lives to smell the flowers of the spring, 'you may promise yourself 500 autumns'. Yet this brave King is thinking of again shaking Italy with war, and is spurred on by Trivulcio and other exiles.[37]

Over the last fifteen years, Ferdinand had been Catherine's anchor outside England, the link to her homeland, her mother, her childhood, her identity, even her language. The relationship had been a complex one, developing in the last decade into a blend of paternal feeling alongside political statecraft although, awkwardly for Catherine, the interests of Spain and England had not always overlapped. Yet Ferdinand had been a constant presence, through his letters and gifts, even his decisions and machinations, and the final cornerstone of the family unit she had belonged to as a child, to the lives of her surviving sisters and the scenery of her youth. Catherine had now been in England as long as she had been in Spain. Ferdinand's passing refined her current status and identification as an established English queen, a woman who belonged in her new land, who had been welcomed by its people, steered them to victory, weathered personal and political storms and had now delivered its heir. The following March, another family connection was lost with the death of Catherine's sister Maria, Queen of Portugal. As nothing before had quite managed with the same significance, the ties binding Catherine to Spain were symbolically cut. There would be no more juggling two interests or mediating the men's disputes: now she was singularly and wholeheartedly committed to England.

Ferdinand's death represented the end of a phase in Spanish history, and of Europe moving forward, as old certainties crumbled and the face of Western religion was poised on the verge of irrevocable change. As well as preaching at court against war in 1512, John Colet had attacked the Church with the notion that those convicted of heresy were not nearly as 'pestilent and pernicious' as 'the evil and wicked life of priests'.[38] Four years later, Thomas More published his *Utopia*, perhaps being inspired by the climate of recent exploration to site his imaginary island in the middle of the Atlantic Ocean. Depicting an ideal place, More uses the mouthpiece of a traveller to address such questions as how advisers might raise difficult questions with rulers, such as the tendency of kings to start wars and waste money. More had been moving upwards in political circles, having been appointed Privy Councillor and Master of Requests in 1514, a job which involved hearing the suits and problems of servants of the king and the poor. His writing does not evade some of the thornier humanist questions regarding kingship and its role in the emerging new world. At the time, it was considered to be a mirror to all the ills of society, with Erasmus writing to inform More that 'a burgomaster at Antwerp is so pleased with it that he knows it all by heart'.

Utopia presents a Platonic model of the world as the ideal and states that the study of philosophy was essential for those in power to prevent themselves from being corrupted by evil ideas.

That very corruption, and the lust for martial glory, was the reason that another leading humanist had left England. More's friend Erasmus had escaped for Switzerland, disappointed by Henry's policies and finding that the reality did not live up to the expectations he had entertained of the new reign in 1509. In Basel, he published a Greek translation of the New Testament and *Sileni Alcibiadis*, a direct commentary on the need for Church reform and targeting the greedy, lewd and power-hungry priests, who should simply be God's servants rather than spending his riches on themselves. Criticisms of the old ways, of unquestioning faith and martial kings, had taken hold across Europe.

The humanist interest in history and the classics also inspired reflection on recent events. Royal printer Robert Pynson brought out the first edition of Robert Fabyan's chronicle after the sheriff and alderman had died in 1512, having related the story of England from the arrival of the mythical Brutus of Troy to the death of Henry VII. 1515 had seen Albrecht Durer produce his famous woodcut of the rhinoceros, after one had been shipped to Lisbon from India, the first to appear on European soil since Roman times. In Rome, Leonardo da Vinci's patron Guiliano de Medici died, and the artist accepted the invitation of Francis I to retire to France, moving to spend his last years at Clos Lucé, a house in the grounds of the royal Château d'Amboise. When he arrived that May, he brought the *Mona Lisa* with him and, although he could no longer paint because his arm was paralysed, he was treated as a celebrity, an icon of the Italian renaissance that was so admired by the French. Both the Northern and Southern Renaissances lost key figures when Hieronymus Bosch died that August and Venetian artist Giovanni Bellini followed at the end of November.

Mary was christened on Wednesday 21 February in the church of the Friars Observant at Greenwich. The route was railed and hung with arras, gravelled and strewn with rushes, and a 'house' erected at the church door was also hung with tapestries to protect the baby as her godparents the Duchess of Norfolk, Countess of Devon and Cardinal Wolsey paused there while she was given her name. She was carried inside by the Countess of Surrey under a gold canopy, with the dukes of Norfolk and Suffolk assisting, through the embroidered hangings encrusted with jewels, and dipped into water from the silver font that had been brought up from Canterbury. All the rituals of the Catholic Church were carried out, with salt placed upon her tongue, holy oil used to anoint her and a linen chrisom cloth placed over her forehead. Afterwards her confirmation was carried out, for which Margaret Pole was sponsor. When all was complete, her titles were announced and trumpets sounded. *Te Deums* were sung by the king's chaplain before the procession returned to the palace.

Three or four weeks later, Catherine would undergo a similarly elaborate ceremony of purification as she was churched, approaching the same church in a veil, perhaps with a lighted taper between her hands, in order to be spiritually cleansed in order to re-emerge into public. Both women would cling to their religion in the coming years, as Europe was shaken to the core by the most critical, defining moment of the Reformation. At the time of Mary's christening, a German monk named Martin Luther was working on a new translation of the fourteenth-century text *Theologia Germanica*, arguing that man could become one with God through a life of goodness and the renunciation of sin. The following year, his ideas would change the world as Catherine knew it.

With her young daughter thriving in her nursery under the care of Lady Bryan, Catherine had the company of both her sisters-in-law for a brief time. Mary had given birth to her first child that March, just a month after Catherine had delivered her namesake, and had been churched and returned to court in time to enjoy the May Day jousts Henry planned in honour of Margaret Tudor's return. It was an interesting triumvirate of three queens, of England, France and Scotland, all strong women who had made decisive choices in life. That Margaret was lodged for part of that time at Catherine's property of Baynard's Castle suggests that the two women were on good terms. On 19 May, Henry, Brandon, the Earl of Essex and Nicholas Carew answered all challengers in the lists, dressed in black velvet covered with embroidered honeysuckle made from fine, flat gold damask, 'cunning and sumptuous' with every leaf moving. The challengers were dressed alike in blue velvet and cloth of gold. The next morning, the king and his party had changed into purple velvet costumes with rose leaves of gold, with their attendants in yellow velvet and satin, edged with gold and the challengers in white satin. When the knights had exhausted themselves, they retired to a banquet in honour of Margaret.[39]

Margaret and Catherine were both guests of honour at the festivities held that Christmas, also at Greenwich, when a garden of hope was wheeled into the great hall, surrounded by railings held in place by the four towers in the corners. Upon the artificial banks inside were flowers made of silk, gold and green satin, all around a golden pillar of the antique style, topped with an arbour in which sprouted red and white roses and a pomegranate bush. There was much dancing, banqueting and afterwards, Henry left the women together while he 'exercised him selfe muche in hawkynge'.[40] It was a pleasant idyll for Catherine, with the company of two fellow queens, the love of her husband, a healthy child in the nursery and the hope of more still to come. Even her contemporaries would look back to this time with nostalgia, considering it to be 'merry' England, with its jousts and woodmen in green, its church bells ringing and candles flickering before shrines. All was well, but it would not remain so for long.

PART FIVE

European Queen 1517–1524

15

Extremes 1517–1519

I

Martin Luther had been born just over two years before Catherine, in Eiselben, Saxony, part of Maximilian's Holy Roman Empire. Having rejected an education that was designed to prepare him for the legal profession, he took holy orders in 1505 and lived as an Augustinian monk, spending hours in prayer and pilgrimage, confession and fasting. It was a regime that Catherine would have approved of. In 1508, he was invited to the newly founded university at Wittenburg, a centre for progressive learning, founded by Archduke Frederick the Wise, who wished to embrace the new tenets of humanism, the study of history, the classics, moral philosophy, rhetoric, poetry and grammar, to equip the people for a useful civic life. Having found law too uncertain, offering no assurances about life, Luther sought out empirical evidence, setting aside reason in favour of divine revelation and the teaching of the Scriptures. In 1517 he protested against the sale of indulgences after the Pope sent pardoners to Germany to raise money for the rebuilding of St Peter's Basilica. An indulgence was a pardon for sins that the bearer had committed, such as theft and adultery, meaning they did not have to undergo the usual process of confession, absolution and punishment. Luther had been preaching against indulgences for at least three years and became concerned when his parishioners travelled great distances to purchase them and returned confident in the belief that they no longer needed to make changes in their lives or to resist sin. Luther drafted up a number of arguments, known as his ninety-five theses, against this practice, which he sent to various significant figures in the Empire. He also nailed a copy to the door of All Saints Church. It would be the catalyst to permanent change.

Luther took issue with some of the central tenets of Catherine's faith. He saw the Church as a corrupt institution that removed worshippers from a true connection with God, by distracting them with icons, greed and false promises. He rejected the sort of relationship that Catherine had with Fray Diego, dependent as it was upon the friar's intercession, with the queen seeking his guidance and approval, with only him able to offer her forgiveness for her sins. Instead, he argued for justification by faith, a direct personal connection with God, and that faith and righteous acts were enactments of God's will, rather than personal choices. Luther attacked private confession and the majority of the sacraments upon which Catherine routinely depended, retaining only baptism, communion and absolution. He preached that individuals should take direct inspiration from the word of God in the Bible, rather than seeking others to interpret it for them; Catherine would have been horrified at the thought of a Bible being translated into English and accessible to anyone who was literate. Taking its cue from the Pope, English Catholicism was disseminated to the people in Latin, by trained mediating clergymen, following the 1408 Constitutions of Oxford, which had forbidden the translation of the Bible in response to a previous attempt by John Wycliffe. No printed Bible in English would appear until 1526, when Henry would ban William Tyndale's version. Catherine would have completely rejected the thought that her subjects might be able to read and interpret the word of God in their own homes.

Luther's teachings found two other immediate enemies in England in Thomas More and Cardinal Wolsey, who worked hard to prevent the spread of his message. In Rome, Luther's words were seen as not just a criticism of indulgence selling, but a dangerous attack upon the power of the Pope. The Catholic Church attempted to prevent him preaching against indulgences, with the Pope requesting that his Augustinian Order ensure his silence. The Dominican Friar Sylvester Mazzolini, a teacher of theology at the University of Bologna, prepared *A Dialogue Against Martin Luther's Presumptuous Theses Concerning the Power of the Pope*, which was to be used in a trial against him. The original pardoner he had criticised, Johann Tetzel, called for Luther to be burned as a heretic, and when he refused to cease his preaching he was excommunicated.

Catherine was well equipped to understand and reject Lutheran teaching. Erasmus considered her to be at least the equal of Henry when it came to education and intellect. In 1518, he wrote that 'the queen is well instructed – not merely in comparison with her own sex – and is no less to be respected for her piety than her erudition'. That May, Erasmus was coming under attack in Switzerland for his reputed connection to Luther, although, as he wrote to Wolsey, he had 'dissuaded' the publication of the offensive books, 'as the friends of Luther can bear witness'. Instead, Erasmus advised them to 'moderate their freedom of speech and abstain from references to the heads of the Church'.[1] By the following year, Henry was reading Luther's theses for himself and preparing his response, sharing his thoughts on it with Wolsey as early as June 1518. Others at court saw the attack upon religion as a threat to the heart of English life and identity. As Thomas Howard, who had fought alongside his father Surrey at Flodden, reflected, harking back to pre-reformation days, 'it was merry in England afore the new learning came up'. In 1517, Luther may have seemed an immediate and obvious enemy to Catherine, but his views would surface later, unexpectedly, when she was at a crisis in her life.

II

While the threat of Lutheran teaching continued to gain ground on the Continent, chaos of a different kind erupted in England. The outburst of anger against Spaniards in 1514 had been uncomfortable for Catherine, but it seemed a temporary aberration as London had always been a thriving mix of foreigners, especially merchants, who arrived from all over Europe and beyond. Many settled in Lombard Street, literally named after the resident Lombards, which John Stow described as the place where 'straungers of diverse nations assemble ... twice every day', or in Tower Hill, St Katherine's, Westminster or St Martin's Le Grand in Aldersgate behind Cheapside. From

1407, Englishmen trading overseas in cloth had been under the protection of the Guild or Company of Merchant Adventurers of London, with a charter renewed by Henry VII, but those foreign traders resident in the city had less protection and the mistrust of strangers left them vulnerable. Among the records of foreigners seeking letters of denization or paying taxes in the decade prior to 1517 were three merchants of Venice – Nicholas Duodo, Stephen Fexano and Nicholas Balby – as well as a number of other Italian, Spanish and German traders.[2]

The seeds of conflict had been growing for a while, with apprentices and their masters resenting the way that their market was being dominated by those who had not been subject to the strict laws that meant a man must train and join a guild before being allowed to sell his wares. Edward Hall captured some of the xenophobic feeling in London, claiming that the Genovese, French and 'other strangers ... boasted themselves to be in such favour with the kyng and his counsayll, that they set naughte by the rules of the citie: and the multitude of strangers was so great about London, that the poor English artificers could scarce get any lyvyng. And most of all the straungers were so proude that they disdained, mocked and oppressed the Englishmenne, which was the beginning of the grudge.' He cited the case of one carpenter called Williamson, who was about to purchase two stock doves in Chepe, whereupon 'a Frenchman tooke them out of his handes, and said they were not meate for a carpenter'. When Williamson protested, the strangers complained to the French ambassador and the carpenter was sent to prison, as 'no Englishemen should denye that they Frenchmen required'.[3] In another case, a Lombard named Francis de Bard enticed an Englishman's wife to come to his chamber bearing her husband's plate, and when the man demanded her return he was told that he would have neither and was arrested for the cost of his wife's board.[4] When this erupted into violence in the spring of 1517, it fulfilled the threat one member of the Mercers' Company had made against 'whoreson Lombards ... by the mass, we will one day have a day at you'.[5]

On Easter Tuesday, a Dr Bell made an inflammatory speech at St Paul's Cross, at the urging of a London broker, John Lincoln. Bell called on 'all Englishmen to cherish and defend themselves, and to hurt and grieve aliens for the common weal'.[6] Sebastian Giustinian wrote to the Doge of Venice with more details, including the claim of the discontented that foreigners were not only depriving 'them of their industry ... but disgraced their dwellings, taking their wives and daughters' so that the intention was to 'cut them to pieces and sack their houses'.[7] With rumours flying of intended attacks upon May Day, Mayor John Rest called an emergency meeting at the Guildhall at which Thomas More was present in his capacity as a Sheriff of London. The debate went on too long and it was late in the day when Rest asked permission to impose a curfew with military support. That night, as More was patrolling the streets, he encountered a large gang of rioters and attempted to dissuade them from attacking local businesses and properties in Cheapside and St Martin's Le Grand. Just as he appeared to be having success, the residents began to retaliate in their defence, throwing stones and tipping boiling water out of their windows. Giustinian put the number of rioters at around 2,000, bracketing them together as apprentices and bandits, although a number of London citizens also joined the fray. Barricading the city gates, they forced the mayor to release prisoners from the gaols before they

> attacked the French and Flemish quarters, and sacked the houses. They proceeded to the French secretary (Meautis), sacked his house, and would have killed him had he not escaped up the belfry of the adjoining church; then to the Italian merchants, but as they were well armed, the mob did little damage. Sebastian's own house was not attacked at all. Much greater mischief would have occurred but for the measures adopted by the Cardinal and the lords, who came by several roads to the city gates, which had been locked by the rioters.[8]

The rioting escalated and Henry was woken from his sleep at Richmond to be informed of the event, dispatching Wolsey, the Duke of Norfolk and his son the Earl of Surrey to quell the insurrection. Order was restored to the streets at three in the morning. Incredibly, no one was killed, but something between 70 and 300 rioters were arrested.

It must have been difficult, as a Spaniard, for Catherine to hear of the attacks upon foreigners. Even though she was an anointed queen, recent events had proved that her position as a Spaniard was a sensitive one. Now she chose to act as an advocate for the rioters, soothing the difficult mood in the city by ensuring that they had to thank a foreigner for the restoration of their freedom. Henry made an example of the ringleaders, so that around a dozen were hanged at the city gates and their body parts distributed throughout the city. After that, on 14 May, around 400 men and 11 women were summoned to Westminster Hall with halters around their necks, crying in the belief that they were about to be hanged. It must have been an imposing sight, hung with arras tapestries and peopled with the king's council and lords of the realm. This was clearly an effective piece of theatre staged by Henry and Catherine, to play on their different roles and strengths. With tears in her eyes, she knelt to ask the king to pardon the offenders, for the sakes of their wives and children, which was echoed by Wolsey. Henry allowed himself to be visibly moved and ordered the prisoners' release, upon which they 'took the halters from their necks and danced and sang'. Word soon spread around the capital and Catherine's popularity soared, described by the papal nuncio as 'our serene and compassionate queen'.[9]

III

On 7 July 1517, Catherine was at Greenwich for a banquet held on St Thomas' Day, to celebrate Henry, King Charles I of Spain and the Emperor Maximilian forming a league for the defence of the Church. The details of service, including a hand-drawn seating plan, give a glimpse into the ceremony and planning of such events, the guests and who was chosen to serve them. It seems strange to a modern reader that the most high-born noblemen should be the ones serving the dishes rather than enjoying them, but it was a considerable mark of honour to be trusted enough to bring the king and queen their food, so Sir David Owen would have been pleased to carve for Henry that day. Owen was the illegitimate son of Owen Tudor and thus the king's great uncle, who was now aged around fifty-eight and, although he had settled in Sussex, provided a link with the king's Welsh heritage. Of Henry's jousting partners, Sir Nicholas Carew was the cupbearer and Sir William Kingston the server. Two men were assigned to hold the doors while the plates were brought in, sixteen to hold torches while the diners ate, two to keep the barriers at the stairhead and four lords to hold torches while the king washed. The Earl of Surrey, Lord Clinton and Lord Grey were to bear towels and basins along with a dozen others and a sergeant of the scullery was to wait behind the door with a basket to receive the dirty silver dishes. Sir Christopher Garnish and four others were to wait upon the French ambassador, while the Spanish ambassador, the Bishop of Spain and the Provost of Castile were to be served by four men each. At least ten messes were expected per course, and it was standard for such a feast to comprise three courses or more. Catherine was seated in the plan with Henry, Mary and the Imperial ambassador. Also present at the feast were Lady Mountjoy, Lady Elizabeth Boleyn, Lady Elizabeth Stafford and Lady Willoughby, Catherine's former lady-in-waiting Maria de Salinas.[10]

The occasion was also described by Francesco Chieregato, writing on 10 July to Isabella d'Este, Marchioness of Mantua. The Spanish delegation 'were accompanied by so noble a train of men and horses, that had the king of Spain himself come in person, he could not have been more honourably attended'.[11] The entourage included a hundred horses and twenty-four wagons. Henry had sent a delegation of 400 to meet them and conduct them to Greenwich, where they recorded their impression of the English court. The king 'was dressed in stiff brocade in the Hungarian fashion, having a collar of inestimable value around his neck'. Catherine appeared in a style that her mother would have approved, 'in cloth of gold, with chains around [her] neck, everything glittered with gold'. On one occasion they dined privately with the king and queen, in Henry's chambers, and after dinner he 'took to singing and playing on every musical instrument and exhibited part of his very excellent endowments', as well as dancing and giving away gifts.[12]

On St Peter's day they attended chapel to hear mass with the king, who wore 'royal robes down to the ground, of gold brocade lined with ermine, and another different collar of very great value, and his train was carried. All the rest of the court glittered with jewels and gold and silver, the pomp being unprecedented.'[13] On the day of the St Thomas feast, a joust was also held, for which Henry was 'dressed in white damask, in the Turkish fashion, with the above-mentioned robe all embroidered with roses made of rubies and diamonds, in accordance with his emblems, a most costly costume; his scimitar was all embroidered with pearls and precious jewels'. His armour was covered by a surcoat of cloth of silver, 'wrought through with emblematic letters', each ending in a pearl worth 30 to 40 ducats. The gentlemen jousters, also in white embroidered with the letters 'H' and 'K', must have 'cost the king a mint of money as during the last four months all the London goldsmiths have wrought nothing but these trappings'.[14]

The ambassadors also attended a buffet given by Henry, the table being thirty feet long and twenty feet wide, set with dishes, bowls, goblets and basins of pure gold, all for show, while the guests ate from smaller plates. The guests remained at table for seven hours, watching as each course was brought out to the king 'by an elephant, or by lions, or panthers, or other animals, marvellously designed; and fresh representations were made constantly with music and instruments of divers sorts'. Chieregato's detailed account presents a vivid view of Henry and Catherine's court:

> The removal and replacing of dishes the whole time was incessant, the hall in every direction being full of fresh viands on their way to table. Every imaginable sort of meat known in the kingdom was served, and fish in like manner, even down to prawn pasties [*fino alli gambari de pastelli*]; but the jellies [*zeladie*], of some 20 sorts perhaps, surpassed everything; they were made in the shape of castles and of animals of various descriptions, as beautiful and as admirable as can be imagined.
>
> In short, the wealth and civilization of the world are here; and those who call the English barbarians appear to me to render themselves such. I here perceive very elegant manners, extreme decorum, and very great politeness; and amongst other things there is this most invincible King, whose acquirements and qualities are so many and excellent that I consider him to excel all who ever wore a crown; and blessed and happy may this country call itself in having as its lord so worthy and eminent a sovereign, whose sway is more bland and gentle than the greatest liberty under any other.[15]

The occasion was also witnessed by Giustinian, who commented that the youth and beauty of one of the ambassadors caused Catherine and her ladies to pay him as much honour 'as if he was a sovereign'.[16] The occasion was marked by the king's chaplain, Dionysius Memo, whose 'instrumental music' lasted four hours, 'to the extreme delight of all the audience and especially of the king'. He noted that at the feast Henry sat between Catherine and his sister Mary, with a sumptuous repast and dancing until two in the morning.[17]

It was the last occasion that some of those present were to celebrate. Just days later there was an outbreak of the sweating sickness, the same illness Catherine had suffered from in 1502 and which may have contributed to, if not caused, Arthur's death. Henry had a further season of pastimes planned, but suddenly the illness raged through the court, with the first ominous note being sounded in a letter from Cuthbert Tunstall on 13 July, which concluded with the stark news that 'Lord Fiennes is dead'.[18] The twenty-seven-year old Thomas, also known as Lord Clinton, died at Richmond, as did Thomas, Lord Grey of Wilton, aged around twenty-one, and others of Henry's gentlemen. The malady, claimed Hall, was so cruel that it 'killed some within three hours, some within two hours, some mery at dinner and dede at supper'.[19] Unsurprisingly, Henry took flight. He and Catherine did not attend the christening of Mary and Brandon's daughter Frances on 17 July at Bishop's Hatfield, with Lady Elizabeth Boleyn standing in for the queen. Instead they hurried into seclusion in the countryside to wait until the danger had passed. Oxford and Cambridge suffered such losses that the Michaelmas term was cancelled and 'the kyng kept himself ever with a small company and kept no solempne Christmas', lamenting the deaths of his people.[20]

Among the losses that August was Henry's Latin secretary, the Italian humanist, Andrew Ammonius, who was 'carried off in eight hours'.[21] His death was greatly lamented in verse by Erasmus, described by the Bishop of Worcester as 'the king's faithful servant and the ornament of the Latin tongue',[22] and whose canonry of Westminster went to Thomas Linacre. Giustinian reported that Henry was 'keeping aloof' at Windsor with his physician and three favourite gentlemen. 'No one is admitted on account of the disease, which is now making great progress'. Wolsey had been ill, apparently for the fourth time, explaining why Giustinian could never get an audience with him, but was beginning to recover[23] and in thanks vowed to undertake a pilgrimage to Walsingham. When they finally met, Giustinian found him 'with a troubled countenance and bent brow' and judged that his appearance 'in addition to his mental perturbation' indicated so, as did his 'profuse perspiration'.[24] The Venetian ambassador and Sagudino had also pulled through the sickness, while Francis Chieregato had gone so far as to leave England for Rome to avoid the sweat.[25] Thomas Spinelly, Henry's ambassador to the Low Countries, wrote in alarm to Wolsey on hearing incorrectly of the death of the Duke of Norfolk, but was correct that 'other great noblemen of England are dead'.[26] That November, Henry's aunt Princess Bridget Plantagenet, his mother's youngest sister, died at thirty-seven, the same age as Elizabeth of York. Bridget had been a nun in Dartford Priory, and while the cause of her death is unclear, she may well have been another victim of the epidemic.

The sickness was raging through Europe, too, with the Bishop of Durham, Cuthbert Tunstall, in Bruges finding 'his retinue ... so poisoned with the foul odours of the country that by strict fast of several days he was barely able to keep off an attack of fever. Before he left three of his servants had been struck down; and had he not sent them away, upon the advice of his physician, none of them would have recovered. He is not alone in this respect; many of the court were seized, and it is a mercy the King escaped.'[27] Charles had finally sailed from Burgundy to Spain, but arriving in the Bay of Biscay in mid-September could not find a safe place to land because the sickness was so rife. In London, Henry's absence led to worrying developments, causing Giustinian to flee:

> Has left London to avoid the plague. Has heard of another conspiracy of the mob to murder the strangers and sack their houses. Thinks it was suggested by the absence of the King, Cardinal and other lords, who have gone in the country. The city is prepared: 3,000 householders are under arms. Three of the ringleaders have been arrested. Desires to return home.[28]

On 15 October, the same day as he reported the death of Lord Grey, Richard Pace, Wolsey's secretary, was admitted for an hour to see Henry at Windsor. Otherwise, the king and queen were living in quiet seclusion, hawking and hunting, although Henry was finding time to spend 'part of the day in study, in this differing entirely from those who imagine that kings have no business with learning and philosophy'.[29] It was that November that Pope Leo X wrote to both Henry and Catherine on behalf of her old chaplain, Alessandro Geraldini, 'a great historian [who] had written much that is approved of by men of learning' and was a 'most zealous trumpeter of the king's praises'. Geraldini was hoping to return to England and build bridges with Catherine, and Leo reminded her that the bishop 'had been in great favour with Ferdinand and Isabella, and employed in the education of Catherine' and her siblings but she was unable to forgive his betrayal of 1502, and refused to acknowledge him. Even if she had been minded to overlook his treachery, visitors were still being denied access at Windsor, 'through fear of the plague', including the newly arrived Bishop of Paris.[30] The illness was still claiming victims, as some of the pages who slept in the king's chamber had recently died, and his staff was still reduced to the bare minimum of three gentlemen and a doctor.[31] To enable Windsor to be cleaned, Henry and Catherine travelled twenty-five miles south-west to Farnham Castle, home of the Bishop of Winchester. But the deaths kept coming. On November 25, Sir Thomas Allen reported the demise of Thomas Parr, Comptroller of the king, a former protégé of Margaret Beaufort and now the father of a little girl who was to become Henry's sixth wife. He also reported that the king and queen were to pass Christmas at Windsor 'if it please God to save [them] from the sickness'.[32]

In January 1518, Catherine received a letter from Passamonte in Santo Dominigo, the treasurer-general of the Indies, appointed by Ferdinand, who appears to have known her during her childhood. He had heard from Sir John Stile, the English ambassador in Spain that she was in 'good health and prosperity' which gave him 'great pleasure' as he had always intended to come and kiss her hands and feet, which he still hoped to do. Passamonte sent her gifts of a grand gown and a side saddle but did not send parrots, as he feared they could not stand the climate. He hoped 'she will have a prince from whom a numerous progeny may spring'.[33] The following month, Catherine did conceive again.

IV

The summer of 1518 saw the first visit to England of a man who was to play a significant role in Catherine's life a decade later. Cardinal Lorenzo Campeggio was then in his forties, a graduate of Bologna University who had been awarded the red cap by Leo X for his attempts to unite Europe against the threat of the Turks. Erasmus described him as 'one of the best and most learned men living'.[34] Now the Pope wanted Henry to join his league too. Wolsey saw this as an opportunity, advising Henry to tell the Pope that it was not the English custom to admit such officials, but that Campeggio was welcome if Wolsey was also made a papal legate, to share his power. Leo had little choice if he wanted to further his plans, so agreed to the suggestion, granting Wolsey the position on 17 May. Campeggio wrote to Henry eleven days later to confirm he was bringing the bulls of the legateship with him.[35] A knight was dispatched to Calais to bring the cardinal safely to England and, in the meantime, Wolsey wrote to the Bishop of Worcester that

> there is no king in the world who is more ardently loved and respected by his friends, nobles and subjects than the King of England. His very look strikes terror into evildoers. As for Wolsey and his administration, the kingdom never was in greater harmony and repose than now.[36]

Erasmus agreed when it came to Wolsey's influence, comparing the cardinal to Ptolemy for his 'patronage of learning and collection of books'.[37]

Campeggio made a good impression upon Henry. He landed at Deal on 23 July and was met by a deputation of local lords who accompanied him to Sandwich, before heading on to Canterbury, where he was received in the cathedral by Warham. Campeggio 'kissed certain relics' and visited the shrine of St Thomas, before being conducted to lodgings in nearby St Augustine's Abbey. The next day, although it 'thundered, lightened and rained sore', he set off for London via Sittingbourne, Otford, Lewisham, Greenwich and Blackheath, where he changed his clothes in the king's tent and headed for the city. He received a splendid welcome, with all the clergymen of London turning out to welcome him, Thomas More making an oration, crosses and censors held aloft amid crammed streets and more holy relics presented to kiss at London Bridge, before reaching his lodgings at Bath Place. On the following Sunday, 3 August, Wolsey and Campeggio took a barge to Greenwich, and Henry, 'royally apparelled and accompanied', gave them a warm welcome.[38] A surviving diagram shows where their chairs of cloth of gold were placed, on Henry's right hand, under his cloth of estate of gold tissue. They listened to an oration given by Campeggio's brother in the king's presence chamber, to which one of Wolsey's servants replied that the king would not neglect his Christian duty, although he had no need to be reminded of it,[39] then they heard Mass and dined before returning to London.

Campeggio would have seen Catherine too, and perhaps had the opportunity to talk to her on that occasion or later in his visit. When he returned to England a decade later, she would greet him as an old friend. She was clearly capable of matching any man when it came to debate and logic, with Erasmus paying her the compliment of raising her above gender expectations of the time, narrow as they were: 'a woman of such learning, piety, prudence and constancy that you would find nothing in her that is like a woman, nothing indeed that is not masculine, except her gender and her body'.[40] It was one of the highest compliments that could be paid to the queen, according to the mores of the day, to equate her with a man in terms of ability, and gave further validity to Catherine's own desire to be an equal ruler with Henry.

He would dedicate his 1526 *Institution of Marriage* to her, with its thoughts on the raising of daughters, and praised her again in his 1529 *On the Christian Widow.*

In the early stages of her pregnancy, that March, Catherine had undertaken a pilgrimage to the shrine of St Frideswide in Christ Church Cathedral in Oxford. The relics of the seventh-century saint had been transferred there in 1180 and had been attracting pilgrims ever since, especially women, for whom she was considered a healing saint, curing the blind, dumb and lame. No doubt Catherine prayed there and left an offering, perhaps even touching the holy relics and whispering up her prayers. She was to be one of the last visitors in the shrine's four-hundred-year history. Just six years later St Frideswide's Priory would be dissolved by Wolsey, and in 1538 her shrine would be destroyed and Catherine's gift gathered up among all the rest and shipped off to fill the royal coffers.[41]

Henry was also thinking about his own mortality. The loss of so many members of his household must have weighed upon his mind as he began to draw up plans for a tomb that was along the same lines as that of his parents. He was still seeing himself and Catherine as conforming to the example they had set, by planning that they would lie side by side in effigies of white marble and black touchstone, made by the same artist, Pietro Torrigiano, who was now 'resident in the precincts of St Peter's'.[42] The project was to be overseen by Wolsey, to cost no more than £2,000 and be completed in four years, although a significant point was that it was to be made 'one-fourth larger than that which he has already made for Henry VII'.[43] In the event, neither Henry or Catherine would be laid to rest in Westminster, or under the work of Torrigiano or anything similar. The Italian artist began work early in 1519, as instructed, and even tried unsuccessfully to enlist the help of Benvenuto Cellini, but the tomb was never completed and the bronze work was melted down under the Commonwealth, along with, ironically, Wolsey's tomb. Not long afterwards, Torrigiano returned to Italy.

With the sweat still raging, Catherine and Henry were keeping out of the public eye. Thus her fifth pregnancy was only announced that summer, by the time she was mid-term. They had made a brief appearance in London in January but after that, had intended to stay at Windsor until Easter. However, by the middle of March, Henry was at Richmond, 'in trouble' as 'three of his pages have died of the plague'[44] and Easter was observed instead at Abingdon.[45] On 12 April, Richard Pace, Wolsey's secretary wrote that 'it is secretly said that the queen is with child' and he 'prays God heartily it may be a Prince, to the surety and universal comfort of the realm'.[46] The one other person who had known about the development early on was Wolsey, in whom Henry was increasingly confiding, explaining that he was 'sloth to repair to London ward, by cause about this time is partly of her dangerous times, and by cause of that, I would remove her as little as I may now'. Nor was he certain of her condition then, adding that it was 'not ... an assured thing, but as a thing wherein I have great hope and likelihood'.[47] Giustinian had only realised the queen was pregnant when he heard court gossip to the effect in June, when she was already four months gone. By July, though, there was no doubt about her condition, when Henry returned to Catherine at Woodstock Palace, where she welcomed him 'with a goodly belly'.[48] On the eleventh, it was reported that two of their servants at Woodstock had died of the sweat, while others were infected, so they left at once for Ewelme, with a small household who were lodged nearby at Wallington. From there, Richard Pace wrote to Wolsey that they were already moving on to Bisham Abbey because 'they do die in these parts in every place, not only of the smallpox and measles, but also of the great sickness'.[49] Next, they went on to the Manor of the More in Rickmansworth, Hertfordshire, where Catherine went hunting in a nearby park belonging to Sir John Pechy.[50] It is unlikely that she would have undertaken any strenuous exercise, being around mid-way through her pregnancy, so perhaps this was hunting with hawks, which she greatly enjoyed, or riding gently while others pursued the hart. At the end of August, the Bishop of Worcester reported that the Pope was delighted to hear she was expecting another child and hoped it would 'be a prince who will be the prop of the universal peace of Christendom'.[51]

Catherine was now thirty-two and had high hopes for this pregnancy. After all, there was proof in the royal nursery that she was capable of bearing a healthy child. The first woman to oversee baby Mary's upbringing was Elizabeth Denton, who had been Henry's nurse back in the 1490s, but her death in 1517 led to Lady Margaret Bryan being awarded her annuity of forty pounds for 'services to the princess'.[52] Catherine paid close attention to her daughter's upbringing from the start, even though she was not permitted to breastfeed her as this would have interfered with her ability to conceive again, and Catherine's entire existence as queen was geared around conception and pregnancy. She would, though, have liaised closely with Lady Bryan about the choice of wet nurse for her daughter, and her diet once she was weaned. Lady Catherine, wife of Leonard Poole, was appointed for the former task, as 'nutrici Marie filie Regis', being awarded an annuity of £20 on 2 July, suggesting the princess had been weaned at around sixteen months.[53] Lady Catherine, *née* Bridges, of Cubberley in Gloucestershire, was then aged around twenty, and had borne her first child, Giles, around the same time as the queen delivered her daughter. Giles would later serve in Mary's parliaments as a 'safe Catholic' on whom she could depend.[54] After she had been weaned, Mary was allowed one messe, or serving, of meat for her lodgings, with sufficient bread and drink for all her attendants.[55] Her laundress, Avis Woode, was paid 33*s* 4*d* per half year, while

£10 was given to one of her gentlewomen, Alys Baker, and 6*d* a day to her chaplain and clerk of her closet, Sir Henry Rowte.[56]

At New Year 1517, Mary's first such celebration, she received gifts from a number of those close to Catherine: Cardinal Wolsey gave her a cup of gold, her aunt Mary a golden pomander and the Duchess of Devonshire a gold spoon, while the Duchess of Norfolk gave her a primer, Lady Mountjoy a smock and Lady Darrell some pears.[57] Her household was based at Enfield but at Christmas she was moved to Datchet, just over the Thames from where her parents were celebrating at Windsor, presumably to allow for visiting. In July 1518, while her parents kept on the move to escape the sweat, there was a scare when one of the women in Mary's household fell ill 'of a hot ague'; Henry summoned his daughter to be brought to Bisham Abbey and on to the Manor of the More, in Rickmansworth, Hertfordshire. The woman recovered but the king 'wishes the princess to be removed, notwithstanding', until they heard his further pleasure.[58] Soon after Mary's second birthday, Giustinian saw her at court, and was able to draw near as she was carried in her nurse's arms:

> After this, Princess Mary, who is two years old, was brought in. The Cardinal and Sebastian kissed her hand, the greatest marks of honor being paid her, universally, more than to the Queen herself. The moment she cast her eyes on the Reverend Dionisius Memo, who was there at a little distance, she commenced calling out in English 'Priest!' and he was obliged to go and play for her.[59]

Giustinian also left descriptions of Mary's parents. In the ambassador's words, King Henry was

> much handsomer than any other Sovereign in Christendom, a great deal handsomer than the King of France. He was very fair, and his whole frame admirably proportioned. Hearing that King Francis wore a beard, he allowed his own to grow, and as it was reddish, he had then got a beard which looked like gold. He was very accomplished and a good musician; composed well; was a capital horseman, and a fine jouster; spoke good French, Latin, and Spanish; was very religious; heard three masses daily when

> he hunted, and sometimes five on other days, besides hearing the office daily in the Queen's chamber, that is to say, vespers and compline. He was extremely fond of hunting, and never took that diversion without tiring eight or ten horses, which he caused to be stationed beforehand along the line of country he meant to take. He was also fond of tennis, at which game it was the prettiest thing in the world to see him play; his fair skin glowing through a shirt of the finest texture.[60]

He also appeared to have changed his tune when it came to warfare:

> He was affable and gracious; harmed no one; did not covet his neighbour's goods, and was satisfied with his own dominions, having often said to the ambassador, '*Domine Orator*, we want all potentates to content themselves with their own territories; we are satisfied with this island of ours'. He seemed extremely desirous of peace.[61]

Giustinian also left a brief description of Catherine, although he admitted he had seen her 'but seldom'. She was 'not handsome, though she had a very beautiful complexion. She was religious and as virtuous as words could express.'[62]

In July 1518, Wolsey had been given a commission to negotiate with Francis I for a match between Princess Mary and his newborn son. Catherine would have hoped for an alliance with a prince of Spain or the Empire, but she had embraced England and Henry's wishes, so a 'treaty of universal peace' was concluded with the French on 2 October. The terms were proclaimed at St Paul's, after which Henry hosted entertainments at Catherine's old home of Durham House, including twenty-four masked mummers led by Henry and his sister Mary, followed by 'countless dishes of confections and other delicacies', gambling with ducats and dice until supper, concluded by dancing.[63] The betrothal took place three days later, in the Queen's Great Chamber at Greenwich. The tiny princess was dressed in cloth of gold, with a cap of black velvet and many jewels, as she stood in front of her mother to receive a small ring and be blessed. Mary may have only been four months off her third birthday but the prince was only seven months old; and Catherine may have taken heart that the wedding would not take place for at least fourteen years, during which much could change. She and Henry were also taking a risk, as while Mary remained their only heir, in line to inherit the throne, any husband she took would have become King of England, so this match opened up the possibility of the country being united with France under one pair of rulers, effectively conceding England to the French. It may be that they were counting on the hope that Catherine was about to deliver a son.

Celebrations for Mary's marriage were held at Wolsey's York Place, but Catherine retired early, now in an advanced stage of pregnancy, leaving a masked Henry to partner Bessie Blount in the dancing. It was around this time that the unmarried Bessie, then aged around nineteen, conceived the king's child. Catherine may have noticed that she disappeared from court soon afterwards, although she had plenty to occupy herself with her own approaching confinement. Her apartments at Greenwich were ready, with her bed draped in purple tissue edged in ermine. On October 25, Giustinian observed that 'the Queen is near her delivery, which is anxiously looked for'. He hoped she 'would have a son, that the king may be at liberty to embark in any great undertaking'.[64] However, on the night of 9/10 November, Catherine lost her child. 'This night the Queen was delivered of a daughter, to the vexation of as many as knows it,' Giustinian wrote, as 'the entire nation looked for a prince'. The baby was either stillborn or died soon after birth. It must have been a terrible disappointment for the queen. It is likely that this loss was the catalyst for her adopting a hair shirt, worn under the clothing to 'mortify' the flesh as an act of penance.

The following June, Bessie Blount gave birth to a baby boy at St Laurence's Priory, in Blackmore, Essex. The process was overseen by Wolsey, who made all the arrangements with such discretion that none of the ambassadors commented on the child's existence and Catherine herself may not even have known at this stage. That summer, she accompanied Henry to stay in two of their Essex properties, Havering-atte-Bower, where Catherine hosted a banquet for which Henry 'thanked her hartely', then Beaulieu, later called New Hall. Both were conveniently within ten or twelve miles of Blackmore, so Henry could hear news of the baby's arrival and progress, and perhaps even visit on the pretext of hunting. The boy was christened Henry Fitzroy, a name which left no doubt about his paternity. Perhaps the king simply informed Catherine of the child's existence and she decided to accept it, just as her mother had to accept the illegitimate offspring of Ferdinand. If so, it must have been very painful for her that another woman had succeeded in the one task that she so desired to fulfil. She must have learned about the boy at some point before 1525, when he was invested as duke at court and his identity publicly clear. While Henry Fitzroy's birth was a constant reminder of Catherine's failure, it gave the king cause to think. As the months turned into years it became apparent that the queen would not bear another child, but another woman might. The arrival of his son seemed to confirm for Henry that the problem lay with Catherine, not with him.

16

Goldenness
1519–1524

I

On 23 January 1519, a letter arrived at the English court for Henry. Margaret of Savoy had written 'in great trouble and anguish', as it had 'pleased God to take to his mercy her father, the Emperor, who died at the city of Veltz ... after receiving the sacraments'.[1] The death of Maximilian at the age of fifty-nine meant that the most powerful job in Europe was vacant, and with the new kings of France and Spain being younger and less experienced than him, Henry hoped to take the prize. However, the game of international politics was never that simple.

Relations between the new triumvirate of Henry, Francis and Charles were to change greatly over the coming years, but although Catherine followed her husband's lead, her sympathies were always with her nephew in Spain. On 6 February, Charles entreated Wolsey to 'obtain for him Henry VIII's interest towards his election to the Empire',[2] although the Venetian ambassador reported that Charles had already sent 25,000 crowns to Germany to secure the job[3] and it was the opinion of the Pope that it would 'go to the highest bidder'.[4] According to the French ambassador, Francis was 'doing his utmost to prevent' Charles from being elected and 'therefore meant to favour the Duke of Saxony',[5] although he had already secured the backing of four electors for himself.[6] In turn, Henry wrote to Francis on 8 February, promising 'all his favour and power to obtain for him the Imperial crown'.[7] Yet on 22 February, Charles thanked Henry for writing to the Pope in favour of his election.[8] Campeggio suggested that a good way to prevent either Charles or Francis from being elected would be if Henry himself became Emperor.[9] The manoeuvring of Catherine's husband amongst his allies was worthy of Ferdinand. Henry was staying at Penshurst Place with the Duke of Buckingham on 28 June, his twenty-eighth birthday, when Richard Pace brought news that the electors had determined in favour of Charles.

Although Henry had not won the prize, the fact that he was married to the new emperor's aunt put England in a strong position. It could not help but increase Catherine's worth in his eyes, and those of Europe: suddenly the descendents of Isabella and Ferdinand were back at the centre of politics. In 1520, Henry juggled his friendships with Francis and Charles, arranging to meet the new Emperor before departing for France for a rendezvous with the new Valois king. Catherine was delighted at the prospect of meeting Juana's son, the inheritor of the kingdom on whose behalf she had worked for years, the ruler of her homeland. 'Clasping her hands and raising her eyes unto heaven, [she] gave laud unto God ... that she might behold her nephew, saying it was her greatest desire in the world.'[10] Catherine was 'gratified at his success' but there was also the option that Mary's French alliance, conducted 'against the will of the Queen and all the nobles', would be replaced by one with Spain.[11] Although there was a large age gap, Catherine hoped that one day her daughter might marry Charles and join the kingdoms of England and Spain under one crown.

On 21 May, Catherine left Greenwich at Henry's side to travel down to Canterbury, where they were to await Charles' arrival at the Archbishop's Palace. The city was being prepared in honour, with the streets being sanded, the city officials decked out in new gabardines, or cloaks, and the keys to the Westgate being tied with a new ribbon, in advance of being presented to Charles. They were cutting it very fine, with Henry and Catherine due to be in France on the last day of the month, but terrible conditions in the North Sea kept the imperial ships in harbour on the coast of Flanders. On 26 May, the weather finally allowed Charles to sail and his fleet appeared near Hythe, from where they were conducted safely around the coast to Dover by England's Vice Admiral, Sir William

Fitzwilliam, 'with six of the king's shippes well furnished'.[12] Wolsey was already waiting there to greet Charles and Henry followed swiftly on the heels of his chancellor, meeting the emperor 'under the cloth of his estate of the black eagle all splayed on rich cloth of gold'[13] at Dover Castle.

Catherine's meeting with her nephew had to wait until the next morning. She remained in the Archbishop's Palace, as a guest of William Warham, with its fine wooden panelling, marble pillars, gardens and library, of which only an arched doorway remains. On 27 May, Henry and Charles arrived in the city and attended Mass in the cathedral, to celebrate the feast of Pentecost, before processing along a purple carpet into the palace, where they were greeted by twenty-five of the 'handsomest and best apparelled' court ladies and twenty of Catherine's pages dressed in 'gold brocade and crimson satin in chequers'. It was Charles's intent 'specially to see queen of England his aunt', and Catherine was waiting for them at the top of a flight of fifteen marble steps and wept as she greeted her nephew.[14]

She would have seen a tall, thin young man, physically awkward and with a pronounced lower jaw. His face was long and narrow, with an aquiline nose and thick lips, which his later portraits show is clearly a face of Hapsburg descent. In 1520, though, he was only twenty, more like the image painted two or three years before by Bernard von Orley, or an artist in his school. Although his jaw and lips are thick, almost to the point of deformity, his face is clear and open, his chin cleft, his blue eyes narrowed in focus and his brown hair cut in the fashionable bell of the time, under a wide brimmed black hat adorned by a gold medallion in a surround of pearls. The chain of the Order of the Golden Fleece hangs across his fur-adorned shoulders. Other portraits are less flattering, with one anonymous Flemish picture showing him with an open mouth and more rounded nose and chin, while another makes his jaw appear almost dislocated. Henry had hero-worshipped the young man's father, who had been renowned for his beauty; perhaps there was a charm in Charles, or a resemblance to the Trastámara family in Catherine's eyes.

After their initial greetings, Catherine changed into a dress of cloth of gold lined with violet velvet, a headdress of black and gold decorated with jewels, and a string of pearls about her neck, in the centre of which hung a large diamond. Charles also had the opportunity to meet Princess Mary, then the Duchess of Suffolk and the mother of three children, who, but for the quirks of diplomacy six years before, might have been his empress. The Elizabethan chronicler Holinshed adds 'peradventure the sight of the Lady Mary troubled him, whome he had sometime loved, and yet through fortunes evill hap might not have her to wife'. Charles would have been aware that the 'evill hap' was more down to Henry than fortune, but their new relationship meant that was a thing of the past. The two kings were looking forward to forging a friendship that would be at the heart of Europe. It must have been a happy time for Catherine. After four days of festivities, on 31 May Charles bade farewell to his hosts and departed for Sandwich, from where he sailed to Flanders. That same day, Henry and Catherine headed for Dover, where they boarded ship for Calais, arriving at eleven o'clock that night. What followed would be magnificence on an unprecedented scale, known to history as the Field of Cloth of Gold.

II

As she had learned from her mother, Catherine was determined to look the part. She understood that colours, fabrics and jewels were the foundation stone of majesty, the costume by which she decked herself with the symbols of power and authority. Just like her mother, her favourite was gold. An entry in the State Letters and Papers for 1520 gives an idea of the nature and opulence of her wardrobe at this time, in advance of her diplomatic roles. During the months of April and May, a Louis Harpsifield had been paid almost £150 for providing her with two pieces of white satin at over eighty-six yards long, fifty-eight yards of green velvet, seventy-three yards of green Bruges satin, yellow and russet velvet, black velvet, crimson velvet and green cloth of gold. It seemed that Catherine's servants shopped in London's Chepe Street, parallel with the river, its very name deriving from the Old English term for 'market'. Stow's survey of London described it as the centre of the city's wealth, with goldsmiths and merchants occupying houses that could rise as high as five storeys. With their shopfronts filled with luxury goods, these traders attracted custom from the court. In spring 1520, Barker 'of Chepe' supplied the queen with more white satin and his neighbour, Barton 'of Chepe', sold her black sarcenet and green and russet velvet.[15]

Catherine would not have gone to buy these items in person. Overseeing these purchases was the man in charge of her wardrobe, Ellis Hilton, who settled the bills and delegated purchases to other servants and traders. An agent named George Bryggus purchased 14*s* 4*d* worth of crimson velvet for her from 'Colier of Chepe', who also received an order for yellow damask from the Lord Chamberlain for the queen's use. Her servants also shopped further afield. A John Norris in Friday Street supplied linen cloth, Master Smith of Watling Street gave red kersey, and broad grey cloth was bought from an unspecified vendor at Blackwell Hall. New bedding was also bought for Catherine, perhaps in readiness for her departure to France, as on such occasions it was customary for royalty to dismantle and export their own high-status beds. Over seventy-seven yards of blue sarcenet was purchased to make bed curtains, perhaps in anticipation of being embroidered with gold fleur-de-lys.[16] On 10 May, the mercer William Lock had supplied the queen with cloth of silver for escutcheons and arms, red satin and yellow damask for lining her chairs and violent satin for lining a gold valance, all 'paid by me, Elys Hylton'.[17]

Ellis Hilton also made a number of other purchases on behalf of his queen, including green cloth from a Mr Wilkinson in Candlewick Street, to make coats for the her guard; Catherine did not like them, however, and they were given away.[18] Generally, members of the queen's retinue were well catered for, with payments made for their coats and doublets in the Tudor colours of white and green, for an embroiderer named Ebgrave to sew the motif of feathers onto their clothes and for crimson velvet to line their cloaks. Milan bonnets were bought for them from Gerard the capper at 6*s* each; the account includes bucklers, swords, shirts and points, as well as orange-coloured boots at 4*s* 3*d* a pair, spurs at 6*d* a pair, coifs of gold for the queen's ladies at 10*s* each, while eighteen shirts cost 8*s* each to be made.[19]

Catherine's travel arrangements are also recorded in detail for the month, with a Roger Brown being paid 20*s* for taking the stuff of the guard from London to Canterbury, and a man named Parker receiving 53*s* 4*d* for painting the 'close car'. More of her henchmen's 'stuff' travelled by barge to Gravesend at a cost of 5*s*, then on to Canterbury by road at 2*d* per mile, for twenty-six miles. Her clothes and linen were likely to have been transported in the five spruce chests with hanging locks which cost 32*s* 8*d* and her tailor Thomas Kelevytt made garments for the queen's use at a price of £28 3*s* 4*d*. Some of Catherine's items were washed at Dover before she embarked for France, which cost 16*d*, but the carrying of the same items from the ship to her lodgings in Calais cost 14*d*.[20]

As befitted her status, Catherine took a large retinue with her to France. It was headed by Thomas Stanley, Earl of Derby, who was Henry's cousin through their mutual descent from the Wydevilles. As his personal allowance, Derby had six gentlemen, three chaplains, twenty-four servants and twenty horses: his wife Anne also attended among the queen's party of ladies. Catherine had three bishops accompanying her: John Fisher, Bishop of Rochester; Charles Booth, Bishop of Hereford; and Jorge de Athequa, a Spaniard who had come with her to England in 1501, now Bishop of Llandaff. Each of the three had four chaplains, six gentlemen, thirty-four servants and twenty horses. She had four barons: William Blount, Baron Mountjoy, who had been married to Catherine's Spanish lady Agnes de Venegas, who had died before 1515; William Willoughby, Baron Willoughby d'Eresby, the husband since 1516 of Catherine's companion Maria da Salinas; Thomas Burgh, Baron Cobham, future father-in-law of Catherine Parr; and Henry Parker, Baron Morley, future father-in-law of George Boleyn. Each had a retinue of their own of chaplains, gentlemen and servants, as did Catherine's thirty-one knights.

The most senior of Catherine's ladies accompanying her to France was the Duchess of Buckingham, Lady Eleanor Percy, followed in precedence by seven countesses, those of Stafford, Westmorland, Shrewsbury, Devonshire, Derby and Oxford, as well as the Dowager Countess of Oxford, each of whom had seven servants. Among her sixteen baronesses were Elizabeth, Lady Fitzwalter, whom Henry had sent away from court after her interference in the affairs of her sister Anne, Lady Hastings, who was also present; Anne, Lady Grey; Elizabeth, wife of Sir Arthur Plantagenet, an illegitimate son of Edward IV; Lady Elizabeth Boleyn, Henry's future mother-in-law; and the wives of the barons in her company. Additionally, Catherine was served by eighteen knight's wives, including Lady Compton, Lady Guildford and Lady

Parr and twenty-five gentlewomen, among whom were Mistress Carew, Mistress Parker, Mountjoy's new wife Alice and Mary Boleyn, Mistress Carey. She had three chamberers, who were each entitled to take a servant, fifty yeomen of the chamber, with twenty servants between them and sixty people to take care of her horses.

The king's equally extensive retinue included Thomas Wolsey and Thomas Boleyn, who had masterminded the event, plus the Duke of Buckingham, ten earls, four bishops, twenty-one barons, three Knights of the Garter, and a hundred knights including his court favourites Sir William Compton, Sir Nicholas Carew, Sir Francis Bryan along with Sir Thomas More. There were ten chaplains, two secretaries, two clerks of the signet, two clerks of the privy seal, twelve sergeants-at-arms, two hundred yeomen of the guard, seventy servants of the king's chamber with one hundred and fifty others at their disposal, two hundred and sixty-six members of the king's household, assisted by a further two hundred and six, with two hundred and five in the stable and armoury, and an unspecified number of minstrels and trumpeters. These figures give some idea of the vast scale of the operation, as well as the minimum numbers thought necessary to maintain the king's dignity on such an occasion. It must have made a splendid sight, this long train of people, horses and wagons, progressing slowly through the French countryside, glittering with jewels.

The well-known image in the Royal Collection of Henry arriving at the Field of Cloth of Gold was painted in around 1545. It conveys a sense of the transformation that had taken place in a field outside the little French town of Guines and the expense that had gone into creating what was, in effect, a temporary city. One Italian observer thought that even Leonardo da Vinci, who had died the previous year, could not have improved upon it.[21] The painting of 1545 simultaneously contains the highlights of the visit, showing Henry's entry surrounded by his retinue, with Calais, the Channel and a distant England behind; there is also a panoply of tents set up in camps, some white, some decorated, some gold, fountains flowing with wine, a huge temporary palace and glimpses of Henry and Francis at key moments: wrestling, jousting and feasting. It was the zenith of both their reigns. Henry features as the central figure, but Catherine is only glimpsed in symbolic form. She was definitely present to observe the joust, but her portrait is so small that no detail can be identified; she may also be among the women dining in one of the small tents. A clear choice has been made not to place her among the initial procession, alongside the king and Thomas Wolsey. It is a stark reminder that by the time the picture was painted Catherine had been edited out of Henry's life.

The Field of Cloth of Gold, as it came to be known, must have been dazzling to behold. Its centrepiece was a temporary palace, built in three months by 600 English and Flemish workers, with foundations of stone and a framework of timber imported from the Netherlands. The windows were made of real glass but the walls and roof were of painted canvas. It was described by chronicler Hall as 'the most noble and royal lodging before sene', in the shape of a 'quadrant' 328 feet long. Before the entrance gate, on a green, stood a fountain of gilt and fine gold, decorated with antique work, topped by a figure of Bacchus and running with red and white wine. On the other side of the gate stood a pillar wrapped in gold, decorated by the faces of lions and topped with a sculpture of Cupid, with his bow and arrows ready 'to stryke the young people to love'. The arched entrance gate 'of great and mighty masonry' included windows depicting men of war, above statues of Hercules and Alexander richly lined with gold.[22]

The gate led into a courtyard with bay windows on every side. From there, a range of doors marked the extent of the chambers within, which were 'long and large and well proportioned, to receive light and air', with white floors and roofs made of silk. They were decorated with rich cloths of silver, knit and fret with cuts and braids, 'like bullions of fine burned gold' with roses set in lozenge shapes, so that 'no living creature might but joy in the beholding thereof'. Each room was hung with cloth of gold, tissue and rich embroidery, with chairs covered in the same fabrics, decorated with golden pommels and great cushions from Turkey. Inside the palace was a chapel with two closets, decorated in cloth of gold and tissue with roses, and an altar with gold candlesticks, three rich crosses and all the requirements for Catholic ceremony, in gold and pearls. The first closet was for the use of the king, with a crucifix, an image of the Trinity, an image of the Virgin Mary, two gold candlesticks and twelve other images of gold and precious stones on the altar. The second was for Catherine, with an altar 'so richly apparelled that there lacked neither pearls nor stones of riches', with twelve great images of gold on the altar.[23] These exquisite closets, glittering with gold and gems, serve as a reminder of the intense Catholic faith and ritual of the king and queen and its centrality to pre-Reformation life.

The royal party was lodged in four suites inside the palace, one each for Henry, Catherine, Mary, Duchess of Suffolk, and Thomas Wolsey. There were also a number of administrative offices, for the Lord Chamberlain, the Lord Steward, Lord Treasurer of the Household, the Controller and office of the green cloth, wardrobes, jewel house and the offices of service, including the ewery, confectionary, pantry, cellar, waffry, saucer, buttery, spicery, pitcher house, larder, poultry and all other offices for the craft of 'viands' such as ovens, chimneys and ranges.[24] Other offices and members of the court were lodged in a sea of tents sprawling out behind the palace. Surviving plans in the British Library depict a variety of complex constructions, echoing the layout of Tudor palaces, with a series of connected galleries leading to a number of private apartments, made up of large and small tents subdivided with curtains. Dressed in red and blue cloth, or green and white, they are fringed with mottoes, sewn and topped with gold, with ridgeboards on the roof bearing golden fleur-de-lys and Tudor roses. The tent poles are topped with heraldic beasts, holding standards with crowns, royal arms and other heraldic devices.[25] In total, tents outside the palace and small town of Guines provided lodgings for 820 people, 'which was a goodly sighte'.[26]

While Henry and Catherine were establishing themselves in their camp outside Guines, Francis I and his wife, Queen Claude, were settling into their royal lodgings in nearby Ardres. The suave, sophisticated Francis, with his eye for fashion and the ladies, was twenty-five to Henry's twenty-eight. He had a 'very tall stature and presence … a regal majesty … on account of his virtues, valour, great deeds and high merit, as were once Alexander, Pompey and others'.[27] Edward Hall described him as 'a goodly prince, stately of countenance, merry of chere, brown coloured, great eyes, high nosed, big lipped, fair breasted and shoulders, small legs and long feet'.[28] A Welshman in Henry's household who accompanied him to France in 1520, Ellis Griffiths, noted that Francis was six feet tall, almost as tall as the king of England, and

> his head was rightly proportioned for his height, the nape of his neck unusually broad, his hair brown, smooth and neatly combed, his beard of three months' growth darker in colour, his nose long, his eyes hazel and bloodshot and his complexion the colour of watery milk. He had muscular buttocks and thighs, but the legs below the knees were thin and bandy, while his feet were long, slender and completely flat. He had an agreeable voice and, in conversation, an animated expression, marred only by the unfortunate habit of continually rolling his eyes upwards.[29]

Francis was a lot like Henry in many ways, combining intellect with a love of sport and action. He loved hawking, riding and mock battles, fighting duels with wild boar and hunting. Certainly they admired each other with a mixture of love and loathing, and engaged in rivalry that was deeper than the superficial sparring or wrestling suggested. Each was determined not to be outshone by the other, making for an uneasy mood of tense camaraderie at Guines that summer.

His wife, counterpart of the thirty-five-year-old Catherine, was Claude, daughter of the old king, Louis XII, once the stepdaughter of Mary Tudor and also Francis's cousin. She was only twenty, very short, and suffered from scoliosis, but she had already borne four children, three of whom were still living and two of which were boys. That June, she was heavily pregnant with a fifth, a daughter, who would arrive on 10 August. But there was another woman waiting to emerge from the shadows behind the unimposing Claude. Among her retinue of ladies was Anne, the younger daughter of Sir Thomas Boleyn, who was a couple of years younger than the queen and may have acted as her translator. Dark-haired, elegant and well educated, Anne had been abroad since 1513, acquiring a European polish at the court of Margaret of Savoy at Malines before coming to France for Mary's marriage to Louis, after which she had stayed on to serve Claude. If Catherine had previously seen the Boleyn's younger daughter as a child, this would have been at least seven years ago and Anne was now a grown woman. The Field of Cloth of Gold also provided an opportunity for Anne to be reunited with her mother, Elizabeth Boleyn, and sister, Mary Carey, who had been married earlier that year to Privy Chamberer William Carey. The queen probably paid little attention to two more of the many attractive young ladies present at the festivities, but the Boleyn girls would prove impossible to avoid in the years to come.

Catherine and Claude were not present at the initial encounters between the two kings, who met and banqueted in a tent between the two camps. Hall gives us a glimpse of Henry as 'the moost goodliest Prince that ever reigned over the Realm of England', dressed in cloth of silver of damask, ribbed with cloth of gold, 'marvellous to behold' and riding a horse likewise trapped in gold. The queens finally met on 1 June, at a field that was decorated with a pageant of two trees. Catherine and Claude saluted each other 'right honourably' and took their places on a stage to watch the men engage in a tournament 'so valiantly that the beholders had great joy'.[30] The women sat in a 'glazed gallery, hung with tapestry and talked about the tourney' and many in their company were obliged to use the services of translators, as they could not understand each other. More days of entertainments continued, with feats of strength and skill including wrestling, fighting with weapons, archery and darts presided over by the queens, with Claude presenting Henry with his prizes and Catherine doing the same for Francis, interspersed with talks and banquets. On 13 June, a treaty was ratified for the marriage of the dauphin to three-year-old Princess Mary, left behind at Richmond under the care of Margaret Pole. This cannot have been Catherine's first choice, as she was still hoping for a Spanish match for her daughter.

While Henry dined with Claude, Catherine and Mary, Duchess of Suffolk, received Francis on 17 June, 'with all honour that was according'. On display, there was a 'multitude' of silver and gold plates and vessels, and the finest ingredients had been sourced from local 'forests, parks, field, salt sea, rivers, moats and ponds', for which men were well rewarded for finding great delicacies.[31] When the plates were cleared away, masked dancers performed and women acted as mummers. A provisional menu survives for the occasion and, although it does not represent the final order of service, it gives a fair idea of the kinds of dishes that were consumed that evening. The first of three courses contained boiled capon, cygnets, carpet of venison, pike, heron and hart, followed by pear pies, custard, cream and fruit. Secondly, kid, capon, sturgeon, peacock, pigeons, quails and baked venison prefaced similar sweet dishes, before a final course introduced storks, pheasants, egrets, chickens, gull, haggis, bream and green apples, followed by oranges, fruit, creamy towers and a cold banquet.[32]

Estimations in advance for the consumption of the king and queen in France had allowed for £420 worth of wheat, £770 of wine, £27 of sweet wine, £560 of beer, £24 for Hippocras wine, £624 for 340 pieces of beef, £33 for four hogs, £6 for mutton, £200 for veal, £300 for salt and freshwater fish, £440 for spices, £1,300 for all kinds of poultry, £300 for table linen and cloths, £200 for wax, over £26 for white lights, £300 for pewter vessels, £200 for braising pans, turning spits and other essentials, and £40 for rushes. Twenty cooks were to be hired at the fee of 20*d* a day, twelve pastillers at the same salary, twelve brewers and twelve bakers, both at a daily rate of 8*d* again.[33]

In comparison, the expenses paid after the event proved a lot more detailed. Among some of the most evocative entries were 20*s* 10*d* paid to Thomas Tayllor for cream for the king's cakes, John Rogers received 5*s* for two hundred pippins (apples), John Busshe was paid 25*s* for strawberries and junkets, a Mr Dosson received 12*d* for making a lock and key for the spicery door, Antony Carleton carried two loads of the queen's wardrobe from Guines to Calais for a fee of 5*s* 4*d*, though these were not all of Catherine's clothes, as a Jasper Cope was paid 8*s* for carrying twice the amount from Guines to the camp. 2*s* was paid for a casket for wafers and 12*s* for two pairs of wafer irons, 9*s* 1*d* was paid for fourteen sticks of sugar candy, 6*s* went to a Margery Bennett for fanning and washing hempseed and 14*d* to Robert Constantin for supplying line and cord to hang the quails' cages.[34]

On 23 June, a chapel was erected on the field which had witnessed the tournaments, where Wolsey sang High Mass and issued an indulgence, a pardon for any sins, to all present, including both sets of kings and queens. Part way through, a huge artificial dragon appeared in the sky from the direction of Ardres, four fathoms long and full of fire, which scared many of those assembled. It passed over the chapel 'as fast as a footman can go',[35] and while some thought it a comet or a monster, it was part of the festivities, either as some huge firework or balloon, recorded for prosperity in the corner of the 1545 painting. Following this, Catherine, Claude and Mary, Duchess of Suffolk, dined together before retiring for the night, when guns were fired to mark the vigil of St John the Baptist.[36]

On 24 June, Henry and Francis formally concluded the festivities with the exchange of gifts: a collar of diamonds for the French king and a bracelet of great price for England. Catherine gave a gift of horses to Claude, who responded with the gift of a cloth of gold litter and mules. It had been a great diplomatic success. As remarked by Martin du Bellai, the spectators believed they had witnessed 'an amity so entire that nothing could ever alter it'.[37] However, they were mistaken. Henry and Catherine were already riding back into the arms of Francis's enemy, the emperor. Consequently, the Field of Cloth of Gold has been referred to by one historian as 'the most portentous deception on record'.[38]

On 10 July, after resting at Calais, Catherine and Henry took a fraction of their entourage to Gravelines, on the French coast, just to the east, over the border into Flanders. There, Charles greeted them, with 'such semblant of love',[39] along with his aunt Margaret of Savoy, whom Catherine had not seen since her childhood when Margaret had been married to her brother John. Returning with the English king and queen to Calais, Charles and Margaret were lodged at the Hall of the Staple, in anticipation of the completion of an eighty-foot banqueting house built using the masts of ships. Strong winds prevented it from being completed, though, so the banquets and masques were relocated into the Chequer and the Staple. An agreement was reached that both powers were 'to have the same enemies and the same friends' and neither would enter a treaty without the knowledge and consent of the other. On 14 July, Catherine bid farewell to her family before boarding ship and setting sail again for England.

III

Catherine returned from France to find Princess Mary thriving and healthy. Margaret Pole told her of the little girl's beautiful playing on the virginals to impress a group of French visitors at Richmond Palace, where the guests were amply entertained with four gallons of Hippocras, wafers and fruit, at a cost of 35*s* 3*d*, and departed full of praise for the little princess. Other recent payments had been made to individuals for contributing to Mary's larder, for bringing quails and rabbits, chickens and a pig, puddings and bread, strawberries and cherries to supplement her larders. The household accounts also reveal that Mary's establishment contained six gentlemen and nine valets, six grooms of the chamber and twelve grooms of the household, as well as the ladies charged with her daily care.[40]

Mindful of her daughter's intended future, Catherine wrote to Queen Claude after their meeting at Guines, in response to her 'good and affectionate letters'. She had been 'very greatly consoled' to hear the 'good news, health, estate and prosperity in [which is my] very dear and most beloved good son, and yours, the dauphin'. She expressed the 'good love, friendship and fraternal intelligence and alliance which is now between the two kings our husbands and their kingdoms, which I hold inseparable and pray God that it may continue'.[41] However, the French betrothal proved even shorter than Catherine may have anticipated, being broken the following January in favour of Mary's betrothal to Emperor Charles. As Henry explained to Bishop Cuthbert Tunstall, then on a diplomatic visit to attend the Diet at Worms, 'our daughter will be of age before the French king's, and will be a more advantageous match than the other, by possibility of succession'.[42] In opening imperial negotiations, Henry was mindful of his daughter's worth: 'It is to be considered that she is now our sole heir, and may succeed to the crown; so that we ought rather to receive from the Emperor as large a sum as we should give with her if she were not our heir.' However, the king was still hopeful that Catherine would conceive again, two years and two months after her last delivery. Henry specified that 'if we have a male heir hereafter', he was willing to give Mary as great a dowry as he had to his sister.[43]

On Valentine's Day 1521, the six-year-old princess was given a brooch of gold and jewels bearing her fiancé's name, which was noted by the Imperial Ambassadors and reported back to Charles, along with Mary's 'beauty and charms'.[44] She also performed a dance, twirling 'so prettily that no woman in the world could do better ... then she played two or three songs on the spinet' with the 'grace and skill ... and self-command' that 'a woman of twenty might wish for'.[45] The considerable age gap meant that they would be unable to wed for at least eight years, so Catherine set out equipping her daughter with the skills she would need for her future life as Holy Roman Empress, ensuring that she learned to dance and sing as well as the more scholarly pursuits she had followed in her own childhood.

The following May, Mary had a chance to meet her fiancé when Charles visited England again. He arrived at Dover on the afternoon of 27 May and Henry, who had been awaiting him at Canterbury, went to greet him and conduct him to London via Sittingbourne, Rochester and Gravesend. From there, on 2 June, they took a barge to Greenwich, arriving at around 6 p.m.[46] At the entrance to the great hall, Charles was reunited with Catherine and Princess Mary, expressing 'great joy' to see the pair of them, especially the princess. He was lodged in Henry's apartments by the river, which were so richly hung with tapestries that the visitors marvelled at them. Jousting, feasting and disguisings followed, in which a masked Henry was among those who 'toke ladies and daunsed', and rode in the lists among those dressed in gold and silver, with plumes on their heads. Catherine and Charles stood in the gallery to watch as Henry broke the lances of the challengers clothed in russet velvet.[47]

From Greenwich, the party headed towards London. Just outside the city they encountered a rich tent made of cloth of gold, where Sir Thomas More made an 'eloquent oration' on the love between the two princes 'and what a comfort it was to their subjects to see them in such amity'.[48] A series of nine pageants followed, full of historical, mythical and allegorical symbolism for the alliance, with Hercules and Samson guarding London Bridge before a castle painted to look like black-and-white marble.[49] Beyond it was Jason and his golden fleece, beside a fiery dragon and Medea with two bulls. At the Conduit in Gracechurch Street sat actors representing Henry and Charles, the former being handed the sword of triumphant victory by Charlemagne, who then gave Charles the sword of justice. Where Leadenhall met Bishopsgate, a huge pageant of eighty feet by thirty-eight featured John of Gaunt, from whom Henry, Catherine and Charles were all descended, sitting in a tree which featured them on its branches. At the Conduit in Cornhill, Catherine and the party were met by a representation of King Arthur, a solemn moment for the queen, before they passed into a beautiful arbour of roses, lilies and other flowers, birds and beasts.

After visiting Westminster Palace, where they saw Henry VII's chapel, including the tombs of Henry's parents, they travelled on to the Brandons' home at Southwark, then Richmond Palace, then had 'grete chere' at Wolsey's residence at Hampton Court before going on to Windsor, where they passed nine days, between 11 and 20 June. On a Sunday night they assembled to watch a pageant in the great hall, featuring a 'proud horse which would not be tamed nor bridled'[50] representing Francis I, until the arrival of prudence and policy, force and puissance (power). Catherine would have been a participant in the hunting and disguising, even perhaps watching Henry and Charles play tennis, but the council chamber doors were closed upon her while the two men discussed business, which would result in the Treaty of Windsor. However, the queen was delighted at its outcome, as it committed Charles to marry Mary within eight years and that once she had reached her twelfth birthday, in 1528, the emperor, who would then be twenty-eight, would send a proxy to London for the first formal wedding ceremony. Wolsey sealed the deal with his authority as a papal legate by adding the condition that if either man broke it they would automatically be excommunicated. Charles sailed from Southampton on 7 July, having spent six weeks in England.

When Mary was seven, Catherine invited the Spanish humanist scholar Juan Luis Vives to England to act as tutor to the princess, and commissioned him to write *The Education of a Christian Woman,* a groundbreaking book about female learning. His dedication to her read:

> I dedicate to you this book, Noble Queen, like a painter who designed your portrait; in the canvas you would find an image of your body, in my book you will encounter a likeness of your soul. As a young girl, a spouse, a widow and now a wife, for many years to come, as I hope and pray, you have left to all women in every way of life a magnificent example.
>
> I know you would prefer to have feminine virtue praised, rather than yourself. Difficult as it is, I will try to obey you in this respect and avoid mentioning your name in every page. Let it be known however that everything I praise in this book is an eulogy of my queen.[51]

Vives was then thirty and had been born in Valencia, in Spain, but had left after his family were executed by the Inquisition as Jews who pretended to convert to Christianity. A friend of Erasmus, who had rediscovered some of his enthusiasm for Henry VIII's kingship, Vives was inspired by his friend to dedicate his 1522 commentary on Augustine's *De Civitate Dei* to the English king. It was Erasmus, too, who praised Vives to Thomas More as early as 1520 for his 'elegant scholarship',[52] but a student in Paris, Nicholas Daryngton, also praised Vives in 1522 as 'no mean scholar' and attended his classes on cosmography.[53] More recently he has been considered the father of psychology.

When Vives arrived in England, he was lodged at Christ Church College, Oxford, where he lectured in philosophy and was made Doctor of Law while composing his work for Catherine. He had some advanced ideas about the nature of intelligence and learning, believing that environment, health and well-being contributed to the ability to absorb and apply knowledge, centuries before Maslow framed his hierarchy of needs. He compared the feeding of the mind to the feeding of the body, nourishing both for purpose and wrote that the personality of the teacher, choice of books and sensory experience of the classroom in the early years mattered greatly. He also argued that the state had a responsibility to provide training for unskilled workers and financial relief for the poor. This is perhaps what attracted Catherine to his work, rather than his views on the ability and proper sphere of women.

By 1524, when the work was complete, six years had elapsed since the queen's last pregnancy and she was on the verge of the menopause, so her commission to Vives illustrates the seriousness with which she was considering Mary as Henry's sole heir, as a future queen of England. A woman had never previously inherited the English throne and ruled alone in her own right, but Catherine's mother had proved it was not just possible but desirable, uniting a troubled country, making it strong and pioneering in exploration and religion. All the contemporary stereotypes of weak, unlearned, unwarlike women had been exploded by Isabella, who had educated her daughters in the same model. Yet Vives had questions about the exercise of female authority over men, writing, 'I give no license to a woman to be a teacher, nor to have authority of a man, but to be silent.' He followed the biblical line of advocating female silence and dismissed the need for Mary to learn rhetoric and oratory. If Mary was to become queen, he believed, she would rely on her male counsellors who would explain things simply to her 'as women may yet be informed by a few words'. Instead, he insisted the woman's role was to wage war on vices and advocate moral excellence and religious devotion, peddling the traditional notion of woman-as-Eve, leading man astray.

It seems a strange paradox for the daughter of Catherine of Aragon, the victor of Flodden, the granddaughter of Isabella of Castile who had admired Joan of Arc, to be asked the question by Vives, 'What should a maid do with armour?' and to hear that some books were forbidden. A surviving fragment in the State Letters and Papers for the end of May 1525 sets out a dialogue on the question of 'whether the mother of a king, being a woman, [was] qualified to act as a regent'. The identity and gender of the writer are unknown, although it is signed 'Hanybal', but the conclusion drawn is a positive one, justifying 'the fitness of women to rule by the instance of the dame De Beaujeau, sister of Charles VIII and Elizabeth [Isabella] of Spain, mother of our Queen Catherine'.[54] Vives' work also highlights the difference in upbringing for Mary, who would crave a husband, and her half-sister Elizabeth, not a pupil of Vives, who would reject marriage. Catherine would also give her approval to Vives' other book, *The Institute of a Christian Marriage*, and when her own marriage was challenged she would summon him for assistance.

17

A Queen's Identity 1521–1525

I

The early 1520s raised key questions about Catherine's identity, striking at the very heart of her nationality, purpose and faith. European perceptions of Spaniards in the 1520s varied widely, with poets and chroniclers praising them for their bravery and loyalty, while Antoine de Lusy saw another side and described them as 'presumptuous and vainglorious'.[1] The Venetian Gasparo Contarini, who travelled in Spain at this time, found them to have a 'melancholy disposition' which led them to be reserved and prudent, while others saw a tinge of drama and cruelty in the Spanish administration of justice.[2] In 1530, Cornelius Agrippa described Catherine's people as being cheerful, effective speakers, well dressed, pleasant towards strangers, cultivated yet boastful. In addition, he thought that they were impatient in love. Baldassare Castiglione's 1528 *Book of the Courtier* saw more subtle shades behind the stereotypes, admitting that, while there were some arrogant Spaniards, 'those who are highly esteemed are, for the most part, extremely modest' and 'instinctively witty'.[3] A decade later, the Venetian ambassador in Spain portrayed its people as 'patient in adversity, sober and restrained in eating and drinking and careful in their dress and appearance' while also being rather avaricious.[4]

Just how far was Catherine defined by her Spanishness? It was a 'difference' perceived by others, especially in her early years in England, when her clothing was unusual and she had not yet mastered the English tongue. Yet it was also a state of mind that had formed her character and her values, and predetermined her reactions. No doubt accounts of national character tell us just as much about the person doing the observing, and will typically divide along patriotic lines, but amid this mixed bag, something of Catherine's character emerges. At court with her husband and ladies, dancing, hunting and playing, she could certainly be cheerful, even high-spirited and witty in her youth. She understood from her parents the importance of being well dressed and employing drama to good effect to create a sense of majesty, and there was no doubting her loyalty and faith. As the 1520s progressed, her world began to change in a number of ways, firstly on a religious and cultural level as the new learning spread through Europe – although as a Christian queen she would have risen to this challenge, seeing it as her own crusade against heresy, as her parents had against the Jews and Muslims. More damaging for her was the personal change in her husband and their marriage, which drew out her melancholy and stubborn aspects as she tried to cling to her position and resist change, refusing to admit that she had lost in the marital stakes and been ousted from her position.

Worrying news came from Spain in the summer of 1521: the Navarrese were attempting to reclaim their country, which Ferdinand had annexed to Castile nine years before. A surprise attack mounted by Henry II of Navarre, with troops of around 12,000 men, had initially been successful, taking a garrison at Pamplona. The young Ignatius Loyola was wounded here, and the incident proved to be the catalyst for his conversion; thirteen years later he would found the Society of Jesus, also known as the Jesuits. The Spanish retaliated against the Navarrese in the Battle of Noáin, and the territory was decisively recaptured. That September, with the support of Francis I, Henry II attempted to retake other areas in the north and Navarre's access to the Atlantic. Catherine and Henry backed Charles's Castilian interest, and Catherine herself wrote in support of their efforts. Her words do not survive but a response does from the Duke of Alva in Vitoria on 28 December. He 'kissed her hands' for her letter and was 'much obliged by what she says concerning the dead in this her house', and that she had 'shown herself such a true Castilian'. Alva paraphrased some of the contents of Catherine's letter, saying that she 'rejoiced at what the grandees and knights have done in defence of the crown', winning two battles and bringing back the allegiance of two kingdoms.[5] A number of foreigners in her service were also granted letters of denization, obtaining certain rights as a resident, including her Spanish sewer Francis Philippo in February[6] and her Italian physician Balthasar de Guercis in March.[7] Catherine might have been resident in England for twenty years, and its queen for twelve, but she had not forgotten her original loyalties and her status as a foreigner. Her Spanishness was not just geographical, cultural and political, it was also a state of mind that manifested itself in her loyalty, the depths of her commitment, passion, drive, conviction and faith.

Catherine was deeply wedded to the old ways of worship, of sacraments, pilgrimages, shrines and relics. As queen, she was particularly devoted to the cult of the Virgin Mary, which was strong as ever in Spain even as it was on the verge of crumbling in England. In the late Middle Ages, Spanish pilgrimage sites like Santiago de Compostela had made the country more popular with religious visitors than Rome itself.[8] Robert Langton, Archdeacon of Salisbury, visited shortly before 1522, when he published his account, stating that if pilgrims 'wished to behold holy relics, whatever is venerated in all Europe will appear before your eyes'.[9] In Oviedo, he saw Christ's swaddling clothes, his tunic, manna from the desert, bread from the last supper, fish left over from feeding the five thousand, the apostle's fishing baskets and John the Baptist's honeycomb.[10] Italian visitors in 1538 listed a number of different pilgrim routes through the country incorporating visits to Granada, Zaragoza, Guadalupe, Cadiz, Jaén, Valencia, Burgos and Finisterre, as well as Santiago itself, where the head of St James was on display every morning, accompanied by descriptions in Spanish, French and Italian. As late as 1599, 600 pilgrims were being fed daily at the Marian Shrine of Montserrat, and 4,000 on feast day.[11] As the Protestant Reformation took hold in northern Europe, Spain remained one of the few countries where it was possible to worship in the old ways and thus continued to attract rising numbers of foreign pilgrims as well as its own citizens.[12]

In the 1520s, England too was a country bursting with relics. Catherine had kissed them at Canterbury, Walsingham, Westminster and St Paul's, and followed Elizabeth of York's example of going into labour clutching the birthing girdle of the Virgin Mary. And these relics were accessible to the people in small parish churches, not just in the large cathedrals and monasteries. In Shelford visitors might see phials of Mary's milk and part of her churching candle, in Kaldham the finger bone of St Stephen was on display, in Burton-on-Trent pilgrims might see the staff of St Modwena, and part of the shirt of St Thomas could be found at Derby. Clothing, girdles, combs, hair, bones and bodily fluids could be found housed all around the country as an essential component of pre-Reformation Catholicism, accessible, powerful and defining. Catherine was an important religious leader in England, teaching by example. Among the artefacts that accompanied her on her travels were pictures of Mary and her mother, St Anne, and St Elizabeth, who must have had particular resonance for Catherine, as she had miraculously conceived and given birth to a child even after the onset of her menopause. As late as 1538, while shrines across the country were being dissolved, 600 visitors a day were flocking to offer their prayers to the Virgin at St Asaph in Flintshire.

In the early 1520s, Henry stood by his wife in her unshakeable Catholicism. Like Ferdinand and Isabella, they prayed together and took a stand against heresy together. After the impact of his ninety-five theses, Martin Luther composed a further attack upon the papacy and the sale of indulgences, for which he was excommunicated. He was summoned to appear before the Diet of Worms in April 1521, presided over by Catherine's nephew Charles, to answer charges of heresy. Charles intended to treat them severely: just a few years later he wrote that he was 'bitterly annoyed' at the conduct of Luther's followers and intended to 'exterminate' them.[13] On the verge of being condemned for owning certain books and refusing to recant of his beliefs, Luther fled under the protection of Frederick III to Wartburg Castle in Eisenach. In his absence he was declared an outlaw, his books were banned, a warrant was issued for his arrest and his potential murder was legalised.

Not to be outdone, Henry reacted by writing his own rebuttal in his *Defence of the Seven Sacraments*, which called for Catholics to reject such heretical views:

> Do not listen to the Insults and Detractions against the Vicar of Christ which the Fury of the little Monk spews up against the Pope; nor contaminate Breasts sacred to Christ with impious Heresies, for if one sews these he has no Charity, swells with vain Glory, loses his Reason, and burns with Envy. Finally with what Feelings they would stand together against the Turks, against the Saracens, against anything Infidel anywhere, with the same Feelings they should stand together against this one little Monk weak in Strength, but in Temper more harmful than all Turks, all Saracens, all Infidels anywhere.

John Foxe later wrote that although the book carried the king's name, 'yet it was another that administered the motion, another that framed the style'. Luther himself objected to the book on the grounds that it was not written by Henry, blaming Wolsey for its existence. It is possible that Wolsey, More or even John Fisher contributed to the final work, although as early as 1517 Henry had been composing his thoughts before sharing them with his advisers. With her education and intelligence, it is difficult to believe he did not discuss the matter with Catherine. In 1521, Pope Leo X awarded Henry the title of Fidei Defensor, or Defender of the Faith. Wolsey presented the king with the papal bull, with a speech drawing on the observations of John Clerk, Henry's ambassador to Rome, who had initially presented Leo with the work. It had been 'beautiful to hear with what exultation the Pope and Cardinals broke out in praise of Henry, declaring that no one could have composed a better antidote to the poison of heresy'. With 'great eloquence', Henry had 'completely refuted Luther by reason, Scripture and the authority of the fathers … and shown an example to Christian princes'.[14] To make the point at home, Luther's works were publicly burned at St Paul's Cross, London, Oxford and Cambridge.

Catherine was also seen as being an influential figure who might influence her husband and her people. The new Pope, Adrian VI, wrote to her directly in 1523, shortly before the fall of Rhodes, to invoke in her the spirit of her parents:

> All the world knows the zeal of the late King and Queen Catholic [Ferdinand and Isabella] in behalf of the Catholic faith, whose

> footsteps Katharine [*sic*] has followed. Is writing to the King her husband touching the oppression of Christendom by the loss of Rhodes. Begs she will give effect to his exhortations like a good Catholic, and induce him to peace, or at least some good truce, by means of which the power of the Turk may be repressed.[15] Recommends public prayers and processions in England, on account of the sins of Christendom. Henry should act up to his title of Defender of the Faith against the present dangers, which are of more consequence than the schism, which he has almost extinguished.[16]

And there were indeed 'present dangers' in England. Groups of heretics flourished at the Inns of Court, including More's son-in-law William Roper, who was persuaded out of his new beliefs, but others continued to meet at the White Horse Tavern in Cambridge, including Robert Barnes and William Tyndale. In 1523, Tyndale's controversial views got him into trouble when he debated Lutheran teaching with local Gloucestershire clergy and translated a tract by Erasmus arguing for a personal and direct relationship between man and God. Summoned to appear before the bishop's court, he followed Luther's example and fled, seeking shelter with Cuthbert Tunstall, Bishop of London, who rejected his proposal to translate the Bible into English. The following year, Tyndale set sail for Germany. Heresy trials led by Wolsey in 1526 and 1529 would stifle the new Lutherans in England. Robert Barnes was charged with twenty-five counts of heresy based on a sermon he preached on Christmas Eve in St Edward's Church, Cambridge. He recanted and was arrested, but escaped and sailed to Antwerp, as did John Frith who was imprisoned for owning heretical books. Also in Wolsey's sights was Thomas Bilney, who had preached against pilgrimage and the veneration of saints and relics; he was imprisoned in the Tower until he recanted and was released.

As early as 1521, steps were also being taken to reform abuses in the Church by closing corrupt or superfluous religious institutions. One of the first to go was Higham Nunnery, which had originally contained sixteen nuns but now held just three; the last prioress, Anchoreta Ungothorpe, had died that year. Agnes Swayne, Elizabeth Penney and Godliff Laurence remained, and 'the last two were convicted of gross immorality by several witnesses'.

The nuns resigned and the properties went to St John's College, Cambridge, all confirmed by a papal bull. On 3 March 1522, at Windsor, William Moleyns led an inquisition to expose the true nature of the Benedictine nunnery of St Margaret at Bromehall, with similar results. The prioress, Joan Rawlyns, had resigned and two other nuns had left because it had become a 'profane place'. As a result it was dissolved and all its possessions reverted to the king.[17] Early in 1525 more minor establishments had been dismantled, with Wolsey being forced to defend the actions of his agents. Pensions were issued in March to Katherine Welles, late prioress of Littlemore; John Bigge, lately in charge of Daventry; William Yong and William Benson of Wallingford; Peter Stace of Tonbridge; John Blakemore; and John Clemond of Lessonnes.[18] But although many of these were closed as the result of corruption, there was not yet a wider ideology behind it. It was an economic decision to dissolve a number of smaller houses and absorb their wealth in order that Wolsey could found Cardinal College, Oxford, now known as Christ Church College. The cardinal knew he had his critics, but he took pains to assure Henry that all was by the book, and for the king's glory:

> Though 'some folks, which be always more prone to speak evil', may have informed the King otherwise, Wolsey has taken no steps in the suppression of the monasteries without fully satisfying those who had right or interest in the same. In the foundation of his colleges, intended for the King's honor, the advancement of learning, and the weal of his soul, he will be sorry to acquire anything ex rapinas [by violence].[19]

Catherine would have approved of the closure of a religious institution that had lost its way, but she had no idea how this process would escalate in the coming years and sweep away the very foundations of her faith. She may have had some doubts, or even clear objections, to the location of Wolsey's new college, which was to stand on the very spot of St Frideswide's shrine,[20] where Catherine had so recently prayed and asked for assistance. Did the king and queen discuss this move? Did Catherine voice her displeasure, or did she support her husband's wishes? For the time being, Henry and Catherine believed they had made England a safe haven from the spread of northern European heresies, but their success was only a temporary measure. The centuries-old monasteries of England would fall, one by one, and Tyndale, Barnes, Frith and Bilney were all to become influential martyrs for the Protestant cause.

II

Around the same time that Navarre was struggling with Castile, Catherine may have become aware that Henry was having an affair. In the recent lists, while his wife looked on from the gallery, the king's old motto of Sir Loyal Heart and his devices of arrow sheafs, pomegranates and Castilian castles had been replaced by embroidery bearing the legend 'she hath wounded my heart'. Did Catherine notice this as Henry rode past? If not, surely court gossip must have brought it to her ears. Did she question him about it, or did she bite her tongue and smile at the crowd, secure in the knowledge that, while her husband might have a new mistress, she was his established queen?

The woman in question was a daughter of the diplomat Thomas Boleyn, who along with Wolsey had helped mastermind the arrangements for the Field of Cloth of Gold. His newly married daughter Mary had been present in France, and if the liaison had not begun by then, it certainly had by the spring of 1522. She made a dazzling appearance at Wolsey's home of York Place on the night of Shrove Tuesday, 4 March, in an entertainment for the Imperial ambassadors. A pageant of a castle had been prepared, a *Chateau Vert*, painted green and decorated with leaves and banners hanging from three towers, topped with three more thinly veiled declarations of love. The first banner bore the image of three hearts, torn in half, the second showed a lady's hand gripping a man's heart and the third showed another female hand 'turning' a man's heart. Taking her place to watch the performance begin, what must Catherine have made of these coded messages? Eight ladies waited inside the castle, dressed in Milan bonnets and gowns of white satin, each with their role, all abstract virtues, embroidered in gold. The part of Beauty was taken by Mary Tudor, Duchess of Suffolk, and Honour was played by Gertrude Blount, the Countess of Devonshire. The daughter of Lord Morley, Jane

Parker, was Constance, and Mistress Browne, Mistress Dannett and the daughters of Sir Thomas Boleyn also took roles. The elder Boleyn girl, Mary, who had served Mary Tudor in France, either chose or was assigned the part of Kindness, while her sister Anne, recently returned from the court of Queen Claude, played the role of Perseverance.

More figures appeared from under the castle, but these were a grotesque parody of the courtly women trapped within. Played by choristers of the Chapel Royal, attired 'like to women of Inde', or India, they represented the negative qualities of lovers: Danger, Disdain, Jealousy, Unkindness, Scorn, Strangeness and Malbouche, or harshness of tongue. Eight lords then entered the hall, dressed in blue capes and golden caps, yet none was so dazzling as their leader, who took the role of Ardent Desire in a costume of crimson satin adorned with burning flames of gold. For once, Henry was not so unsubtle as to take this role in front of his wife. It was probably played by William Cornish, who was nearing the end of a long career as actor, musician and master of the Children of the Chapel Royal. Accompanying him were Love, Nobleness, Youth, Devotion, Loyalty, Pleasure, Gentleness and Liberty. A mock battle followed, an allegory for the overcoming of a lover's scruples, in which the ladies wished to yield to Ardent Desire but were dissuaded by Scorn and Disdain. In their defence the women threw rose water and comfits, while the men replied with dates and oranges and the suggestive 'other fruits made for pleasure'.[21] With the women surrendering and being led from the castle by their suitors, Henry was hoping that life would imitate art. The signs suggest that it was around this time that his affair with Mary Boleyn began.

And yet there is a chance that Catherine knew nothing about it at all. With the assistance of the gentlemen of his chamber and the existence of separate households for the king and queen, Henry was able to be so discreet that the entire affair was almost lost to history. Our knowledge for this liaison rests on the shoulders of a nineteenth-century historian, John Lingard, as Henry ensured that very little evidence survived to establish the extent of their relationship. In 1817, Lingard cited a letter written by Cardinal Pole in 1535 in which Henry was forced to admit to the affair in order to clarify the terms on which he would marry Mary's sister Anne Boleyn. When accused of having previously slept with Mary and her mother, he famously replied, 'Never with the mother.' However, Lingard's evidence was swiftly rejected by his contemporaries. One reviewer of his work suggested the theory was borne out of 'a spirit of determined hostility' towards Anne Boleyn, 'in order to fix a character of greater odium on her marriage with the king' and to present Henry's rejection of Catherine of Aragon in a less favourable light. But this was never the historian's intention. In response to this criticism, Lingard defended his position by quoting Pole's response to Henry regarding Anne: 'For who is she? The sister of a woman, who you had long kept as a mistress ... whose sister you have carnally known yourself ... the sister of one who has been your concubine.' As Lingard stated in his defence, Pole's 'language is that of a man who asserts nothing of which he is not assured, and who neither fears nor expects to meet with contradiction'.[22] This leaves little doubt that Mary and Henry were lovers and that their relationship was of some duration. Whether or not Catherine knew for certain, or even suspected, cannot be certain. If she was aware, she drew a regal veil over it.

Apart from the pageant, no surviving evidence of Henry's affair with Mary dates from the early 1520s. No whisper, no rumour, no accusation or gossip survives to shine any light on their connection. It can scarcely be considered the open secret that some historians have suggested, with not a single shred of proof that it was known outside the most intimate court circles. Henry would have put his trust in a few men; as the facts show, his close relative Cardinal Pole was aware of the affair, and Wolsey's role in the birth of Henry Fitzroy suggests he would also have been Henry's confidant. An interesting case is that of the Franciscan Friar William Peto, who mentioned Mary when he spoke out against Henry's divorce in 1532. Peto was close to Catherine and her daughter, being appointed as confessor to Princess Mary, so may also have been trusted as a confidante outside the confessional. It is interesting to ponder, though, whether he had learned this information from the king or from Catherine herself.

It has been speculated by historians that one or both of the children Mary bore in the 1520s was fathered by the king. Her first was a daughter named Catherine, possibly named out of deference to the queen, whose arrival may have taken place any time between 1522 and 1526, although the date preferred by most historians is 1524. Her son, Henry, was conceived that year and arrived on 4 March 1525. This does not mean, though, that the King's paternity is guaranteed; in fact, it may imply that Mary herself was not certain about the identity of her children's father, which helps explain the fact that Henry did not acknowledge these potential illegitimate offspring. There are also the possibilities that Henry did know Catherine was his but did not feel the need to own her, due to her gender, or that he knew for certain that she and her brother were not, as the affair had already ended or the dates of their encounters were decisively against it. Additionally, it was a completely different thing to acknowledge a love child born to an unwedded mother, than it was to admit to sleeping with a married woman. In Mary's case, the paternity of any children she bore was automatically ascribed to her husband and would require lengthy legal wranglings and a degree of scandal for Henry to own them as his. He already had one illegitimate son and had little to gain in the 1520s by acknowledging the pair.

It would have rubbed salt in Catherine's wounds to know that Henry may have fathered more children. She was approaching her fortieth birthday and had not conceived for six years. In 1525 she sat for a portrait by the Flemish artist Lucas Horenbout. He had previously been employed at the court of Margaret of Savoy, but was in England by September, when he was referred to as a 'pictor maker', although much of his work was in miniature form and on illuminated manuscripts. Catherine is dressed in the fashion of the day, opting for an archaic English gable hood, wired to look like the gable end of a house, usually draped with a long embroidered lappet framing the face and a hood hanging down the back. Catherine's gable-end was gold and studded with gems, with a thick red lappet sewn with diamond, or diaper, shapes, pinned up at either side and the traditional thick black hood. Not an inch of her hair shows except for the shadow, a suggestion at the very top of her head. It was a conservative choice, favoured by older ladies over the lighter, smaller version or the round French hood Catherine favoured as a young widow when she had sat for Michael Sittow. She wears a brown velvet bodice, with the entire length of the square neckline sewn with pearls and gold ornaments, revealing the very edge of her smock, which appears to be embroidered in blackwork. Her wide over-sleeves are folded back at the elbow to reveal the delicately patterned golden sleeves beneath, with their lace cuff. Her hands are bare and white; she wears no rings but in her right one she clasps a cluster of brown-grey feathers or a bunch of herbs. On a gold chain around her neck hangs a five-part pendant, with three drop pearls dangling below. A second jewel of gold is attached to her bodice. Her face is pale and serene. It has lost the round sort of girlishness of Sittow's image, but the cheeks are rosy, the red lips set determinedly, the chin heavy, the nose straight and the dark eye hooded as she stares off to the left. It is certainly a regal portrait, with nothing of the vulnerability she displayed in 1502.

This was the point when Catherine's ladies-in-waiting noticed that her erratic monthly periods had ceased altogether. The arrival of her menopause was a significant watershed in the life of both the queen and the king, signalling that there would be no more children. Yet Henry was still only in his mid-thirties and, without being aware of any medical impediments, might have anticipated another decade of fertility. It has been suggested that Henry stopped frequenting her bed as a result, but this is not certain, although he may have visited her far less, with the objective of physical satisfaction alone. Although the poet Lydgate's *Dietary* advised that 'with women agyd, flesschly have not to do', canon law still advised post-menopausal wives to yield up the marital debt, to prevent their husbands straying into sin.

The idea of the conjugal debt in canon law related to the husband as well as the wife, but by 1524 Henry wanted to free himself from this obligation. Apostle Paul stated that 'you must not refuse each other, except perhaps by consent, for a time, that you may give yourself to prayer, and return together again lest Satan tempt you for you lack self-control'. Catherine had taken her marriage vows with sincerity and endured her husband's humiliating infidelities. Setting aside the question of her queenship and the rights of her daughter, she was not about to give her consent that Henry might refuse his marital obligations. Sterility or old age were not considered valid impediments to a marriage in medieval law, although the case of a king in need of a male heir was more complicated. It was around this point, as Catherine waited in vain to see if her menstruation would return, that the idea must have been implanted in Henry's mind that he would have to upset the status quo if he were to father

1. Isabella of Castile. Catherine's mother is one of the most significant women in Spanish history, pursuing her domestic, foreign and religious policies with an absolute conviction and determination. Her influence extended over the entirety of her daughter's life. (Courtesy of Luis Garcia under Creative Commons)

2. Ferdinand of Castile. A military genius and cunning statesman, Catherine's father was the model used by Machiavelli when writing his political tract, *The Prince*. In later years, Catherine was her father's ambassador at the English court, but Ferdinand did not always have her best interests at heart. (Courtesy of Luis Garcia under Creative Commons)

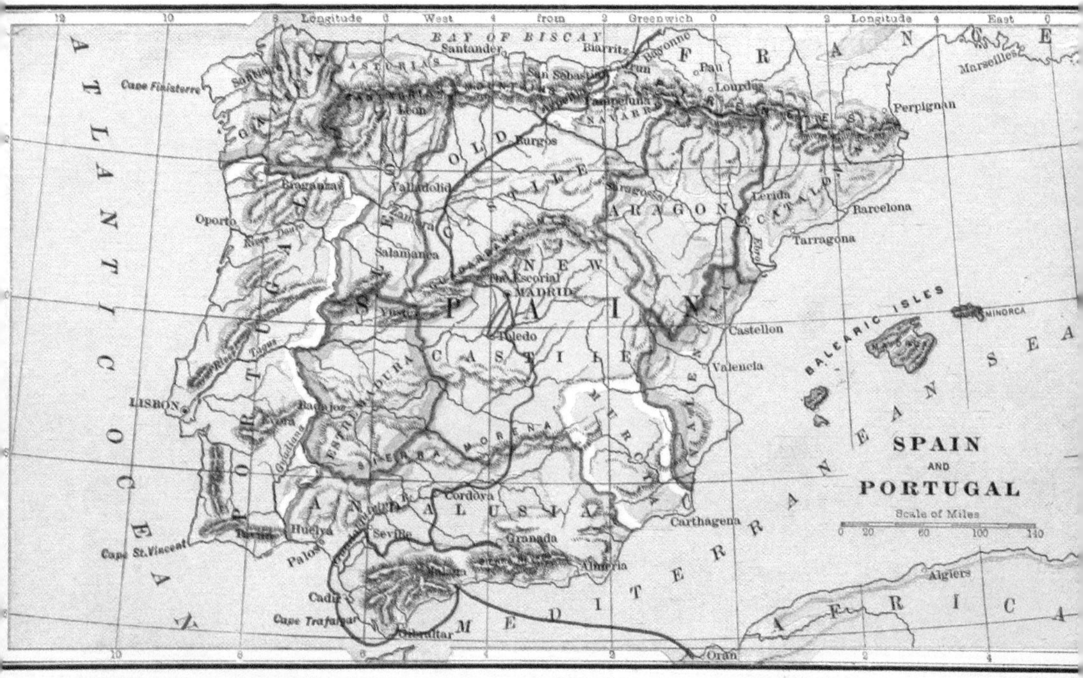

3. A map of old Spain, showing the different regions. Castile is the large region in the centre, with Aragon to the top right. (Courtesy of the British Library)

4. Joint arms of Ferdinand and Isabella. The union of Catherine's parents brought together a large percentage of old Spain and made them a formidable team. It was a successful and happy marriage, with each bringing different skills to their attempt to create a new Jerusalem. (Courtesy of the British Library)

5. Arevalo Castle. Catherine's maternal grandmother and mother lived here in the 1450s, when the young Isabella of Castile was influenced by the nearby monks and their library. (Courtesy of J. Pilar under Creative Commons)

6. The Palace at Alcala de Henares, where Catherine was born on December 15, 1485. (Courtesy of M. Peinado under Creative Commons)

7. The Alhambra in Granada, symbol of the ancient Moorish regime in Spain, which Catherine's parents occupied in 1492. (Courtesy of mcxuro under Creative Commons)

8. Statue of Catherine as a young woman at Alcala de Henares. She carries a book under her arm, as a reminder of her learning and intelligence. (Courtesy of Patrick Williams)

Above: 9. Henry VII. Catherine's father-in-law hurried to meet her after her arrival in England, casting aside protocol. He was often solicitous for her health and happiness, but this was balanced by disputes about her dowry and maintenance. (Courtesy of Elizabeth Norton)

Right: 10. Elizabeth of York. Catherine's mother-in-law may have proved a friend at the English court, but for her premature death in childbirth in 1503. (Courtesy of Amanda Miller)

Above left: 11. Prince Arthur. Catherine's first husband was fifteen at the time of their wedding. Raised to be king, and in expectation of this marriage, he wrote fond letters to her in Spain before their wedding. Whether or not they consummated the match was a question that would cast a long shadow over Catherine's later life. (Courtesy of David Baldwin)

Above: 12. Catherine of Aragon as queen. (Courtesy of Ripon Cathedral)

Left: 13. Henry VIII in middle-age, from a sketch by Hans Holbein. (Courtesy of Jonathan Reeve JR951b53p505)

Right: 14. Pomegranate carving in a linenfold panel; Catherine adopted the fruit as her personal device, the symbol of Granada, when she became Princess of Wales. (Author's collection)

Below: 15. Ludlow Castle, where Catherine and Arthur spent the brief months of their married life, and where Arthur died, on 2 April 1502. (Author's collection)

Bottom: 16. Another view of Ludlow Castle. (Author's collection)

Left: 17. Map of Westminster. The seat of court and government, Catherine would have frequently visited the complex around Westminster Palace and Abbey during her widowhood and her early years as queen. (Courtesy of Jonathan Reeve JRCD2b20p769)

Below: 18. The Jewel House. Most of Westminster Palace burned down in a huge fire in 1513, but this portion of the old palace still survives, giving an impression of the complex Catherine would have known. (Author's collection)

19. Greenwich, a later artist's impression of the rural palace where Catherine and Henry were married, on 11 June 1509. (Courtesy of Sarah Morris and Natalie Grueninger)

20. The surviving gatehouse of Richmond Palace. Rebuilt by Henry VII, Catherine spent much time here as a young woman, but the rest of the palace as she knew it has been destroyed. (Author's collection)

Left: 21. Westminster Abbey. Jousting, tilting and other celebrations were held before the Abbey for Catherine's wedding to Arthur in November 1501. After years of uncertainty, Catherine was finally crowned there in June 1509. (Author's collection)

Below: 22. Lady Chapel, Westminster. Built by Henry VII to be the most splendid resting place for his dynasty, it now houses his magnificent tomb, as created by Italian artist Pietro Torrigiano. (Author's collection)

Above: 23. Dover Castle. Catherine stayed here in 1513 when she accompanied Henry to the coast before his campaign in France. She saw Dover again in 1520, on the way to and from the Field of Cloth of Gold. (Author's collection)

Right: 24. Thomas Wolsey. Rising from humble origins, Wolsey's abilities and readiness to please soon made him indispensable to Henry, but his rise to power displaced Catherine from her position as her husband's chief adviser. She respected Wolsey but the pair were never close. (Courtesy of Jonathan Reeve JR1169b2p7)

Left: 25. Anne Boleyn. By 1526, Henry had decided to replace Catherine with Anne, thus beginning the seven years of negotiations by which he would announce his first marriage invalid. (Courtesy of Elizabeth Norton)

Below: 26. Henry and Anne at Wolsey's York Place. Soon Henry's relationship with the diplomat's daughter became common knowledge, meaning that Catherine was obliged to endure the presence of her rival at court. (Courtesy of the Library of Congress)

27. Desiderius Erasmus. Impressed by Henry as a youngster, the humanist scholar had high hopes for England upon his succession in 1509. He later found the King's choices difficult and was horrified by his treatment of Catherine and respected Catholics at court. (Courtesy of daarwasik under Creative Commons)

28. Martin Luther. Having nailed his theses to the door of Wittenburg's church in1517, Luther was responsible for kick-starting the Protestant Reformation. Henry initially rejected Luther, writing a treatise against him, but later came to see him as a potential ally, who had also rejected orthodox Catholicism. (Author's collection)

Left: 29. Thomas More. As a young student of the law, More witnessed Catherine's arrival in London in 1501. Later to serve as Henry's Chancellor, he refused to swear the Act of Succession which would displace the queen and her offspring. He was executed in 1535 for his loyalty to Catherine. (Courtesy of the British Library)

Below left: 30. Letter from Catherine to Wolsey. In spite of her dislike of Wolsey, Catherine would have witnessed his fall from grace in 1529–30 with trepidation. It illustrated just how ruthless the king could be in the rejection of his former favourites. (Courtesy of Jonathan Reeve JR962b20p895)

Below: 31. Woodcarving of Catherine at the Blackfriars trial of 1529, being harangued on both sides by Campeggio and Wolsey. Here, Catherine gave the performance of her life, prostrating herself at Henry's feet and never deviating from her position that she was his lawful wedded wife and queen. (Courtesy of Jonathan Reeve JR977oldpc 15001600)

Right: 32. Thomas Cranmer became Archbishop of Canterbury after the death of Catherine's supporter William Warham in 1532. Cranmer was swift to pronounce her marriage invalid, paving the way for Henry to marry Anne later that year. (Courtesy of Elizabeth Norton)

Below: 33. Tomb of Ferdinand and Isabella, in the royal chapel next to the cathedral in Granada. When Isabella died in 1504 and Ferdinand in 1516, Catherine lost two powerful advocates and her connection with her homeland. (Courtesy of the Library of Congress)

34. Tomb of Catherine of Aragon in Peterborough Cathedral. After Catherine's death in January, 1536, Henry was adamant that she would be buried as a dowager Princess of Wales instead of a queen. Her modest tomb still attracts visitors today. (Courtesy of Elizabeth Norton)

35. Queen Mary I. Eighteen years after her mother's death, Catherine's only surviving daughter became Queen of England and attempted to restore the country to the pre-Reformation Catholicism her mother had cherished. (Courtesy of Ripon Cathedral)

a legitimate son. He began to question why his marriage had not been blessed with healthy children, seeking out some impediment and debating the possible cause in secret with his confessor, John Longland, Bishop of Lincoln. In the meantime, his thoughts turned to his illegitimate son.

On 18 June 1525, Henry Fitzroy was thrust from the privacy of his secluded childhood onto the political stage. He was brought to Bridewell Palace and invested as Duke of Richmond and Somerset in a public ceremony that included many members of the court and clergy. It was no longer possible for Catherine to remain in ignorance of his existence and, had she previously been unaware of it, this event would have proved a rude awakening. A private letter written by Lorenzo Ohio, the Venetian Ambassador, described the event and the return of the party to Windsor on a cold morning, wearing gowns lined in lynx fur. He provides the first evidence that the boy was a cause of tension between Henry and Catherine: 'The Queen resents the earldom and dukedom conferred on the King's natural son and remains dissatisfied, at the instigation, it is said, of three of her Spanish ladies, her chief counsellors, so the King has dismissed them [from] the court, a strong measure, but the Queen was obliged to submit and to have patience.'[23]

Still, Ferdinand had brought his illegitimate offspring to the Spanish court, where they had been known to his wife and children. The boy posed no threat to Catherine's status as queen, nor did Bessie Blount, but he definitely endangered the future inheritance of Catherine's daughter. Fitzroy's elevation to the peerage had historical significance too, as the title had been devised for Edward, the Black Prince and had previously been bestowed on John Beaufort, Henry's Lancastrian great-grandfather, who had been born out of wedlock but later legitimised. This was a clear indicator that Henry was considering making the boy his formal heir at some future point. Having narrowly escaped death in a jousting accident in 1524, the king was probably pondering his mortality and the condition of the realm should he die at this point, leaving only his nine-year-old daughter to sit on the throne. Adding to the insult to Catherine, Fitzroy was given his own London establishment at her former home of Durham House.

Yet Henry had not forgotten about Mary, who was still his only legitimate child. Following the custom for the male heir of the last three generations, the princess was sent to Ludlow Castle, the traditional training place for the heir to the throne. Catherine's memories of her marriage to Arthur and brief life there must have left her in constant fear for her daughter's good health, as well as the considerable pain of separation. Henry's response made it clear that she had no choice but to accept the situation and bite her tongue. For the time being, she complied. Her situation required it.

III

In February 1525, shocking news arrived at the English court. Francis I had occupied Mirabello Castle, near Pavia, Lombardy, when thousands of Imperial troops broke through the defensive wall at dawn and streamed into the park and the surrounding woods. The Battle of Pavia was fought over the course of around twelve hours, during which it is estimated that between 6,000 and 15,000 Frenchmen lost their lives. Almost all the nobility was killed or captured, and Francis was knocked from his horse and received two wounds in the hand and face.[24] He was captured by De la Mota, Maitre d'Hotel of the Duke of Bourbon, and taken to the castle of Cremona. Charles's general, Charles de Lannoy, wrote in person to Henry VIII the same day, announcing the news.[25]

Amid the defeat, Francis was able to compose a letter to his mother, Louise of Savoy:

> To advertise you of my unfortunate chance. Nothing is left but the honor and the life that is saved; and because some other news shall recomfort you, I have desired to write to you this letter, the which liberally hath been granted to me, beseeching you to regard the extremity of yourself, in ensuing your accustomed wisdom. For I hope that at length God will not forget me; to you recommending your little infants and mine, supplying you to give safe-conduct, to pass and return from Spain, to this bearer that goeth toward the Emperor, to know in what wise I shall be intreated; and thus right humbly to your good Grace I have me recommended. This subscribed by your humble and obedient son.[26]

Henry and Catherine reacted to the news with joy. The order was given for trumpets to be sounded, bonfires lit and wine to flow from the London conduits. Moreover, Richard de la Pole, the last Yorkist claimant, nephew to Edward IV and Richard III, also known as the White Rose, had been killed fighting for the French. Francis's defeat represented a wonderful opportunity for England. With help from Charles, Henry could now launch a proper invasion of the kingless country and claim the glorious titles and spoils he had been promised in 1513. It was exciting for Catherine too, as the culmination of her hopes to see the two countries she loved, the two men she loved most, standing shoulder to shoulder to conquer Europe. John Clerk, the English ambassador to Rome, wrote privately to Henry that the Italians were pleased to see the French defeated but that they feared 'being left a prey to Spaniards, who for their cruelty are most hated of all nations'.[27] He would not have dared voice such opinions to Catherine. Other notes of caution were sounded across Europe, too. In Bruges, scholar John de Fevyn wrote, 'I fear the insolence of the Emperor' to Franciscus van Cranevelt, Justice of the Great Council of Mechelen, to whom Thomas More also wrote, in the fear that 'the madness of war prevails everywhere'.[28] Had Henry been less delighted by the fact that his rival had been humiliated, he might have reflected on the implications of one European king imprisoning another, forcing him under great duress to sign treaties and substituting his young sons as prisoners for his royal person.

A jubilant Henry wrote to congratulate Charles on his victory and for capturing Francis; if it had not been for the great distance, he stated, he would have sent Wolsey in person with his congratulations.[29] Instead he sent Cuthbert Tunstall and Richard Wingfield with detailed instructions, in which Henry framed the opportunity to conquer France as an obligation to God. They were to 'insist on [Henry's] desire to do service to Christendom, the increase of Lutheranism, and the confusion that has arisen mainly from the pride of the French king; and if the present occasion be not followed, God's indignation is to be feared'.[30] They were also to remind Charles 'of his secret promise made to the King's highness and Wolsey at sundry times and places, all tending to the expulsion of the king of France, and setting up the King in his place'. Their charge was nothing less than to 'treat with Charles V. for a joint personal invasion of France during the present year, for the recovery of the crown, unjustly withheld from the kings of England by those of France, and for the partition of the kingdom between Henry and Charles'.[31]

To sweeten the deal, Henry was even prepared to arrange 'delivery to him of the princess Mary, even before marriageable age if expedient'.[32] Was Catherine aware that Henry had made this offer? Mary had just turned nine years old and if Henry was considering sending her off to the emperor imminently, it could only mean that he intended to father another son, or for Henry Fitzroy to rule England. However, Henry's ambassadors advised against this, for the very reason that Mary was the sole heir and there was little sign of Catherine bearing any more children. They wrote jointly on 8 July from Toledo:

> She was your only child at this time in whom your Highness put the hope of propagation of any posterity of your body, seeing the Queen's grace hath been long without child; and albeit God may send her more children, yet she was past that age in which women most commonly are wont to be fruitful and have children. Besides, as the Princess is not much more than nine years old, it might greatly endanger her health and growth if she were transported into an air so different from that of England.[33]

Tunstall and Wingfield also insisted that if Mary was to be a future empress and Queen of Spain, there was no one better to raise her for the job than her mother:

> For bringing her up, 'if he should seek a mistress for her to frame her after the manner of Spain, and of whom she might take example of virtue, he should not find in all Christendom a more meet than she now hath, that is to say, the Queen's grace her mother, who is comen of this house of Spain, and who, for the affection she beareth the Emperor, will nourish her, and bring her up as may be hereafter to his most contentation'.[34]

As it transpired, all the excitement turned to disappointment. Charles proved unwilling to support the English endeavour, saying that 'if the English wish war, [he] leaves them to it'.[35] In the event, neither the marriage nor the war would take place. Henry and

Catherine were disappointed to hear the following January that Charles had signed The Treaty of Madrid with Francis, by which the French king practically sold his soul under duress to be granted his hard-won freedom. Henry's vision for France would never come to pass. Instead, he began to see a new future for himself that did not contain Catherine.

PART SIX

Things Fall Apart 1525–1529

18

The Rival 1525–1526

I

1525 was a year full of turbulence in a world poised on the verge of great change. The Battle of Pavia had upset the European dynamic and marked a watershed moment in the long-running Italian Wars at the same time as the Turkish Sultan, Suleiman the Magnificent, had begun a more virulent campaign against Europe after successfully taking Rhodes. A dashing figure who led his armies in Hungary, Greece and modern Serbia, the most famous of all Turkish emperors was an eastern counterpart to Henry, Francis and Charles, establishing laws and presiding over a court of gold. At a time when his fortunes reached their lowest ebb, Francis outwitted his European enemies by forming a Franco-Ottoman alliance with the very power the Pope had been urging them all to repel. The all-powerful Suleiman was ruthless in dealing with threats and rivals, dispatching them as he pleased, even ordering the strangulation of his heir and circumventing the problems of dynasty by fathering at least ten children with three consorts to whom he was married simultaneously. Henry would have deplored such heathen practices.

In 1525 the German peasantry rose in revolt, fuelled by the rise of Protestantism and economic hardship. In the south-west and Alsace they took up crude weapons, having realised from Luther's teachings that their crippling burdens were not simply the will of God, but harsh impositions from the aristocracy. A pamphlet called *Twelve Articles* was published in Memmingen, containing the first outline of human rights ever to be seen in Europe. It stated that preachers should be elected and deliver the gospels simply and directly without translation, and that in accordance with the Scriptures all men should be free and none enslaved. The meadows and woods should belong to all and be used by all as a resource for firewood and game. Taxes and fines should be fairly applied and fixed at reasonable amounts. Luther rejected all connection with the rebels, siding with the authorities and writing his response in *Against the Murderous, Thieving Hoard of Peasants*. However, as with most class wars, the peasants were brutally suppressed by mercenaries in a number of encounters culminating at the Battle of Frankenhausen.

In the year that Catherine turned forty, Michelangelo designed the Laurentian Library in Florence, Segovia Cathedral was rebuilt and work continued on St George's Chapel, Windsor, begun by Henry's grandfather, Edward IV. The queen would also have heard the sad news of the death of Michael Sittow, her parents' court painter, who had succumbed to the plague in Reval, now Tallinn, in Estonia. In exile in Germany, William Tyndale defied the authorities and translated the New Testament into English. A first attempt was made to print it in Cologne but was halted on a wave of anti-Lutheran sentiment, so the text was successfully brought out in the sympathetic Worms, then in Antwerp. Soon smuggled copies would arrive in England, to be roundly condemned by Cuthbert Tunstall, Bishop of London and Lord Keeper of the Privy Seal. Printers and booksellers up and down the country were warned to be on their guard against its appearance and copies were symbolically burned in public. In Zurich, the pastor of the Grossmunster, Huldrych Zwingli, was speaking out against the practice of fasting in Lent and the use of images in worship, later introducing common liturgy to replace the Mass, using wooden cups and plates, with the congregation seated at tables. That June he opened a school in Zurich to retrain members of the clergy when the city's churches were reorganised and the monasteries converted into hospitals. At the same time, in France, the father of a teenaged John Calvin enrolled his son in the University of Orléans, to train him to become a lawyer.

In Basel, Erasmus published his *Institution of Marriage*, dedicated to Catherine, extolling her union with Henry as 'most sacred and fortunate', an exemplary match from which others might learn. The chief source of happiness, Erasmus advised, was the 'appropriate choice of partners, whose virtue and compatibility will ensure lasting happiness'. It was important to marry an equal but this was 'not be measured simply in terms of wealth but of every kind of attribute', meaning the attributes of the mind and morals. A potential spouse should also have a 'temperament that will make for a harmonious union', with differences in character that would complement each other's strengths and weaknesses, instead of being too similar. Most of all, it was important that spouses shared the same approach to their parents and religion; but, Erasmus added, 'if true piety agrees an agreeable flexibility, superstition means a harsh inflexibility, and it tends to infect women more than men'. Catherine was both pious and superstitious, but with her 'exemplary' marriage about to unravel, Henry was to discover just how inflexible she could be.[1]

In almost all ways, Catherine and Henry were perfectly matched. Erasmus was not wrong to elevate them as a shining example of contemporary royal matrimony, only he was about a decade too late. Raised by parents who had fought for their thrones, acting as pioneers of their dynasties, they had both experienced the extremes of privilege and uncertainty. At times it had been doubtful whether either of them would wear a crown, with Henry being a younger son and Catherine a widow, but from the sidelines they had witnessed the means by which such power was projected and exercised. Both had seen challenges to their family's dynastic legacy dealt with harshly and understood the balance of public and private that was an essential component of their position. They were equal in majesty, in terms of their physical presence and bearing, their instinctive dignity, and were both regal in their shared Lancastrian descent. Each had been educated during a time of new knowledge and discoveries, amid a wave of exciting changes to the world and a questioning of old values by some of the leading minds in their parents' courts – courts that really valued learning and exploration for their own sake. As a woman, Catherine could more than equal her husband's understanding of literature, law, theology and the classics, but she was also wise enough to play the female role and defer to his masculinity. Gender stereotypes were too entrenched to dissolve because of the existence of a few extraordinary women like Catherine and Isabella, even had they chosen to embrace some sort of proto-feminist vision, which they didn't. The early passion Catherine and Henry shared had been genuine, their vision of a merry England brought their youthful court to life, and their journey together as partners and parents had demonstrated many instances of real concern and devotion to each other. They were united in their love of sports, music and books, and in their faith, with Catherine's reserve and caution contrasting Henry's boyish high spirits and her experience supporting his youth. In turn, he had been strong enough for her to lean on when they suffered disappointments in international politics and in the nursery. Catherine was everything that Henry wanted in a woman. He wanted to love her; he had chosen her, woven myths of chivalry and romantic love around her, hoped to father children with her and respected her. They were an ideal couple in every way except one.

By the end of 1525, Henry was confiding in Wolsey that he had been experiencing doubts about his marriage. He had witnessed Catherine's attempts to bear children and believed she could not be blamed, having done her best, yet still he did not have the son he needed. Searching outside the marriage for a reason, he questioned whether this might be God's judgement for some legal impediment, arising from Catherine's former union with Arthur. No doubt Henry and Wolsey debated the points of theology behind closed doors, but the king's increasing dependency upon the cardinal aligned him more closely with his minister than his wife, who was kept in the dark. As they celebrated Christmas at Eltham with the usual religious observance, the pageants and feasting, the queen had little awareness of just how deeply the rot had set into her marriage, or the role that her husband's chief adviser was then taking. Catherine had always preserved a distant respect in her relations with Wolsey, but around this time, as he soared past her to the pinnacle of his career, his attitude towards the queen changed. In his eyes she was no longer Henry's cherished spouse, the figurehead of adoration, the courtly symbol of reverence; she was an inconvenience which he needed to find a way to remove. Yet Wolsey was not the driving force, he was the able servant fulfilling Henry's will. None of this would have happened had Henry not wished it to be so. Part of the king's process of redefinition included turning the lens of investigation upon his household and Catherine's, a task which he put into Wolsey's capable hands.

At the end of 1525, Catherine opened up her establishment to the exacting eyes of her husband's chief minister. Ever conscious of status, exactly what the queen thought of being scrutinised by a man of such humble origins is unclear, but if she had disliked de Puebla for his uncouthness and low birth, she would have loathed Wolsey. As ever, though, she complied with Henry's wishes and laid the mechanics of her household bare for his pen to evaluate and scratch out in ink. In minute detail, the Eltham Ordinances listed exactly who was fed what and when, how much money was allocated to each of the various household offices, where the supplies came from and at what cost. Not a single herring or a half-burned candle went unaccounted for. Ordinances were a fairly common part of aristocratic life, helping to save money and keep control over large households. Numbers of them survive from the previous century. It was part of a wider attempt to reform abuses in religious and secular establishments, but it was also symbolic of Henry's domestic redefinition through the agency of Wolsey's ability. Once this task had been achieved, they would apply themselves in a similar way to analysing and redrawing the lines of his personal life.

One benefit of the Eltham Ordinances is the amount of detail it contains on those familiar faces who surrounded Catherine on a daily basis. Wolsey provides a list of those 'ordinary' members of the queen's establishment who were entitled to eat in her chamber. Her carver was Henry Semer, probably Henry Seymour, one of the less well-known brothers of the King's third wife, who was then in his early twenties and, as yet, unmarried. Catherine's sewers were Robert Warner and Nicholas Frogmorton, whose brother was her cup-bearer, Clement Frogmorton. With the erratic, phonetic spelling of the era, these were probably members of the Throckmorton family, the young sons of Sir George, who had served with Henry in France in 1513 and been present at the Field of Cloth of Gold. Henry Webb was the Gentleman Usher of Catherine's Privy Chamber, and in addition she had four gentlemen ushers and three gentlemen waiters. All of these men were entitled to draw a salary of £11 8*s* 1*d* and to have bouche of court, or be fed at the court's expense. Catherine's household contained an additional three servers of the chamber who received a wage but no entitlement to food.[2]

Also well rewarded were those of the queen's personal waged servants who received bouche of court and an allowance of meat. They included William Herper or Harper, her Clerk of the Court on £6 15*s* 3*d*, and her groom porter, William Uxenbridge, who drew 11*s*. She had three men overseeing her robes, the yeoman Ralph Worsley on £4 11*s* 3*d*, the groom Thomas Firten on 11*s*, and the page Arthur Belfield on 26*s* 8*d*. A similar triumvirate governed her beds. Yeoman of her beds was Edward Floyd on £4 16*s* 3*d*, his groom Thomas Neverell, or Neville, received 11*s*, and the page, Thomas Harrison, got 26*s* 8*d*. Bouche of court was also granted to the queen's laundress for wood and lights.[3] In addition, Catherine had twenty-two yeomen of the chamber, drawing a salary of £15 4*s* 2*d*, five grooms of the chamber who received £2 but no food and four pages who only got £1 6*s* 8*d*. A higher value was placed on her messenger, John Grove, whose reward was £4 2*s* 3*d*. Eight others were listed as having no manner of allowance within the queen's household: her surveyor, auditor, attorney, solicitor, Clerk of the Council, Clerk of the Wardrobe, Clerk of the Closet and Sergeant at Arms.[4] Arrangements were all made for the provision of food for those entitled to eat in the queen's chamber. Catherine herself made do with only one serving at breakfast, with two to be shared between her attendant ladies; this still came in at an annual cost of £70. Sitting in her chamber while she ate, her Lord Chamberlain, her Vice Chamberlain and 'other' of her council shared one 'mess' or course. A further three messes were to be divided between her four chaplains, her ushers, waiter, sewers and a handful of other officials. Her ladies were granted seven messes to share and her maidservants only three.[5]

If Catherine chose to dine or sup outside the hall, then she would be fully attended by a specified number of servants and no others should be 'suffered to tarry' nearby. All servants, rascals, boys and other foes would be expelled from the place outside the doors and the area was to be kept clean, with no 'ale, water, broken meat or other thing conveyed out of the royal chamber be cast or remain there to the filthiness and annoyance' of Henry, so that a 'large passage to the Queen's chamber' was created.[6] The final point about passage to the Queen's Chamber is an interesting one. Following on from comments about cleaning up after meals, the implication is that Henry may wish to visit Catherine in the hours of the evening or night. Undoubtedly, the king was entitled to attend the queen for discussion and company, but there may have been an implication that Henry was still sharing Catherine's bed at the time the ordinances were drafted, or else that he did not wish to contradict the belief that he was. In reality, Henry was trying his very best to bed another woman. That other woman was well known to Catherine: in fact she was right under her nose, being one of her ladies-in-waiting.

II

Had circumstances been different, the dark-eyed and fascinating Anne Boleyn might simply have become another one of Henry's mistresses, like her sister Mary. She may even have been his first maîtresse-en-titre, a title the king offered her inspired by the court of his rival Francis I. Perhaps she would have reigned at court for half a dozen years, borne a couple of illegitimate children and died at a comfortable old age. But by the time Henry fell in love with her in 1526, Catherine's childbearing days were over and he had already made the decisive mental leap to reject his wife and queen and replace her with a younger, fertile model. Anne's charms were probably the final proof he required to convince himself that Catherine was not his legal wife and that they had been living in sin for seventeen years. Perhaps Anne's will and ambition were also a driving force in this monumental shift; the hostile Richard Pole certainly thought so, claiming that the experience of her sister had taught Anne how 'fleeting' the king's affections were, so 'she herself sent her chaplains, grave theologians, as pledges of her will ... not only to declare to [Henry] that it was lawful to put [Catherine] away but to say that [he] was sinning mortally to keep her as [his] wife even for a single moment'.[7] After some initial reluctance, personified by the silver statue she sent Henry of a woman in a ship tossed on stormy seas, Anne was as keen for the marriage to take place as Henry was. Yet ultimately, it would not have happened had it not been the king's will.

Anne's birth is usually given as 1501, although some historians have placed it as late as 1507, after Mary but before their brother George. Arriving at Blickling Hall in Norfolk and raised at Hever Castle, Kent, Anne was around twelve years old when she was sent to the court of Margaret of Savoy in the Netherlands, conveyed there by a Claude Bouton, Captain of the Guard to Charles. They arrived in the summer of 1513, shortly before Henry himself on his campaign against the French. Anne may even have glimpsed him there. The young girl clearly impressed Margaret, as she wrote to Sir Thomas Boleyn that she was 'more beholden to you for sending her to me, than you to me'.[8]

Although Margaret owned considerable properties across the Netherlands, her main residence was in the Hof van Savoye in Malines, a building she was expanding and developing, with its decorative red-and-white brickwork, steep, sloping roofs and dormer windows with gable decoration. Anne was exposed here to new waves of learning, to European influences and fashions, that would define her unique style. Margaret had turned her impressive new Renaissance palace into a centre for leading humanist scholars, artists, musicians and thinkers. In her extensive library was the *Trés Riches Heures de duc de Berry*, her art collection included Van Eyck's Arnolfini portrait and she retained Gerard Horenbout as her illuminator and miniaturist before he travelled to England with his son Lucas and daughter Susannah. Margaret had also employed Erasmus, poet Jean Second and physician Cornelius Agrippa, among a host of talented men in a range of fields, including Adrian of Utrecht, who had been tutor to Prince Charles. Castiglione referred to her as one of the 'noblest' examples of contemporary womanhood, who governed her state 'with the greatest wisdom and justice'.[9] The extent of Margaret's learning was outlined by her court poet, Jean Lamaire:

> Besides feminine work of sewing and embroidery, she is excellently skilled in vocal and instrumental music, in painting and in rhetoric, in the French as well as Spanish language; moreover, she likes erudite, wise men. She supports good minds, experts in many fields of knowledge and frequently she reads noble books ... yet not content merely to read, she takes pen in hand

> and describes eloquently in prose as well as in French verse, her misfortunes and admirable life.[10]

Anne was educated alongside Prince Charles's sisters, the nieces of Queen Catherine. Eleanor had been born in 1499, Isabel in 1502 and Mary in 1505, in the nearby Hotel de Bourgoyne on Keyershof.[11] Antonio Beatis, a papal secretary visiting the city in 1517, only three years after Anne's residence, described it as 'a superb city, very large and well fortified. Nowhere have we seen streets so spacious and elegant ... a number of canals whose waters follow the movement of the oceans traverse the city.'[12] He described Margaret herself as 'not unpleasant looking and her appearance is truly imperial and her smile full of charm'.[13] These influences, stemming from a formidable mentor, placed Anne at the heart of the European humanist Renaissance, at a stage of her life when her opinions and tastes were being decisively formed. When Henry was planning to marry his sister to Louis XII, Anne had been recalled to France to attend the ceremony.

Anne was reunited with her father and elder sister in France, although it is not clear whether she arrived in time for the wedding. After Louis' death, both girls remained to serve Queen Claude but Anne stayed longer, after Mary had departed for England at the end of 1519. It is likely that during her time at the French court Anne encountered another significant humanist scholar, a highly educated and accomplished woman, Marguerite of Navarre, sister to Francis I. Best known today as the author of the collection of short stories called *The Heptameron*, she was described by Erasmus as possessing 'prudence worthy of a philosopher, chastity, moderation, piety, an invincible strength of soul, and a marvellous contempt for all the vanities of this world'. In service to Claude, Anne would have visited the chateau of Blois, which Francis was improving, and may even have seen Leonardo da Vinci, when he was presented to the court at Amboise in 1516.[14] One of Anne's earliest surviving possessions was a Latin book of hours from Bruges, dating from 1450; later she would build a considerable collection of evangelical works in English and French. In January 1519, Sir Thomas was posted to Paris as ambassador and would have seen both his daughters frequently. That March he stood in for Henry at the christening of Francis and Claude's fourth child and would soon begin work on the arrangements for the Field of Cloth of Gold that would reunite all his family members. By 1521, when relations between England and France had soured, Boleyn left Francis for the court of the Emperor, and it seemed expedient to withdraw Anne in the developing political climate. That November, he had a suitable marriage for her in mind, writing to Wolsey from Bruges to try and hasten arrangements so that Anne could leave, which she did the following January. She made her court debut on 4 March 1522, in the pageant of the *Chateau Vert*, although Henry's attention was then focused upon her sister.

It seems to have been the consensus among her contemporaries that Anne was not a conventional beauty, as Catherine had been in her youth. Her best feature, according to the Venetian diplomat Sanuto, was her 'black and beautiful' eyes; apart from these, he described her as having a 'swarthy complexion, long neck, wide mouth, bosom not much raised'. The French diplomat de Carles agreed that her eyes were 'most attractive' and that she knew how to use them to good effect, to send flirtatious messages. The poet Thomas Wyatt referred to Anne in poetry as 'brunet', and the following century his grandson, George Wyatt, echoed the idea of her dark colouring and added that she had several small moles and the 'little show of a nail' upon one little finger, perpetuating the myth that Anne had six fingers. This, and examples such as Thomas Wolsey's private name for her, 'the night crow', in contrast with the comment from one of his servants that Anne 'stood out for her excellent grace and behaviour', illustrates just how far she was able to divide opinion among her contemporaries.

Anne's physical attraction lay in her exotic difference from the English concept of curvaceous, blue-eyed, blonde- or red-gold-haired beauty to which Catherine had conformed. Where the queen was decidedly Spanish in identity, accent and style, Anne wore the most up-to-date French styles, setting trends among the ladies of Catherine's household. According to French courtier Brantôme, although she devised new clothes that were copied by other ladies at court, Anne was still 'the fairest and most bewitching of all the lovely dames'.[15] George Wyatt elaborates: 'In this noble imp, the graces of nature graced by gracious education ... a beauty not so whitely as clear and fresh above all we may esteem, which appeared much more excellent by her favour passing sweet and cheerful

... her noble presence of shape and fashion representing both mildness and majesty.'[16] Anne had a European polish and charm, an intelligence, wit and humanist education and an unquantifiable sexual appeal that many would have found irresistible.

Henry appears to have fallen in love by early February 1526. At the Shrovetide jousts, held at Greenwich, he dressed in embroidered gold and silver, bearing the device of a 'mannes harte in a presse, with flames about it', with the motto 'declare, I dare not'. His opponents, headed by the king's cousin, Henry Courtenay, Marquis of Exeter, were dressed in green and red velvet, decorated with the image of burning hearts, over which was a woman's hand 'commyng out of a cloud, holdyng a garden water pot, which dropped silver drops on the harte'. The symbolism revealed a new object of affection, the pain of concealed love and the remedy, within the reach of the right woman. Henry 'did service' to the queen and her ladies, including Anne, to whom his cryptic message was directed. Experienced as she was at decoding such symbols, Catherine might already have suspected the relationship that was developing under her nose, although it is unlikely that she could guess just how serious it would become. However, almost as if to foreshadow the coming years, the joust took a violent and shocking turn. In an event reminiscent of the jousting accident Henry himself had endured in 1524, when a lance splintered against his visor, Sir Francis Bryan was injured by the 'chance shivering of the spere'.[17] He lost an eye and would always wear a patch as a consequence. It was another reminder about the fragility of life and how death and accident could strike at any time. If the king was to meet an untimely end, the kingdom would be left in the hands of a ten-year-old girl. It made him all the more determined to secure his future.

On 10 March 1526, Emperor Charles married Isabella of Portugal, the daughter of Catherine's sister Maria. Improvements were being made to the magnificent cathedral at Seville, the largest in the world, where the four-year-old Catherine had witnessed the proxy marriage of her eldest sister, another Isabella. The breathtaking great altarpiece, or *retablo mayor*, with its intricately carved wooden figures was completed in time for the ceremony, after having been begun in the time of the bride and groom's shared grandparents. In recent years there had also been a new great dome, choir and transept vaults, all behind the imposing façade that witnessed the joining of the cousins. Bringing a dowry of 900,000 crowns, Isabella was also quite beautiful, as captured in her portrait by Titian, and Charles was keen to hurry the match through as soon as he set eyes on her. The wedding took place just a week after she had arrived in Spain.

The match had the advantage of maintaining the old connection between Spain and Portugal, which Ferdinand and Isabella had prized so highly, and that at twenty-three, Isabella was fully able to consummate the match and, as later proved, equally able to act as regent of Spain during Charles's absence. She bore her first son, Philip, in May 1527, while Mary herself was still only a child of eleven. Ironically, it was this Philip who would go on to become Mary's husband in the 1550s. The news was an immense blow for Henry, as Charles had previously refused to assist him in his plans to conquer France, and now he rejected Mary and the union of England with Spain. It provided Henry with another excuse to turn away from Spain and seek greater friendship with Francis I and all those who favoured France – and that dichotomy was typified in the choice of Anne over Catherine, new over old, France over Spain. But Charles was not yet finished; later that year his actions would further complicate Henry's chances of gaining his marital freedom.

III

In 1526, a new Spanish ambassador arrived at the English court. Inigo de Mendoza was then aged around fifty, a cleric and the grandson of a nobleman who had fought against the Moors with Catherine's parents. His father, the Count of Miranda, had been Spain's general of the sea when Ferdinand dispatched him to help Juana and Philip return from England in 1506, and later Viceroy of Navarre. Catherine is likely to have known the viceroy's son before she left for England, as a relative of her mother's favourite Cardinal Mendoza, so when he was appointed Imperial ambassador by Charles, she would have expected to greet him as an old friend. Especially at this time, she needed all the friends she could get.

The new ambassador's journey turned out to be a trial. Mendoza was captured en route and detained in France for four months, while the French attempted to ascertain his business and locate his papers. They had no luck. Mendoza was convinced this was a plan devised by Wolsey and the French regent, Louise of Savoy, in order to intercept letters between Catherine and her nephew. As he explained to the Emperor,

> I have reasons to believe that my arrest has been planned between the Cardinal of England [Wolsey] and Madame the Regent [of France], for they understand each other perfectly. Thinking I was the bearer of despatches, such as the King of England naturally expects to receive in the present condition of affairs, and that my mission had a different object, they imagined that by seizing my person and papers they ensured also the success of their plans. But if they hoped thereby to establish friendly relations with the English King, they must have been sadly disappointed, for, as I said before, I destroyed not only my instructions, but the very letters I had for the King and Cardinal of England.[18]

Having outsmarted the French, the ambassador was sent on his way, annoyed by the treatment he had received and predisposed to dislike Wolsey before he even crossed the Channel. When he finally arrived in England late in 1526, Mendoza went to Greenwich to offer his introduction. As he arrived, he witnessed Henry emerging from his private chamber in splendour to go and hear Mass, so instead he went to pay his respects to Catherine.[19] He soon realised he had made a mistake, as he was summoned away by Wolsey to be questioned by the king over Charles' allegiances and intentions. It was a tense interview, as Mendoza related, in which 'many unpleasant things were said' which the ambassador chose to pass over. However, he did pass on the fact that Henry insisted the Emperor was 'not his friend' as he had reneged on so many of his promises, such as the invasion of France. Henry appeared so angered by the Emperor's various betrayals that he was considering marrying Mary to the now syphilitic thirty-two-year-old Francis I, an option that Catherine must have deplored. Mary had just celebrated her eleventh birthday, so could legitimately become a bride in two or three years' time, particularly if consummation was delayed. 'The queen,' wrote Mendoza, 'is very dissatisfied with these proceedings, though little of it is communicated to her.'[20] Henry would not relinquish the idea, though, and by the following

February it was being reported that the negotiations 'were very much advanced and on the verge of being closed'.[21]

Very little was being communicated to Catherine on any topic, and the ambassador quickly realised that Henry was controlling her visitors and communication, as well as what information she was being given. To his surprise, after his initial meeting Mendoza was not permitted to see Catherine alone, 'though she desires it, and has tried for an interview'. Henry clearly wished to prevent them having opportunities to discuss her situation, or her receiving advice from Charles, knowing that he would only succeed by dividing his wife from her powerful nephew. Instead, Mendoza was only able to pass messages to her with the help of her confessor, Jorge de Athequa, and was finally granted an interview only on the condition that Wolsey was present. Mendoza was warned in advance to stick to small talk, and 'must not let it appear that he has any political communication to make to her, but merely messages and commendations from former friends in Spain'. He assured Wolsey that 'as he had been formerly in waiting on the queen herself, and on her mother, he had many things to say to her respecting old friends and things in which she took interest'. Even then, their meeting was drawn to a close quickly when they were 'suddenly interrupted by the cardinal', saying that 'the king has many things to tell you. Her Highness will perhaps excuse us if we take leave and go. You shall have audience another time.' But Her Highness had no say in the matter and it must have been as painful for Catherine to be dictated to by Wolsey as it was to go from being Henry's closest confidante to this level of mistrust. Both the queen and Mendoza agreed that without Wolsey's consent it would be 'impossible for them to communicate in future'. The ambassador got the sense that Catherine was unhappy at the way she was being marginalised by the cardinal and that the occasion represented 'a pre-concerted plan to prevent any conversation between the Queen and himself'. Catherine and her friends were walking a difficult line:

> Her suspicions are raised, as she sees that they do not tell her truth in these and other matters. She would very much like, if an opportunity offered itself, to speak to the ambassador on these subjects, and knows quite well that he [Mendoza] is equally

> desirous to inform her of the present state of affairs. She would do everything in her power to preserve the old alliance between Spain and England, but in reality, though her wishes are strong, her means of carrying them out are small.[22]

Eventually Mendoza and Catherine arranged a private meeting, which exposed just how far the queen was being kept out of politics, including those affecting her own nephew. The ambassador thought it wisest to communicate this to the Emperor in code:

> Related to her all that had passed between the King, her husband, and the Emperor, touching the mediation for the settlement of peace, and also the terms brought by him [Mendoza] for the King's especial gratification. The Queen replied as one who would fain make every possible effort to preserve the former good understanding between the King and the Emperor. Judging from the pleasure which the Queen seemed to receive on hearing the flattering words contained in the Emperor's letter, he [Don Iñigo] thinks she must have been previously misinformed respecting the Emperor's real sentiments in this affair.[23]

The days when Catherine had advised Henry over his foreign policy, even ruled in his absence, were long gone; but this shift was indicative of a far more sinister change in her marriage. She was being marginalised to make way for her rival. Henry intended not just to replace her in his affections but to deny her very status as his wife and her position as queen.

19

Queen on Trial
1527–1528

I

On 17 May, Wolsey convened a secret ecclesiastical trial at York Place to investigate the validity of the royal match. Henry had been debating the question with him for months, and now the time had come for action, to shine a light upon all the legal aspects of the royal union and seek a solution to this 'great matter'. On hearing this news, everything fell into place for Mendoza, who wrote to the Emperor after suffering months of rudeness at the cardinal's hands that it was 'the finishing stroke to all his iniquities'. It should have been a fairly quick and simple matter, given the precedents. Louis XII's first marriage had been annulled to allow him to make a better dynastic match, and only that March the Pope had done the same for Henry's own sister Margaret, who wished to be released from her marriage to the Earl of Angus and cited his earlier pre-contract as an excuse. Wolsey and the king had every reason to believe that Pope Clement would readily do in May what he had in March. The trial should really have just been a formality. They didn't reckon with the daughter of Isabella of Castile.

In a clever piece of theatre, Wolsey and Archbishop Warham summoned Henry to the court 'to justify' his marriage, casting the king in a defensive role. With Henry seated beside him, Wolsey raised doubts about Catherine's first marriage to Arthur all those years ago, and quoted a passage from Leviticus that condemns marriage to a brother's wife as unclean and destined to remain barren: 'If a man shall take his brother's wife, it is an unclean thing: he has uncovered his brother's nakedness. They shall be childless.' Although a contrary verse existed in Deuteronomy, stating that 'the wife of the deceased shall not marry to another, but his brother shall take her and raise up seed for his brother', Henry's council advised that Leviticus took precedence over Deuteronomy in canon law. Nor were Henry and Catherine exactly childless, with the existence of Princess Mary, but this was conveniently overlooked by the substitution of lacking male issue. Wolsey declared that the issue had been raised by the President of Paris during the negotiations for a match between Francis and Princess Mary, thus neatly absolving Henry, who appeared horrified, ready to spring to his wife's defence. The court cast doubt upon the validity of the dispensation issued by Julius II in 1503, for which Ferdinand and Isabella had pushed so hard, but was essentially political rather than religious in intent. After hearing these doubts, Henry had expected Wolsey to deliver a simple recognition that the union had never been valid, leaving the king free to remarry at once and would remove any need for further examination. Yet this would have established a dangerous precedent whereby a cardinal had the authority to overturn the ruling of a Pope, in this case the dispensation issued by Julius II. The court met four times in total over the course of two weeks.[1] At the end of May, Wolsey lost his nerve and referred the case to Rome. The next day, some devastating news arrived in England.

Having found her 'Sir Loyal Heart' to be fickle, Catherine had turned to her nephew. Charles had been fighting in Italy when she lamented in a letter to him on 10 May that he was neglecting her. Now his mutinous army took decisive steps that would block any attempts Henry might make to manipulate the Pope into granting his request. Hundreds of miles away from Wolsey's court, over 30,000 Imperial soldiers attacked the walls of Rome and burst into the city, embarking on a campaign of destruction, murder and pillage that would last for days. Symbolically, the tomb of Julius II, the very pope who had issued the dispensation for Henry and Catherine back in 1503, was ransacked and his bones scattered. By the time Henry's secret court met, Pope Clement, on whom he was depending, had already been driven to flee to safety in the Castel Santangelo; effectively the Pope was now Charles's prisoner.

This made the Emperor the most powerful man in Europe. Under different circumstances, Henry's first marriage might have been quickly swept away, but the conjunction of these events on the European stage tied a Gordian knot of diplomacy and legal wrangling that would take years to unravel.

The destruction of Rome had a far greater significance for Henry, though, and for the western world. As the seat of the Pope and the epicentre of Christian worship and legislation, it was emblematic of centuries of faith, illustrated by its practices, its status and its architecture. The physical destruction of the city, with attacks upon palaces, statues, graves and consecrated ground was a violation, a de-consecration of an institution that had acquired a hegemonic status by the advent of Henry's reign. No one was above the Pope, as God's representative on earth, even though the office was riddled with corruption and nepotism, especially under the Medicis. The invasion of Rome paralleled the danger to the Christian faith of the teachings of men like Luther but it also highlighted the vulnerability of the Pope as a man, one who was not above the onslaught of progress and change. If the Emperor could imprison the Pope, Henry could reject his decisions. If Rome had lost its sanctity, he would turn to Canterbury instead.

The sack of Rome bought Catherine some time to think. Initially she blamed herself for Henry's rejection of her, believing 'that the principal cause of all that she is made to suffer is that she identifies herself entirely with the Emperor's interests', allying with Spain when Henry favoured France. Mendoza asked for the Pope to be 'put on his guard in case any application should be made to Rome against this marriage; also that His Holiness should tie the Legate's hands, and by having the cause referred entirely to himself, should prevent him from taking part in it, or appointing judges in this kingdom'. This is exactly what Charles would do, forbidding Clement from making any ruling and attempting to delay Henry's investigation into the marriage in any way that he could. After discussion with the queen, the ambassador believed that if Henry met with any success, he would soon make the affair public, but 'should the king see that he cannot succeed, he will not run the risk of any of the preliminary steps being known'. Until then, 'the Queen desires perfect secrecy to be kept in this matter, at least for the present'.[2] It was to Catherine's advantage for Henry to believe her in ignorance of his plans, but she was currently unaware of his great secret: his desire to make Anne his wife.

It came as no surprise to Catherine that Henry had doubts concerning their marriage, but it must have been an unpleasant shock when he approached her at Windsor on 22 June to voice them. Up until this point, the pair had been carefully skirting round the issue, with Henry hoping to find the least painful resolution and Catherine hoping it would go away. While the matter remained unspoken between them, she could almost turn a blind eye, shut it away in her mind as she had done with his former affairs and escape into her regality. It was what a good queen did. For her husband to broach the silence, to speak openly of separation or annulment of the marriage, to threaten to remove her from his side after all these years, was a dramatic wake-up call for Catherine.

This does not mean she was not prepared. Catherine had probably thought of little else since the rumours had first reached her in the weeks before the trial.[3] In the meantime, she had been discreetly gathering support to the extent that Mendoza was convinced most of the court would chose to side with her against Wolsey, 'both because she is much beloved here, as because the Legate, who is suspected to be at the bottom of all this, is universally hated'. Outlining the questions of conscience that had been troubling him, the king informed his wife that they had been living in mortal sin since 1509 and that they must separate, with her retiring to a convent. Catherine replied that she had never consummated her marriage to Arthur and that she was Henry's lawfully wedded wife. But Henry would only repeat his position and asked her to choose a place where she would like to retire. This interview convinced her that he was serious. This was final. To be confronted with Henry's desire to part in this way, for it to have finally become an acknowledged reality, must have been devastating for Catherine.

The *Spanish Chronicle* includes an account of events composed by an author who was possibly an eyewitness at court during the 1520s and 30s, or who had access to someone who had been. Into the mouth of the 'sainted Queen Catherine' on 22 June, the writer puts this reasoned speech:

> My good Henry, I well know whence all this comes, and you know that the King, Don Ferdinand, when he gave me in

marriage with the Prince of Wales, was still young, and I came to this country a very young girl, and the good Prince only lived half a year after my coining. My father, the King Don Ferdinand, sent at once for me, but King Henry VII wrote and asked my father that I might marry you. You know how we were both agreed, and how my father sent to Rome for the dispensation, which the Pope gave, and which my father left well guarded in Spain.[4]

Other sources claim that Catherine burst into tears. At the very least it must have been an emotional encounter on both sides, after their long history together and given what was at stake. Henry asked her to keep the matter between themselves, little knowing that it was already the worst-kept secret in Europe, but this suggested to the queen that any separation was still merely theoretical at this stage. She still had time; she might be able to change his mind. Mendoza even doubted that the separation would go ahead at all, but he was still sceptical of the ability of the people to prevent it:

> Not that the people of England are ignorant of the Kings intentions, for the affair is as notorious as if it had been proclaimed by the public crier, but they cannot believe that he will ever carry so wicked a purpose into effect. However this may be though people say that such an iniquity cannot be tolerated, he [Mendoza] attaches no faith to such popular asseverations, especially as they have no leader to guide them, and therefore should this King carry out his design, and the suit now commenced go on, the people will most probably content themselves with grumbling.[5]

In the event that Henry persisted, Mendoza had a plan for Spanish assistance, because he did not think the English would stand to see their queen treated so badly and Princess Mary declared illegitimate:

> There is so much feeling expressed here about the Queen's divorce, not only on her account, but because, in the event of these proceedings being carried out, her daughter the Princess would be declared illegitimate [*bastarda*], that should six or seven thousand men land on the coast of Cornwall to espouse the cause

> of both mother and daughter forty thousand Englishmen would at once join them.[6]

With one failure under his belt, Wolsey resorted to unpleasant methods to discredit the queen. He wrote to his representative in Rome, Gregory Casale, that sexual relations were now impossible between Henry and Catherine, as 'certain diseases in the queen defying all remedy, for which, as well as for other causes, the king will never again live with her as a wife'. Some intimate illness, Wolsey suggested, meant that Henry was 'utterly resolved and determined never to use' her again and that 'danger ... may ensue to the king's person by continuing in the queen's chamber'.[7] This was quite a dramatic claim. It implied that Catherine had some infection, illness or condition that affected her sexual organs and that this might be transmitted to her husband, or that the queen was capable of doing direct or indirect violence to Henry. Was this really true, or were Henry and Wolsey prepared to use whatever weapon they thought might prove successful in severing the king from his wife? Considering that Wolsey also lied to the Pope that the bloodstained sheets from her 1501 wedding night had been sent to Spain and defamed Catherine as frenzied with desire for sex, his argument about her disease appears in a less credible light.

At the end of the month, the Emperor gave his view on the matter in a letter to Mendoza. 'You may well imagine,' wrote Charles, 'how sorry we were to hear of a case so scandalous in itself, and entailing such lamentable consequences for the future, from which evils innumerable must inevitably arise, especially at the present juncture. We cannot desert the Queen, our good aunt, in her troubles, and intend doing all we can in her favour.'[8] He counselled that the matter should be dealt with privately and moderately, as 'it would still be a more honourable proceeding to keep the matter secret and work out its remedy privately, if necessary', although he was unable to believe there were motives for such a breach, upholding the royal marriage as something of a shining example, as Erasmus had:

> Knowing his [the King's] great personal virtues, his elevation of mind, his good and righteous intentions, and the perfect love he has always borne towards us and our affairs, we cannot in any

> manner be persuaded to believe in so strange a determination as this on the part of His Serenity, a step which would so astonish the whole world, were it to be earned into execution. Nor can we believe it possible, considering the good qualities of His Serenity and of the Queen, his wife, and the honesty and peace in which they have lived for so many years so much to the fame and reputation of both parties, as is notorious throughout the Christian world – the Queen herself being so good and virtuous, loving so much His Serenity, having always conducted herself towards him in so irreproachable a manner, and being of such Royal blood, that such a design can be entertained. To which we may add that having, as they have, so sweet a Princess for their daughter, it is not to be presumed that His Serenity would consent to have her or her mother dishonoured, a thing so monstrous of itself and wholly without precedent in ancient or modern history.[9]

In October 1527, Emperor Charles defied Henry to declare that he would support his aunt in her refusal to submit and demanded that Pope Clement took no further steps towards granting an annulment. Effectively, Charles had his uncle in checkmate. After his failure to pronounce definitively at the York House investigation, Wolsey had been sent to Rome to try and find a solution, but his mission turned out to be something of a wild goose chase. When he returned to England in September, knowing that another ambassador had been dispatched to Rome and having worn out his ill body, there was no welcoming committee. Worse still, when he arrived at Richmond to speak privately with the king, Anne Boleyn was the one to summon him to Henry's presence and accompanied them into the closet for the duration of the interview. Just as Wolsey had used his power to marginalise Catherine, he was now at the mercy of a more powerful royal favourite.

It is not clear exactly when Catherine became aware that Henry was intending to replace her with Anne Boleyn. It may have been as early as the summer of 1527, perhaps in August, when Henry applied for a dispensation to remarry, although no new wife is specifically named. Or it may have been the following February, when the Venetian ambassador became aware of her existence, writing that Henry was repudiating Catherine because the dispensation covering her initial marriage to Arthur was 'defective and invalid' and intended, 'for the maintenance and welfare of his realm', to wed 'Thomas Boleyn's daughter, who is very beautiful'.[10] After eighteen years of marriage, Catherine must have become adept at reading her husband's moods and observing the development of his affairs, but lately she had been denied the kind of intimate access to him that would have enabled her to read and influence him. Early on in the marriage, and again with the elevation of Henry Fitzroy, she had been reminded by Henry that he would not tolerate her commenting upon certain aspects of his personal life and, if Wolsey's biographer Cavendish is to be believed, she had learned to keep her enemies close, almost to appreciate them, holding Anne in 'great estimation' and accepting 'all things in good part and with wisdom and great patience'. She had weathered the storm thus far and would refute these allegations with obstinate certainty. As an anointed queen, stepping aside to enter a convent was insult enough; leaving the throne empty for her lady-in-waiting was unthinkable. Catherine was the daughter of two monarchs, with Plantagenet blood in her veins and connected to the great ruling houses of Europe; Anne was the descendent of a merchant. There was also the question of religion and the supremacy of the Church. Catherine represented the old faith, with its Catholic ritual and the guidance of papal authority; Anne's background was reformist, 'more Lutheran than Luther himself'. She leaned towards France rather than Spain and the Holy Roman Empire. Thus, she represented a threat to the entire world that had produced and nurtured Catherine, which she had proudly represented for decades. Anne could not replace Catherine. Such a move would redefine England.

II

Despite Catherine's popularity with her subjects and at court, her presence created a degree of uncertainty. Hearing rumours of the imminent change in her status, some of Henry's servants chose to ally themselves with the rising star of the Boleyns. Others were uncertain how much deference was still due to the queen, especially those whose interests were represented by the new faction. On 25 May 1527, the hesitant French ambassadors at court needed to take their cue from the king when it came to sharing information in front of his wife. The incident appears to show Henry being solicitous for Catherine's feelings, but it also exposes that significant secrets were being kept from her at court. It was Henry himself who sent them up to the queen's chamber after dinner, where 'they talked about the king's prosperity and the friendship of the two monarchs [Henry and Francis]'. But then Catherine started asking questions, requiring the bishop to tell her whether they intended 'to treat for a universal peace'. He answered cryptically, saying that 'the object for which they had come must precede, but did not state what it was, as he did not know whether it ought to be mentioned to the queen'. That was when Henry stepped in, 'smiling, to her, that he was speaking of the marriage of the princess'.[11] Catherine would not have been fooled by the show of harmony, knowing how her husband was working against her behind the scenes.

In public, Anne was now taking over the ambassadorial role that Catherine had long enjoyed. Renowned for her fluency in French and her Continental grace, she would have been indispensable at the reception of Lord Montmorency at Greenwich that autumn. The Grand Master of France had been at Francis's court since 1515 so it is likely that Anne already knew him and would have been selected from among Catherine's attendants to form part of the official welcoming party. The reception took place at Greenwich, followed by jousts and a feast in a new banqueting hall hung with gold embroidered with satin silver, which was so bright it seemed that the fabric leaves were growing. Henry, Catherine and the ambassadors sat down together and were served with ninety dishes before a pageant of a white marble fountain flanked by hawthorn and mulberry trees, set with gold gargoyles and winged serpents. If Anne's powers of translation had served their purpose by the end of the meal, she may have been one of the eight 'fair ladies in straunge attire' of cloth of gold slashed with silver, with whom the king and his companions danced 'very lustily'.[12]

Incredibly, Henry continued to house both women together under the same roof at Greenwich. They had separate establishments within the large complex and could have used them to maintain a degree of privacy but encounters would have been unavoidable in the public arena, such as at chapel and on the occasions that the three chose to dine together in the same hall. In fact, it seems that the queen went out of her way to meet Anne and Henry, singly and together, using her presence in an attempt to divide them. According to George Cavendish, Catherine employed various methods to keep the lovers apart, 'the oftener had her at cards with her, the rather that the King might have the less her company', on which occasion Catherine reputedly uttered the ironic line that Anne had 'good hap to stop at a king, but you are not like others, you will have all or none'.[13] Otherwise, chronicler George Wyatt suggests that she behaved impeccably, never showing 'any spark or kind of grudge or displeasure'. Perhaps Catherine decided it was safest to keep her enemy close and that her presence would prove restrictive to the pair, like a chaperone, preventing them achieving greater intimacy or plotting her downfall behind her back. Also, she would have maintained that, as England's anointed queen of eighteen years, it was her right and her duty to be visible at court, in the palaces she had been inhabiting for so long, accessible to the people and served at table according to her due. She may have hoped that her presence would be enough to provoke Anne to shame or drive her away. It did not.

Again, time played to the queen's advantage, allowing her to take advice, communicate further with Charles and prepare her case. Early in the New Year, though, news arrived in London that Clement had escaped from captivity, walking out past his guards disguised under a long beard. Finally he could act independently of the Emperor, although it was symbolic that he was now sheltering in the wreckage of his former palace. He immediately agreed to two draft bills allowing Henry to remarry once he was free from Catherine, even if his choice fell on a woman forbidden to him by a former connection with a relative of hers. The second endorsed bigamy, simply allowing him to take a second wife. Perhaps this, or Catherine's stubbornness, acted as a catalyst. In February 1528, Wolsey applied for a commission to allow proceedings to go ahead for the trial in London, in order to appease Henry's 'troubled conscience'. In response, Catherine sought the advice of a number of religious experts, including William Warham, Archbishop of Canterbury, John Fisher, Bishop of Rochester, Dr Henry Standish, Bishop of St Asaph's, Cuthbert Tunstall, Bishop of London, and John Clerk, Bishop of Bath and Wells, to defend her against the papal legate Henry had requested to come to England and hear his case. Henry then made a shocking U-turn that illustrates just how far his thinking had changed. He appealed to Martin Luther.

Luther was living at the Black Cloister, part of a former monastery in Wittenberg, and, despite his religious vows, had married a former nun, Katharina von Bora. Back in 1525, in the belief that the English king had become 'inclined towards the Gospels',[14] Luther had written to Henry to apologise for attacking him and for the accusation that Wolsey had written his book. He even begged Henry for his forgiveness and friendship, praying 'that God who has begun it, will cause your Majesty to grow and increase in the attainment of the inclination towards the Gospel' and that the king would ignore the 'flatterers and sweet-spoken hypocrites' that called Luther a heretic. In his defence, Luther summed up his teachings as 'charity towards one's neighbour, obedience to secular authority and mortification of the sinful flesh'. He also deplored the 'abuse and tyranny of the bishops ... who chase after tithes, rents, splendour, lusts of the flesh, yea after kingdoms, empires'.[15] Luther appealed to Henry as an outcast from society, placing himself beyond the restrictive laws of a corrupt society, a law unto himself, 'answerable only to God'.[16]

Yet at that moment in time, Henry had not been receptive. He saw Luther as 'wretched, vile and detestable, provoking the world to mischief, encouraging the world to sin'.[17] In response he wrote criticising Luther's marriage, having taken a nun and 'openly abused her in sin', and deplored the reforms that meant nuns and monks were forced to leave their establishments, the 'good religious folke [who] be dayly by your meanes expelled oute of their places in whiche they were determyned in chastity, prayer and fastynge to bestow their lyves in goddess [God's] service'.[18] In 1525 Henry had no intention to dispute further with Luther and wrote that he would leave him to his lewdness. It is a measure of just how much Henry's views were changing that a few years later he attempted to enlist Luther's support for the dissolution of his marriage, and would himself begin a programme to expel most of England's monks and nuns from their religious houses.

Henry came to see Luther as another pioneer who was prepared to defy the religious establishment, to break with the conventions of the Church and act according to his conscience. He would have rejected Lutheranism completely, even been outraged at the suggestion that the two men had any theological common ground, but it suited him to use aspects of Luther's status in the late 1520s when support for his case was thin on the ground at home. Henry had been disappointed when his new chancellor, Thomas More, had refused to speak against Catherine or advocate the royal separation. It was another former enemy, the exiled heretic Robert Barnes, who was charged with the task of winning Luther over to Henry's cause. But Luther would completely oppose the notion of divorce, only considering it permissible in cases of adultery, desertion or incapacity. Catherine would always remain Henry's wife and queen, as the existence of Princess Mary proved, and Henry's attempts to prove otherwise were in Luther's eyes a violation of God. His actions would make 'the mother as well as the daughter into incestuous women'.[19] It was not what Henry wanted to hear.

In the meantime, Catherine still entertained hope. She had seen other rivals come and go before, and that June another formidable enemy made an appearance, which might have been the answer to her prayers. The dreaded sweating sickness broke out again in London, and while Henry and his wife left for the country, Anne sought the shelter of her family home at Hever. Slipping back into the old daily routine, with Catherine sewing Henry's shirts and the two attending Mass and confession together, it may have seemed to the queen that the mistress was out of sight and out of mind. The public façade continued. Yet, as Henry's letters indicate, he was still in regular contact with Anne and was soon writing out of concern for her health, having heard 'the most afflicting news' and saying he would 'willingly bear the half of yours to cure you'. He sent her one of his own physicians and beseeched her to 'be guided by his advice'.[20]

When Anne fell ill with the sweat, it must have seemed like a convenient answer for Catherine, perhaps even a divine judgement for her ex-servant's immorality. Such terrible epidemics, often claiming hundreds of lives apparently at random, could only be explained in the sixteenth-century mind as an act of God, as a reaction to sin. The queen would not have needed to look far to identify what that sin might be. At Hever the physicians might have employed some of the most popular remedies of the day, including the liberal application of vinegar and treacle, the dosing of patients with a concoction called Imperial Water and the use of nosegays made from wormwood, rosewater and crumbs of brown bread. Henry himself was something of an expert on medical cures, having escaped former outbreaks, and now advised Wolsey, when he fell ill, to eat lightly, drink very little wine, take 'pills of Rasis' and the herb 'manus Christi', which the king enclosed with his letter.[21] At Tittenhanger Manor near St Albans, the air was 'purged daily with fyers and other preservatives, that neither (Henry) nor the quene nor none of their company was enfected', although they did hear of the deaths of Sir William Compton, Mary Boleyn's husband William Carey and Sir Francis Poyntz, the English ambassador in Spain.

Catherine and Henry both awaited news from Hever with very different hopes. It would have been understandable if the queen secretly speculated that with her rival neatly removed, the marriage might have a chance of recovery. The passage of a few years might even lessen the pain and erase the memory. But Anne did not die. The prospect of losing her prompted Henry to keep her even closer. As the danger faded, he ordered that new apartments be prepared for Anne at Greenwich, close enough to allow access to his but not so close to create a scandal. Catherine might have argued that the scandal had already broken.

III

Lorenzo Campeggio had been appointed by the Pope to investigate the case, and although he left Rome in June 1528, his poor health dictated that his return journey to England was long and tortuous. On 24 October, three weeks after his arrival, Catherine and Campeggio finally met again at Bridewell Palace. He was carried there on a red velvet litter borne by four men, as he was in too much pain to walk.[22] Hoping to find a supporter, the meeting would have been a disappointment for her. She resisted his attempts to persuade her to enter a convent, saying that she 'intended to live and die in the state of matrimony, to which God had called her, that she would always remain of that opinion and that she would never change it'. Yet Campeggio would not give up, afterwards writing to the Pope's brother-in-law, Jacopo Salviati, that although it was 'difficult and more than doubtful', he did not despair and hoped to encourage the Emperor to persuade her to retire from the world.[23] He argued that as she was 'nearly fifty' (she was forty-two), she would 'lose nothing whatever and much good would ensue'. He could not understand her refusal, as it would be 'less scandalous and more secure' but Catherine cared little for scandal. What was scandalous to the queen was the way in which Henry was treating her.

At this point, Catherine was being offered the only real solution which would permit her to retire with her dignity intact. Given her piety and age, it would not have been an unreasonable suggestion for a widow, as many former queens had taken this route to end their days in quiet contemplation, away from the theatre and dangers of politics. But Catherine was not a widow. She may have been devout, but above all she had been raised to be a Queen of England and she would never deviate from this stance. She considered it to be the will of God. Retiring to a convent might have saved her much heartache, but it was more than stubbornness and desire to retain her status that made her dig her heels in. For Catherine, this was personal as much as it was political. It was about her and Henry. She was his equal, not a subject to be discarded and not to be treated as less than the daughter of Isabella of Castile. Her stance owed as much to outrage that her husband dared take this line with her, that he dared to contradict the path that God had chosen for her.

The question of Mary's future had to be considered. If Catherine agreed to withdraw voluntarily, it would also mean that her marriage and any subsequent marriage made by the king would both be legal and her daughter would retain her legitimate status and inheritance. Although Catherine did not wish to step aside, this option was in Mary's best interests and would guarantee her future. It is easy to look back at this moment with hindsight, knowing the terrible distress that Mary would go through in the coming years, even fearing for her life and the toll it took upon her health, and to consider this as a critical failure of care on her mother's part. Yet Catherine did not know how events would play out, or that Henry would make the choice to treat his daughter badly. As time went by, her husband would punish Catherine by taking out his wrath on Mary and keeping the pair apart. The queen may have thought it was in her daughter's best interests for her to retain her position, as she may have been less able to influence future decisions about Mary's life and marriage if she was removed from the heart of the court. However, it is unavoidable for a modern historian to dwell on the question of just how far Mary's welfare featured in Catherine's decision-making. Drawing conclusions, though, is far more difficult and probably not advisable. Catherine loved her daughter deeply and did not intend to harm her, but she found herself in an unprecedented situation and did not have the benefit of hindsight in 1528. And Catherine was not one to go back on her word. When she refused to enter a convent, her word was final and she would not change her mind. Perhaps she was too stubborn, perhaps she was brave. She sincerely believed that she was obeying God's calling, and in preventing her husband's remarriage she was saving him from sin.

Campeggio's mandate was limited. He had been instructed by the Pope to delay proceedings as long as possible in order to try and win Catherine over to the idea of entering a convent. Beyond that, though, he had little power. As Mendoza realised, the Pope and Henry were attempting to 'frighten the Queen, so that she should of her own accord enter religion' but the Pope had 'secretly intimated to Campeggio' that 'if she refuse, no further use shall be made of the commission which he publicly bears'.[24] The legate recognised that Catherine could 'obtain all she chose to desire', retaining her status, 'dowry, rents and ornaments' if she did not 'attempt this course of [going to] trial but content herself with a chaste profession of living in the service of God, and in tranquillity of mind and conscience'.[25] Wolsey visited him while his gout confined him to bed and they 'argued the question for three or four hours together', but Campeggio found the cardinal as inflexible and immovable as if he had been speaking to a rock.[26] When the ambassador warned that the situation would cause 'mortal war with the Emperor' and ruin all hope of a universal peace, Wolsey's reply that this would be avoided because it would be 'determined with so much benefit and honour to the queen' seems almost delusional. It was even suggested that a marriage between Mary and her illegitimate half-brother Fitzroy would solve the problem, but Catherine must have been horrified at the idea, not merely for the close blood connection but because she had higher hopes for her daughter.[27] The assertion that she was being treated honourably would have been refuted by the queen.

Catherine was given the opportunity to defend her position with the assistance of a range of legal and religious minds. Henry permitted her to have William Warham, Archbishop of Canterbury, John Fisher, Bishop of Rochester, John Clerk, Bishop of Bath and Wells, Cuthbert Tunstall, Bishop of London, her confessor, various other bishops and the Chancellor of Ely. He did not want her to have Spanish advice, but did grant her wish to recall Juan Luis Vives, who was then resident in Flanders. Vives was duly dispatched by Margaret of Savoy on 17 November, to be accompanied by Catherine's servant Ochoa de Salzedo.[28] Of course Margaret, just like Catherine, was the Emperor's aunt, and, as such, was prepared to back her through this difficult time. The French ambassador du Bellay believed, correctly, that Fisher and Tunstall were 'of the Queen's opinion', but feared they would not win as even if all the cardinals 'past time and the present approved the marriage, that they could not have made it valid', because it was proven that Catherine had lain with Arthur and 'God has long ago himself passed sentence on it'.[29]

For Catherine, such a matter was far from proven. Two days after meeting Campeggio, she visited him again at his lodgings at Bath Place, where he was again incapacitated by illness. Henry had agreed to them meeting on the pretext that she was going to him in order to make a confession, but her words can hardly have been those the king had hoped she would utter. Catherine 'affirmed on her conscience that from her marriage with Prince Arthur ... she had not slept in the same bed with him more than seven nights and that she remained as intact and uncorrupted as the day she left her mother's womb'. As in the years of her widowhood, duress pushed Catherine to dramatic extremes, embracing the notion of martyrdom, claiming that 'although she might be torn limb from limb, should compel her to alter this opinion; and that if after death she should return to life, rather than change it, she would prefer to die over again'.[30] Campeggio believed her. However, he would be less certain about her next move.

Catherine now produced what she considered to be her trump card. The sons of the long-dead Spanish ambassador from her youth, Rodrigo Gonzalez de Puebla, had uncovered a crucial piece of evidence among his papers. It was a papal brief, a copy of the original dispensation that had been issued allowing Henry and Catherine to marry, which she now presented as irrefutable evidence that the marriage had been legitimate, as this paperwork even covered the eventuality that consummation had taken place. Yet although this brief was reputedly a copy, it actually predated the original to 26 December 1503. Thus, Henry's scruples should be eradicated regarding the legality of the match, which Catherine maintained was unnecessary anyway, as no prohibitive affinity had been established between her and Arthur.

The existence of this brief clearly troubled Henry. On the same day, Henry sent Warham and Tunstall to interrogate her, on the pretext that there had been a plot reported against the king's life. If any harm came to Henry, they told her, the intention would be reputed to her. This was an unexpected move that must have shocked the queen profoundly. Worse still, while Henry was 'pensive and troubled' by the state of their marriage, Catherine was then accused of frivolity. Her behaviour, her attempt to remain cheerful, was taken as evidence that she wished the king ill, and while he attempted to repudiate her on one hand, he accused her on the other of not being loving enough. Henry practically expected her to go into mourning for him and was piqued when she proved stronger than that:

> The King takes this very earnestly, and doubts the more because she does not show such love to him, neither in [nor] yet out of bed, as a woman ought to her husband. 'What was [in] bed between both your Graces we pass over', but openly she does not behave suitably; for though the King is in great pensiveness on this account, she is not so, but shows many signs and tokens to the contrary.
>
> 1. She exhorts other ladies and gentlemen of the court to dance and pass time, though it would be better for her to exhort them to p[ray] that God would set some good end in this ma[tter].
> 2. She shows no pensiveness in her countenance, nor in her apparel, nor behavior.
> 3. She shows herself too much to the people, rejoicing greatly in their exclamations and ill obloquy, and by beckoning with her head and smiling, which she had not been accustomed to

> do in times past, rather encouraged them in their so doing than rebuked them, as she ought to have done.
> 4. She ought to have informed the King of the brief which she pretends to have had for a long time, and not to have kept it close, for the exhibition thereof might have given much ease.[31]

Henry used this as an excuse to keep Catherine at a distance from him and to prevent her from seeing her daughter:

> Considering all this, the King cannot persuade himself that she loves him as she ought, but that she rather hates him; and therefore his Council think it not safe for the King to be conversant with her either at bed or at board, specially after the beginning of the process. Think that if the King has such fear, he may lawfully withdraw from her company, and for like suspicion he will not suffer the Princess to come into her company; which should be a very grievous thing to the Queen, as the Princess should at her age be near her for her better education.[32]

IV

On 7 November, Catherine made a declaration at Bridewell Palace in the presence of William Warham, the Archbishop of Canterbury, who had presided over her marriage, and John Fisher, Bishop of Rochester. In swearing an oath upon the Gospels that she had been a virgin on her marriage to Henry, she rejected the clause that had been inserted in the brief in 1503 to allow for the possible consummation of her first marriage. She did this 'of her own volition', being 'neither asked nor required to do so'. Those who had inserted the original clause to allow for the possibility of her first marriage being consummated were, she declared, 'following the presumption of the law rather than what actually happened'.[33] This oath is the most compelling evidence in Catherine's case, given the strength of her faith. Whatever may or may not have happened regarding the papal brief, she was not about to publicly and voluntarily swear an untruth upon the Gospel and risk her immortal soul.

Popular support for Catherine was also at an all-time high. Henry had good reason to be concerned because the royal marriage had become a topic for discussion up and down the country.

Many subjects, particularly women, were being rather vocal in their defence of Catherine, not just due to her long-standing popularity, but because she was seen as a more universal symbol of womanhood being wrongly treated by man. Hall relates how the people said 'that the king for his own pleasure would have another wife and ... be divorced from his queen'. The 'common people' may have supported Catherine with 'many folishe words'[34] and rumours, but support her they did. Now that the secret had well and truly been exposed, Henry needed to create an opportunity to spread his version of events among the people, only at one remove from actually making a declaration at the cross or in the market place.

The very day after Catherine made her oath, Henry summoned the mayor and aldermen of London, the Privy Council and lords to Bridewell Palace. There he delivered an impromptu defence of his actions, and in an attempt to win support extolled Catherine's virtues as a queen. He also did a remarkable job of trying to absolve himself from any suggestion that he had instigated or desired to separate from his queen. Although it had 'pleased God to send him a fair daughter', he declared, 'of a noble woman and me, begotten to our great comfort and joy', he had been informed by 'divers great clerks' that Mary was not 'our lawfull daughter nor her mother our lawfull wife but that we live together abominably and detestably in open adultery'. These words, he urged the assembly to believe, touched his body and soul and troubled his conscience and vexed his spirits 'daily and hourly'. If it was 'adjudged by law of God that she is my lawfull wife, there was never thyng more pleasant or acceptable to me'. He went on to assure his audience that 'beside her noble parentage ... she is a woman of moste gentleness, of most humilitie and buxumnes, yea and of all good qualities appertaining to nobilitie, she is without comparison', so that if he could choose her again, he would do so above all women.[35] He would 'sorrow from departing from so good a lady and loving companion, but muche more lament and bewaile' that they had lived in adultery. Those assembled were to be his ambassadors among the people, 'as our trust and confidence is in you to declare to our subjects our mynde and entente accordyng to our true meaning, and desire them to pray with us that the very truth may be knowen for the discharge of our conscience and the savyng of our soule'.[36] The reaction was mixed. Some 'sighed and said nothing', while others expressed concern that the king was so troubled. Those who were in favour of Catherine 'much sorrowed that this matter was now open' and 'every man spake as his heart served him'.[37] But French ambassador Jean du Bellay reported with some disbelief that Henry had been threatening, saying that if 'any man should speak of it in other terms than he ought to speak of his prince, he would let him know that he is master' and that 'there was not a head so dignified that he would make it fly'.[38] The king was riled. His court understood that he was serious.

The papal brief raised more problems than it solved. Straightaway Wolsey was quick to call it a fake and Campeggio was inclined to believe him. Whether or not they thought Catherine was responsible for it or if she had been duped was a thorny area they deliberately left vague. In a combined letter to the Pope, the pair explained 'that the Queen has exhibited a copy of the brief of Julius II., dated at the same time as the bull, but they suspect its genuineness. Besides its unexpected appearance on such an occasion, it seems incredible that such a document should have been obtained.'[39] They also shared what they believed to be Henry's motives:

> Those who think the King is moved by hatred of the Queen, or by the desire of another wife, err greatly. As neither disagreeable manners nor the despair of future offspring could impel the King's mind to hatred, so no one could think him to be so weak as, for the pleasures of sense, to wish to break a connexion in which he has spent his life since his youth. He is influenced by a fear of divine law and a respect for human law.[40]

Catherine would have been disappointed at this step and perhaps at the role Campeggio played in it, if she was aware of it. When she protested, she was 'compelled' by Wolsey 'to swear solemnly that she would use every effort' to get the original brief, which was then in the hands of the Emperor, 'as urgently as if her life depended on it'. Mendoza wrote to warn Charles that this had been done by the queen 'under compulsion'.[41] This makes it sound as if Wolsey believed that Catherine had initiated the forgery, although she argued that it had been given to her by the sons of de Puebla, having been found among his effects. They had passed it on to Mendoza who had given it to her six months before. Catherine warned Mendoza that he was likely to be questioned about its existence and provenance, and he planned his answer 'that it may not disagree with the queen's declaration, nor make it appear as if she had stated an untruth'.[42] It is impossible now to know whether or not the queen believed the brief to be genuine, but it should not be forgotten that her parents had forged a dispensation allowing them to marry and Catherine herself understood that such papers were necessary political stepping stones to smooth the way to greater acts. It is also questionable why she did not present it at her first meeting with Campeggio, instead waiting until two days later, or even why she did not mention it in the previous six months. Catherine stated in her defence that she did not think it would be required, although this may stretch credulity. Perhaps she chose to present the brief to Campeggio rather than Henry or Wolsey in the belief that they might make it disappear. In placing her faith in it, she was clinging to it as a life raft. The more Catherine refused to comply with Henry's wishes, the more she was mistrusted, her movements curtailed and her every action and letter observed by the spies Wolsey had placed in her household. It was sad that her life had come to this, but Catherine was not just the daughter of Isabella of Castile. She was also the child of Ferdinand, the model for Machiavelli's *The Prince*. She knew something about subterfuge.

20

The Blackfriars Court 1528–1529

I

Catherine's most intimate details were now being discussed right across Europe. As Henry had turned to Luther and appealed to the universities of Italy and France for a ruling on his case, Catherine sought out her own humanist champion in Juan Luis Vives. From being a guarded secret, the marriage was suddenly propelled into international politics and almost everyone had an opinion on it. Henry now wanted to open up the entirety of their relations, and those of Catherine with Arthur, to public scrutiny, sending scholars out to scour libraries and bookshops for relevant precedents, even penetrating the archives of the Vatican. This was to embed the question of the 'divorce' firmly amid the new wave of European reform, debated in houses of learning just like the question of the marriage of priests. It was fairly groundbreaking that such a domestic, personal question should take on such widespread political importance.

Help was on its way. Catherine had set much personal store in the belief that Juan Luis Vives could help her out of her marital predicament. Vives was thirty-five and had recently completed his work on provision for the poor, identifying the causes of urban poverty and proposing methods by which the state might support the impoverished, in his *De Subventione Pauperum Sive de Humanis Necessitatibus*. More recently, he had actually been in England in 1527, between April and June, just as the rumours about the royal marriage were beginning to spread and it was then that Catherine had asked him to return that autumn and instruct Princess Mary in Latin. While back at home in Bruges, in the summer of 1527, Vives had sent Henry a copy of Erasmus's *Adagia,* his annotated collection of Latin and Greek proverbs, along with his thoughts on Henry's response to Luther. Having heard about Wolsey's mission to Rome, Vives had expressed his wish that the Cardinal might 'reach a settlement worthy of your Majesty, the most kind, the most learned, the most pious of all princes'. The correspondence of Vives' friends that summer, however, shows a less respectful view of the proceedings which blamed Wolsey, with Fevyn writing that the 'insane Cardinal' was pushing Henry into a divorce. Vives, Fevyn and Cranevelt were convinced that Wolsey was attempting to divide the king from Catherine in order to push him into the arms of the French, suggested by Wolsey's negotiation of the Treaty of Amiens that August.[1] But that scenario did not take into account the existence of Anne Boleyn. If Wolsey was pushing for a divorce, it was because Henry required him to do so.

Having left Flanders by 17 November at the latest, Vives had arrived in England by 8 December,[2] and was finally allowed an audience with the queen at Greenwich. It was an uneasy season at the palace, with the king and queen keeping open house 'as it used to be in former years', except that 'Mademoiselle de Boulan is there also, having her establishment [*son cas*] apart, as, I imagine, she does not like to meet with the Queen'.[3] Catherine was delighted to see an ally appear, to the extent that she tried to encourage Vives to send for his wife, dispatching presents and affectionate letters to Margaret Vives in Flanders.[4] But Vives would not bring his wife into the hostile atmosphere he sensed at once. He had only been in England for a few weeks when he realised that Wolsey's spies were following him and that his life was threatened; he was cross-questioned by Wolsey.[5] Yet Catherine felt able to confide in him. She confessed that she was 'afflicted about this controversy as to her marriage' and, believing Vives to be 'well read in morals and consolation' as well as being 'her countryman who spake the same language', she opened up about her 'great distress' that 'the man whom she loved more than herself should be so alienated from her that he should think of marrying another'. Her feelings for Henry were not in doubt: 'Her grief was the greater in proportion as she loved him.' Vives offered his consolation, adding that she was 'dear to God' and that all would praise her moderation, as all she desired was for her 'sister's son not to suffer her to be condemned without a hearing'.[6] Then, worse still, Vives was compelled by the now 'wholly unscrupulous' Henry to reveal the subject of his conversations with the queen. He was outraged, as 'a servant trusted by a mistress whose fidelity to her husband is undoubted'.[7] After having been virtually kept under house arrest for six weeks, Vives added that he did not 'willingly meddle with the affairs of princes'.[8] As soon as he could, Vives escaped home again to his wife in Flanders, never to return to England. There, he would produce the book *De Officio Mariti*, or *On the Duties of the Husband*, which went into fifty-six editions.

At the end of 1528, Anglo-Spanish relations were at a low. Henry had swung from his jubilation at the defeat of Francis three years earlier, to signing a perpetual peace with France in the Treaty of Amiens. When a fleet of six Spanish merchant ships were 'encountered' off Rye, one of the Cinque Ports on the tip of East Sussex, by a French fleet captained by La Barre in a galleon called *Lartigues*, they were driven to land and 'compelled to surrender'. This resulted in the arrest of both the Spanish and French parties and their sails being confiscated. Believing their treatment to have been too harsh, Mendoza took up their cause, adding his voice to theirs as they made complaint to Wolsey.[9] The ambassador wrote again on 9 December, calling the detention of Spanish vessels to be too harsh and 'the reasons for their non-restitution are frivolous, as it is not at all likely that Spanish merchant vessels with a valuable cargo would fire upon French men-of-war'.[10] The following month, while they still languished in prison, John Hacket, the English ambassador to the Low Countries, wrote to voice the concerns of Margaret of Savoy: 'My Lady recommends herself to Wolsey, to whom she has written in favour of the Spaniards, marvelling that the French are allowed to drown Spanish ships, kill the men, and plunder the goods in the King's jurisdiction, as has lately happened in the Camer port.' She asked for 'restitution'.[11]

It must have been difficult for Catherine and her supporters not to read a wider symbolism into the arrest of the merchant ships and wonder if the Spanish merchants had been targeted because of their nationality and on account of the new friendship between England and France. Catherine was not in a position to help them, being barely able to help herself. She was 'surrounded by spies in her chamber' and she had 'so little liberty' that she could not find messengers to dispatch upon necessary tasks.[12] She wrote to Charles on 9 January, begging him 'for the love of God to obtain justice'. She was certain her nephew 'would regret to see her parted from her husband and her child prejudiced' and asked him to send the original of the brief she had shown Campeggio, because then she would be able to 'demand her rights by law'.[13] After receiving her letter, Charles wrote to the Bishop of Burgos, asking him to 'labour in this behalf in the Queen's name at Rome' and expressed how deeply the situation grieved him, believing Henry was under the influence of 'sinister persuasion of some who are about him'.[14] Aware that the king was planning to hold a Legatine court in England to try the case, Charles knew that Catherine would dare not object and was 'not allowed advocate, nor proctor, nor writings to defend herself'. Thus, he thought it unreasonable that the matter 'should be determined in England in which the king himself is a party'. He was unable to send Catherine the original of the papal brief, as it was a 'matter which touches the validity of the dispensation and the authority of the Holy See'.[15] He believed that Catherine had made the request 'under constraint' and that she wrote 'at the king's dictation', having been forced to swear to write no private letters.[16] It was the Emperor's opinion that the Pope ought to revoke the matter to Rome and recall Campeggio. But this did not stop Henry going ahead planning his court, in the hope of hearing that his marriage was invalid.

Nor was Henry pleased that Catherine was appealing to Charles for help. Where it had once been a useful diplomatic connection that she was the aunt of the Emperor, now it had become an inconvenience. Henry hoped to set aside the personal aspect of their relationship in the hope of dealing directly with Charles as one king to another. At Greenwich, he led Mendoza aside to a window, where he issued an indirect warning to the Emperor to not get involved:

> As to the Queen, who wished him alone to defend her, the King said that, for this reason, and in order that the truth of this matter might appear the more plainly, he had assigned to her such a

> council for her defence; that he had no need for the defence of the Emperor or of any other prince, seeing that he did not interfere in the affairs of others, and that no one ought to meddle with his.[17]

Mendoza replied that Henry was mistaken if he thought Charles would be influenced 'more by menaces and threats' than by the love of Christendom. If he had interfered in Catherine's marriage, it was in the hope 'that they might live in the same concord and harmony in which they had always lived' not to create any 'discord'. He continued

> that Charles, in acting thus, believed he was acting in accordance with his conscience and his honor, and with the authority of his person and that of the Queen, to whom he was so greatly bound. That if, on Charles's part, anything had been done for the said defence, it had been done with so much moderation as to be evidently done out of love for the King.[18]

This response made Henry furious. With 'great wrath', and 'in rather an angry tone, and with greater passion than was consistent with his royal dignity', he told the ambassador that he 'wished Charles to know that the more he defended the queen the more he would injure her cause'. Mendoza replied that the Emperor would never abandon his aunt's cause, 'even if the queen desired it; and on this account the queen did not merit any greater ill-treatment, for it was not in her power to prevent Charles from acting as he did'.[19] Shortly after this, Henry advised Mendoza that it was better if he retire and return to Spain on account of his ill health. Mendoza was indeed ill, but he also felt defeated by the current situation, so he put in an application for his passport and left London seventeen days later.[20]

Pope Clement was of no use, however, being so ill during these months that his life was despaired of. He was even thought to have died one night, only to 'recover' in the morning, and rumours of his demise flew around Europe. Henry saw an opportunity in this, asserting that in his incapacity the Pope should deputise his decision on the case to Wolsey and Campeggio. He added, for good measure, that it may be argued that the Pope's authority did not extend to 'degrees prohibited by the divine law' and that it was 'expedient that the succession to the kingdom should be fixed and incontestable' and his own conscience quieted. As a highly illuminating parting shot, he urged that 'the Pope should grant his desires on account of his merits'.[21]

As the months advanced, the atmosphere at the English court became more tense. The expectation was weighing on Catherine, and she was, as Margaret of Savoy told Charles, 'so perplexed that she can do no more' and there was 'no person who dares to meddle in this affair contrary to the King's pleasure'.[22] An anonymous document written in Spanish, now among the State Letters and Papers of Henry's reign, reports some of the scurrilous rumours that were flying about the city, even fears for Catherine's life:

> He told me, moreover, that they had expressly spoken about poison, saying that if the King were not such a good man, servants would not be wanting. I said that the Queen was ready to incur this danger rather than be a bad wife, and prejudice her daughter, and that if such a course were resorted to the Emperor would avenge it; moreover I was ashamed that they should hold such language before his Holiness.[23]

It may be that in the weeks leading to the convening of the legatine court Catherine genuinely believed her life was in danger, if not from the assassin's hand then from a verdict she would find impossible to bear. The notion of a secret poisoner waiting to lace her food was fairly dramatic and Italian, almost Machiavellian, but it was not outside the realms of possibility. She may have feared that some zealous friend or servant of the Boleyn family would act secretly on their behalf. On the brink of losing her position, forbidden from seeing her daughter and already estranged from her husband, she began to prepare for the greatest performance of her life.

II

On 31 May 1529, Wolsey and Campeggio assembled in the Parliament Chambers at Blackfriars Priory, to the east of Bridewell Palace. The venue had been established in the 1270s as a home to London's Dominican community, whose distinctive garb had given them their alternative name. By the mid-fifteenth century,

Blackfriars had a large church 'richly furnished with ornaments' and a number of other buildings, including a hall that was frequently being used for meetings by Parliament. Charles had been lodged there on his visit in 1522, and seven years later there still stood a long gallery of over seventy feet that had been built to connect the site with nearby Bridewell Palace. As the players prepared themselves to enter the spotlight for what they anticipated would be a dramatic piece of political theatre, it was ironic that Henry also chose Blackfriars in 1529 as the new location of his Office of the Revels, so that costumes and props were stored there. Fifty years later, a long time after the friary had been dissolved, the site became a location for one of London's first theatres.

On the last day of May, the proceedings were begun by John Longland, Bishop of Lincoln, the confessor in whom Henry had confided his first doubts about his marriage and one of the most driven advocates of his annulment. Longland presented the papal commission to Wolsey and Campeggio, which was then read aloud by the notary Florian Montini, before a company of abbots, notaries, archdeacons and bishops. In it, the Pope declared that it had 'frequently been related to him by trustworthy persons that there was a question about the validity of the marriage' between Henry and Catherine and 'because of the importance of the matter a rapid judgement was required'. He urged the court to proceed 'summarily and plainly, without judicial fanfare and form' to determine whether the marriage was valid or invalid. Then, if one of the parties were to request it, they were to 'confirm the marriage or declare it null'.[24] Thus the proceedings were cleverly framed as if they were an independent inquiry prompted by the Pope rather than the king, who was equated with Catherine as one of the parties under investigation. The two cardinals then appointed Longland and John Clerk, Bishop of Bath and Wells, to summon the king and queen to appear before the court on the morning of 18 June, between the hours of nine and ten.[25]

On 1 June Catherine was in residence at Bridewell Palace, as was Henry. Built on the site of the old St Bride's Inn, next to the Fleet River, it had begun as one of Wolsey's projects before being turned into a palace under the king's instructions, purpose-built for him and Catherine from around 1515 onwards. It stood three storeys high around two courtyards, the inner and outer court, from which the gallery led over the Fleet to Blackfriars, with gardens stretching down to the Thames, flanked by a 200-foot-long gallery culminating in a Water Gate. The king's double-storied presence chamber and watching chamber overlooked the gardens, with his privy chamber at right-angles to the north. Catherine's lodgings were on the other side of the courtyard, on the first floor.[26] The fires would have been burning in the grates at Bridewell, as Campeggio reported 'we are still wearing our winter clothing and use fires as if it were January'. He had 'never witnessed such inclement weather' and reported to James Salviati, papal legate in France, that the plague had re-emerged and fresh outbreaks of the sweat were also feared.[27]

Even the first day of June, which might have been anticipated as warm, proved disappointing. On that day, Longland and Clerk requested an audience from Henry and Catherine and presented them each with their summons to appear at the court. Catherine's response as recorded by Hall stresses the personal blow that this represented: 'When she heard the cause of their coming, no marvel that she were astonished as it touched her very near.' She paused before she answered, then directed herself to the bishops, asking whether it was now a question if she was the king's lawful wife or not and why nothing had been raised on the matter in the last twenty years. She considered it a 'great marvel' that in spite of the existence of many prelates and learned men during that time, no one had ever questioned her position before. It had always been thought 'lawful and honest', which had now become 'detestable and abominable'. She invoked their dead fathers, thinking the proceedings strange considering 'what a wise prince the king's father was and also the natural love and affection that King Fernando' had borne her. She could not believe that either of their fathers had been 'so uncircumspect, so unwise and of so small imagination' that they might have made a mistake over this marriage, especially given that they had sent to Rome 'and there after long suit, with great cost and charge, obtained a licence and dispensation'.[28] According to Hall, she then turned on Wolsey, saying she wondered at his 'high pride and vainglory, abhorre[d] his voluptuous life and abominable lechery and little regard to his presumptuous power and tyranny' which had made him 'kindle this fire' out of malice.[29] It seems out of character for Catherine to let her regal mask slip enough to attack an enemy so directly and openly, even someone she hated as much as the cardinal. Hall's account may well owe more to hindsight because, as it happened, Wolsey's downfall was just around the corner.

Three days before the court was due to convene, Catherine went to visit Campeggio, who was bed-bound due to his gout. She was, in his words, 'very anxious and perplexed about her affairs'. She had been expecting the arrival of two lawyers from Flanders who were to plead her case, but they had not arrived because the Emperor had told them it was not safe to do so. She now found herself in the position of having no one to plead for her, as despite having certain figures assigned to her by the king, she did not trust them not to have a 'greater regard to the king's pleasure than to her necessity'. Campeggio advised her to pray and 'keep a good heart, to rely upon the King's justice, and upon the conscience and learning of those prelates who have been assigned to her for counsellors, and to rest sure that nothing inconsistent with justice and reason would be done by us Legates'. She then repeated her refusal to take religious vows, a matter she regarded as 'the great solace of her mind and the firm foundation of her righteousness', and reminded the cardinal of her confession at an earlier meeting, that she had been a virgin when she married Henry. Catherine had granted him, as her confessor, the right to lift the veil of silence that his role required and share her secrets with the court. It was a master stroke. From Campeggio she 'went to her lodging here in London and there met her counsellors'.[30] Nobody was quite sure how the queen was planning to react when she stood before the court, with the cardinal recording that 'some think she will object to the place, some to the judges; some think to both. Others think she will not appear ... within three days we shall know for certain.'[31]

Catherine chose to make a pre-emptive strike. By 16 June, she had left Bridewell Palace and was staying at Baynard's Castle. There she called a meeting of her chief supporters, including William Warham, Cuthbert Tunstall, John Clerk, John Fisher, Nicholas West, Henry Standish, Jorge de Athequa and her almoner Robert Shorter. Catherine solemnly appealed the case from the legates to the Pope, refusing to recognise the authority of the court.

When Catherine arrived at Blackfriars two days later, she found it had been decked out in splendid detail, as if the end of the marriage required as much display as the start. Campeggio and

Wolsey were seated on two chairs of cloth of gold, with cushions of the same, before a table with a railing around it, covered in tapestry, like a 'solemn court'.[32] Henry's chair was to the right, made of rich tissue under a cloth of estate, while Catherine's, on the left, was simply a 'rich chair'.[33] Little reminder was needed that this was an ecclesiastical court, with the cardinals and their entourage arriving with crosses, pillars, axes and 'all the ceremonies belonging to their degrees'. The commission was read again and then Henry and Catherine were both summoned by name. The queen was accompanied by four bishops and a large number of her ladies and gentlewomen. She stood before the legates and issued a formal protest, as well as submitting a written one which she had prepared in advance, then she exhibited her appeal to the Pope and asked for it to be recorded and the documentation returned to her. Her initial challenge to the court was that her judges were disqualified from hearing her case because of their close association with Henry, as both Wolsey and Campeggio had been promoted by Henry. She demanded that her case should be heard by impartial judges and then swept out of the hall.

On 22 June, Catherine was represented in court by John Fisher, Bishop of Rochester, and John Clerk, Bishop of Bath and Wells. Fisher was approaching his sixtieth birthday, having begun his long career under Margaret Beaufort, becoming her chaplain and confessor in 1497. Having been educated at Cambridge University, he had become a Doctor of Sacred Theology and then the university's vice-chancellor before holding the position of the Lady Margaret Professorship of Divinity. Henry VII had appointed him as Bishop of Rochester in 1504 and five years later he had preached at Margaret Beaufort's funeral. Most recently he had given open-air orations at St Paul's while copies of Tyndale's translated Bible were burned. He had been responsible for the interrogation of Thomas Hitton, a heretic who had been captured on his return to England in order to distribute Tyndale's work, and along with Warham, Fisher would condemn him to be burned at the stake in 1530. The long-sighted bishop also foresaw the dangerous path along which this court might lead – towards a break with Rome and huge upheaval in the Catholic Church – so for him it was as much about protecting his conservative religious values. When Henry claimed he had the backing of all the bishops, Fisher indignantly denied that he did and declared himself willing to die as a martyr for the cause of true matrimony, just as John the Baptist had, implying a parallel between Henry and King Herod.[34] Henry would never forgive him.

Further, Fisher added that he was present that day before the assembled lords in order 'not to procure the damnation of his soul, and in order not to be unfaithful to his King, or to fail in doing the duty which he owed to the truth, in a matter of such great importance'. Aware that he was jeopardising Henry's good will and his future career, Fisher declared eloquently 'and with forcible reasons to demonstrate to them that this marriage of the King and Queen can be dissolved by no power, human or divine; and for this opinion he declared he would even lay down his life'.[35] A conservative intellectual, religious principle and absolute truth mattered far more to Fisher than the service of his king. Conversely, Wolsey had built his career on the opposite pretext, placing Henry's wishes above everything. Neither strategy would pay off. Both men were to lose everything as a result of the king's pursuit of his desires.

John Clerk was a younger man by a margin of eleven years, another Cambridge graduate who had studied in Bologna University and entered the household of Cardinal Bainbridge after becoming a Doctor of Canon Law. Returning to England, he served in Wolsey's household in a variety of roles before becoming Dean of the Chapel Royal and Dean of Windsor, then Bishop of Bath and Wells in 1523. He had also recently been a judge in the Star Chamber and Master of the Rolls. It was Clerk who had the job of personally handing a copy of Henry's refutation of Luther to the Pope. Now he nailed his colours to the mast and stood alongside Fisher to support Catherine over her husband. Their argument was that because Catherine was indeed Henry's lawful wife, it was their duty to prevent Henry from falling into mortal sin.

There is some confusion as to exactly when Catherine delivered the most important speech of her life. Some sources place it on 21 June, prior to Fisher and Clerk's defence, while others place it a week later. First Catherine sat down before the audience to listen to the 'scruples' Henry claimed to have felt 'from the beginning' but had not raised for the 'great love he had, and has, for her'. Henry claimed he desired 'more than anything else, that the marriage should be declared valid, and remonstrated with the judges that the Queen's request for the removal of the cause to Rome was unreasonable, considering the Emperor's power there; whereas this country is perfectly secure for her, and she has had the choice of prelates and lawyers'.

Catherine knew what she had to do. Rising from her seat, she knelt before Henry, addressing him only, appealing to him as her husband and as the only other person in the court of equal rank:

> Sir, I beseech you for all the love that hath been between us, and for the love of God, let me have justice. Take of me some pity and compassion, for I am a poor woman, and a stranger born out of your dominion. I have here no assured friends, and much less impartial counsel. Alas! Sir, wherein have I offended you, or what occasion of displeasure have I deserved? I have been to you a true, humble and obedient wife, ever comfortable to your will and pleasure, that never said or did any thing to the contrary thereof, being always well pleased and contented with all things wherein you had any delight or dalliance, whether it were in little or much. I never grudged in word or countenance, or showed a visage or spark of discontent. I loved all those whom ye loved, only for your sake, whether I had cause or no, and whether they were my friends or enemies. This twenty years or more I have been your true wife and by me ye have had divers children, although it hath pleased God to call them out of this world, which hath been no default in me. And when ye had me at first, I take God to my judge, I was a true maid, without touch of man, and whether it be true or no, I put it to your conscience. If there be any just cause by the law that ye can allege against me either of dishonesty or any other impediment to banish and put me from you, I am well content to depart to my great shame and dishonour and if there be none, then here, I most lowly beseech you, let me remain in my former estate and receive justice at your hands. The King your father ... and my father, Ferdinand, King of Spain ... thought then the marriage between you and me good and lawful. Therefore, it is a wonder to hear what new inventions are now invented against me, that never intended by honesty ... I most humbly require you, in the way of charity and for the love of God, who is the just judge, to spare me the extremity of this new court, until I may be advised what way and order my friends

> in Spain will advise me to take. And if ye will not extend to me so much impartial favour, your pleasure then be fulfilled, and to God I commit my cause![36]

Henry attempted to raise Catherine from her knees twice but she would not move. Finally, she rose, curtseyed, and turned to walk straight out of the courtroom. An official called to her to return, but she responded that 'it makes no matter, for it is no impartial court for me, therefore I will not tarry. Go on!' With her head held high, she never returned to the courtroom. Henry, moved by her performance, echoed that she had indeed 'been to me as true, as obedient, and as conformable a wife as I could in my fantasy wish or desire. She hath all the virtuous qualities that ought to be in a woman of her dignity ... she is also a noble woman born.'[37] But he went on to outline his suspicions, after 'all such male issue as I have received of the queen died incontinent after they were born, so that I doubt the punishment of God in that behalf'. He explained that he wished to 'take another wife in case that my first copulation with this gentlewoman were not lawful, which I intend not for any carnal concupiscence, ne for any displeasure or mislike of the queen's person or age, with whom I could be as well content to continue during my life, if our marriage may stand with God's laws, as with any woman alive'.[38]

The account of the French ambassador Jean du Bellay predates Cavendish's account, and although it is shorter, still gives a ring of truth to Catherine's dramatic performance. Yet here it comes across more as a debate between the king and queen:

> The Queen appeared in person, and the Dean of the Chapel for the King. The Queen refused the judges. The King desired them to determine the validity or nullity of his marriage, about which he had from the beginning felt a perpetual scruple. The Queen said that it was not the time to say this after so long silence. For which he excused himself by the great love he had and has for her. He desired, more than anything else, that the marriage should be declared valid, and remonstrated with the judges that the Queen's request for the removal of the cause to Rome was unreasonable, considering the Emperor's power there; whereas this country is perfectly secure for her, and she has had the choice of prelates and

> lawyers. Finally, she fell on her knees before him, begging him to consider her honor, her daughter's, and his; that he should not be displeased at her defending it, and should consider the reputation of her nation and relatives, who will be seriously offended; in accordance with what he had said about his good will, she had throughout appealed to Rome, where it was reasonable that the affair should be determined, as the present place was subject to suspicion, and because the cause is already at Rome.[39]

Retiring to Bridewell Palace, Henry was angered by Catherine's behaviour, believing her rejection of the court and appeal to Rome would at best complicate, at worse jeopardise, his chances. He wrote on 23 June to his agents in the Vatican, framing her decision to appear to undermine her faith in her own cause, already anticipating that the Pope would side with the Emperor and block or halt the proceedings:

> The Queen, trusting more to the Imperialists than the justice of her cause, put in her protest, and appealed to the Pope, alleging the avocation of the cause. The judges allowed her till the 21st, when we both appeared, and her protestation was refused; but she persisted in her appeal, and, when they proposed to proceed, left the court. Being thrice summoned to appear without effect, she was pronounced *contumax*, and cited to appear on Friday next. As she will make all efforts to impeach the cause, we have thought good to advertise you of the same, that you may prevent the Pope from granting anything to stay process; and if the Imperialists should attempt it, you shall signify to him the dishonor he will do to his legates, his own commission, and his promises, and any other motive you can devise. We doubt not the Pope will act like a loving father, and not do anything displeasant to us, knowing how inconvenient it would be for this cause to be decided at Rome, which is now in the Emperor's power.[40]

In this developing situation, Thomas Wolsey was sharp enough to see the seeds of his own downfall. By 24 June, he was 'greatly troubled' to hear that the Pope was unwilling to make any concessions and refused to fulfil any of the promises Wolsey had made to the king. The Pope had greater need of Henry than Henry had of the Pope, the cardinal attempted to argue to Gregory Casale in Rome, as 'the King has great reason for abandoning the Pope, and leaving him to be excluded from the forthcoming league'. Wolsey promised to 'use my efforts that he shall be honorably treated; and I believe that such is his Majesty's generosity that he will not fail to comply with my intercession, provided that his Holiness does nothing to the King's injury, especially in the avocation of the cause'. Wolsey knew that this, 'among other evil effects, will cause my ruin' but he also foresaw Henry's break with the papacy. Clement was in danger of losing Henry and destroying Wolsey's 'authority, reputation, and life itself'.[41] Even Catherine recognised the inevitable, writing to Mendoza after he had left England that 'she perceives that all the king's anger at his ill success will be visited on Wolsey'.[42] Within months, the first of Wolsey's grim predictions would come true.

There was a sense at the court, not just from Wolsey, that their proceedings would be groundbreaking and that things would be different after this, not just for Henry and Catherine, but also for many of the individuals involved. Campeggio had been thrown by the strength of Bishop Fisher's advocacy of the marriage and could not see what the future might hold for him: 'This affair of Rochester was unexpected and unforeseen, and consequently has kept everybody in wonder. What he will do we shall see when the day comes. You already know what sort of a man he is, and may imagine what is likely to happen.'[43] Yet beyond the implications for individuals, the questions being debated at Blackfriars, even the existence of the court itself, had national implications that would prove the catalyst for far more wide-reaching questions of religion, kingship and nationhood.

In Rome, the Pope foresaw the likelihood of a future breach between the Vatican and England brought on by the English king's impending disappointment. Henry was pressing ahead in the belief that he was just days away from a sentence being pronounced that would leave him free to remarry at once. Yet this had never been Clement's intention and his delaying and avoiding the awkward matter was bound to make Henry into an enemy.

The Pope understood that the English king wanted a quick solution. Henry only desired the sentence to be pronounced by the legates and was not willing to wait for confirmation from Rome in order to immediately contract a new marriage. Clement was at a loss to know how Henry can have reached this conclusion, unless from Campeggio, as he was in a queue. Clement had several other commissions to execute before any process could be made. Yet he knew this procrastination would anger Henry; he was quite correct that he 'will be able to excuse himself for not having granted their previous requests; but if he does so again, he will produce inextinguishable hatred in the King's mind'.[44]

And inextinguishable hatred was something of a speciality for Henry, whose views towards former friends who fell from grace was implacable. It was not difficult to predict just how explosive Henry's anger would prove when the court failed to deliver the verdict he required, nor the lengths to which the king might go. A letter in code written by Peter Vannes, Dean of Salisbury, on 30 June, appears to present a piece of gossip or unguarded comment made by Wolsey, perhaps on the occasion when he and Vannes travelled together in France. Vannes reports that 'Wolsey at one time said that unless the Pope complied with the King's request, he would find some means to make his Holiness repent, and certain other expressions were used about privation. It would be good to frighten him thus, if he could be moved by threats.'[45] If Henry had privately voiced an intention to threaten the Pope, Wolsey would have been the man to know about it, and it is entirely fitting that such explosive material should be communicated in cipher. The Henry of 1521, who received a papal title for writing in defence of the faith, was no more. That young zealous Catholic had undergone a transformation from seeing the papacy as an institution of veneration to one that had little relevance for his personal faith or rule. It was partly the influence of the sack of Rome and the character of Clement VII, but largely the result of Henry's developing awareness of questions raised by the new learning which he could harness in the hope of reaching his own goals.

Therefore, Henry's defence put forward twelve articles against the marriage at Blackfriars on 25 June. These were largely general, establishing what was already known, such as the degree of relationship between Henry and Arthur, Catherine's two marriages and subsequent children with Henry. The eighth article, though, stated that in 1509 there had been 'a grave, immense and widespread scandal ... amongst the clergy and the people of England and in other places concerning such a marriage and that obloquy and insistent murmuring against it arose amongst the nations'.[46] This simply was not true. Warham was the only one to raise any brief objection, the people had welcomed and celebrated it, and, as for other nations, the marital histories of Catherine's own sisters showed that it would never be a problem in Burgundy, Spain or Portugal. Catherine and Henry were summoned to appear before the court on 28 June, with the paperwork delivered to Catherine in her chamber at Greenwich, but the queen did not return to Blackfriars.

III

The debate rumbled on without resolution. In mid-July, Campeggio and Wolsey visited Catherine again to make one last attempt to convince her that she must retire from life and enter the convent of her choice, but they found her adamant. Receiving them in her rooms at Bridewell Palace, the queen appeared with a skein of white thread about her neck, as she had been interrupted sewing with her ladies, 'thinking full little of any such matter' as the steps they urged her to take. She appealed to their better natures, claiming, 'I am a poor woman lacking both wit and understanding sufficiently to answer such approved wise men as ye be both, in so weighty a matter … I am a simple woman, destitute and barren of friendship and counsel here in a foreign region.'[47] Yet Catherine was anything but a simple woman.

Amid the heartbreak and uncertainty she was feeling, she threw herself into maintaining the legitimacy of her marriage and the justification of her position as Henry's wife, Mary's mother and her country's representative of the Church of Rome. Having questioned the court's authority, Catherine refused to return and was declared contumacious, or wilfully disobedient.

In Catherine's absence, the investigation continued for a further two months. Henry attempted to prove that Catherine and Arthur's marriage had been consummated, but Bishop Fisher proved a formidable opponent, countering the king's arguments with the queen's sworn statements of virginity and corresponding passages from the Bible. As he had done by inventing the disease Catherine was reputed to be suffering from, Wolsey decided to fight with whatever weapons he could. He now drew on a number of statements he had gathered from those who had been witness to the 1501 marriage as servants, pages and companions: those placed to repeat the worst kind of gossip that can arise out of the bawdy jokes and tone of the moment. The chief witness was Charles Brandon, who spoke of Arthur's boast the following morning at being tired after spending the night 'in the midst of Spain'. Wolsey also found William Thomas, who had helped Arthur to undress and accompanied him to Catherine's chamber, although this could only prove that he passed the night there, not that the pair had actually had sex. Eventually, it was concluded that what had transpired between Catherine and Arthur could not be proven either way, especially in the light of the queen's sworn statements.

It is worth remembering that the Legatine court was divided between those who had been alive or in England at the time of Catherine's first marriage, and those who had not. The testimony of Richard Foxe, Bishop of Winchester and Lord Privy Seal, had been recorded in Wolvesey Castle, Winchester, on 6 April 1527, eighteen months before his death. Foxe died shortly before the trial began but had been an important figure during the early years of Catherine's life in England, and his words were permitted to stand from beyond the grave. They also served to reinvoke the queen's history and the honour that was afforded to her in former times:

> Says he is 79 years old; and it is now 41 years since he knew Henry VII. Knew prince Arthur, who was born in the priory of St. Swithin's, Winchester, and baptised in the monastery; he being secretary to Henry VII., and present. Says he baptised Henry VIII. in the Church of the Observants at Greenwich. Remembers the entry of queen Katharine into London, and met her in St. George's Fields, and conducted her into London.[48]

On the technical details of the original marriage Foxe was less helpful, but that did not stop him from asserting that Catherine and Arthur were man and wife together:

> Does not remember anything of the matrimonial contract between her and Arthur. Was present at the solemnization at St. Paul's. Thinks the contract was passed some time before. Thinks the

> Prince was of sufficient age for marriage, but cannot remember how old he was. Says they cohabited in the palace of the bishop of London, near St. Paul's, for about 14 days, and after that resided in Wales, to the Prince's death.[49]

Foxe believed that Catherine's second marriage had been the work of de Puebla, which was to overstate the late ambassador's influence somewhat. He recalled that dispensations had been needed and that the match caused much discussion, although the 'impediment' he identifies that caused Henry VII anxiety in 1502 was that of Arthur's age:

> Frequent deliberations took place between the King's councillors, of whom he was one, in reference to the impediment. Thinks there was a contract between the two. Does not know the express age of the Prince. Is certain that a bull was obtained from the Pope, which was then thought sufficient for contracting the marriage and removing the impediment. Believes that various bulls were obtained, two of which remain in England, and one or two in Spain, all of the same tenor. On a copy of the bull being read to him, stating that Henry desired the marriage, and yet at the time of the bull he was a minor, believes the suggestion was a true one, so far as the peace of the two kingdoms was concerned; but whether the King desired the marriage at the time of the bull, says he does not know what the King's mind was.[50]

On 13 July, after much lengthy deliberation, Pope Clement reached the decision that the legatine court at Blackfriars must be suspended and had the formal announcement made three days later. The news reached the two cardinals in London on 22 July, and Wolsey must have been aware that he had just received warning of his own downfall. As yet, nobody else knew. The same day the Bishop of Bayonne had written confidently that until lately 'matters were almost as the king wishes' and that a verdict had been imminently expected, but now, having heard Clement's news, Campeggio seemed less keen. The bishop could not understand the change. At the end of the month, Campeggio prorogued the court on the pretext that papal business was suspended over the summer and that it would reconvene on 1 October. But this was never his intention.

In the meantime, the court's suspension seemed like a victory for the queen's cause. Henry was not going to be taking a new wife anytime soon. That August, the Imperial ambassador to Rome, Miçer Mai, wrote to Charles that Catherine's cause was now safe, for two main reasons. Firstly, the queen's own appeal on the grounds of the court's authority created a case for *litis pendentia* (conflicting pending suits) and secondly, because the proceedings were considered unwarranted.[51] Thus it was in consequence of Catherine's response that the Pope had been able to find grounds to disregard the proceedings against her. She must have been pleased to hear this. Mai added that the king was trying to 'hurry on the affair' although he had not reckoned with the reasoning of Catherine's most vocal advocate. In the words of John Fisher, 'a very learned and holy man', only God could dissolve the match. He had been brave enough to speak out against the king publicly, giving a speech to the effect that 'he was now an old man, and had studied this cause, and for discharge of his conscience he declared it a valid marriage, which only God could dissolve. Many affirmed the same opinion; and it may be that, seeing this, they will hesitate to proceed in the sentence.'[52] According to Fisher, it would be canonically wrong for Henry to leave Catherine or take another wife.

Clement VII agreed. Having recently been so ill that his death had been reported across Europe, andhaving endured the sack of Rome, he was beginning to find Henry's marital trials irritating. The Pope's tactic was always to delay, to buy time and hope for the issue to resolve itself. Reports of Henry's relationship with Anne made it sound so volatile that Clement may have been hoping their passion would burn itself out, or else be consummated, while they waited. There was some wisdom in this tactic. Louis de Praet, formerly Charles's ambassador to England, wrote to the Emperor on 12 August in a letter that exactly illustrates the cunning papal subterfuge that was preventing the Blackfriars court from reaching a verdict:

> A courier has come from England in nine days with a duplicate of the Queen's procuration, and the process made. They say

> that sentence has been prorogued to the 1st Oct.; which is good, because meanwhile the inhibition and revocation will arrive.[53]

Clement and Charles hoped that Henry would reflect in the interim and come to his senses, or find a solution without further need for legal proceedings. The King of England was suffering from a temporary madness, an obsessive delusion, a devastating passion, yet all those concerned knew him to be an intelligent, pious, educated man. Surely a little more time was all that was needed to bring him to his senses? The Emperor was certain that a period of reflection would 'afford the King of England an opportunity of coming to a good understanding ... if he is so minded'.[54] But Henry was not so minded. He wanted a definite answer so that he could go ahead and marry Anne at once.

He was not to receive that answer. On 1 September, to Henry's great frustration, the cardinal referred the question back to Rome. Six days later, de Praet wrote that it was suspended from Christmas to Easter. This wasn't acceptable to the king. From Windsor, Henry wrote in exasperation to the Pope, urging a final judgement in his favour as soon as possible. He had wished that all things would have happed in correspondence with his expectations, not because he had developed these desires rashly, but because he had been encouraged by Clement's promises. In a veiled threat, he promised that he would repay such an act with kindness. The implication was that if his wish were refused he would cease to be kind and would not forget what had passed. Henry was now less the young man who had been painted in 1520, bejewelled and mild of expression, looking off to the sidelines, and more the bombastic famous figure of Holbein's later portrait, hand assuredly on hip, eyes staring straight into those of the viewer, commanding and defiant. The Legatine court was the turning point between those two images. In the summer of 1529, the relationship between Henry and the Pope was at an all-time low. The king's tone in this letter to Clement is incredulous, disappointed and forceful:

> As it is, we are compelled to regard with grief and wonder the incredible confusion which has arisen. If the Pope can relax Divine laws at his pleasure, surely he has as much power over human laws. Complains that he has often been deceived by the

> Pope's promises, on which there is no dependence to be placed; and that his dignity has not been consulted in the treatment he has received. If the Pope, as his ambassadors write, will perform what he has promised, and keep the cause now advoked to Rome in his own hands, until it can be decided by impartial judges, and in an indifferent place, in a manner satisfactory to the King's scruples, he will forget what is past, and repay kindness by kindness.[55]

But in the battle of wills the Pope was just as stubborn as the King of England. In reply, Clement wrote that the case was 'suspended' and that the original papal ruling on both Catherine's marriages remained valid. Moreover, to Henry's annoyance, Clement was disposed to believe Catherine's sworn oath. This was still her most valuable bargaining point. If the queen, 'as she affirms, was not known by Prince Arthur, there is no doubt that the dispensation was perfectly sound', Clement pointed out to Henry. If Henry rejected this, he would be calling his wife a liar. He would never do this. Clement then attempted to appeal to the English king's conscience, to concentrate on wider issues and resume his role as a Christian Prince in Europe, by begging him 'to consider the danger in which Christendom stands from the Turks, and how much it is enhanced by this dispute'. But Henry had decided that his allegiance to Rome was at an end. In his opinion, the Turks were not 'going to do such serious mischief'.[56] The king felt he had been misled and let down by Clement in what he thought should have been a straightforward case. He summoned what would come to be called his Reformation Parliament, which would alter the face of religion in England.

Catherine had not quite finished either. She wanted to ensure that such a proceeding would never take place again. At her request, the Imperial ambassador John Antony Musettula entered a petition to the Pope that the matter should never be reopened. She asked Clement to 'impose on him perpetual silence, or at least to commit the judgement to Cardinals at the court of Rome, or papal auditors'. It was 'notorious', according to Musettula, 'that the Queen cannot be defended or obtain justice in England', so he hoped the Pope would 'forbid anything to be done prejudicial to the cause' or to allow a new 'marriage to be contracted by the King, under the penalties of ecclesiastical censure, to be assisted by the secular arm, if need be'.[57] It sounds very much as if this petition was inviting some sort of force to be at least threatened against Henry, perhaps in unison with the Emperor, to prevent him from taking a new wife.

The failure of the legatine court was a victory for Catherine, temporarily halting the possibility of Henry marrying Anne, but it was a pyrrhic victory. It did not make the king wish to return to her and resume their life together, nor did it solve the long-term problem of Anne Boleyn, or another future woman. She knew that her husband would continue to seek ways to leave her, and that must have been heartbreaking. Had it been a straightforward political union, the queen might have found it less painful but still reprehensible to be cast aside. It is a testament to the strength of her feelings, her genuine love for Henry, that the matter touched her on such a personal level. Catherine found comfort in the fact that her marriage had been vindicated by the papacy, that the last two decades of her life, and the seven years of struggle before it, had not been in vain. Since the age of three she had been raised to be Queen of England, wife to the country's king, mother of its heir. She was not prepared to see that taken away from her. There was also another mission to be fulfilled: Catherine may have lost her husband, but she was confirmed in her continuing mission to try and bring about his salvation. He may no longer want her to be his wife, but she was determined to prove his saviour.

21

Exits and Arrivals 1529

I

While Catherine's marriage had been debated, the world had not been standing still.

That summer, a European alliance was reached when the Peace of Cambrai was signed between France and Spain on 5 August. It was actually Francis's mother, Louise, and her sister-in-law, Charles' aunt Margaret of Savoy, who negotiated the deal, but now there was no other resistance to the growing dominion of the Emperor, with whom Henry was still having to tread the fine line of trying to maintain friendly diplomatic ties while attempting to keep Charles from interfering in his personal life. Thomas More, Cuthbert Tunstall and John Hackett were sent to conclude the English aspect of the deal. Also that August, the Turks were advancing west under the leadership of Suleiman the Magnificent. They took the city of Buda on 8 September and sailed up the Danube, hoping to capture Vienna. The city blocked its gates, dug out a defensive ditch and erected huge walls and ramparts. After a siege of several weeks, suffering from illness and a lack of supplies and facing the approach of winter, the Turkish army were forced to withdraw and the walls of the capital of the Hapsburg Empire were not breached. Had Suleiman strode into St Stephen's Cathedral in his embroidered kaftan, the face of Europe in the sixteenth century might have been considerably different.

At Henry's court, an invasion of another kind had taken place. Just before the first sitting at Blackfriars, there were worrying reports that heretical texts 'of an evil sort' had arrived 'thick and threefold' in London.[1] Some had been smuggled in by the priest George Constantine, who had helped Tyndale with his translations in Antwerp and read more Lutheran texts in Paris, denouncing the Catholic Church. Campeggio reported that he was endeavouring to obtain one of these words but had been unsuccessful, although he heard the works contained promises by Lutherans to reject all heresies and to follow the Divine Law if Henry and Charles were to work together 'to reduce the ecclesiastical state to the condition of the primitive church, taking from it all its temporalities'. Campeggio warned Henry that 'this was the Devils dressed in angels' clothing, in order that he might the more easily deceive' and that the Lutherans' real intention was to 'seize the property of the church'. Their ensuing debate shows how the king was beginning to be receptive to reformed ideas, as the cardinal stated that councils and theologians had 'determined that the Church justly held her temporal goods', but Henry replied that the Lutherans said those decisions had been made by ecclesiastics, 'insinuating that now it is necessary for the laity to interpose'. Campeggio argued that this would be directly against the king's interests because 'as matters now stood, he obtained large sums of money' which he would lose, and if the laity held Church property, 'they would probably grow rich and rebellious'. Henry replied that the laypeople accused the clergy, especially those in Rome, of living 'very wickedly' and having 'erred in many things from the Divine Law'. Campeggio conceded that there were sins committed in Rome 'because we are but men' but that the 'Holy See had not deviated a jot from the true faith'. Henry concluded by reassuring the cardinal that he 'had been and always would remain a good Christian' but simply wanted to pass on what others had told him. The critical and exploratory nature of the king's thinking on Church property, as well as his excuse that he was merely repeating the views of the heretics, indicates a further step along the road of monastic suppression.

It may have been at this time that another influence was affecting Henry's religious perspective. In contrast to Catherine's Catholicism, Anne Boleyn was very much a reformer; not perhaps 'more Lutheran than Luther' as she was later described, but certainly a follower of the new learning, especially as it had been manifest in France in recent years, and an evangelical in her adherence to the direct interpretation of the Scriptures. She was in favour of reform and supported those whose agreement with these views led them into trouble. Around this time, Anne owned a copy of very same translation of the Bible by Tyndale that Henry had recently ordered to be burned, and she also had in her possession his more recent book, which she lent to her lady-in-waiting Anne Gainsford. Published the previous year, Tyndale's *Obedience of a Christian Man* proved to be a critical text for the development of Henry's beliefs about himself, the State, the Church and God. After the book ended up in the wrong hands, Anne asked Henry to intervene with Wolsey to ensure its return and she 'besought his grace most tenderly to read it'. Tyndale's view that there was no higher earthly authority than a king meant that rulers were not obliged to owe any allegiance to the Pope. For Henry this was a liberating idea, confirming his current frustrations with Clement's slowness and deliberate obfuscations and his increasing disillusionment with Rome. By contrast, Catherine's Catholicism deepened, as she celebrated Mass on her knees, fasted, donned her hair shirt and rose in the early hours to pray. It must have been difficult for her to learn that Anne Boleyn had not just stolen away her husband's affections, but that she was also corrupting his faith. Yet this is exactly why Catherine remained devoted to her husband, in the belief that his soul was in peril and that her purpose was to bring him back to the true faith.

Over in Freiburg, Catherine's old friend Erasmus, who had fled from England in disappointment early in Henry's reign, wrote to Cuthbert Tunstall in January 1530 about the changing political times. He approved of the criticisms being made of the Church, but also that devout voices were no longer being listened to and respected among the reforming zeal:

> To all appearance the long war of words and writings will terminate in blows. But for his soul's health would rather be in the camp from which he fled; but Heaven forbid, that, for the little life remaining to an old man, with a stone, which is certain death, in his bladder, he should desert the unity of the Church. As to what its ministers may decree concerning his writings, that is

their affair. If the rulers of the Church were men like Augustine, Erasmus would agree with them excellently; but if Augustine himself were to write now what he has written, or what the age requires, he would be as badly thought of as Erasmus. It is true what you say, that fire is not put out by fire; but it is not right to endure a charge of impiety. Can adduce hundreds of passages, both in Augustine and in St. Paul, which would now be denounced as heresies. Monks and schoolmen are deceived if they think this is the way to secure the peace of the Church. They throw oil upon the flames. Does not congratulate More, although he does not grieve for him. England he does congratulate, and himself, not a little.[2]

Another of Catherine's long-serving friends was on the verge of leaving the country. Despite poor health and very restricted circumstances, Don Inigo de Mendoza had done his best to serve Catherine in his capacity as ambassador, but in 1529 he was preparing to leave England. After taking his leave of the king, who remained angry at what he perceived to be Imperial interference in his private affairs, Wolsey then asked to see Mendoza alone and tried to convince him to stay, saying that his departure at the current time would be prejudicial to the cardinal's cause. Yet Mendoza would not stay, assuring Wolsey that the Emperor would 'soon send a personage as liege ambassador to reside in England'. He departed seventeen days later, leaving when his passport arrived. The following year, Mendoza was made a cardinal and was at Bologna to witness the long-delayed coronation of Charles as Holy Roman Emperor. He died in 1535.

The 'new personage' Mendoza had promised Wolsey arrived in the form of Eustace Chapuys, a native of Savoy. He was around five years younger than Catherine, making him almost forty at the time of his arrival in England in late August 1529. Having been educated at the universities of Turin, Valence and Rome, he was a good choice for Catherine's difficult situation, being Doctor of Canon and Civil Laws. In September, Chapuys reported back to the Emperor on the situation in the English court, listing the dukes of Norfolk and Suffolk, Sir Thomas Boleyn and his son George, Lord Rochford, as 'the king's most favourite courtiers and the nearest to his person'. He had observed that 'the King's affection for La Bolaing [Boleyn] increases daily. It is so great just now that it can hardly be greater; such is the intimacy and familiarity in which they live at present.'[3] Yet there was no chance of a marriage taking place, as certain modifications by the legatine court had been 'carefully preserved, because should the King in the meantime attempt anything new, or actually marry another woman, this second matrimony be null, under the 'litis pendentia' and express inhibition'.[4] Catherine could rest assured there would not be another queen at court just yet. However, more worryingly, Chapuys picked up a rumour in October about Princess Mary, who was then thirteen, approaching marriageable age and being kept apart from her mother: 'I have just heard from a very good source that this King is so blindly and passionately fond of his Anne, that he has, at her persuasion, consented to treat of a marriage between the princess Mary, his daughter, and the son of the Duke of Norfolk, who is a near relative of the lady.'[5] Fortunately for Catherine, no more came of this story.

In Wolsey's absence from court, Anne and her faction were responsible for transacting 'all state business' and, according to rumour, it was 'entirely in their power … to remain in office'. He continued that Anne Boleyn would soon be responsible for the dismissal of Wolsey, 'for she happens to be the person in all this kingdom who hates him most, and has spoken and acted the most openly against him'.[6] In cipher, he added:

> I cannot say what will be the upshot of all this, certain it is that from this moment the affairs of the said Cardinal are beginning to take a very bad turn. Formerly no one dared say a word against him, but now the tables are turned, and his name is in everybody's mouth, and what is still worse for him, libellous writings, I am told, are being circulated about him.[7]

At first, the new ambassador was not able to see the queen. She sent him a message which was delivered by her physician, Fernando de Victoria, 'to say how pleased and comforted she was by my coming'. She wrote that she had 'felt more joy at the news than she had experienced for a long time' and that his arrival 'could not be more opportune'. However, she warned him that he was not to see her without the king's permission, instead allowing Victoria, 'a very trusty man', to be their messenger, enabling her to keep Chapuys up to date with affairs.[8] True to Catherine's word, Victoria arrived at the ambassador's lodgings and accompanied him and his escort through the streets of London, giving him a summary of recent events. Catherine also had plans for the next stage of the proceedings, wishing Chapuys to 'consider and calculate the best means of promoting the advocation of the cause to Rome', given that Henry 'opposed it violently'. Although the king had been more pleasant towards her lately, having 'for the last three or four days put on a better mien than was his wont', Chapuys was not to spare 'such flattering and conciliatory words as might, without prejudice to my commission', when he met Henry, 'or influence his nature, which is more accessible to persuasion than to threat'. The atmosphere of mistrust was still strong, as indicated by Victoria's decision to leave Chapuys 'as late as possible in the evening to avoid observation'. Catherine herself would also soon tell him that there were 'matters upon which I dare not, surrounded as I am, speak to you in detail'.[9]

It was 18 September before Chapuys was granted an audience with Catherine. She was grateful to receive the new ambassador, who struck the right note with her at once:

> After dinner the King, to whom I had expressed my wish of being introduced to the Queen, and presenting her with the Emperor's letter, bade one of his chamberlains to conduct me to her apartments. Having exhibited my credentials, and delivered the letter, I went on to explain the substance of my instructions, and the conversation I had had with the King, her husband, and what I myself had replied to the King's arguments. She seemed very glad, and said to me that I could not have said more in her favour; but that the room being full of people at the time, she could not do more than express her gratitude and assure me that an ambassador from the Emperor at such a time was a great comfort in the midst of her tribulations.[10]

The ambassador's account also gives a glimpse into the methods Catherine was forced to employ in order to ensure her privacy. When speaking of Wolsey, she spoke 'in such a low tone of voice that nobody but myself could hear her, and I doubt even whether the courtiers in the room could see her actually move her lips. After this she raised her voice to its usual pitch, and inquired where 'Your Majesty was, and whether your health was good, and so forth'. Catherine was aware just who she could and could not trust among those in her chamber, right under her nose.[11] She was also able to convey to Chapuys that she was 'concerned and frightened' at the imminent sitting of the Parliament that Henry had called, believing he would try and use it as a vehicle to achieve what the legatine court had failed to do. She feared that 'something may be brewed there against her' and that Henry had 'played his cards so well' that he was likely 'to get a majority of votes in his favour'. Chapuys doubted it would come to this, having seen 'the affection of the English' for their queen.[12] Catherine was so upset about the opposition of Henry's council that she again appealed to the Emperor, through Chapuys, who wrote on 8 October that her fear had 'so perplexed her of late that she actually hesitates as to the best course to follow'. Her only resolution was to 'inform Your Majesty, through me, of her perplexity and fears' and to beg that 'the matter be taken entirely out of her hands and placed' into Charles's.[13]

II

But Catherine was not to be the first victim of the Reformation Parliament: that honour went to Thomas Wolsey. The cardinal and numerous other observers had already foreseen his demise as a consequence of the failure of the Blackfriars court. Accustomed to having all his desires satisfied for the last two decades, Henry needed someone to blame when it all went wrong. As far back as January, Mendoza reported that the king confided in him that 'he has begun to lay the blame upon his cardinal, who, he says, has not fulfilled his promises in the matter'.[14] Chapuys summed up the problem neatly upon his arrival, seeing at once that 'the cause of this misunderstanding between the king and the cardinal can be no other than the utter failure of the measures taken in order to bring about the divorce, on which failure those parties, who for a long time have been watching their opportunity to revenge old injuries, and take the power out of the cardinal's hands, have founded their attacks to undermine his influence with the king, and get the administration of affairs in their own hands'.[15]

Yet in outward appearances, Wolsey seemed to be thriving. His programme of suppressing minor monasteries in order to fund his Cambridge college and Ipswich school was pressing on, being granted a papal bull to dissolve those houses whose revenue did not exceed 8,000 ducats the previous November,[16] and as late as 29 June 1529, while the court was still in session at Blackfriars, he was contemplating what would have been a far more wide-reaching reform of religious practice in England. Writing to Gregory Casale regarding the 'union of monasteries', Wolsey desired 'to have the power of uniting small monasteries, as well as annexing them to greater. The bull for erecting cathedrals only empowers him to enquire and report concerning monasteries and other matters, but the King thinks that authority for completing the matter is needed.'[17] In January, Wolsey had been planning the building work for his new colleges, requesting stone to be brought from a quarry in Caen, Lower Normandy and transported to his sites 'for the perfection of the said edifices' although he did not wish to have to pay any 'duty thereupon'.[18] At the end of May, just before the legatine court convened, he received confirmation of a papal bull for the suppression of Snape, Dodnesh and other places, and 'dismemberment of the same, for the benefit of the said college'.[19]

This was not simply an economic matter to fund his institutions, as his correspondence with the young Richard Rich shows. Rich was then a lawyer in search of a patron, writing to the Cardinal knowing his 'great zeal for reform' and begging 'to be called before him that he may declare the abuses that are daily used and suggest remedies'.[20] Even a list of gifts made to Wolsey in a five week period concurrent with the court shows that, at the very least, people still had confidence in his importance and influence. He received four pheasants, two beefs and two gulls from Sir John Rogers, a beef from Sir Thomas More, fifteen herons and five shovellers from Sir Edward Willoughby, a beef and ten mutton from Sir William Woodall and numerous other gifts of meat and game from individuals and institutions.[21] He was still in possession of his household and expensive clothing, still with access to the king, treated almost like royalty, in fact, but his failure to deliver the verdict Henry required sealed his fate. However, the king found it difficult to let go.

In September, Henry was staying at Grafton in Northamptonshire, where Wolsey and Campeggio travelled in order for the Italian to bid the king farewell before returning to Rome. Henry greeted his servant warmly, raising him from his feet and discussing with him earnestly. Yet, on 21 September, the king sent the dukes of Norfolk and Suffolk to demand that the cardinal leave court and surrender the great seal. The following day he seemed to change his mind again, sending the cardinal a ring as a sign of his favour, by which token Wolsey believed himself to have a chance of salvation. It was not to be.

One evening, a week later, the dukes of Norfolk and Suffolk arrived in the gallery of his house at Westminster, to remove the great seal from his possession and take an inventory of his goods before they were confiscated. According to the report of the newly arrived Imperial ambassador, Eustace Chapuys, Henry and Anne returned by water secretly, to pick over Wolsey's possessions, 'and found them much greater than he expected'. The list includes a range of items, from the religious to the luxurious, which typifies Wolsey's dual existence; it gives a sense of the life lived by the man who built Hampton Court, who was briefly the most powerful subject in the country. Among them were hundreds of wall hangings and tapestries, intended to line a large number of rooms of great dimensions. Made of cloth of gold and velvet, say and buckram, they depicted biblical, historical, mythological and symbolic scenes, with one eight-piece set including 'Priamus, Parys and Atchilles, Jupiter, Pluto and Ceres, Hanyballe, Virtue, and hunting'. Otherwise the tapestries featured a fairly random mix: 'the emperor Octavian, with Our Lady and son appearing in a sunbeam; woodcutting, and a man shooting at a heron; a woman with a banner and a helmet; a king, with a lady holding a cup; a king in his pavilion, and a lady in red kneeling; a fountain, and a lady in her hair standing by it; a lady putting a black shoe upon a man's foot; one king crowning.'[22] He also had the choice of 78 feather beds or 157 woollen mattresses, 32 of which were covered with Holland cloth and intended for Wolsey's personal use. His pillow covers were of black silk with gold *fleur-de-lys* or white sile with the design in red. He owned thirteen close stools, or portable toilets, covered with scarlet and black velvet.[23]

One curious entry lists 'saints' apparel', which appear to have been items used to dress statues, a feature of the high Catholic cults of interceding saints that was already being widely criticised as a diversion from a direct, personal relationship between man and God:

> Saints' apparel: 2 coats for Our Lady, crimson velvet guarded with cloth of gold and set with counterfeit pearls; and black damask, guarded with crimson velvet, and bordered with white satin; a cloth of blue satin of Bridges, embroidered with gold flowers and stars, to hang before Our Lady; a launde kerchief for her; a coat for her son, of black velvet, guarded with cloth of gold; a coat of blue damask for St. John; a coat for him, of tinsel satin guarded with crimson satin.[24]

Some of Wolsey's items were also monuments to the recent past, including six hangings of arras, each nine yards by four and a half, featuring the arms of England and Spain, as well as a bed of rich tissue, made for Wolsey's time at the Field of Cloth of Gold. Some of his chairs were decorated with cardinals' hats and pomegranates. He also owned lengths of blue and crimson velvet featuring an image of St James, from Compostela, edged with the traditional pilgrim's scallop shell in green and silver, which may have arrived with the Spanish in 1501. Among his treasury there was a golden salt cellar featuring red and white roses and the initials H and K, as well as a 'gilt layer of Spanish work', featuring naked children and wild beasts.[25] When Wolsey's effects were divided up, Thomas More was sent a set of six bowls featuring cardinals' hats and pomegranates, considered a suitable gift by Henry, but within a few years, they were to prove something of a poisoned chalice.

Catherine might have privately rejoiced in the downfall of her enemy, but she was shrewd enough to see parallels between Wolsey's fate and her own, understanding just how completely Henry could turn on those he had formerly loved. On 8 October, she would have heard how Wolsey was stripped of his titles and officially charged with *praemunire*, of placing his allegiance to the Pope above his loyalties to Henry. Two weeks later, in the privy chamber and Greenwich, the king formally handed the great seal to Thomas More, 'a good servant of the queen', who agreed to fill the job of chancellor. More was now fifty-one and had gained considerable experience by acting as Henry's secretary and adviser. The famous portrait of the Mores had been completed by Hans Holbein in 1527, showing the statesman seated at the heart of his household, which was unusual in its advocacy of female education, as the picture is for depicting a Tudor family group. He was a conservative Catholic and deplored the criticisms of the reformers and the move towards Protestantism on the Continent. He had worked with Wolsey in recent years to prevent the importation of heretical books and in questioning booksellers and doubters; under his regime as chancellor, some of the leading English heretics would be tracked down and burned at the stake.

Ill and abandoned, the king's most able and devoted servant was heartbroken at his fall from grace. Writing pitifully to Henry, Wolsey cried 'daily to [Henry] for mercy', and beseeched the king 'that you will not think it proceeds from any mistrust I have in your goodness, nor that I would molest you by my importunate suit. The same comes of my ardent desire, that, next unto God, I covet nothing so much in this world as your favour and forgiveness. The remembrance of my folly, with the sharp sword of your displeasure, have so penetrated my heart.' Cardinal Jean du Bellay visited Wolsey 'in his troubles' and judged him to be 'the greatest example of fortune that one could see'. He wept and prayed, with his countenance having 'lost half its animation' so that even his enemies 'could not help pitying him, yet they do not desist from persecuting him to the last'. He was prepared to 'give up everything, to his shirt, and to go and live in a hermitage, if this King will not keep him in disfavour'.[26] But it was the king's rising favourite whom Wolsey had most offended, as he acknowledged, writing that 'none dares speak to the King on his part for fear of Madame Anne's displeasure'.[27] Finally, on 27 October, Wolsey was 'definitively condemned by the Council, declared a rebel, and guilty of high treason for having obtained a legatine bull, whereby he had conferred many benefices in the King's patronage. He has been deprived of his dignities, his goods confiscated, and himself sentenced to prison until the King shall decide.'[28] In Freiburg, rumours of Wolsey's arrest had reached Erasmus, who sent to enquire after him with the comment, 'Oh, the slippery turns of this world!'[29] Wolsey would die on the way to his trial the following year.

III

In spite of everything that had happened, the pretence of harmony was being maintained at court. The tensions erupted at times when Henry and Catherine came together, such as an occasion Chapuys relates in early October 1529 which arose after dinner. Henry turned to his wife and said that she wished to serve her interests 'and defend the validity of the dispensation' by claiming that Arthur had never consummated his marriage, which was 'well and good, but no less was our marriage illegal'. It was an admission that Catherine was speaking the truth when she repeatedly claimed to have gone to Henry's bed a virgin, which he never refuted. However, Henry's new line of argument was that 'the bull [did] not dispense' with the clause of public honesty, the fact that Catherine and Arthur had been legally man and wife, and therefore, Henry continued, he intended 'disputing and maintaining against all people that a dispensation thus conceived is insufficient'.[30]

Chapuys considered this argument to be on 'very brittle footing' and related Catherine's response that 'whatever arguments were used to convince her that she was not his lawful and legitimate wife would be of no avail; she considered herself such. That was not the time or place to dispute about such matters, and that they had better go to Rome, and have the question determined by the Pope.'[31] A few more weeks of sharing meals like this, and royal tempers were wearing thin.

For Catherine, at least, the Greenwich ménage á trois was proving an impossibly difficult arrangement. She was deeply upset at still being parted from Princess Mary, who was being kept at Windsor as a punishment for the queen resisting the authority of the Blackfriars court. This state continued 'to the great sorrow of the Queen, her mother, who would wish to have her by her side'. But the question of the marriage had come to a standstill, as Chapuys reported: 'On that point, however, hardly a step has been gained. Of her business not a word is said, she has lately sent two of her secretaries, members of her Council, to confer with me, and shew a paper written in her defence, which, I must say, is very commendable.'[32]

Once Catherine had returned to Greenwich, Chapuys related to the Emperor that he had visited her with some of the other ambassadors and found her in a state of depression:

> We all called at the apartments of the Queen, whom we found in great sorrow, so much so that she could hardly suppress her tears in our presence. We told her that, according to Your Majesty's letters, Mr. de le Sauch, there present, had consulted on her case with several of the Parisian doctors, all of whom had given their opinion that it was quite impossible to dissolve the marriage, and that neither the king of France himself nor any other prince in the World had the power of making the university give a contrary opinion. This assurance, and the hope and trust which the Queen has in Your Majesty's exertions in her behalf, somewhat relieved her from her anguish, and her countenance gladdened; but as there were many in the room she dared not say much, nor did we venture to speak to her on the subject. She, however, promised to write or let me know her wishes by private and verbal message. And so she did, for on the following day she wrote me a letter through her physician [Fernando Victoria], explaining the King's behaviour towards her, which, she says, is still the same, and begging me to report upon it, and particularly to recommend her poor case to Your Majesty.[33]

The pressure was becoming too much for Catherine, and when Henry dined with her on St Andrew's Day, 30 November, her composure snapped. She told her husband that 'she had long been suffering the pains of Purgatory on earth, and that she was very badly treated by his refusing to dine with and visit her in her apartments'. Henry replied that she had no cause to complain, as she was 'mistress of her household' and could 'do as she pleased'; furthermore, that he had been busy recently cleaning up the mess that Wolsey had left. He added that 'as to his visiting her in her apartments and partaking of her bed, she ought to know that he was not her legitimate husband, as innumerable doctors and canonists, all men of honour and probity, and even his own almoner, Doctor Lee, who had once known her in Spain, were ready to maintain'. He was only waiting for the opinions of the Parisian doctors in order to forward them to Rome and if the Pope did not conform and declare the marriage null and void, 'then it that case he [Henry] would denounce the Pope as a heretic and marry whom he pleased'.[34] It must have been very shocking for Catherine to hear that Henry was actually planning such a decisive religious step, which she believed could only lead to the damnation of his soul.

Catherine replied that Henry knew full well 'that the principal cause alleged for the divorce did not really exist, because she had come to him as a virgin, 'as he himself had owned upon more than one occasion'.[35] She went on to challenge him that she cared not for the opinion of his almoner, who was not her judge: the Pope was, and 'for each doctor or lawyer who might decide in your favour and against me, I shall find 1,000 to declare that the marriage is good and indissoluble'.[36] After a 'good deal of talking and disputing', Henry abruptly left Catherine at the table and headed off to sup with Anne, 'very disconcerted and downcast'. But he did not receive a warm welcome there, being berated by his mistress about the control Catherine still exercised over him. Reputedly, Anne was annoyed at the delay and its implications for her future. Nor did she like Henry spending so much time with Catherine, so she reminded him:

> Did I not tell you that whenever you disputed with the Queen she was sure to have the upper hand? I see that some fine morning you will succumb to her reasoning, and that you will cast me off. I have been waiting long, and might in the meanwhile have contracted some advantageous marriage, out of which I might have had issue, which is the greatest consolation in this world; but alas! farewell to my time and youth spent to no purpose at all.[37]

This may have been the occasion that prompted Henry to send Catherine away from court, although it might also have been as the result of a case of plague locally. It was a foreshadowing of Catherine's final expulsion from Henry's life eighteen months later, but this time it was simply for a few weeks, in order for the king to placate Anne Boleyn. As Chapuys noted, it was not Catherine who had Henry under her control, but Anne, who was growing increasingly impatient as the months ticked past without resolution. The king was so much in love with her, thought the ambassador, that he was no longer listening to reason: 'As far as I can hear and judge, this King's obstinacy and his passion for the Lady are such that there is no chance of recalling him by mildness or fair words to a sense of his duty.'[38] This was especially frustrating as Catherine and Chapuys had just received copies of the papal brief forbidding Henry from taking another wife while his divorce case was pending.[39]

The queen was obliged to leave Greenwich and go to Richmond. 'The Queen's treatment is worse than ever,' complained Chapuys. 'The King is always away from her as much as possible, and is here with the lady, whilst the Queen is at Richmond. He has never been so long without paying her a visit, and makes his excuse that one has died of the plague near her residence. He has renewed his attempts to persuade her to become a nun, to which she will never consent.'[40] There was a reason for Henry keeping away from Catherine for so long. During her absence from court, on 8 December, the king elevated Anne's father Thomas Boleyn to the positions of Earl of Wiltshire and Ormond. This had been followed by a feast at which Anne was seated at the king's right hand, placed above Henry's sister Mary and 'occupying the very place allotted to a crowned queen, which by the by is a thing that was never before done'.[41] Such dancing and 'carousing' followed that there had been nothing wanting, said Chapuys, 'except for a priest to give the nuptial ring and pronounce the benediction'. Seven miles away, he added, the 'poor queen' was holding her 'own fête of sorrow and weeping'.[42] Catherine indeed had every cause to complain, the ambassador continued, because of 'the king's indifference to, and neglect of her', which he claimed was 'increasing rapidly in proportion to his passionate attachment' to Anne. Chapuys urged the Emperor to act:

> At no time was his love of this latter more apparent or his intention to carry out the unrighteous and scandalous act of forsaking her, and taking the other for his wife more manifest. As I have had occasion to inform Your Majesty, it is to be feared that he may do this sooner than is anticipated unless God inspire him with repentance, or Your Majesty interfere actively to prevent.[43]

Catherine was permitted to return for the Christmas season, which was traditionally presided over by the King and Queen together. And Henry was not quite ready to dispense with traditions, either religious or marital; he would need a couple more years for that. Hall related that the season was observed 'in great triumph ... with great plenty of viands and diverse disguisings and interludes, to the great rejoicing of his people'[44] but it was definitely not a triumph for Catherine. To observers, it seemed that Henry was being pleasant to Catherine, showing his wife 'more consideration than was his wont', and with Anne not making an appearance.[45]

However, all was less than harmonious behind the scenes. On Christmas Eve, after her return, Henry had told Catherine that even if the Pope declared their marriage lawful, he still intended to divorce her and he would get his way, as the Church of Canterbury was more important than Rome and he would declare the Pope a heretic. Something must have broken in Catherine to hear this. She had, related Chapuys, 'lost all hope of bringing him to a sense of right and duty'[46] and never could think that her affairs would fall so low as they are at present. She always fancied that the king, 'after pursuing his course for some time, would turn away, and yielding to his conscience, would change his purpose as he had done at other times, and return to reason'.[47] She had been wrong.

Yet the queen had also been working behind the scenes. She might have been down but Catherine was nothing if not an indefatigable fighter, so she was not yet out. In the knowledge that Henry was hoping for the French and Italian universities to confirm his view of his marriage, Catherine set out to counter his efforts. She was more than a match for him intellectually and in terms of character, but in her present restricted circumstances there was little she could do, being excluded from the political process as the Reformation Parliament met for the first time. Appealing to the universities was something positive that she hoped might influence the council. The same Edward Lee, Henry's almoner, had informed the king that nobody in Spain apart from the Emperor 'cared a straw' whether or not the marriage was dissolved, so Catherine asked Charles to ask the Spanish universities to write in her defence, along with her niece, Empress Isabella. She hoped that if the Archbishop of Toledo could gather their responses, 'her case might be considerably improved'. She also wrote to Margaret of Savoy with the same request, and 'wherever else it may be considered expedient', as it was the only thing now she thought might 'stop the king in his course'.

Catherine feared that her husband was 'so blind as passionate in these matters, that it is much to be feared that one of these days he will take steps which may perhaps induce his people and the Commons ... to consent to the divorce'.[48] She begged Henry for permission to consult her council of advisers, and was granted permission for them to attend her at Richmond.[49] However, this kindness may have only been conferred 'in order to discover whether she had received a recent dispatch from Rome'. In fact, Henry's new parliament would not yet discuss Catherine and her marriage in its coming session; instead they were setting about the process of undermining the ties that bound England to Rome.

The Reformation Parliament had met for the first time on 3 November 1529. Its intentions were the removal of Wolsey and the reform of ecclesiastical abuses. The first was easily accomplished and the second began a three-year process of legislature that gradually curtailed papal powers in England without yet any decisive break taking place. Until this point, clergymen had enjoyed the privilege of being tried for their crimes in ecclesiastical courts, but this resulted in serious crimes going unpunished as it was usually a more lenient body who would excuse first offences. This was now abolished, meaning that the clergy were to experience the same implementation of justice as all their flock, and certain serious crimes such as murder and robbery would lead to forfeiture of all former privileges. Certain fees such as those payable to a mortuary or in probate were to be carefully regulated and altered according to the financial situation and status of the payer. Clerics were forbidden from holding more than one office or from engaging in trade, and any papal legislation challenging these resolutions, past or future, was automatically invalidated. Householders of great benefices were living well and spending nothing on their flock, while some occupied farms as stewards, thus keeping out genuine tenants.[50] It may have been symbolic that the court met at Blackfriars, where Henry's hopes had been thwarted by the Pope and where he now intended to build up the independence of the English Church in contrast. There was also a strong message being sent to any resistant clergy that while they remained in England, the king was ultimately in charge of their lives and professions, not the Pope. One of the lone voices speaking against these changes was John Fisher, Bishop of Rochester, who used his position in the House of Lords to predict that such measures could only result in the complete destruction of the Catholic Church.

Catherine could see what was coming. Chapuys recorded the following February that 'the clergy have been compelled, under pain of the said law of *praemunire*, to accept the King as head of the Church, which implies in effect as much as if they had declared him Pope of England ... This Act has very much astonished the queen, who, seeing that the king is not afraid to commit such enormities, notwithstanding the promises which have been made to the contrary, which were only to lull suspicion, has no doubt that now the king's lady is as much delighted as if she had gained paradise.'[51] The following April the queen wrote to Dr Ortiz, the Emperor's Proctor at Rome, warning him that the heretics in England were predicting that the 'Head and Protector of the Church will give the Church a great fall'. She could do no more, she stated, than trust to God and write to tell Clement the truth 'and show him the evils which are imminent'. If all that failed, she would 'complain to God, because there is neither faith nor charity in his ministers on earth'. Her learned advisers informed her that she required 'a stronger medicine to cure her wound'. Only a favourable final ruling regarding the divorce could make her well again.[52]

PART SEVEN

The Martyr 1530–1536

22

Abandonment 1530–1531

I

By 1530, Henry was determined to separate from Catherine no matter what the cost. Yet it seems that the cost was going to be huge. Dr Pedro Garay, a doctor of theology who was appointed to oversee the discussions about the divorce at the University of Paris, wrote to Charles V with prophetic words, saying that 'the king of England is making such efforts to procure the divorce as are enough to set the world on fire'.[1] He was not alone in this thought, as in January the Emperor wrote to his brother, Archduke Ferdinand, that Henry's current course of action was likely to provoke a war. 'The king of England,' he stated, 'is on the point of abandoning our aunt without the Pope's consent. Perhaps, if he sees that I am at peace in Italy, he and the king of France will beware of creating new war.' Yet if Henry persisted, Charles was considering declaring war on him as he was now in a good condition in terms of military strength 'for, besides having Naples undisturbed, I have 12,000 Spaniards and 9,000 Germans in Italy, which I can keep up until April'.[2] As Chapuys reported, rumour was running high: 'They say the king of England already holds his mistress as his wife, and maintains that, whether the Pope will or no, he will make her so.' He suspected this would not end well: 'He treats the Pope as a heretic, and says he might be degraded. On one hand, the Pope would not consent, the affair being too scandalous; on the other, he does not like to incur disgrace and the loss of Henry's obedience. Suspects he will commit some folly. In any case this will be a sufficient cause of new war.'

Sympathy for Catherine was widespread. Chapuys added that matters for her 'can hardly be worse than they are at present' because such was 'the blind passion of the King for the Lady [Anne]'. The ambassador feared that 'one of these days some disorderly act will take place'.[3] The Venetian Rodrigo Nino, Imperial ambassador, wrote to Charles V to remind him how little Catherine's treatment was in line with her heritage, a fact which should unite 'the King and Mother Church' and 'all Christendom' to 'take up the cause as their own against' Henry. It must be settled, added Nino, because 'she is the daughter of queen Isabel, and the Emperor's aunt' and he hoped 'that the King will think well before he executes his design, as the Queen is so important a member of his kingdom; for that would be to forsake such a person as the queen of England, and for what, except to marry as he pleased?'[4] Neither was Princess Mary being given the consideration due her according to her birth. She was currently being housed at Windsor and, Chapuys had heard, 'not very well treated considering her rank and birth'. Catherine was trying to communicate with the ambassador, but it was difficult and required subterfuge. She had lately sent Chapuys a message 'to say that she was thinking and planning how I could go to her apartments without being noticed' as there now was 'no chance' of going 'thither openly and by daylight', as it would 'greatly displease the king' and 'would not profit' the queen.[5] When Chapuys was finally summoned to Catherine's presence, he was given reluctant approval by Henry so long as he was accompanied by Anne's father, the newly created Earl of Wiltshire. The earl attempted to persuade the ambassador that 'she was absent from home and had gone to hear a sermon' but Chapuys persisted and 'found her, however, sitting in her room'. Soon Catherine was left behind at Greenwich while Henry went to London, where Anne Boleyn played the role of queen for the departure of the French ambassadors.[6] Nothing gave the king 'greater satisfaction' than to see the deference and respect of the French towards Anne, Chapuys noted, and believed that Henry was still in the city at the end of January 'to be at a greater distance from the Queen'.[7] Catherine rarely saw Henry now but when she did, he used it as an opportunity to attempt to persuade her to change her mind. As Chapuys reported to the Emperor in February:

> The Queen is treated as badly and even worse than ever. The King avoids her company as much as he can. He is always here with the Lady, whilst the Queen is at Richmond. He has never been half so long without visiting her as he is at present, giving as an excuse or pretence that someone has died of the plague near her residence. He has also resumed his attempts to persuade her to become a nun; this, however, is but a delusion and loss of time, for the Queen will never condescend to consent to it. The continued trouble and annoyance which she has to undergo compel her to be importunate both by her own letters and by mine; nor will she cease to do so until her suit is brought to a final conclusion, which she hopes will take place before Your Majesty's departure from Italy.[8]

Two months later, the queen's situation had not improved. Henry was angry to learn that Catherine had been in communication with the Emperor but she remained 'comparatively calm and indifferent' in response. He gave orders that she should be removed to Windsor, and although he had recently passed near the castle, did not visit her and had not seen her for weeks. Since having divided Catherine and Mary, Henry had also attempted to punish his wife further by not providing her with a proper household of her own. Instead she was being waited on by the king's own attendants, perhaps in order to better diminish her privacy and increase her dependency upon Henry's goodwill. In April, he remedied this situation, but the ambassador was unable to guess why unless it was something more sinister, for 'as she is not allowed to receive visitors it may be that they intend watching her more closely than before, or that they think by such gentle means to induce her to consent to some measures which they desire'.[9] Finally, that May, Henry relented and allowed Catherine to see her daughter. Princess Mary was then fourteen and had been suffering from ill-health and anxiety about the state of her parents' marriage and her mother's future. She had been staying at Alton, but was now permitted to make the journey to Richmond, where they spent five or six days together and invited Chapuys to go and stay with them.[10]

By the end of May, Henry, Catherine and Anne were back under the same roof at Hampton Court. The relationship between the king and his mistress had always been a tempestuous one, with tears, arguments and scenes of high drama followed by emotional reconciliations, worsened by the pressure the pair was experiencing as their desires for marriage were continually thwarted. The New Year had been stormy, with Henry sending Anne a valuable present and asking her family to intervene to bring them back together. Catherine may have seen it as an opportunity to try and regain her husband's favour, but if she made any attempts of that nature then they were unsuccessful. Once Henry's mind was made up it was fixed, inviolable, and Catherine was not able to compete with Anne's promise of a son. The real nature of Henry's new relationship sparked much controversy at the time and continues to do so today, as to whether the pair were sleeping together at this point, or when that intimacy began. It is impossible to say for certain that they were lovers in the physical sense in 1530, but the implications for Henry's succession if Anne fell pregnant and bore a son before they had the chance to wed might suggest abstinence. Their behaviour certainly suggested intimacy, even in public, and must have been a source of embarrassment to the long-suffering Catherine. Henry was showing 'great favour' to Anne 'every day', and when riding from Windsor he took the 'most unusual proceeding' of making 'her ride behind him on a pillion' which 'greatly called forth people's attention'. Two bystanders were even sent to prison for having commented upon it.[11] Catherine was also at Windsor at Whitsun, without Mary, and perhaps it was rumours such as these that encouraged her to speak to him, to try and make him mend his ways.

On 14 June, Catherine had an audience with her husband that lasted for some time. It shows that her mission was more than simply personal, but that she was acting as a queen, with dignity and concern for her country and the soul of its king, the man she had married and still loved. She exhorted him to 'be again to her a good prince and husband, and to quit the evil life he was leading and the bad example he was setting, and that even if he would shew no regard for her, who was, as he well knew, his true and lawful wife, that he should at least respect God and his conscience'. She added that Henry should not ignore the words of the Pope in forbidding him to remarry until their case had been judged. After 'many words and much commendation of those who had written in his favour', Henry replied that the Pope was simply 'compelled to act as the Emperor wished' and then 'left the room abruptly without saying another word'.[12]

Another incident from the same month illustrates the tension under which the three were living. Chapuys related how Catherine was still making Henry's shirts, a task she had always willingly done, as her mother had for her father. When Henry sent her some cloth, 'begging her to have it made into shirts for him', Anne sent for the bearer of the cloth, one of Henry's gentlemen of the bedchamber, and interrogated him. 'Although the king himself confessed that the cloth had been taken to the Queen by his order,' the ambassador explained, 'she abused the bearer' in Henry's presence, threatening to have him severely punished. There was also talk at court of some of the officers of the Royal Household being dismissed to please Anne, following on from the dismissals at Anne's request of three women from Catherine's household 'in whom she found more comfort and consolation than in any others'.[13] Then, in mid-July, Chapuys reported that 'the queen is to accompany the king on the hunting expedition as usual'.[14] This constant change between 'the usual' and 'the new' put an unbearable strain on Catherine. There were times, at dinner, at Christmas, out hunting, when the old protocol was observed and she was permitted to fulfil the role of queen, only to be distanced from Henry again when Anne asserted her personal hold over the king. The situation had now been dragging on for three years, and for Catherine it was a public and private limbo.

II

If the Pope was going to refuse to recognise that Henry's marriage had been invalid, then Henry would seek other authorities. Having appealed to the European universities, to the great thinkers of his age, he scoured the libraries to find works of theology and canon law that might determine his case. The humanist scholar Richard Croke was sent to search for manuscripts in Italy and the abbots of Reading, Gloucester, Spalding, Ramsey and Evesham supplied him with books, so many that they were transported en masse with his furniture as he moved from house to house.[15] The Duke of Norfolk wrote to the Spanish ambassador that Henry was so bent upon his cause that he did not 'think anyone but God could turn him aside', as he was now convinced it was 'imperative for the welfare and tranquillity of his kingdom that he should marry again for the sake of having male succession'. He had convinced himself 'from the books he had read on the subject and the discussions he has instituted throughout his kingdom' that his union with Catherine was 'from the beginning illegitimate'.[16]

Henry was convinced that 'learned doctors of this kingdom' would come out in his favour, even those who had taken Catherine's part at the beginning, who had 'since acknowledged their mistake'. Chapuys argued that he knew 'many among the most learned of this country who maintained their first opinion as strongly as ever' but that even if all his subjects entirely agreed with him, it was 'insufficient for the decision of the case', because they were 'natives of this country' and, therefore, 'might and ought to be considered suspect'. He recommended that Henry take the 'opinions of the first universities in Christendom' before 'attempting a divorce between two persons of such exalted rank, whose union has lasted so long and from whom there is issue'. Henry did not like this response. He stated that there were plenty of honest men in his kingdom, well acquainted with such matters, well read and writing well, who had quietened his conscience. Suddenly the universities were 'the only judges in this matter, not the Pope'. Henry's determination was 'unalterable'; Chapuys firmly believed that 'no living man could ever persuade him to change his opinion or to return to the Queen even if he were to lost everything through persisting in this purpose'.[17]

Of course, Henry also requested that the case of the marriage should be heard in the universities of Oxford and Cambridge. He sent his confessor, John Longland, Bishop of Lincoln, to Oxford, and Dr Edward Foxe, Bishop of Hereford, to Cambridge to obtain the two seals of the universities. However, they did not receive a warm welcome. At Oxford, Longland and his party were 'driven away by the women of the place and pelted with large stones', so that they required reinforcements from the Duke of Suffolk, who committed the women to prison and was 'eagerly following up the King's commission in order to obtain the seal' by bribes or threats.[18]

Rumours flew around 'on sufficiently good authority' that while the matter was being debated at Cambridge, 'there was a squabble and a fight, six or seven of them being left dead on the spot'.[19] Chapuys was unsure whether or not to believe it, but concluded that 'if the fire, however, should be thus lit, there will be hereafter more harm done and more execrable deeds perpetrated than the parties immediately concerned in the affair foresee'.[20] Henry would wring consent out of the universities 'by fair means or foul' and control the spread of dissent among his people. To that effect, he wrote to the vice-chancellor of Cambridge on 5 May, desiring him to appoint 'twelve of the best learned men in divinity ... to meet a like number from the University of Oxford to examine certain English books commonly read among the people, containing erroneous and pestiferous words, sentences and conclusions, which might pervert their judgments, and occasion division and contention in the chief points and articles of our faith and religion, whereon is like to ensue, unless it be repressed, the dissolution of our commonwealth'.[21] Despite all this, the English universities offered the king little help. At Cambridge, after consultation, examination of the Bible and public discussion, they reached the unanimous decision that Henry and Catherine's marriage was 'not forbidden by divine right and natural for us Christians',[22] while at Oxford it was decided that divine and natural law forbade a Christian to marry his deceased brother's wife.

In March 1530, news reached the Pope that Henry was making claims that he would soon remarry. In response, Clement issued an inhibition forbidding him to do so, to be fixed on the doors of English churches, 'under the penalty of the greater excommunication and interdict to be laid upon the kingdom'.[23] Two weeks later a papal bull followed, banning all ecclesiastical judges, doctors, notaries, advocates and others to 'speak or write against the validity of the marriage between the king and queen of England under pain of excommunication'.[24] This was rather too little too late when it came to the rulings of the universities, nor did it prevent further discussion from taking place. Yet the paradox at the heart of this whole question was that of Henry's personal faith. While he rejected the rule of Rome and called the Pope a heretic, he still considered himself more than ever to be a true Catholic, a defender of the faith: it was the Vatican and the corrupt clergy who were in the wrong. Henry saw himself as a reformer, defending his people from the dangers of corruption and leading them towards the light, as the head of the Church of England.

To this end, the assembly Henry had summoned of divines from Oxford and Cambridge was to advise him on the approval or rejection of certain 'pestiferous' religious texts, newly arrived in the country. After discussion, it was agreed that 'the books entitled *The Wicked Mammona*, *The Obedience of a Christian Man* (Tyndale), *The Supplication of Beggars*, *The Revelation of Anti-Christ*, *The Summary of Scripture*, and others printed beyond sea, contain pestiferous errors and blasphemies. All persons are therefore cautioned, under pain of the King's displeasure, not to buy or receive such books, either in English, or in French, or Dutch.'[25] If anyone was already in possession of a copy, they had fifteen days to hand the books in to a bishop or priest, or else be brought before the King's Council. In addition, 'no person hereafter shall print new books in English concerning Holy Scripture until they have been examined by the ordinary of the diocese, and the name of the examiners shall be printed with the books'. Henry had also asked the scholars to debate the question of the Bible in the vernacular, 'who have come to the conclusion that it is not necessary to have the Scriptures in English in the hands of the common people, but that the permission or denial thereof should depend upon the discretion of the superiors; and, considering the malignity of the present time, a translation into English would tend to the increase of error'. Instead, the people should continue to have the Scriptures read to them by preachers in their sermons and that all translations must be handed in.[26]

In July 1530, the University of Paris found in favour of the king. One hundred doctors had spoken in favour of his cause, so the institution had given its seal to the divorce, although some information about the decision-making was initially suppressed. It was bad news for Catherine, with Chapuys anticipating that 'the king will become more arrogant than ever, and have their names and votes proclaimed through his kingdom'. However, there were some who questioned the decision, including Catherine's chaplain, who was called before the king's council for having said in several places that 'all those who advised the king to take any other wife than the queen were very wicked people'. On being questioned, he 'boldly confirmed that statement, and added that since the Church had approved of this marriage for so many years, and since the Pope had threatened excommunication to all those who should countenance the second, anyone abetting the king in this unrighteous act was ... a traitor to God and to the king'. He went on to assert that 'no trust could be placed in the seal of the [University of] Paris owing to the corruption which had prevailed there, in spite of which 44 doctors among the most learned and honoured in Christendom, the list of whom he then and there produced, had voted in favour of the queen'. Having seen the lists of names, even the Duke of Norfolk was forced to admit that 'it is a most wicked and treacherous act on the part of the French to have stated that the consent of the university was unanimous'. The chaplain was banished from court at once and Anne's faction called for punishment, but

> the Queen replied that justice was entirely in the King's hands, but that it would not be justice to make anyone suffer for having acted rightly. The Queen had meditated giving notice of the brief on this occasion, but out of love and reverence for the King she refrained, and has hitherto delayed writing again to the Pope, however much I have urged her to do so.[27]

Chapuys confirmed in a letter to the German humanist Cornelius Agrippa that 'the truth has come to light at Paris; and though many of the doctors of the Sorbonne were suborned to pass judgment against the queen, many of pure life and sounder learning dared to oppose them; and one of them, either in his own name, or that of all, has written a book to testify his opinion'. Chapuys sent a copy to his friend, 'though Agrippa does not need such compositions: it is like adding water to the sea'.[28]

After this incident, Chapuys related that Catherine 'had never been firmer in purpose than since hearing of what has passed in Paris, and did not care a straw for all that has been done there in favour of the King; and, in my opinion, she is quite right, for I have certain information that one of those who went over to agitate for the king has said the same since his return from that capital, and expressed his great surprise that there should have been so many distinguished men in that university ready of their own accord to speak out so boldly and firmly in support of the Queen's cause.[29] Yet Catherine was also 'amazed' at the debacle of the Parisian university information, believing quite rightly that information was being deliberately kept from her. The ambassador thought it would give her great comfort if those who had voted in favour of her marriage had the opportunity to present their findings to the king 'with some words of remonstrance'. It was not an opportunity Henry was willing to grant them.

In response to the Paris ruling, though, Anne Boleyn was becoming bolder. Chapuys also warned the Emperor that she informed Henry that Charles 'had it not in your power to do him any harm' and that her family alone would provide 10,000 men for his service at their expense. She also cited that Charles had not 'suffered any qualms of conscience' in marrying his first cousin, so could not 'decently ask others to be more scrupulous in this matter'. Henry replied that Anne was 'under great obligation to him' as he was making enemies and causing offence everywhere for her sake. Anne then brought up one of the ancient prophecies so beloved of the people, which foretold that 'at this time a queen shall be burnt: but even if I were to suffer a thousand deaths, my love for you will not abate one jot'.[30] This made Emperor Charles angry. On 13 August, he gave Chapuys the commission 'to act and protest on the queen's behalf in the matter of the divorce'.[31]

In 1531, after much deliberation, the opinions of the universities were published in the pamphlet *The Determinations of the Most Famous and Most Excellent Universities of Italy and France, that it is so Unlawful for a Man to Marry his Brother's wife, that the Pope hath no Power to dispense therewith*. Overall, fifty-three ruled that the marriage was unlawful, forty-two disagreed and five were unsure but ruled that the Church would uphold the marriage.[32] Although the difference was a mere margin of six, and therefore fairly inconclusive, Henry technically had his victory. The Spanish universities of Salamanca and Alcala found in favour of Catherine as expected, but Padua, Bourges, Venice, Verona, Bologna and most of the Italian institutions sided with the king.

The following July, the Pope passed the Parisian Dr Ortiz an anonymous book that had been written in favour of the king's divorce based upon the findings of the universities. He made a savage and sweeping criticism of the work as being based on the 'worthless' conclusions of the universities of Orleans, Angers, Poitiers, Bologna, Pavia and Toulouse, which had 'no foundation in reason whatever' and had evidently been 'got up in great haste, without proper knowledge of the cause itself'. He suggested that 'bribery and corruption' had been used, 'in complete opposition to the integrity which ought to rule in affairs of this kind, in the deliberation of matters concerning faith and in the scrutiny of votes'. Dr Ortiz stated that the process of judgement undertaken by the universities had been deeply flawed, as it was well known that in some cases 'there were only two or three doctors to vote', and where they were numerous, as in Paris, 'the most learned and moral' of them voted for the queen, 'as they could not well be corrupted by bribery and threats as the others'.[33] The book's author, 'whoever he may be', had relied too heavily upon 'rhetorical flowers' instead of engaging with the arguments and would have done better to go to Rome to dispute with Dr Ortiz, who would have set him straight.[34]

III

Understandably, the impasse was taking its toll on Catherine's health. Early in September she had a fever for two or three days, but she recovered after her physicians bled and purged her. She was also under constant pressure from observers, as Anne had forbidden certain of her friends from visiting her 'and had placed some women about her to spy and report anything she may say or do, so that she can hear but few news and those with great difficulty'.[35] The Duchess of Norfolk may have been one of those whom Anne intended to convey information regarding the queen's activities. Chapuys reported that she had sent Catherine a present of poultry and an orange, enclosing a letter from Gregory Casale, English ambassador to the Emperor. Catherine believed that 'the duchess did this out of regard for her' – and the duchess was indeed not on the best of terms with Anne, rowing about the arrangements for her daughter's wedding to Henry Fitzroy, which would finally take place in 1533. However, Chapuys feared 'it was done with the knowledge of her husband, as a means of entering into some secret communication with her Majesty more easily'.[36] When Catherine had been afraid at the sitting of the Reformation Parliament, the Duchess of Norfolk was the one sent to tell the queen that her opponents were trying to draw her over to their party, but that if all the world were to try it she would remain faithful to her. She also desired the queen to be of good courage, for her opponents were at their wits' end, being further off from their object than the day they began.[37] It must have been difficult for Catherine to trust anyone, even those she had known for years.

In November 1530, Catherine was ill again at Richmond and remained behind there when Henry and Anne went to York Place and then on to Hampton Court. The news also reached London of the death of Cardinal Wolsey, who had passed away at Leicester following his arrest. It meant there would be no trial. Catherine had recovered and arrived at Greenwich in time for the Christmas celebrations and those at Twelfth Night, dining with Henry and sitting beside him in estate in the great hall, 'whereas were divers interludes, rich masks and disportes, and after that a great banquet'. Briefly, the appearance of royal harmony was resumed. However, Anne was not going to accept defeat, and as Chapuys wrote to Charles on 1 January, he had just heard from a 'well-informed man that this marriage will undoubtedly be accomplished in this Parliament'. This mood of buoyancy produced an air of defiance in Anne Boleyn, who was now 'braver than a lion' and dared to say to one of Catherine's ladies that she wished all the Spaniards in the world 'were in the sea' and she 'did not care anything for the queen and would rather see her hanged than acknowledge her as her mistress'.[38]

In spite of Catherine's isolation, there was considerable feeling against the divorce at this time. One figure at the English court remained openly and vociferously loyal to Catherine throughout, unafraid of the wrath of Anne Boleyn and willing to take his chance with Henry's displeasure. The ageing John Fisher was not just steadfast in his support but had been preparing his own book in defence of Catherine's marriage to answer her critics. The Parisian Dr Ortiz was effusive in his praise of Fisher's work, commenting that

> many thanks are due to God for the many virtues and sound learning with which he has endowed that prelate, who may rightly be called the true beacon that in our days has lighted the Church. Indeed, his answer is so clear, so learned, and so full, shewing the

> true path through which this suit may be gained, that it leaves no point untouched and very little, if any, work to do for those who like him [Ortiz] are to plead in the Queen's defence. No lawyer, however ignorant, can fail to find in the book sufficient arguments to defeat his opponents, and that is the reason why the learned Bishop is deserving of so much praise and thanks.[39]

Ortiz also drew the Emperor's attention to a second book which had also been published in Catherine's defence, this time by Juan Gines de Sepulveda, a native of Cordoba:

> Master Sepulveda, who is his friend, wrote some time ago a treatise in favour of the most serene queen of England, a work of much sound learning. Having found that besides its elegant style the treatise contained excellent doctrine, and such as would lead to the perfect knowledge of the case, and demonstrate the clear justice of the Queen's cause, he [Ortiz] advised him to have it printed, which has been done.[40]

According to Chapuys, there was an appetite among the people to see the book, and to 'discuss freely this matter of the divorce'. Fisher, however, had some anxiety about his authorship being made public, although he had taken 'great pains' to write it and Chapuys believed that 'sufficient testimony is afforded by the works themselves; his great learning, and his good and pious life, well known at Rome and elsewhere', which could not fail to 'add authority and credit to his opinion'. No wonder Fisher was concerned, as there was a powerful groundswell of popular feeling in favour of Catherine, which he knew Henry would find difficult to accept. As Chapuys also recorded, the general opinion was that Henry was intent on his 'evil designs' and that, in response, Anne had adopted the device '*ainsi sera groingne qui groingne*', meaning 'grudge who grudges, this is how it will be'. All this bad feeling sparked superstitions. The people, 'seeing that mischief is likely to ensue', resurrected 'some idle prophecies, to which they attach much faith', which foretell that around this time, this 'kingdom will be destroyed by a woman'. According to the ambassador, they were 'greatly agitated' by it and some English merchants had approached him to ask about relocating to Flanders or Spain.

Anne Boleyn was also the target of one swell of feeling in London, according to a report that reached Venice. Reputedly a mob of 7,000 or 8,000 women, and men dressed as women, gathered in London and stormed the house on the river where Anne was staying. It was rumoured that they intended to kill her, and apparently Anne escaped downriver just in the nick of time.[41] The veracity of this event cannot be established with certainty, but the very real existence of the mob of women who threw stones at John Longland in Oxford makes it seem possible. There may have been a smaller number of rioters, who may have targeted Anne's house, or perhaps her servants thought it prudent to move on an occasion when there was discontent in the city. What is significant, though, is that there was sufficient feeling against Anne for the report to have been repeated as credible. It is also interesting that when reports of this nature surface, it is usually women who were the perpetrators, suggesting that there was considerable support for Catherine as a wronged wife.

An exception to this gender bias is proven by the case of a Roger Dycker who was imprisoned in the Marshalsea for slander, although the account of his words have the ring of innocent disbelief. Just like the two men who had been arrested for commenting when Henry and Anne rode together on one horse, Dycker's case shows that the king was not prepared to tolerate any criticism or anything that even sounded remotely like it. The sixty-nine-year-old Dycker and two others went to the house of their vicar, Sir Roger Page, in Derbyshire, to welcome him home, presumably from London. Page gave them the news that 'the king was about to marry another wife, and that Dycker knew the woman and that her father was Sir Thomas Boleyn'. 'Dycker then said that her name was Mrs. Anne Bullan, and he was sure it was but tales, for so noble a lady, so high born, and so gracious, he would not forsake and marry another.' An accusation was the brought against him, despite his age and the fact that he 'has been sore bryssyd in the King's wars, and they do all this to undo him utterly'.[42]

Another result of this mood of discontent was that pamphlets and placards bearing 'defamatory libels' were posted on the door of Canterbury Cathedral. They attacked Archbishop Warham, his chancellor, Henry and the Privy Council 'on account of this divorce, setting out the evils which might arise therefrom'.[43] Henry's response was to order that all similar items would be seized and burned.[44] In December, one anonymous book referred to in a pamphlet had been addressed to Henry himself, 'touching the divorce affair and other matters connected to him and his kingdom', and was written 'in a masterly and most complete manner'. Chapuys knew it was doomed, though, as it 'tells the truth too plainly to please the King'. Henry was in no mood to tolerate 'truth-tellers' or anyone who spoke out against his wishes, and that put Fisher in the firing line.

One Sunday before Christmas, Archbishop Warham summoned Fisher to his house, where Cuthbert Tunstall, Henry's chaplain Edward Lee and Dr Edward Foxe were also waiting for him. Together they 'most earnestly besought him to retract what he had written in favour of the queen, and take the side of the king, who, they said, had sent them to convince him by argument of the error of his opinion'. Fisher refused to be bullied. He replied 'with much prudence and moderation' that 'the matter was in itself so clear that no arguments upon it were needed' and that because the Pope was the 'sole judge and arbiter', the case could only be properly argued at a court in Rome. In response, Tunstall accused him of being 'self-willed and obstinate' and said that in spite of this the king was summoning twelve doctors to debate the case, at which occasion Fisher would be obliged to appear.

While Fisher's support for Catherine only strengthened, one of her council had recently changed his mind in favour of the king's cause. William Warham, Archbishop of Canterbury since 1504, had been the sole dissenting voice at Catherine's 1509 wedding, although he put these views aside in order to marry the pair on Henry's wishes. In 1530 he had turned eighty, and although Chapuys commented that 'old age had abated his constancy and discretion', he was still intellectually sharp enough to draw up two articles protesting that the case should never had been heard by the legates Wolsey and Campeggio but should have been tried by himself in his capacity as archbishop and head of the English Church. Anticipating that Warham would head an English court and pronounce her divorced, Catherine clung all the more tightly to Chapuys, who felt despair about his inability to help her: 'The Queen, fearing lest I should when the action for the divorce begins ask for my recall, as I should much like to do, has begged me to dismiss all thought of leaving this country, as she says she will have more need of my services than ever. I do not know how can stay here, nor of what service I can be in the midst of the boiling vortex likely to be opened here.'[45]

In her desperation, Catherine wrote at length to the Pope. Having been protected by him to an extent, she was beginning to feel despair at his procrastination and complained that he had abandoned her cause. The letter is worth quoting in full, to give an insight into her state of mind, her strength and faith, as well as her continuing loyalty to Henry at the end of 1530:

> *Most holy father,*
> The great need in which my troubled affairs stand of Your Holiness' redress and help (upon which the service of God and my own repose, and the salvation of my soul, as well as that of the King, my Lord, depend), obliges me to be thus importunate with Your Holiness that I may be heard on that very account, even had I an ordinary claim to ask what I have so long and so affectionately prayed for, and so frequently urged; much more now that the justice of my cause is so great before God, who knows my perfect sincerity and innocence, do I hope that Your Holiness will see that God, in His great mercy, wishes to declare it. In public I believe Your Highness to be well informed that there is no learned or conscientious person acknowledging the power and authority of that Apostolic See who does not say and maintain that the marriage between the King, my Lord, and me is indissoluble, since God only can separate us. I cannot then do less than complain that my petitions, both true and just, should have been so long disregarded by Your Holiness. One thing only comforts me in the midst of my tribulations, which is to think that God wishes to punish me for my sins in this world, and that therefore Your Holiness, His vicar on earth, will not forgive me. I humbly beg Your Holiness to have pity on me, and accept as though I had been in purgatory the penance I have already suffered for so many years, thus delivering me from the pains, torments, and sudden fears, to which I am daily exposed, and which are so great and so numerous that I could not possibly bear up against them had not God given me strength to endure

the same; God, in whom all my hopes are concentrated, sure as I am that He will not abandon me in this cause, in which justice is so clearly with me.

The remedy [I allude to] lies in the sentence and determination of my case without any delay. Any other course short of that will do more harm than good, as appears quite evident from the evils which the delay has already produced. Should the sentence be still deferred, Your Holiness will perceive that the delay in this matter will be the cause of a new hell [upon earth] the remedy for which will entail more disastrous measures than have ever yet been tried. I have been informed that my enemies demand a new delay. I beg Your Holiness not to grant it to them, for, in so doing, the greatest possible injury will be done to me, sure as I am that everything proposed in that quarter is for the worst, as it might come to pass justice would suffer through it, and that from the purgatory in which I now am I should be cast down into a temporal hell, from the bottom of which I should be continually raising my voice to God, and complaining of the small amount of pity and mercy Your Holiness has granted me. Again I beg and entreat Your Holiness not to allow any further delays in this trial, but at once pronounce final sentence in the shortest way. Until this be done I shall not cease importuning Your Holiness, as did the Samaritan to Jesus Christ, on whom her remedy depended.

Some days ago Miçer Mai, the ambassador of His Imperial Majesty, and my solicitor in this case wrote to say that Your Holiness had promised him to renew the brief which Your Holiness issued at Bologna, and another one commanding the King, my Lord, to dismiss and cast away from him this woman with whom he lives. On hearing of it, these 'good people' who have placed and still keep the King, my Lord, in this awkward position, began to give way, considering themselves lost. May God forgive him, who was the cause of the briefs not being delivered, for the news only of the preparation produced a most marked improvement in my case; besides which, had the potion, though disagreeable to their palates, been administered at the right time, that which I hope Your Holiness keeps in store for them would have been comparatively sweet. I am, therefore, deeply grieved at the injury which was inflicted upon me by the withdrawal of the promised briefs; but I bear all this with patience, waiting for the

> remedy to the evils of which I complain. This can be no other, I repeat, than the sentence I am expecting every day and hour. One thing I should like Your Holiness to be aware of, namely, that my plea is not against the King, my Lord, but against the inventors and abettors of this cause. I trust so much in the natural goodness and in the virtues of the King, my Lord, that if I could only have him two months with me, as he used to be, I alone should be powerful enough to make him forget the past; but as they know this to be true they do not let him live with me. These are my real enemies who wage such constant war against me; some of them that the bad counsel they gave the King should not become public, though they have been already well paid for it, and others that they may rob and plunder as much as they can, thus endangering the estate of the King, my Lord, to the risk of his honour and the eternal perdition of his soul. These are the people from whom spring the threats and bravadoes preferred against Your Holiness; they are the sole inventors of them, not the King, my Lord. It is, therefore, urgent that Your Holiness put a very strong bit in their mouths, which is no other than the sentence. With that the tongues of the bad counsellors shall be stopped, and their hope of mischief vanish; the greedy thieves shall no longer devour him on whom they have been feeding all this time; they will set him at liberty, and he will become as dutiful a son of Your Holiness as he was in former times. This to me will be the greatest charity that ever Your Holiness bestowed on a human being; it will restore peace and happiness among the Christian princes, and set a good example [for the future] to the whole of Christendom.[46]

Around the time that she wrote this letter, news reached Catherine of Thomas Wolsey's death. Following his disgrace, the cardinal had retreated north to Cawood Castle while his fate was decided. He had been summoned to London to appear in his trial and had fallen ill on the way and died at Leicester. He was fifty-seven. He is reputed to have spoken the famous last words that if he had 'served God as diligently as I have done the King, he would not have given me over in my grey hairs'. Henry and Catherine left Hampton Court to spend a solemn Christmas at Greenwich. On Twelfth Night there were interludes, 'rich masks and disportes' followed by a banquet. After that Henry left Catherine behind and travelled to London, staying at York Place.[47]

In the first days of 1531, news arrived in London of the death of Margaret of Savoy. As Catherine's former sister-in-law, by virtue of her brief marriage to John of Asturias, Margaret had once been considered an ally by Henry. He had been a guest at her court in Malines in 1513, the very court where Anne Boleyn had been educated, but by virtue of her relationship with her nephew Charles, Henry had come to see her as the enemy. His response to her death was crass in the very least. 'The death of Madame [Margaret] is regretted by those who have intercourse with Flanders,' Chapuys wrote to console Charles, who was his aunt's sole heir. 'I am told the king of England said it was no great loss for the world. He delights in everything that is to the disadvantage of your Majesty; but these are not things to take notice of, for the blindness of his miserable *amour* makes him talk indiscreetly. One reason why he is glad of Madame's death is because she took great interest in the Queen's matter, and also because she was the real means of concluding the amity with France.'[48] No doubt Catherine mourned Margaret's loss sincerely.

Other news from abroad pleased Henry even less. Luther's thoughts about the marriage were not what he had hoped to hear from a religious rebel, overlooking the fact that the monk's private life was one of devoted marital fidelity: 'Before I should approve of such a repudiation,' Luther stated, 'I would rather let him (Henry) marry a second queen ... Even if there should be a divorce, Catherine will remain Queen of England, and she will have been wronged before God and man ... No, my friend, if you are bound to a woman, you are no longer a free man; God forces you to stay with wife and child, to feed and rear them.'[49] Then Henry heard from another of Catherine's supporters, Juan Luis Vives, writing from Burges, who framed the danger of the king's situation within a European context:

> Has not heard from him for three years, nor from the Queen for a long time, but heartily desires to see them both. Sends the books which he wrote about his marriage when in England at the desire of the cardinal of York. Begs him to consider the danger of his present course, and of incurring the enmity of the Emperor now

> that the Turk is victorious. If the King's object is to have a son as heir to the Crown, he might choose a suitable person to marry his daughter.
>
> If he were to marry another wife, there is no certainty that he would have a son, or that a son would live. A new marriage would leave the succession doubtful, and afford grounds for civil war. Is moved to write by his duty to the King, love to England, where he was so kindly received, and anxiety for the quiet of Christendom.[50]

Vives was fortunate to be out of the country. The continuing vocal support given to Catherine by Bishop John Fisher may have been enough to provoke an attempt on his life in March 1531. Chapuys related that everyone who had eaten a batch of pottage that had been served in the bishop's household, 'that is nearly all the servants, were brought to the point of death, though only two of them died', along with some poor people to whom it had been given in alms. Fisher had not tasted the dish, but the implication was reasonably made that it was intended for him. In the ambassador's version, the cook, Richard Roose, was 'immediately seized [and] confessed he had thrown in a powder, which he had been given to understand' would merely upset the servants without doing them harm. In Chapuys' opinion, Henry could not 'wholly avoid some suspicion, if not against himself', whom the ambassador thought was above such a thing, but 'at least against the lady and her father'. Fisher was suffering ill health for unconnected reasons, but had arranged to leave his house despite his suffering, as Chapuys speculated that he may fear 'there is some more powder in reserve for him'.[51] An early biographer of Fisher related more details of the incident, stating that Roose had added poison to the gruel, which had claimed the lives of 'one gentleman, named Mr. Bennet Curwen and an old widow, [who] died suddenly, and the rest never recovered their health till their dying day'. On discovery, Roose attempted to pass his actions off as a jest, claiming to have thought the powders were laxatives, but he was arrested and an Act of Parliament was hastily passed to enable him to suffer the gruesome death of being boiled alive. He never received a trial and the sentence was enacted on 5 April. As for Bishop Fisher, Chapuys was correct that Henry had not intended to poison him in 1531. When the king did choose to take his life, four years later, it would be through a legal process, with the sentence conducted in public.

Early 1531, Henry made the unprecedented move of attempting to charge Fisher and Catherine's other supporters with *praemunire*, before deciding to open up the charge to the entire English clergy. This was intended to be leverage to ensure they all swore his new oath of allegiance to himself as Supreme Head of the Church. He demanded £100,000 for their collective pardon, refusing their request to pay this over a five-year term, and insisted that they agree to five articles. These required them to recognise him as 'sole protector and Supreme head of the Church and clergy of England', that he had complete spiritual jurisdiction and the powers of the English Church were only upheld where they did not detract from the laws of the realm or the king's prerogative. Bishop Fisher was not prepared to accept this and inserted into the articles the clause 'as far as the law of God allows'. When it was discussed in the chamber nobody dared speak against it, and when Warham observed that those who were silent seemed to consent, one clergyman replied, 'Then we are all silent.' The bill was passed in March, making the decisive shift of ultimate power from the Pope to the king, giving Henry unprecedented powers. Religion in England would never be the same again. It was not the only dramatic break that would take place at this time.

In the summer of 1531, Catherine's life would change forever. It seems a fitting point to reflect upon her former self, through the comparison of two versions of the same portrait of the queen. Just as little as six years earlier, when she had no intimation of any intended divorce, Horenbout had painted her as a stately queen. In 1531, that image was reworked by an unknown artist with a different purpose. Almost in reference to Renaissance works like da Vinci's *Lady with an Ermine*, the queen is portrayed holding a rare capuchin monkey, which holds flowers in one hand and appears to play with her brooch with the other. But the allegory is more subtle; the 'capuchin' or religious monkey, playing on the notion of a monk of the same name, is rejecting a coin offered by the queen and her brooch is in fact a crucifix, indicating the true holy path is to reject wealth in favour of salvation. The species has been identified as a Macgrave's capuchin, now very rare, which had been imported to Spain from Portuguese traders in the New

World, making it a symbol of her home and its empire as well.[52] Catherine wears black, with wide ermine sleeves turned back over black sleeves slashed with white and a chemise buttoned up to her neck. The familiar gable headdress and black hood sit on her head but her features are far closer to those of the young Catherine.

At this point in time, Mario Savorgnano, an Italian naval commander, left descriptions of Catherine and her daughter when he visited England. He had a brief interview with Henry, who was off hunting, judging him to be 'tall of stature, very well formed and of very handsome presence, beyond measure affable'. Savorgnano believed Henry to be the best-disposed king he had ever seen and 'most generous and kind', almost 'perfectly good' if he had not been on the verge of repudiating his wife 'after having lived with her for twenty-two years'. This matter, said the Italian, 'detracts greatly from his merits, as there is now living with him a young woman of noble birth, though many say of bad character, whose will is law to him'. The people were opposed to it, he added, 'nor during the present queen's life will they have any other queen in the kingdom'.[53] Savorgnano went on to meet Catherine afterwards, whom he described as 'not of tall stature', being instead 'rather small' and 'if not handsome she is not ugly ... somewhat stout and has always a smile on her countenance'. Although she was not tall either, Mary was 'well proportioned' with a 'very beautiful complexion' and 'pretty face'. At sixteen, she could speak Latin, Spanish and French and had a good grounding in Italian and Greek.

Later that year, the Venetian ambassador in London, Lodovico Falier, also wrote in glowing terms about Henry, describing him as combining 'such corporal and mental beauty' that would 'astound' all men, and possessing a stature that gave 'manifest proof of that intrinsic mental superiority which is inherent in him'. He was more 'angelic' than handsome, pious in hearing two Masses daily, a natural athlete who also believed it 'monstrous for a prince not to cultivate moral and intellectual excellence', although he had become too 'allured by his pleasures'. Catherine was 'of low stature, rather stout, with a modest countenance; she is virtuous, just, replete with goodness and religion; she is beloved by the islanders more than any queen that ever reigned; she is about forty-five years old', and Mary was a 'handsome, amiable and very accomplished princess, in no respect inferior to her mother'.[54]

By the summer of 1531, the painful triangle of Catherine, Henry and Anne had reached an impasse. Something had to give and, predictably, it was the queen. Recently, her situation had appeared to improve, with Henry dining with her more frequently and visiting her chamber in order to give the appearance that he was not separating from her through choice. Chapuys was able to report on 14 May that 'there was nothing but courtesy and kindness on the part of the king', although the following day he refused to consent to Catherine's request that Princess Mary visit her mother at Greenwich, saying that the pair might meet elsewhere.[55]

Then, late on a June evening, Henry made one last attempt. Shortly before bedtime, Catherine was interrupted in her chambers by a delegation of thirty noblemen and clergy who made a concerted effort to persuade her to submit to her husband's demands. They were led by the dukes of Norfolk and Suffolk, Anne's father the Earl of Wiltshire and a handful of bishops, in an attempt to overwhelm the queen through their numbers and persistence, and to break her will. Norfolk presented her with two charges from Henry: that she had lived with Arthur as his wife and consummated the marriage, and that she had humiliated her husband by having him summoned to appear before a court in Rome. The duke demanded that in the name of the king she must abandon her appeal to the Pope and allow her case to be heard in England by impartial judges. He made the dramatic claim that her failure to do so would imperil England, and had the presumption to remind her that she had always been treated honourably as the country's queen and that England had assisted her father and nephew on a number of occasions. Catherine had no cause for complaint, Norfolk stressed.

Catherine disagreed. Refusing to be intimidated by the crowd of her opponents, she rose to the opportunity. She replied that she was Henry's lawful wife and would 'never consent to it as long as she lived' and would continue to obey her ultimate sovereign, the Pope. When Dr Lee attempted to accuse her of having slept with Arthur, and therefore having consistently lied, she cut him down to size as a man more interested in flattering the king than knowing the truth, and recommended that he went to Rome, where he could debate the matter with a man who could demonstrate to him that he had not read every book on the topic. She also dismissed Dr Sampson's argument that she may as well give up as any papal verdict would be overturned, adding that he had no knowledge of the extent to which she had suffered since the proceedings had begun. Bishop John Longland then tried to break her with the comment that she must have been living in sin with Henry, as God had punished them by the loss of their children. Catherine merely repeated that she was the king's lawful wife and she was surprised that so many honourable men of power and influence were required to call on a poor, friendless and defenceless woman at such an hour.[56] She finished by giving them a clear message to take back to Henry. She would obey him in everything save for those which touched her two greater allegiances: God and her conscience.

Catherine's response was praised by Dr Ortiz, who recounted the event to Charles:

> Is thankful to God that the Queen behaves so prudently as she did in the answers she gave to the persons sent to her by the King. It is clear that the Holy Ghost spoke through her mouth. She answered like St. Katharine when the doctors came to dispute with her. The Pope and Cardinals highly appreciate the behaviour of the Queen, and say that her answers deserve to be printed, for the glory of God, and in justice to the virtues of the Queen.[57]

By elevating Catherine to this saintly status, making her the mouthpiece of the Holy Ghost, all of which was consistent with the abuses that Henry was reforming in the Church, Ortiz breached the gap between the queen being merely a mortal in distress and becoming a martyr for her cause. It was a suggestive and dangerous move for someone as dedicated to her cause as Catherine.

By the middle of July, the court was at a Windsor. Henry and Anne rose early one morning and rode away to Woodstock, ostensibly on a hunting trip. Catherine was left behind, without having had a chance to say goodbye. She did not know it then, but she would never see her husband again.

23

The Spanish Inquiry 1531–1532

I

Catherine may not have set foot in Spain for thirty years but she was still a daughter of Ferdinand and Isabella, the parents of the nation as it now was, united under their grandson Charles and granddaughter Isabella. Spain was not prepared to stand by and see an insult done to a descendent of its illustrious leaders without putting up a degree of legal resistance at the least. After all, Catherine's parents had been responsible for patronising the very institutions of learning and new thinking that had trained the next generation of students in canon law. Thus a court was convened in 1531 at Zaragoza, on papal authority, under the guidance of Miguel Jiminez de Embun, Bishop of the Cistercian Abbey at Veruela. Once the monks of Veruela had honoured England, replicating the cloisters of Westminster Abbey in the building of their chapter house. Now they sought to question the heart of its religious and legal processes and to succeed where Wolsey and Campeggio had failed.

On Sunday 11 June 1531, in front of a packed congregation in Zaragoza Cathedral, Salvador Felipe read aloud a summons to Henry VIII, King of England, to appear in the court. The court's intention was to gather evidence in the case of the royal marriage and reach a verdict about its legitimacy. If Henry wanted to offer his defence, he was bound to travel to Spain and appear before the dignitaries assembled. Since it was physically impossible for the king to appear within the three days stipulated, the court would automatically proceed in his absence. It had not been a simple journey to reach that point, though.

Given that thirty years had elapsed since Catherine's first wedding, the chances of tracking down those who had been witnesses to the event did not initially seem very likely. However, due to the youth of the bride and groom, it was their more direct contemporaries, such as the young ladies- and gentlemen-in-waiting, now in their forties and fifties, who seemed the most likely survivors. With an unquestioning dedication to the Spanish princess who had left her country at the age of fifteen, the Empress's servants set about tracking down those who travelled with her on her long journey to the coast and over the stormy Channel to her new life and her first husband. There was Catalina, once the queen's slave, who used to make her bed and attend to other services of the chamber, who had been married to a morisco named Oviedo, a crossbow-maker at Valdezcaray. They had lived in Malaga, but after being widowed, she had gone with her daughters to live in her home town of Motril. She had formed part of the royal household when the said queen and her husband, Henry, met for the first time in 1501. There was also Catherine's former lady-in-waiting Katarina Fortes, now a nun in the convent of Madre de Dios, at Toledo, and a niece of treasurer Morales, who had been much in the confidence of her mistress. Equally trusted by Catherine at the time was Doña Maria de Rojas, the wife of Don Alvaro de Mendoça. In 1531 she was living close to Najera, or near Vitoria, and used to sleep in the queen's own bed after the death of her first husband, Arthur. Catherine's former treasurer Juan de Cuero had passed away, but his wife was found living in Madrid; she had once been a maid in their household. Likewise, Catherine's Master of Hall, Alonso de Esquivel, was dead but his servant Fornizedo was found, then being resident at Seville; he had once been groom-in-waiting to Her Highness. There was also a notary named Tamayo, before whom the marriage contract between the queen and King Henry passed, and who attested it. Thirty years before, he had lived with the ambassador de Puebla, but was now resident with the Marquis of Tarifa, whom he accompanied on his pilgrimage to Jerusalem. Finally, there was even Diego de Fernandez, Catherine's old confessor, dismissed from England in shame in 1515. He was to be found and cross-questioned to discover the name and description of the secretary or notary who signed the contracts and settlements for Catherine's marriage to Henry.

It was Charles's wife, Emperor Isabella, the daughter of Catherine's sister, who issued the instructions for the Spanish investigation into the marriage. The questioning was to be rigorous and detailed. Her servants were to travel all over Spain in the effort to track down those who might help the queen's cause and the relevant paperwork. First, they were to

> go to Calatayud, where Juan Perez de Almaçan, the lord of Maella and son of secretary Almaçan now resides, and if you should not find him there you shall go to Çaragoça [Zaragoza], or wherever he or the rest of that Secretary's heirs may be at present. You shall exhibit to him, or to them, the letters where of you are now the bearer, as well as this present instruction, and try to ascertain from them whether among the papers of the said Secretary, their sire, any of the following papers can be found:
>
> 1st. The marriage contract between king Henry VIII. of England, and Her most Serene Highness queen Katharine, his wife, our most beloved aunt, after the decease of Arthur, prince of Wales, or the treaty made with the King, his father [Henry VII] for the said marriage.
>
> 2nd. The receipt or receipts given for the dowry of the said most Serene Highness, now queen [of England] upon her second marriage.
>
> 3rd. The deed of settlement, or donation 'propter nuptias', that was made or promised to the said Queen at the time.
>
> 4th. Any other deeds, contracts, or letters relating to that event in Latin, Spanish, French, or any other language whatsoever.[1]

After that, the servants were to head to Tarazona and Valencia, to the old homes of secretary Pedro de Quintana, nephew of d'Almaza, and ask similar questions to his widow and heirs about the location of the papers. They were to seek out the agents of Martin Cabrero in Zaragoza and request to see his papers and those of his uncle Juan Cabrero, the chamberlain. After that, they were to track down Luis Caroz, the first Spanish ambassador of Henry's reign, in Valencia, and record any information that he might have about the marriage.[2]

The witnesses were to be asked a series of questions:

1. If they know of any deeds, contracts, or other papers relating to the marriage of the Most Serene Highness the Queen of England, and if so, where, and in whose hands they now are?
2. How long did the said Queen live with Arthur, Prince of Wales, and whether the councillors of the king of England [Henry VII] were of opinion that the said Queen and Arthur, her first husband, did not consummate matrimony, owing to his extreme debility, and to the act being exceedingly injurious to his health?
3. Whether it be true that the said Arthur was very young and thin, delicate, and of a weak complexion, and unfit for a woman, and whether he looked as if he were impotent for marriage?
4. Whether it was said at the time, and considered as a fact among the people of the Royal household, Spaniards as well as Englishmen, that the said Prince Arthur had not consummated his marriage with the said Queen
5. Whether it is true that after the death of Prince Arthur the queen was in bad health and crippled, emitting bad humours from the mouth, and that a consultation of several eminent physicians took place respecting her illness, all of whom, after careful examination of the symptoms, and information received from the queen herself, declared the cause of the complaint to be no other than the non-consummation of the marriage, and that if she were to many another man she would speedily recover her health. And whether she did not on her subsequent marriage with king Henry recover her health and spirits, and was not stouter and better looking?
6. Whether it be true that when she was married to king Henry the said Queen was a virgin, and it was so stated among the courtiers, and among people of the Royal household, who believed it, king Henry her husband having also publicly stated the fact?
7. Did not king Henry shew a great desire to marry the queen, and did he not immediately after his father's death send his ambassadors to the said Queen, urgently requesting her to take

him for her husband, and pressing his application until the marriage was effected ?
8. Did not Henry's grandmother and those of the Council of England advise the said Henry, and indeed press him, to marry the sister of the king of France, and not his present Queen; and did not king Henry, against the advice of the said parties, determine to marry the said lady Queen, as he actually did some time after?
9. Do they know of any person or persons likely to furnish information on such points?[3]

The court struck lucky with several witnesses. Firstly, Ruiz de Puebla, the son of the former Spanish ambassador to England, gave evidence regarding the recent papal brief that had been sent to Catherine that she had presented to Campeggio in 1529. His evidence confirms that the brief had not been a forgery as suspected by Wolsey and even Campeggio:

> The Emperor being at Burgos at the time of the challenge, in the year 1528, he (Ruiz de Puebla) and his brother the archdeacon of Malaga, gave to His Majesty in his own hand the original brief [of pope Julius II] dispensing for the marriage of Katharine queen of England, and this present King Henry VIII., as well as the copy of a bull granted by the same pope for that purpose, and besides a letter of acknowledgment and receipt of the dower taken by the Queen on marriage.[4]

The commissioners also found Juan de Gamarra, the twelve-year-old boy who had slept in the room beside Arthur and Catherine on their wedding night. He related how the prince had risen 'very early' the following morning, 'which surprised everyone a lot', and upon entering Catherine's chamber Juan had found that the atmosphere was one of 'concern for Catherine and disappointment with Arthur'. He related how Catherine's dresser, Francesca de Carceras, was sadly telling the others that 'nothing had passed between Prince Arthur and his wife, which surprised everyone and made them laugh at him'.[5]

Then there was the nephew of the licentiate Alcarez, the man who had been Catherine's doctor in 1501. The doctor had since died but the youth who travelled to London with him vividly recalled that his uncle had been shocked to see Arthur's physical frailty, saying his 'limbs were so weak that he had never seen a man whose legs and other bits of his body were so thin'.[6] He went on to say that the prince had been 'denied the strength necessary to know a woman, as if he was a cold piece of stone, because he was in the final stages' of his deadly illness.

Also to give evidence was Juan Vinyol, a Spaniard who had travelled to England in 1510 and had witnessed Henry and Catherine's early happiness. He deputed that the king 'loved the queen his wife greatly ... stating publicly in French that his Highness was happy because he was owner of such a beautiful angel and that he had found himself a flower'.[7]

In May 1531 a letter was rediscovered, written by Catherine's father Ferdinand to his ambassador in Rome, Francisco de Rojas, which appeared to change everything. Catherine must have been excited to hear that it confirmed that Arthur had not consummated the marriage but that Rojas was to apply for a dispensation anyway in order to satisfy the English. The letter had been written in Barcelona on 23 August 1503, and the relevant section read:

> In the clause of the treaty which mentions the dispensation of the Pope, it is stated that the Princess Katharine consummated her marriage with Prince Arthur. The fact, however, is, that although they were wedded, Prince Arthur and the Princess Katharine never consummated the marriage. It is well known in England that the Princess is still a virgin. But as the English are much disposed to cavil, it has seemed to be more prudent to provide for the case as though the marriage had been consummated, and the dispensation of the Pope must be in perfect keeping with the said clause of the treaty. The right of succession depends on the undoubted legitimacy of the marriage.[8]

These statements, along with the verification of others, was sufficient to prove to the court at Zaragoza that the marriage of Catherine and Henry was a legal one and had, in fact, once been a happy one. Catherine was pleased to hear the result. From Windsor, she wrote to Charles at the end of July:

> The testimony to my virginity from Spain will be of great use. I cannot but complain of the Pope, who, by the delay, keeps the King in bondage [*tiene preso al Rey mi seor*]. Meanwhile they are making new inventions, and gaining new hope. They cause the King to do things which lessen his honor and fame, and imperil his conscience. The Pope is the cause of all this, by his refusal of justice. Commendations for the Ambassadors.[9]

II

It was not apparent to Catherine at first that Henry had left her for good. She remained at Windsor Castle that summer, wondering where her husband and Anne were, when they might return, or whether she might get a summons to attend the king somewhere else. It had been a long-standing custom between the king and queen that they would visit each other every three days, so when the end of the month arrived with no word from her husband, Catherine sent to enquire after his health. She expressed her concern that she had not been able to speak with him when he left, to bid him goodbye, and that she was deprived of the pleasure of his company. However, she added dutifully, it was 'for her to show obedience and patience'.[10] Henry was not pleased to receive the message. He summoned Norfolk and Dr Stephen to a meeting and emerged to summon the messenger 'in great choler and anger', to impart a return message for the queen. Coldly, he told Catherine he had

> no need to bid her adieu, nor to give her that consolation of which she spoke, nor any other, and still less that she should send to visit him, or to inquire of his estate; that she had given him occasion to speak such things, and that he was sorry and angry at her because she had wished to bring shame upon him by having him personally cited; and still more, she had refused (like an obstinate woman as she was) the just and reasonable request made by his Council and other nobles of his realm; that she had done all this in trust of your Majesty, but she ought to consider that God was more powerful than you; and, for a conclusion, that henceforth she must desist from sending him messengers or visitors.[11]

Catherine refused to ignore such a decisive rejection. She replied that she was sorry for the 'anger and ill will he had against her without cause' for she had done everything 'for the honour and discharge of their consciences'. Her hope, she stated boldly, 'did not depend upon [his] Majesty, nor on any prince alive, but only on God, who was the real protector of truth and justice'. Henry did not reply for three days. When he did, it was merely to repeat that she was obstinate to swear she had never known Prince Arthur and to have 'preached' it to the world. Catherine was, he stated, 'very much deceived if she founded herself upon that' as he would 'make the contrary quite evident by good witness'. She would do more wisely 'to employ her time in seeking witnesses to prove her pretended virginity, than to waste it in holding such language to the world as she did'. It was better for her to attend to her own affairs instead of sending him messages.[12] Worse still, the letter bore no address, as if the king's councillors were unsure of what title they should afford Catherine and doubted whether they might still refer to her as queen. This was very ominous and caused Catherine such 'great alarm' that Chapuys had to persuade her that it did not indicate Henry had received a positive ruling from the Pope.[13]

It seemed that Henry and Anne were preparing for marriage and that the king was taking steps to establish his new love in the eyes of the world as a replacement for Catherine. That July, Chapuys reported that Anne was declaring her 'marriage to the king will take place in three or four months at the latest'. She was making provisions for her royal position and had appointed an almoner and several officers, and was now accompanying Henry on hunting trips without any female attendants of her own. This, related the ambassador, was 'exceedingly aggravating to the queen', not only because of her separation from the king but because 'she fancies that his object in taking the Lady with him to such hunting parties is that he may accustom the lords and governors of the counties and districts he traverses on such occasions to see her with him', and that he may 'better win them over to his party when Parliament meets again'.[14] Catherine was not wrong in this supposition.

In the same letter, Chapuys provides an assessment of Catherine's character which remains the most compelling argument in favour of her assertion that she never slept with Prince Arthur. 'The queen is so virtuous, devout, and holy, so truthful,' he wrote, 'and

God-fearing that for naught in this World would she tell an untruth, but would prefer to die a thousand deaths rather than perjure herself to the detriment of a third party, or live in the unlawful state which such a case would entail.'[15] This was the simplicity of Catherine's case. Known for her piety and devotion, having sworn oaths to this effect and made the content of her confessions to Cardinal Campeggio public, she would never have committed such a heinous crime in the eyes of the Church as to have continued to practise a deception on such a critical matter. Her soul would have been damned eternally; yet that was the very fate she was fighting to save Henry from.

With Henry and Anne elsewhere, even if they were planning their marriage, Catherine was able to invite Princess Mary to Windsor at the end of July. Mary's presence, Chapuys told the Emperor, 'will make her forget her grief for the absence of the king', and they were amusing themselves by 'hunting and visiting the royal houses round Windsor' and hoping for good news from Rome. It must have been a happy time for them both, finally spending some proper time together despite their ongoing pain regarding the royal marriage. As they rode in the park and hunted together, they made the memories that would help sustain them in the coming years. But this summer marked a turning point in the king's determination, and therefore his cruelty, towards those who refused to comply with his wishes. Henry would never permit mother and daughter to see each other again.

In mid-August Henry ordered Catherine to leave the castle on the grounds that he wanted to use it for hunting. She was to relocate to The More while Princess Mary went to Richmond. 'Many think this very strange,' commented the ambassador, 'and think it an extreme determination for the divorce', but he thought it a punishment in order to 'induce the queen to consent that the cause may be tried here'. The More was a red-brick building in Rickmansworth, Hertfordshire, centred around a single courtyard that sat in a wide moat, with a base court lying to the south and a privy garden to the north. In 1527, Jean de Bellay had thought it a comparable house to Hampton Court, perhaps even better, but Catherine objected loudly to being sent there, calling it one of the worst houses in England and claiming she would rather have been lodged in the Tower. 'She is exceedingly sorry that the king has refused her certain houses to which she wished to retire, and has commanded her to go to one of the worst,' wrote the Spanish ambassador.[16] In addition, it had formerly been owned by Wolsey and so had the unhappy connotations of a former favourite fallen from grace. Chapuys explained the move to the Emperor by saying it was 'owing to some of her own maids of honour being taken sick',[17] but added that 'she has been but scantily visited by the king's courtiers, nor has she received from them such consolation as her case requires'.[18] However, according to the visiting Venetian Mario Savorgnano that August, it was large enough for her to retain a court of around 200 people,[19] although she confided in Chapuys that she would rather have been locked in the Tower because at least everyone would have been aware of her misfortune and 'would pray God to give her patience, and inspire the king to treat her better'.[20] She wrote to Charles that her 'tribulations are so great, my life so disturbed by the plans daily invented to further the king's wicked intention' and, although she had offended neither 'God nor the king', they continued to treat her in a way that 'is enough to shorten ten lives'.[21] Dr Ortiz heard that Catherine had left her own household in some distress.[22]

In October Dr Lee, the Earl of Sussex and Dr Sampson visited Catherine at The More. Their message was the same, although they attempted a gentler approach on this occasion, making a 'long discourse of the inconvenience which must arise if the difference between the king and herself proceeded according to the rigour of justice'. It would be much better, they urged, if all could be concluded amicably.[23] Again, Catherine was adamant, answering with 'sweetness and frankness' but repeating her previous arguments in favour of the validity of her marriage and queenship. She also introduced a new point, assuring the gentlemen that initially she had believed that Henry was acting according to 'a scruple of conscience' but now she was convinced that he was motivated 'by mere passion, [so] she would not be so ill advised as to consent to the compromise which the king required, especially here, where everybody, either for fear or subornment, would say black was white, and that the king ought not to doubt that she would pursue the process commenced by him, seeing that she had done everything by his leave'.[24] Hearing this, the deputation fell to its knees before her, 'begging her for the honour of the king, the great good of the princess, the peace of the kingdom, and her own repose, and that the king might treat her better than he had ever done before, that she would allow the process to be decided here, either by justice or amicably'.

The queen's reaction was equally as dramatic. She 'likewise threw herself upon her knees, praying them, for the honour of God and his Passion, for discharge of the king's conscience and her own, to remove such a scandalous example from Christendom for the good and peace of the realm'. She implored them to persuade the king to return to her, 'as he knew that she was his true and lawful wife; or, if he had any scruple, he would allow it to be cleared at Rome, where it could not be supposed that your Majesty had employed any violence or practice, for you were a very just prince'. Her opponents were not prepared for this and did not know how to answer, especially as all Catherine's people were present, and while the complaints were made against her in 'a low tone', she spoke loudly so all could hear. There were 'few of them that did not shed tears'. As they left, the lords informed her that Henry gave her the option of remaining where she was 'or retiring to a small house of his, or to an abbey'. The queen replied that 'it was not for her to choose, and that wherever the king commanded her, were it even to the fire, she would go'.[25]

Catherine's willingness to embrace martyrdom demonstrates her complete belief in her cause and her absolute refusal to relinquish her anointed position. She was obeying a higher authority than her husband. However, his wishes still counted for something, as on 13 November an awkward situation arose when both Henry and Catherine attended a feast for the serjeants-at-arms at Ely House. The king managed to avoid his queen by insisting they dine in separate rooms, and Catherine went away again without having seen him.[26]

A letter written by the queen that month, desperate in tone, gives an insight into her state of mind:

> My tribulations are so great, my life so disturbed by the plans daily invented to further the king's wicked intention, the surprises which the king gives me, with certain persons of his Council, are so mortal, and my treatment is what God knows, that it is enough to shorten ten lives, much more mine. As far as

> concerns this business, I have offended neither God nor the king, to whom I have always shown obedience as a true wife, and sometimes more so in this affair than my conscience approved of. Yet they treat me in such a manner that I do not know what to do, except to complain to God and your Majesty, with whom my remedy lies, and to beg you to cause the Pope to make such a speedy end of the matter as my truth merits. I pray God to pardon the Pope for his delay. In this world I will confess myself to be the king's true wife, and in the next they will know how unreasonably I am afflicted.[27]

Chapuys agreed that Catherine was almost at the end of her tether when he wrote to Charles on 25 November that her affairs 'proceed from bad to worse'. She had been forced to recognise that there was 'now no appearance that she will ever be recalled by the king', but would instead 'be further separated from him' because Anne Boleyn 'governs all' in the belief that she would soon be queen.[28] Just a week later, the ambassador followed this with another letter that the queen's physician, probably Dr Victoria, had informed him 'that it had been proposed in the Council to recall the queen to court'. Although this 'took not effect', it was determined that she 'should be not removed further, as she was afraid'. As a response to this ripple of sympathy, Henry ordered her to have 'greater provision than usual for the festivals'.[29]

Catherine was still at The More by the time Christmas arrived in 1531. Henry observed the season with Anne at Greenwich 'but all men said there was no mirth ... because the queen and the ladies were absent'.[30] In the list of New Year's gifts for 1532, Sir Thomas Boleyn and George, Lord Rochford received gilt bowls, goblets and cups, and the Countess of Wiltshire, Anne's mother, along with Bessie, Lady Tailboys and Mary Rochford, were given gifts from a range that included gilt cruets, bottles, cups, salts and goblets. In return, Anne's parents gave their future son-in-law a box of black velvet with a steel glass set in gold and a coffer of needlework containing three silver collars and three gold, while the widowed Mary Boleyn gave Henry a shirt with a black collar. In the records, a space was left by the queen's name. Henry gave Catherine no gift for the first time that year, and had forbidden her to send him anything for Christmas. However, he had not mentioned anything about New Year, so Catherine sent him a gold cup 'with honourable and humble words'. However, her gift was intercepted before the official presentation and therefore went unrecorded in the privy accounts. A couple of hours after receiving it, Henry 'praised its fashion' but returned it to her with the message that because they were no longer married, it was not an appropriate gift for her to have sent.[31] Anne gave Henry a set of rich and exotic boar spears or darts from the Pyrenees, and 'in return, he gave her a room hung with cloth of gold and silver, and crimson satin with rich embroideries. She is lodged where the Queen used to be, and is accompanied by almost as many ladies as if she were Queen.'[32] Henry had made no gift to Princess Mary either, a situation which Chapuys believed 'will lower the state of both [Catherine and Mary] unless there is speedy remedy'.[33] Not receiving a gift from Henry was symbolic enough, but it was not as bad for Catherine as having been banished from her husband's presence for an entire six months.

24

The New Queen 1532–1533

I

The year 1532 was a dark one for Catherine. Banished to the country, she was spared the painful sight of watching as Anne took over the role of queen at court and began to live openly with Henry as his wife. Clement wrote angrily to Henry for defying his ruling, hoping that the rumours were false and that the king would come to realise just 'what a scandal this is to the Church and how unworthy a religious prince, and how unbecoming to decide in his own cause'. The Pope tried to appeal to whatever was left of that youthful Henry who had spoken out against Luther and been rewarded with the title of Defender of the Faith. Hitherto, Clement wrote, Henry had 'been the Church's most zealous defender and the Pope would remonstrate with him as a loving father before assuming the function of a judge'. He told Henry that upon hearing that Catherine was put aside in favour of Anne, true Catholics would grieve while heretics rejoiced. He reminded the king that Catherine was 'the daughter of kings and the aunt of the Emperor and the king of the Romans'. Finally, Clement tried to appeal to the king's sense of justice, saying that he was convinced Henry would not have approved of such actions among his subjects, but would have punished such immorality. He hoped Henry 'will take Catherine back again and put away

Anne'.[1] Henry had no such intention. Nor did he plan to listen to anything that the Pope had to say.

The same month, Henry defended his position as England stood on the verge of schism. He had been informed 'by virtuous and learned men', he wrote to the Bishop of Durham, that 'considering what the Church of Rome is, it is no schism to separate from it and adhere to the words of God'. He had decided that 'the lives of Christ and of the Pope are very opposite, and therefore to follow the Pope is to forsake Christ',[2] and had an answer for each of Tunstall's concerns. In justifying his unprecedented move, Henry did not believe that any Christian princes would abandon England or 'withdraw their benevolence' because they had chosen to obey Christ. In his eyes, the Church of Rome was 'usurped' and no Christian should be bound to those who feared man more than God, a sentiment of which Catherine would have wholeheartedly approved. The Pope, wrote Henry, 'has already divided from the most part of Christendom and is now in no such credence as once he was'. He trusted that 'the papacy will shortly vanish away if it be not reformed' and that he would never separate from 'the universal body of Christian men'.[3]

Hearing of Henry's rejection of the papacy, the Cardinal of Osma wrote that he was much concerned, as the Pope had intended to cure Henry of his infatuation 'by delay', but the scheme had backfired. Osma identified that three 'evils' had arisen from this delay: the king was now a public adulterer, the 'queen was robbed of her rights by force' and Henry had 'lost all respect for the Apostolic See'.[4] Right under Henry's nose, his archbishop also launched an objection. On 24 February, in the presence of witnesses, William Warham made an official protest 'against all enactments made in the Parliament commenced in the Blackfriars ... in derogation of the Pope's authority, or of the ecclesiastical prerogatives of the province of Canterbury'.[5] Henry would have been furious at such a betrayal, but Warham was a sick man, and in August, before any action might be contemplated against him, he died. Thus the man who had married Henry and Catherine and had seen the tempestuous journey of their life together failed to see its final act, although his death left an important vacancy. Henry could now seek to appoint someone to the archbishopric who would be more sympathetic to his cause.

The king's first choice for the job was the pro-Boleyn Reformist Thomas Cranmer. Now in his early forties, Cranmer had risen from comparatively humble origins to benefit from a Cambridge education and had been the first to suggest that Henry might canvass the opinions of the universities on his marriage back in 1529. He was a controversial choice, having just married the niece of the Lutheran scholar Andres Osiander, who had edited a version of the translated Bible and attended the 1530 Diet of Augsburg, convened by the Emperor to address the spread of Protestantism. Cranmer was definitely a progressive thinker, backed by the Boleyn faction, and would go on to crown Anne less than a year later. He was travelling through Italy as Henry's ambassador to the Imperial court when he received a letter on 1 October 1532 informing him that he had been appointed as Warham's replacement. Cranmer must have known what expectations Henry had of him. Now that the Pope would not give Henry the divorce he wanted, he was resolved to break with Rome and head his own Church of England, where all such matters would be referred to his sympathetic appointees.

In the meantime, Catherine's popularity remained high, but those who dared to speak in her favour continued to be punished. An anonymous preacher, examined by the council for speaking out against the divorce, said he was 'moved to do so by the truth, the service of God and the honour of the king'. Another who attempted to preach in favour of Henry's cause 'in the bishopric of Cardinal Campeggio' was stopped in his tracks because 'the women and others would have treated him very ill, if it had not been for the authority of justice'.[6] At Easter, a preacher at the Friars Minors at Greenwich dared to deliver a critical sermon in front of Henry, saying that the 'unbounded affection of princes and their false counsellors deprived them of the knowledge of the truth'. When the king questioned the man afterwards, he 'heard words which did not please him', especially the warning that he was 'endangering his crown … for both great and little were murmuring at this marriage'. When the king found the man unwilling to change his views, he had him dispatched to Toulouse, in the south of France.[7]

Henry also made a direct response to the Pope. He was 'astonished and troubled' that Clement 'should persist in this fancy of wishing him to recall the queen; for if his Holiness said the queen was his wife, it was not his business to meddle with the way he punishes her for the rude behaviour she daily uses to him'. He also repeated that the 'punishment of his wife was his affair, and not the affair of anyone else', implying that Catherine's treatment was the result of her wilfulness and obstinacy. As the result of this, he had 'ordered the queen to remove after these holidays to a house much farther off than where she now is, and with bad accommodation'.[8] Henry angrily declared in public that he would 'not allow the Pope to treat him as he had done' and that Clement 'had no power over him'. He would 'celebrate this marriage in the most solemn manner possible' and began to fill the offices for Anne's coronation. The reaction was a horrified silence, as 'no one dared say a word, and most of the Court are scandalized, fearing that the king will carry out his intention, which is incredible'. Chapuys 'informed the queen, and will not fail to keep watch, and prevent it if possible'.[9]

In May 1532, Henry ordered Catherine to leave The More and move to Hatfield, in Hertfordshire, 'a house much farther off than where she now is, and with bad accommodation. The queen is vexed, because the house belongs to the Bishop of Lincoln, who has been the principal promoter of these practices', but as Charles's special envoy in England, Montfalconet, pointed out, she was retaining her dignity: 'The queen, although surrounded by vile persons devoted to the king, has never in any way given any occasion for slander, and even those who endeavor to damage her in the estimation of the king are struck with admiration for her virtue.'[10] Hatfield was around eighteen miles to the north-east of The More, and had been built around a central courtyard in 1497 by John Morton, Bishop of Ely. It had impressive decorative red brickwork and a banqueting hall and would later be used as a home for Princess Mary and the rest of Henry's children, but it represented the increasing isolation of a queen who was considered an inconvenience. Montfalconet also reported in the same month that when Henry asked Parliament for a subsidy for fortifying the border with Scotland, he was given the reply that 'if he would live with the queen as formerly, he should have no cause to complain, and that if he kept the friendship of the Emperor he would find himself strong enough, without any additional defences'. Henry would not stand for this, though, and they soon 'altered their tone'.[11] That month, support for Catherine grew – 'all love the queen' – and her supportive clergymen, including John Fisher, Bishop of Rochester, 'preached daily in her favour', even though some ran the risk of arrest, with her chaplain Thomas Abel publishing a book, *Invicta Veritas*, in English, in her favour. He was sent to the Tower while Henry tried to procure all the copies and had the book examined by the University of Oxford, but they did 'not know what to take hold of, and it is certain that if the book had not been prohibited there would have been a danger of commotion'. Even Charles Brandon, the king's closest companion and brother-in-law, whose wife's dislike of Anne Boleyn was an open secret, declared that it was time for Henry to be talked out of his folly.

Thomas More had been an active force against Luther and the spread of heresy, seeing it as a holy war. He was unwavering in his campaign to hunt down, interrogate and punish heretics, believing that 'the clergy doth denounce them ... the temporality doth burn them. And after the fire of Smithfield, hell doth receive them where the wretches burn forever.'[12] He confided in Erasmus that he found 'that breed of men [heretics] absolutely loathsome' and intended to be 'as hateful to them as anyone can possibly be'.[13] More had devised his own list of banned books and ruled that seeking out heresy must be the top priority of those who held clerical office. Under his regime, Thomas Hitton had become the first Reformation martyr in England after smuggling in translations of an English psalter by Luther's colleague George Joye. After Hitton, Cambridge scholar Thomas Bilney was burned in August 1531, and that December he was followed by another Cambridge alumnus, Richard Bayfield, who brought works by Luther, Zwingli and Philip Melanchthon into the country from Flanders. He also issued warrants for the arrest of the exile John Frith, who had been responsible for distributing works by Tyndale, although this would come into effect after More's tenure as Chancellor, with Frith being burned in 1533.

The details of the interrogation of James Bainham in December 1531 expose the questions that lay at the heart of the English Reformation, questions that were central to Catherine's own beliefs. The process was conducted by John Stokesley, Bishop of London, at More's house in Chelsea. Bainham was a lawyer from the Middle Temple who owned works by Tyndale and Frith and, according to John Foxe's later *Book of Martyrs*, was subject to imprisonment and flogging by More before being sent to the Tower to be racked. More denied such claims in his *Apology*. Bainham was asked if he believed in Purgatory, whether departed saints were to be honoured and if departed souls were in Heaven.[14] Next his interrogators wanted to know if he thought that confession to a priest was necessary and if it was true that he had commented that the 'truth of the Scriptures had lain hid till now'. He replied that, until lately, under the preaching of Reformers such as Hugh Latimer of Cambridge, no man had 'preached the word of God sincerely and purely'. When asked if he knew anyone who lived 'in the true faith of Christ' he named Richard Bayfield, whom he thought had died 'in the faith of Christ'. When asked about Luther's marriage, Bainham refused to denounce it as lechery and confessed he did not think he offended God by owning Tyndale's translated Bible, nor a number of other books that had been banned. He said he 'never saw any errors in them; but if there were any, if they were corrected, it was good the people had the books. He thought the New Testament in English was utterly good. Apparently he did not know that Tyndale was a naughty fellow.'[15] He was burned at the stake on 30 April 1532.

At the end of 1531, Stephen Vaughan, a merchant in the service of Wolsey's protégé Thomas Cromwell, wrote to him from Antwerp. He had heard that 'divers men and women of the Lutheran sect' had fled out of England 'for fear of punishment' and that as a result, 'new Tyndales will grow, or worse than he'. The interrogations were spreading a climate of fear and distrust, even among the faithful. Vaughan was afraid of being implicated by association, by the 'untrue report of any evil disposed person' who might 'spit out any venom against me to escape himself'. As a result, Vaughan refused to 'meddle' with the heretics, to prove that he was not one of them and had 'not so corrupt a mind, evil a conscience, nor so little understanding'.[16] Cromwell was the rising man, stepping into Wolsey's shoes to make himself indispensable to the king and supporting Henry's assertion of royal supremacy. In the summer of 1532, he was moving into position to become the king's chief minister in direct opposition to More.

When the third session of the Reformation Parliament was dissolved in the summer of 1532, the Chancellor deplored the direction in which things were moving and was forced to recognise that the royal marriage could no longer be saved. After only three years as Chancellor, More decided it was time to go. He complained to Erasmus of the 'rapid progress of heretical doctrines, notwithstanding the efforts that have hitherto been made to repress them. Incorrect versions of the Scriptures, and heretical books of all kinds, make their way from Flanders into England.'[17] More resigned his position that May and surrendered the great seal, handing it over in a white leather bag to Henry in person in the gardens of York Place.[18]

In July 1532, Anne and Henry headed north on an extended hunting trip, which included a five-day stay at Waltham, where the French ambassador accompanied Anne, hunting and watching the deer run. Henry was concerned for their privacy, as later Privy Purse payments show 40*s* being paid 'to the smith, for bolts and rings to the king's chamber door all the time of the progress';[19] was this more to repel potential intruders, or to keep the secret of what was going on within? Although 'great preparations' had been made, the trip was unexpectedly cut short and the party returned quietly to London. According to Chapuys, 'some say the cause is that, in two or three places that he passed through, the people urged him to take back the queen, and the women insulted the Lady' (Anne).[20] Yet if Henry and Anne were daunted by this, they were planning a far more significant conquest in the form of Francis I.

II

Sunday 1 September 1532 was another quiet day in Catherine's existence of exile, of alternate hope and despair, of prayers to God to help alleviate her suffering. Perhaps she knelt in the chapel at Hatfield or walked through its flat green parkland, or wrote to her daughter wondering whether her letter would reach her. It is difficult to know just how much information she received in her seclusion, or whether she was aware of More's resignation or Warham's death. She probably did not know that Suleiman was leading another army against Hungary or that the most famous painter of the English Renaissance, Hans Holbein, had arrived in England to work at Henry's court. Had she heard that Tyndale had translated the Torah, which was being printed in Antwerp to be distributed in England, or that the creator of future sublime music at the English court, Thomas Tallis, was the new organist at Dover Priory? Henry and Anne may well have heard him play that autumn as they headed to and from France. Perhaps word reached her of the death of her contemporary Spaniard, Diego de Ordaz, who had taken part in expeditions to Mexico and been one of the first Europeans to climb to the top of the volcano Popocatepetl.

The stillness and silence at Hatfield was in great contrast to the pomp and ceremony taking place thirty miles to the south, at Windsor Castle. The officers of arms, the dukes of Norfolk and Suffolk and other noblemen led out the figure of Anne Boleyn, wearing her long, dark hair loose, and dressed in a surcoat of crimson velvet furred with ermine and long straight sleeves, attended by two ladies. Brought before the king, she knelt to receive her patent, which was read aloud by Stephen Gardiner, Bishop of Winchester, before she was invested with her mantle and coronet, making her Marquesse of Pembroke. It was a significant moment, intended to raise Anne to a level of nobility that would pave her way to a meeting with the King of France and, perhaps, to becoming Henry's wife.

Catherine would certainly have interpreted Anne's elevation as a statement of intent. She was on the receiving end of another such directive at the end of that month when the Duke of Norfolk arrived at Hatfield to claim Catherine's jewels, which were needed to adorn Anne for the coming visit. Her collection of gems included some state pieces, gifts from her husband and inheritances from other family members, but also some that she had brought with her from Spain. They were far more than just wealth; their possession was a critical indicator of status and a connection to her past, both as queen and the legacy of her parents; they were also heirlooms for her daughter. Catherine responded with righteous passion, refusing to 'give up my jewels for such a wicked purpose as that of ornamenting a person who is the scandal of Christendom'. She replied with dignity that she would only relinquish them if Henry issued a direct order, so Henry did exactly that and was 'exceedingly pleased and happy' when Catherine complied with his wish.[21]

Henry's sister and other royal ladies had also been asked to yield up their jewels for the benefit of Anne, but the records indicate a number of items that were clearly Spanish in origin or had been created to honour Catherine's weddings. Besides the jewels and pearls, however, a wider confiscation of the queen's goods was going on, as Cromwell arranged the transportation of a number of items from Greenwich to Hampton Court, where the carved initial 'Ks' in the stonework were being chiselled away and replaced with the letter 'A'. There was a collar of Spanish work and a gold chain, Spanish fashion, enamelled red, white and black, a gold cup and cover with an image of St Catherine enamelled white with a wreath of pomegranates and four glass goblets wrought with roses, bearing the initials 'H' and 'K'. There were candlesticks engraved in the same way, and others decorated with carved arrow sheaves, a golden salt cellar called 'The Moresdaunce' depicting five dancing Moors, and more salt cellars, cups, basins and spoons bearing initials, roses, royal arms and pomegranates. There was also a silver-gilt tabernacle of Spanish work, a gospel bearing the royal arms and Catherine's devices and a gilt cup of Spanish fashion. Catherine would never see them again.

It was another humiliation for the queen in a long line of humiliations; she was permitted to keep a small gold cross that reputedly contained a shard of wood from the real cross, but the knowledge that the rest had gone to her rival, who was about to be feasted and treated as a queen in France, must have made a bitter day indeed for her. As Chapuys anticipated, 'it would much distress [Catherine's] conscience were she to deliver up her jewels for so bad a purpose as that of decorating a woman who was a scandal to the whole of Christendom, and a cause of infamy to the king himself who dragged her after him to such an assembly'.[22] But Chapuys also reported that Henry had met Mary while out riding, although he 'did not stop or converse long with her, asking only about her health' and promising to see her more in the future. The ambassador believed that the king did not 'dare' to invite Mary to wherever he was living with Anne, as she had 'already declared that she will not have it nor hear of her' and that he would have remained longer to speak with his daughter had Anne not 'sent two of her own suite with the king, that they might hear and report what he said to her'.[23] It was arranged that Mary would live at Windsor during Henry's absence in France, while Catherine was relocated to Enfield.[24] Worse still, her friend of longest standing, Maria de Salinas, Lady Willoughby, who had been with Catherine since her arrival in England, was ordered to leave the household and not contact her again. From this point forward, her life would become increasingly closed, quiet and lonely, as she was cut off from those she loved, restricted and moved further and further away from court. It was a personal tragedy for the daughter of Isabella, who had ruled the country at the time of its great victory at Flodden.

Now buried under north London's sprawl, Enfield Manor House was once a fortified property developed by the fourteenth-century de Bohun family. It was enclosed by a moat named Camletmoat, which was measured to stretch 160 yards by 135, while the grounds beyond contained a park and fish ponds. Catherine was resident there by 13 September, when she wrote to Charles V, apologising for disturbing him while he was busy resisting the Turks, although she believed her affairs were 'perhaps equal in the offence they cause to God'. She reported that 'books are being printed here full of falsehoods and filth touching the Faith' and that the marriage question was to be settled in England, 'the details are so foul and unreasonable, and dishonorable to her husband, that she does not like the Emperor to know them from her, and the Ambassador will tell him'.[25] Catherine may have been alluding to Henry and Anne's imminent departure for Calais, which she saw as a milestone in their relationship. As Chapuys explained, 'the queen was very much afraid that the king would marry the Lady at this meeting; but the Lady has assured some person in whom she trusts, that, even if the king wished, she would not consent, for she wishes it to be done here in the place where queens are wont to be married and crowned'.[26]

Henry's departure was delayed by ten days, though, due to an outbreak of plague in Dover.[27] Chapuys had his own concerns about the number of people going and the speed with which the trip had been organised. He had heard the French ambassador du Bellay assert 'that no ladies would be present' although he believed that 'lady Anne will be there, considering the preparations of ladies and servants to accompany her'.[28] Chapuys was correct that Anne was with Henry at Calais, but the Frenchman was right that no women would be present at the formal meeting between Henry and Francis. Du Bellay believed that Henry did not wish to take Catherine because 'he hates the Spanish dress', but there was no chance of the queen being invited at all. Anne was going to play a limited role in order to avoid the awkwardness of having to meet Francis's second wife, Eleanor, who was the sister of Emperor Charles and thus Catherine's niece. Henry had also requested that 'two types of men' be removed from the court: Imperialists and those 'who have the reputation of being mockers and jesters, who are as much hated as any people by this nation'.[29]

That November, while Henry and Anne were out of the country, Catherine wrote again to Charles to congratulate him on repelling the Turks from Hungary. Again, she pleaded her own cause as being of equal significance, hoping that 'with the grace of God, his Holiness will slay the second Turk, which is the business of the king, my lord, and my own'. She explained that she called 'it the second Turk, because the ills which have followed, and still follow every day, owing to his Holiness not putting an end to this cause in time, are of so great and such evil example, that I do not know which is the worst, this business or that of the Turk'.[30] However, it was difficult to ignore the comparison between the infidel in the east and the infidel who was destroying the Catholic Church and living an immoral life in England. Catherine related how the Pope's 'delay has occasioned her so much suffering' and begged Charles, 'for the love of Christ', to continue to work in her favour, otherwise she would 'enter another purgatory'.[31] But again things were to get worse. Catherine was about to be cast out of purgatory and into hell. She did not know that Henry and Anne were married in secret upon their return to Dover on 14 November, the very same date that she had become Arthur's wife. A second ceremony was carried out at the end of January. Nor did she know that within weeks Anne was pregnant and was promising Henry the one thing that Catherine had been unable to give him. Henry was preparing himself for the arrival of his son.

III

In March 1533, Catherine was moved on again. It is likely that she learned the news of Anne's pregnancy after she had arrived at Ampthill Castle in Bedfordshire. The castle had been built in the late fifteenth century, covering an area of around 220 square feet, with a large court in front and two smaller ones behind. There were two square projecting towers at the front and nine smaller ones all round the sides. Henry had often stayed there on hunting trips, praising the location in 1528 for its 'clearness of air'. In 1770, long after the place had gone into decline, a stone cross was erected on the site in memory of Catherine's stay, with verses attributed to Horace Walpole:

> In days of old here Ampthill's towers were seen,
> The mournful refuge of an injured Queen;
> Here flowed her pure but unavailing tears,
> Here blinded zeal sustain'd her sinking years.
> Yet Freedom hence her radiant banner wav'd,
> And Love aveng'd a realm by priests enslav'd;
> From Catherine's wrongs a nation's bliss was spread,
> And Luther's light from Henry's lawless bed.[32]

From this point, things began to speed up. Henry opened a new session of parliament in February with the Act in Restraint of Appeals to Rome, forbidding his subjects from making appeals to the Pope. Catherine was summoned by Thomas Cranmer to attend a court at Dunstable Priory, which was to examine her before pronouncing a final sentence upon her marriage. She refused to attend. In her absence, the momentous step that Henry, Anne and Catherine had been preoccupied with for so long was taken: as head of the new Church of England, Cranmer fulfilled his king's expectations and pronounced that Henry's first marriage was null and void, making Anne his first legitimate wife. Contrary to the descriptions of popular history, Henry's separation from Catherine was never a divorce; the marriage was annulled on the grounds that it was invalid from the start. The vote went overwhelmingly in the king's favour, with 197 to just 17, one of which was John Fisher. Cranmer pronounced Henry and Catherine's marriage to be null and void. Three days later, on 5 April, a ruling was passed that the Pope did not have the authority to dispensate against the Leviticus verse forbidding the marriage of a man with his dead brother's wife. Again, Fisher voiced his objections. On the following day, which was Palm Sunday, the loyal bishop was arrested and placed under the custody of Stephen Gardiner, Bishop of Winchester. There is no doubt that Fisher was the king's most formidable opponent. As Chapuys recognised, 'there is no one here of whom the Lady is more afraid than the bishop of Rochester [Fisher], for he is just the man who without fear of any sort has always defended and upheld in the most unanswerable manner the queen's cause'.[33] On 9 April, the dukes of Suffolk and Norfolk arrived at Ampthill to urge Catherine to give up her cause and give her permission for the marriage to be tried in England. When she refused they informed her that Henry had already remarried.

It must have been with a sense of foreboding that Catherine received William Blount, Lord Mountjoy, her chamberlain since 1512, at Ampthill on 3 July. He found her 'lying on a pallet', as she had 'pricked her foot with a pin and could not stand', and was also suffering from a cough.[34] He was charged with delivering to her the news that Anne had been crowned queen on 1 June and that, as a result, Catherine was no longer to be referred to as queen, but must revert to the title of Princess Dowager, her status on the death of Arthur. Mountjoy was instructed to inform her that Henry had found his 'conscience violated, grudged, and grieved by that unlawful matrimony contracted between him and the Dowager', but now that it had been 'defined and determined by a great number of the most famous universities and clerks of Christendom to be detestable, abominable, execrable, and directly against the laws of God and nature', he was lawfully divorced, by the advice of all his nobles, bishops and the commons of the realm. Therefore, he was now legally married to Anne, who was now the queen. There could not be two wives or two queens, so Catherine must no longer 'persist in calling herself by the name of queen', but was to be satisfied with the name of Dowager and should 'beware of the danger if she attempt to contravene it'. If she chose to ignore these instructions because of her vehement arrogancy, the king would be 'compelled to punish her servants, and withdraw her affection from his daughter. Finally, that as the marriage is irrevocable, and has passed the consent of Parliament, nothing that she can do will annul it, and she will only incur the displeasure of Almighty God and of the king.' If this was not bad enough, Princess Mary was forbidden from contacting her mother.[35]

It must have been a difficult message for Mountjoy to deliver, having been close to Catherine for so many years and having witnessed her long journey, with all its highs and lows. Knowing her so well, he could also probably predict her reaction. Catherine refused to comply. She insisted on still being referred to as queen and scribbled out any written references to her as a dowager princess. She stated that she was the king's true wife, that her children were legitimate and 'that the cause was not theirs but the Pope's to judge. To other arguments, that she might damage her daughter and servants, she replied she would not damn her own soul on any consideration, or for any promises the king might make her.'[36] A number of her staff supported her loyally, stating they had taken an oath to serve her as 'queen' and would be committing perjury if they now referred to her by another title.[37] Finally, Catherine retreated into her nationality, claiming 'if anything in the report was prejudicial to her cause, she protested against it, considering she was no English woman, but a Spaniard, and might err in her words if she had no counsel'.[38]

Mountjoy reported back to Cromwell that a number of the members of Catherine's household had 'never ceased to call her by the name of queen', thus showing their defiance to the king. The officers of her council and household were prepared to call her princess but her gentlewomen and her chaplains could not see how they could 'discharge their consciences ... as they were sworn too her as queen'. Their names were recorded and sent to London. But, as Mountjoy recorded, it was not possible for him 'to be a reformer of other folk's tongues, or to accuse them', because he truly believed them to be loyal to Henry. Neither could he bring himself to 'vex and disquiet' Catherine, as she had kept 'herself true to the king, as he knew no other'. Therefore, in view of his respect for her and their long association, he begged, 'without the king's displeasure', that he may 'be discharged of the office of chamberlain'.[39]

Queen or not, Catherine now feared most for her daughter, as Chapuys related, certain that while 'this cursed Anne has her foot in the stirrup' she would do the queen 'all the injury she can and the princess likewise'. Now she and her daughter were stripped of their former titles, they were vulnerable to all kinds of abuses, including being made to conform to positions that were below their fitting rank. The ambassador reported Anne's boasting that she would have Mary for her lady's maid, in order to 'make her eat humble pie' or to marry her to some varlet, although it is very unlikely Henry would have done so, later swearing that she would never marry during his lifetime. Yet the ambassador also feared the 'scandal which will arise from this divorce, and likewise to prevent the kingdom from alienating itself entirely from our Holy Faith and becoming Lutheran'.[40] In Catherine's downfall, he foresaw the downfall of the Catholic Church of England. Therefore, he took the dramatic step of urging the Emperor to invade England, or at least to declare war on Henry and capture Calais:

> The attempt would be easy, for they have no horse, nor men to lead them, nor have they the heart of the people, which is entirely in favour of you, the Queen, and the good Princess, I may say not of the mean, but of the higher classes, except Norfolk and two or three others. It will be right that the Pope should call in the secular arm; and meanwhile, in support of the censures already executed, you might forbid negotiations in Spain and Flanders, and so induce the people to rise against the authors of this cursed marriage.[41]

This is where the first real concerns arise about Catherine's life, either as the result of poison, neglect or even execution, which were to be a theme through her remaining years. Charles asserted that 'many think the queen ought to leave England on account of the danger to her life' and debated the question of an invasion with his council.[42] Even the Pope suggested that 'unless the queen was very sure of her servants that they would not give her poison, she should leave the kingdom'.[43] Catherine, though, was firmly against leaving or any notion of a war as being disloyal to her husband and her country. 'Seeing the bad disposition of affairs here, I have attempted to learn the queen's intention,' wrote Chapuys to Charles, 'in order to find some remedy, since kindness and justice have no place. But she is so scrupulous, and has such great respect for the king, that she would consider herself damned without remission if she took any way tending to war.'[44] So Chapuys put aside such thoughts and tried to reason again with Henry.

Next, the plucky ambassador went to court to request an audience with the king. After several denials, he was finally permitted to see Henry and laid out his arguments regarding Catherine's case. First, he referred the king to five popes who had given dispensations in similar cases and stated there was not a doctor in his kingdom, 'if it came to the point, that would not confess the truth'. Next, he spoke about the debacle of the Paris University vote, 'on which he rested much', desiring to show the king the letters and names of those on Catherine's side, but Henry refused to see them. Chapuys continued to urge that there was not a single prelate or doctor in Spain who supported Henry's view, nor did many in England, again offering his collected letters of proof, which Henry would not see. Then, when the ambassador raised the question of Catherine's virginity, saying that the king had often confessed that she had come to him untouched and could not deny it, Henry finally 'admitted it, saying it was spoken in jest, as a man, jesting and feasting, says many things which are not true'. Leaving the ambassador stunned with his callousness, the king diverted the conversation by saying that he wished to have a successor to his kingdom, whereupon Chapuys made a quick recovery to observe that 'he had a daughter endowed with all imaginable goodness and virtue and of an age to bear children', and that because he had received the 'principal title to his realm by the female line, nature seemed to oblige him to restore it to the princess'. When Henry asserted that he knew better than his daughter and wanted more children and Chapuys ventured to suggest that this was by no means a certainty, the king asked him three times 'if he was not a man like other men' and said that Chapuys was not privy to all his secrets. By this, the ambassador 'clearly understood that his beloved lady [Anne] was enceinte' (pregnant).[45] This was the ultimate blow to Catherine.

Nor were the English people content with the new marriage, if Chapuys' account to Charles is to be believed. When an Augustinian prior urged his congregation to pray for Queen Anne, 'they were astonished and scandalized, and almost every one took his departure with great murmuring and ill looks, without waiting for the rest of the sermon'. Henry was furious to hear of it and sent word to the mayor that 'on dread of his displeasure he should take order that nothing of the kind happened again, and that no one should be so bold as to murmur at his marriage. The Mayor hereupon assembled the trades and their officers of the several halls, and commanded them, on pain of the king's indignation, not to murmur at his marriage, and to prevent their apprentices from so doing, and, what is worse and more difficult, their wives. The King in vain forbids and makes prohibitions, as it only makes the people speak more against it in private, and these prohibitions only serve to envenom the heart of the people.'[46]

Henry was very sensitive to the possibility of being mocked by his subjects. That May, one example emerged of him and Anne being a laughing stock to the common people, as one John Coke, Secretary to the Merchant Adventurers, related to Cromwell. A 'naughty person' from Antwerp had sold images and pictures on cloth at the Easter market at Barowe, some of which depicted the king. He pinned upon it the image of a 'wench' holding a pair of scales, with two hands on one side and a feather on the other. A script above it stated that 'love was lighter than a feather', which 'pleased the Spaniards and others of the Dutch nation', who 'jested and spoke opprobrious words against the king and queen'. The miscreant was arrested and questioned, but said he meant no harm, and was let off on pain of the confiscation of his merchandise and further punishment.[47] Even more damning were the words of Sir Rauf Wendon to Sir Thomas Gebons, priest, of King's Sutton in Warwickshire, who had said that the queen 'was a whore and a harlot and that there was a prophecy that many should be burned in Smithfield and he trusted it would be the end of Queen Anne'.[48]

Nor were these isolated incidents, as Henry was furious to discover. The Earl of Derby wrote directly to him regarding the 'arrest of a lewd and naughty priest', one James Harrison, 'who has spoken slanderous words about your Highness and the queen's grace'. The miscreant was examined at Ley, in Lancashire, for having stated that 'Queen Catherine should be queen and as for Nan Bullen, that whore, who the devil made her queen?' He also said, with irony, 'this is a marvellous world. The King will put down the order of priests, and destroy the sacrament; but it will be … that it cannot reign long, for he saith that York will be London hastily.'[49]

The voice of dissent was also raised close to home. Elizabeth Amadas was a relative, perhaps the wife, of Henry's jeweller Robert, although her ramblings of 1534 read more like the product of a deluded and confused mind than deliberate heresy or treason. That mattered little to Henry, though. She believed that Anne Boleyn 'should be burned, for she is a harlot', and that the king's gentleman Henry Norris and Anne's father were 'bawd between the king and her' and that Henry had slept with both Anne's sister and mother. To this accusation, it will be recalled that the king famously replied, 'Never with the mother.' Elizabeth believed that 'there was never a good married woman in England except prince Arthur's dowager, the Duchess of Norfolk, and herself', and in a coming battle of priests, 'the king would be destroyed, England would be divided into four and there would be no more kings'. According to those who knew her, she defamed the king daily because he has 'forsaken his wife', and was reputedly encouraging Elizabeth's husband to do the same. She also predicted that if Anne was not 'burnt within this half year, she will be burnt herself'.[50]

Even the Duke of Norfolk, Anne's own uncle, was 'very much grieved' by the treatment of Catherine, finding out on the eve of Anne's coronation that 'the arms of the queen had been not only taken from her barge, but also rather shamefully mutilated'. In response, he had 'rather roughly rebuked the Lady's chamberlain, not only for having taken away the said arms, but for having seized the barge, which belonged only to the queen, especially as there are in the river many others quite as suitable'.[51] Likewise Thomas Cromwell commented to the ambassador of the many 'virtues of the queen, the great modesty and patience she had shown, not only during these troubles, but also before them, the king being continually inclined to amours'. He also hoped that 'the king would not diminish her dower, of about 24,000 ducats, assigned to her in the time of prince Arthur, if she would content herself with the state a widow princess ought to keep'.[52]

IV

On 11 July, Chapuys reported that certain key members of Catherine's household, including her chamberlain, almoner, secretary, purveyor and master of the horse, were given instructions by the king to 'make divers remonstrances to her' that it was 'great arrogance and vainglory on her part to usurp the title of queen'. She was deceiving herself, or pretending ignorance, that they were not 'lawfully divorced' and he was 'duly married to another, who had since been crowned'.[53] If she would submit to him, Henry declared, he would 'treat her well', otherwise 'he would punish her as his subject' and, if she persevered in her obstinacy, she would 'create parties in the kingdom, and confusion in the succession', from which would arise 'enormous bloodshed and great destruction of the kingdom, to the burden of her conscience'. Henry clearly had in mind the state of the country under his grandfather's rule, when disputed claims led to civil war, but the situation was hardly the same. These were not battles between fully grown men, but the threats of a thwarted man to his discarded wife. Worse still, Henry then moved to threaten his neglected daughter, which must have appalled Catherine as much as it terrified her. If she persisted, 'the king would ill-treat the princess, and those who spoke of it, and all her other servants, would incur the king's indignation'.[54]

In the face of these threats, Catherine replied 'openly and courageously' that she knew 'assuredly she was the king's true wife' and would 'never call herself otherwise than Queen, or answer to any other name, to any person in the world'. She absolutely refuted the claim that this was due to arrogance or vainglory, 'for she would be much more proud to be called the daughter of her father and mother than to be the greatest queen in the world, if she could not conscientiously use the title'. When it came to the question of the king not taking her back, 'she had perfect confidence that He who in a moment converted St. Paul, and turned him from a persecutor into a preacher, would inspire the king's conscience, and not permit such a virtuous prince long to continue in error, to the slander of Christendom and ecclesiastical authority. As to the division of the kingdom, and the confusion of the succession, those only were to blame who had persuaded this new marriage, because the king had already lawful succession acknowledged by the whole kingdom; and from such an abominable marriage there could only arise a perverse offspring, which would throw all into confusion that allowed it to reign.' When it came to Princess Mary, 'the king being her father could do what he pleased. No doubt she would be sorry to see her ill-treated, and also that her servants should incur the king's indignation; but neither for that, nor for any death, would she damn her soul or that of the king her husband.'[55]

It was often the case that Catherine's 'disobedience' was followed by the downsizing of her household or a change of properties. Provisions ordered for Catherine's household at Ampthill in May show that yet another move was being planned for her. Rhys ap Howell was charged to provide her with flour, William Shaw with oxen and sheep, John Stone with capons, hens, wildfowl, butter and eggs, John Reynolds hay and litter for the stables, George Hill with fresh and sea fish and John Turner, yeoman porter, 'to provide carts and horses at the removal of the princess'.[56] Just weeks after asserting herself as queen that July, Catherine was removed from Ampthill to Buckden House in Cambridgeshire, a property twenty miles away, owned by the Bishop of Lincoln. Yet this provided an unintended opportunity for her supporters to express their devotion. As she prepared to leave, 'all the neighbourhood' gathered outside the house as she left, to 'see her and pay her honour' and affection 'along the whole route'. The loyal Chapuys painted rather a dramatic picture of the occasion: 'They begged her with hot tears to set them to work and employ them in her service, as they were ready to die for the love of her', and even though it was 'forbidden on pain of death to call her queen', they 'shouted it at the top of their voices, wishing her joy, repose and prosperity and confusion to her enemies'.[57]

Before she moved, Catherine would also have heard of the death of Henry's sister Mary, the companion of her youth, with whom she had often found consolation during the difficult years of her widowhood. Having married Charles Brandon, Duke of Suffolk, and borne him four children, she had remained a staunch supporter of Catherine's until the end, refusing to recognise Anne Boleyn as queen. She had died in Suffolk on 25 June, at the age of thirty-seven. Another important friend and link with Catherine's past was gone.

Catherine had taken up residence at Buckden Place, in Cambridgeshire, by 16 July 1533. Situated on the Fens, it was 'surrounded by deep waters and marshes' and quite possibly, according to Chapuys, even though it had been recently reworked, 'the most unhealthy and pestilential house in England'. The fortified red-brick gateway still survives, through which Catherine would have ridden to the new buildings inside, which had replaced the old wooden structures as recently as 1475. It is likely that she arrived with a reduced household, too, as Henry was renewing her officers, allowing her 30,000 crowns out of which 12,000 was available to her, although she had to pay her ladies out of that. Catherine was not happy with the change, writing to Chapuys that 'sooner than consent to it, even if they gave her 7,000,000 cr., she would die, or go and beg for God's sake, thinking that if she consented to any change in her treatment she would prejudice her right and her conscience'.[58] On the occasion of his last visit, Catherine had announced to Mountjoy that if Henry was aggrieved at the cost of her allowance, she would scale down her household, being satisfied with what she had 'and with her confessor, physician, apothecary, and two women, and go wherever he wished'. The ambassador advised her that 'considering the protests already made, and that she was compelled to have patience, repeating her protestation, she could not possibly injure her cause; and that I thought, as she could obtain nothing better, that it would be safer not to go to extremes'.[59] It was not the king's doing, Chapuys added, as he was not 'ill-natured', but it was 'this Anne who has put him in this perverse and wicked temper and alienates him from his former humanity'. He fully believed that she would never cease 'until she has seen the end of the queen, as she has done that of the Cardinal, whom she did not hate so much'.[60]

In addition, an inventory was taken of the plate remaining with the 'Princess Dowager' for her daily service. She was permitted to keep gilt candlesticks, a holy water sprinkler, basins, a Spanish crucifix and, controversially, given the spread of reformed views, several images of saints, as well as a number of items 'of her own' that she had brought from Spain.[61] Her pantry was stocked with golden salt cellars and gilt and white spoons, her cellar with pots and bowls of gold and gilt, decorated with enamel, her ewery with basins, some bearing the king's arms and a number of chandeliers. She was left with eight white spice dishes, eleven white sauce pits and over seventy white plates in her scullery. It was a modest legacy, even for a dowager princess.[62]

Yet Henry could not prevent rumours of Catherine's ill-treatment from spreading, even across Europe, to the friends of his former wife. Ambassador Hawkins reported such murmurings at the Imperial court, prompting Henry to declare himself 'surprised that the Emperor or his Council should believe anything about his proceedings but what is godly and honorable'. He felt himself well able to refute this allegation on the grounds that 'the lady Katherine's house, offices, and servants are arranged as well as can be devised, and the same of the lady Mary'.[63] Charles's correspondence shows that he believed himself to have won a victory, though, as Henry had 'arranged for a restitution of her old servants', which had been caused by 'the Emperor's having urged on the English ambassador that the queen ought to be restored to her ancient dignity'.[64] Charles was also concerned about his cousin Mary's health, hearing that 'the princess has been a little unwell, but has recovered, and removed yesterday from a house of the Archbishop of Canterbury, where she had been more than a year, to one belonging to the king, about forty miles from this'. In turn, Henry had been 'pleased to send her the queen's physician and apothecary', and permitted Catherine to 'send to her' as often as she liked.[65]

In August, amid a summer in the midst of the flat Fens, a messenger rode up to Buckden Palace. Finally, after years of deliberation, the Pope had taken decisive action. Clement had issued a bull commanding Henry to restore Catherine and 'put away Anne' within ten days, on pain of excommunication. In case of disobedience, he called upon Charles V and all other Christian princes, as well as Henry's own subjects, 'to assist in the execution of the bull by force of arms'.[66] Chapuys reported that 'the king's great affection to the Lady appeared to have cooled, in consequence of the sentence passed at Rome, and that he seemed somewhat to recognize his position'. However, Henry was not so easily defeated and summoned a meeting of his learned doctors, 'who have given him to understand that great wrong has been done him, and that even if they annul the second marriage, that sentence would not confirm the first'.[67] At Buckden, Catherine waited for news. The ten days elapsed. Nothing changed. Instead, she waited for the next letter from court, which would no doubt contain news of the son that Anne Boleyn was about to bear.

Anne was due to enter confinement at the end of August 1533. The last royal pregnancy had been fifteen years earlier, and although she was miles away, Catherine would have recalled all the steps of protocol as the chambers were prepared and furnished with their colourful cushions and hangings, the prayers said and anticipation mounted. Perhaps her ladies conspired to keep from her any news that they would have understood to be so painful, but the impending birth became impossible to ignore when Anne requested that Catherine hand over the 'very rich triumphal cloth which she brought from Spain to wrap up her children with at baptism', which Isabella herself had placed in Catherine's trousseau. This was a step too far. Catherine replied that 'it has not pleased God she should be so ill advised as to grant any favor in a case so horrible and abominable'.[68]

Henry was certain that Anne's child would be a healthy boy. It had to be, in order to justify him putting aside Catherine and breaking with Rome. His physicians and astrologers confirmed his hopes, so he planned 'rejoicings and solemn jousts' with horses ordered from Flanders and the bed of the Duc d'Alençon brought out of the royal treasury for Anne's use. Perhaps Chapuys passed on court rumours that Anne had cause to be jealous of a new rival at court and, during a heated argument in which she used 'some words' that displeased Henry, had been warned by him to 'shut her eyes and endure as well as more worthy persons' had done before her.[69] The ambassador certainly saw hope for Catherine's cause amid such tensions, as Henry continued:

> She ought to know that it was in his power to humble her again in a moment more than he had exalted her. By reason of which words there has been some grudge, and *faon de faire*, so that the king has been two or three days without speaking to her. No doubt these things are lovers' quarrels, to which we must not attach too great importance, yet many who know the king's disposition consider them a very favourable commencement for the recall of the Queen.[70]

On 7 September, at about three in the afternoon, Anne gave birth to a daughter, Elizabeth. Chapuys wrote with glee to the Emperor that it was 'to the great regret both of [Henry] and the lady, and to the great reproach of the physicians, astrologers, sorcerers, and sorceresses, who affirmed that it would be a male child. But the people are doubly glad that it is a daughter rather than a son, and delight to mock those who put faith in such divinations, and to see them so full of shame.'[71] Although the long-awaited boy was, in fact, a girl, her existence as the legitimate heir had implications for Catherine and Mary. Henry sent members of his council to inform Mary that she must forbear using the title of princess, 'which belongs to the one who was lately born, and not to her'. The seventeen-year-old Mary took the same line as her mother, replying that she would be obedient to her father in all things, but she had no right to renounce or derogate from the titles and prerogatives that God, nature, and her parents had given her; that, being daughter of the King and Queen, she had a right to be styled princess'.[72] Chapuys suspected that 'by thus treating the princess he hopes to bring over the queen; but he is mistaken ... Or, perhaps, his evil star brings him to this, in order the more to incur the indignation of God and the world.' He also worried that Henry might wish to send his eldest daughter to a nunnery or marry her off against her will, and he persuaded Catherine to prepare her arguments in advance, should either eventuality arise.[73] That October, when Mary received a letter asking her to move from Beaulieu to Hertford Castle, she objected to the fact that it was addressed to 'the lady Mary, the king's daughter'. Writing to her father, 'marvelling at this', she asserted that surely, Henry was 'not privy to it, not doubting but you take me for you lawful daughter, born in true matrimony'.[74] But there had been no mistake. Soon, to her horror, and that of her mother, Mary's household was disbanded and she was brought to attend upon the baby Elizabeth as her lady's maid.[75] The loyal Margaret Pole offered to stay with her and serve her at her own expense, but she was told that this was out of the question.

When Catherine wrote to Chapuys that November, she could not keep back her tears, 'to think of her innocence and separation from the king', who had left her and remarried 'without any divorce except what he has arranged and ordered'. She fully expected that 'she and her daughter will be martyred at the next Parliament'.[76] As news spread to her native land, an Englishman in Valladolid called John Mason asked, 'What will this tragedy come to, God wot? if that may be called a tragedy which began with a marriage.'[77] As the terrible year of 1533 drew to a close, it was a question that was much on Catherine's mind.

25

Dark Days 1534–1536

I

On 20 April 1534, a woman named Elizabeth Barton was taken along with five other men from the Tower of London to Tyburn, where they were publicly denounced for maintaining 'the false opinion and wicked quarrel of the queen against the king'. Having gained a name as a prophetess at Henry's court, Barton, also known as the Holy Maid of Kent, had lost the king's favour by foretelling his downfall within a month of his marriage to Anne Boleyn.[1] She was also charged with using superstition to 'prevent the Cardinal of York from proceeding to give sentence for the divorce, as he had resolved'[2] and had received instructions to command 'that infidel prince of England ... to amend his life' and to 'destroy these new folks of opinion and the works of their new learning'. Reputedly, an angel had told Barton to 'bid him take his old wife again, or else'.[3] She had been arrested and examined by Cranmer the previous summer, but released and then re-arrested by Cromwell in the autumn. This time there was no escape; she was condemned for treason and heresy. She and her associates were hanged and beheaded before the crowd at Tyburn, and Barton's became the first female head to grace the spikes on London Bridge.

Perhaps as the spring arrived at Buckden, Catherine heard news of the Nun's fate, or of the other voices of dissent which were speaking out in her favour across the country. One Dr Powell had spoken against Henry's second marriage, saying it was not lawful, and composed a book against it.[4] There was also a priest called Sir John Warde, from Maldon in Essex, who said in front of witnesses that Henry 'was no king of right',[5] and a captain in Antwerp who told three merchants heading to England, 'I give you knowledge that if your King take not his Queen again within 30 days I would advise you nor none of your nation to pass this ways, but to keep you at home; for if you do, I woll take you as good prise.'[6]

With such outspokenness in favour of Catherine, Henry was quick to clamp down on his wife and daughter, to the extent that Chapuys and Charles were increasingly concerned about their welfare, and even their lives. It seemed a diabolically logical step that if Henry's subjects were being persecuted for supporting the 'old' queen and her daughter, their removal would provide a simple solution to the problem. Always fearing the worst, Chapuys warned that 'this cursed lady will arrange to get quit of her',[7] adding that 'the French ambassador said he was astonished that good guard was not kept about the princess to keep her from being carried away, as it would totally ruin the king if she were to cross the sea. This agrees with what I have already written, that the king did not care to marry her on the other side of the sea.'[8] Dr Ortiz of Paris was also deeply concerned about the 'tribulations with which the queen has been visited'. He 'eulogises her virtues and the honour she acquires by her martyrdom [but] wished the princess were out of England, for he fears that with the cruelty of Herod they will either kill her, or force her to enter religion or marry some base person, though such a profession of religion or marriage would be worth nothing'.[9] Nor would Catherine or her daughter play the game in order to make their lives easier; it simply wasn't in their characters, being completely convinced of their right to the titles of legitimate princess and queen. On first hearing that she was to be deprived of her title of princess, Mary answered that the title belonged 'to herself, and to no other', making many very wise remonstrances that what had been proposed to her was strange and dishonorable.[10] When Anne Boleyn went to visit Mary, to urge her to reconcile with her father and to honour her as queen, Mary replied that 'she knew no queen in England except her mother', but that she would be much obliged if the king's mistress would do her that favour. In response, Chapuys reported that Anne had threatened to 'bring down the pride of this unbridled Spanish blood', and anticipated that 'she will do the worst she can'.[11]

Chapuys's concerns were fuelled by a period of illness Catherine experienced in the winter of 1533–4, being very unwell just before Christmas so that 'the physicians had given her up'.[12] However, there were suspicions that this was just a rumour, put around to prepare the ground for an attempt upon her life, as Charles conveyed to his ambassador in France: 'As to the report spread by the king of England that the queen our aunt is ill, you are to take an opportunity of telling him that she is in very good health of body, notwithstanding her ill treatment, and that the spreading of such a report is very suspicious.'[13] He believed that this, coupled with the fact that 'they have put her in a very unhealthy habitation, and taken away her physician, and almost all her servants, so that the *essai* of viands is no longer made', pointed to a conscious attempt to starve or intimidate Catherine, or otherwise bring about her death.[14] Du Bellay reported that Henry had been to visit Princess Elizabeth, but had not seen Mary, who was a member of her household, 'on account of her obstinacy, which came from her Spanish blood'. When the ambassador commented that Mary had 'been very well brought up', tears came into the king's eyes and he 'could not refrain from praising her'. This display of emotion was dangerous, thought Chapuys, who saw it as a cause of animosity from Anne, who knew the true depths of the king's feeling for his elder daughter. 'A gentleman told me yesterday,' wrote Chapuys to Charles, 'that the earl of Northumberland told him that he knew for certain that she [Anne] had determined to poison the princess.'[15] He was also convinced that Henry 'has great hope in the queen's death. He lately told the French ambassador that she could not live long, as she was dropsical, an illness she was never subject to before.' As the ambassador warned the Emperor, 'it is to be feared something has been done to bring it on'.[16]

Hearing of these events, Catherine wrote a moving letter to her daughter, who was still in Princess Elizabeth's household at Hatfield. She advised Mary to follow the same path she was taking, to accept whatever God had planned for her while maintaining her loyalty to Henry as far as possible. Anticipating that things would now not turn out well for either of them, Catherine urged

Mary to be resigned to her fate, to be brave and strong in the face of opposition, in fact to adopt the mindset of the martyr, devoted to the last. She must be brave in the years ahead, 'for we never come to the kingdom of Heaven except though troubles'. In the meantime, she was to remain devout, study the Latin texts her mother had sent her, take care of her health and try to relieve some of the tension of her situation by keeping up her music.[17]

Another move was on the cards for Catherine. Henry planned to send her to Somersham Palace, also in the Cambridgeshire Fens, fifteen miles to the east of Buckden. It was a place surrounded by marshes, thought to be very unhealthy, which fed Catherine's fears that her very life was in danger. Indeed the records of disputes between the bishops of Ely and Abbots of Ramsay regarding the site do describe the nearby Crowlodemoor and Hollode as 'marshes',[18] which might explain the place's rapid recent decline. The Tudor palace had been constructed on the site of an earlier manor with extensive gardens by James Stanley, Bishop of Ely, whose 1515 tomb records that 'he builded Sommersome the byshoppe's chief manor'. It quickly fell into disrepair after his death, though, and by 1520 the palace was in a state bordering on the dangerous. The next incumbent, Bishop Nicholas West, described it as his 'poor house at Somersham', and in a letter to Wolsey said that he was so surrounded with water that he could not leave and no one could go to him without great danger except by boat. The banks were in 'great danger of collapsing and five hundred men were working on them to prevent the low country there from being drowned, while a further hundred watched at night, in case the water should break through'.[19] West had died in April 1533, and accumulation of building material at the property at that time indicates that preparations were being made to patch over the problems in readiness for the royal arrival, but Catherine had other ideas.

The Duke of Suffolk was charged to deliver the news at Buckden that Somersham was being made ready for Catherine's arrival. He arrived after dinner and made the announcement in the great chamber, 'before all the servants of the house'. Catherine protested 'with open voice' that she was Henry's queen and would rather 'be hewn in pieces than depart from this assertion'. She resisted the move to Somersham 'because of her health', even though Lord Mountjoy and her almoner, Dymock, also tried to persuade her to comply. Suffolk asked to know 'the king's pleasure, as she will not remove to Somersham, against all humanity and reason, unless we were to bind her with ropes. She also refuses the service of those men sworn to her as Princess Dowager, and by her wilfulness may feign herself sick, and keep her bed, or refuse to put on her clothes, or otherwise order herself by some imagination that we cannot now call to remembrance.'[20] To Cromwell, Suffolk wrote that 'we find this woman more obstinate than we can express',[21] sentiments he repeated to the Duke of Norfolk, along with the conclusion that 'there is no other remedy but to convey her by force to Somersham'.[22]

Chapuys was able to give an account of the occasion that was closer to Catherine's perspective, presumably having heard it from her. They had, he wrote to Charles, 'used much sharp language to her' and then 'proceeded to take away her chamberlain, chancellor, almoner, master of the horse and other chief officers', who were refusing to swear an oath to acknowledge that Catherine was no longer queen. Her confessor, Bishop Athequa, her physician Miguel de la Sá, her Burgundian gentleman-in-waiting Bastian Hennyocke, her apothecaries John Sota and Philip Greenacre, along with Anthony Rocke refused to swear, as did eight of her ladies. When Suffolk attempted to remove Athequa, Catherine explained that she was only able to make her confession in Spanish and there was no one else in the house equipped to hear her. Suffolk made do with removing her chaplains, a man named Barker and Thomas Abel, who had published in favour of Catherine's marriage. In the Tower, he was charged with spreading the lies of Elizabeth Barton, the recently martyred Nun of Kent, and with encouraging Catherine to 'obstinately ... persist in her wilful opinion against the same divorce and separation'. He would languish in the Tower for six more years, outliving Catherine, and carving his personal device of the letter 'A' above a bell, until his sentence was carried out in 1540.

As Chapuys explained to Charles, Suffolk had been 'commissioned to bring the queen by force to a house surrounded with deep water and marshes, which is, as she is informed, the most unhealthy and pestilential house in England and she, seeing the evident danger of it, refused to go except by force'. It was the opinion of the ambassador that 'the king, at the solicitation of the Lady, whom he dares not contradict, has determined to place the queen in the said house, either to get rid of her, or to make sure of her, as the house is strong; and, besides, she is seven miles from another house situated in a lake, which one cannot approach within six miles, except on one side'.[23] This makes the choice of Somersham sound like a deliberate attempt at incarceration, if nothing worse. Chapuys believed that it had been decided between Henry and Anne 'to seek all possible occasions to shut up the queen within the said island, and, failing all other pretexts, to accuse her of being insane'. He had also heard rumours that Henry intended that his next parliament should pass an Act declaring the princess illegitimate and to remove her from the succession, and that 'all the appointments of the queen shall be revoked, and then he will openly take, at the Lady's dictation, all the queen's goods, and deprive her of the power to spend a single penny'.[24]

The reality of the encounter between Suffolk and Catherine at Buckden was far more dramatic. When Henry's officials arrived to load her baggage and evict her, the ex-queen locked herself in her room and challenged them, through a hole in the wall, to break the door down and carry her away. 'This they dared not do,' related Chapuys, 'as one of them has confessed, through fear of the people that had assembled there, weeping piteously and lamenting at such cruelties'.[25] She was told that if she proved obstinate, 'the king would be compelled to show her that he was not satisfied with her, and would clip her wings by taking from her, her state and her servants, and shut her up in the house mentioned in my last, using many bitter and discourteous words, protesting that she might be the cause of great trouble in Christendom and effusion of human blood'.[26] Next, they made 'rough menaces' and removed her servants:

> When the Commissioners left her they summoned before them all her servants, dismissing some, and making prisoners of others, as two priests who were brought here to the Tower, where they are now. They used great harshness to those whom they drove away, commanding them to avoid the place the same day on pain of death. They debated on taking away her confessor, a Spanish bishop; but on the Queen saying that she never confessed, nor knew how to do it, except in Spanish, they left him, and said

> nothing to her physician and apothecary, who are Spaniards. They took away almost all her *femmes de chambre*; but as the Queen affirmed she would not have any others, and would sleep in her clothes, and lock the gate herself, they returned two of them, but not those that the Queen wished. All her present servants, except the confessor, physician, and apothecary, who cannot speak English, have been sworn not to address her as Queen, and for this she has protested before the Commissioners that she will not regard them as her servants, but only her guards, as she is a prisoner.[27]

Suffolk and the other commissioners remained at Buckden for six days in the hope that Catherine would crumble under the pressure, but she did not. This was a serious test of her strength and status: there was no guarantee that Henry's servants would not carry out such an act of violence. Yet Catherine's birth, her years as their queen and their respect for her prevailed. Waiting behind her locked door, she heard them ride away. It was a small victory. Catherine would never live at Somersham, but Henry was intent on breaking her by moving her to another, less convenient place. He offered Catherine Fotheringhay Castle in Northamptonshire, which she refused, but soon afterwards settled on a new location, and this time his former wife was given no choice but to comply.

This incident represented the lowest point to which Catherine had so far been pushed, the desperation of an abandoned woman against the will of a husband who was able to exercise the full power of a king, even if his servants obeyed his commands unwillingly. She was once again an outsider, the disenfranchised Spanish princess fighting for her independence, her health, her name and her right, as if she had been transported back to the difficult times of 1502–9. But Catherine had learned from that period, and she was no longer the naïve girl who was dependent upon the will of powerful men. Since then she had learned much about queenship, statescraft and dignity. She was not prepared to be the victim of Henry, or Anne; she was going to fight every step of the way, resist every change and every challenge, rise to every occasion and cling to each small victory. She would dig in her heels and discover exactly what lengths they were prepared to go to, and to what depths they were prepared to sink. In this, she had the advantage over her husband: there were limits to the conditions he might impose upon the captive daughter of Ferdinand and Isabella, and his retaliation to gossip shows he certainly feared reprisals and the comments of his subjects. Knowing his former wife as well as he did, Henry must have seen that now her nerve outstripped his. However far he pushed her, she was willing to defy his ruling and never give up on her position as his wife and queen. Her contemporaries knew the extent of her strength: 'The Lady Catherine is a proud, stubborn woman of very high courage. If she took it into her head to take her daughter's part, she could quite easily take the field, muster a great array and wage against me a war as fierce as any her mother Isabella ever waged in Spain.'[28]

Stripped of all her comforts and her daughter, she had little more to lose other than her life, and her willingness to embrace death for her cause must have privately terrified Henry. On one level, it would conveniently remove her and all the problems of his marital situation, but if somehow she was perceived by the people to have died a martyr, there might be catastrophic consequences for his reign. And she certainly was prepared to die a martyr, writing to Cromwell of her 'fixed determination to die in this kingdom; and I offer my person as security that if such a thing be attempted he may do justice upon me as the most traitorous woman that ever was born'.[29] It almost seemed like Catherine was willing death to arrive, rushing to embrace it, as an end to her sufferings and a grand religious gesture of martyrdom. Chapuys wrote to the Emperor almost a month after Suffolk's departure that 'the queen has not been out of her room since the Duke of Suffolk was with her, except to hear Mass in a gallery. She will not eat nor drink what the new servants provide. The little she eats in her anguish is prepared by her chamber women, and her room is used as her kitchen. She is very badly lodged. She desires me to write to you about it.'[30]

At this low ebb, Catherine may have heard that an upsetting new witness emerged to give testimony about her marriage to Arthur. A woman called Margaret had come forward, wife to a Thomas Clarke who had formerly been a servant to Sir George Wolleston at Hapthorpe in 1502. Margaret was then forty-five, so she would have been only thirteen when she spent six months under Wolleston's roof, but across the intervening thirty-two years, she recalled overhearing a question that her master asked of Sir

Davy Phillips regarding the cause of Arthur's death. Phillips replied that 'as far as he could perceive, it was the oft accompanying with the Lady Catherine, which the physicians dissuaded' and that although she was 'kept from his company for a time', this could not be continued 'without his high displeasure'. Davy added, '(Woe) worth the time that ever the lady Katharine came into this realm, for she was the cause of the death of the most noble prince.'[31]

Catherine would have been deeply upset to hear of her husband's next move. Henry moved to suppress the monasteries of the Observant Friars, who had long been close to Catherine's heart and had been a favourite of her mother since her childhood at Arévalo. She had always chosen her confessors from the order, had been married in their Greenwich church, and two of her children, the short-lived Prince Henry and Princess Mary, had been baptised there, as indeed had their father. This also represented a significant break with the past, as Henry had previously honoured the Greenwich establishment as being founded by his grandfather and developed by his father, but the friars had come out in support of Catherine, and as a result they were to be disbanded. Her former confessor Brother John Forest had been based at Greenwich, where he preached against the divorce. In 1533, he had been arrested and taken to Newgate prison, where he was sentenced to death, although the sentence had not yet been carried out when Catherine wrote to him the following spring.

Forest was preparing himself for martyrdom. Catherine wrote that she had 'no doubt he is ready to die for Christ' and encouraged his resolution. She deeply regretted that she would 'lose her spiritual father, who was beloved by her in the bowels of Christ' and would rather 'go before him with the greatest tortures than follow him'. She begged Forest to pray for her 'that she might follow him with a constant mind'.[32] She entrusted her letter to a servant named Thomas, who was able to bring one back to Buckden for Catherine. Forest replied that he was 'happy to find her constant in the faith of the Church' and begged her 'not to be afflicted on his account'. He was expecting his imminent death, having been informed that he had only three days to live, and hoped that, at the age of sixty-four, he would not be inconstant in his devotion. Looking back on forty-three years as a friar of St Francis, he had learned to 'despise earthly things' and sent Catherine his own rosary as a legacy.[33] A woman named Elizabeth Hammon, who was clearly a close associate of Catherine at this time, also wrote to Forest. She wished to pass on the 'intense grief of the queen and herself at his sufferings', adding that Catherine 'weeps and prays without intermission'. Hammon urged Forrest that 'if he sees any chance of escape by help of his friends, that he will not leave them comfortless, for she feared that it may be fatal to the queen, especially considering the king's anger'.[34] As it happened, Forest would outlive Catherine by two years, eventually dying a martyr's death by burning at the stake in 1538.

II

Then, in March 1534, came the news that Catherine had most been dreading. The new session of parliament passed Henry's Act of Succession, declaring Princess Mary to be illegitimate as her mother's marriage was invalid and that the true heir of England was Princess Elizabeth. As Chapuys related to Charles in more detail, 'It is decided to exclude the princess, and the succession to go to the king's issue by Anne Boleyn, and in default to the nearest of kin.' It had also been determined that 'if the king dies before his lady, she shall be regent and absolute governor of her children and the kingdom, and that applying the title of queen or princess to anyone except the said Anne or her daughter shall be considered high treason'. All Henry's subjects were obliged to swear the oath. The penalty for refusing to do so, or acting to contravene it, was to be the 'confiscation of body and goods is also threatened to all who conceal this crime or murmur against the acts of this parliament, even those in favour of the second marriage and against the papal authority'. Chapuys found this to be 'strange and tyrannical' and reported that 'for greater security the king wishes to appoint commissioners to take oaths from the people'.[35] After 1 May, it was also to be an offence of treason for any person to question the validity of Henry's marriage to Anne Boleyn. The net was closing in on Catherine: to maintain her position that she was Henry's wife and queen was now to make her a traitor. Would Henry take the final step and make her undergo a traitor's death? Or would someone else, if the king was unwilling?

In a sensational letter to the Emperor, Chapuys sets out his terrifying vision for Catherine's future. Although it must be remembered that there is no evidence to suggest that Anne Boleyn was in any way planning her rival's demise, and that the ambassador is frequently citing court gossip, his belief in the threat to Catherine taps into an emotional truth about her fears and the state in which she was living. Rejected and depressed she may have been, but Catherine was not overreacting to believe herself on the verge of arrest and death. Such a step would be unprecedented but so many old certainties had been torn away in the space of only a few short years. If the husband who had loved and protected her for two decades could remarry; if the Defender of the Faith could reject the Pope as a heretic and destroy the very foundation stones of centuries-old religious practices, and shatter the very heart of what her parents had fought to uphold, then he might do anything. It was reasonable to suppose that he may order Catherine's execution on the grounds of treason. Wolsey had already gone; chaplains and priests were being arrested, heretics burned, and in just a year's time Henry would put to death two more of his loyal servants. And although Catherine would not know it, just two years later, Henry would indeed go so far as to order the execution of his queen. In the summer of 1534, though, Chapuys feared that if Henry were to leave the country, leaving Anne as regent, she would act swiftly to remove her rival:

> I am informed by a person of good faith that the king's concubine had said more than once, and with great assurance, that when the king has crossed the sea, and she remains *gouvernante*, as she will be, she will use her authority and put the said Princess to death, either by hunger or otherwise. On Rochford, her brother, telling her that this would anger the king, she said she did not care even if she were burned alive for it after. The Princess quite expects this, and thinking that she could not better gain Paradise than by such a death, shows no concern, trusting only in God, whom she has always served well and does still better now. Having spoken to the Queen, by her advice I will make remonstrances; but I know not if they will do any good.[36]

One by one, Catherine's supporters swore the oath, unwilling to become martyrs to Henry's latest cause. Cuthbert Tunstall, Bishop of Durham, who had formerly sat on Catherine's council, reluctantly explained that he had 'hitherto maintained the cause of the queen both by word of mouth and by books, but now, not wishing to be a martyr or to lose such a benefice, which is worth more than 15,000 ducats, he has been compelled to swear like the others, although it is said with certain reservations, by which he thinks to satisfy his conscience'. Tunstall had become concerned to hear that two days after he left his house 'certain commissioners of the king entered it, opening everything and cataloguing all his goods, and every letter that they found was brought to the king'.[37] Henry was determined to use the oath as an opportunity to remove his enemies and to bring doubters back into his service. In May 1534, he chose Tunstall to accompany Edward Lee, Archbishop of York since Wolsey's demise, to deliver his message to Catherine.

Catherine had just moved house again, this time to Kimbolton Castle in Cambridgeshire. This was a far less hazardous residence than Somersham or Fotheringhay, even if it was not a suitable location for a woman who still considered herself England's queen. Work in the 1480s had improved the original twelfth-century castle, and in 1521 it was described as 'a right goodly lodging contained in little room, within a moat well and compendiously trussed together in due and convenient proportion, one thing with another, with an inner court ... lodgings and offices for keeping a duke's house in stately manner'. However, like Somersham, the place desperately needed some essential repairs 'by occasion of the old wall, the hall there well-builded is likely to perish; and through the said castle is and will be great decay, by occasion there is no reparations done'. Sir Richard Wingfield was granted the castle by Henry in 1522 and rebuilt the affected areas as well as adding to the building, allowing Leland to report that 'the Castelle is double dyked and the building of it is ... strong ... [with] new fair lodgings and galleries upon the olde foundations of the Castelle'. Later inventories list a 'great hall with screens, a long gallery, a chapel, dining room, drawing room, upper round chamber, lower round chamber, Queen's Chamber, and many other rooms, a gatehouse, stables, the Castle Court, Dial Court, the Great Garden, and the Little Fountain Garden'.[38] The bedchamber and closet allocated to Catherine are reputed to have survived the castle's later modernisation. With the former queen out of sight, Henry could anticipate the arrival of his next child by Anne. Aware of the impending arrival, it must have been a low point for Catherine, still separated from her daughter, the court and the majority of her servants and friends. Would Henry finally get his legitimate son?

On the very same day that the Act of Succession was being passed, news arrived from Rome. On 23 March, Clement VII and the Consistory of Cardinals had met to give their verdict on Catherine's case, five years after she had submitted her appeal. After much discussion, the sentence was pronounced that the marriage of Henry and Catherine had been lawful, as it had not been prohibited by divine law. It gave Catherine the essential defence that she was to require, sooner than she had anticipated. Henry was striking at her closest supporters. Tunstall might have buckled under the pressure, but John Fisher and Thomas More stood firm and refused to swear the oath. Both were sent to the Tower.

Tunstall and Lee were Catherine's first visitors at Kimbolton. It must have been with some awkwardness, if not downright reluctance, that they asserted their familiar commission, that her marriage to Henry was invalid, that carnal knowledge between her and Arthur had been effectively proven, that she was urged to give up the title of queen and acknowledge the king's new marriage. Their task was to 'inform her' of the new act, 'lest she should incur a penalty by ignorance'. At this, they observed Catherine had fallen into a 'great choler and agony', frequently interrupting them. When she finally had the opportunity to answer, she replied that her marriage was a true one and she would 'always account herself [Henry's] lawful wife', that it was a false lie to assert that she had ever had 'carnal knowledge' of Arthur, that she was not bound to stand by a divorce pronounced by that 'shadow', Cranmer, and that the Pope, Christ's vicar, had pronounced in her favour. She refused to ever stop using the title of queen, refused to acknowledge Henry's marriage to Anne and denied that she was bound by any Acts of Parliament, as she was 'Henry's wife and not his subject'.[39]

After the departure of Tunstall and Lee, Catherine wrote to Chapuys of the 'rude and harsh words' they had used to her, and their express threats regarding 'the penalties contained in the ... statute, telling her it involved death'. While they had hoped 'to stagger her' she had 'remained all the more firm', replying 'among other things that if there was any one who had come to do such an execution let him come forward' as she wished for nothing more.

Although, she added, if she was to die, 'it should be in public and not in a chamber or other secret place'.[40] Hearing this, Chapuys had serious concerns that 'some ill turn will be done to the queen, seeing the rudeness and strange treatment to which she is daily subjected, both in deeds and in words' but found this 'monstrous and difficult to believe'. He also related how Thomas Audley, the new Chancellor in place of More, became angry at 'three or four of the principal foreign merchants, [and] told them that if they were to be trusted, all the foreigners in this kingdom would be treated as they deserved, and that they would cut off very great ones, which the said merchants interpreted to mean the queen'.[41] The ambassador noted that 'the queen and some others have lately thought it better to show the king their teeth a little' but he feared this will do them more harm than good.[42]

That July, Catherine was ill and requested that Chapuys come to visit her. It was partly due to her health, but also partly a diplomatic game, to make a show of Imperial support and prove that she had not been forgotten. 'I cannot imagine why the queen has been so very urgent that I should go to her,' he wrote to Charles, 'as she has sufficient opportunities of writing or sending to me, unless it be to let all the world see, especially her well-willers, that your majesty had [not] forgotten her, as the opposite party has given people to understand.' He considered Catherine to be 'more a prisoner than before, for not only is she deprived of her goods, but even a Spanish lady who has remained with her all her life, and has served her at her own expense, is forbidden to see her'. This was probably Maria da Salinas, who was denied permission to visit Kimbolton by Henry. By contrast, Catherine now only trusted five or six of her servants and considered the rest to be her 'guards to keep her prisoner'. So, in order to make a show of allegiance, Chapuys set out from London with a huge entourage of sixty horses, carrying his own men and 'certain Spanish merchants here'. He was stopped just five miles away by a messenger commanding him to turn back, as he was forbidden 'to enter where the queen was or speak with her'.[43] Chapuys continues:

> To ascertain more expressly the wish of the said chamberlain and steward, I sent one of my men to them, to whom they held the same language. As my man was returning he met one of those

> sent by the king last year into Germany, who is a cunning fellow, and was going where the Queen was. I waited all day to see if he would send to tell me anything, and also to understand meanwhile the Queen's pleasure, who sent to me to say that she held herself as well satisfied with my journey as with any service I could have done her, and was greatly bound to me for it; and as to going further to Our Lady of Walsingham, she left that to my discretion, and that she had no opportunity to write to me at Present, but would soon do so at great length. One of her chamber gave me to understand that, although she did not dare to declare it, he knew well she would have great pleasure if part of the company were to present themselves before the place; which they did next day, to the great consolation, as it seemed, of the ladies with the Queen, who spoke to them from the battlements and windows; and it seemed to the country people about that Messiah had come.[44]

In a similar mood of reverence towards their former queen, a number of her subjects persisted in their outspokenness despite the penalties. Sir George Cydrowe, a parish priest of Kettering, was also a curate to one of Catherine's former chaplains, who was reported for saying that 'it was a pity the king was not buried in his swaddling clothes, and whosoever would call the queen that now is, queen, at Bugden, where his master dwells, should be knocked to the post'. He said he hoped to see Lady Anne brought full low, and we should have no merry world till we had a new change, 'for the king will not leave while it is well'. He said he knew also what the Bishop of Canterbury was: 'he was a hostler'.[45] Angered by this continuing loyalty, Henry commanded that Catherine's close servants were not to speak to her 'except in the presence of people and not in any other language than English'.[46] Her expenses from this time show that she was living moderately, far below the huge sums Henry claimed she was costing him. For an entire year, her bakehouse spent £187 6*s* 4*d*, her buttery £547 16*s*, her kitchen £877 16*s* 10*d*, her stable just over £140, her wardrobe £345. Including other offices, her yearly living costs were £2,951, more than £37,000 less than Henry stated.[47]

Wardrobe accounts that survive for Catherine dating from 14 February 1535 give a fascinating insight into the material effects of her life in transition, in an age when status and power were measured by the quantity and quality of fabrics, styles and jewels one might wear. The record was made by Sir Edward Baynton at Henry's command, of all Catherine's effects that remained behind at Baynard's Castle, which had been designated as her official wardrobe store in happier times. The Princess of Spain who had once awed the crowd with her wide white farthingale was now reduced to wearing old clothes and having those frequently mended, while the glad rags of her time as queen were assessed and recorded, probably to be passed on, or dismantled to contribute to new dresses for other women. Just as she had been robbed of her jewels, she was stripped of her former finery in a move that was no less poignant for having been a small act of bureaucracy. What makes it all the more significant is that such inventories were usually taken after someone's death. In many ways, Catherine had already undergone a symbolic death in that she no longer existed as Henry's wife and queen in his eyes; this calculated assessment of her material worth underlined that the old Catherine was no more. Wrapped up among her hangings and bedlinen were the moments she had most cherished in the past: laughter and love, magnificence and ceremony, dressing carefully to present herself at Henry's side, the object of adoration for Sir Loyal Heart. Now they were little more than folded fabrics, stored away with herbs to keep out the moths.

Among Catherine's effects at Baynard's Castle were seven velvet hangings, with red and green panels bearing the arms of England and Spain topped by an Imperial crown and bordered with roses, fleur-de-lys and pomegranates. Her tapestries told the stories of Jason and Hercules' labours, or bore small flowers, crowned trees, the falcon and fetterlock of the House of York, roses and suns. Her beds had been draped in blue velvet and cloth of gold or silver, with white damask, yellow cloth of gold and crimson velvet. A little cradle, in anticipation of the birth of a child in the winter months, had been decked out in velvet finery. She had canopies, cloths of estate and curtains bearing the English and Spanish arms, carpets, cushions and downy pillows, sheets of Holland cloth and featherbeds on which she had once lain in Henry's arms. Two of her hand towels made of Holland cloth, wrought at both ends with Venice gold and fringed with silk, were set aside to be delivered to the king. Inside her devotional closet were needlework tablets for altars bearing more royal arms of Spain and an image of the virgin and child, with others depicting St Francis, St Anne, St John the Baptist and, ironically, the martyrdom of St Catherine. Henry also took a vellum primer covered with cloth of gold, with silver-gilt clasps depicting Christ's baptism in gold thread and two ivory chess sets. A horn cup with a cover, garnished with 'antique work' and with a foot and knot of ivory, as well as a dozen wood trenchers and two little ivory stools were delivered to Anne Boleyn. Catherine had also once owned gaming tables, seven pairs of Spanish slippers, corked and garnished with gold, a broken branch of coral, which would have been used as a baby's teether, childbirth smocks, two looking glasses, a pin cushion, a pair of scales, twenty books, seven tapers of wax and kitchen utensils.[48] Henry must have judged that his wife no longer had need of them.

III

As the autumn of 1534 arrived, Catherine learned of the death of Clement VII, who had succumbed to a fit of apoplexy at the age of fifty-two. There is no doubt that Clement's procrastination had contributed significantly to Catherine's situation and that she recognised this. He may have been acting out of the best motives in hoping that Henry would come to his senses, but his unwillingness to act decisively and pronounce in favour of Catherine's marriage back in 1529 had eroded Henry's respect for the papacy and opened the door to new ideas and reforms in England that otherwise might not have been tolerated. Catherine also had respected him as the Pope, as 'Christ's vicar', but had become frustrated by his slowness. No doubt as a symbol of her faith she grieved his loss, but she would have had high hopes for his successor, the more robust and decisive Paul III.

Henry rejoiced at the loss of Clement and proposed to burn all the bulls, briefs and provisions formerly granted by the Vatican. He appointed Dr George Brown, an Augustinian friar who had married him and Anne, to preach a sermon directed at the bishops, stating that those who refused to comply 'deserved very severe punishment'. Henry also added to his titles 'that of Sovereign Head of the Church of England on Earth', considered re-baptising everyone who had undergone the rite under papal jurisdiction and dismissed the 'bishop or idol of Rome' as a 'limb of the devil'.[49] But he had bigger plans on the horizon, being overseen by his new right-hand man, Thomas Cromwell.

In January 1535, Henry appointed commissioners to create a survey of all the ecclesiastical bodies in England, being sent out the entire length of the country to assess monasteries, priories, abbeys and nunneries. Their findings would become the huge document Valour Ecclesiasticus, which Henry would use to close all these institutions, inflicting permanent change on England in cultural and social ways, as well as the centuries-old practices of worship. For not only were these religious centres, but they were also providing essential services as hospitals, refuges, for social care, alms, libraries, the creation of manuscripts, the keeping of records, accounts and histories and for the understanding and practices of herbal medicine. All this was to go. His commissioners were to enquire into the 'lives and morals' of the abbots, with powers to remove and punish those they found to be in fault. Each was issued with a series of questions to ask, including whether divine service was strictly observed, the numbers of residents, the founders, the conduct of those concerned, the increase of lands, the rent, the rules of the house, the presence of women, visitors, behaviour and confessions.[50]

One of the first great houses to fall was that of the Augustinian friars in London. They were found to be deficient in the celebration of the Mass, sitting instead in the beer house from six in the morning until ten at night, more 'like courtiers and drinking Flemings' and entertaining harlots. During services, the friars walked about the church with merchants, they were in debt, dined in parties and despised the prior's authority, with no more rules kept than 'in hell among devil'.[51] Elsewhere, Sir William Courtney reported to Cromwell that the abbot of Hartland had no 'learning sufficient to rule', and his answers at interview made them laugh out loud.[52] In other cases, they met with resistance to the new oath. A Robert Lawrence, prior of the Charterhouse at Bevall, Notts, and Augustine Webster, prior of the Charterhouse at Hexham, Lincolnshire, said 'they could not agree that the king is supreme head of the Church of England, according to the statute'. Richard Reignolde, brother of the Order of Recluses of St Bridget, of the monastery of Sion, could not take the king to be supreme head under Christ and refuse the Pope as head of the Universal Church.[53]

Catherine was often named in these 'heresies', each case making her existence a little more precarious. John Leek, clerk of Syon, deposed that Mr Reignoldes and he agreed that the princess dowager was the true queen, and that the king could not be supreme head of the Church.[54] Sir Thomas Kinge, vicar of the chapel of St Andrew's in St Albans, declared to Cranmer that Catherine was the true queen and that Henry's marriage to Anne was invalid, and had been convincing people that they were 'bound under pain of damnation to obey the Pope'.[55] Depositions were also taken against Guilliaum Cowschier, a skinner of St Omer's, for saying 'that our sovereign lord king Henry was a wretch, a caitiff and no Christian man, having two wives and a concubine', while a Nicholas Delanoy said that, 'pity it was of the king's life to forsake the noble blood of the Emperor and to take a poor knight's daughter'.[56]

Catherine herself remained defiant when it came to her religious observance, as Sir Edward Chamberlain reported to Cromwell:

> We have just learnt that the Princess Dowager intends to keep a Maundy, in spite of the king's order of last year to the contrary. She says she will keep it secretly in her chamber, and wishes to know if she may go to the parish church, where we think she will try and keep it if prevented from doing so privately.[57]

Incredibly, Henry was prepared to concede, but only up to a point, saying that he was content if she was 'willing to keep her Maundy in her chamber in the name of the princess dowager' but not in the name of queen, otherwise she would be guilty of high treason and not permitted to make her observances at all.[58] As well as keeping her own observances, Catherine wrote to Charles, asking him to 'bear in mind our Holy Catholic Faith, and the peril in which this realm is standing for want of it. I entreat for this as earnestly as possible; for, as a Christian woman, I am bound to do so, seeing the need for it that I do.'[59] In the belief that her husband had gone astray in his faith, she maintained her positon as the true queen of England and a symbol of the old religion.

Yet Henry was cracking down on other methods Catherine had used to worship. A book was printed under royal licence against the use of images, the Mass and canonical hours, and rumours followed that he was to follow in the footsteps of Luther and allow the marriage of priests who had left their institutions.[60] 'He will do stranger things still,' commented Chapuys, quite correctly. One of Cromwell's chief investigators, Richard Layton, sent his findings from Glastonbury to Henry. They included a host of relics, two flowers wrapped in black and white sarcenet that were reputed to spring into bud and bear blossoms on Christmas Eve, a part of God's coat, the Virgin's smock, part of God's supper, as well as the Virgin's girdle, used by women in labour, and more.[61] Next, Henry visited Winchester, the location his father had chosen for Arthur's birth and the seat of the myths that he had spun for the Tudor dynasty. There, just like at all the other religious houses, an inventory was being made of the church's treasures, from which the king confiscated 'certain fine rich unicorn's horns ... and a large silver cross adorned with rich jewels'.[62] He turned out any monks and nuns who had made profession of their calling before the age of twenty-five, leaving the rest to remain or leave, apparently as they wished. His methods of persuasion were indirect but definite. 'It is true they are not expressly told to go out,' explained Chapuys, 'but it is clearly given them to understand that they had better do, it, for they are going to make a reformation of them so severe and strange that in the end they will all go; which is the object the king is aiming at, in order to have better occasion to seize the property without causing the people to murmur.'[63]

Watching these changes in Europe, reformers were hopeful that England was becoming open to a 'purer' religion. Luther's close friend Philip Melanchthon wrote to the German classical scholar Joachim Camerarius that a stanger had been sent to him from England, 'talking only of the king's second marriage' as Henry 'cared nothing, as they say, about the Church matters', but, importantly, 'no cruelty is exercised against those who are zealous for better doctrine'. This, he reported, had made the French furious.[64] Melanchthon also wrote to Henry from Wittenburg, full of hope at the changing tide:

> Although there were urgent reasons why he should write to the king, yet shame would have deterred him had it not been for Dr. Antonius. who has been so loud in the king's praises. Much is

> due from students and men of his order to the king. Never has England produced so many men of genius. Letters in Germany are despised by the prejudices of men, and are brought into odium in consequence of religious controversy. Hopes the king will use his influence for good, as certain abuses have crept into the Church, and monarchs have not used their efforts for establishing a simple and certain form of doctrine. Antonius has asked his opinion on certain articles on which he sends his judgment in writing.[65]

In the spring of 1535, with More and Fisher imprisoned, monasteries being dissolved and the oath of Supremacy hanging over the queen's head, Chapuys and Charles discussed possible ways to help Catherine and Mary escape England. Afraid for their lives, and for the changing religious climate, the pair proposed that Spain would be a safe haven for the women, at least to ensure they did not fall victim to further abuses or worse. Chapuys really was convinced that if any outbreaks of resistance erupted, 'the king would not be too hasty to use violence to those ladies', and although Henry did not, the ambassador's fears must be taken seriously. It would be easier if Catherine was in the Tower, Chapuys deduced, rather than the closely guarded confines of Kimbolton, as she would be accessible by river. The practical questions might prove the most difficult: 'If the wind be not favourable for her departure,' mused Chapuys, 'there would be no fear of the great ships here, because she could leave by the same wind as others did. But as it is proposed to change her lodging, we must wait to know where her residence will be fixed, and devise other expedients accordingly.'[66] A dangerous prophecy was also in circulation, tapping into the unstable mood at court, as Anne Boleyn suffered her second miscarriage following the birth of Elizabeth:

> The concubine has suborned a person to say that he has had a revelation from God that she cannot conceive while the said two ladies are alive. Doubts not she has spoken of it to the king, and she has lately sent the man to Cromwell. She constantly speaks of them as rebels and traitresses deserving death, and Cromwell would willingly say what Caiaphas did.[67]

Just as Catherine was suffering isolation and privation, with the fear of imminent martyrdom hanging over her head, so was her most loyal advocate. The sixty-five-year-old Bishop Fisher was being kept in appalling conditions in the Tower because his conscience would not allow him to swear the Oath of Succession. He wrote in desperation that he 'had neither shirt not sheet nor yet other clothes that are necessary for me to wear, but that he ragged and rent too shamefully'. He might have tolerated his nakedness if he had been able to keep himself warm, but his diet was 'slender' and 'in mine age my stomach may not away but with a few kind of meats, which if I want I decay forthwith, and fall into coughs and diseases of my body, and cannot keep myself in health'. He was being maintained by his brother 'out of his own purse, to his great hindrance', and wrote in the hope of release 'from this cold and painful imprisonment'. He had no priest to hear his confession and longed for some books 'to stir his devotion more effectually'.[68]

Fisher's fate was sealed when Pope Paul III nominated him as a cardinal in the December of 1535. Gregory Casale wrote to Cardinal du Bellay that he was 'very sorry' to hear of the nomination, as it would 'completely ruin him'. He urged du Bellay to get Francis to intercede with Henry and explain that the Pope had not known about Rochester's incarceration, or that Fisher should be allowed to go to Rome.[69] That May, Fisher's cardinalate was confirmed, perhaps in the hope that it would save the old man's life. Dr Ortiz explained the situation of the bishop and More to the Empress, as having been 'arrested for the same reason and their defence of the queen'. Both were 'ordered to recant their opinions ... in eight days but, animated with the same constancy ... replied that they want no time to deliberate, but [were] prepared to die for the Catholic faith'.[70] Writing on 31 May, he supposed that Fisher and More were 'already martyred' and that Catherine, 'who suffers a continual martyrdom', had 'sent them before her to heaven'. Surely, thought Ortiz, the Lord 'will have given [Fisher] the true red hat, the crown of martyrdom', and he implored the Empress to pray for Catherine and Mary.[71]

More and Fisher were not dead when Dr Ortiz composed his letter. Not just yet. Fisher went to his death on 22 June, 'a man of great sanctity of life and wonderful liberality to the poor', being calm and dignified at the end. He was executed on Tower Hill and, according to Henry's instructions, his body stripped and left on the scaffold until that evening. It is reported that his head, 'when fixed on London Bridge, instead of shrivelling, grew more florid and life-like, so that many expected it would speak, as we read has been the case with other martyrs. The rumour, however, was suppressed, and lest the same thing should happen with More's head it was boiled in water'.[72] Pope Paul wrote to Ferdinand, King of the Romans, the Emperor's younger brother and Catherine's nephew. He was 'much moved by' Fisher's death and had believed that 'his promotion ... would procure his safety and liberation, not his death'. He compared Henry's conduct to that of Henry II, who had made a martyr of Thomas Becket, although Paul felt the king had surpassed his ancestor and asked assistance in order to deprive Henry of his kingdom, 'in the execution of justice'.[73]

More followed Fisher to the scaffold on 6 July. The measured speech he gave in explanation, before the sentence was carried out, summarised his objections to the oath and his incredulity that it had come to this:

> 'Since I am condemned, and God knows how, I wish to speak freely of your Statute, for the discharge of my conscience. For the seven years that I have studied the matter, I have not read in any approved doctor of the Church that a temporal lord could or ought to be head of the spiritualty.'
>
> The Chancellor interrupting him, said, 'What, More, you wish to be considered wiser and of better conscience than all the bishops and nobles of the realm?'
>
> To this More replied, 'My lord, for one bishop of your opinion I have a hundred saints of mine; and for one parliament of yours, and God knows of what kind, I have all the General Councils for 1,000 years, and for one kingdom I have France and all the kingdoms of Christendom'.
>
> Norfolk told him that now his malice was clear.
>
> More replied, 'What I say is necessary for discharge of my conscience and satisfaction of my soul, and to this I call God to witness, the sole Searcher of human hearts. I say further, that your Statute is ill made, because you have sworn never to do anything against the Church, which through all Christendom is one and undivided, and you have no authority, without the common consent of all Christians, to make a law or Act of Parliament or Council against the union of Christendom. I know

well that the reason why you have condemned me is because I have never been willing to consent to the king's second marriage; but I hope in the divine goodness and mercy, that as St. Paul and St. Stephen whom he persecuted, are now friends in Paradise, so we, though differing in this world, shall be united in perfect charity in the other. I pray God to protect the king and give him good counsel.'[74]

The deaths sent shock waves around Europe. Gulielmus Covrinus Nucerinus wrote to Philippus Montanus that More's death was deplored on account of his virtues, 'his candor, urbanity, and kindness', who was friendly to all nations, to 'Irishmen, Frenchmen, Germans, and Hindoos. His kindness so fixed itself in all minds that he is lamented as a parent or a brother. I have myself seen many shed tears for him who had never seen him or had anything to do with him. Tears fall even from myself unwillingly while I write this. What will Erasmus now feel, whose friendship was so close that they seemed to have but one soul?' Nucerinus added that he 'would have liked to persuade the king to show less severity to these lights of Britain'.[75] A letter from the Bishop of Faenza helped spread the news, and the condemnation of it, to the 'infinite grief of the people of London'. He had heard that 'the people are so angry that some just trouble might easily succeed some day in the kingdom, in consequence of those cruelties'.[76] Yet London did not rise, perhaps fearing its own damnation, or a traitor's death. When there was finally a full-scale rebellion against the changes Henry was making, it would take place in the north, nine months after Catherine's death.

The deaths of Fisher and More must have been a watershed moment for Catherine. No doubt she wept and prayed for her old friends, in the certainty that she would be reunited with them soon in Heaven. Her physician informed Chapuys that she was terrified of being asked to swear the oath and as a result of refusing would be 'put in perpetual prison or beheaded'.[77] While Henry turned his back on Rome and Europe, forcing England to stand alone, she continued to seek assistance from her relatives, as part of a wider Empire to which England had always belonged. Her letter to Queen Mary of Hungary shows her desperation, her compulsion 'by the offence given here to God, the danger of her husband's conscience, and the scandal to Christendom, to implore the persons who can help to remedy it'. Mary was soon to meet with the Empress and Catherine to beg her 'to use her influence with the king her husband to be a good friend to Henry in getting him to abandon the sin in which he stands'.[78] She also appealed to Paul III, hoping to intercede for the soul of the husband who had treated her so cruelly. Dr Ortiz wrote in acknowledgement of 'the warfare in which she is engaged against the enemies of the faith'.[79] Although he had repudiated her, Catherine was still fighting a religious crusade on Henry's behalf:

> Has forborne to write to his Holiness as her letters are full of complaints, although not without scruple, as matters in this kingdom require greater diligence. For one thing, however, she gives thanks to Christ for having given Christendom such a vicar in a time of so great necessity. Begs him to have special consideration for this kingdom, for the king her husband, and her daughter; for, if a remedy be not applied with all speed, there will be no end to the loss of souls or to the making of martyrs. The good will be constant and suffer, the lukewarm perhaps fall away, and the rest stray like sheep without a shepherd. Writes to his Holiness plainly for discharge of her conscience as one who expects death along with her daughter. Has some comfort to think she will follow those holy men in their sufferings, though she grieves that she cannot imitate their lives.[80]

Dr Ortiz also wrote to the Empress twice, in great concern that

> the state of England is getting more and more disorderly. It is publicly said that mass is a great abuse; that Our Lord is not in the Sacrament of the Eucharist, and only was so when He consecrated it; that saying the *Ave Maria* is folly; and that Our Lady cannot help those who pray to her and invoke her aid, for she is only a woman like others. Blasphemous words are said of images. The rents of many churches are taken away, and it is said that they will take away images, shrines, and the principal temporalities of the Church. Is much grieved at the danger to the lives of the Queen and Princess, and begs the Empress to have continual prayer made on their behalf. Sees no remedy if [*Charles*] does not take them out of the kingdom.[81]

His second letter made it explicit that he believed in Catherine's imminent death: 'The King has twice said that the queen and princess are traitors, and despise the statutes, and that though he lose his crown they shall suffer the same penalty as others. The ambassador declares most seriously that they are in great danger.'[82] Catherine herself believed it, preparing herself for death on 22 November by sending letters to Chapuys 'as her last testament, because, considering her present state and the orders made in the Parliament of this November, it appears likely that she and the princess will be sentenced to martyrdom, which she was ready to receive in testimony of the Holy Faith, as the cardinal of Rochester and other holy martyrs had done. She only grieves that her life has not been as holy as theirs, and she is in great sorrow for the multitude of souls who are daily condemned.' Dr Ortiz also reported that Anne Boleyn had said of Mary 'that it is the princess who causes war, and that it will be necessary to treat her as the cardinal of Rochester has been treated'.[83]

That winter, it was with a complete lack of irony that Cranmer wrote to Lord Lisle in Calais regarding a case of immorality there:

> I understand that one Thos. King, now abiding in Calais, has left his wife Eleanor Saygrave, and lives with another woman, denying his former marriage. I have therefore sent my commissary to see them both punished, in which I desire your assistance.[84]

Thomas King of Calais might have been punished for leaving his wife and living with another woman because he was merely a subject. Apparently the actual king could do the same and expected to escape censure.

IV

Amid this climate of fear, amid the anticipation of further suffering and martyrdom, as she begged Europe for help and prepared for her end, Catherine, was, in fact, dying. Chapuys heard the first news of it from Cromwell in December 1535, after a servant had just been dispatched to inform Henry that Catherine was 'very sick'. The ambassador immediately asked for leave to go and visit her, and was given permission to send a letter, although a visit would need to receive Henry's approval. As he was leaving Cromwell, Chapuys relates, a letter arrived from Catherine's physician saying that 'with God's help, her illness would be nothing at all'. He was wrong.

In the middle of the month, Dr Ortiz described how Chapuys had been forbidden from visiting Catherine or Mary and that they were surrounded by 'guards and spies, not servants, for they have sworn in favour of Anne' and refused to call Catherine queen or to serve her 'with royal state'. So, Ortiz wrote to the Empress, in order 'not to give them cause to sin, the queen has not left her chamber for two years; and perhaps if she wished to, it would not be allowed'.[85] Near Christmas, Chapuys heard again from the physician, John de la Sá, stating that Catherine had relapsed and was worse than before, and was asking to see him. Convinced by this, Henry agreed that Catherine, to whom he was only referring now as Madame, 'would not live long' and that if she did, the ambassador would 'have no cause to trouble yourself about the affairs of this kingdom'. As Chapuys tried to leave, further news arrived at court that 'the queen was in extremis' and that he 'should hardly find her alive'. He was recalled by Suffolk, who confided in him that 'this would take away all the difficulties between your Majesty and him', as if Catherine was a mere inconvenience and her removal would eradicate her poor treatment and the religious changes Henry had made. Chapuys requested that Mary might be permitted to see her mother, and although Henry refused the request at first, he then agreed to 'take advice' on the subject.[86]

As the Christmas season advanced, Catherine's apothecary Philip Greenacre reported that 'the queen is very ill ... she gets worse every hour'. For the last two days and nights she had been unable to eat or drink, as nothing would remain in her stomach, and she had not slept for more than an hour and half because of the pain. She begged Chapuys to 'come as quickly as possible', for she had 'lost all her strength'.[87] Another old friend keen to be by Catherine's side was Maria de Salinas, Lady Willoughby, who had been denied permission to attend her two years earlier. Now she wrote to Cromwell, 'for I heard that my mistress is very sore sick again. I pray you remember me, for you promised to labour with the king to get me licence to go to her before God send for her, as there is no other likelihood',[88] as did Sir Edmund Bedingfield, who had heard that 'the princess dowager is in great danger of life' but would take advice from no other physician 'but only commit herself to the pleasure of God'.[89]

Bedingfield reported Chapuys' arrival at Kimbolton on Sunday 2 January 1536, seeing the encounter from the outside. The ambassador arrived after dinner and visited Catherine in her chamber for a quarter of an hour, during which time Bedingfield and her chamberlain were present. They were closely observed: 'He saluted her in Spanish, which I do not understand, but Mr. Vaghan, who was present, can declare to your Mastership the effect of their communication.' Later, at around five, Chapuys was with her alone for half an hour save for his steward, and then again for an hour from seven. 'We can find out nothing about these two later times,' Bedingfield reported, 'for no one was present except the persons mentioned and her old trusty women, who, I think, do not understand Spanish, or if the matters were of importance we should get [some manner] of knowledge by them. We do not know how long he will remain.' He also reported that Maria de Salinas had arrived at Kimbolton on New Year's Day and tricked her way inside by claiming to have fallen from her horse. Catherine's doctor reported that 'she hath somewhat taken comfort upon the coming of these folks' and had rested more that night, but he feared it would be 'a long continual sickness'.[90]

Chapuys' own account presents the meeting from the other side. Upon his arrival, Catherine had called him to her at once and told him she thought it best to allow the others to witness their first meeting, so that 'it might not be supposed her sickness was feigned' and because Bedingfield had been sent to 'spy and note all that was said and done'. Chapuys kissed her hands and she thanked him for the 'numerous services [he] had done her hitherto and the trouble (he) had taken to come and see her', which she had 'ardently desired'. If it 'pleased God to take her', she would be consoled to die in his arms, and 'not unprepared, like a beast'. The ambassador 'gave her every hope, both of her help and otherwise', saying that Henry had offered her new houses to move to, and that her arrears would be paid. He also added, quite untruthfully but kindly, that 'the king was very sorry for her illness' and he begged her to get well because 'the union and peace of Christendom depended upon her life'. He and Catherine employed a little subterfuge, relating arguments that had been prearranged with the help of a third party, perhaps Maria, to satisfy the spies. Then Catherine sent him away to rest after his journey, and was able to have a little sleep herself.[91]

Soon after, though, Catherine sent for the ambassador again. They spent 'full two hours' in conversation, and although he was wary of wearying her, she told him it was 'so great a pleasure and consolation'. Over the next four days, they spent the same period of time together, during which she enquired about the health of the Emperor, Mary and 'the delay of remedy by which all good men had suffered in person and in goods, and so many ladies were going to perdition'. Chapuys assured her that Charles had done all he could, but that now the new Pope had declared, on account of Fisher's death 'and other disorders', to seek a solution. When she expressed concern about the number of heretics, the ambassador replied pragmatically that 'there must of necessity be heresies and slanders for the exaltation of the good and confusion of the wicked, and that she must consider that the heresies were not so rooted here that they would not soon be remedied'. Catherine was glad to hear this, as she had previously 'had some scruple of conscience because [the heresies] had arisen from her affair'. After four days, when he saw that she was again able to sleep and retain food, Catherine's physician considered her out of danger. Chapuys decided to return to London, 'so not as to abuse the licence the king had given me' and to request that she be sent to a 'more convenient house'. She was 'very cheerful' as he took his leave of her, even laughing two or three times and requesting some games or pastimes from one of her gentlemen. She gave Chapuys a list of her wishes regarding her burial and some letters as testaments, as she considered herself still a married woman and, therefore, legally forbidden to compose a will. The following morning, he was informed that she had slept well and should have no fear of departure. The physician would recall him with all diligence, should her health take a further turn for the worse.[92] Chapuys would never see her again.

Chapuys left Catherine on 5 January. The next day, Epiphany, she was able to comb and tie her hair and dress her head without assistance. About an hour after midnight, she began to ask the time, hoping that it was near day, because she wanted to hear Mass and celebrate the sacraments but would not do so until dawn. Her confessor, the loyal Jorge d'Athequa, who had been with her for years, offered to celebrate Mass at four in the morning, but she refused. Finally, she celebrated at dawn with 'the utmost fervour' and continued to 'repeat some beautiful orisons and begged the bystanders to pray for her soul'. She was certain that God would pardon Henry 'the wrong he had done her' and that the 'divine goodness would lead him to the true road and give him good counsel'. Then she received the last rites.[93]

Catherine did have the opportunity to jot down some thoughts about the disposal of her meagre effects after her death. She requested that her body be buried in a convent of Observant Friars, but this wish was not honoured. Nor was the plea that 500 Masses be said for her soul or that some soul undertake a pilgrimage on her behalf to the shrine of Our Lady of Walsingham, which was to be suppressed in 1538 and its statue of the Virgin burned, probably by Thomas Cromwell. She left small sums of money to loyal friends: £200 to Mrs Darel for her marriage, £100 to Mrs Blanche, £40 each to Mrs Margery and Mrs Whyller. Her physician's wife, Mary, received £40, as did Isabel, the daughter of a Marguerite and Francisco Philippo. Her physician, goldsmith, washerwoman and apothecary each had their accounts settled and an additional year's wages, while Mr Whyller was paid for making her gown and got an extra £20. Philip, Anthony and Bastian received £20 a head and the 'little maidens' got £10. Her lady, Isabel of Vergas, was given £20, while her daughter Mary received a gold collar she had brought from Spain.[94]

Catherine's last letter to Henry, dictated after Mass on the morning of 7 January, was dignified and restrained, but remained steadfast to the belief that she was his lawful wife and that he had committed sin in the eyes of God:

> My most dear lord, king and husband,
> The hour of my death now drawing on, the tender love I owe you forceth me, my case being such, to commend myself to you, and to put you in remembrance with a few words of the health and safeguard of your soul which you ought to prefer before all worldly matters, and before the care and pampering of your body, for the which you have cast me into many miseries and yourself into many troubles.
>
> For my part, I pardon you everything, and I wish to devoutly pray God that He will pardon you also. For the rest, I commend

> unto you our daughter Mary, beseeching you to be a good father unto her, as I have heretofore desired. I entreat you also, on behalf of my maids, to give them marriage portions, which is not much, they being but three. For all my other servants I solicit the wages due them, and a year more, lest they be unprovided for.
>
> Lastly, I make this vow, that mine eyes desire you above all things.[95]

Yet it is by no means certain that this is a genuine letter, surviving in a later document rather than the State Letters and Papers. Some historians have questioned its veracity, even resolving that it is a later forgery[96] or part of a dramatic work. Catherine's final wish of seeing Henry again came too late, even if he had been minded to set out at once for Kimbolton. Four and a half years since their last meeting, Catherine can hardly have expected a deathbed reconciliation, although the years she had spent at his side, as his queen and love, may have led her to hope in vain. She died at two in the afternoon of the same day, at the age of fifty.

Chapuys heard of Catherine's death from Cromwell the day after he had returned to court. It was the 'most cruel news that could come to me', especially as he feared that the grief might kill Mary or provide Anne with the opportunity to act against her. Given the nature of the suspicions and rumours of the last few years, and the fact that she had seemed to rally before his departure, it was logical for Chapuys to ask Catherine's doctor if there were any grounds for suspecting that she had been poisoned. He thought that there were, explaining that she had seemed to deteriorate after drinking some Welsh beer, which led him to conclude 'it must have been a slow and subtle poison'. He could discover no evidence of 'simple and pure poison' but believed that indications would be found when the post-mortem was conducted.[97]

On the evening of the same day, Catherine's body was opened on the command of Edmund Bedingfield, on behalf of the king. No other person was allowed to be present, 'not even her confessor or physician, but only the candle-maker of the house and one servant' and the 'companion', the man who opened her. They were not surgeons, according to Chapuys, 'yet they have often done such a duty', and upon examining her remains, reached a conclusion about her death. That conclusion remains controversial, then and now. Their leader told Athequa 'in great secrecy as a thing which would cost his life', that he had found all Catherine's internal organs 'as sound as possible except the heart'. Catherine's heart was 'quite black and hideous, and even after he had washed it three times it did not change colour'. Upon dissection, it was seen to be the same throughout, with some 'black round thing which clung closely to the outside of the heart'. When the physician was asked 'if she had died of poison, he replied that the thing was too evident by what had been said to the Bishop her confessor, and if that had not been disclosed, the thing was sufficiently clear from the report and circumstances of the illness'.[98] The ambiguity of this statement allows for many interpretations and 'what had been said to the Bishop her confessor' is not known. The reply is synonymous with saying that the cause of death was apparent, which might be a confirmation that poison was suspected. A black heart containing a 'black round thing' sounds very much like a cancerous tumour or blood clot, although the apparent health of her other organs suggests any cancer had not spread.[99] Equally, this was simply the report that was made to Athequa, who did not see the body himself, in conditions of great secrecy. Why was such secrecy required? Was the ambiguity deliberate, in order to conceal or reveal the possibility of the death by poison that Catherine and her friends had been fearing for years? The actual cause of Catherine's death cannot be established with certainty. As such, we cannot rule out poison administered over a period of time.

After this, Catherine's body, handed over to the embalmers, who would proceed to disembowel the body and enclose it in lead. Then it was 'seared, trammelled, leaded and chested with spices' in advance of its burial.[100] A groom of the chamber was reputedly 'able to sear her', which might account for the 'servant' recorded among the three who saw the body. Any evidence was quickly destroyed. In an undated letter, Bedingfield wrote to Cromwell that 'the bowelling and cering [searing] is already done in the best manner. The leading and chesting is prepared for, and shall be finished with all speed.'[101] So, who exactly was this Edmund Bedingfield who had overseen Catherine's end, made the arrangements for the opening of her body and its readiness for burial, reporting all back to Thomas Cromwell in London?

Edmund's father, also called Edmund, had been a Yorkist during the Wars of the Roses, knighted by Richard III and building a family seat at Oxburgh. He had adapted to the Tudor regime, however, and entertained Henry VII at his new moated manor house in 1487. His eldest son, Thomas, inherited his estate and was knighted at the coronation of Henry VIII, but it was another son, Edmund, born in around 1479, who oversaw Catherine's final years, described as the 'steward of her household'. He had been knighted for bravery in France by the Duke of Suffolk, and after marrying Grace Marney had fathered a son named Henry. He inherited the family estate from his elder brother and passed in on to his own son when he died in 1553.[102] Otherwise he is a shadowy figure in the records, barely mentioned in the State Letters and Papers for the reign of Henry VIII. Might he simply have been a reliable servant chosen for a specific job, or else a younger son, looking for advancement, willing to undertake the difficult and unpopular job of acting as the gaoler of a woman who had once been beloved but was now ill, separated from her daughter, and increasingly difficult? Might he have taken a bribe? Might he have turned the other way while poison was administered?

By the end of January, Chapuys had another possible murderer in his sights:

> Many suspect that if the Queen died by poison it was Gregory di Casale who sent it by a kinsman, of Modena, named Gorron, who came hither in haste, and by what he told me the night before he returned, he had come to obtain letters in behalf of the Prothonotary Casale. He said the king and Cromwell would speak to me about it, but they have not done so. Those who suspect this say the said Gregory must have earned somehow the 8 ducats a day the king gave him, and to get a slow poison which should leave no trace, they had sent for him, which Chapuys cannot easily believe, as there would be too great danger of its being made known.[103]

Exactly what led him to suspect Casale, who was Henry's ambassador to the Vatican, is unclear. Very little other evidence survives about Casale's life and career. Did Chapuys think he was acting on the instructions of Henry? And how exactly had he administered the poison to Catherine, or whom had he paid to do so? He does not appear to have even been in the country at the time, being recorded on 18 January as a resident of Naples[104] and was on 13 February in Rome.[105] Who was the mysterious Gorron?

Such questions are pure speculation and would not have arisen had Chapuys not maintained a constant stream of doubts about the queen's safety. Nor would this be sufficient grounds for suspicion in itself, except that Catherine herself was convinced that her enemies were plotting to remove her. It would be easier to remove the former queen to increasingly more distant isolation, separate her from friends and trusted servants, than to summon her to the executioner's block and make a public martyr of her in the style of Fisher and More. Certainly the Emperor, his brother Ferdinand and the Pope would have launched a joint attack upon England had Catherine's head appeared on London Bridge. Henry was certainly not foolish or desperate enough to have even contemplated it. Then there is the circumstance of Fisher's cook, a known attempt to poison the bishop for his resistance to the divorce. The case that Catherine of Aragon was poisoned is circumstantial. But just as it is unproven, so it cannot be dismissed. What is perhaps more remarkable is just how quickly the possibility was dropped in both England and Europe at the time, and by historians since.

V

News of Catherine's death soon spread. Henry, hearing the news on Saturday, remarked that 'God be praised that we are free from all suspicion of war', and dressed, the following day, all in yellow, with a white feather in his bonnet, and paraded Princess Elizabeth at court. After dinner, he joined the ladies dancing 'and there did several things like one transported with joy'.[106] Anne was initially joyful, but then her mood rapidly changed, according to 'various quarters' that Chapuys did not consider very good authorities, 'that notwithstanding the joy shown by the concubine at the news of the good Queen's death, for which she had given a handsome present to the messenger, she had frequently wept, fearing that they might do with her as with the good queen'.[107]

Chapuys encouraged Princess Mary to show 'good heart and constancy ... great sense and incomparable virtue and patience' to bear the loss of 'such a mother to whom she bore as much love as any daughter ever did to her mother, who was her chief refuge in her troubles'.[108] Then there were the English people. From what Chapuys had heard, 'the grief of the people at this news is incredible, and the indignation they feel against the king, on whom they lay the blame of her death, part of them believing it was by poison and others by grief; and they are the more indignant at the joy the king has exhibited'.[109] Catherine's nephew Charles wrote to his wife, Catherine's niece Isabella, explaining that there were 'different accounts of her illness'. While some held that it was a 'disease in the stomach and lasted more than 10 or 12 days', others were saying that 'the evil began one time when she drank, not without suspicion that there was in it [the drink] what is usual in such cases'. He did not want to be responsible for spreading the rumour of poison, 'but the popular judgement cannot be suppressed'. He ordered the Imperial court into mourning and obsequies were performed.[110] The Empress also received a letter from Dr Ortiz, enclosing a copy of one from 'that glorious martyr' Catherine herself 'by which the Empress will see the perfection and heroic virtues to which she attained'. Catherine would be a 'true patroness and advocate of the Empress in Heaven'.[111]

Chapuys reported that 'great preparation' was being made for Catherine's funeral, informing the Emperor that it would be 'so magnificent that even those who see it all will hardly believe it'. He had heard that Henry meant to dress around 600 people in mourning, including himself, upon whom Cromwell kept pressing lengths of black material for his funeral attire. In the end, Chapuys did not attend, because after having taken advice, he concluded that he could not endorse a ceremony in which she was not buried as a queen. She was to be laid to rest as the Dowager Princess of Wales, the wife of Arthur, not with the honour due to one who had shared Henry's bed and throne for two decades. Splendid preparations had begun at Peterborough Cathedral, thirty miles to the north of Kimbolton, but then it had unexpectedly ground to a halt: 'The king had intended, or those of his Council, that solemn exequies should be made at the Cathedral Church of this city, and a number of carpenters and others had already been set to work to make preparations, but, since then, the whole thing has been broken off; I do not know if it was ever sincerely intended, or if it was only a pretence for the satisfaction of the people, to remove sinister opinions.'[112] One reason for the interruption might have been disagreements over protocol. Cromwell's secretary Ralph Sadler had been tasked to arrange details with Henry for the event, but received a curt reply to the suggestion of a hearse. The king declared that it was neither 'requisite or needful', and when Sadler pointed out that Henry's sister Mary had one in 1533, he received the reply that 'she was a queen, and as the princess Dowager' was to be buried in Peterborough, not London, there was no need of one.[113] Bedingfield was responsible, along with Sir Edward Chamberlain, for arranging the lights to burn around the body, the blacking to be hung and draped, the appointment of personages as mourners, their clothing, the chariots to follow the corpse, the number of prelates to be present, the dole to be paid and where the body was to be interred.[114]

Directions for the event were recorded under the heading 'A remembrance for thenterrement of the right excellent and noble Princesse the Lady Catherin, Doughter to the right highe and mighty Prince Ferdinand, late King of Castle, and late Wief to the noble and excellent prince Arthur, Brother to our Soveraign Lorde King Henry the viijth'.[115] There were to be torches lit in all the towns though which her body would pass, and nine lights in the cathedral, with the body attended by three mutes, various noblemen and four knights to bear a canopy over it, while six knights bore it, assisted by six barons. Catherine was to lie under a pall, with a 'puffed image of a princess', but no wooden effigy like that which had topped the coffins of Elizabeth of York and Henry VII and their predecessors. The chief mourner was to be Henry's niece, Suffolk's eldest daughter, Frances Brandon, who was almost the same age as Princess Mary. Eight ladies were to ride behind her on palfreys trapped in black cloth, followed by two chariots of others.[116] Chapuys was not happy about the location of her tomb, being 'far removed from the high altar, and much less honorable than that of certain bishops buried there; and even if they had not taken her for princess dowager as they have done in death and life, but only as simple baroness, they could not have given her a less honourable place, as I am told by men acquainted with those matters'.[117] He was clearly bitter and disappointed at the final treatment of a woman he had come to consider a martyr: 'Such are the great miracles and incredible magnificence which they gave me to understand they would put forth in honor of her memory as due alike to her great virtues and to her kindred. Possibly they will repair the fault by making a becoming monument in some suitable place.'[118]

The funeral took place on 29 January 1536. On the same day, Anne Boleyn miscarried a foetus of around three and a half months. It had the appearance of a boy. Chapuys foresaw her doom in it, as perhaps did Anne. In fact, there was already another rival on the scene in the form of Jane Seymour, whom Anne had disturbed in the king's company, leading to a terrible row. Chapuys linked the event with Anne's loss:

> Some think it was owing to her own incapacity to bear children, others to a fear that the king would treat her like the late Queen, especially considering the treatment shown to a lady of the Court, named Mistress Semel, to whom, as many say, he has lately made great presents. The Princess's *gouvernante*, her daughters, and a niece, have been in great sorrow for the said abortion, and have been continually questioning a lady who is very intimate with the Princess whether the said Princess did not know the said news of the abortion, and that she might know that, but they would not for the world that she knew the rest, meaning that there was some fear the king might take another wife.[119]

Anne's tenure as queen was to last a mere three months more. On 1 May, she was arrested and taken to the Tower of London. Accused of adultery and incest, and also reputed to have ensnared the king with witchcraft, she was condemned to death and beheaded eighteen days later. The terrible fate that had haunted Catherine, the execution of a queen on the order of her once loving husband, had come to pass. Catherine had narrowly avoided it, but the full force of Henry's wrath descended upon the head of her rival. The following day, Henry was engaged to be married to Jane Seymour and she became his third wife before the month was out. She would give Henry his longed-for legitimate male heir, the future Edward VI, whose reign would see Henry's reforms pushed even further towards the heresies of Protestantism.

1536 was something of a watershed year in Henry's reign, as well as in the wider world. Hans Holbein painted an upper-torso portrait of the English king, newly head of his own Church, where the king stares off to the right, resplendent in slashed doublet, furs, jewels and a feathered hat. Just a year later he was to create the most iconic image of Henry, standing square, larger than life, staring the viewer challengingly in the eyes, defiant, majestic and compelling. In July 1536, Erasmus died, at the age of sixty-nine, of an attack of dysentery while visiting Basel. Just two months later, on 6 September, William Tyndale, the translator of the Bible, died a heretic's death by being strangled and burned at the stake in Vilvoorde, near Brussels, despite the efforts of Thomas Cromwell to intercede and soften the Imperial court's verdict. Also that year, the French humanist John Calvin published *Institutes of the Christian Religion in Geneva*, which would become a seminal work of the Protestant Reformation. Juan Luis Vives lived on until 1540, dying at the age of forty-seven in Bruges. After years of escaping those who sought to condemn him, Martin Luther died in his bed in February 1546 at the age of sixty-two. Eustace Chapuys continued in the Imperial service until forced to retire through ill health in 1545, and used his retirement to set up schools in his home towns of Savoy and Annecy before dying in January 1556.

Henry died in January 1547, believing himself a devout and complete Catholic. Catherine's daughter, Princess Mary, would become Queen of England after a bloodless coup against the Reformers in 1553.

Notes

Prologue

1. Bucholz, Robert and Key, Newton, *Early Modern England, 1485–1714: A Narrative History* (Wiley-Blackwell, 2nd edn, 2009)
2. Unknown, *Life in the Middle Ages*, University of California Press http://content.ucpress.edu/chapters/11633.ch01.pdf
3. Ibid

1 Catherine's Roots, 1447–1453

1. Pendrill, Colin, *Spain, 1474–1700 The Triumphs and Tribulation of Empire* (Heinemann, 2002)
2. Liss, Peggy K., *Isabel the Queen: Life and Times* (Oxford University Press, 1992)
3. Ibid
4. Liss
5. Giladi, Avner, *Muslim Midwives* (Cambridge University Press, 2014)
6. Ibid
7. Ibid
8. Rubin, Nancy, *Isabella of Castile: The First Renaissance Queen* (New York: St Martin's Press, 1991)
9. Round, Nicholas Grenville, *The Greatest Man Uncrowned: A Study of the Fall of Don Alvaro de Luna* (Tamesis Books, 1986)
10. Ibid
11. Ibid

2 Isabella of Castile, 1454–1485

1. Downey, Kirstin, *Isabella the Warrior Queen* (Knopf Doubleday, 2014)
2. Liss
3. Rubin
4. Liss
5. Phillips, William D., 'Isabel of Castile's Portuguese Connections' in Weissberger, B. (ed.), *Queen Isabel I of Castle: Power, Patronage, Persona* (Tamesis, 2008)
6. Downey
7. Liss
8. Rubin
9. Rubin
10. Lanz
11. Rubin
12. Liss
13. Rubin
14. Kagan, Richard L., *Clio and the Crown: The Politics of History in Early Medieval Spain* (JHU Press, 2010)
15. Rubin
16. Ibid
17. Ibid

18. Elliott, J. H., *Imperial Spain 1469–1716* (Penguin, 2002)
19. Cowans, Jon, *Early Modern Spain: A Documentary History* (University of Pennsylvania Press, 2003)
20. Ibid
21. Tremlett, Giles, *Catherine of Aragon: Henry's Spanish Queen* (Faber and Faber, 2010)
22. Ibid
23. Palonen, Kari, Ihalainen, Pasiu and Pulkkinen, Tuija, *Redescriptions: Yearbook of Political Thought and Conceptual History* (LIT Verlag, 2005)
24. Tremlett
25. Rubin
26. Ibid

3 Childhood, 1485–1492

1. Tremlett
2. Earenfight, Theresa, 'Two Bodies, One Spirit: Isabel and Fernando's Construction of Monarchial Partnership' in Weissberger, Barbara F. (ed.), *Queen Isabel I of Castle: Power, Patronage, Persona* (Tamesis, 2008)
3. Liss
4. Ford, Richard, *A Handbook for Travellers in Spain. Part One: Andalucia, Ronda and Granada, Murcia, Valencia and Catalonia* (John Murray, 1855)
5. Howe, Professor Elizabeth Theresa, *Education and Women in the Early Modern Hispanic World* (Ashgate Publishing, 2013)
6. Ibid
7. Nauert, Charles G., *The A-Z of the Renaissance* (Scarecrow Press, 2006)
8. Howe
9. Watson, Foster (ed.), *Tudor School-Boy Life: The Dialogues of Juan Luis Vives* (London: J. M. Dent, 1908)
10. Ibid
11. Howe
12. Coolidge, Dr Grace E., *Guardianship, Gender and the Nobility in Early Modern Spain* (Ashgate Publishing, 2008)
13. Howe
14. Rubin
15. Ibid
16. Fox, Julia *Sister, Queens* (Weidenfeld and Nicolson, 2011)
17. Neale, J. M., *A History of Portugal* (Joseph Masters, 1846)
18. Liss
19. Cowans
20. Machiavelli, Niccolò, *The Prince* (1513)
21. Whitechapel, Simon, *Flesh Inferno: Atrocities of Torquemada and the Spanish Inquisition* (Creation Books, 2003)
22. Cowans
23. Ibid
24. 'Blood and Gold: The Making of Spain' presented by Simon Sebag Montefiore (BBC Four, December 2015)
25. Rubin
26. Nauert, Charles G., *The A-Z of the Renaissance* (Scarecrow Press, 2006)
27. Lanz, Eukene Lacarra, *Marriage and Sexuality in Medieval and Early Modern Iberia* (Psychology Press, 2002)
28. Ibid

4 Negotiations, 1489–1499

1. Williams
2. Ibid
3. CSPS Vol. 1 1489 p. 20–6
4. Ibid
5. Ibid

6. CSPS Vol. 1 1490 pp. 26–35
7. CSPS Vol. 1 1495 p. 57
8. Liss
9. Williams
10. Rubin
11. Williams
12. Fox
13. Rubin
14. CSPS Sept. 1493 p. 85
15. Madden, Frederic, *Documents Relating to Perkin Warbeck, with Remarks on His History* (J. B. Nichols and Son, 1837)
16. CSPS Oct. 1496 p. 163
17. Williams
18. CSPS 17 July 1498 p. 203
19. CSPS June 1499 p. 265
20. Ibid p. 266
21. Ibid p. 280
22. CSPS July 1498
23. Williams
24. CSPS 23 March 1501 p. 293
25. Netherton, Robin and Owen-Crocker, Gale R., *Medieval Clothing and Textiles 10* (Boydell and Brewer, 2014)
26. Weir, Alison, *The Six Wives of Henry VIII* (Vintage, 2007)
27. Calendar Lynn Emerson
28. CSPS 29 June 1500 p. 282
29. Williams
30. Tremlett
31. CSPS May 1501 p. 294
32. Ibid
33. Weir
34. Riddell, Jessica Erin, *'A Mirror of Men': Sovereignty, Performance and Textuality in Tudor England 1501–1559* (Unpublished PhD, Queens University, Canada, 2009)
35. Gairdner, James (ed.), *Letters and Papers Illustrative of the Reigns of Richard III and Henry VII* (Longman, Roberts and Green, 1861)
36. CSPS 21 May 1501 pp. 299, 300
37. CSPS 5 July 1501 p. 302
38. Tremlett

5 First Impressions, 1501

1. Sneyd, Charlotte Augusta, *A Relation, or Rather a True Account, of the Island of England: With Sundry Particulars of the Customs of these People and of the Royal Revenue under King Henry VII, Around the year 1500* (Camden Society, 1884)
2. CSPS Vol. 1 p. 305
3. Ibid
4. Sneyd
5. CSPS Vol. 1 p. 305
6. Sneyd
7. Ibid
8. http://www.legendarydartmoor.co.uk/weather_moor.htm
9. Sneyd
10. Leland, John, *Antiquarii de Rebus Collectanea* (Thomas Hearne)
11. Kipling, Gordon (ed.), *The Receyt of the Ladie Kateryne* (Oxford University Press, 1990)
12. Tremlett
13. Sneyd
14. Erasmus, Desiderius, *Epistles from Erasmus: From his Earliest Letters to his Fifty-First Year*, ed. Nichols, Francis Morgan (Longman, Green & Co, 1901)
15. Sneyd
16. Leland
17. Cunningham, Sean, *Prince Arthur: The Tudor King Who Never Was* (Amberley, 2016)
18. Riddell
19. Tremlett
20. Leland
21. Tremlett
22. Vergil, Polydore, *Anglia Historia* (1555)
23. Erasmus' Epistles

24. Andre, Bernard, *Life of Henry VII*, ed. Gairdner, James (*c.* 1502; Italica Press, 2011)
25. Cunningham
26. www.englandsimmigrants.com
27. Ibid
28. Riddell
29. Sanok, Catherine, *Her Life Historical: Exemplarity and Female Saints' Lives in Late Medieval England* (University of Pennsylvania Press, 2009)
30. Ibid
31. Receyt
32. Fox
33. www.british-history.ac.uk/vch/london/vol1/pp491-495
34. Receyt
35. Ibid
36. Riddell
37. Benson, Pamela Joseph, *Invention of the Renaissance Woman* (Penn State Press, 2010)

6 The Wedding, November 1501

1. Thurley, Simon, *The Royal Palaces of Tudor England* (Yale University Press, 1993)
2. Penn, Thomas, *Winter King: HenryVII and the Dawn of Tudor England* (Simon and Schuster, 2013)
3. Benham, William, *Old St. Paul's Cathedral* (Seeley and Co Ltd, 1902)
4. Bowman, Karen, *Corsets and Codpieces: A Social History of Outrageous Fashion* (Pen and Sword, 2015)
5. Tremlett
6. Receyt
7. Ibid
8. Ibid
9. Ibid
10. Ibid
11. Tremlett
12. Howell, Thomas Bayly and Howell, Thomas Jones, *A Complete Collection of State Trials and Proceedings for High Treason and other crimes and misdemeanors from the earliest period to 1783* (Longman and Co, 1816)

7 Man and Wife? 1501

1. Receyt
2. Ibid
3. Leland
4. Ibid
5. Ibid
6. Anglo, Sydney, *Images of Tudor Kingship* (Seaby, 1992)
7. Leland
8. Thurley
9. Receyt
10. CSPS vol. 1 pp. 310–13
11. CSPS Supplement 1 p. 1
12. Ibid
13. Ibid
14. Ibid
15. Ibid
16. CSPS vol. 1 p. 313
17. Receyt
18. Leland

8 Aftermath, 1502–1504

1. CSPS vol. 1 p. 314
2. CSPS vol. 1 p. 322
3. CSPS vol. 1 pp. 316–8
4. CSPS vol. 1 p. 321
5. Nicolas, H., *Privy Purse Expenses of Elizabeth of York* (William Pickering, 1830)
6. CSPS vol. 1 p. 322
7. Nicolas
8. CSPS vol. 1 p. 322
9. CSPS vol. 1 p. 325
10. CSPS vol. 1 p. 327
11. Nicolas
12. Ibid

13. CSPS vol. 1 p. 360
14. Ibid
15. Receyt
16. CSPS vol. 1 p. 364
17. Ibid
18. Thurloe
19. CSPS vol. 1 p. 398
20. Ibid
21. CSPS vol. 1 p. 395
22. CSPS vol. 1 p. 397
23. CSPS vol. 1 p. 398
24. Penn
25. CSPS vol. 1 p. 401
26. Ibid
27. Ibid
28. CSPS vol. 1 p. 413
29. Rubin
30. Fox

9 Potential Spouses, 1505–1507

1. CSPS vol. 1 p. 430
2. CSPS vol. 1 p. 431
3. CSPS vol. 1 p. 435
4. CSPS vol. 1 p. 437
5. Ibid
6. CSPS vol. 1 p. 447
7. CSPS vol. 1 p. 437
8. Tremlett
9. Ibid
10. CSPS vol. 1 p. 427
11. Ibid
12. CSPS vol. 1 p. 446
13. CSPS vol. 1 p. 448
14. CSP Venice vol. 2 p. 865
15. Williams
16. CSP Venice vol. 2 p. 865
17. CSP Venice vol. 2 p. 842
18. Starkey, David, *Six Wives of Henry VIII* (Vintage, 2004)
19. SLP Henry VIII vol. 1 p. 451
20. Starkey
21. CSPS vol. 1 p. 452
22. Tremlett
23. CSPS vol. 1 p. 455
24. Ibid
25. CSPS vol. 1 p. 490

10 Solace in the Church, 1507–1509

1. Waller, Gary, *The Virgin Mary in Late Medieval and Early Modern English Literature and Popular Culture* (Cambridge University Press, 2011)
2. Erasmus, Desiderius, *Handbook of a Christian Knight* (1501)
3. CSPS vol. 1 p. 459
4. Ibid
5. CSPS vol. 1 p. 484
6. Ibid
7. CSPS vol. 1 p. 491
8. CSPS vol. 1 p. 506
9. Ibid
10. CSPS vol. 1 p. 517
11. CSPS vol. 1 p. 513
12. The letter was mistakenly addressed to Arthur, Prince of Wales, despite the fact he had died three years earlier.
13. Hutchinson, Robert, *Young Henry: The Rise of Henry VIII* (Hachette, 2011)
14. CSPS vol. 1 p. 532
15. CSPS vol. 1 p. 527
16. CSPS vol. 1 p. 541
17. CSPS Supplement 1 p. 2
18. Ibid
19. Ibid
20. CSPS Supplement 1 p. 3
21. Ibid
22. Ibid
23. CSPS Supplement 1 p. 4
24. Ibid
25. Ibid
26. Penn
27. CSPS vol. 1 p. 552
28. CSPS vol. 1 p. 588
29. Ibid
30. CSPS vol. 1 p. 603
31. Ibid
32. CSPS Supplement 1 p. 4
33. Ibid
34. CSPS vol. 1 p. 603

35. CSPS vol. 1 p. 604
36. Erickson, Carolly, *Great Harry: The Extravagant Life of Henry VIII* (Robson Books, 1998)
37. Penn
38. CSPS vol. 2 p. 1
39. Ibid
40. Hutchinson
41. CSPS vol. 1 p. 588
42. CSPS vol. 1 p. 586
43. SLP Venice vol. 1 p. 906
44. SLP Venice vol. 1 p. 909
45. Hutchinson
46. Ibid
47. Penn
48. SLP Henry VIII vol. 1 May 1520
49. SLP Henry VIII vol. 1 p. 20
50. Ibid

11 Wife and Queen, 1509

1. Hall
2. Erasmus, *Letters*
3. SLP Henry VIII vol. 1 p. 101
4. Williams
5. SLP Henry VIII vol. 1 p. 50
6. SLP Henry VIII vol. 1 p. 51
7. CSPS vol. 2 p. 14
8. SLP Henry VIII vol. 1 p. 101
9. Hall
10. Page, William (ed.), *A History of the County of Kent*, Volume 2 (Victoria County History Series, 1926)
11. Ibid
12. SLP Henry VIII vol. 1 p. 17
13. Weir, *Six Wives*
14. Brooke, in 'Archaeologia: Or Miscellaneous Tracts Relating to Antiquity', *The Society of Antiquaries of London*, IV (1777)
15. Hall
16. Ibid
17. SLP Henry VIII vol. 1 p. 37
18. Fox
19. Hall
20. Ibid
21. SLP Henry VIII vol. 1 p. 82
22. Ibid
23. Starkey
24. Hall
25. Stow, John, *The Survey of London* (1598)
26. Ibid
27. Hall
28. Ibid
29. SLP Henry VIII vol. 2 p. 83

12 Queen of Hearts, 1509–1511

1. SLP Henry VIII vol. 1 p. 112
2. Ibid
3. Ibid
4. SLP Henry VIII vol. 1 p. 20
5. See Licence, Amy, *The Six Wives and Many Mistresses of Henry VIII* (Amberley, 2014)
6. SLP Henry VIII vol. 1 p. 23
7. SLP Henry VIII vol. 1 p. 28
8. SLP Henry VIII vol. 1 p. 29
9. CSPS vol. 2 p. 29
10. SLP Henry VIII vol. 1 p. 253
11. CSPS vol. 2 p. 32
12. Hall
13. SLP Henry VIII vol. 1 p. 249
14. SLP Henry VIII vol. 1 p. 473
15. CSPS Supplement 1 p. 7
16. CSPS Supplement 2 p. 7
17. SLP Henry VIII vol. 1 p. 8
18. SLP Henry VIII vol. 1 p. 7
19. SLP Henry VIII vol. 1 p. 8
20. Ibid
21. Hall
22. SLP Henry VIII vol. 1 p. 8
23. Ibid
24. Ibid
25. SLP Henry VIII vol. 1 p. 474
26. Ibid
27. SLP Henry VIII vol. 1 pp. 505, 506, 510, 511
28. Hall
29. SLP Henry VIII vol. 1 p. 528
30. SLP Henry VIII vol. 1 p. 540

31. SLP Henry VIII vol. 1 p. 563
32. SLP Henry VIII vol. 1 p. 555
33. SLP Henry VIII vol. 1 p. 587
34. Thurley
35. Hall
36. Ibid
37. SLP Henry VIII vol. p. 578
38. SLP Henry VIII vol. 1 p. 647
39. Hall
40. SLP Henry VIII vol. 1 p. 670
41. SLP Henry VIII vol. 1 p. 675
42. SLP Henry VIII vol. 1 p. 678
43. SLP Henry VIII vol. 1 p. 671
44. SLP Henry VIII vol. 1 p. 698
45. SLP Henry VIII vol. 1 p. 1025
46. SLP Henry VIII vol. 1 p. 968
47. Hall
48. Ibid
49. SLP Henry VIII vol. 1 p. 707
50. Ibid

13 The Ferdinand and Isabella of England, 1511–1513

1. SLP Henry VIII vol. 1 p. 728
2. SLP Henry VIII vol. 1 p. 734
3. SLP Henry VIII vol. 1 p. 730
4. CSPS vol. 2 p. 39
5. SLP Henry VIII vol. 1 p. 45
6. CSPS vol. 2 pp. 54, 55
7. SLP Henry VIII vol. 1 p. 795
8. CSPS vol. 2 p. 45
9. CSPS vol. 1 p. 62
10. SLP Henry VIII vol. 1 p. 1132
11. SLP Henry VIII vol. 1 p. 1161
12. SLP Henry VIII vol. 1 p. 1160
13. SLP Henry VIII vol. 1 p. 1162
14. SLP Henry VIII vol. 1 p. 1144
15. SLP Henry VIII vol. 1 p. 1195
16. Tremlett
17. SLP Henry VIII vol. 1 p. 1422
18. Ibid
19. Ibid
20. SLP Henry VIII vol. 1 p. 1458
21. CSPS vol. 2 p. 68
22. SLP Henry VIII vol. 1 p. 1460
23. CSPS vol. 2 p. 12
24. Tremlett
25. SLP Venice vol. 2 p. 211
26. Williams
27. Mackail, J. W. (ed.), *Erasmus Against War* (The MerryMount Press, 1907)
28. Ibid
29. SLP Henry VIII vol. 1 p. 1985
30. Tremlett
31. Ibid
32. SLP Henry VIII vol. 1 p. 2120
33. Ibid
34. SLP Henry VIII vol. 1 p. 2138
35. CSPS vol. 2 p. 122
36. SLP Henry VIII vol. 1 p. 2330
37. Starkey, *Six Wives*
38. SLP Henry VIII vol. 1 p. 2138
39. SLP Henry VIII vol. 1 p. 2162
40. SLP Henry VIII vol. 1 p. 2207
41. Fox
42. SLP Henry VIII vol. 1 p. 2226
43. SLP Henry VIII vol. 1 p. 2330
44. SLP Henry VIII vol. 1 p. 2268
45. Erasmus *Letters*
46. SLP Henry VIII vol. 2 p. 331
47. Ibid
48. Dixon, William Hepworth, *History of Two Queens, Catherine of Aragon and Anne Boleyn*, Volume II (B Tauchnitz, 1873)
49. SLP Henry VIII vol. 1 p. 2394
50. SLP Henry VIII vol. 1 p. 2440
51. Mackail
52. SLP Henry VIII vol. 1 p. 752
53. Sweetinburgh, Sheila, *Late Medieval Kent 1220–1540* (Boydell and Brewer, 2010)
54. SLP Henry VIII vol. 2 p. 943

14 Maternity, 1514–1516

1. SLP Henry VIII vol. 1 p. 2741
2. SLP Henry VIII vol. 1 p. 3009
3. SLP Henry VIII vol. 1 p. 2982
4. SLP Henry VIII vol. 1 p. 3027
5. SLP Henry VIII vol. 1 p. 3018

6. SLP Henry VIII vol. 1 p. 3041
7. Ibid
8. SLP Henry VIII vol. 1 p. 3151
9. SLP Venice vol. 2 p. 456
10. CSPS vol. 2 p. 201
11. Fraser, Antonia, *The Six Wives of Henry VIII* (Weidenfeld and Nicolson, 1992)
12. CSPS vol. 2 p. 201
13 Ibid
14. Ibid
15. SLP Henry VIII vol. 1 p. 3440
16. SLP Henry VIII vol. 1 p. 3581
17. CSPS vol. 2 p. 231
18. CSPS vol. 2 p. 238
19. Ibid
20. CSPS Supplement 1 p. 9
21. Hall
22. SLP Henry VIII vol. 2 p. 15
23. SLP Henry VIII vol. 2 p. 227
24. SLP Henry VIII vol. 2 p. 409
25. SLP Henry VIII vol. 2 p. 411
26. Ibid
27. SLP Henry VIII vol. 2 p. 410
28. Hall
29. Ibid
30. Ibid
31. Ibid
32. SLP Venice Vol. 2 p. 690
33. CSPS vol. 2 p. 245
34. SLP Henry VIII vol. 2 p. 1563
35. CSPS vol. 2 p. 238
36. SLP Henry VIII vol. 1 p. 4382
37. SLP Henry VIII vol. 1 p. 3435
38. Wilson, Derek, *The English Reformation* (Robinson, 2012)
39. Hall
40. Ibid

15 Extremes, 1517–1519

1. SLP Henry VIII vol. 1 p. 4173
2. www.englandsimmigrants.com
3. Hall
4. Ibid
5. Wilson
6. Rappaport, Stephen, *Worlds within Worlds: Structures of Life in Sixteenth Century London* (Cambridge University Press, 2002)
7. SLP Henry VIII vol. 1 p. 3204
8. Ibid
9. Fox
10. SLP Henry VIII vol. 1 p. 3446
11. SLP Venice vol. 2 p. 918
12. Ibid
13. Ibid
14. Ibid
15. Ibid
16. SLP Venice vol. 2 p. 920
17. Ibid
18. SLP Henry VIII vol. 1 p. 3472
19. Hall
20. Ibid
21. SLP Henry VIII vol. 1 p. 3645
22. SLP Henry VIII vol. 1 p. 3657
23. SLP Henry VIII vol. 1 p. 3641
24. SLP Henry VIII vol. 1 p. 3655
25. SLP Henry VIII vol. 1 p. 3645
26. SLP Henry VIII vol. 1 p. 3656
27. SLP Henry VIII vol. 1 p. 690
28. SLP Henry VIII vol. 1 p. 3697
29. SLP Henry VIII vol. 1 p. 3864
30. SLP Henry VIII vol. 1 p. 3788
31. Ibid
32. Ibid
33. SLP Henry VIII vol. 1 p. 3871
34. Erickson
35. SLP Henry VIII vol. 1 p. 4193
36. SLP Henry VIII vol. 1 p. 3973
37. SLP Henry VIII vol. 1 p. 4173
38. Hall
39. SLP Henry VIII vol. 1 p. 4366
40. Ward, Allyna, *Women and Tudor Tragedy: Feminizing Counsel and Representing Gender* (Rowman and Littlefield, 2013)
41. Schmitt, Miriam and Kulzer, Linda, *Medieval Women Monastics: Wisdom's Wellsprings* (The Liturgical Press, 1996)
42. SLP Henry VIII vol. 3 p. 7
43. Ibid

44. SLP Henry VIII vol. 1 p. 4009
45. SLP Henry VIII vol. 1 p. 4035
46. SLP Henry VIII vol. 1 p. 4074
47. SLP Henry VIII vol. 1 p. 4279
48. SLP Henry VIII vol. 1 p. 4288
49. SLP Henry VIII vol. 1 p. 4320
50. SLP Henry VIII vol. 1 p. 4326
51. SLP Henry VIII vol. 1 p. 4398
52. SLP Henry VIII vol. 1 p. 3802
53. Madden, Frederic, *Documents Relating to Perkin Warbeck, with Remarks on His History* (J. B. Nichols and Son, 1837)
54. www.historyofparliamentonline.org/volume/1509-1558/member/poole-sir-giles-1517–89
55. Madden
56. Ibid
57. Ibid
58. SLP Henry VIII vol. 1 p. 4326
59. SLP Henry VIII vol. 1 p. 3976
60. SLP Venice vol. 2 p. 1287
61. Ibid
62. Ibid
63. SLP Henry VIII vol. 1 p. 4481
64. SLP Henry VIII vol. 1 p. 4529

16 Goldenness, 1519–1524

1. SLP Henry VIII vol. 3 p. 38
2. SLP Henry VIII vol. 3 p. 61
3. SLP Henry VIII vol. 2 p. 1145
4. SLP Henry VIII vol. 2 p. 1148
5. SLP Henry VIII vol. 2 p. 1154
6. SLP Henry VIII vol. 3 p. 70
7. SLP Henry VIII vol. 3 p. 1163
8. SLP Henry VIII vol. 3 p. 88
9. SLP Henry VIII vol. 3 p. 137
10. Tremlett
11. SLP Venice vol. 2 p. 1520
12. Hall
13. Ibid
14. Fox
15. SLP Henry VIII vol. 3 p. 852
16. Ibid
17. Ibid
18. Ibid
19. Ibid
20. SLP Henry VIII vol. 3 p. 852
21. Weir, *Six Wives*
22. Hall
23. Ibid
24. Hall
25. Ibid
26. Ibid
27. Knecht, R. J., *Francis I* (Cambridge University Press, 1984)
28. Hall
29. Knecht
30. Hall
31. Ibid
32. Jerdan, William (ed.), *Rutland Papers: Original Documents Illustrative of the Courts and Times of Henry VII and Henry VIII* (Camden Society, 1842)
33. Ibid
34. SLP Henry VIII vol. 8 p. 919
35. SLP Henry VIII vol. 3 p. 920
36. Hall
37. Rutland
38. Pollard, A. F., *Henry VIII* (London, 1913)
39. Hall
40. SLP Henry VIII vol. 3 p. 970
41. *Letters of Illustrious Women*
42. SLP Henry VIII vol. 3 p. 1150
43. Ibid
44. Fox
45. SLP Henry VIII vol. 3 March 10 p. 1522
46. Hall
47. Ibid
48. Ibid
49. Ibid
50. Ibid
51. Norena
52. SLP Henry VIII vol. 3 p. 838
53. SLP Henry VIII vol. 3 p. 2052
54. SLP Henry VIII vol. 3 p. 1367

17 A Queen's Identity, 1521–1525

1. Gunn, Stephen, Grummit, David and Cools, Hans, *War, State and Society in England and the Netherlands 1477–1559* (Oxford University Press, 2007)
2. Hillgarth, J. N., *The Mirror of Spain 1500–1700: The Formation of a Myth* (University of Michigan Press, 2000)
3. Ibid
4. Ibid
5. SLP Henry VIII vol. 3 p. 909
6. SLP Henry VIII vol. 3 p. 2074
7. SLP Henry VIII vol. 3 p. 2108
8. Hillgarth
9. Ibid
10. Ibid
11. Hillgarth
12. Ibid
13. SLP Henry VIII vol. 3 p. 1453
14. SLP Henry VIII vol. 3 p. 1659
15. SLP Henry VIII vol. 3 p. 2848
16. SLP Henry VIII vol. 3 p. 2849
17. SLP Henry VIII vol. 3 p. 2080
18. SLP Henry VIII vol. 4 p. 1138
19. SLP Henry VIII vol. 3 p. 1063
20. SLP Henry VIII vol. 3 p. 1499
21. Hall
22. Licence, Amy, *The Six Wives of Henry VIII* (Amberley, 2014)
23. SLP Venice vol. 3 p. 1053
24. SLP Henry VIII vol. 4 p. 1124
25. SLP Henry VIII vol. 4 p. 1121
26. SLP Henry VIII vol. 4 p. 1120
27. SLP Henry VIII vol. 4 p. 1131
28. Norena
29. SLP Henry VIII vol. 4 p. 1211
30. SLP Henry VIII vol. 4 p. 1212
31. Ibid
32. Ibid
33. SLP Henry VIII vol. 4 p. 1484
34. Ibid
35. SLP Henry VIII vol. 4 p. 1213

18 The Rival, 1525–1526

1. Rummel, Erika, *Erasmus on Women* (University of Toronto Press, 1996)
2. Eltham Ordinances
3. Ibid
4. Ibid
5. Ibid
6. Ibid
7. Erickson
8. Ives, Eric, *The Life and Death of Anne Boleyn: The Most Happy* (Blackwell, 2005)
9. Licence, *Six Wives*
10. Ibid
11. Warnicke, Retha, *The Rise and Fall of Anne Boleyn* (Canto, 1991)
12. Licence
13. Ibid
14. Denny, Joanna, *Anne Boleyn: A New Life of England's Tragic Queen* (Piatkus 2004)
15. Grueninger, Natalie and Morris, Sarah, *In the Footsteps of the Six Wives of Henry VIII* (Amberley, 2016)
16. Norton, Elizabeth, *Anne Boleyn: Henry VIII's Obsession* (Amberley, 2008)
17. Hall
18. CSPS vol. 3 part 1 p. 619
19. CSPS vol. 3 part 2 p. 8
20. CSPS vol. 3 part 2 p. 18
21. Ibid
22. CSPS vol. 3 part 2 p. 7
23. Ibid

19 Queen on Trial, 1527–1528

1. Erickson
2. CSPS vol. 3 part 2 p. 69
3. Erickson
4. The Spanish Chronicle, quoted in Licence, *Six Wives*
5. CSPS 3 part 2 p. 113
6. Ibid
7. Tremlett

8. SLP Henry VIII vol. 3 part 2 p. 131
9. Ibid
10. SLP Venice part 4 p. 236
11. SLP Henry VIII vol. 3 p. 3105
12. Hall
3. Norton
14. Doernberg Erwin, *Henry VIII and Luther: An Account of their Personal Relations* (Stanford University Press, 1961)
15. Ibid
16. Ibid
17. Ibid
18. Ibid
19. Whitford, David M., *A Reformation Life: The European Reformation through the eyes of Philipp of Hesse (*ABC-Clio, 2015)
20. SLP Henry VIII vol. 4 p. 4383
21. Erickson
22. Hall
23. SLP Henry VIII vol. 4 p. 4875
24. SLP Henry VIII vol. 4 p. 5177
25. SLP Henry VIII vol. 4 p. 4880
26. SLP Henry VIII vol. 4 p. 4881
27. Ibid
28. SLP Henry VIII vol. 4 p. 4943, 4946
29. SLP Henry VIII vol. 4 p. 4899
30. SLP Henry VIII vol. 4 p. 4875
31. SLP Henry VIII vol. 4 p. 4892
32. SLP Henry VIII vol. 4 p. 4981
33. Kelly, H. A., *The Matrimonial Trials of Henry VIII* (Wipf and Stock, 2004)
34. Hall
35. Ibid
36. Ibid
37. Ibid
38. SLP Henry VIII vol. 4 p. 4942
39. SLP Henry VIII vol. 4 p. 4980
40. Ibid
41. SLP Henry VIII vol. 4 p. 5211
42. Kelly

20 The Blackfriars Court, 1528–1529

1. Norena
2. SLP Henry VIII vol. 4 p. 5016
3. SLP Henry VIII vol. 4 p. 5063
4. Norena
5. Ibid
6. SLP Henry VIII vol. 4 introduction
7. Ibid
8. SLP Henry VIII vol. 4 p. 4990
9. SLP Henry VIII vol. 4 p. 5016
10. SLP Henry VIII vol. 4 p. 5017
11. SLP Henry VIII vol. 4 p. 5137
12. SLP Henry VIII vol. 4 p. 5255
13. SLP Henry VIII vol. 4 p. 5154
14. SLP Henry VIII vol. 4 p. 5266
15. SLP Henry VIII vol. 4 p. 5301
16. Ibid
17. SLP Henry VIII vol. 4 p. 5687
18. Ibid
19. SLP Henry VIII vol. 4 p. 5657
20. Ibid
21. SLP Henry VIII vol. 4 p. 5377
22. SLP Henry VIII vol. 4 p. 5599
23. SLP Henry VIII vol. 4 p. 5441
24. Kelly
25. SLP Henry VIII vol. 4 p. 5613
26. Thurley
27. SLP Henry VIII vol. 4 p. 5636
28. Hall
29. Ibid
30. SLP Henry VIII vol. 4 p. 5681
31. Ibid
32. Hall
33. Ibid
34. Williams
35. SLP Henry VIII vol. 4 p. 5732
36. Cavendish, George, *The Life and Death of Cardinal Wolsey* (Houghton, Mifflin and Co., 1905)
37. Ibid
38. Ibid
39. SLP Henry VIII vol. 4 p. 5702
40. SLP Henry VIII vol. 4 p. 5707
41. SLP Henry VIII vol. 4 p. 5711

42. SLP Henry VIII vol. 4 p. 583
43. SLP Henry VIII vol. 4 p. 5732
44. SLP Henry VIII vol. 4 p. 5725
45. SLP Henry VIII vol. 4 p. 5740
46. Kelly
47. Cavendish
48. SLP Henry VIII vol. 4 p. 5791
49. Ibid
50. Ibid
51. SLP Henry VIII vol. 4 p. 5827
52. Ibid
53. SLP Henry VIII vol. 4 p. 5846
54. SLP Henry VIII vol. 4 p. 5909
55. SLP Henry VIII vol. 4 p. 5966
56. SLP Henry VIII vol. 4 p. 6618
57. SLP Henry VIII vol. 4 p. 5969

21 Exits and Arrivals, 1529

1. Hall
2. SLP Henry VIII vol. 4 p. 6179
3. CSPS vol. 4 part 1 p. 135
4. Ibid
5. CSPS vol. 4 part 1 p. 182
6. CSPS vol. 4 part 1 p. 136
7. Ibid
8. CSPS vol. 4 part 1 p. 160
9. Ibid
10. CSPS vol. 4 part 1 p. 152
11. CSPS vol. 4 part 1 p. 160
12. Ibid
13. CSPS vol. 4 part 1 p. 182
14. SLP Henry VIII vol. 4 p. 5177
15. CSPS vol. 4 part 1 p. 133
16. SLP Henry VIII vol. 4 p. 4902
17. SLP Henry VIII vol. 4 p. 5639
18. SLP Henry VIII vol. 4 p. 5212
19. SLP Henry VIII vol. 4 p. 5594
20. SLP Henry VIII vol. 4 p. 4937
21. SLP Henry VIII vol. 4 p. 5746
22. SLP Henry VIII vol. 4 p. 6184
23. Ibid
24. SLP Henry VIII vol. 4 p. 6184
25. Ibid
26. SLP Henry VIII vol. 4 p. 6011
27. SLP Henry VIII vol. 4 p. 6076
28. SLP Henry VIII vol. 4 p. 6026
29. SLP Henry VIII vol. 4 p. 6090
30. CSPS vol. 4 part 1 p. 182
31. Ibid
32. CSPS vol. 4 part 1 p. 211
33. CSPS vol. 4 part 1 p. 224
34. Ibid
35. Ibid
36. Ibid
37. Ibid
38. CSPS vol. 4 part 1 p. 160
39. CSPS vol. 4 part 1 p. 162
40. SLP Henry VIII vol. 4 p. 6199
41. CSPS vol. 4 part 1 p. 232
42. Ibid
43. CSPS vol. 4 part 1 p. 232
44. Hall
45. Ibid
46. Fox
47. Ibid
48. CSPS vol. 4 part 1 p. 224
49. SLP Henry VIII vol. 5 p. 73
50. SLP Henry VIII vol. 4 p. 6183
51. SLP Henry VIII vol. 5 p. 105
52. SLP Henry VIII vol. 4 p. 6337

22 Abandonment, 1530–1531

1. SLP Henry VIII vol. 4 p. 6321
2. SLP Henry VIII vol. 4 p. 6142
3. CSPS vol. 4 part 1 p. 228
4. SLP Henry VIII vol. 4 p. 6422
5. CSPS vol. 4 part 1 p. 228
6. CSPS vol. 4 part 1 p. 250
7. CSPS vol. 4 part 1 p. 255
8. CSPS vol. 4 part 1 p. 257
9. CSPS vol. 4 part 1 p. 265
10. CSPS vol. 4 part 1 p. 302
11. Ibid
12. CSPS vol. 4 part 1 p. 354
13. Ibid
14. CSPS vol. 4 part 1 p. 373
15. Erickson
16. CSPS vol. 4 part 1 p. 249
17. CSPS vol. 4 part 1 p. 265
18. CSPS vol. 4 part 1 p. 270
19. Ibid
20. Ibid

21. CSPS vol. 4 part 1 p. 270
22. SLP Henry VIII vol. 4 p. 6259
23. SLP Henry VIII vol. 4 p. 6256
24. SLP Henry VIII vol. 4 p. 6279
25. SLP Henry VIII vol. 4 p. 6487
26. SLP Henry VIII vol. 4 p. 6487
27. CSPS vol. 4 part 1 p. 396
28. SLP Henry VIII vol. 5 appendix 17
29. CSPS vol. 4 part 1 p. 396
30. CSPS vol. 4 part 1 p. 373
31. SLP Henry VIII vol. 4 p. 6560
32. Harpsfield, Nicholas, *A Treatise on the Pretended Divorce between Henry VIII and Catherine of Aragon* (Camden, 1878)
33. CSPS vol. 4 part 2 p. 766
34. Ibid
35. CSPS vol. 4 part 1 p. 422
36. SLP Henry VIII vol. 4 p. 6738
37. SLP Henry VIII vol. 5 p. 73
38. SLP Henry VIII vol. 5 p. 24
39. CSPS vol. 4 part 2 p. 779
40. Ibid
41. Erickson
42. CSPS vol. 4 part 2 p. 628
43. CSPS vol. 4 part 2 p. 547
44. CSPS vol. 4 part 2 p. 539
45. CSPS vol. 4 part 2 p. 547
46. CSPS vol. 4 part 2 p. 548
47. Hall
48. SLP Henry VIII vol. 5 p. 24
49. Oberman, Heiko, A *Luther: Man Between God and the Devil* (Yale University Press, 2006)
50. SLP Henry VIII vol. 5 p. 46
51. SLP Henry VIII vol. 5 p. 120
52. Dimmock, Matthew, Hadfield, Andrew and Quinn, Paul (eds), *Art, Literature and Religion in Early Modern Sussex: Culture and Conflict* (Ashgate Publishing Ltd, 2014)
53. Williams
54. Ibid
55. Ibid
56. Ibid
57. CSPS vol. 4 part 2 p. 766

23 The Spanish Inquiry, 1531–1532

1. SLP Henry VIII vol. 5 p. 570
2. Ibid
3. SLP Henry VIII vol. 4 p. 527
4. Ibid
5. Tremlett
6. Ibid
7. Ibid
8. CSPS vol. 1 p. 370
9. SLP Henry VIII vol. 5 p. 355
10. SLP Henry VIII vol. 4 p. 361
11. Ibid
12. Ibid
13. CSPS vol. 4 part 2 p. 775
14. CSPS vol. 4 part 2 p. 765
15. SLP Henry VIII vol. 5 p. 375
16. SLP Henry VIII vol. 5 p. 416
17. SLP Henry VIII vol. 5 p. 401
18. CSPS vol. 4 part 2 p. 786
19. Williams
20. SLP Henry VIII vol. 5 p. 416
21. SLP Henry VIII vol. 5 p. 513
22. SLP Henry VIII vol. 5 p. 492
23. SLP Henry VIII vol. 5 p. 478
24. Ibid
25. Ibid
26. SLP Henry VIII vol. 5 p. 531
27. SLP Henry VIII vol. 5 p. 513
28. SLP Henry VIII vol. 5 p. 546
29. SLP Henry VIII vol. 5 p. 563
30. Ibid
31. SLP Henry VIII vol. 5 p. 696
32. Ibid
33. Ibid

24 The New Queen, 1532–1533

1. SLP Henry VIII vol. 5 p. 750
2. SLP Henry VIII vol. 5 p. 820
3. Ibid
4. SLP Henry VIII vol. 5 p. 835
5. SLP Henry VIII vol. 5 p. 818

6. SLP Henry VIII vol. 5 p. 879
7. SLP Henry VIII vol. 5 p. 941
8. SLP Henry VIII vol. 5 p. 1046
9. SLP Henry VIII vol. 5 p. 1202
10. SLP Henry VIII vol. 5 p. 1059
11. Ibid
12. Wilson
13. Ibid
14. SLP Henry VIII vol. 5 p. 583
15. Ibid
16. SLP Henry VIII vol. 5 p. 618
17. SLP Henry VIII vol. 5 p. 1094
18. SLP Henry VIII vol. 5 p. 1075
19. SLP Henry VIII vol. 5 p. 1202
20. Ibid
21. SLP Henry VIII vol. 5 p. 802
22. Ibid
23. Ibid
24. SLP Henry VIII vol. 5 p. 1377
25. SLP Henry VIII vol. 5 p. 1311
26. SLP Henry VIII vol. 5 p. 1377
27. SLP Henry VIII vol. 5 p. 1292
28. SLP Henry VIII vol. 5 p. 1256
29. SLP Henry VIII vol. 5 p. 1187
30. SLP Henry VIII vol. 5 p. 1520
31. Ibid
32. BHO Victoria County History
33. SLP Henry VIII vol. 5 p. 805
34. SLP Henry VIII vol. 5 p. 760
35. SLP Henry VIII vol. 5 p. 391
36. SLP Henry VIII vol. 5 p. 760
37. Williams
38. SLP Henry VIII vol. 5 p. 765
39. SLP Henry VIII vol. 5 p. 1252
40. SLP Henry VIII vol. 6 p. 324
41. Ibid
42. SLP Henry VIII vol. 6 p. 774
43. SLP Henry VIII vol. 6 p. 863
44. SLP Henry VIII vol. 6 p. 391
45. Ibid
46. Ibid
47. SLP Henry VIII vol. 6 p. 518
48. SLP Henry VIII vol. 6 p. 733
49. SLP Henry VIII vol. 6 p. 964
50. SLP Henry VIII vol. 6 p. 923
51. SLP Henry VIII vol. 6 p. 556
52. Ibid
53. SLP Henry VIII vol. 6 p. 805
54. Ibid
55. SLP Henry VIII vol. 6 p. 805
56. SLP Henry VIII vol. 6 p. 571
57. SLP Henry VIII vol. 6 p. 918
58. SLP Henry VIII vol. 6 p. 1018
59. Ibid
60. SLP Henry VIII vol. 6 p. 351
61. SLP Henry VIII vol. 6 p. 340
62. Ibid
63. SLP Henry VIII vol. 6 p. 1053
64. SLP Henry VIII vol. 6 p. 1054
65. SLP Henry VIII vol. 6 p. 670
66. SLP Henry VIII vol. 6 p. 953
67. SLP Henry VIII vol. 6 p. 1018
68. SLP Henry VIII vol. 6 p. 918
69. SLP Henry VIII vol. 6 p. 1069
70. Ibid
71. SLP Henry VIII vol. 6 p. 1112
72. SLP Henry VIII vol. 5 p. 1249
73. Ibid
74. SLP Henry VIII vol. 6 p. 1207
75. SLP Henry VIII vol. 6 p. 1392
76. SLP Henry VIII vol. 6 p. 1453
77. Hillgarth

25 Dark Days, 1534–1536

1. SLP Henry VIII vol. 6 p. 1468
2. SLP Henry VIII vol. 6 p. 1460
3. SLP Henry VIII vol. 6 p. 1466
4. SLP Henry VIII vol. 7 p. 28
5. SLP Henry VIII vol. 6 p. 1492
6. SLP Henry VIII vol. 6 p. 1493
7. SLP Henry VIII vol. 7 p. 171
8. Ibid
9. SLP Henry VIII vol. 7 p. 184
10. SLP Henry VIII vol. 6 p. 1528
11. SLP Henry VIII vol. 7 p. 296
12. SLP Henry VIII vol. 6 p. 184
13. SLP Henry VIII vol. 7 p. 225
14. Ibid
15. Ibid
16. SLP Henry VIII vol. 7 p. 83
17. Williams

18. BHO Victoria County History, Cambridgeshire
19. Ibid
20. SLP Henry VIII vol. 6 p. 1541
21. SLP Henry VIII vol. 6 p. 1543
22. SLP Henry VIII vol. 6 p. 1542
23. SLP Henry VIII vol. 6 p. 1558
24. Ibid
25. SLP Henry VIII vol. 6 p. 1571
26. Ibid
27. Ibid
28. CSPS vol. 5 part 1 p. 142
29. SLP Henry VIII vol. 6 p. 1126
30. SLP Henry VIII vol. 7 p. 83
31. SLP Henry VIII vol. 7 p. 128
32. SLP Henry VIII vol. 7 p. 129
33. SLP Henry VIII vol. 7 p. 130
34. SLP Henry VIII vol. 7 p. 131
35. SLP Henry VIII vol. 7 p. 393
36. SLP Henry VIII vol. 7 p. 871
37. SLP Henry VIII vol. 7 p. 690
38. Leland
39. SLP Henry VIII vol. 7 p. 695
40. SLP Henry VIII vol. 7 p. 726
41. Ibid
42. SLP Henry VIII vol. 7 p. 393
43. SLP Henry VIII vol. 7 p. 1013
44. Ibid
45. SLP Henry VIII vol. 7 p. 559
46. SLP Henry VIII vol. 7 p. 1193
47. SLP Henry VIII vol. 7 p. 1208
48. SLP Henry VIII vol. 8 p. 209
49. SLP Henry VIII vol. 8 p. 122
50. SLP Henry VIII vol. 8 p. 79
51. SLP Henry VIII vol. 7 p. 1670
52. SLP Henry VIII vol. 7 appendix p. 37
53. SLP Henry VIII vol. 8 p. 565
54. Ibid
55. SLP Henry VIII vol. 8 p. 589
56. SLP Henry VIII vol. 8 p. 324
57. SLP Henry VIII vol. 8 p. 432
58. SLP Henry VIII vol. 8 p. 435
59. SLP Henry VIII vol. 8 p. 514
60. SLP Henry VIII vol. 8 p. 357
61. SLP Henry VIII vol. 8 p. 168
62. SLP Henry VIII vol. 8 p. 434
63. Ibid
64. SLP Henry VIII vol. 8 p. 375
65. SLP Henry VIII vol. 8 p. 384
66. SLP Henry VIII vol. 8 p. 327
67. SLP Henry VIII vol. 8 p. 431
68. SLP Henry VIII vol. 8 p. 1095
69. SLP Henry VIII vol. 8 p. 747
70. SLP Henry VIII vol. 8 p. 786
71. Ibid
72. SLP Henry VIII vol. 8 p. 1097
73. SLP Henry VIII vol. 8 p. 1095
74. SLP Henry VIII vol. 8 p. 996
75. SLP Henry VIII vol. 8 p. 1097
76. SLP Henry VIII vol. 8 p. 1104
77. SLP Henry VIII vol. 8 p. 684
78. SLP Henry VIII vol. 9 p. 48
79. SLP Henry VIII vol. 10 p. 11
80. SLP Henry VIII vol. 9 p. 588
81. SLP Henry VIII vol. 9 p. 681
82. SLP Henry VIII vol. 10 p. 10
83. SLP Henry VIII vol. 9 p. 964
84. SLP Henry VIII vol. 9 p. 996
85. SLP Henry VIII vol. 9 p. 983
86. SLP Henry VIII vol. 9 p. 1036
87. SLP Henry VIII vol. 9 p. 1037
88. SLP Henry VIII vol. 9 p. 1040
89. SLP Henry VIII vol. 9 p. 1050
90. SLP Henry VIII vol. 10 p. 28
91. SLP Henry VIII vol. 10 p. 59
92. Ibid
93. SLP Henry VIII vol. 10 p. 141
94. SLP Henry VIII vol. 10 p. 40
95. Vergil
96. Tremlett
97. SLP Henry VIII vol. 10 p. 59
98. Ibid
99. SLP Henry VIII vol. 10 p. 59
100. SLP Henry VIII vol. 10 p. 37
101. SLP Henry VIII vol. 10 p. 41
102. Dictionary of National Biography
103. SLP Henry VIII vol. 10 p. 200
104. SLP Henry VIII vol. 10 p. 123
105. SLP Henry VIII vol. 10 p. 297
106. SLP Henry VIII vol. 10 p. 59

107. SLP Henry VIII vol. 10 p. 199
108. SLP Henry VIII vol. 10 p. 59
109. Ibid
110. SLP Henry VIII vol. 10 p. 230
111. SLP Henry VIII vol. 10 p. 212
112. SLP Henry VIII vol. 10 p. 59
113. SLP Henry VIII vol. 10 p. 76
114. SLP Henry VIII vol. 10 p. 38
115. Ibid
116. Ibid
117. SLP Henry VIII vol. 10 p. 282
118. SLP Henry VIII vol. 10 p. 282
119. Ibid

Acknowledgements

Thanks go to Jonathan Reeve for commissioning this book and to Jonathan Jackson for his support and for being flexible when I overran my deadline. Thanks also to the team at Amberley, and to Hazel and Philip for their work in promoting this book, and others. Many thanks to my editor, Alex Bennett, for displaying such patience and being so easy to work with, and also to Aaron Phull, for producing such a beautiful cover. I have been particularly blessed to have some wonderful friends: thank you to Anne Marie Bouchard, Sharon Bennett Connolly, Jonathan Howell, Magdalen Pitt, Tim Byard-Jones, Geanine Teramani-Cruz, Kyra Kramer, Karen Stone and Harry and Sara Basnett for keeping me sane during the writing of this book. There have been significant others. Particular thanks go to Sharon Bennett Connolly for her enthusiastic and close reading of this book in manuscript. Many thanks to Dr Sean Cunningham, for being so generous in sharing his work and ideas on Prince Arthur. Also to my godmother 'Lady' Susan Priestley, for her kindness and support. Thanks also to all my family, to my husband Tom and my sons Rufus and Robin, to Paul Fairbrass, Sue and John Hunt. Most of all, it is for my mother for her invaluable proof-reading skills and for my father for his enthusiasm and open mind: this is the result of the books they read me, the museums they took me to as a child and the love and imagination with which they encouraged me.

Bibliography

Calendar of State Papers Spain Volumes 1–5 Bergenroth, G. A., Mattingly, Garrett, Gayangos, Pascual de, 1865/1947

Calendar of State Papers Venice Volumes 1 and 2 Rawdon Brown, London 1864

State Letters and Papers Henry VIII Volumes 1–10 J. S. Brewer, Gairdner, James London 1887/1920

Andre, Bernard *Life of Henry VII* (ed.) Gairdner, James *c* 1502 Italica Press, 2011

Anglo, Sydney Images of Tudor Kingship Seaby 1992

Anonymous Editor, *The Will of Henry VII*, London 1775

Benham, William Old St. Paul's Cathedral Seeley and Co Ltd, London 1902

Benson, Pamela Joseph *Invention of the Renaissance Woman* Penn State Press 2010

Bowman, Karen *Corsets and Codpieces: A Social History of Outrageous Fashion* Pen and Sword 2015

Brooke, (unknown) in 'Archaeologia: Or Miscellaneous Tracts Relating to Antiquity', *The Society of Antiquaries of London*, IV (1777)

Bucholz, Robert and Key, Newton *Early Modern England, 1485–1714: A Narrative History* Wiley-Blackwell, second edition 2009

Cavendish, George *The Life and Death of Cardinal Wolsey* Houghton, Mifflin and Co 1905

Coolidge, Dr Grace E. *Guardianship, Gender and the Nobility in Early Modern Spain* Ashgate Publishing 2008

Cowans, Jon *Early Modern Spain: A Documentary History* University of Pennsylvania Press 2003

Cunningham, Sean *Prince Arthur: The Tudor King who Never Was* Amberley, 2016

Denny, Juana *Anne Boleyn: A New Life of England's Tragic Queen* Piatkus 2004

Dimmock, Matthew, Hadfield, Andrew and Quinn, Paul (eds) *Art, Literature and Religion in Early Modern Sussex: Culture and Conflict* Ashgate Publishing Ltd 2014

Dixon, William Hepworth *History of Two Queens, Catherine of Aragon and Anne Boleyn*, Volume II. B Tauchnitz 1873

Doernberg Erwin *Henry VIII and Luther: An Account of their Personal Relations*. Stanford University Press 1961

Downey, Kirstin *Isabella the Warrior Queen* Knopf Doubleday 2014

Earenfight, Theresa 'Two Bodies, One Spirit: Isabel and Fernando's Construction of Monarchial Partnership' in Weissberger, Barbara F. (ed.) *Queen Isabel I of Castle: Power, Patronage, Persona*. Tamesis 2008

Elliott, J. H. *Imperial Spain 1469–1716* Penguin 2002

Erasmus, Desiderius, *Epistles from Erasmus: From his Earliest Letters to his Fifty-First Year* (ed.) Nichols, Francis Morgan, Longman, Green and Co. 1901

Erasmus, Desiderius, *Handbook of a Christian Knight,* 1501

Erickson, Carolly *Great Harry: The Extravagant Life of Henry VIII* Robson Books 1998

Ford, Richard *A Handbook for Travellers in Spain. Part One: Andalucia, Ronda and Granada, Murcia, Valencia and Catalonia* John Murray 1855

Fox, Julia *Sister Queens* Weidenfeld and Nicolson 2011

Fraser, Antonia *The Six Wives of Henry VIII,* Weidenfeld and Nicolson 1992

Gairdner, James (ed.) Letters and Papers Illustrative of the Reigns of Richard III and Henry VII. Longman, Green, Longman, Roberts and Green, London 1861

Giladi, Avner *Muslim Midwives* Cambridge University Press 2014

Grueninger, Natalie and Morris, Sarah *In the Footsteps of the Six Wives of Henry VIII* Amberley 2016

Gunn, Stephen, Grummit, David and Cools, Hans *War, State and Society in England and the Netherlands 1477–1559* Oxford University Press, 2007

Harpsfield, Nicholas *A Treatise on the Pretended Divorce between Henry VIII and Catherine of Aragon* Camden 1878

Hillgarth, J. N. *The Mirror of Spain 1500–1700: The Formation of a Myth* University of Michigan Press 2000

Howe, Professor Elizabeth Theresa *Education and Women in the Early Modern Hispanic World* Ashgate Publishing 2013

Howell, Thomas Bayly and Howell, Thomas Jones, *A Complete Collection of State Trials and Proceedings for High Treason and other crimes and misdemeanors from the earliest period to 1783* Longman and Co, London 1816

Hutchinson, Robert *Young Henry: The Rise of Henry VIII* Hachette 2011

Ives, Eric *The Life and Death of Anne Boleyn: The Most Happy* Blackwell 2005 (1988)

Jerdan, William (ed.) *Rutland Papers: Original Documents Illustrative of the Courts and Times of Henry VII and Henry VIII* Camden Society 1842

Kagan, Richard L. *Clio and the Crown: The Politics of History in Early Medieval Spain* JHU Press 2010
Kelly, H. A. *The Matrimonial Trials of Henry VIII* Wipf and Stock 2004
Kipling, Gordon (ed.) *The Receyt of the Ladie Kateryne* Oxford University Press 1990
Knecht, R. J. *Francis I* Cambridge University Press 1984
Lanz, Eukene Lacarra *Marriage and Sexuality in Medieval and Early Modern Iberia.* Psychology Press 2002
Leland, John *Antiquarii de Rebus Collectanea* Thomas Hearne 1776
Levin, Carole and Stewart-Nunez, Christine (eds) *Scholars and Poets talk about Queens* Springer 2015
Liss, Peggy K. *Isabel the Queen: Life and Times* Oxford University Press 1992
Machiavelli, Niccolò *The Prince* 1513
Mackail, J. W. (ed.) *Erasmus Against War* The MerryMount Press, Boston 1907
Madden, Frederic *Documents Relating to Perkin Warbeck, with Remarks on His History.* J. B. Nichols and Son 1837
Madden, Frederic *Privy Purse Expenses of the princess Mary, daughter of King Henry VIII* W. Pickering 1831
Mattingly, Garrett *Catherine of Aragon* Jonathan Cape 1942
Mulgan, Catherine *The Renaissance Monarchies 1469–1558* Cambridge University Press 1998
Nauert, Charles G. *The A-Z of the Renaissance* Scarecrow Press 2006
Neale, J. M. *A History of Portugal* Joseph Masters 1846
Netherton, Robin and Owen-Crocker, Gale R Medieval Clothing and Textiles 10 Boydell and Brewer 2014
Nicolas, Nicholas Harries *Privy Purse Expenses of Elizabeth of York* William Pickering, London 1830
Norena, Carlos G. *Juan Luis Vives* Springer Science and Business Media 2012
Norton, Elizabeth *Anne Boleyn: Henry VIII's obsession* Amberley 2008
Oberman, Heiko, A. *Luther: Man Between God and the Devil* Yale University Press 2006
Page, William (ed.) *A History of the County of Kent*, Volume 2, Victoria County History Series, London 1926
Palonen, Kari, Ihalainen, Pasiu and Pulkkinen, Tuija *Redescriptions: Yearbook of Political Thought and Conceptual History LIT Verlag Münster* 2005
Pendrill, Colin *Spain, 1474–1700 The Triumphs and Tribulation of Empire* Heinemann 2002
Penn, Thomas *Winter King: HenryVII and the Dawn of Tudor England* Simon and Schuster 2013
Phillips, William D. 'Isabel of Castile's Portuguese Connections' in Weissberger, B. (ed) *Queen Isabel I of Castle: Power, Patronage, Persona.* Tamesis 2008
Pollard, A. F. *Henry VIII* London 1913

Prescott, William H *History of the Reign of Ferdinand and Isabella, the Catholic, of Spain* Volumes 1, 2 and 3 Routledge, Warne and Routledge, London 1854, 1862
Pulgar, Hernando del *Cronica los senores Reyes Catolicos Don Ferdinand y Doña Isabel de Castilla y de Aragon* Benito Montfort 1780
Rappaport, Stephen *Worlds within Worlds: Structures of Life in Sixteenth Century London* Cambridge University Press 2002
Riddell, Jessica Erin *'A Mirror of Men:' Sovereignty, Performance and Textuality in Tudor England 1501–1559* Unpublished Phd, Queens University, Canada 2009
Round, Nicholas Grenville *The Greatest Man Uncrowned: A Study of the Fall of Don Alvaro de Luna* Tamesis Books 1986
Rubin, Nancy *Isabella of Castile: The First Renaissance Queen* St Martin's Press, New York 1991
Rummel, Erika *Erasmus on Women* University of Toronto Press, 1996
Sanok, Catherine *Her Life Historical: Exemplarity and Female Saints' Lives in Late Medieval England* University of Pennsylvania Press 2009
Schmitt, Miriam and Kulzer, Linda *Medieval Women Monastics: Wisdom's Wellsprings*, The Liturgical Press, Collegeville, Minnesota 1996
Sneyd, Charlotte Augusta *A Relation, or Rather a True Account, of the Island of England: With Sundry Particulars of the Customs of these People and of the Royal Revenue under King Henry VII, Around the year 1500.* Camden Society 1884
Starkey, David *Six Wives of Henry VIII* Vintage 2004
Stow, John *The Survey of London* 1598
Sweetinburgh, Sheila *Late Medieval Kent 1220–1540* Boydell and Brewer 2010
Thomas, Hugh *Rivers of Gold: The Rise of the Spanish Empire*
Thurley, Simon *The Royal Palaces of Tudor England* Yale University Press 1993
Tremlett, Giles *Catherine of Aragon: Henry's Spanish Queen* Faber and Faber 2010
Unknown, Life in the Middle Ages, University of California Press http://content.ucpress.edu/chapters/11633.ch01.pdf
Vergil, Polydore *Anglia Historia* 1555
Waller, Gary *The Virgin Mary in Late Medieval and Early Modern English Literature and Popular Culture* Cambridge University Press 2011
Ward, Allyna *Women and Tudor Tragedy: Feminizing Counsel and Representing Gender* Rowman and Littlefield 2013
Warnicke, Retha *The Rise and Fall of Anne Boleyn* Canto 1991
Warren, Nancy Bradley *Women of God and Arms: Female Spirituality and Political Conflict* 1380–1600 University of Pennsylvania Press 2011
Watson, Foster (ed.) *Tudor School-Boy Life: The Dialogues of Juan Luis Vives* J. M. Dent, London 1908
Weir, Alison *Henry VIII: King and Court* Jonathan Cape 2001
Weir, Alison *The Six Wives of Henry VIII* Vintage 2007

Whitechapel, Simon *Flesh Inferno: Atrocities of Torquemada and the Spanish Inquisition* Creation Books, 2003
Whitford, David M. *A Reformation Life: The European Reformation through the eyes of Philipp of Hesse* ABC-Clio 2015
Williams, Patrick *Katharine of Aragon* Amberley 2013
Wilson, Derek *The English Reformation* Robinson 2012

Index

Tudor History from Amberley Publishing

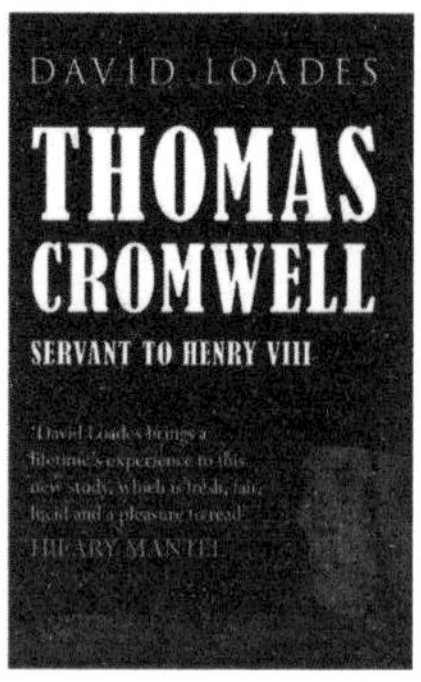

THOMAS CROMWELL
David Loades
'Fresh, fair, lucid and a pleasure to read' ***HILARY MANTEL***
£9.99 978-1-4456-4001-3 368 pages PB 27 col illus

TUDORS: THE ILLUSTRATED HISTORY
Richard Rex
'The best introduction to England's most important dynasty' ***DAVID STARKEY***
£25 978-1-4456-4371-7 256 pages HB 200 col illus

KATHARINE OF ARAGON
Patrick Williams
'Forty years' familiarity with the Spanish archive gives Williams the courage to march in where most biographers have feared to tread – notably in the bedroom' ***SARAH GRISTWOOD, BBC HISTORY MAGAZINE***
£9.99 978-1-4456-3592-7 512 pages PB 40 col illus

IN BED WITH THE TUDORS
Amy Licence
'Explores what really went on in Henry VIII's bedroom … a fascinating book' ***THE DAILY EXPRESS***
£9.99 978-1-4456-1475-5 272 pages PB 30 illus, 20 col

HENRY VIII
David Loades
'David Loades' Tudor biographies are both highly enjoyable and instructive, the perfect combination' ***ANTONIA FRASER***
£12.99 978-1-4456-0704-7 512 pages PB 113 illus, 49 col

CATHERINE PARR
Elizabeth Norton
'Norton cuts an admirably clear path through tangled Tudor intrigues' ***JENNY UGLOW***
£9.99 978-1-4456-0383-4 312 pages PB 49 illus, 30 col

Available from all good bookshops or to order direct
Please call 01453-847-800 or go to www.amberley-books.com